NONSTATE WARFARE

Nonstate Warfare

THE MILITARY METHODS OF
GUERILLAS, WARLORDS, AND MILITIAS

STEPHEN BIDDLE

A COUNCIL ON FOREIGN RELATIONS BOOK
PRINCETON UNIVERSITY PRESS
PRINCETON & OXFORD

Published by Princeton University Press
41 William Street, Princeton, New Jersey 08540
99 Banbury Road, Oxford OX2 6JX

press.princeton.edu

All Rights Reserved
First paperback printing, 2022
Paper ISBN 978-0-691-21666-9
Cloth ISBN 978-0-691-20751-3
ISBN (e-book) 978-0-691-21665-2

LCCN: 2020040045

British Library Cataloging-in-Publication Data is available

Editorial: Bridget Flannery-McCoy and Alena Chekanov
Production Editorial: Mark Bellis
Jacket/Cover Design: Karl Spurzem
Production: Erin Suydam
Publicity: Kate Hensley and Kathryn Stevens
Copyeditor: Kathleen Kageff

Jacket/Cover Credit: Northern Alliance fighters ride on a T-62 tank on the motorway 3 km north of Kabul, Nov. 13, 2001. REUTERS / Yannis Behrakis

The Council on Foreign Relations (CFR) is an independent, nonpartisan membership organization, think tank, and publisher dedicated to being a resource for its members, government officials, business executives, journalists, educators and students, civic and religious leaders, and other interested citizens in order to help them better understand the world and the foreign policy choices facing the United States and other countries. Founded in 1921, CFR carries out its mission by maintaining a diverse membership, with special programs to promote interest and develop expertise in the next generation of foreign policy leaders; convening meetings at its headquarters in New York and in Washington, DC, and other cities where senior government officials, members of Congress, global leaders, and prominent thinkers come together with CFR members to discuss and debate major international issues; supporting a Studies Program that fosters independent research, enabling CFR scholars to produce articles, reports, and books and hold roundtables that analyze foreign policy issues and make concrete policy recommendations; publishing *Foreign Affairs*, the preeminent journal on international affairs and U.S. foreign policy; sponsoring Independent Task Forces that produce reports with both findings and policy prescriptions on the most important foreign policy topics; and providing up-to-date information and analysis about world events and American foreign policy on its website, www.cfr.org.

The Council on Foreign Relations takes no institutional positions on policy issues and has no affiliation with the U.S. government. All views expressed in its publications and on its website are the sole responsibility of the author or authors.

This book has been composed in Arno

For Tami

CONTENTS

List of Figures   ix

List of Tables   xi

List of Maps   xiii

Preface   xv

1   Introduction   1

2   The Fallacy of Guerilla Warfare   22

3   Materially Optimal Behavior   46

4   Politically Achievable Behavior   74

5   Hezbollah in the 2006 Lebanon Campaign   107

6   The Jaish al Mahdi in Iraq, 2003–8   147

7   The Somali National Alliance in Somalia, 1992–94   182

8   The ZNG, HV, and SVK in the Croatian Wars of Independence, 1991–95   224

9   The Vietcong in the Second Indochina War, 1965–68   263

10   Conclusion and Implications   292

Appendix   315

Notes   337

Index   425

FIGURES

2.1. A Fabian-Napoleonic spectrum of military behavior 40

3.1. Distribution of military personnel strength among states 49

3.2. Distribution of military personnel strength among armed nonstate actors 49

3.3. Artillery range 57

3.4. Artillery lethal area 57

3.5. Attack aircraft combat radius 57

3.6. Attack aircraft bomb loads 58

3.7. Mean penetration range of heavy US antitank systems 58

3.8. Force-to-space ratio, state actors (semilog scale) 66

3.9. Force-to-space ratio, nonstate actors (semilog scale) 69

5.1. Hezbollah internal organization (from Hamzeh, *In the Path of Hizbullah*, 46) 124

10.1. Expected frequency of war-fighting methods 298

10.2. Distribution of US capability across enemy war-fighting methods 303

A.1. Predicted military behavior as a function of institutional makeup and technology, assuming high stakes $(s=1, f=0.25)$ 332

A.2. Predicted military behavior as a function of institutional makeup and technology, assuming low stakes $(s=0, f=0.25)$ 334

A.3. Predicted military behavior as a function of actor-to-opponent numerical imbalance and technology, assuming high stakes and mature natural order institutions $(s=1, i=3)$ 335

TABLES

2.1. Determinants of Actors' Position on the
Fabian-Napoleonic Spectrum   39

4.1. Taxonomy of Nonstate Institutional Makeup   98

4.2. Key Predictions—How Fabian?   105

10.1. Case Study Results   295

A.1. Coding Rules   325

A.2. Institutional Makeup Coding Rules   330

MAPS

5.1. Southern Lebanon   111

6.1. Iraq   150

6.2. Baghdad   151

7.1. Somalia   184

7.2. Mogadishu   187

8.1. Croatia   228

9.1. South Vietnam   266

PREFACE

HOW DO MILITARIES FIGHT? What strategies, tactics, and operational methods will a given force employ in battle? A central theme in the last generation of research on military effectiveness has been the importance of nonmaterial variables for combat outcomes, and among the most important of these variables are the methods and behavior adopted by combatants on the battlefield.

The methods of nonstate actors in particular warrant special attention. Nonstate fighters are widely expected to adopt a distinct military style very different from that of state armies. Whereas interstate warfare is widely expected to feature uniformed, heavily armed formations employing massed firepower to destroy one another as a means to take and hold ground, nonstate actors are expected to wage irregular warfare using lethal but militarily unsophisticated "asymmetric" means such as suicide vests, roadside bombs, snipers, assassinations, and car bombings; to seek out densely populated areas and to intermingle indistinguishably with civilian communities; and to combine these tactics with sophisticated information strategies using the internet and transnational cable news networks to influence world and regional opinion rather than taking and holding ground or seeking decisive battle.

This expected difference in methods underpins a widespread assumption that state and nonstate warfare are profoundly different phenomena with fundamentally divergent requirements for success. The category error of treating an internal war like an interstate conflict is often blamed for American defeat in Vietnam and the more recent struggles of the US military in Iraq. A generation of US military modernization, force design, doctrine development, and training after 2001 focused heavily on reorienting US forces away from the perceived needs of interstate war and toward those of intrastate conflict. Academic research on civil warfare has expanded dramatically since 2001, creating a sub-subfield whose distinctiveness lies in the expectation that civil war is different. At the heart of this categorical distinction is an assumed difference in military methods: if state and nonstate actors fought about the same way, the same military policies would mostly suit either conflict type, and academic studies of civil war would be based on a distinction without a difference.

Yet this assumed distinction is overstated at best. Some nonstate actors do use methods similar to the standard assumption, but many do not, and almost none follow the expected playbook in all its particulars. The more closely one studies the actual behavior of nonstate actors, the less clear the ostensible category distinction with state conventional war making becomes.

In fact there is nothing intrinsic to state status in the conduct of war. All combatants, whether states or not, must respond to a common set of incentives created ultimately by the nature of weapon technology. And since at least 1900, all sound war-fighting systems, whoever adopts them, have had to combine features commonly associated with both "conventional" and "irregular" warfare—the very categories themselves are artificial heuristics that appear in their pure form only as rare extrema on a continuous spectrum in which almost all real actors occupy points somewhere in the middle. This does not mean the resulting differences of degree are unimportant—in fact they have major policy implications. But the range of typical variance is narrower, the differences that matter are subtler, the underlying similarities are more important than commonly supposed, and the policy implications that follow from this are different from those commonly assumed in the public debate. To treat state and nonstate military methods using categorical distinctions of kind is an oversimplification with potentially serious consequences for policy and scholarship.

This book is intended to explore these military methods in detail, to describe more carefully the differences of degree that distinguish the real battlefield behavior of state and nonstate militaries, and to explain the variations one observes when doing so. The explanation I propose focuses on differences in the internal political makeup of different nonstate actors—especially their varying internal institutions and perceived stakes in the wars they fight—as central causes of their observed behavior. I contrast this political theory of nonstate military behavior with common alternative views that focus on nonstate material disadvantages or tribal culture, and I argue that internal politics, in interaction with the nature of available technology, offers a more successful explanation.

I base this argument on a combination of deductive causal theory construction and a series of historical case studies of nonstate actors selected to enable the greatest possible theoretical leverage for distinguishing the competing accounts. These case studies use a variety of evidence types but make particularly extensive use of field research involving a total of 137 interviews with combatants and officials who either fought as members of a nonstate military or were in a position to observe directly the behavior of nonstate combatant foes. These interviews enable the kind of detailed, in-depth, granular description of combat methods, battlefield events, and political details that I need to evaluate the theories under study here but which are often absent from secondary historical accounts.

The book's text presents my central ideas in natural language and is intended to be accessible to a wide range of audiences. For the full technical details, however, specialists will want to consult the appendix, which formalizes the new theory's causal claim in mathematical language, presents detailed criteria for coding independent and dependent variables empirically, and summarizes the theory's comparative statics graphically. Many readers will find the narrative presentation in the text sufficient, but the book is designed to enable those who want a more rigorous articulation to find this via the technical appendix.

I am grateful for the assistance and support I have received from a great many people and organizations in developing this argument. I would particularly like to thank the Smith Richardson Foundation, which provided grant support; the Council on Foreign Relations, which supported the book's early development and much of the travel that enabled its field research, and especially the war zone travel in Iraq and Afghanistan; the Multinational Force Iraq headquarters in Baghdad, which facilitated my travel and interviews in Iraq; the International Security Assistance Force headquarters in Kabul, which facilitated my travel in Afghanistan; the Dado Center for Interdisciplinary Military Studies in Tel Aviv, which facilitated my travel and interviews in Israel, and particularly its then commanding officer Brigadier General Itai Brun; the staff of the US Embassy in Zagreb who facilitated my travel and interviews in Croatia; the Strategic Studies Institute of the US Army War College, which provided funding for research travel in Israel under its External Research Associates Program; and the US Army Command and General Staff College at Fort Leavenworth, Kansas, which facilitated interview access to US Army returnees from combat duty in Iraq. Richard Haass, James Lindsay, Amy Baker, Dominic Bocci, Patricia Dorff, and Natalia Cote-Munoz of the Council on Foreign Relations have been particularly instrumental in supporting the project intellectually and administratively.

Jeffrey Friedman, Michael Johnson, Brian Lowe, Julia MacDonald, Ryan Baker, Chana Solomon-Schwartz, Daniel Eem, and Samantha Weiss provided outstanding research assistance. Dima Adamsky, Dan Fayutkin, Radmila Jackovich, Charles Lewis, Moran Maymon, Elena Papageorghiou, Martin Peled-Flax, Maureen Shaldag, and Nathan Toronto kindly assisted in arranging interviews. Maps for the book were created by Erin Greb of Erin Greb Cartography.

Michael O'Hanlon, Ken Pollack, Dan Reiter, Paul Staniland, and Caitlin Talmadge read the entire manuscript and provided incisive comments. I have also benefitted from extensive conversations and comments on the book's argument and related issues with Alexei Abrahams, Daniel Altman, Nir Artzi, Mark Bell, Peter Bergen, Eli Berman, Richard Betts, Max Boot, Daniel Byman, Sarah Chayes, Fotini Christia, Luke Condra, Ben Connable, Anthony Cordesman, Conrad Crane, Catherine Dale, Ketti Davison, Etienne de Durand, James Dobbins, Alexander Downes, Jeffrey Eggers, Andrew Exum, James Fearon, Peter Feaver, Joe Felter, Carl Forsberg, Gian Gentile, Charles Glaser, Seth Jones, Fred Kagan, Kim Kagan, Whitney Kassel, Terry Kelly, David Kilcullen, Esteban Klor, Christopher Kolenda, David Laitin, Carter Malkasian, Dan Markey, Kimberly Marten, John Martin, H. R. McMaster, Thomas McNaugher, Michael McNerney, Dipali Mukhopadhyay, Ronald Neumann, Aaron O'Connell, Ivan Oelrich, Angela O'Mahony, Kevin Owens, Gerard Padró i Miquel, Luis Peral, Jeffrey Peterson, Stacie Pettyjohn, Aaron Prupas, Joel Rayburn, Alissa Rubin, Senada Selo Sabic, Idean Salehyan, Jon Schroden, Jacob Shapiro, Martin Stanton, Ray Takeyh, Alex Thier, Charles Van Bebber, Oliver Vanden Eynde, Barbara Walter, Nils Weidmann, Michael Yankovich, Yuri Zhukov, and seminar participants at Harvard, Yale, Princeton, the University of Chicago, Duke, the University of California at Berkeley, George Washington University, the US Army War College, the RAND Insurgency Board, and the Defense Intelligence Agency. I am particularly grateful to the many participants and teaching colleagues who have joined me every summer since 1998 at the Columbia University Summer Workshop on the Analysis of Military Operations and Strategy (SWAMOS)—many years of stimulating conversation and debate on a wealth of issues including but not limited to the military behavior of nonstate actors have honed my ideas and enriched my summers in a uniquely productive way, and I thank all for their intellectual comradeship.

My daughter, Emmy Biddle, withstood long parental conversations about nonstate actors for many years and tolerated her father's time away in Iraq and Afghanistan. Her joyous greetings when I returned were the highlight of every trip.

Finally, my wife, Tami Davis Biddle, has been both my bulwark and a remarkable intellectual partner for the last 32 years. She is a military historian by training but an interdisciplinary scholar of strategy by trade, and I have learned much from her over our many years together. She was a crucial sounding board for every idea in this book, a voice of encouragement when things went slowly, and a source of joy when the work progressed. It is a great blessing to be able to share our lives together, and I dedicate the book to her.

NONSTATE WARFARE

1

Introduction

ARMED NONSTATE ACTORS, civil warfare, and the challenges these pose have dominated the US national security debate for most of the last 20 years. Nonstate fighters have been central features in large-scale American wars in Afghanistan and Iraq. They have been US targets or allies in a host of smaller-scale interventions in civil wars ranging from Syria to Somalia to the Philippines to Nigeria to Ukraine. The perceived requirements of fighting nonstate enemies have inspired major modernization programs for counterinsurgency, and multiple revisions of US military doctrine and training. In many ways, the US military of 2020 is now a product of a nearly two-decade focus on armed nonstate actors.[1]

Whether this focus should continue has become one of the most important ongoing debates in US defense policy. As the US role in Afghanistan and Iraq winds down, many would now shift emphasis away from nonstate enemies and civil wars and back toward the great power threats and interstate warfare that dominated military planning before 2001.[2] Arguments for such a shift sometimes cite the rising importance of Russia or China, but many frame their case around the military difficulties of civil warfare against nonstate enemies—which they often see as insurmountable at a cost Americans will be willing to pay.[3] Others, however, disagree, arguing that nonstate enemies in civil warfare will remain an important problem for the US military in the future and that the country cannot simply opt out of preparing to meet such challenges.[4] Still others say critics overstate the difficulty of defeating nonstate foes, and that hard-earned lessons from Afghanistan and Iraq enable more effective counterinsurgency at a more manageable cost.[5] And some argue that nonstate threats can be met with "balanced" forces not designed for a preclusive focus on civil warfare and counterinsurgency.[6]

Academics, too, have been paying attention to nonstate warfare. Since 2001, civil warfare involving nonstate actors has attracted a large and growing literature in international relations and comparative politics. Inspired partly by the public concerns raised by Afghanistan and Iraq, partly by the new availability of high-quality data on the conduct of these wars, and partly by the scale of human suffering created by such conflicts, the subject has drawn scholars and research that have now produced in excess of 275 published papers, more than 80 scholarly books, and a recognized sub-subfield: courses on civil war are now taught in most elite departments of political science in the United States.[7]

Yet for all this diversity in today's defense debate, and all the focus in the last generation of scholarship on civil warfare, most analysts share a critical underlying assumption. For most on all sides of today's debate, it is assumed that nonstate actors fight very differently than states do.

In particular, interstate warfare is usually seen as high-intensity, conventional combat in which large, uniformed, heavily armored formations maneuver in the open on substantially rural battle spaces away from large populations of innocent civilians, employing massed firepower to destroy one another as a means to take and hold ground. By contrast, nonstate actors are widely expected to wage irregular warfare using lethal but militarily unsophisticated "asymmetric" means such as suicide vests, roadside bombs, snipers, assassinations, and car bombings; to seek out densely populated areas and to intermingle indistinguishably with civilian communities; and to combine these tactics with sophisticated information strategies using the internet and transnational cable news networks to influence world and regional opinion rather than taking and holding ground or seeking decisive battle.[8]

In fact it is this underlying assumption about the distinctiveness of state and nonstate war fighting that drives the whole debate. Those who want US defense planning to shift away from nonstate war fighting and toward interstate warfare advocate this because they believe the two domains differ profoundly in their nature and requirements. Much of the opposition to this camp accepts its basic assumptions for nonstate warfare even while opposing their policy prescriptions as impractical. Even those who argue that nonstate enemies can be beaten with the same US forces and tactics that work against state armies still usually assume that the enemy will fight very differently if they are a nonstate warlord militia or guerilla insurgency than if they are a state army; for advocates of "balance" the issue is still one of balancing the demands of two very different styles of military opposition. The existence of a scholarly subliterature on "civil war" presupposes a category distinction: if state actors in interstate warfare and nonstate actors in civil wars all behaved about the same way, there would be no reason to teach courses or write books about a distinction without a difference.[9]

Yet there are good reasons to suspect that this widespread assumption is oversimplified at best. While some nonstate actors do fight in much the way the standard assumption describes, others do not.

In 2006, for example, the nonstate Shiite militia Hezbollah met an Israeli state offensive with a remarkably conventional defense in southern Lebanon. Armed with modern, precision-guided antitank weapons and disposed in depth among a system of fortified villages astride critical lines of communication, Hezbollah defended ground against Israeli armor, infantry, and artillery through a 34-day campaign using methods not unlike those of German defensive doctrine on the Eastern Front from 1942 to 1945. The Israeli Army, for its part, had begun a low-tech transformation process to improve its effectiveness in irregular warfare and had reoriented its training and doctrine away from conventional combat by 2006. When it instead faced a surprisingly state-like defender in Hezbollah the result was unexpectedly heavy casualties and near defeat for a well-equipped Westernized state; the ensuing political unrest in Israel contributed to the fall of the Kadima government and cost the military chief of staff his job.[10]

Nor is Hezbollah in Lebanon the only such example. Al Qaeda fighters in 2001–2 at Bai Beche, Highway 4, and the Shah-i-Kot valley in Afghanistan used surprisingly conventional methods with considerable skill, as did Chechen militiamen in Grozny in 1994–95, Croatian separatists in the Balkans in 1991, and Rwandan rebels in 1994. And these conventional methods enabled nonstate actors either to defeat ill-prepared state armies (such as the Russians in the First Chechen War) or to sell their lives dearly in hard fighting at close quarters against even well-prepared state militaries (such as America's in 2002).[11] Not all nonstate opponents will be capable of this. But some already are—and others will be.

Nor do all *states* follow the expected playbook very closely. Saddam's state military in 2003 augmented its mechanized regulars with a variety of irregular Fedayeen militia organizations patterned after the Somali gunmen that nonstate warlord Mohammed Farah Aideed had used against American Rangers in Mogadishu in 1993. Much of the actual combat in 2003 took the form of attacks by these Saddam Fedayeen irregulars, who used a combination of rocket-propelled grenades, small arms, and civilian cars or motorbikes to assault heavily armored US ground forces on the outskirts of Iraqi cities.[12] In

2011, Libyan strongman Muamar Gaddafi quickly realized that his state military could not counter NATO airpower using concentrated formations of tanks and artillery in the open and instead abandoned such conventional methods for intermingled operations among the population waged by mostly irregular formations of dismounted infantry with a substantial involvement by hired foreign mercenaries.[13] In Crimea in 2014 the Russian state deployed foot soldiers in unmarked green uniforms that were meant to blur the line between state regulars and nonstate forces.[14] The Iranian state security forces today combine regular mechanized formations with irregular paramilitary militias with a combination of internal, border security, and possibly irregular warfare missions.[15]

Just how different, then, *are* state and nonstate war making? Is the widespread assumption of radical difference correct most of the time but with occasional, rare, exceptions? Or are the exceptions increasingly the norm? Is the accuracy of the standard assumption changing over time? If so, why? What determines how any given actor will fight? Are these determinants themselves changing? And what implications follow for the future of warfare and the proper design, structure, equipment, or doctrine of US or other militaries?

Their importance notwithstanding, these questions have been surprisingly little studied. There are enormous, sprawling literatures on nonstate actors, future conflict, and irregular warfare. But little of this tries to explain variance in nonstate actors' military strategy and tactics in any theoretically systematic way.

The counterinsurgency literature, for example, is built around the exigencies of defeating nonstate insurgents—but tends to assume a prototypically "asymmetric," irregular fighting style for insurgents and makes little effort to explain systematic variance in insurgent methods theoretically.[16] Official intelligence assessments are rarely based on systematic theoretical foundations; the intelligence community tends to rely on rich reporting on particular cases, interpreted via the professional judgment of intelligence officers. The results depend critically on the skills and experience of the individuals involved, and the classified nature of most such data and findings typically precludes open assessment of the results.

The scholarly literature on civil warfare is extensive and growing, but its focus has typically been the onset, termination, and settlement of such wars, not their military conduct. Where the methods of civil warfare are studied at all the issue is usually whether combatants will target civilians, commit atrocities, employ indiscriminate force, or use sexual violence—not whether their methods will be conventional or asymmetric.[17] (Some civil war scholars have recently distinguished "irregular" from "symmetric nonconventional" and "conventional" civil wars wherein some nonstate actors use conventional methods; but systematic theories of conventional nonstate war making remain uncommon, and to date the distinction has often been coded by actors' equipment rather than their behavior or methods.)[18] Analysts and historians have considered individual conflicts or particular actors, but largely in isolation.[19] Political science more broadly has amassed a large body of research documenting nonstate actors' growing importance in international politics, explaining this growth, and assessing its implications for traditional notions of sovereignty, the incidence of conflict, and international relations more broadly.[20] An overlapping literature prescribes policy responses for the United States and others.[21] Very little of this, however, is based on any explicit analysis of how such actors will behave militarily; the assumption of asymmetric methods is widespread, but rarely examined or evaluated.

In the absence of sustained direct research, analysts' expectations for nonstate military behavior usually rest on implicit and largely unexamined assumptions about cause and effect. For most in today's debate, these underlying causal assumptions fall into one (or both) of two broad schools.

The first sees the expected nonstate preference for asymmetry as a reflection of material structural constraints. In this view, states are too large and too strong for smaller, weaker, nonstate actors to beat them in conventional warfare, so the weak resort to irregular methods as a rational response to inferior materiel.[22]

A smaller school sees nonstate war making as a reflection of nonmaterial cultural distinctions. This argument usually emphasizes tribalism as a source of cultural norms that are expected to promote irregular warfare and make conventional war fighting too alien for effective adoption by some nonstate actors.[23]

Both schools expect irregular methods for most of today's nonstate combatants. But the difference in their underlying assumptions about cause and effect matters: the two may yield the same expectations for *today*, but they imply very different predictions for the future, and therefore different policy prescriptions.

Most materialists, for example, assume that states' advantages in military wherewithal are simply too great for nonstate actors to overcome, and hence today's preference for irregular warfare is stable, because the material imbalance is stable.[24] But others see new technology as leveling the playing field for the future. They see nonstate actors acquiring precision weapons that were once the preserve of states, and gaining access to new communications media for mass broadcasting in the form of the internet and transnational satellite television networks. At the same time, these analysts see declining state strength in the developing world resulting from environmental or demographic stress. The basic materialist causal logic would lead one to expect nonstate actors to adopt more state-like methods under such conditions. And in fact, a new school of "fourth-generation" or "hybrid" warfare theorists now predict that the combination of better nonstate materiel and weaker state opposition will lead states and nonstate actors to converge onto a common military model that blends high technology with irregular methods, creating a new form of warfare in the process.[25]

By contrast, a tribal culture argument would imply more limited change. While technology can be transferred quickly and state administrative effectiveness can collapse quickly, underlying cultural norms change more slowly. If tribal culture is the most powerful shaper of military behavior, then warfighting methods are unlikely to be transformed simply because new weapons or communications technologies become available, or simply because opponents weaken. Few culturalists would see norms as completely invariant, but most see them as more stable than military materiel and less volatile over time. Hence a tribal culture approach would predict a continuing preference for irregular methods with limited adoption of alien doctrines typical either of historical state warfare or of some new "fourth-generation" or "hybrid" alternative.

Neither of these approaches, however, have been as systematically developed, tested, and debated as their importance would warrant. Given the stakes in the debate they underpin, it is essential that they receive the searching examination needed to put this debate on the strongest possible analytical foundations.

The purpose of this book is thus to provide such an examination: a direct, systematic analysis of the determinants of nonstate military behavior.

My central findings are that neither materiel nor tribal culture offers an adequate explanation for the observed pattern of nonstate war making—and that the commonplace assumption of distinct state and nonstate methods is unsound. Instead, I argue below for a different causal model, a political theory of nonstate war making, which implies a different pattern of future warfare.

This new explanatory model begins by rejecting the widespread assumption that "conventional" and "guerilla" or "irregular" warfare constitute autonomous, exclusive categories of distinct military conduct.[26] Real actors' actual military behavior is so interpenetrated by the intuitive elements of each as to make the distinction mostly misleading. Of course there are differences of degree that matter. But the important differences are almost all matters of relative degree, not kind. The new theory thus begins by framing its dependent variable, its outcome to be explained, as a continuous spectrum of military methods, only the extremes of which resemble pure versions of intuitively "conventional" and "guerilla" war fighting. These extrema, moreover, are empirically very rare: almost all real warfare for at least a century has been closer to the blended middle of the spectrum than either extremum, and many current actors—both states and others—have been moving further toward this middle for the last half a century or more. Hezbollah's nonstate defense of southern Lebanon in 2006 bore little resemblance to the massed, exposed armored legions of popular "conventional" imagination—but neither did the US Army's state military defense of Saudi Arabia in Operation Desert Shield in 1990 fit this model. The popular model just isn't very helpful in characterizing the actual methods of real militaries in the modern era, whether these be states or not—there are meaningful differences between Hezbollah's methods and the US Army's, or between the Vietcong's and the Wehrmacht's, but a simple categorical dichotomy between "conventional" and "guerilla" doesn't get us very far in understanding those differences or their causes. On the contrary, the tendency in the debate to chop this continuum of shades in blended methods into exclusive categories of "guerilla" and "conventional" promotes misunderstanding: it exaggerates superficial epiphenomena, conceals underlying commonalities, and obstructs theorizing that might illuminate the real, incremental change now ongoing in all actors' methods. I thus begin the new theory with a different taxonomy of behavior to be explained: not which of two dichotomous categories (or three, if we include a third category of "hybrid") an actor occupies, but where an actor lies on a continuum that positions actors by their relative distance from empirically rare extrema that I will call *Fabian* and *Napoleonic* military styles, to avoid confusion with the artificially stark categories now so deeply embedded in the existing literature.

The new theory explains any given nonstate actor's position on this spectrum with an argument that emphasizes the actor's internal politics. In particular, the theory advanced here emphasizes combatants' institutional development and perceived stakes in the war, both of which vary widely across nonstate actors. The importance of internal politics derives from the complex cooperation among interdependent specialists needed to implement military methods near the middle of the Fabian-Napoleonic spectrum. Properly exe-cuted, such midspectrum methods are the superior choice for a wide range of combatants. But proper execution requires complex interdependence of a kind that creates inherent collective action problems fundamental to this style of warfare. Actors whose political institutions are weak and whose decision mak-ing is personalized find these collective action problems very hard to over-come and thus face strong incentives to resort instead to less powerful but simpler Fabian or Napoleonic methods that rely much less heavily on complex cooperation among specialists. And even highly institutionalized actors some-times prefer not to spend the resources needed to master such difficult mid-spectrum war fighting; where the stakes are limited—and especially in wars over divisible economic spoils—the cost of achieving midspectrum profi-ciency can exceed its likely payoff. Actors whose stakes are limited will thus often resort to simpler Fabian or Napoleonic methods even if their institutions would permit midspectrum war fighting.

This is not to say that materiel or tribalism are irrelevant. Materially over-whelmed actors have no choice but to adopt more-Fabian war fighting, and tribal culture can sometimes constrain institutional development. But ongoing changes in technology have been leveling the material playing field between states and nonstate actors for half a century or more. And many apparently tribal cultures of the kind some cultural theorists expect to adopt irregular methods have nevertheless adopted significantly more Napoleonic military styles. Materiel in particular can shape military behavior in important ways—but its effects work in close interaction with its users' politics. The scale of resources needed to wage state-like midspectrum warfare has now shrunk to the point where many nonstate actors can fight effectively in this style—*if* their institutions are up to the job. And the ongoing spread of sophisticated weap-ons means that actors' politics, and not their materiel, is increasingly the bind-ing constraint on their methods.

This new theory has significant implications. It predicts, for example, faster change for many actors than tribal culturalists would expect, but not the scale of convergence that many fourth-generation or hybrid warfare theorists an-ticipate. Technology is spreading rapidly, but actors' internal politics vary and will continue to do so. Because politics are an important constraint on actors' military methods, this means that war-fighting methods are unlikely to con-verge as fast as technology does, and that technology will be a weak predictor of nonstate actors' behavior. Nonstate combatants *with permissive internal politics* will be able to exploit modern weapons to wage increasingly state-like midspectrum warfare—but others will not, regardless of how modern or lethal their equipment becomes. The net result is thus likely to be increased variance, as some nonstate actors' war fighting comes increasingly to resemble that of states, but others retain older irregular styles even as they acquire modern weapons. And the chief determinants of how any given enemy will fight are shifting away from their weapon holdings, their numerical strength, or the scale of assistance they receive from state patrons, and toward their *politics*— the job of anticipating future opponents' methods is thus increasingly the social science challenge of understanding actors' internal political dynamics rather than the traditional military task of counting weapons or assessing technology per se.

These expectations for future opponents in turn pose implications for US defense policy. Since the early 1990s, a fixture of the defense debate has been a series of calls to "transform" an ostensibly out-of-date, legacy military for radically new conditions of future warfare. From the early 1990s to roughly 2005, transformation advocates chiefly sought a much smaller, faster-moving, higher-technology, information-enabled force built for high-firepower stand-off precision warfare against massed fleets of enemy tanks and armored vehicles; existing forces were criticized as too manpower heavy, too slow, and too oriented toward low-tech close combat.[27] As the Iraq insurgency intensified after 2005, the debate flipped: new transformation advocates saw the existing US military as too capital intensive, too small, and too firepower dependent to cope with dispersed, population-intermingled insurgents using guerilla methods; "transformation" now meant a move away from high-tech standoff precision capital intensity and toward a more labor-intensive, dismounted, lower-firepower force better suited to persistent population security.[28] As the Iraq and Afghan insurgencies have wound down, the debate has now flipped back again, with "transformation" advocacy returning to its pre-2005 emphasis on high-tech standoff precision warfare enabled by new networked information technologies.[29]

Yet neither of these transformation agendas is a good fit to the threat environment the new theory projects. High-tech, standoff-precision forces perform well against massed, exposed, near-Napoleonic foes but perform poorly against better-concealed, midspectrum enemies—and the new theory predicts fewer of the former and more of the latter over time as many nonstate actors join astute state militaries in moving toward the middle of the

Fabian-Napoleonic spectrum. And a standoff military would be radically ill suited for the highly Fabian methods that will persist among those nonstate actors who lack the internal politics for midspectrum war fighting. Conversely, a force transformed for low-tech, low-firepower population security would lack the lethality needed against midspectrum enemies, whether these be states or the nonstate actors who will be increasingly capable of such methods in the future.

Perhaps ironically, the force best suited to the future might be one that looks much more like US forces of the past. In land warfare against midspectrum enemies, the ideal force would be a balanced, medium-weight alternative with more dismounted infantry than the high-tech transformed force but more armor and artillery than the low-tech transformed force—in fact, this ideal force bears more than a passing resemblance to the structure of the legacy US land forces of the Cold War. By contrast, the futuristic high-tech standoff alternative is optimized for fighting a kind of enemy that is likely to become less common in the future, not more: massed, exposed, highly vulnerable Napoleonic state armies. The low-tech transformed alternative has an opposite but analogous problem: it is optimized for fighting the highly Fabian nonstate irregulars that will not disappear, but will probably also become less frequent in the future as more nonstate actors shift toward the middle of the Fabian-Napoleonic spectrum. Of course the ultimate design of the US military depends on more than just the nature of likely opposition. But the threat environment does matter, and the new theory suggests, paradoxically, that both of the futuristic, ostensibly forward-looking "transformation" agendas in today's debate are actually built around backward-looking threat projections for either state or nonstate actors in future land combat.[30] If sound, the new theory thus suggests that the best design for future US land forces may be among the least radically transformational.

For scholars, the new theory casts doubt on the widespread tendency to isolate studies of civil war, with ostensibly distinctive dynamics, from research on interstate warfare. In fact, military behavior by nonstate actors in civil warfare differs only by degree along a continuum from that of state actors in international warfare, and the study of each can profit from systematic exposure to the other. By helping to unify these phenomena as special cases of more general causal dynamics the new theory sheds light on both domains. And in the process, the results help develop an understudied topic in the civil war literature via a systematic account of participants' combat methods and their military rationale.

To make this case, the balance of this chapter will first define some critical terms and delimit the theory's scope. It then presents the book's methodology and justifies this choice. It concludes with a description of the book's organization and structure and provides a roadmap for what is to come.

Scope and Definitions

The book seeks to explain the military behavior of nonstate actors in warfare involving numerically superior state opponents since 1900. Several of these terms require careful definition.

First, by "nonstate actor" I mean any entity other than a sovereign state as defined in international law. The 1933 Montevideo Convention defines a sovereign state as an institution with "(a) a permanent population; (b) a defined territory; (c) government; and (d) capacity to enter into relations with other states."[31] Hence nonstate actors would include, inter alia, insurgent groups; ethnic separatists; internationally unrecognized armed forces such as warlord militias; mercenaries or private military firms; armed religious or ideological extremists; criminal syndicates; or any other user of armed force other than Montevideo Convention states.

But while I define "nonstate actor" expansively, I do not aspire to explain *any* use of violence by actors other than sovereign states. Labor riots, family violence, petty crime, or looting in the aftermath of natural disaster, for example, are all important in their own right but play little role in the national security debate. I thus limit consideration here to *warfare*, which I define as organized violence exceeding 1,000 total battle deaths with at least 100 deaths on each of at least two sides.[32] This includes some campaigns often described as "terrorism" (such as Al Qaeda's conflict with the United States) and others sometimes described as "criminal" (such as the FARC's narco-insurgency in Colombia)— my distinction is based on the scale of violence, not its purpose or motives.

This domain includes warfare between nonstate actors in wars where states are active participants (for an example, see the discussion of the Croatian War of Independence in chapter 8), and it has implications for purely nonstate conflicts as well (for an example, see the discussion in chapter 7 of the Somali SNA's warfare against other militias before the US intervention). But inter-nonstate warfare is not its focus, and the analysis is not meant to be dispositive for all such examples.

The theory's temporal domain extends from 1900 to the mid-21st century, and its scope includes continental warfare but excludes war at sea. This focuses the analysis on the era of industrial- and information-age warfare that extends through today and into the midterm future, thus accommodating the most policy-relevant subset of the empirical record. I exclude piracy or other maritime conflict per se but include most other forms of large-scale armed violence in the 20th and 21st centuries.

The universe of potential cases thus includes all continental wars from 1900 to the mid-21st century involving at least one state and at least one armed nonstate actor.

The unit of analysis is the nonstate actor's modal military behavior in a given conflict year. Of course there will be subunit variance under this specification: different formations' commanders will use their fighters differently; the same commanders will change their behavior at irregular intervals. I argue, however, that internal politics will tend to shape relatively common behavior across commanders, and over time, for a given internal political configuration.

The dependent variable for the theory below is the behavior of military actors. Of course, combatants in war perform thousands of tasks and do so in thousands of ways; some subset must be specified if the analysis is to be tractable. Given the policy debate around which the book is framed, the natural approach is to focus on the subset of behavior most closely associated with the intuitive distinction between putatively "conventional" state and "irregular" nonstate styles of fighting. However, I treat these not as exclusive categories but as a continuum defined by an actor's modal distance from a *Napoleonic* extremum framed as a pure version of the popular intuition of "conventional" war fighting, and a *Fabian* extremum framed as a pure version of the "irregular" or "guerilla" category. These terms are defined in greater detail in chapter 2 and the appendix, but for now, the characteristics of pure *Fabian* methods include an absolute unwillingness to defend ground via decisive engagement at any point in the theater; dispersed operations with no local concentrations in excess of the theaterwide combatant density; insistence on concealment obtained via intermingling with the civilian population; exclusive reliance on coercion rather than brute force; and rejection of heavy weapons, even when available, in favor of light arms and equipment more suitable to concealment among the population. By contrast, the characteristics of pure *Napoleonic* methods include an insistence on decisive engagement to defend or seize ground that will not be voluntarily relinquished; local concentration to shoulder-to-shoulder densities at a point of attack where ground is contested; use of uniformed forces on battlefields removed from urban population centers; exclusive reliance on brute force rather than coercion; and preferential employment of the heaviest weapons available to maximize firepower and armor protection. Of course few real actors fit either of these extrema; below I present an index measure that adjudicates varying combinations of observable correlates of these traits to code any given actor on a continuous $(0, 6)$ scale, with 0.0 corresponding to the Fabian extremum, 6.0 corresponding to the Napoleonic extremum, and values in between denoting admixtures whose balance is increasingly Napoleonic as values increase from zero to six.

I explain this dependent variable via two classes of independent, or explanatory, variables: materiel and politics; and I contrast this new theory with prior views emphasizing materiel per se and tribal culture. Here, too, the variables are operationalized in more detail in chapters 2 through 4 and, especially, the appendix. For now, however, *materiel* encompasses both the quality of actors' military equipment (in terms of the lethality of its technology), and its quantity, in terms of the numbers of fielded combatants. *Politics*, like military behavior, comprises a potentially infinite variety of subdimensions; below I consider two: actors' institutional development (to what degree is leadership personalized and informal or impersonal and bureaucratized?) and their perceived stakes in the war (are these limited and divisible or existential and indivisible?).

Tribal culture is not an explanatory variable for the new theory, but, given its salience in the nonstate military literature, I treat it as an alternative explanation in the case studies below. Culture is a richly multidimensional phenomenon with a wide range of potentially important subdimensions and consequences; its role in the nonstate military behavior literature, however, tends to focus on the claim that tribalism is inconsistent with conventional war fighting.[33] In this literature, *tribalism* is a cultural trait in which much of social interaction is shaped by family lineage and descent patterns. In strongly tribal cultures, it is held, trust and cooperation are strong within the family unit but attenuate rapidly beyond it, making commerce, dispute resolution, and collective action progressively more difficult the more remote the perceived bonds of common descent. This in turn is held to produce distinctive patterns of military behavior: tribal societies are expected to field small, decentralized fighting units with often fierce motivation to defend others of close common descent but difficulty cooperating in larger formations that cross lines of family lineage. Loyalties are held to be fluid and command arrangements loose, reflecting the segmented nature of tribal lineage relationships; "me against my brother, my brother and I against my cousin, and all of us against the stranger" is a perhaps apocryphal Bedouin aphorism often cited to describe the realignments that an emphasis on family group can promote when action is shaped by the relative closeness or distance of kinship.[34] And these patterns are in turn expected to promote tactics that emphasize small-unit raids, ambushes, and quick hit-and-run strikes rather than sustained defense of positions. As Richard Shultz and Andrea Dew put it:

> Traditional societies do not have standing professional armies in the Western sense. Rather, all men of age in a tribe, clan or communal group learn through societal norms and legacies to fight in specific ways, and to fight well, if required. . . . these traditional concepts invariably take protracted, irregular, and unconventional forms of combat.[35]

In other parts of the political science and strategic studies literature, "culture" can have a wide variety of other meanings, referring, for example, to patterns of behavior within organizations, or to broad national systems of value or perception.[36] I do not seek in this book to advance a general claim about the causal role of culture in this broader sense. But given the role of arguments about tribalism per se in the nonstate military debate I do thus address this aspect of culture in the case studies and findings below.

Approach, Method, and Cases

The theory below is motivated by a detailed deductive causal argument. This argument focuses on the relative military advantages and disadvantages of more-Fabian and more-Napoleonic methods and holds that for almost all actors, midspectrum blends of the two are militarily superior but extremely complex. I then develop the internal political requirements of fielding forces able to cope with this complexity.

The deductive argument below draws heavily on the experience of both state and nonstate militaries in modern war. Indeed, one of my central claims is that the putative category distinction between the two is largely an illusion; to sustain this claim requires a sustained exploration of both. The tendency to separate interstate and nonstate warfare into distinct, stove-piped literatures is part of the reason for the widespread misunderstanding of these underlying commonalities: if one studies nonstate warfare by looking only at nonstate actors then its similarities with interstate combat will never be seen. I argue that modern technology creates common military incentives that affect all actors alike—my theoretical discussion of these incentives thus makes extensive use of the modern military history of interstate as well as nonstate warfare, as a means of shedding unique light on the features of nonstate warfare per se. Strictly speaking my findings pertain to nonstate actors per se, but the deductive discussion draws heavily on observations of both.

The result is a rationalist theory. None of this means that warlord commanders are cool, emotionless, Enlightenment calculators who evaluate all options in the way Adam Smith or John Stuart Mill might have done, and choose the one best suited to their mathematical objective functions. The causal mechanism here does assume, however, that the reality of warfare disciplines behavior by imposing disproportionate cost on those who make poor choices. War is an unforgiving enterprise. Those who misunderstand its dynamics will be exploited by those with stronger perception, and the result will be destruction or defeat of the obtuse at the hands of the astute: selection effects will remove, through death or conquest, those who consistently choose badly. In the crucible of war, trial and error will thus cause surviving combatants to vector in on something resembling the result of an objective calculation even if it never occurs to them as such. At any given time, some warriors will be in the process of elimination, hence not all will behave as a rationalist optimal behavior model would expect. But if the theory below is sound, then in steady state, most combatants at most times will display behavioral choices that mirror those the logic below suggests are optimal—and those who do not should suffer for their failure. The explicit calculations in the theory below thus short-circuit the process of experiential learning by real combatants in war, but they should predict about the same outcomes if the military logic below is correct.[37]

The result is a deductive theory of military behavioral choice. This deductive theory is then tested via a series of detailed historical case studies of campaigns chosen to create maximum leverage for assessing the theory's validity.

These case studies use a variety of sources but make particular use of field research involving a total of 137 structured interviews with state and nonstate participants in critically selected military campaigns. This field research was conducted in Iraq, Croatia, and Israel, and in the United States with participants who had returned from Iraq and Somalia. It included interviewees who either fought as nonstate combatants (in Croatia) or were in a position to observe directly the behavior of nonstate combatant foes (in Lebanon, Iraq, and Somalia), at military ranks from private to major general, and ambassadorial rank in the Department of State, and it enabled detailed, in-depth, granular description of combat methods, battlefield events, and political details important to the theories assessed here but absent from typical secondary historical accounts. Throughout, military participants were asked to address only factual events they observed themselves (or performed themselves); wherever possible, multiple participants' accounts of the same events were solicited to insulate the findings against observer bias to the greatest degree possible.[38]

Case method permits the depth of analysis needed to characterize variables that have not heretofore been included in large-n data sets, especially military behavior. It also allows process tracing to help distinguish real causation from mere coincidence. This is especially valuable where a deductive theory with a detailed causal mechanism enables multiple observable hypotheses to be deduced for a single case—the more substantively detailed the deductive theory, the more points of tangency there will be between its claims and the historical events of any given case, and thus the more powerful the case can be as a test of the theory.

This depth of detail, however, makes it impossible to consider more than a handful of cases. No such sample can exhaust the range of possible empirical variation, especially for a theory whose dependent variable (and some independent variables) are continuous and real-valued. For a theory specified in continuous variables, there is literally an infinite number of points that make up the relevant theoretical space—this cannot be exhaustively surveyed to see whether prediction and observation match at each possible point. Nor could even the largest plausible large-n data set accomplish this. To test the theory here thus requires some act of selection to create a sample of observations chosen to create the greatest possible leverage for evaluating the theory given the scale of research needed to characterize fully all the relevant variables for any given case.

Given this, the cases considered here have been chosen to meet several important, theory-driven selection criteria designed to produce the most challenging test possible from an inherently limited sample.[39] First, they must enable direct observation of all independent and dependent variables; cases where the documentary record is insufficient or where participants are unavailable for interviewing are thus not suitable. Second, they must collectively show variance on all three classes of explanatory variable—materiel, tribal culture, and internal politics. Third, they should collectively explore as many distinct regions of the relevant theoretical space as possible (that is, they should approximate a stratified sample from that space). Fourth, they should present conditions for which the respective theories predict different outcomes, enabling the case to distinguish between them in their ability to explain the evidence. Finally, they should provide maximum benefit of the doubt to the preexisting prototheories, and stack the deck against the new theory to the degree possible. Small-n case testing cannot prove or disprove theories. But if case testing shows the new theory outperforming its competition under conditions deliberately chosen to benefit the competition, this unusual result would merit a greater shift in confidence than would otherwise be warranted from such a small sample of cases.

The cases examined here are Hezbollah in the 2006 Lebanon campaign; the Shiite Jaish al Mahdi (JAM) militia in Operation Iraqi Freedom from 2003 to 2008; Mohammed Farah Aideed's Habr Gedir militia in Somalia from 1992 to 1994; the Croatian nationalist ZNG and Croatian Serb SVK in the Croatian Wars of Independence of 1991–95; and the Vietcong in the American phase of the Second Indochina War from 1965 to 1968.

Hezbollah in 2006 offers an opportunity for a controlled comparison with the Jaish al Mahdi in Iraq. Both were drawn from Shiite Arab communities that were much more tribal than those of their state opponents; both faced materially superior Westernized state militaries; and both had external support from the same Iranian patron. The 2006 campaign also approximates an Ecksteinian critical case for the hybrid materialist subschool: it is the single most prominent example of hybrid or fourth-generation warfare in the literature; for the theory to have much merit, it must account for Hezbollah in 2006. The two actors' internal politics, by contrast, were very different: Hezbollah had a stable, elaborately developed formal institutional structure and saw its conflict with Israel as existential, whereas the JAM's leadership was personalized and divided, with multiple factions turning increasingly to economic predation as the Iraq War continued. Orthodox materialist theories would thus predict similar, highly Fabian methods for both actors; tribal culture theories would do much the same, albeit with some expectation for more Napoleonic war fighting for the JAM (tribal norms were stronger in rural southern Lebanon than in urban Baghdad where the JAM was strongest). The new theory, by contrast, predicts substantially state-like midspectrum behavior for Hezbollah but more Fabian methods for the JAM—and this is in fact what the case evidence shows. The case also shows important variance between the details of Hezbollah's methods and the particular expectations of hybrid materialists: whereas the latter see hybrid warfare as a combination of high-tech weapons and irregular tactics, Hezbollah's tactics were no more irregular than those of most states.

Mohammed Farah Aideed's Somali National Alliance (SNA) militia approximates an Ecksteinian critical case for tribal culture theorists: if the theory is ever going to work anywhere, it should work here. Tribe and clan were the central organizing principles both for Somali society in general and for the competing warlord militias in the aftermath of the Siad Barre government's fall. And in fact the Somalia case plays a prominent role in the tribalist literature on nonstate warfare, which treats this as almost the defining case of tribally determined irregular war fighting. The material imbalance here, by contrast, was more modest than in many cases of nonstate warfare. For over a year and a half, the war pitted rival militias against one another, with no state military engaged; neither the SNA nor its enemies enjoyed a decisive material edge. Only when American forces arrived after December 1992 did the SNA face a material disadvantage, and even here the material balance was less favorable to the Western forces than in cases such as Iraq: the SNA had access to a substantial arsenal of sophisticated weapons inherited from the Siad Barre state military, and the SNA fielded an unusually large combatant force for the size of its operating area. Materialist theories would thus expect Aideed's methods to change over time, with little need for the SNA to adopt highly Fabian irregular methods prior to 1993, but with increasingly Fabian "asymmetric" war fighting after that; neither period, however, should display a historical extremum of the kind that tribal culture arguments would expect. The new theory, by contrast, predicts change in SNA behavior over time, but in the opposite direction. The SNA's political organization was personalized and highly informal throughout. Its stakes, however, changed dramatically by mid-1993. Before that, SNA war aims were limited and economic, but when American admiral Jonathan Howe declared in August 1993 that his goal would be Aideed's capture and imprisonment and began targeting Aideed and his chief lieutenants, the war suddenly took on existential stakes for the SNA's leadership. For the new theory, the SNA's weak institutionalization would preclude highly complex midspectrum warfare throughout, but the radical change in stakes should motivate movement in that direction even for a nonstate militia—hence the new theory would predict *less* Fabian war fighting after the American intervention, not more (as materialists would expect), and not stasis (as culturalists would predict). In fact the case shows change, and change in the direction of an increasing effort by the SNA to hold key territory after August 1993. At no point did this amount to truly state-like midspectrum warfare, but neither was it the extremum of irregular methods predicted by tribal culture arguments, and the direction of change was toward the Napoleonic end of the spectrum after the United States intervened and the material balance worsened for the SNA—not the opposite, as materialist logic would imply.

The Croatian Wars of Independence present two different nonstate separatist groups, the Croatian nationalist ZNG and Croatian Serb SVK, together
with a variety of associated militias. None were strongly tribal. The nationalist
ZNG initially faced a materially preponderant state opponent in the Jugoslav
National Army (JNA) in 1991; Serb militias aligned with the JNA enjoyed
important material advantages over their ZNG rivals. This balance then reversed when the nationalists achieved international recognition and state status, Croatian Serbs did not, and the JNA withdrew—by 1995, Croatian Serbs
were the materially inferior side. Throughout, Croatian Serb politics were
highly personalized and subject to bitter factional disputes; their stakes were
nominally existential, but until the very end their leadership assumed that the
JNA would return to defend them—the expected outcomes for Croatian Serb
elites varied mostly with respect to patronage and seniority in a regime they
believed others would defend. Croatian nationalists, by contrast, saw unlimited stakes in a self-help war that they expected would yield brutal oppression
in the event of failure. Nationalist institutions were much more formal and
extensive than the Serbs' but remained highly personalized at the most senior
levels as President Franjo Tudjman relied on cronyism to secure his own position. By 1995, however, this personalized institutional system was augmented
via a different kind of nonstate actor: the private military firm MPRI, whose
advisory services circumvented some of the normal politico-military problems of cronyism. In this setting, tribal culture theories would predict state-like
"conventional" behavior for all parties. Materialist theories would expect
highly Fabian irregular warfare for the nationalist ZNG in 1991 and for the
outnumbered nonstate SVK when large-scale fighting reignited in 1995, but
more Napoleonic methods for the materially superior Serb nonstate militias
in 1991. The new theory identifies simpler, more Fabian methods as the best
choice for poorly institutionalized actors like the Serbs with limited perceived
stakes, and it implies that better-institutionalized parties like the nationalists
should be able to field midspectrum militaries quickly when motivated by
existential stakes; cronyism at the top should limit high-level coordination,
especially in large-scale offensive action, but not tactical cooperation within
small units. Observed behavior in the case fits the new theory but contradicts
the others for the nationalist ZNG. The Serbian SVK fits none of the theories
perfectly but follows the causal logic of the new theory even where the outcome is not exactly as predicted: the Serbs' weak institutional foundation and
limited stakes left them incapable of the complex cooperation needed for midspectrum warfare; the theory assumes they would thus choose simpler, more

Fabian methods better suited to their limited skills. When they instead tried to implement complex midspectrum methods beyond their proficiency, the result was military disaster in August 1995 when the Croatian state army crushed the Serbs in a brief, four-day campaign.

The Vietcong from 1965 to 1968 were perhaps the paradigmatic nonstate irregular force in the eyes of most Americans, and their methods had a profound influence on subsequent policy and scholarship; any theory of nonstate warfare must account for the Vietcong. The case also offers a theoretically important opportunity to observe nonstate warfare prior to the advent of precision firepower—in fact, the 1965–68 era in Vietnam offers one of the last examples of warfare before the dawn of modern precision weaponry, which was introduced by the United States in the war's latter campaigns. The chief finding from the case is to corroborate the new theory's account of technology's role in nonstate war fighting. The Vietcong faced existential stakes and had remarkably formal, mature institutions. There is good reason to believe they could have mastered the complexity of modern midspectrum warfare. Yet they chose mostly very Fabian methods instead—and suffered gravely when they departed from this pattern as in the 1968 Tet Offensive. I argue that their inability to use midspectrum methods successfully was due to their low-lethality weapon technology, which combined with the difficult jungle terrain of their primary operating areas to leave them unable to control territory on the necessary scale even though they deployed a large combatant force. With only light, low-firepower weapons at their disposal, the VC could not prevent their American, and to some extent South Vietnamese, state opponents from massing overwhelming combat power at chosen points. The problem here was not numerical imbalance per se, or even technological asymmetry—Hezbollah and the Croatian ZNG both proved able to control ground with midspectrum methods under comparable numerical and technical inferiority. But whereas Hezbollah and the ZNG had modern weapons lethal enough to force better-equipped state enemies to disperse, yielding manageable local imbalances at the critical points, the VC did not. The Vietcong's 1960s-era light weapons and small arms could cause gradual attrition over time, but they could not stop a massed state offensive from crushing their defenses at any given point. Nor could the Vietcong take ground against state armies' positional defenses with such arms. Their only option was thus to resort to highly Fabian warfare, notwithstanding the VC's existential motivation and mature institutions. Later nonstate actors with more advanced weapons were able to make different choices even when faced with materially superior state opponents.

Plan of the Book

Chapter 2 presents the theory's dependent variable—a continuous, Fabian-Napoleonic spectrum of military behavior—and distinguishes this from the treatment of "conventional" and "guerilla" warfare in the existing literature.

The theory to explain this dependent variable is presented in chapters 3 and 4. Chapter 3 treats the role of materiel, arguing that material military incentives have been driving both once-Napoleonic state militaries and once-Fabian non-state forces toward the midspectrum middle for more than a generation. Chapter 4 treats the role of internal politics, arguing that political constraints shape any given nonstate actor's ability to act on this material incentive and implement the complex methods required. An appendix formalizes the theory's coding scheme for these variables and its functional form for interrelating them, and it presents comparative statics to identify the theory's predictions with greater precision.

Chapters 5 through 9 present the case studies of historical campaigns and their relationship to the theories under test. These cases show a pattern of closer correspondence with the new theory than either its materialist or its tribal culture competitors even under conditions chosen to place those competitors on their strongest analytical ground. Of course, this neither proves the new theory nor disproves the others—proof or disproof is beyond the capacity of case method. But it does establish a degree of empirical plausibility for the new claims. And it does so under conditions that should have offered easy, unambiguous predictive successes for preexisting theories if the latter were correct. Empirical findings are necessarily provisional pending large-n research that is possible only with the development of new data, but the unusual conditions in the cases chosen warrant a greater shift in confidence toward the new theory than would otherwise be warranted from a small sample of cases.

Chapter 10 concludes the book. It provides a more detailed summary of my main arguments and findings; most of the chapter, however, develops their implications for scholarship and policy, and it contrasts these with the views now typically held on the basis of current understandings. I argue that these contrasts are quite sharp, and that neither scholarship nor policy can be conducted on a sound basis without a more systematic consideration of the real determinants of nonstate military behavior.

2

The Fallacy of Guerilla Warfare

NONSTATE WAR MAKING is often misunderstood. Among the more common misconceptions is a tendency to treat state and nonstate military methods as autonomous, mutually exclusive categories. States fighting other states, many assume, wage "conventional" warfare whereas nonstate actors wage "guerilla" or irregular warfare with radically different aims, methods, and principles. Recently some have added a third category of "hybrid" warfare falling somewhere between guerilla and conventional war. But even the hybrid warfare literature frames war making in discrete categories of contrasting methods—they just add one to the other two. Nor are these distinctions treated merely as superficial differences of appearance or degree. The whole point of distinguishing nonstate "guerilla" from state "conventional" war making is that the categories are thought to reflect profoundly different underlying causal dynamics: even for greatly superior armies, to mistake one for the other is often said to court defeat—a widespread criticism of US war fighting in both Vietnam and Iraq has been the charge that Americans committed the category error of failing to recognize that their enemy was waging guerilla rather than conventional war, leading to military failure in one or both cases.[1]

Yet this division of warfare into distinct state and nonstate categories is misleading. Of course many nonstate actors do fight differently than many states, and misunderstanding hostile methods can certainly produce failure. But the distinctions that count are matters of degree, not kind. Modern firepower poses demands on all combatants that create broadly similar requirements for anyone who wants to survive long enough to accomplish any meaningful mission. Varying local conditions encourage differences at the margin in actors' methods, but the underlying calculus is shared, with more principles in common than not. Attempts to chop the resulting continuum into exclusive categories of "guerilla" and "conventional" exaggerate superficial epiphenomena, conceal underlying commonalities, and obstruct theorizing that might illuminate the real, incremental change now ongoing in all actors' methods.

In fact there is nothing intrinsic to nonstate status in the conduct of war. And nonstate status is both a less important signpost to meaningful differences of degree than often assumed, and one that matters less with every passing year. Some nonstate actors already use intuitively state-like "conventional" methods with greater efficacy than do many states, and this is likely to grow more common over time. Conversely, some states have long sponsored terrorism; others rely increasingly on intuitively nonstate "guerilla" or irregular methods for fighting both state and nonstate rivals. As these trends mature, future variance in methods *within* the state and nonstate categories could easily exceed the variance in methods between them.

In an important sense, the commonplace intuitive picture of nonstate "guerilla" warfare is thus a fallacy. Like many myths, it is not without an important grain of truth—some nonstate actors' methods have sometimes approximated the intuitive model. But many others have not. And the category conceals as much as it reveals: it exaggerates the real distinctions between state and nonstate war fighting, it masks trends that are changing each by degree over time, it distorts scholarship in the study of both civil and interstate warfare, and it can lead to defense policy choices that leave Western states ill prepared for the demands of future warfare. Chapters 3 and 4 will present a theory to explain observed variance in the military methods of nonstate actors in particular. But to do this it is first necessary to overturn the myth of guerilla warfare and to develop instead an alternative characterization of military methods as a continuous difference of degree between two rare polar extremes, with almost all real military practice falling closer to the middle than to either archetypal end point.

I do this in three steps. First, I address the common claim that state and nonstate actors differ systematically in the end purposes for which they wage war—I argue that this is mistaken, and that almost all real actors have long pursued similar, Clausewitzian ultimate goals and will continue to do so. Second, I turn to the means used to pursue these ends. I argue that while these have often differed for state and nonstate actors, the differences are matters of degree, not kind, and are best considered as points along a continuum between two uncommon extremes—what I will call *Fabian* and *Napoleonic* military archetypes—but where almost all actors have long combined elements of each. As such, a categorical treatment leads to ambiguity at best and error at worst. An appendix presents a series of observable indicators and coding rules that can be used to specify any actor's position on this spectrum, thus operationalizing the dependent variable for the theory to come in chapters 3 and 4 as an actor's relative distance from these contrasting Fabian and Napoleonic end point extrema. I close this chapter, however, with a series of brief descriptions of historical actors and their placement on the resulting spectrum as a means of illustrating both the range of variance in the dependent variable for the theory to come—and the perils of treating "guerilla warfare" as a category apart, populated only with nonstate warriors.

Nonstate Actors and the Purposes of Military Action

Many now see a major difference in the purposes served by state and nonstate war making. In particular, states have long been assumed to follow the Clausewitzian dictum that war is a means to political ends; in Clausewitzian interstate warfare, the aim is to topple or defend rulers, seize or defend provinces, or extract political concessions from foes who would contest these political stakes.[2] Nonstate actors, by contrast, are often said to wage war for nonpolitical, post-Clausewitzian purposes such as the pursuit of profit, hatred, honor, religious duty, or cultural self-expression. And these novel, nonpolitical aims are held to promote systematically different means than the conventional tactics of traditional interstate warfare; this putative difference in underlying ends thus underpins for many the need to distinguish state conventional from nonstate guerilla or irregular means.[3]

Nonstate actors often do use different methods than states do. And war aims do indeed have a powerful effect on war making. But the critical distinction is not between obsolescent "political" ends and modern alternatives— almost all warfare by almost all actors remains "political" in Clausewitz's terms. The real issue concerns the *magnitude* of the political stakes, and especially the distinction Clausewitz himself drew between wars fought for limited as opposed to existential political objectives. I return to this distinction in chapter 4; for now, it is enough to clarify that even for modern, nonstate actors, the purpose of military action is normally the political one of controlling the collective decisions of civilian populations over the distribution of power and resources.

Consider wars of profit. Wealth is produced by human economic activity; war for profit normally involves warriors controlling some population to divert its production to the warriors' benefit. To be effective, a war for profit must thus shape the collective choices of human groups to change the flow of resources. Some argue that unlike states, nonstate actors can gain wealth from lootable resources such as diamond mines without large-scale cooperation from the population, and that this wealth can be attained during protracted war without actually winning. Diamond mines or coca fields can be exploited economically with less labor than oil fields or steel mills, but even here the requirement is not zero: human labor is still required for extraction, and some degree of complicit public tolerance is still required for shipment. The difference in the *scale* of public involvement needed can be important for some nonstate actors' choices between discriminate and indiscriminate violence, but in all cases the cooperation of some living civilians must be secured for wealth to be extracted—and securing this cooperation, whether via coercion or co-optation, is ultimately a political aim.[4]

Consider hatred. Hatred could in principle be expressed by pure killing without any control over the living. Yet few actual combatants have ever waged war without important agendas for control of the survivors: even Al Qaeda has an elaborate political program for a new Islamist caliphate to govern large populations now under others' rule; Al Qaeda's violence, while indiscriminate, is not a nihilistic end in itself but an instrumental means to political control over the living.[5]

Religious or ethnic violence more broadly is normally a means to control populations and alter their choices. Iraqi Shiites in 2006, for example, fought to dominate rival Sunnis (and vice versa), not to literally exterminate them all. Sectarian cleansing in Baghdad was achieved chiefly by coercing the survivors to leave, as was the ethnic cleansing of the Balkan Wars in the 1990s.[6] Joseph Kony's LRA (Lord's Resistance Army) in East Africa fights for goals that include implementation of his own warped understanding of Christian theology (and advancement of his own personality cult), but the LRA's aims prominently include the overthrow of the Museveni government in Uganda, a profoundly political objective.[7]

Consider honor or self-expression. These could theoretically be sought by gratuitous displays of courage or ritualistic demonstrations without meaningful coercive potential. Yet it is hard to identify examples. Pashtun society celebrates martial virtues, yet Pashtun combat is normally aimed at coercing concessions from rivals, deterring them from future offenses, or protecting kinsmen from domination by outsiders.[8] Hezbollah terrorism is sometimes described as expression of a cultural norm of resistance, yet Hezbollah has explicit political goals for the control of populations in Lebanon and Palestine.[9]

Modern warriors may not always seek the literal territorial conquest typical of Clausewitz's day, but they almost always use force as an instrumental means to control populations of living civilians, whether these populations are large and broadly distributed, or small and localized.[10] Political aims, in this fundamental sense of politics as the collective decision making of civilians, are thus nearly universal in war regardless of the actor involved—they are not a unique property of states.

The Methods of Military Action: A Fabian-Napoleonic Spectrum

How do combatants pursue this common goal? The literature typically assumes "guerilla" methods for nonstate actors—but strict definitions of the term are rare. Many are satisfied with a mostly intuitive, Potter-Stewart-like definition-by-example: "guerilla" warfare is something like what the Vietcong did in the mid-1960s, whereas "conventional" warfare looks like the World Wars in Europe or North Africa. For recent "hybrid warfare" theorists, this new category looks like either Hezbollah in 2006 or sometimes the Russians in Crimea in 2014.

Maybe Chief Justice Stewart really did know pornography when he saw it.[11] But this is an awkward basis for a rigorous theory of nonstate military behavior.

The chief problem is that the commonplace intuitive notions of "conventional" and "guerilla" warfare are actually very difficult to parse into consistent, mutually exclusive categories. Almost all real combatants combine elements from both intuitive models—the more closely one examines real combat, the fewer truly unique features one can find in either intuitive style. Even the German Wehrmacht in 1944 displayed strikingly "guerilla-like" methods in important respects; even the Vietcong in 1965 did many things that most people associate with "conventional" war fighting. In fact the real differences are all matters of degree and relative emphasis among an array of *shared* requirements for survival against modern firepower. To capture this kind of variance, a handful of discrete categories is an awkward approach; the theory in chapters 3 and 4 thus uses a continuum, not a discrete set of categories, to describe military behavior.

To see why, it is useful to consider several of the commonplace intuitive features of "guerilla" warfare in greater detail. In particular, many analysts distinguish "irregular" or "guerilla" from conventional warfare by reference to differences in combatants' emphasis on stealth; by reference to their different intentions to hold ground; by citing different levels of concentration and dispersion; by contrasting strategic emphases on coercion as opposed to brute force; or by discussing combatants' choices to fight "symmetrically" as opposed to "asymmetrically." In fact, all these are relative distinctions of degree, not kind, and all are functionally linked to shared underlying requirements for surviving modern firepower long enough to accomplish meaningful military missions.

Stealth

Stealthiness is the single trait most commonly associated with guerilla or irregular warfare. Outnumbered, outgunned guerillas are typically assumed to require concealment in order to survive in the face of superior government militaries.[12]

Yet even in conventional warfare, exposure frequently means death. The modern battlefield is so lethal that it has been suicidal to allow massed formations to be caught exposed in the open since at least 1914. In fact, concealment— and the techniques needed to provide it as technology has changed—has arguably been the single most important theme in the history of modern *conventional* tactics.[13] A distinguishing feature of post-1914 conventional warfare has been the "empty battlefield" that resulted from the widespread adoption of cover and concealment in modern high-intensity combat; soldiers in such wars commonly develop an instinctive suspicion of conditions that "seem too quiet" precisely because conventional defenders are commonly invisible to attackers much of the time.[14] Of course, there are differences in the *way* conventional armies and guerilla forces obtain the needed concealment— although both use the natural complexity of the terrain to conceal themselves (indeed guerillas classically exploit mountains, jungles, or other unusually complex terrain for this purpose), guerillas also typically try to conceal themselves via intermingling with an indistinguishable civilian population. Classical guerilla tactics assume either that the government will be loath to harm apparently innocent civilians, or that the government will suffer politically from doing so. Hence many guerillas wear civilian clothing and live, train, and fight among civilian populations as a means of rendering themselves as difficult as possible to distinguish from those civilians.[15] Conventional armies, by contrast, wear distinguishing uniforms, occupy distinct bases, and often fight in rural areas away from civilian population centers. But even here, the difference is often less clear than it seems. Urban warfare has long been a major feature of even conventional combat (Stalingrad, Berlin, Caen, and Aachen were among the many cities destroyed by ground warfare in World War II); villages and other built-up areas are traditionally exploited as favorable defensive ground in conventional warfare precisely because of the superior concealment and cover they offer; civilians are often killed in greater number than uniformed soldiers in conventional combat because even the use of uniforms does not always enable combatants to distinguish or discriminate from a distance or in the heat of battle; and all this is becoming increasingly characteristic of conventional warfare as cities grow and economies urbanize around the world.[16] Concealment is thus critical in all modern warfare, guerilla or conventional, and the difference between an emphasis on terrain for such purposes in conventional warfare and on civilian intermingling in guerilla warfare is more a difference in emphasis and relative incidence than a sharp distinction of kind.[17]

Holding Ground

An intention to hold ground is another trait often held to distinguish conventional from guerilla warfare. Conventional armies are normally expected to take and hold ground; guerillas, by contrast, are typically assumed to favor hit-and-run methods in which retention of ground is not attempted and in which the guerillas' orientation is to the enemy, not the terrain as such. That is, the classical guerilla chooses terrain based solely on its potential to enable casualty infliction on the enemy, not for its control per se. Guerillas are expected to melt away when attacked by superior government forces rather than to stand their ground and accept decisive engagement, and they often prefer booby traps, mines, roadside bombs, or harassing rocket or mortar fire meant to inflict casualties without denying the opponent access to an area.[18]

All these techniques, however, are standard elements of orthodox conventional doctrine, too. Delaying actions, for example, are a normal element of any theater defense. In a delaying action, defenders trade space for time, weakening the attacker as it advances, disrupting the attacker's formations, and if possible demoralizing its troops—but without accepting decisive engagement and without expecting to retain any particular piece of ground.[19] Some of the most prominent, and successful, defenses in conventional interstate military history took the form of a trade of space for time, in which ground was not to be retained for its own sake—including the Russian defeat of Napoleon in 1812 and the Soviet defeat of Nazi Germany in World War II. Mobile defense, one of the three basic forms of defensive maneuver in orthodox conventional doctrine, orients the defender on the enemy's forces rather than on particular terrain; terrain is chosen to facilitate the destruction of the enemy, which is the primary objective. Mobile defenses normally involve delaying actions along the attacker's axis of advance; delays without decisive engagement are also central to the conduct of conventional covering force operations in the forward sectors of prepared defenses in depth.[20]

Ambush, moreover, is a standard technique in orthodox defense, in which defenders strive to remain hidden and undetected until attackers have entered a designated kill sack where they can be surprised and taken under sudden and concentrated fire. Such defenders may or may not hold their positions until decisively engaged.[21] Harassing fires from mortars or artillery are common means by which conventional defenders seek to disrupt or interdict enemy movement in otherwise apparently safe rear areas; mines are sometimes used to defend ground that must be retained, but they are also used elsewhere to delay, disrupt, or inflict casualties on attackers in transit without denying them access directly.[22] Orthodox conventional defense by state armies thus commonly includes many actions that do not hold ground per se or accept decisive engagement.

Of course, there are normally geographical limits to delay and harassment in conventional defense; conventional defenders will not allow an invader access to the entire national territory without making a stand somewhere. Ultimately, a conventional defense is intended to leave the defender in control of the country. But even guerillas often have limits on their willingness to allow an enemy to move: critical locations such as base camps or weapon caches can sometimes be defended by fighters who accept decisive engagement in such locations.[23]

Dispersion

Dispersion and the apparent absence of distinctions between a contested front and a safe rear area are other traits commonly associated with guerilla warfare. Guerillas are normally assumed to avoid concentration and instead to spread themselves over large areas in small, independent formations, using stealth, concealment, and infiltration to afford them access to any part of a theater and often choosing preferentially to attack "soft" logistical or support targets in nominal rear areas.[24] Yet dispersion, like concealment, has been a central theme in the history of modern conventional tactics. As early as 1917, conventional militaries discovered that they could not exploit the potential cover inherent in rural terrain while operating in large, concentrated formations. The natural complexity of the earth's surface provides an enormous amount of potential cover from enemy fire, but such "dead ground" is irregularly distributed and often broken into tiny patches. To take advantage of this potential, massed linear formations had to be broken down into small groups with only handfuls of soldiers, sprinting from cover to cover on the basis of the vagaries of the ground rather than the progress of their neighbors. Movement in the presence of the enemy came to depend increasingly on working small groups forward unobserved, using a combination of concealment and suppressive fire to keep them from being annihilated by enemy fire en route. The resulting techniques have sometimes been called "infiltration tactics" as a result, and infiltration per se, often at night, is a standard movement method for infantry in orthodox conventional state armies.[25] Coupled with the increasing depth of modern defenses—the Soviet defensive system at Kursk in 1943, for example, extended over a distance of more than 100 miles from the front line[26]—this dispersion has often resulted in deliberately porous defensive systems in which individual positions have had to be prepared for 360-degree defense and in which friendly and hostile forces are often intermingled in ways that blur the distinction between front and rear. The increasing reach of standoff fires, moreover, has extended the threat of attack even further away from the nominal front. For Germans on the western front in 1944, for example, no location was truly safe from Allied air attack: Erwin Rommel was famously wounded during an administrative movement in a nominal rear area in France during the Normandy campaign when his staff car was strafed by an Allied fighter.[27] Even superpowers with complete air supremacy must expect deep attack against rearward positions in modern interstate war: in the 1991 Gulf War, an Iraqi Scud missile struck an American barracks in Kuwait, killing 28 US soldiers and wounding 98; in the 2003 Gulf War another Iraqi missile struck a US command post south of Baghdad, killing 2 soldiers and wounding 15.[28] And involuntarily bypassed defenders or designed stay-behind forces that allow themselves to be bypassed can pose lethal threats well to the rear even in conventional interstate war: in 2003, a convoy of the US 507th Maintenance company was ambushed by Iraqi state military forces well behind friendly lines, resulting in the deaths of 11 soldiers and the capture of 6.[29] In today's era of deep strike by

precision air or missile forces and rapid movement of battle fronts over confused battlefields, even conventional interstate warfare offers much less
guarantee of safety in the rear than it once did.

Coercive Strategic Intent

Contrasts in strategic intent are another distinction often drawn between guerilla and conventional warfare. In particular, conventional strategy is often seen
as an exercise in what Thomas Schelling termed *brute force*; nonstate guerilla
strategy is usually seen as *coercive* (and sometimes *persuasive*). Coercive strategies work by convincing the enemy to give you what you want by threatening
pain if they do not (persuasion strategies use positive inducement rather than
negative sanction). Brute force strategies work by taking what you want
through force without requiring any meaningful decision on the enemy's
part.[30] Guerillas, in the typical view, are too weak to prevail by outright brute
force destruction of the enemy, hence they must resort to manipulating others'
decision calculus via some combination of persuasion and coercive pain infliction as their only real options—they aim either to convince civilians to oppose
the state, or to kill enough state soldiers or destroy enough state value for the
government (or its foreign backers) to decide that the cost exceeds the stake
at issue in the war, yielding political concession to guerilla demands. States
engaged in conventional warfare, by contrast, are thought to have the material
resources to pursue their aims by brute force and to prefer this.[31]

Coercive intent, however, is hardly unique to nonstate actors or irregular
warfare. On the contrary, if the ultimate goal of almost all warfare is to control
the choices of living civilians then the causal mechanism must ultimately be
coercive for all: the way combatants control the collective decisions of civilian
populations is by shaping their expectations of future violence and reward,
which is the very definition of coercion. There is obviously a great deal of brute
force in the conduct of many wars, this brute force can be critical to the outcome, and variation in the relative incidence and employment of brute force
and coercion is a critical issue for the conduct of any war. But as Schelling
points out, the role brute force plays, even in conventional interstate land war,
is normally to enable eventual coercion of civilians by destroying the enemy
forces that would deny coercive access to the population.[32] And even the destruction of a conventional army in the field typically involves a mix of brute
force and coercion at different levels of war. To encircle a hostile army, for
example, an attacker must first displace defenders in their path at the initial

point of penetration; this can be done by killing them all (pure brute force), but it is normally achieved by killing some and persuading the others to withdraw via the threat of death if they remain (coercion), opening thereby an avenue of advance for exploitation and encirclement. It is possible for war to be purely coercive: Schelling, for example, argues that intercontinental nuclear warfare in an era without missile defense is a contest in pure coercive pain infliction.[33] It is not possible, however, for nongenocidal warfare to be *purely* brute force—if the behavior of survivors has anything to do with combatants' war aims, then coercion is ultimately required to secure these, even for states, and even in nominally "conventional" wars. And most interstate conventional wars involve a great deal of coercion indeed, and at levels of war far beyond the tactical.[34]

As an illustrative example, Allied strategy in World War II involved a great deal of brute force (the intended destruction of Axis militaries)—but it also embraced a strategic bombing campaign whose intent was largely coercive. That is, it was hoped that the destruction of hostile economic assets and population centers would impose so much pain on enemy societies as to convince their leaders to make peace in order to halt it. Many Allied leaders hoped that this could be accomplished without brute force land invasions of Germany or Japan, and in fact Japan surrendered before the home islands were conquered.[35] American strategy in 1991 was a mix of brute force in the ground war to drive Saddam out of Kuwait, and coercion in a strategic bombing campaign intended to increase Saddam's costs by destroying valued assets within Iraq until and unless he agreed to withdraw.[36] NATO strategy in 1999 was chiefly coercive, with the primary aim being to impose financial and political pain on Slobodan Milosevic by bombing valued economic assets in Serbia until and unless he halted ethnic cleansing in Kosovo.[37]

Nor is strategic bombing the only form of coercion in conventional interstate warfare. In almost all such wars, the weaker power must ultimately rely on a coercive logic to prevail. As noted above, in World War II Japan realized it had no chance of destroying the US military—American population, wealth, and industrial advantages were too great, enabling America to crush Japan militarily if it chose to mobilize fully and pay the price. Japan's only hope was to raise the price of doing so to one that Americans would not pay: by killing enough US soldiers, sailors, and Marines in a tenacious defense of their Pacific conquests, the Japanese hoped to convince the Americans to accept a negotiated peace that would preserve Japanese expansion rather than fighting on until Japan was destroyed.[38] Germany is among the states most often cited as relying on brute force battlefield annihilation of military opponents rather than political coercion.[39] Yet German strategy in both world wars came to rely increasingly on political coercion rather than military brute force once the tide of battle turned against them. By 1917, for example, no rational German could conclude that an Allied coalition including the distant United States could be militarily destroyed; the only option was to raise the cost of continuing the war to the point where at least some key opponents would accept a negotiated settlement tolerable to Germany, and German strategy increasingly reflected this.[40] In World War II, even Hitler no longer hoped to destroy Allied armies outright or to deny them access to German soil by 1944; instead German strategy hoped to exploit Western war weariness by inflicting casualties, using a form of coercive cost imposition to split the Allied coalition and persuade Western governments to accept a separate peace that would leave Hitler in power.[41] In all three examples—imperial Japan, Wilhelmine Germany, and Nazi Germany, state governments in "conventional" world wars pursued strategic logics that were centrally coercive. In fact this is such a common great power strategy in major conventional warfare that Clausewitz treats it as a fundamental feature of war per se and discusses it as such explicitly and at length in *On War*.[42] In practical terms, the only meaningful distinction between classically "state" and "guerilla" methods on this score is thus the relative emphasis between coercive and brute force elements of strategies that always involve both.

"Asymmetry": Combatant Distinguishability and Front/Rear Distinguishability

Another distinction often drawn between state and nonstate war making is that states are held to fight one another "symmetrically" (using similar forces, methods, and purposes) whereas nonstate actors fight states "asymmetrically"—using forces, methods, and aims deliberately chosen to differ from those of their state enemies.[43] The claim that nonstate actors use coercion whereas state actors use brute force is one dimension of this asserted asymmetry, but others include the expectation that nonstate actors will field lightly armed guerillas or will resort to terrorism against civilian targets whereas states will field heavily armed formations of uniformed soldiers who seek out combatants rather than civilian targets, or that nonstate actors will employ the hit-and-run tactics of ambush, assassination, and suicide bombing whereas state armies will prefer offensive sweeps, positional defenses of fortified areas, or presence patrolling by maneuvering formations of coordinated infantry.[44]

This distinction is problematic in light of the considerable use by state ac-tors of coercion, concealment, dispersion, and ambush as noted above—these are not literally distinct or characteristic of one class of actor. That said, actors' relative degree of reliance on such methods varies a great deal; perhaps a system-atic difference in the degree of such reliance is a categorical feature of nonstate war fighting. But if so, this cannot be boiled down to a distinction between nonstate "asymmetrical" methods defined as war making preferences that dif-fer from their state opponents' and interstate "symmetrical" warfare in which the combatants' preferences are the same or nearly so. In fact, almost all war-fare is asymmetric in this sense: two combatants will almost never use the same strategy and tactics, whether they are states or not.

The largest interstate war in modern history, World War II, involved major differences in methods and approaches between combatants at all levels of war. In tactics, for example, the German invaders of France in 1940 emphasized combined arms whereas their French and British opponents used armor in-dependently in concentrated, all-tank formations.[45] Both sides had tanks, but their employment was hardly "symmetrical." In theater strategy, the Japanese knew they could not destroy American war-making potential and thus sought to impose coercive pain to wear down American will to fight; the United States, by contrast, aimed chiefly to crush the Japanese military and overrun Japanese-controlled territory outright.[46] Both sides fought for possession of Pacific island chains, but the strategic intent was very different. In grand strat-egy, the Axis powers were originally expansionist, whereas the Allies began the war with status quo objectives.[47] Even in an interstate world war, very little of its conduct involved two sides using literally the same methods; strictly speaking, there is no such thing as truly "symmetric" warfare, and "asymme-try" of some kind is almost universal in war.[48] In literal terms, "asymmetric" warfare is thus meaningless as a distinction.

In practical terms, most of those who use the term "asymmetric warfare" have a much narrower meaning in mind. The asymmetry of interest is usually that between a strong actor (typically a state) using "regular" or "conventional" forces and methods and a weak actor (usually not a state) using "irregular," or "guerilla," or "terrorist" approaches.[49] In this interpretation, it is not a condi-tion of difference per se, but a specific difference characteristic of nonstate guerillas fighting state conventional armies that makes the former "asymmet-ric." But given the lack of bright lines in actual methods between state and nonstate armies as noted above, for this to be meaningful requires a definition based on identity rather than behavior—that is, some clear definition of an "irregular" actor who fights only against a clearly defined "conventional" actor. Yet this is no easier to define than for behavior. Most such attempts to define "irregular" actors focus on either what they wear or where they fight. That is, some try to define an "irregular" (or partisan, or *franc tireur*) fighter as one who wears civilian clothing without distinguishing insignia or uniforms, or one who fights away from an identified battle front, or one who does both. These distinctions are no more helpful than those based on the behaviors of stealth, ground holding, dispersion, or coercion.

International law, for example, defines "irregular" combatants as those who do not wear identifying insignia or carry their arms openly.[50] Yet many historical nonstate actors normally seen as guerillas have done both: the Vietcong, for example, deployed main force fighters who wore khaki-and-green uniforms, and visibly carried assault rifles.[51] The US Defense Department unhelpfully defines irregular combatants as those that are not "regular"; no formal definition of the latter is provided. Irregular warfare, in turn, is defined essentially as whatever nonstate actors do.[52]

Nor is it much help to define an "irregular" warrior as one who fights away from an identified battle front in an undifferentiated theater of war. A standard mission of US Special Forces and elite commando units in most great power state militaries is to penetrate deeply behind enemy lines and operate there for extended periods; few would see the uniformed, highly trained, specially equipped US Green Berets or British Special Air Service commandos as "irregulars" whose distinction from other state soldiers would make their methods un-state-like owing to asymmetry.[53] Nor are operations in great depth the sole province of commandos: when the "front" can be anywhere from 100 miles deep, as at Kursk in 1943, to the depth of the entire theater, as it has become since the dawn of the airplane and the long-range missile, then even areas that would normally be considered the rear can be arenas of highly intense "conventional" combat. While many state armies articulate a highly differentiated theater architecture that distinguishes not just "front" and "rear" but a communications zone, a forward battle area, and a main battle area, this does not mean that combat occurs solely along an identified frontline trace even for great power militaries—hence it is impossible to identify as uniquely "irregular" any warrior who does not fight at the front.

Even this narrower intuitive notion of asymmetry thus breaks down when pressed: it is very hard to define a meaningful concept of "asymmetric" warfare that cleanly distinguishes state from nonstate war making.

A Spectrum between Fabian and Napoleonic Extrema

In fact there are very few, if any, features of modern warfare that are literally, or even mostly, unique to nonstate actors as opposed to state armies. Yet this is not to say that state and nonstate military methods are identical. There *are* important distinctions, but these are interpenetrated matters of degree rather than kind, and the common language of "conventional" and "guerilla" or "irregular" is unhelpful as a vehicle for explaining them—for too many observers, these terms connote discrete, mutually exclusive alternatives. Given this, I instead frame variance in state and nonstate military methods on a continuous spectrum between rarely seen extremes that I will describe as *Fabian* and *Napoleonic*.

These end points represent abstract archetypes—pure versions of the intuition reflected in the terms "guerilla" and "conventional" without the overlapping, shared traits that actual modern militaries display. As such, they will rarely if ever be observed in modern combat. Their role is instead to enable real militaries to be coded in terms of their relative distance from these two abstract extrema.

The *Fabian* archetype is named for the Roman dictator and general Quintus Fabius Maximus Verrucosus (280 BC–203 BC), whose strategy of avoiding battle with the superior Carthaginian army of Hannibal Barca focused on raids and harassment against the Carthaginian's extended lines of communication to exhaust them rather than on destroying them. The term "Fabian strategy" has subsequently become associated with methods of delay and protraction without decisive battle; I use it here to signify a pure version of the intuition behind modern "guerilla" war. As such, I define it as an absolute unwillingness to accept exposure or to defend ground via decisive engagement at any point in the theater; dispersed operations with no local concentrations in excess of the theaterwide combatant density; exclusive reliance on coercion; insistence on concealment obtained via intermingling with the civilian population and rejection of heavy weapons, even when available, in favor of light arms and equipment more suitable to concealment among the population; and a spatially undifferentiated, uniform distribution of forces across the theater without an identifiable front or rear.[54]

Methods of this kind impose stark trade-offs on their users. Fabian methods can radically reduce one's vulnerability to hostile fire (especially so against armies unwilling to target civilians); they can enable small, lightly armed forces to survive long enough to inflict cumulative casualties on the enemy that can eventually become severe; and they can lengthen the war and impose cumulative financial and political costs on opponents that may exceed the enemy's political stake in the conflict. But these advantages come at a heavy price. Unwillingness to accept decisive engagement in defense of terrain, for example, means that no point in the theater can be held—not even critical logistics caches, command posts, or communications nodes, and certainly not concentrations of sympathetic civilians. Dispersed operations with only light weapons and no local concentrations in excess of the theaterwide combatant density mean that pure Fabian raids will be small, unlikely to destroy heavily defended positions, and limited largely to soft targets such as unescorted convoys, isolated posts, economic infrastructure, or civilian gatherings. Concealment among the population risks exposure via informants and heavy casualties to sympathetic civilians if enemy forces attack. Exclusive reliance on coercion allows the enemy to choose whether to continue or concede; it leaves the power to end the war in others' hands. Warfare at the Fabian extreme is thus extremely costly for its users as well as its targets—and it imposes its costs not just on its armed participants but on the civilians whose political allegiance and cooperation are the aim of almost all war making. This approach is uncommon for a reason.

Conversely, the *Napoleonic* archetype is named not for one of its earliest proponents but one of its latest: the French emperor Napoleon Bonaparte, whose armies conquered most of Europe in the early 19th century. Bonapartist Napoleonic warfare emphasized massed formations maneuvering in the open on rural battlefields to destroy hostile armies in brief decisive battles. I use the term here to signify an extreme version of the intuition behind modern "conventional" war. As such, I define it as exposed formations relying on massed firepower in decisive engagement to defend or seize ground that will not be voluntarily relinquished; packed local concentration to shoulder-to-shoulder densities at a point of attack where ground is contested; exclusive reliance on brute force rather than coercion; use of uniformed forces on battlefields removed from urban population centers with preferential employment of the heaviest weapons available to maximize firepower and armor protection; and a spatially differentiated theater of war with clear, mutually exclusive distinctions of front and rear, and with combat limited to identifiable front lines.[55]

As with Fabian warfare, pure Napoleonic methods as framed here impose harsh trade-offs. Napoleonic war fighting maximizes one's short-term firepower and can swiftly annihilate targets exposed to that firepower; it can thus seize or withhold defended stakes and impose political terms on its wielder's timetable. But it makes concealment from enemy fire virtually impossible: its radical exposure makes acceptance of enemy fire the price of projecting one's own. Against better-concealed enemies with high-firepower weapons or even exposed foes of greater size, Napoleonic massed exposure in the open can easily yield suicidal casualty rates. Since industrial-age firepower matured in the early 20th century, few real combatants have been able to survive with such methods long enough to accomplish meaningful military missions; pure Napoleonic war fighting as defined here is thus rare in post-1900, high-firepower warfare for a reason.[56]

Almost all real militaries thus reject both extremes and instead choose varying admixtures of Fabian concealment and Napoleonic firepower—real warfare almost always occupies points well to the interior of this spectrum between pure Fabian and Napoleonic extrema. Nor do state and nonstate actors sort themselves into contiguous, nonintersecting subsets of this continuum. In fact some nonstate actors already employ methods more Napoleonic than those of some states—and some states employ methods more Fabian than some nonstate actors.

The appendix presents a coding system for translating observed characteristics of military behavior in the field into a continuous, real-valued (0, 6) scale of relative adherence to these Fabian and Napoleonic archetypes; this coding system is used in the case studies and empirical illustrations below to identify where on the Fabian-Napoleonic spectrum any given actor's behavior lies. On this scale, the zero extremum corresponds to a (rarely observed) purely Fabian style, the maximum value of six corresponds to a (rarely observed) purely Napoleonic style, and the more commonly observed values in between present relative gradations of increasingly Napoleonic interminglings of archetypical behaviors as the score increases. The coding system does this by distilling from the popular intuition of "guerilla" and "conventional" warfare as described above a series of concrete, specific, observable behavioral correlates, and using their relative prevalence in the always-interpenetrated reality of actual military practice to produce a score for a given military in a given campaign. These observable behaviors correspond to the six intuitive features outlined above and summarized in table 2.1: stealth, holding ground, dispersion, coercion, and the issues of civilian intermingling and theater organization that most meaningfully represent the popular intuition of "asymmetry" in nonstate warfare. The list of specific observable behaviors, the rationale for their inclusion, and the methodology for scoring them are presented in detail in the appendix; for now, it is chiefly important to note that the more a given actor's behavior reflects the popular intuition of "guerilla" or "irregular"

TABLE 2.1. Determinants of Actors' Position on the Fabian-Napoleonic Spectrum

1. Stealth: how covered and concealed are the actor's forces?

2. Holding ground: how often does the actor accept decisive engagement to contest territory?

3. Dispersion: how dispersed are the actor's forces?

4. Coercion: how coercive is the actor's strategy?

5. "Asymmetry": how distinguishable are the actor's forces from civilian noncombatants?

6. "Asymmetry": how uniform and functionally undifferentiated is the actor's organization of the combat theater?

warfare, the lower the index score and the more Fabian the coding; the less a given actor's behavior reflects these features, the higher the index score and the more Napoleonic the coding.

Actors on the Fabian-Napoleonic Spectrum

Figure 2.1 presents a graphic representation of this spectrum, with a variety of illustrative examples of post-1900 combatants—both states and nonstate actors—plotted using the coding system described in the appendix. (Of course this is not an exhaustive coding of the historical universe of such actors; it is illustrative rather than exclusive.)

The Ulster Volunteer Force (UVF) in 1975 represents an intuitively irregular or guerilla force. Its tactics consisted chiefly of assassinations, bombings, ambushes, and raids of brief duration, with small groups of fighters quickly melting away into urban Ulster to avoid government firepower. Their strategy was purely coercive: an attempt to impose costs on the British occupiers without any meaningful prospect of destroying the occupation force or driving them from territory by brute force, in a theater with no meaningful front or rear. But even the UVF departed from the archetype in some respects: larger attacks were mounted at times, demanding greater local concentrations of force. And the UVF adopted distinctive black clothing that visually differentiated its members from noncombatant civilians.[57] By the scoring system in the appendix, its combination of traits yields a value of 0.3—unusually close to the Fabian extreme, but not conforming to the intuitive model in all respects even so.[58]

The RUF (Revolutionary United Front) in Sierra Leone in 1995 was another intuitively irregular guerilla force, with a ragtag mix of equipment and

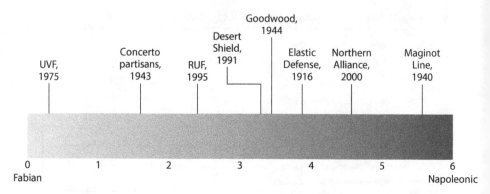

FIGURE 2.1. A Fabian-Napoleonic spectrum of military behavior

clothing and operating chiefly in small formations with an emphasis on ambushes and raids. Yet the RUF nevertheless adopted a number of traits commonly associated with conventional war fighting. Its fighters' clothing and
equipment was polyglot but clearly military in nature. There was an identifiable frontline that moved toward the capital of Freetown as the RUF's fortunes
improved, with relatively secure rear areas away from this and with most fighters concentrated at the front. They sought to capture Freetown by intimidating
government forces into withdrawal, advancing to take ground in a form of
brute force, and they tried to hold ground they had taken against government
counterattack.[59] By the scoring system in the appendix, this combination of
traits yields a value of 2.4—more Fabian than Napoleonic, but further from
the Fabian archetype than the UVF.[60]

The Afghan Northern Alliance of 2000, by contrast, was a nonstate actor
but hardly one that fit the intuitive model of irregular guerilla forces—in fact,
its military methods were more "conventional" in important respects than
those of many states. A coalition of warlords who opposed Taliban rule, the
Northern Alliance waged a static positional defense of a contiguous territory
that encompassed about 15 percent of the country's land area. Their defenses
featured rural entrenchments, wire obstacles, a clear distinction between front
and rear, a clear concentration of combatants at the front, and polyglot but
often clearly military clothing and equipment. They retained territory against
Taliban attack by brute force and used heavy weapons such as tanks whenever
available.[61]

Conversely, some state military organizations have employed decidedly
unconventional methods. The Soviet Union, for example, deployed a

conventional mass military in World War II, but it also fielded an enormous force of irregular partisans who fought German invaders behind German lines. In Operation Concerto in the fall of 1943, over 200,000 such combatants launched an attack on German lines of communication in western Russia. Some wore elements of military uniform; others did not. They relied on ambush, sabotage, and quick hit-and-run raids while avoiding sustained contact with German forces, and they melted away into the civilian population or the surrounding forests when challenged. Their entire area of operation was to the rear of the conventional front, but their purpose was to erase the distinction between a combat front and a safe rear in their operating areas. Yet these apparent guerillas were state combatants operating under a Soviet state military chain of command, and in coordination with the Soviet conventional military's brute force operations.[62] The net result is a state military organization in a world war whose methods were closer to the Fabian extremum than were those of nonstate actors such as the RUF.

A state military much closer to the intuitive archetype of "conventional" warfare in figure 2.1 was the French defense of the Maginot Line in 1940. The Maginot Line was a fixed, positional defense of the French-German border from Switzerland to Luxembourg, with heavily fortified underground concrete bunkers for command, billeting, supply storage, and combat; with armored turrets for artillery and machine guns; and with elaborate wire obstacles overseen by firing positions. Its garrison were uniformed soldiers on a clear front line whose mission was to sustain close combat against attacking forces as long as necessary to defend their positions by brute force. Yet for all that, even the Maginot Line did not conform perfectly to the pure Napoleonic model. In particular, its designers were unwilling to abandon Fabian stealth altogether in the pursuit of Napoleonic firepower: though its fortifications were mostly static, they were sited and designed to provide as much local concealment as possible, with extensive camouflage that included hydraulic mounts to allow entire gun turrets to disappear below grade when not in use. And those positions were not simply massed on the border—instead they were dispersed across a zone distributed over an average depth of 4 kilometers but with some rearward positions more than 20 kilometers from the border.[63] Not even the Maginot Line conforms perfectly to the archetypical conventional model.

Many other state militaries have adopted more substantial elements of the Fabian archetype, and especially its emphasis on cover, concealment, and dispersion. As early as 1916 it had become apparent to all European great power militaries that massed forces in exposed positions could not survive modern firepower. The great trench stalemate on the western front produced preparatory artillery barrages of literally nuclear magnitude: the 10-day Allied bombardment before Messines in July 1917 dropped about 1,200 tons of explosives—in nuclear parlance, more than a kiloton, or more explosive power than the US W48 tactical nuclear warhead—on every mile of German defensive frontage.[64] Not even thoroughly dug-in static defenses could withstand firepower on such a scale—the only solution was to disperse into depth, conceal fighting positions from hostile observation, and rely increasingly on camouflage and mobility rather than concrete—all of which represented a systematic, progressive shift, in multiple state militaries, toward the Fabian end of the spectrum in figure 2.1.

For example, the resulting German "elastic defense" concept of 1916–18 obtained concealment via the terrain and disposed its forces largely around the nature of the terrain rather than the enemy's locations, but was distributed over a depth of 5 to 15 kilometers and was built around the assumption that ground would not be held to the death. In fact, the Germans referred to this doctrine as the *An-sich-herankommen-lassen*, or "invitation-to-walk-right-in," system: attackers would be allowed to advance into the depths of the defense, where they would eventually be halted and repulsed by counterattack. The larger intention was still to retain ground in the end, but it was expected that the means to this end would be fluid and dispersed, involving a heavy emphasis on stealthy movement by small teams, counterattack, and a deemphasis on decisive engagement in static defenses of specific points.[65] This is still a long way from the UVF, but it was substantially less "conventional"—less Napoleonic—than the Maginot Line.

German World War II defensive doctrine was still less intuitively "conventional." The German defenses opposing the British offensive in Operation Goodwood of July 1944, for example, were distributed over a depth of more than 15 kilometers and built around a series of fortified French farming villages whose civilian buildings and outworks were exploited for concealment. Most of the defensive system's combat power was held in mobile reserve still further to the rear, and success rested on the assumption that the prepared positions would merely delay an attack while this large reserve maneuvered fluidly to its flanks for the counterattacks that were expected to halt the attacker; forward defenses were not expected to hold ground to the last cartridge but were to break contact and withdraw if possible in order to reinforce other defenses to their rear.[66]

The US defense of Saudi Arabia in Operation Desert Shield of 1990 was even less like the Maginot Line. Here, a covering force of under 50,000 troops was expected to fight only a delaying action, withdrawing gradually from covered and concealed positions through a zone 130 kilometers in depth without accepting decisive engagement while setting the stage for a climactic action to be fought in a main battle area extending back to 240 kilometers from the frontier. On the critical coastal sector, a total defensive force of less than 170,000 troops was dispersed over more than 30,000 square kilometers (or an average density of under three soldiers per square kilometer) and was expected to fight a fluid, distributed action oriented largely to the enemy rather than the peculiarities of the ground.[67]

In a previous book, I argued that a particular pattern of military behavior, what I called the "modern system," had proven centrally important to success in mid-to-high-intensity continental state warfare since at least 1918.[68] That book excluded nonstate actors from its explanatory domain. But in fact there are powerful elements of underlying commonality between the state "conventional" warfare I treated in *Military Power* and the nonstate military methods under study here. In an important sense, the modern system's birth and subsequent evolution amounted to the adoption of increasingly Fabian methods by state militaries in major warfare for precisely the reasons many assume that nonstate guerillas fight this way: to survive against enemies with radical firepower. To draw a bright line between this and the dispersed, high-concealment methods of many traditional nonstate actors and to call the one "conventional" and the other "guerilla" is thus to miss the fundamental underlying commonality between the functional logic of both. The German defense at Goodwood in 1944 or the American defense of Saudi Arabia in 1990 certainly differed from the UVF's or RUF's methods (or the Vietcong's or those of many others)—but the differences are in degree and are responses to military requirements that are ultimately more similar than different in kind.

(In fact, in an important sense the resulting scale represents a generalization and expansion of the characterization of state military behavior, or "force employment," that I presented in *Military Power*. Whereas *Military Power* treated behavior, or force employment, as an independent variable and used it to explain combat outcomes, here I treat military behavior as a dependent variable and seek to explain it by reference to other causal variables. And whereas *Military Power* focuses on the range of behavioral choices typical of great powers in the post-1918 era—that is, roughly, the two-to-five neighborhood of the spectrum in figure 2.1—here I must treat a wider range of choices, and especially, the theory here must consider explicitly the more Fabian behaviors represented by the zero-to-two neighborhood in figure 2.1. This requirement, plus the theoretical challenges of a dependent variable as multidimensional as the treatment of force employment in *Military Power*, encourages a reframing of military behavior, yielding the treatment presented in this chapter. This reframing, however, does not supersede or invalidate its predecessor: the component elements of the modern system as presented in *Military Power* can be mapped into the Fabian-Napoleonic spectrum here in a way that makes the modern system a special case of this broader Fabian-Napoleonic range.[69])

In all, then, what figure 2.1 shows is thus clearly not a simple, neat, categorical distinction between state conventional and nonstate guerilla warfare. Some states employ military methods that are intuitively close to the Fabian "guerilla" intuitive archetype—as with Soviet state partisans in Operation Concerto, whose conduct fit the Fabian model more closely than did the nonstate RUF. Conversely, some nonstate actors fight in ways that fit the Napoleonic "conventional" intuitive archetype more closely than do many state armies—as the nonstate Northern Alliance demonstrated in Afghanistan. And most state militaries have long adopted major elements of the ostensibly nonstate Fabian archetype, and especially its emphasis on stealth, cover, concealment, dispersal, and rejection of static positional defenses, in favor of fluid movement and counterattack. Nor is there any obvious place to chop the spectrum in figure 2.1 into internally consistent baskets—if one split the difference between the RUF and Desert Shield and declared a value of, say, 2.7 as the boundary between a "guerilla" category of lower scores and a "conventional" category of higher scores, the result would be to lump together actors like the UVF and the RUF, whose methods are actually more different from one another than the RUF is from the state "conventional" methods of Desert Shield.

The more one breaks down the actual conduct of war by state and nonstate actors, the less autonomous or internally consistent either nominal category thus appears. In fact, the typical categorical distinctions are misleading in important respects. There is nothing intrinsic to state status in the conduct of war; there is great variance in the actual military behavior of both state and nonstate actors; and there is important and growing overlap in the methods of nominally "conventional" and nominally "guerilla" warfare. The most interesting and important part of the spectrum is not the conceptually pure extrema—rather it is the conceptually intermingled middle. And the most important developments in military behavior over the last century of warfare have been a series of variations by degree in the behavior of actors whose methods are substantially removed from either simple archetype. To do justice to these developments thus requires us to move beyond the guerilla warfare stereotype and to treat military behavior as a continuous spectrum between uncommon extrema.

In the next chapter, I thus take as my dependent variable this continuous Fabian-Napoleonic spectrum and develop a theory to explain where on this spectrum any given nonstate actor's methods will fall.

3

Materially Optimal Behavior

CHAPTER 2 PRESENTED the theory's dependent variable: military behavior, operationalized as an actor's choice of methods along the Fabian-Napoleonic spectrum. The next two chapters present a theory to explain this choice, using a rationalist causal logic with four independent variables: two that describe materiel (numerical imbalance, and technological sophistication), and two that describe internal politics (institutionalization, and stakes).

The causal logic that interconnects these variables posits that material conditions create a militarily optimal behavioral choice. But not all actors can implement it—internal politics create important constraints on military behavior. Early in the 20th century, the materially optimal behavior for nonstate actors was highly Fabian and easy to implement. Changing technology, however, has moved this optimum toward the middle of the Fabian-Napoleonic spectrum over time, creating increasingly difficult implementation requirements. Nonstate actors with permissive internal politics have been able to meet these requirements and have changed their behavior over time to reflect the changing material optimum. Nonstate actors without permissive politics, however, have been unable to implement complex midspectrum methods and so have retained simpler (but less powerful) highly Fabian methods even as the material military optimum changed. The result has been increasing variance in nonstate behavior over time, as some have, but others have not, been able to respond to changing material military incentives.

The purpose of this chapter is to explain this relationship between materiel and actors' militarily optimal behavioral choice, and to show that over time this optimum has moved toward the middle of the Fabian-Napoleonic spectrum. The purpose of the next chapter is to present the political constraints that can interfere with implementing this material optimum, and to show how variations in stakes and institutions have enabled some nonstate actors, but

MATERIALLY OPTIMAL BEHAVIOR   47

not others, to respond to these material incentives and adopt midspectrum military behavior.

In particular, I argue in this chapter that at any given time, the materially optimal nonstate behavior is determined by the competing demands of the firepower needed to control territory and the cover needed to survive. These virtues are inherently in tension. The best resolution of this tension varies with an actor's usable material superiority or inferiority relative to its enemy. Actors with a usable material advantage can afford the exposure needed to project firepower and control territory; the greater the usable material advantage, then the more the optimal behavior choice favors exposure, firepower, and territorial control, and hence the more Napoleonic is the optimum. Actors inferior in usable materiel cannot survive as much exposure and must accept less ability to control territory as the price of the cover they need to survive; the greater the actor's disadvantage in usable materiel, then the more the optimal behavior choice favors concealment and sacrifices territorial control, and hence the more Fabian is the optimum.

Material advantages derive from both quantity (numbers) and quality (technology), but their relationship has changed over time—which has shifted over time the best resolution of the tension between firepower and cover, shifting in turn the militarily optimal behavioral choice for materially inferior nonstate actors. As time has passed, technology has proliferated, and numerical preponderance has become less usable in battle. These changes have reduced the usable material superiority of states over smaller, poorer, nonstate actors—and this in turn has shifted the material military optimum for such nonstate actors away from the Fabian extremum and toward midspectrum methods.

This reduction in the usable military utility of numerical preponderance—and the associated shift in nonstate military material optima—derives from the growing lethality of increasingly proliferated modern weapons. Modern weapons are lethal enough that even a handful of surviving shooters can annihilate massed enemies in the open; because even a few survivors can accomplish this, it has become harder for technologically superior states to preempt nonstate enemies' ability to punish massed exposure by state forces where nonstate actors deploy modern weapons and use them competently. Instead, states facing such opposition have been forced to demass: to disperse their forces to enable them to find cover. Ever-greater requirements for dispersion, however, have progressively reduced the payoff to numerically large armies. Increasingly, the real limiter on viable troop strength in a combat zone is the ability of the terrain to provide adequate cover to dispersed forces, not

the number of troops theoretically available in a fully mobilized state population. And this has systematically reduced over time the value of one of the
most important material advantages states enjoy over nonstate rivals: numerically superior forces. Of course it always helps to be numerically preponderant, and it always helps to be technologically superior. But technological
change has progressively tilted the playing field over time, constraining states'
ability to exploit their full material advantages, and progressively increasing
the number of nonstate actors with the material wherewithal to compete with
the forces that their state rivals can actually bring to bear.

The net result has been a material military incentive for all actors to move
toward the middle of the Fabian-Napoleonic spectrum. Numerically preponderant, once-Napoleonic states have an incentive to become more Fabian in
the search for cover against increasingly lethal weapons; numerically inferior,
once-Fabian nonstate actors have an incentive to become less Fabian as real territorial control becomes more realistically possible for them. Of course, not all
nonstate actors have the political prerequisites to respond to this incentive—a
point I develop in detail in chapter 4.

This chapter develops its argument in four steps. I begin by identifying the
distinguishing features of nonstate actors as a special case of combatants in
general—and especially their often-smaller resource base. I then discuss the
relationship between lethality (firepower) and survivability (via cover and
concealment) and the tensions between them. I then turn to the theory's two
material variables, technology and numerical preponderance, and explain how
technological change has progressively eroded the utility of numerical superiority. I conclude the chapter by arguing that these material trends have created progressive incentives for both state and nonstate militaries to move
toward the middle of the spectrum in figure 2.1.

Material Differences between State and Nonstate Actors

Weber famously defined the state as a territorially based system of binding
administrative order enforced by a monopoly of legitimate force.[1] Certainly
territorial control, administrative efficiency, and a monopoly of violence
ought to be militarily relevant. And in fact they do give rise to some important differences in the typical material endowments of states and nonstate
actors.

Consider, for example, the number of armed fighters that actors mobilize for
war. Figures 3.1 and 3.2 present histograms for state and nonstate participants'

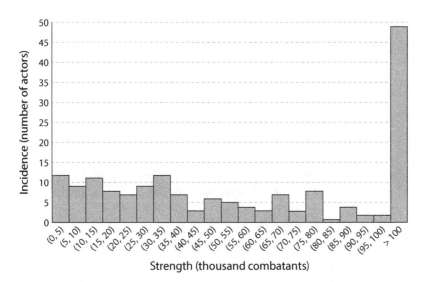

FIGURE 3.1. Distribution of military personnel strength among states

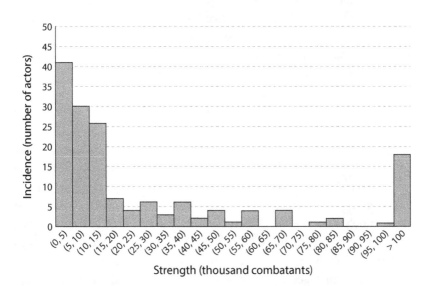

FIGURE 3.2. Distribution of military personnel strength among armed nonstate actors

numerical strength in 160 civil wars between 1914 and 2006.[2] The results suggest two important findings.

First, most states field larger combatant forces than most nonstate actors. The median personnel strength for nonstate actors in these wars was a little over 12,000; the median strength for state combatants was 54,000, or more than four times the median nonstate actor's. In only 52 of the 160 wars studied were nonstate forces even half the size of their state rivals; in 32 cases the state army was more than 10 times larger than the nonstate actor's. This is not surprising. The Weberian state model is premised on contiguous territorial control and administrative capacity; though many states fall short of the full Weberian ideal, state status presumably conveys on average a greater population, tax base, and revenue potential than most actors who lack this status, and this should imply a greater ability to raise and field military forces on average. Indeed this central tendency underlies much of the orthodox literature on nonstate military actors, who are widely assumed to lack the material resources of states and to resort to "asymmetric" or "guerilla" methods as a result.

Second, there is nevertheless a great deal of variance in the size of both state and nonstate armies. The typical nonstate actor fields much smaller forces than the typical state army, but some nonstate forces are much larger than others. In fact, the largest nonstate military in the data set, Mao's Chinese People's Liberation Army in the Chinese civil war, fielded more than two million troops in 1945—making it larger than all but one of the 160 state militaries studied. In fact, almost 20 percent of the nonstate militaries were larger than the median state army; one-fourth of all nonstate armies were within 30 percent of the median state military's size. Not all nonstate militaries are tiny forces dwarfed by much larger state rivals—some are; others are not.

The equipment of state and nonstate actors displays similar trends. Most nonstate actors' tax bases and revenue are smaller than most states', hence their ability to field highly capitalized and heavily armed forces will be less. (They may also *choose* not to use heavy equipment even when available, but that is a behavioral choice—and hence an element of my dependent variable—not a material constraint. Here I focus on material availability alone.) As I note in chapter 5 below, even Hezbollah, an unusually well-funded nonstate actor, nevertheless spent an annual defense budget less than 10 percent of that of its Israeli state rival; the nonstate Croatian ZNG spent far less than one-third as much as did their Jugoslav state opponent in 1990–91.[3] These differences in resources translated into significant differences in capitalization, as described in more detail below.

But this central tendency masks substantial variance among both state and nonstate forces. In particular, almost all nonstate actors have long had potential access to prevailing military technologies via some combination of aid from state patrons, capture from state stocks, smuggling, or the open international arms market. Hezbollah in 2006, for example, deployed modern precision-guided antitank weapons, armed drones, guided antiaircraft missiles, and encrypted communications technology.[4] The Croatian ZNG in 1991 deployed tanks, heavy artillery, armored personnel carriers, and wire-guided antitank missiles.[5] Ukrainian separatist rebels in 2015 fielded T-64 tanks, SA-11 guided antiaircraft missiles, and modern reconnaissance drones.[6] Even the Vietcong of 1965, a force much noted for its absence of heavy weapons, nevertheless equipped essentially its entire force with fully automatic small arms of a lethality that state militaries' infantry had not routinely attained before the 1950s.[7] Such equipment is rarely on the very cutting edge of technological possibility for its day—the state innovators whose arsenals push the technical envelope rarely export their most sophisticated weapons, even to close state allies. But the best weapons fielded by actors such as Hezbollah or the ZNG were broadly representative of what most states were fielding at the time even if their arsenals as a whole were less heavily capitalized than their state rivals."[8]

More broadly, the median nonstate actor has never had access to the quality of equipment fielded by the contemporary median state—but the difference in actual fielded weapon quality between the median state and the median nonstate actor is probably not radically different from the imbalance in their fielded quantity of troops. And the variance in quality within the state and nonstate categories, like the variance in troop quantity, has long been substantial.

On average, most nonstate actors are thus weaker materially and institutionally than most states. But this is a central tendency in categories that display a great deal of internal variance, not an absolute, mutually exclusive distinction or an intrinsic difference between all states and all nonstate actors.

The Trade-Off between Lethality and Survivability

The militaries who use this materiel must both inflict and survive violence. These needs, however, are in tension. To wield the sword, one must emerge from behind the shield, enabling the enemy to land a counterblow. This tension gives rise to a basic trade-off between lethality and survivability—the firepower needed to kill the enemy, versus the cover and concealment needed to survive return fire—whose resolution shapes much of military behavior in war, and especially the distinction between archetypically Napoleonic and Fabian warfare.

In fact, the heart of the distinction between the methods of pure Napoleonic and pure Fabian warfare lies in the tension between the demands of

inflicting and surviving violence: the Napoleonic extremum radically privileges the former at the expense of the latter; the Fabian extremum does the
opposite. Yet both are important, and both must be combined to achieve the
ultimate political purpose of warfare. And it is this need to combine two conflicting virtues that gives rise to the interpenetrated nature of almost all real
combat: armies that need to coerce or protect civilian populations cannot afford to choose either perfect survivability with zero lethality or perfect lethality
with zero survivability and must instead reach some compromise between the
two extremes.

To understand the nature of that compromise and its relationship to materiel and politics, it is first necessary to explore the reasons for the tension in
somewhat greater detail.

Any military actor can reduce its vulnerability to enemy fire by changing its
behavior—but this change normally reduces its ability to kill the enemy, other
things being equal, at any given moment. In conventional wars, for example,
infantrymen can protect themselves from hostile fire by sheltering in foxholes.
But complete protection makes it impossible for them to fire their rifles; to fire
they must expose their head and shoulders above the parapet. Fire requires
exposure. Mortar crews can protect themselves by taking positions behind
hills or buildings, exploiting their weapons' high trajectory to reach over such
obstacles. But the act of firing risks giving their position away—the sound can
be detected, and sophisticated enemies can sense the projectiles themselves
with radars, computing the firing location from the shells' path. Artillery and
long-range missiles face similar dilemmas: their range enables a degree of security by standing back from the enemy, but firing creates detectable sound,
flash, smoke, or moving projectiles, any of which can in principle be sensed
and used to direct return fire. And the very distance that helps protect the
shooter also reduces the effectiveness of its fire: for a constant aiming error,
increased range implies greater miss distance at the target. Even terminally
guided weapons, whose accuracy is potentially independent of range, need
information on the target's location, and this need for a sensor that can detect
the target creates a vulnerability in the form of a platform whose performance
is itself proportional to its proximity to the target, and thus its exposure to fire
from that target. The only way to ensure survival of the firing system as a whole
is to remain silent in hidden locations without firing.

Sometimes these risks can be very low, but they are never zero. When opponents are very mismatched materially, the more advanced combatant can

sometimes seem invulnerable even when killing en masse. Tanks can overrun machine guns that cannot penetrate their armor; modern jet aircraft can drop guided bombs from altitudes beyond the reach of simple handheld air defense weapons. But even the most advanced modern tank can be destroyed by light weapons aimed against vulnerable flank or rear armor surfaces if enemies are given a clean shot at the right range.[9] Even a pilot flying too high to be hit by an unsophisticated enemy still takes a risk that engine failure over hostile territory could lead to capture. Such extrema are very low risk, but even they are not *zero* risk.[10] Most interactions in war are far less one-sided.

Tanks, for example, have almost never been literally invulnerable. Effective antitank weapons appeared within months of the tank's appearance in 1916; by August 1918, rapidly improving antitank technology had contributed to loss rates as high as 98 percent for Allied tanks in the Battle of Amiens.[11] Doctrines for armored warfare since 1918 have regularly reinforced the importance of cover and concealment on the battlefield even for tanks.[12] Aircraft with precision guided weapons can strike ground targets at increasing ranges, but ground-based antiaircraft weapons that can benefit from cover and concealment amid complex terrain have systematic advantages that have given rise to growing concerns with "anti-access/area denial" threats that could make penetrating defended airspace prohibitively expensive.[13] Air warfare has always involved a balance between the potential lethality of aircraft and their potential exposure in the air. For almost all real combatants, survivability in the presence of the enemy requires some degree of concern for cover and concealment.

The same trade-offs are at work whether the combatants have tanks and aircraft or merely assault rifles and roadside bombs. Lightly armed nonstate fighters can protect themselves from government forces by wearing civilian clothing and blending into the community. But to kill soldiers or police they must move weapons or explosives into position, creating a risk of detection by taking actions that innocent civilians would not. If fighters do nothing suspicious, they cannot be detected and killed or captured—but they also cannot kill or damage their opponents. Lethality still requires exposure. Terrorists can reduce the danger of detection by hostile intelligence services if they restrict their movements, limit their communications, and aggressively vet potential recruits. But to conduct attacks they must plan their actions, collaborate with specialists in explosives or infiltration, and move weapons and agents, all of which creates a risk of compromise. To kill others, even terrorists must risk detection and death or capture.[14]

This trade-off is both ubiquitous and continuous: if we hold materiel constant and assume a combatant fighting in a way that minimizes exposure, to increase lethality requires a decrease in survivability and vice versa. Violence requires risk, and the more violence a given combatant metes out, the longer the exposure and the greater the risk. An infantryman who pops above the foxhole's parapet, fires a quick burst, and ducks again is at modest risk but can neither sustain a high rate of fire, nor aim well enough to hit moving targets. Greater lethality demands longer exposure to find targets, aim shots, and fire more rounds, all of which increases the shooter's near-term vulnerability other things being equal. Mortars, artillery, or missile launchers that fire a round then move to another location ("shooting and scooting") limit their vulnerability to return fire directed against the source of the sound, flash, or projectile flight. But the shooters cannot fire accurately while on the move; time spent moving is typically time spent without firing. To increase the rate of effective fire means fewer, shorter moves and more rounds fired in each position, all of which increases the danger of counterfire arriving before the shooter can escape. Nonstate fighters take a risk of detection every time they launch an ambush or lay a roadside bomb; the more ambushes and the more bombs per week, the less time available for planning each one, and the more opportunities to be killed in the act. The more lethal a given combatant chooses to be, the more exposed he or she will be, and vice versa.

To control territory and the choices of the civilians who live there, however, requires lethality. If the ultimate aim of most warfare is to provide some combination of coercive leverage and security reassurance for a civilian population, this cannot be accomplished by combatants who maximize their own survivability with complete cover and concealment: this can neither protect friendly civilians from rivals, nor threaten others. But zero survivability is no better. This may afford great firepower in the short term, but the exposure this requires will normally enable better-concealed enemies to annihilate quickly their exposed tormentors, ending the threat and eliminating its influence over the population. Lethality (or firepower) and survivability (via cover and concealment) are both virtues, but they are in tension and must be balanced to serve the ultimate purpose of war.

How should this balance be drawn? Ceteris paribus, the balance that best serves the ultimate purpose of controlling territory and its civilian inhabitants is shaped by the relative usable material strength of the two sides. The stronger the materiel an actor can bring to bear relative to its foe, the more successfully its fire can kill enemy shooters, preempting their return fire, and the more tolerant of enemy fire an actor can afford to be while either coercing or protecting civilians, and vice versa. Even very superior armies can rarely preempt enemy fire altogether—in land warfare, as I argue below, cover and concealment are too widely available for this—hence some balance between the conflicting virtues of lethality and survivability is almost always best. But usable material superiority shifts the ideal balance in the direction of accepting greater exposure in order to project greater firepower.

The Effects of Technology and Numerical Imbalance

Where does usable material advantage come from? It stems from two interrelated sources: technology, and numerical preponderance. Yet their relationship is not simple and additive. In fact, over time, increasingly lethal technology has been progressively eroding the military utility of numerical preponderance, reducing numerically superior actors' ability to bring their numbers to bear on the battlefield.

Perhaps the most important trend in military technology over the past century and a half has been increasing potential lethality. Above I noted the growing lethality of antitank weapons in World War I, but this reflects a much broader trend.

As I argued in a previous book, industrialization brought a major increase in the firepower of European armies by 1914.[15] In 1812, muzzle-loading brass cannon could fire one 12-pound ball 1,000 yards every 30 seconds; by 1914, steel breechloaders could fire more than twice as many 18-pound shells to 10 times the distance in less than 20 seconds.[16] A Napoleonic infantry battalion of 1,000 men with smoothbore flintlock muskets could project 1,000 rounds to an effective range of 100 yards twice a minute; a bayonet charge by a comparable formation would thus receive about 2,000 rounds before reaching its target, or about 2 shots fired at each soldier.[17] By 1916, an infantry battalion with 1,000 magazine rifles and four machine guns could project over 21,000 rounds to distances of over 1,000 yards every minute.[18] An assault by a comparable unit could absorb over 210,000 rounds in the time needed to close, or more than 200 per targeted soldier—an increase of more than two orders of magnitude. As a result of the enormous increase in iron and steel production over this period, the armies of the 20th century could be equipped with such weapons on a monumental scale. French iron and steel output grew by more than a factor of 15 between 1815 and 1914, enabling France to deploy by 1914 a multimillion-man army capitalized to a level that Napoleon could never have dreamed: in 1815, the French Army deployed around 3 crew-served weapons per 1,000 soldiers; by 1918, the figure had grown to more than 30.[19]

It is widely noted that these developments brought a radical increase in firepower to the battlefields of the First World War; less widely noted is that this expansion in lethality was not limited to World War I. In fact it has been an ongoing, defining characteristic of modern warfare for over a century. Figures 3.3 through 3.7 illustrate these trends in greater detail.

Taken together, they show a clear trend of major, continuing increases across a wide range of lethality indicators over more than a century of technological change. Figure 3.3 presents the reach of the primary firepower source on the 20th-century battlefield, field artillery, over time, for a range of representative European and American weapons. The artillery associated with the great trench stalemate of the western front had an average range of around 10 kilometers; by the end of the century this had increased by a factor of four.[20] Figure 3.4 presents a measure of the destructiveness of the fire that artillery was projecting to those ranges: that is, the lethal area against exposed infantry per round fired. First World War field artillery averaged less than 5,000 square meters of lethal area per round; by the end of the 20th century, weapons with five times that effect were not uncommon.[21] Figures 3.5 and 3.6 give comparable figures for ground-attack aircraft, with very similar findings: technological change since the First World War has increased the reach and payload of air attack by a factor of 5 and 10, respectively.[22]

Of course, as weapons improved so did protective armor. The trend in the modern gun-armor race, however, has strongly favored the gun. As an illustrative example, figure 3.7 presents the weighted mean lethal range for the armor-penetrating weapons in a US armored division when fired against the tanks in a representative opposing division (that is, the maximum range at which one side's antitank weapons could penetrate the other side's tank armor); this measure of net lethality increased by a factor of 10 between 1945 and 2000.[23]

Nor were these trends limited to heavy weapons and aircraft. The small arms carried by all actors' infantry and which constitute a central weapon in many nonstate arsenals saw a comparable increase in performance, and especially in their rate of fire. From the late 19th century through the early 1950s, the standard-issue infantry weapon in all world armies was one or another variant on the bolt-action or magazine-fed semiautomatic rifle. Such weapons had maximum rates of fire that ranged from 10–50 rounds per minute, with the practical rate dependent heavily on the user's training and skill. By contrast, the Soviet AK-47 of 1949, the first widely available fully automatic assault rifle

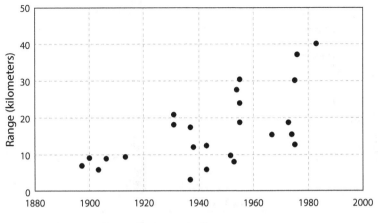

FIGURE 3.3. Artillery range

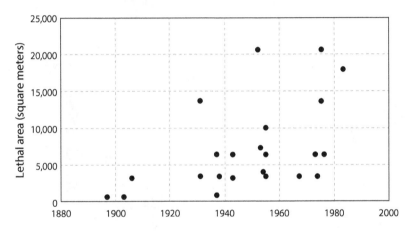

FIGURE 3.4. Artillery lethal area

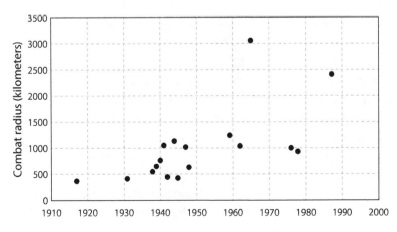

FIGURE 3.5. Attack aircraft combat radius

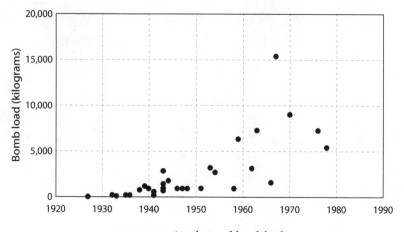

FIGURE 3.6. Attack aircraft bomb loads

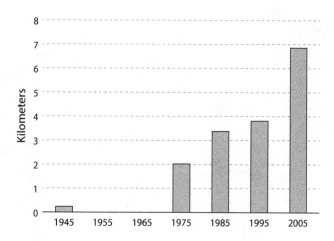

FIGURE 3.7. Mean penetration range of heavy US antitank systems

and perhaps the single most common weapon in modern nonstate arsenals, has a cyclic rate of fire of 600 rounds per minute, or well in excess of 10 times the firing rate of First World War rifles. Moreover, the AK-47 and its imitators required little skill to reach the cyclic rate: simply holding the trigger down was sufficient to expend the magazine at the weapon's maximum theoretical rate of fire.[24]

And as great power weapons in all these categories improved, highly lethal firepower spread outward to other actors. Indirect fire, for example, was largely a state prerogative in World War I; by the 1960s, mortar technology was nearly ubiquitous among nonstate as well as state actors. Early in the 20th century, crew-served machine guns were limited to state armies—and were deployed in relatively small numbers even by the great powers in 1914—but were routine among nonstate arsenals by midcentury.[25] Tanks first appeared on the battlefield in 1916 and still constituted a small fraction of even great power arsenals in 1945, yet by 1990 more than one-fourth of all nonstate actors in the more than 100 civil wars studied by Kalyvas and Balcells deployed tanks, armored personnel carriers, and/or heavy artillery; by 2004, almost half of them did.[26] Nonstate Biafran rebels from 1967 to 1970, UNITA rebels in Angola in 1987, Abkhazian separatists between 1992 and 1994, and Armenian rebels in the Nagorno-Karabakh war of 1991–94, for example, all used heavy armored vehicles that were technologically superior to anything fielded by any of the great powers in World War II.[27] Precision-guided weapons first appeared in sustained combat in 1967 when the US Air Force used them in Vietnam; by 1994, even Somali tribal militias had gained access to Russian-made SA-7 infrared-guided antiaircraft missiles and American-made wire-guided TOW (tube-launched, optically tracked, wire-guided) antitank missiles.[28]

In fact, some nonstate actors have deployed weapons whose sophistication approached—or at times equaled—that of their state enemies. The T-64 tanks fielded in 2015 by the Ukrainian separatists noted above, for example, are also the most common tank model in today's Ukrainian state arsenal; the separatists' Russian-made SA-11 phased-array, radar-guided antiaircraft missiles are often compared to the US Patriot system and are equal to the most sophisticated air defense systems in the Ukrainian state military.[29] Hezbollah in 2006, as noted above, deployed armed drone aircraft, radar-guided antiship missiles, mobile encrypted communications equipment, infrared-guided antiaircraft missiles, and laser-guided antitank weapons, inter alia. While their Israeli state opponents deployed classes of weapon that Hezbollah lacked (such as jet aircraft or tanks), the weapons Hezbollah actually fielded were often comparable technologically to Israel's. Hezbollah's Russian-made Kornet antitank missiles, for example, introduced in 1998, were arguably superior to Israel's American-made TOW-2s (introduced in 1987); Hezbollah's SA-16 antiaircraft missiles, introduced in 1986, were at least as sophisticated as the Israelis' FIM-92A Stinger of 1978.[30] The Croatian separatist ZNG militia in 1991 deployed several hundred T-55 tanks, M-80 infantry fighting vehicles, and wire-guided antitank missiles of identical make and sophistication to those wielded by their Jugoslav national army opponents.[31] The TOW missiles owned by the Somali SNA tribal militia were the equal of any guided antitank weapon in the Israeli, French, or German state arsenals in 1994.[32]

None of this is to suggest that nonstate actors all deploy weapons of comparable sophistication to those of states, or in comparable numbers, or that the cutting edge of superpower weapon technology instantly finds its way into any nonstate actor's arsenal. But there is a surprisingly rapid diffusion of great power weapon technology both horizontally among great powers and vertically from state to nonstate actors. On average, most states' weapon technology at any given time is more sophisticated and more lethal than most nonstate actors'—but here, too, there is substantial variance within each category. And the diffusion process gives many nonstate actors access to weapon technology that would often have been considered cutting edge in interstate warfare only a few years earlier. The net result has been a dramatic increase in the lethality of nonstate, as well as state, arsenals over the last century of warfare.

These technology trends have had important implications for the utility of numerical preponderance. It is always better to outnumber an opponent. But the benefits of preponderance have been shrinking progressively as weapon technology has grown more lethal and as it has proliferated ever more widely.

This is because modern firepower is now so lethal that even small numbers of weapons can quickly saturate whole areas with lethal fires at a density that would kill or wound as many exposed soldiers as an enemy might unwisely try to rush through the killing field. This was not true in Napoleon's day—in 1815, a massed infantry column with sufficient motivation could overrun an outnumbered defense by frontal assault with enough survivors to prevail. Those days are now long gone. As early as 1914, as few as four 75-millimeter field guns could saturate an area the size of a football field with lethal shrapnel in a single volley; the French 1897 Model Soixante-Quinze could do this 15 times in a minute with sufficient ammunition.[33] Machine guns of the 1914 era could saturate the space in front of them with more bullets than attackers could fit bodies.[34] Against modern firepower, even massive numerical advantages are no longer enough to overwhelm even small enemy forces by exposed frontal assaults, as early attempts to do so showed very clearly: on July 1, 1916, for example, the Inniskilling Fusiliers lost over 70 percent of their entire troop strength in just 30 minutes in attempting to charge a handful of surviving German machine guns and artillery pieces on the first day of the Somme offensive.[35]

Tanks are harder to kill than exposed soldiers, but even tanks can rarely overwhelm modern defenses by sheer force of numbers. As Amiens demonstrated in 1918 and as figure 3.7 shows, tanks are hardly invulnerable, and even well-armored tanks can be slaughtered en masse by modern weapons if caught in the open in massed formations. In skilled hands, a battery of six World War II–era 85-millimeter antitank guns, for example, could kill more than 17 exposed midcentury tanks in a single minute of firing at close range; a half dozen midcentury Sagger wire-guided antitank missiles could kill more than 20 exposed tanks in 10 minutes at ranges of up to three kilometers.[36] Small numbers of such weapons can make it prohibitively expensive for even heavily armored attackers to try to saturate such fire with sheer mass in a frontal assault, and armies that have tried this have often suffered gravely. On a single day, October 8, 1973, the Israeli Army lost 180 of 290 exposed tanks that tried to overrun Egyptian antitank positions in the Sinai.[37] In just 40 minutes in 1991, a single US cavalry troop of fewer than two dozen armored vehicles destroyed 69 exposed Iraqi tanks and armored personnel carriers in the Battle of 73 Easting.[38] In July 1944, the British attempted in Operation Goodwood to overwhelm German defenses by concentrating three whole armored divisions on less than a three-kilometer front and rushing them forward against an outnumbered German defense that had just been struck with a 7,900-ton carpet bombing from Allied aircraft; if ever a massed, numerically superior tank attack was going to crush antitank defenses by force of numbers, this should have been the time. Yet the offensive instead failed with ruinous losses: the "death ride of the armoured divisions," as Alexander McKee phrased it, suffered over 400 tank losses, or fully a third of all the British armor on the continent of Europe at the time, in less than three days' fighting.[39] In the face of such slaughter, most combatants quickly abandon any idea of using numerical mass to overwhelm intact defenses by exposed frontal assault.[40]

Nor can counterfire with comparable weapons solve the problem by turning the same technology on the enemy. As early as 1915, most First World War armies had already pivoted from the hasty direct frontal assaults of 1914 to an alternative doctrine in which assaults were delayed while massed preparatory barrages using the attackers' own firepower tried to destroy defenses preemptively. The results were little better. The problem is that modern weapons are so lethal that even a handful of survivors can do tremendous damage to exposed targets in massed formations when these targets eventually appear. Preemptive fires with modern weapons can inflict heavy casualties on defenders, but if defenders are properly dug in then it is very hard for even very lethal fires to kill them all, and even a few surviving defenders with modern weapons of their own can slaughter attackers who try to mass assault forces in the open as Bonaparte and his contemporaries had done.[41]

French defenses at Verdun in 1916, for example, endured a nuclear-scale two-day German artillery barrage equal to about 1,200 tons of explosives. Firepower on this scale killed many of the defenders—but not all, and with modern weapons of their own, the survivors could still halt a massed, exposed German assault.[42] In 1917, German defenses at Messines absorbed more than a kiloton of explosive power per mile of frontage, yet the survivors still halted the ensuing British offensive.[43] Nor did this approach fare any better after 1917. At Cassino on March 15, 1944, heavily outnumbered German positions in the village were struck by 300 tons of bombs in a single day, yet those who lived through the bombing could still halt the associated Allied infantry advance.[44] The 1944 carpet bombing at Goodwood concentrated more than 4,500 Allied aircraft, three corps' worth of artillery, and naval gunfire from two Royal Navy cruisers and the monitor *Roberts* to deliver the equivalent of more than eight one-kiloton nuclear weapons on German defenses at Caen; this inflicted horrific casualties on the German defenders, some of whom went mad from the sheer intensity of the bombing, yet the residual whom the bombing did not kill still prevented a massed, exposed British tank charge from breaking through.[45] As recently as 2002, massive precision-guided US preparatory fires failed to annihilate Al Qaeda defenders of Takur Ghar mountain in Afghanistan's Shah-i-Kot valley in Operation Anaconda; the Al Qaeda survivors fired on the US Special Operations Forces that were subsequently inserted, forcing their withdrawal; four months earlier, in November 2001, more than 48 hours of carpet bombing by American B-52s failed to annihilate Al Qaeda defenders at Bai Beche, who survived in sufficient numbers to drive back US-allied Afghan ground forces with heavy losses.[46]

In fact, neither superior numbers nor even crushing counterfire are adequate solutions in themselves to the problem of modern firepower. And as a result, the progressive increase in lethality over the last century and a half of warfare has thus slowly, progressively eroded the real military utility of numerical preponderance—and forced even well-equipped state armies to adopt behavioral changes, rather than merely material modernization, to accomplish meaningful military missions on the increasingly lethal modern battlefield.

Incentives for Military Behavior

These material trends thus created important behavioral incentives. In particular, they have encouraged all actors to move progressively toward the center of the behavioral spectrum in figure 2.1, other things being equal.

Incentives for State Behavior: Become More Fabian to Escape Modern Firepower

Consider, for example, numerically preponderant state actors and the incentives created for them by changing technology. By as early as 1914, the firepower depicted in figures 3.3 through 3.7 had made exposed, Napoleonic mass movement in the open suicidal for even very preponderant attackers with even the best weapons available. To survive in the face of what Ernst Junger called the "storm of steel" created by post-1900 weapons has thus long required behavioral adaptation.[47]

In particular, states discovered, early in the 20th century, that survival on the modern battlefield required them to reduce Napoleonic concentration and exposure, and to combine preemptive and suppressive fires with some form of cover and concealment to reduce exposure. In an earlier book, I argued that the search for an effective combination of suppressive fire, cover, and concealment produced a transnational body of ideas on the conduct of interstate war that I have termed the "modern system" of force employment.[48] I will not reprise that argument in full here. But it is important to note that modern-system force employment represents an explicit movement toward a more Fabian style of war fighting by advanced state actors waging even interstate world wars. The very heart of the modern system is cover and concealment to reduce exposure to modern firepower—most of its other component elements (such as dispersion, suppression, small-unit independent maneuver, combined arms, depth, and reserves) are merely the means by which state militaries created cover and concealment for themselves while carrying out meaningful military missions. As noted above in chapter 2, cover and concealment are perhaps the two most salient elements of the commonplace intuitive notion of "guerilla" warfare—the adoption by many great power militaries of the modern system in increasingly aggressive form thus represents a progressive movement by states toward the military methods often associated intuitively with nonstate guerilla fighters. And this state adaptation toward increasingly Fabian behavior is at its root a response to the incentives created by technological change and the increasingly lethal firepower this has wrought.

To understand how this evolution in state military behavior has affected nonstate actors' incentives, it is worth considering in detail one particular consequence of the modern system's emphasis on cover and concealment: dispersion.

Cover and concealment deny defenders visible targets. Modern weapons project great quantities of steel, but they still need targets to aim at, and an unblocked line of flight from the launcher or barrel to the target. Concealment thwarts the former; cover thwarts the latter. Both are widely available, even where the terrain is apparently flat and open. The earth's surface is extremely irregular. Hills, gullies, slopes, vegetation, buildings, fences, and walls radically reduce defenders' lines of sight—especially for defenders with their eyes at ground level (as are trench dwellers' when peering over the parapet to fire).[49] Less than two feet of net elevation difference can conceal a prone soldier from a machine gunner dug in with the barrel at ground level. Few of us can keep our entire front lawns under observation from true ground level; the much less regular surfaces of rural battlefields thus offer an enormous amount of potential cover, and especially so after artillery has added shell holes to the natural variation in the terrain. Even virgin land, however, offers ample cover to attackers trained to find it: in the North German plain, more than 65 percent of the ground within 1,000 meters is invisible to a typical weapon position; in the more rolling, broken terrain of the Fulda Gap more than 85 percent is invisible.[50]

This natural cover, though widely available, is very irregularly distributed and often appears in small, noncontiguous patches. Such cover can be very effective in reducing vulnerability to modern firepower, but to exploit it requires breaking up the large, massed formations of Bonaparte's day and spreading out small groups of soldiers over much wider areas. This dispersion is itself useful in reducing vulnerability: the fewer the soldiers in the blast radius of a single shell, the fewer the casualties per round of accurately delivered hostile artillery. But in addition to reducing the victim count per round that hits its target, dispersion is essential for reducing the number of hits by improving armies' ability to find cover and deny their enemies targets at which to shoot.

Consider, for example, Bonaparte's dispositions for his decisive victory at Austerlitz in 1805, the battle that ended the War of the Third Coalition. Austerlitz pitted a total of almost 160,000 soldiers (73,000 French and 85,000 Coalition) on a battlefield of roughly 10 by 11 kilometers.[51] And on this compact battlefield, the troops themselves maneuvered over open ground in exposed, shoulder-to-shoulder formations that would have presented easy, massed targets to modern artillery. In fact, at these densities, the entire French army at Austerlitz could have been wiped out in minutes by less than 100 rounds of 1914-era 75-millimeter artillery fire.[52] If Austerlitz had been fought in 1914 instead of 1805, either these armies would have been slaughtered in the blink of an eye, or they would have been forced to spread out dramatically in order to survive. This is for several reasons. First, they would have had a powerful incentive to put more space between soldiers in any given formation. Let us assume a fairly modest adaptation: an increase to a five-meter spacing between troops (equal to the lethal radius of a modern hand grenade). But this is just a stopgap to reduce the damage if hit—to avoid getting hit one needs cover and concealment. So let us further assume that commanders avoid open ground wherever possible, seek out forests and villages, and avoid filling those forests and villages with so many troops that an enemy could simply barrage them blind and still destroy one's army. To find enough cover for Austerlitz's armies under these assumptions would have required those 160,000 soldiers to distribute themselves over roughly 3,500 square kilometers of the Bohemian countryside—that is, a deployment area over 30 times the size of the 1805 battlefield.[53]

In fact, the need to disperse in order to find cover from modern weapons is a systematic phenomenon and has given rise to a progressive increase in the area occupied by combat forces over time—what is sometimes called a decrease in the average "force-to-space ratio," or fsr. As weapons have grown more lethal, armies have responded with ever lower fsr's.

Figure 3.8 presents on a semilog scale a representative range of force-to-space ratios for battles fought between state armies from 1800 to 2000.[54] In the 19th century, interstate troop densities changed little, with values over a century of warfare lying in a roughly constant band of between 1,000 and 10,000 troops per square kilometer. After around 1900, however, state behavior changes and troop densities begin to fall dramatically. By World War I, typical troop densities had fallen by about a factor of 10 from the 19th-century norm; by World War II they had declined by another factor of 10 to values around 1 percent of typical 19th-century practice. And in Operation Desert Shield of 1991, US troop density had fallen to just 2.3 soldiers per square kilometer, or a value less than one-six-hundredth of Bonaparte's at Austerlitz, or one-three-thousandth of those of the armies at Waterloo in 1815. On average, troop density in interstate warfare has fallen by about a factor of more than 1,000 over the last hundred years of warfare.

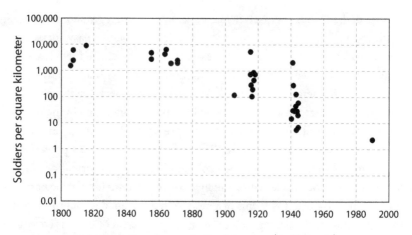

FIGURE 3.8. Force-to-space ratio, state actors (semilog scale)

Taken together, the state military behavior these incentives have encouraged has thus been increasingly Fabian, even in interstate, high-intensity world wars. But the same, technologically driven behavioral changes in state war making have had important, but opposite, effects on nonstate actors' incentives in intrastate civil warfare.

Incentives for Nonstate Behavior: Become Less Fabian to Exploit Opportunity

For materially weaker nonstate actors, the same material trends have encouraged adaptation away from the Fabian extremum as a means of exploiting the opportunities created by the changing behavior of states.

Whereas changing technology has driven large state militaries toward Fabianism, weak actors started there. Against numerically preponderant state foes, 19th-century insurgents had no choice but to adopt highly Fabian methods for survival. In Bonaparte's day, few nonstate insurgents could hope to prevail in a toe-to-toe slugfest against a state army with 4 to 10 times more troops overall and the capacity to concentrate these masses at a point to crush an opponent. Nonstate forces at such a disadvantage could survive only by resorting to highly concealed, intermingled postures with an emphasis on ambush, raids, and other hit-and-run tactics that did not risk decisive engagement with superior state forces. In the 19th century, states could afford to mass troops in the open, but nonstate militaries could not.[55]

Such highly Fabian methods may have enabled insurgents to survive, but they impose enormous political and military costs on their adherents. With no ability to control terrain, Fabian insurgents cannot exclude state armies from access to the civilian population whose decisions both sides seek to influence. Wartime civilian political alignment is strongly influenced by perceptions of future violence, and inability to protect sympathizers or punish adversaries can cede control of a population to rivals who can. Where Fabian nonstate methods preclude real control of ground, superior government forces can punish insurgent collaborators, reward local allies, detain and interrogate suspects, collect taxes, and combine coercive sanction and co-optative assistance as needed. Nonstate fighters can still terrorize hostile civilians unless government forces can literally blanket a population, but it is much harder for outnumbered insurgents to protect friendly civilians from the government if the latter has access to their homes, and governments who can combine such access with superior resources can impose severe costs on insurgents and their supporters. Stathis Kalyvas argues that wartime civilian political alignment often conforms to local military control; for highly Fabian insurgents, lack of such control is a steep price to pay.[56]

Fabian methods also have serious military drawbacks. Just as they cannot deny an enemy access to a civilian population, so they cannot protect friendly base areas, logistical caches, leadership hideouts, or training camps. Periodic raids or sweeps by state armies can thus destroy such infrastructure almost at will. Fabian guerillas can rebuild them unless state forces can sustain a persistent occupation, but each new construction project is at risk just like its predecessors, and the regular loss of capital poses important costs to materially inferior actors whose ability to extract tax revenue is limited by their inability to control access to the population. Insecure base areas also make all other military operations substantially more difficult. Without secure headquarters, planning for complex operations becomes much harder. Without secure training areas, force development becomes much more challenging. Without secure billeting, it becomes much more complicated to provide medical care, reorganization after combat losses, replacement of casualties, and reequipment. Without secure supply dumps, sustaining intense fire or extended maneuver becomes much more difficult.[57]

Truly Fabian warfare in which ground is not controlled is therefore extremely unattractive to most combatants. And the more Fabian the methods, the more unappealing the consequences. In fact, true Fabianism's unattractiveness is the reason so many associate it with materially weak nonstate actors—only actors with no other choice adopt such methods. Whereas some pundits view "guerilla warfare" and insurgency as a juggernaut that will nearly always prevail, very few actual combatants with a real choice adopt it. Anyone could; few do.[58]

As actors grow in strength, their methods thus often move away from the Fabian extremum. This is the reason for Mao's famous dictum that insurgents should move from terrorism and insurgency to destruction of the enemy in conventional battle once the insurgency is strong enough.[59] In principle, Fabian coercion alone can be enough to defeat a state occupier. But to persist in such disagreeable methods longer than necessary is to incur unnecessary politico-military costs.

Taken together, these problems give nonstate actors an incentive, other things being equal, to shift as far away from the Fabian extremum as they can get away with and still survive. And over time, changing state behavior has enabled smaller nonstate forces to survive in progressively less Fabian postures.

Modern firepower gives all actors—state and nonstate alike—an incentive to cover and conceal their forces, and as noted above, this requires space. For materially strong state actors whose large forces would otherwise exceed the carrying capacity of the terrain, this increasing need for concealment has encouraged them to spread out, reducing their density to levels that enable them to find adequate cover. For them, more-lethal weapons encourage more-Fabian methods, even given the political downsides of this. For materially weak nonstate actors, by contrast, their traditional troop strength has rarely exceeded the carrying capacity of the terrain to begin with. Even before weapon technology forced this on them, small armies would have deployed at densities low enough to enable cover simply because they lacked the troop strength to do otherwise. Cover from increasingly lethal weapons thus has rarely required nonstate actors to reduce their operating-area fsr below what it would already have been.

Figure 3.9 illustrates this phenomenon with an illustrative range of fsr's for nonstate actors.[60] Whereas the state fsr's in figure 3.8 began at typical values of 1,000 to 10,000 troops per square kilometer in the 19th century before falling progressively to a range of 1 to 10 by the late 20th century, the nonstate fsr's in figure 3.9 show little change over time and rarely exceed 10 fighters per square kilometer at any point in the interval. In 1949, the nonstate Karen National Defense Organization (KNDO) deployed around 10,000 fighters in an operating area of over 18,000 square kilometers of what is now Myanmar, for an fsr

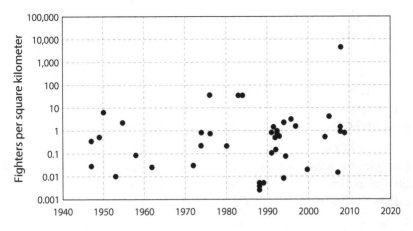

FIGURE 3.9. Force-to-space ratio, nonstate actors (semilog scale)

of around 0.56; in 2004, South Ossetian separatists fielded some 2,000 militia in the 3,900 square kilometers of South Ossetia for an fsr of 0.51. The Philippine Huk insurgency of 1946–54 fielded as many as 50,000 fighters in the 22,000 square kilometers of central Luzon for an fsr of about 2.3; in 1991, Slovenian separatists deployed some 30,000 militia in the 20,000 square kilometers of the Slovenian Jugoslav Republic, for an fsr of 1.5. In fact the nonstate data as a whole show no statistically significant trend over the 60 years of available figures, with most values falling in a range of 0.01 to 5.0 fighters per square kilometer across the interval. Whereas technology has forced large state armies to spread out in order to survive, smaller nonstate forces have long been within the carrying capacity of the terrain and have always been able to find adequate cover without further dispersal. And this has produced gradual convergence in the fielded density of state and nonstate militaries. Whereas the average 19th-century state massed its troops to a density 1,000 times that chosen by most 20th-century nonstate actors, by the 1990s state choices had changed to the point where some nonstate fsr's exceeded those chosen by contemporaneous states, and even the median nonstate fsr differed from US state practice in Operation Desert Storm by less than a factor of four.

This dynamic of ever-lower state densities but stable fsr's for smaller nonstate forces has progressively changed the prognosis for combat between them. Troop density shapes the number of combatants either side can deploy within reach of the enemy—the lower the acceptable density, the fewer the shooters a given army can put in range at any given time, other things being equal. If a large state army with an average weapon range of 1,000 meters can find only enough cover within a kilometer of the enemy to deploy 200 soldiers safely on a 10-kilometer frontage, then it does not matter whether they have 10,000 soldiers available on that front—the other 9,800 will have to be removed to positions beyond weapon range and will be unable to participate in the initial assault lest they be caught in the open and slaughtered to no purpose. This fsr-induced troop ceiling can have a profound effect on large state armies' ability to create favorable local numerical advantages at their chosen points of attack. Attackers typically try to mass a disproportionate fraction of their overall strength opposite a chosen point to create a greater local numerical advantage at that point than they enjoy in the theater as a whole.[61] But the fsr creates a limit on local concentration, which in turn creates a limit on achievable local numerical advantages. Let us assume a large state army attacking a smaller nonstate force. Against a nonstate defender with 15,000 fighters overall and deployed at a density of 2.5 fighters per square kilometer, a state attacker with 60,000 troops would enjoy an overall advantage of 4:1. But if that attacker can safely mass to a density of 5,000 troops per square kilometer at a chosen point (an fsr typical of the mid-19th-century values in figure 3.8), this would enable a local numerical advantage of 1,000:1 for the state army's forces massed on that chosen frontage (assuming weapons of 500 meters effective range). A local superiority on this scale would be crushing; any nonstate attempt to hold ground against such an assault would be suicidal. But if viable troop density falls to 1,000 troops per square kilometer, the same state attacker can now achieve only a 200:1 imbalance at the point of attack. At a maximum density of 100 troops per square kilometer, the achievable local imbalance falls to 20:1. And if the maximum density falls to, say, five troops per square kilometer—a value typical of late 20th-century state armies—the achievable local imbalance falls to just 2:1 even if weapon range increases to 5,000 meters, and this is true even if the state army overall outnumbers its nonstate foe by 4:1 or more. A value of 20:1 would still be crushing, but 2:1 is a value well within the normal range of local imbalances in modern interstate warfare. Many state armies have successfully held ground against attackers who had only a 2:1 local numerical advantage.[62] A two-order-of-magnitude decrease in state fsr's over the last century of warfare can thus have a profound effect on combat outcomes against nonstate forces whose densities now rival those achievable by states.

Of course this has not eliminated all state advantages in combat against nonstate actors. Large state armies enjoy large troop reserves even when they cannot commit them all to battle simultaneously because of fsr constraints; this enables them to grind down smaller foes by replacing losses with unengaged echelons until the weaker side eventually breaks. Most state armies also field better weapons and equipment than their nonstate rivals; an edge in weapon quality can help compensate for reduced local numerical advantages.

But rarely will these differences compensate fully for states' shrinking numerical advantage at the point of attack. In the 19th century, massed state armies could simply crush smaller nonstate foes who tried to stand their ground; by contrast, late 20th-century forces in dispersed postures could eventually exhaust smaller rivals by cumulative mutual attrition, but at much greater cost.[63] Nor has the technology edge enjoyed by most states been enough to offset fully the shrinking utility of superior numbers. If the average technical margin between state and nonstate actors were growing as the utility of state numerical preponderance was falling then it might offset the difference, but many now believe the technical margin is itself shrinking as nonstate actors increasingly acquire sophisticated precision weapons.[64] Victorian state armies could sometimes pit machine guns against African tribal levies armed with spears; such margins are rare in the modern world.[65] Battlefield-saturating firepower has been widely distributed for decades and remains difficult for even superior weapons to preempt fully; surviving nonstate fighters now have routine access to artillery and automatic weapons of a kind that can make exposed movement lethal to even well-equipped state armies. The ubiquitous AK-47, now so common among insurgents that it often features in the iconography of resistance propaganda, is a fully automatic assault rifle with a rate of fire that exceeds that of any standard service rifle in any great power military in either world war.[66] And the increasing availability of sophisticated heavier weapons in nonstate arsenals has left states such as Ukraine, Jugoslavia, and even Israel with little net margin over nonstate rivals in at least some important weapon categories (as noted above). On balance, state weaponry will still normally be superior, but the typical margin of real military supremacy this edge enables is far less today than the crushing advantage once offered by a potential 1,000:1 local numerical imbalance in Bonaparte's day, or even the 20:1 local advantage possible with early 20th-century fsr's. With industrial-scale firepower now widely distributed and still very difficult to wipe out preemptively when properly covered and concealed, later-model weapons in state hands can help but are unlikely to restore the kind of supremacy once enabled by mass concentration of forces.

In effect, this decline in states' achievable local numerical preponderance has thus progressively shifted states' margin of usable material superiority over the median nonstate actor. And this has, in turn, systematically shifted nonstate actors' best resolution of the trade-off between lethality and survivability—and nonstate actors' materially optimal choice on the Fabian-Napoleonic spectrum.

The variance in figures 3.1 and 3.2 has always given a few nonstate actors the numerical strength to challenge states on a relatively even material footing. But as states' ability to exploit their numbers has fallen with changing technology and the growing need to disperse for survival, more and more nonstate actors have become credible contestants for territorial control. And the achievability of this prize has in turn encouraged nonstate aspirants to adopt other elements of intuitively state-like, more Napoleonic methods to facilitate such ambitions.

For example, nonstate actors under a tolerable material imbalance have an incentive to accept decisive engagement more frequently. Nonstate irregulars have always been willing to do this on occasion, when they could overwhelm an isolated local garrison or ambush an overextended column. But when even main-body state forces commonly see local force-to-force ratios in the neighborhood of 2:1, far more nonstate actors can survive decisive engagement and will rationally choose this to control terrain.

Nonstate actors who can plausibly exclude state forces from base areas have an incentive to organize more differentiated combat theaters, with functionally distinguished forward zones with chiefly combat forces, rearward areas with chiefly support elements, and specialized headquarters, communications nodes, supply depots, training areas, and medical facilities.

Nonstate actors who can defend sympathetic civilians have an incentive to disentangle themselves from civilian populations by evacuating noncombatants from combat zones, shifting fighting positions to the outskirts of towns and away from clustered homes and schools, and adopting distinguishably military clothing and markings (both to enable noncombatants to be distinguished and to accentuate nonstate fighters' status benefits as defenders of the people).

Nonstate actors who can destroy enemy forces have an incentive to rely more heavily on brute force and less heavily on coercion, enabling quicker results, greater control of the initiative, and less dependence on enemy choices and decisions for results.

None of this means that nonstate actors can safely move all the way to the Napoleonic extremum: against modern weapons, local concentration beyond the carrying capacity of the terrain for concealment would devastate nonstate forces just as it would state armies. Nor does it mean that the modal state and nonstate army are ever going to adopt identical military methods: weaker forces always have incentives to adopt relatively more Fabian styles than stronger ones do.

But technological change is causing all these differences to shrink over time. As changing technology has progressively discounted one of the greatest traditional military advantages of state status—superior material resources—this has progressively reduced the incentives of materially weaker nonstate actors to accept the politico-military penalties of highly Fabian war fighting. And this in turn is creating an incentive for nonstate actors to shift their methods away from the Fabian extremum over time, and toward military styles ever closer to those traditionally associated with states—other things being equal.

Other things, however, are not always equal. In particular, materially optimal military methods near the middle of the Fabian-Napoleonic spectrum are exceptionally hard to implement effectively. And these implementation challenges pose especially steep barriers for actors with limited stakes and weak institutions—as some nonstate actors have, but others do not. Not all nonstate actors have the internal political makeup needed to act effectively on these behavioral incentives and realize the military potential created for them all by changing technology. The consequences of this internal political variance and the constraints it can pose for military choice are the subject of the next chapter.

4

Politically Achievable Behavior

THIS CHAPTER COMPLETES the new theory by turning to its political variables of stakes and institutions. Chapter 3 argued that material trends have created incentives for all actors to move toward the middle of the Fabian-Napoleonic spectrum over time. In this chapter I argue that midspectrum methods pose unique political challenges that simpler Fabian and Napoleonic approaches do not. Nonstate actors with permissive internal politics (existential stakes and mature institutions) can overcome these challenges and implement complex midspectrum methods effectively; others cannot and face incentives to default to less-powerful but simpler Fabian war fighting.

In particular, I argue that midspectrum war fighting demands much more extensive training than do simpler Napoleonic or Fabian methods. Midspectrum war fighting is also uniquely dependent on complex interaction among mutually dependent specialists. All warfare creates collective action dilemmas for fighters, but these collective action problems are much more severe for midspectrum combatants than for those using simpler Napoleonic and Fabian approaches whose success is less dependent on cooperation among specialist subunits. To implement midspectrum military methods thus demands a much greater allocation of resources to expensive training, and much greater levels of interpersonal trust and cooperation across organizational subdivisions, than do more-Fabian or more-Napoleonic military methods.

I then argue that nonstate actors' internal politics shape their ability to overcome these implementation challenges and execute complex midspectrum methods effectively in the field. Actors facing existential stakes have strong incentives to divert resources from other purposes to mastering complex military skills; actors facing limited stakes often do not. Actors with mature institutions find it easier to overcome collective action dilemmas and enable interunit cooperation; actors with immature institutions find this much harder to do. Stakes and institutional maturity, however, vary widely across nonstate actors. Some face existential stakes with mature institutions; others do not.

This political variation interacts with changing technology to produce important variation in nonstate military methods. Early 20th-century technology created a highly Fabian material optimum for nonstate actors fighting numerically preponderant states. Highly Fabian methods pose few political constraints on implementation; regardless of their internal politics, nonstate actors in the early 20th century would face strong incentives to adopt highly Fabian war fighting when confronting state foes. But as changing technology moved the materially optimal choice toward the middle of the spectrum, nonstate actors with existential stakes and mature institutions would be able to overcome the implementation challenges of the now materially optimal midspectrum war fighting and would be motivated to do so. Nonstate actors without such permissive internal politics, however, would be unable to implement materially optimal but highly complex midspectrum methods effectively and would have a strong incentive to default to less powerful but simpler methods closer to the Fabian extremum even with advanced, late 20th- and early 21st-century technology. And this difference implies increasing variance in nonstate military methods over time, as those with permissive internal politics shift progressively toward the middle of the Fabian-Napoleonic spectrum, but those without a permissive political makeup cannot.

To make this case, I first present a series of implementation challenges posed by midspectrum methods—and especially, a uniquely sharp collective action dilemma created by the military requirements of successful midspectrum war fighting—and I show how these challenges require both technical skill and interpersonal trust to resolve. Second, I discuss the role internal politics plays in enabling some actors, but not others, to overcome these dilemmas and respond to the incentives created by changing technology. I conclude by summarizing the resulting theory, and drawing from it a series of testable hypotheses to be assessed by the case studies in chapters 6 through 9.

Implementation Challenges of Midspectrum War Fighting

Figures 3.3 through 3.7 show weapons' growing technical potential to kill targets. But real militaries vary widely in their ability to realize this potential in the field. At the Battle of 73 Easting in 1991, for example, some US tank crews with modern 120-millimeter stabilized smoothbore guns hit and killed as many as three Iraqi tanks each in less than 60 seconds of firing from moving platforms at ranges of up to 2,000 meters in combat conditions during a sand storm; in all, 182 of 215 shots fired by US attackers in the battle struck their targets, corresponding to a hit rate of 85 percent.[1] By contrast, an Iraqi Republican Guard tank battalion at Objective Montgomery west of Baghdad in 2003 with modern 125-millimeter stabilized smoothbore guns scored zero hits in at least 16 shots against exposed targets at ranges of under 1,500 meters in clear weather during daylight.[2] Technology confers potential lethality, but to translate this into real effects requires skills that some forces have and others lack. Basic marksmanship, moreover, is among the simplest tasks of modern warfare. To realize the full potential of increasingly lethal weapons requires the kind of midspectrum tactics and operations described in chapter 2—but this style of war fighting is exceptionally complex and poses unusually complicated demands on military forces.

This is because midspectrum methods require combatants to combine Napoleonic lethality and Fabian survivability. Lethality and survivability are both virtues in war, but as noted above, they pose conflicting requirements. Extreme choices of purely Fabian or purely Napoleonic war fighting avoid the conflict and enable simple execution—but either extremum sacrifices something militarily critical in the process. To combine the two is much more powerful, but also much harder to do.

Tactics at either extremum are comparatively straightforward. Consider, for example, the technical demands of fighting at the Napoleonic extremum. Some skills are certainly needed, especially accurate firing from simple, exposed, often-stationary firing positions. Basic marching skills also matter, an ability to hold a massed linear formation during an advance is important, and of course personal courage has always been required to perform under fire, and perhaps especially so from such exposed positions. Tactical skill was not irrelevant even in Bonaparte's day; the fog of war, moreover, makes even these apparently simple requirements difficult to execute on a confused and dangerous battlefield. But little is required by way of camouflage or cover, and massed, visible formations simplify control and coordination. The tactics and operations required for this style of fighting are comparatively straightforward, and the training requirements for enlisted soldiers and field grade officers could be met largely through repetitive drill.[3] Against modern weapons, tactics like these are radically ineffective—their extreme exposure yields catastrophic casualty rates. In modern warfare, the ceiling on achievable military power using such methods is thus very low. But that low ceiling is easy to reach with minimum training and skill.

Conversely, at the Fabian extremum the central requirement is camouflage and concealment with less need for sustained accurate fire or marching skills in massed formations. Fabian reliance on gradual coercive attrition allows fighters to sacrifice short-term lethality as necessary to ensure concealment, and this, too, enables comparatively simple tactics. Consider, for example, ambush, assassination, and roadside bombing, all standard elements of modern Fabian practice. Of course any military activity, Fabian or Napoleonic, benefits from rigorous training, specialization of functions, cooperation, and efficient high-level planning. An ideal ambush thus exploits each of these traits: a roadside bomb placed at a carefully reconnoitered choke point triggers combined small arms and supporting mortar fire; ambushing units maneuver to eliminate survivors or to cover withdrawals; hostile reinforcements are blocked by supporting fighters predeployed along the expected approach routes. But a tolerable ambush can be mounted with much less sophistication. Independent subunits of comparable equipment and function can find cover for themselves in the vicinity of a designated engagement zone; some damage can be done by an initial volley of unsupported direct fire; rapid disengagement can enable the shooters to escape before countermaneuver can be organized by the surprised victims. When all are under cover, when all can fire from covered positions, and when all can safely flee after brief engagement, the risk to others if some leave early is bounded. Less damage will be inflicted than in a well-planned, integrated operation, but in a protracted coercive campaign of gradual attrition guerillas can accept lower short-term lethality via less efficient attacks in exchange for safety and survival to fight again another day in a long war.

Fabian assassination and roadside bombing can be accomplished with even less large-scale cooperation if necessary. The ideal assassin or bomber certainly carries out the job with sophistication, planning, and specialization. And even crude roadside bombs require some kind of organization to procure and assemble explosives and detonators or emplace the devices undetected. But here, too, tolerable results can be had with modest inputs. Crude bombs placed at night along remote stretches of road or amid chaotic urban squalor can do serious damage to passing patrols without the bomber necessarily risking return fire of any kind; for simple devices, small cells of guerillas with indifferent training can prepare the ordnance in unspecialized facilities. Drive-by shootings or sniping from windows can pick off individual police or isolated soldiers at limited risk to small parties of fighters even without support. Such methods offer only limited lethality and for this reason are clearly less effective than more sophisticated approaches—but they can be accomplished with limited cooperation and coordination and can still inflict attrition over a long coercive campaign. For combatants without the training or organizational sophistication for more lethal war fighting, they are an available alternative.

To realize the military potential of midspectrum methods, by contrast, is far more demanding. Such methods offer a much higher ceiling in the face of modern technology, but to reach that ceiling is much harder, and such methods are much less forgiving of limited skill than purely Fabian or purely Napoleonic tactics.

In particular, to maintain a significant volume of effective fire without complete exposure, modern weapons must be integrated using combined-arms techniques; movement must be combined with tightly coordinated suppressive fire; and moving elements must be continuously resupplied not just with ammunition but with the fuel, lubricants, and spare parts needed to continue that movement. Each of these requirements is technically very demanding, and to meet them simultaneously is especially so.

Combined Arms in Midspectrum War Fighting

The importance of combined arms for midspectrum war fighting stems from the technical incompatibility of Napoleonic firepower and Fabian concealment in the design of individual weapons. Midspectrum war fighting requires both, but their technical demands are in tension with each other, and the only way to excel at one is to accept weakness in the other. In principle one could try to split the difference and field a single weapon type that offered a bit of both. But given the constraints of engineering design trade-offs this usually produces simultaneous mediocrity in all critical areas.[4] A far better solution is to design multiple weapon types that specialize, each accepting a different weakness as the cost of a great strength, then combine them in tightly integrated operations on the same battle space, enabling the strengths of one to cover for the weaknesses of another and creating a whole that is greater than the sum of its parts.

Artillery, for example, is designed to maximize firepower volume and range, but to do this it must accept weak armor protection, difficult concealment, and the inherent inaccuracy and complex fire direction of long-range fire.[5] Dismounted infantry is easily concealed and can detect concealed enemies, but to do this it must sacrifice armor protection, and weight and volume of fire.[6] Tanks are designed to maximize armor protection and accurate direct firepower, but to accomplish this they give up sensory acuity and stealthiness.[7]

Employed alone, each thus suffers major drawbacks. But if they are used together, the infantry can act as the eyes and ears of the artillery and tanks; the artillery can provide the high-volume suppressive firepower to enable the unarmored infantry to survive dashes in the open between cover; and the tanks can destroy point targets too heavily armored for light infantry weapons to penetrate. This synergistic interaction has been central to all successful great power military doctrines for over a century.[8]

But while powerful in squaring the conflicting demands of Napoleonic firepower and Fabian concealment, this approach is extremely difficult to execute properly: combined-arms tactics are infamously complex. Commanders must know the respective pros, cons, conditions for effective employment, maintenance needs, training procedures, and resupply requirements of a whole range of unique (and individually very complex) weapons; and the closer the integration is to be, the more junior the officers who must master this. Great care must be taken to keep weapons of such different mobility within mutual supporting distance as they move over changing terrain and encounter unexpected obstacles or hostile resistance, and to prevent fratricide (especially when combining rapid maneuver with remote firepower from artillery or aircraft). Finally, the troops themselves often require special training in methods for cooperative operations.[9] Midspectrum combined-arms tactics are much harder to master than simple Napoleonic volley fire or Fabian concealment per se.

If all one needs is Napoleonic exposed short-term firepower with little concern for survivability, combined arms are less important, and this complexity is unnecessary. Conversely, if all one needs is to survive in Fabian hide positions with no concern for sustained lethality, one need not cope with the challenge of integrating armor, infantry, and artillery—it is enough to conceal oneself and wait for opportunities to snipe at unsuspecting targets. But if one chooses to combine significant survivability with significant lethality, as midspectrum methods require, then complicated combined-arms techniques are essential to overcome the technical inability of individual weapon types taken alone to provide both virtues at the same time.

Fire and Movement in Midspectrum War Fighting

Similarly, midspectrum choices that combine survivability and lethality require very careful selection of terrain, custom employment of weapons to overcome inevitable limitations in local terrain, and very careful coordination of forward movement with the use of those weapons to avoid fratricide. This is possible in almost all topography, but to do all this is far more demanding of skill and sophistication than is either a simple Napoleonic advance in the open or a simple Fabian hideout for ambush. The complexity of the earth's surface means that covering terrain of some kind is almost always available. It is easy to find cover that will allow an occasional furtive burst of fire at targets of easy opportunity before hiding again if that is all one needs. At the Fabian extremum, this will suffice. Simple Napoleonic firepower projection in the open is very undemanding of local terrain.

Midspectrum methods, however, require exacting terrain selection and careful coordination of movement and fires over that terrain to sustain effective firepower without debilitating exposure. Ideal midspectrum firing positions require nearby alternate or supplementary firing positions of comparable quality, so shooters can relocate quickly when spotted and reopen fire from suitable positions without extensive delay. Movement to such locations or between them creates a risk of exposure en route. Potential movement routes vary in their relative exposure. And the difference between cover and exposure can depend on complex microvariations in local terrain—two feet of elevation difference can distinguish cover from exposure, and a small rise that covers me from enemies at my direct front may be exposed to enemies further to my right or left—microvariations on this scale are rarely discernible from printed topographic maps and must be discovered by personal reconnaissance combined with military judgment. To exploit the potential of the terrain requires careful scouting, custom tailoring of movement orders, and individual siting of fighting positions to fit the peculiarities of units' immediate surroundings—especially when the weapons to be concealed are large (such as tanks or heavy guns). Forces cannot simply be laid out in standard, textbook formations and marched toward the objective, or deployed in formulaic cookie-cutter defensive layouts; each of the hundreds to thousands of local commanders in a mass army must fashion his or her own unique plans for movement and disposition based on the vagaries of local conditions.

And even the most careful analysis of terrain cannot wholly eliminate exposure if one needs to sustain fires. Eventually, movement to or between sound firing positions will require at least brief periods of exposure during sprints between covered positions. To survive these requires suppressive fires to keep the enemy's heads down while friendly forces are exposed. This combination of suppressive fire and forward movement creates complexity of its own. Suppression must be maintained until the last possible minute but lifted as advancing assault forces overrun the enemy to avoid taking casualties from friendly fire.[10] Sightings of enemy weapons must be communicated to distant supporting units, and suppressive fire redirected as intelligence is developed. The best suppressive weapon type is usually artillery, which is usually deployed well to the rear; as assault units move forward, artillery must eventually cease firing and advance to maintain coverage; if support is not to be lost in the meantime, these moves must be coordinated with both neighboring batteries and forward maneuver elements. Since the pace of an assault varies unpredictably with local terrain or unanticipated enemy action (e.g., discovery of minefields), maintaining continuous suppression thus requires a complex combination of planning, adaptation, and efficient communications between harried commanders at many different echelons.[11] Coordinated fire-and-movement techniques enable maximum cover from terrain without losing firepower effectiveness, but they are much harder to execute than are simple Fabian concealment or Napoleonic exposure.

Logistics in Midspectrum War Fighting

Sustained lethality with modern weapons requires a prodigious supply of ammunition; to provide this without exposure in a midspectrum balance poses complex demands.[12] Convoys of cargo trucks or fuel tankers are much more vulnerable than tank platoons, infantry squads, or insurgent cells. Supply dumps, repair depots, and weapon caches are static, lucrative targets for enemy attack. If high short-term lethality is all that is required and vulnerability is simply accepted, resupply will be less necessary (shooters will either kill the enemy quickly or die trying), and needed munitions can be prestocked in the open near firing positions or carried by the combatants themselves in the limited quantities necessary. Conversely, if maximum concealment is all that is needed, then firing activity will have to be so limited anyway that high logistics throughput will be unnecessary. But for intermediate choices of concealment, where survivability must be combined with substantial volumes of fire, maintaining a resupply system is both more necessary and much harder.[13] Deployment locations must be carefully selected to afford maximum concealment for resupply routes as well as fighting positions. Logistics nodes must be redeployed regularly to stay within effective supporting range of moving combat elements. Changing locations of combat units and resupply points must be communicated regularly between multiple levels of overworked, harried commanders lest rendezvous points be missed in the chaos of combat.

Stockage levels must be monitored continuously as expendables are consumed at varying rates, by a diverse range of weapon types, owned by varying units under varying local conditions, lest combatants be left with oversupplies of ammunition but shortages of fuel, or oversupplies of artillery ammunition but shortages for small arms, or overstockage in one unit while a neighbor runs out. And all this becomes exponentially more complex if the fighters being supported are using combined-arms and fire-and-movement methods: combined arms means that even small units will hold multiple types of deliberately dissimilar weapons and equipment with potentially very different support requirements (e.g., spare parts, lube oil, diesel fuel, and 50-pound guided missiles for tracked, 30-ton armored vehicles; 81-millimeter mortar rounds for light indirect fire support; and food, water, and 5.56-millimeter small-arms ammunition, inter alia, for a single 2010-era US mechanized infantry company); fire-and-movement puts all this in irregular motion and deploys forward elements downrange of friendly shooters who must now distinguish camouflaged, moving friendly units to their front from camouflaged, moving enemy units also to their front, killing only the latter but not the former.

Training Demands for Midspectrum Warfare

To cope with this complexity requires training, which is inherently expensive and burdensome. For mechanized armies and modern air forces, fuel, ammunition, wear and tear on vehicles, and the repair and maintenance required for large-scale training maneuvers impose enormous costs. The United States, for example, spent well over $90 billion on such activities in FY 1998, or over $60,000 per uniformed servicemember that year alone.[14] Large-scale training of large forces also requires space: the US Army's National Training Center at Fort Irwin, California, is almost the size of the state of Rhode Island; the Marine Corps' Twentynine Palms reservation covers nearly as large an area (with a 1,500-building mock city for urban operations that spans 274 acres, or about the size of downtown San Diego); and these are just two of the many such training facilities operated by the US military.[15] Heavy armored vehicles are notoriously hard on the landscape they operate in: tank tracks plow up farm fields and meadows; armored personnel carriers damage buildings and signage when navigating tight turns in narrow urban streets; military convoys snarl civilian traffic. Even lightly armed infantry and insurgent forces impose significant opportunity costs to train: militiamen on maneuvers cannot work to support their families while in the field; guerillas sent to the rear for training are removed from the fight in the meantime. Skills, moreover, are perishable and must be practiced regularly and repeatedly to be maintained, hence training costs are recurring, and the burden of training activity on communities must be sustained in steady state over time if proficient fighters are to be available when needed. Training is thus always expensive—but the more extensive and complex the training needed, the more burdensome the cost.

Interdependence and Collective Action Challenges in Midspectrum Warfare

Even more important, to cope with the complexity of midspectrum methods requires unusual trust and cooperation. All warfare demands trust and cooperation among fighters: if some flee while the others fight, the ones left fighting are imperiled and vice versa. But midspectrum methods raise the stakes substantially.

This is because they are unusually dependent on role specialization and tight interaction between mutually interdependent specialists. It is inherently difficult to combine lethality and concealment; midspectrum methods do this by differentiating military groups into subpopulations of role specialists who can excel in some combat tasks by offloading other tasks onto comrades who will specialize in them instead. If all meet their responsibilities, the whole is greater than the sum of its parts, and the inherent tensions between lethality and concealment can be mitigated to produce reasonable lethality with tolerable vulnerability. But this payoff comes with enormous risks: if any of the specialists fail to play their part, the whole will be much *less* than the sum of its parts, and all will be placed in much greater danger than if they had adopted simpler, lower-risk tactics with lesser demands for specialist interaction—as the simpler methods of very Fabian or very Napoleonic war fighting allow.

Combined-arms techniques, for example, are designed to enable individually vulnerable weapon types to risk advancing across fire-swept ground by relying on others whose complementary strengths cover for one's own weaknesses and vice versa. The very fact of this mutual reliance creates dangerous vulnerabilities if one component attempts such methods but the others they rely on fail to do their jobs.

Recall, for example, the interaction between tanks and infantry noted above. If tanks and infantry work together, the infantry can act as the tanks' eyes and ears to find concealed antitank weapons that armored vehicle crews cannot detect, while the tanks provide the firepower to destroy dug-in positions that dismounted infantry cannot overcome: each can excel at a specialized task that a single generalist could never accomplish, and by combining their efforts they can accomplish all the tasks needed to project lethality while limiting net vulnerability to hostile fire.[16] But to realize this potential, both elements must keep moving in close proximity to one another, and each must divert attention from immediate dangers to itself to communicate with the other about the locations of threats that menace the other much more than oneself. The infantry, for example, are vulnerable to machine gun fire that cannot penetrate tank armor. If infantry respond to a machine gun nest by going to ground and taking cover to protect themselves rather than keeping up with the tanks as they advance, the tanks will often fail to detect this (given the crews' limited visibility from within buttoned-up armored vehicles) and continue to move, soon finding themselves alone and exposed to fire from hidden antitank guns they cannot counter. To keep together, the infantry must be willing to accept risk for the benefit of the tanks, and the infantry's junior leaders must have the presence of mind to divert attention from managing their own troops amid the chaos of battle to coordinate their movements with tanks' commanders who cannot sense the infantry's movements themselves. Conversely, if tanks use their speed to rush through fire-swept ground too quickly, they can leave slower-moving infantry abandoned and exposed. If the beleaguered, harried tank commanders fall back without coordinating carefully with their accompanying infantry, they can literally crush soldiers who have sheltered from enemy fire behind the moving vehicles. If tanks direct their fire only against antitank weapons and leave machine gun nests or pillboxes unengaged, they leave the infantry exposed to threats that dismounted soldiers cannot answer alone.

If infantry can trust their colleagues in the armor to do their part and vice versa, then the combination of infantry and armor thus enables all to advance against enemy fire, balancing lethality and survivability to destroy hostile positions at tolerable risk. But if either suspects that the other will not live up to its part of the bargain, then to attempt such an advance would be extremely dangerous. Either element left alone without the other can be destroyed piecemeal by unassailable enemies, and if caught on the move in disadvantageous positions even large forces can be annihilated quickly by stationary opponents with modern weapons. As noted in chapter 3, in July 1944 a handful of dug-in German antitank guns destroyed almost 10 percent of the entire Allied army's tanks in less than three days when the latter were caught on the move without infantry support north of the Bourgebus Ridge in Operation Goodwood.[17]

Infantry who do not expect tanks to support them are better off staying put and taking cover to protect themselves, privileging self-preservation over identification and suppression of enemy antitank guns and firing only brief bursts through narrow firing apertures to preserve their own concealment. Tank crews who do not trust their infantry to keep up with them are likewise better off if they stay put and seek defilade to protect themselves from enemy fire rather than advancing on foes they will often be unable to detect without their own infantry to find and mark them for engagement. Any of these less trusting solutions represent defection from complex high-ceiling but high-risk mid-spectrum methods to simpler, lower-payoff but lower-risk Fabian concealment per se that depends less on close cooperation from others for one's own survival.

Fire-and-movement techniques pose similar challenges. Firing on the move is inherently less accurate; movement also makes it harder to acquire concealed targets and complicates ammunition resupply (see below). Other things being equal, it is better to fire from a stationary position. But not all positions are equal—locations closer to the target allow more lethal fire, and locations to the flank or above the target can negate intervening cover. To reach the most effective positions thus normally requires movement, but movement reduces firing effectiveness. Fire-and-movement tactics resolve this trade-off by role specialization: they break formations down into sub-elements that remain stationary and concentrate on firing ("overwatch" or "fire support" components) and sub-elements that sprint forward to reach new positions ("bounding" or "maneuver" components) while their stationary comrades cover their movement by firing to keep enemy heads down. Sometimes these roles alternate, sometimes the designations are permanent (artillery, for example, is almost always in a support, rather than maneuver, role), but at any given time there is always a division of labor between maneuver and fire support, and a key requirement for the supporting element is to use its greater fire effectiveness to suppress enemy shooters who would otherwise kill the exposed, moving maneuver elements.

This combination can be very effective if everyone does their job, but if anyone fails then everyone is at much higher risk. Overwatch elements are firing live ammunition over the heads or across the frontage of maneuvering comrades. If this suppressive fire is accurate, sustained, controlled, disciplined, and lifted on cue, it can be critical in surviving an advance into better positions. But if a nervous soldier in overwatch sprays bullets wildly from an assault rifle on full automatic before quickly ducking back into cover, such fire is as likely to hit his or her bounding colleagues in the back as it is to suppress the enemy to the front. If supporting elements fail to fire, or if they failed to clean their weapons properly and the guns jam, or if they cease firing and duck too soon, or if their marksmanship skills are subpar and the suppressive rounds fall wide or long, then bounding elements who have left cover themselves get caught exposed in the open against unsuppressed enemy fire before they can reach safety. Artillery and mortars are commonly used for suppressive fire support but are normally located too far from the front to see the moving fighters they are supporting; if an artillery or mortar crew is hasty or careless or simply miscalculates, they could fire long and miss their targets, leaving bounding fighters exposed, or fire short and hit their own men as they sprint in the open. If artillery crews protect themselves by taking cover against unexpected incoming counterbattery fire, the gap in suppressive fires can leave bounding comrades exposed. Conversely, if bounding elements freeze rather than move, then supporting elements will receive the full attention of enemy soldiers and risk far more lethal return fire when they unmask. If bounding elements inaccurately report their positions or routes, or fail under the pressure and distraction of battle to report at all, then they put supporting artillery crews at risk of causing fratricide if they fire.

If bounding elements can trust their colleagues in overwatch to do their part and vice versa, then their interaction lets them realize the potential of midspectrum methods. But if either suspects that the other will not live up to their part of the bargain, then it would be extremely dangerous to carry out one's own assignment. Being caught in the open or even in assembly areas by fire from one's own forces can be unusually deadly: on July 25, 1944, short bombing by US Army Air Force bombers supporting the assault in Operation Cobra killed 111 US Army soldiers (including General Leslie McNair) and wounded another 490.[18] But far less massive strikes can still be lethal: in August 1968, moving elements of the US Ninth Infantry Division in Quang Tri Province, Vietnam, lost four men killed and four wounded when a single round of supporting US eight-inch artillery landed among their position; on February 26, 1945, at Kirchtraisdorf, Germany, an entire platoon of British mine-clearing tanks was destroyed by US tanks and infantry whose frontage it was clearing.[19] For midconcealment fire-and-movement actions, if either party fails, the other is left much worse off than if they had tried simply to maximize Fabian concealment or to maximize Napoleonic lethality.

The logistical requirements of midspectrum methods create still further interdependencies among role-specialized subunits. Midspectrum war fighting requires extended maneuver in contact with the enemy and sustained heavy fire. The ammunition, fuel, and water this consumes are heavy, bulky, hard to move, and hard to hide. This creates a trade-off between sustainability and combat performance: the more supplies I carry, the longer I can fight, but the greater my load, the lower my agility, the harder I am to conceal, and the less effectively I will fight at any given moment.[20] Modern armies resolve this tension by providing combat units with only modest supplies (a "basic load," or the quantity of supplies carried by individual soldiers or combat vehicles, which is normally designed to last for only about a day of fighting), and replenishing them frequently using noncombat "service support" units with large, clumsy, thin-skinned cargo vehicles. Service support units specialize in resupply and transport but in the process leave themselves unable to fight well; combat units specialize in fighting but in the process leave themselves unable to sustain themselves in extended combat.

Together, the combat units protect the logisticians and in turn the logisticians sustain the fighters. But if either side fails, the other is left badly exposed. To reach engaged combatants, resupply units must move well forward into the combat zone; if truck drivers lose heart and turn back, fighters who expended their ammunition expecting resupply will find themselves defenseless in the face of the enemy. If supply convoy commanders get lost on poorly marked trails at night and fail to rendezvous with moving fighters, or if poorly maintained trucks break down and delay the column, or if staff officers miscalculate consumption rates or unit locations and allow depots to run out of key commodities, the result can be fighters left exposed to enemy fire without ammunition to protect themselves or fuel to escape. Conversely, if the fighters flee the battle unexpectedly, or if they have failed to secure a perimeter and enemy troops infiltrate their lines, or if fighters report their positions inaccurately or fail to arrive at rendezvous points, or if combat units are simply killed or overrun in place, the result can be vulnerable, thin-skinned supply units finding themselves suddenly in combat but in no position to defend themselves.

If fighters and logisticians can trust one another to do their jobs, then their interaction enables the sustained combat intensity needed for midspectrum methods. But if either believes the other will fail, they would be better off avoiding such tactics and choosing simpler, less interdependent highly Fabian or Napoleonic approaches instead. If resupply is not forthcoming, it makes more sense to default to a more purely Fabian solution and hide or dig in, minimize short-term vulnerability, and conserve ammunition rather than firing large volumes of suppressive fire in support of bounding comrades trying to reach superior positions, as midspectrum methods require. Alternatively, low-concealment but high-exposure Napoleonic approaches that maximize short-run lethality offer a chance to destroy the enemy in a short but intense battle before running out of ammunition.

In fact there are many such fighter-supporter interdependencies needed for midspectrum methods to reach their full potential. Infantry and air defense, tanks and engineers, maneuver and signals, or combat and intelligence, to cite just a few, all involve role specialization to enable armies to succeed with midspectrum methods by generating significant lethality without excessive exposure. In each case, less interdependent methods can still generate Napoleonic lethality *or* Fabian concealment, and simpler, less interdependent methods can reach the lower ceilings such near extrema offer. But to meet the complex requirements of balancing substantial concealment with significant lethality requires armies to accept role specialization and tight interdependencies among specialized subcomponents. And this means accepting grave risks if one or another of these specialists fails to do their job. Midspectrum methods are thus unusually demanding of the trust and cooperation needed for highly interdependent networks of specialists to function

This requirement for trust and cooperation creates an inherent collective action problem among wartime combatants. Combat is dangerous, and complex midspectrum methods are technically difficult. A rational fighter who believes that all of his or her comrades will play their assigned parts will profit from playing his or her own, too. But if the fighter expects his or her comrades to fail—whether from error or fear or selfishness or incompetence or some combination—then the fighter will be left far more exposed by carrying out his or her own role faithfully than if he or she held back and protected him- or herself instead. This self-protection can take the form of flight—running from the battlefield, refusing to advance under fire, or hiding instead of firing. Or it can take the form of fighting but defaulting to simpler tactics that entail less dependence on others and hence less risk if those others fail their assignments. Either way, a rational fighter who does not trust all of his or her comrades to cooperate fully and proficiently is thus better served by declining to cooperate him- or herself, too, and instead pursuing self-protection. Each fighter, moreover, knows all the others are subject to the same incentives. If any are untrustworthy, the rational choice for all is to defect to self-protection; only if all can be trusted to cooperate can any be expected to.[21] And the greater the degree of interdependence, the bigger the problem: more interdependent tactics yield greater payoffs if all cooperate, but also greater perils for individuals if others fail in their assignments, and thus the greater the interdependence the stronger the rational incentive to defect if any lack trust in the others.

Internal Politics and Midspectrum War Fighting

The result is that complex midspectrum war fighting requires unusually resource-intensive training and poses serious dilemmas of conflicting interests and collective action, whereas these challenges are much less severe for combatants operating closer to the Fabian or Napoleonic extrema. These dilemmas are rooted in the functional requirements for combining lethality and concealment; they represent rational responses to objective incentives; and they are faced by all combatants who would attempt midspectrum war fighting, whether states or not, rich or poor, large or small.

Yet they are not insuperable, and many militaries do overcome them. For nonstate actors in particular, the primary difference between those who can and those who cannot overcome these challenges is their political makeup— and in particular, their stakes in the conflict (and the war aims that derive from these) and their institutional development. In particular, those nonstate actors with mature institutions and existential stakes face low barriers to cooperation and will typically respond to the pressures of wartime by training troops as needed to remove skill constraints and enable such actors to implement complex midspectrum methods. By contrast, actors with immature institutions and limited stakes face the highest barriers to cooperation and will typically face skill constraints that make effective midspectrum war fighting dangerously impractical, and which encourage them to default to simpler, often more Fabian approaches.[22]

Institutions and Military Cooperation

The collective action problems described above are hardly unique to warfare. The details differ by setting, but the general problem is ubiquitous in human social organization, and institutions are a classical response. Their role in mitigating such problems has been among the more extensively studied themes in the last generation of political science; the large literature on the subject presents them as a means of reducing incentives for free riding and promoting cooperation by substituting iterated interactions for single transactions, providing mechanisms for monitoring and enforcement of collaboration, and facilitating low-cost resolution of internal conflicts. In the process they reduce transaction costs, lengthen the shadow of the future, and reduce the risk that others will exploit cooperative behavior. These traits have been shown to promote cooperation across a wide range of applications characterized by collective action problems, from international trade to legislative bargaining, ethnic conflict, coalition dynamics, democratic transition, economic development, environmental regulation, and more.[23]

Formal institutions in the form of durable organizations also promote technical skill by exploiting division of labor and specialization to build expertise and enable groups to master large, complex undertakings beyond the capacity of individuals or small teams working in isolation.[24] One should thus expect that the presence or absence of formal institutions would play an important role in shaping armed groups' ability to overcome collective action problems and implement complex midconcealment military methods—and I argue that they do.[25]

In fact there is wide variation in the institutional structure of nonstate military actors. Nonstate actors are usually less institutionalized than states, but this central tendency masks wide internal variation within each category.

In the 1980s, for example, the Sri Lankan nonstate Liberation Tigers of Tamil Eelam (LTTE) maintained a civil administrative apparatus with formal ministries of finance, justice, police, economic development, health, and education, all overseen by a standing Central Governing Committee; the LTTE maintained its own legal code and taxation authority and even ran a central bank.[26] The Colombian FARC (Fuerzas Armadas Revolucionarias de Colombia) ran a court system, maintained a police force, organized a financial system to make loans to farmers and businessmen, and administered public works and education programs in their area of control.[27] In 2006, Al Qaeda's Iraqi affiliate ran a bureaucracy that included suborganizations for "movement and maintenance," legal affairs, military affairs, security, medical operations, "spoils," and "media." Its western sector organization included a "mail" section that apparently coordinated the use of couriers, and functional departments for "boats," "relief and depots," and the "Soldiers Chamber (salaries)." These organizations maintained an elaborate system of paper records and reporting requirements for documenting salary payments, expenses, personnel rosters, and policy implementation.[28]

On the other end of the spectrum, the Irish Loyalist UVF in the 1970s was organized around loose "companies" that comprised little more than groups of men who drank in the same bar; UVF leadership was small and centralized, with little formal division of labor and little ability to control often-wanton violence by subordinates.[29] The rebel RCD (Rassemblement Congolais pour la Democratie) in the Democratic Republic of Congo retained the nominal administrative structure of the Congolese government in their territory around Goma but proved unable to make it work, with most civil functions defaulting to the Catholic Church, other NGOs, traditional tribal elders, and trade unions.[30] The RUF (Revolutionary United Front) in Sierra Leone was run by a loose collective leadership with a flat organization centered around independent insurgent brigade commanders coordinated under a war council with little or no formal administrative structure or hierarchy; its cadres were described by the population using a local phrase meaning "riffraffs, lumpens, and unruly youths."[31]

These variations have profound consequences for groups' ability to achieve interpersonal trust and internal cooperation. For personalized, weakly institutionalized groups like the UVF in Northern Ireland, the RCD in Congo, or the RUF in Sierra Leone, cooperation is very difficult to achieve, and factionalism is both an everyday reality and a grave, ongoing threat to life and property.

Elites in such weakly institutionalized groups are endangered not just by state enemies but by their own colleagues internally. In such settings, if economic spoils are misallocated across armed elites, with the balance of rewards failing to match the perceived internal balance of power, the result can easily be schism leading to mutual abandonment or internal violence and outright factional warfare.

And elite rivalry under weak institutions can hinder military cooperation at levels far below that of outright factional warfare. Rivalries based in ethnicity, class, religion, economic interest, institutional interest, personal ties, or ideology can fuel intramural suspicion that sub-elements might nominally follow orders, but without enthusiasm or commitment. Deeper schisms would involve actual disobedience to plenary orders but on small scale and without internecine violence. Still greater divides would produce systematic unwillingness to comply with plenary instructions, occasional internal violence to enforce independence from central control, and, eventually, open factional warfare.

Factionalism of this kind creates systematic barriers to the cooperation and trust needed for effective midspectrum war fighting. Fighters who see rival subgroups willing to pursue their own interests over plenary decisions face powerful incentives to hold back from risky commitments that would place them in mortal jeopardy if complementary specialists who may belong to a rival faction themselves hold back. Rational individuals in a factionalized army will avoid the risky interdependence inherent in midspectrum methods and fall back on the more self-reliant, less specialized methods of highly Fabian warfare. The more severe the factionalism, the stronger the incentive.

At least as problematic are the prophylactic actions leaders in such settings often take to protect themselves from the consequences of factional defection. Where leaders fear assassination, coup, or armed factional uprising, this immediate, personal threat creates a powerful incentive to adopt countermeasures in self-defense. These countermeasures protect the leadership, but they often systematically interfere with low-level cooperation within the military.[32] This trade-off makes sense for leaders with realistic fears of factional violence: an assassin's bullet or a coup conspiracy is usually a more immediate threat than military defeat; first things first. But because these countermeasures are prophylactics adopted in advance of outright defection, they impose their military efficiency penalty even if the feared split never matures into actual disobedience or internal violence. A fighter in the field can undermine midconcealment efficiency if his fear of faction leads him to shirk his duty, but if he grits his teeth and carries on anyway, the factional divide remains a potential rather than an immediate, realized effect. If the *leadership* fears faction, however, their rational countermeasures produce effects on the ground that can block cooperation and sap efficiency in midconcealment warfare even for milder degrees of factional distrust that never reach the stage of outright rebellion.

Among the more important of these countermeasures are divided lines of command; duplicative organization; communication restrictions; internal surveillance; distorted promotion and politicized leadership selection; frequent rotation of officers and breakup of established cohorts; and isolation from foreign training and advising.[33] Taken together, these techniques make it harder for conspirators to reliably control enough force to mount a large-scale putsch; they offer the plenary leadership alternative sources of key capabilities to check any that become unreliable; they increase the odds of detecting defection; they limit rival factions' military influence and access to violence; and they control outside influences that might encourage dissidence or enable outside political interference.

But these very goals are directly antithetical to cooperative, interdependent, technically proficient midspectrum military operations—they cannot succeed in their *internal* purpose without undermining military efficiency against *outsiders*. If the plenary leadership in a factionalized polity allows officers to cooperate, this might improve military effectiveness, but it could also empower an internal faction to overthrow the plenary leadership. Internal divide-and-conquer strategies can discourage this kind of conspiracy by making it harder for conspirators to trust one another and cooperate against the regime, but their very success in suppressing internal violence reduces the military's ability to coordinate midspectrum methods against outside enemies. If commanders are selected for technical competence rather than loyalty, then technically proficient but politically unreliable individuals will find themselves in control of large forces with dangerous consequences for plenary leadership in a factionalized environment. To prevent this means rewarding loyalty over proficiency, but this corrodes combat leadership quality in direct proportion to its effectiveness in installing loyalists in command. If an efficient organization follows a single chain of command and is interdependent without redundant, parallel organizations, then it makes the most of the available resources, but a single dissident element can disable the whole by removing a key supporting function, leaving plenary leadership without the ability to mobilize its military for self-defense against coup d'état or uprising. To retain redundant fallback organizations, however, is to telegraph distrust and encourage some fighters to suspect others. In a factionalized environment, leaders cannot have it both ways: self-defense against the threat of factional violence systematically interferes with the cooperation and trust needed for interdependent midspectrum methods. The more factionalized the organization, the more a rational leadership will have to take precautions—and the less able that organization will be to provide the trust and cooperation needed for effective midspectrum war fighting.

This underlying problem of factionalism and control of armed strongmen's potential for violence is actually ubiquitous and poses arguably the central challenge of political organization generally—for both states and nonstate actors.

Writing in a state context, Douglass North, John Wallis, and Barry Weingast see the primary solution to this problem historically as the development of mature institutions: patterns of rules and shared expectations that govern group behavior and which perform the same functions for the elites that run armed political groups that they perform in so many other social settings. That is, they reduce the transaction costs of internal bargaining; they increase the credibility of sanction for exploitative behavior; they habituate reciprocation; they lengthen the time horizons of the actors involved and discourage short-term defection in favor of long-term mutual benefit; and they promote shared, stable expectations of others' behavior. In the political development context, the emergence of these effects as institutions develop underwrites the evolution of organizationally mediated power-sharing deals in which elites with recourse to violence gradually negotiate among themselves a stable distribution of political authority and economic rents that matches the distribution of violence potential, and then use their power to exclude parties outside the deal from access to its benefits. Only this "double balance" of armed force with political and economic reward protects elites from one another: if a significant subset decides that their arms enable rewards beyond those currently accorded them, internal warfare is always available as a recourse, and only a careful balance between power and reward keeps the peace. It is the growth of stable expectations through increasingly formal, rule-based, impersonal institutions that eventually enabled actors such as Great Britain or the United States to overcome the problems of faction and violence management inherent in political organization.[34]

None of these problems, however, are unique to states—factionalism and the threat of internecine violence among armed elites are at least as serious a threat for nonstate actors today as they were for 18th-century England or America. One should expect nonstate actors to be at least as threatened by such challenges as states are. And one should expect that the importance of institutions for mediating and managing such threats would be at least as important for nonstate actors as it is for states.[35]

In fact I argue that for nonstate actors as well as for states, a central means of mitigating these dangers has been the use of formal institutions.[36] To explain their role, I adapt to nonstate actors the taxonomy of political development in states advanced by North, Wallis, and Weingast in *Violence and Social Orders*. In particular, I adapt three of their four state categories and add a new category unique to nonstate actors: informal natural order.[37]

Nonstate actors with *informal natural order* institutions lack named organizations with written or regularized specialization of labor, or distinct, persistent offices with discrete functions.[38] Perhaps the classic examples would be traditional tribal levies run by councils of elders and chieftains; others would include some kinds of warlord militias and often-small-scale covert militant groups. For such actors, hierarchical command and direction is limited, rarely exceeding two or three layers of functional authority, with few explicit, written rules of procedure or reporting. In the absence of formal, durable organizations, decision making and implementation is personalized, with individuals' traits and relationships rather than offices' authorities shaping outcomes.[39] There are no enforceable legal checks on the behavior of armed elites, who often control economic activity and extract extensive rents. Decision making under informal natural order is often collaborative and consensus based to limit the danger of violence in the absence of formal rules for conflict resolution, but strongman rule by charismatic individuals would also fall into this taxonomic category. And the reason informal natural order decision making is so often collaborative is that the potential for resort to armed violence by dissatisfied parties is ubiquitous.

By contrast, *fragile natural order* refers to actors with multiple named sub-organizations but where these have no meaningful power or capacity, hence decision making and implementation are personalized in ways similar to that of informal natural order actors. Examples might include the RUF in Sierra Leone or the Eritrean Liberation Front (ELF) in the 1960s and 1970s. Here there are nominal offices to handle distinct military and civil functions, with multiple layers of nominally hierarchical officeholders. Armed elites, however, hold all real power, with office titles meaning little beyond the personal authority of the individuals holding them and with no meaningful legal or bureaucratic checks on elite behavior. Elites again typically control economic activity for the extraction of rents. With personalized decision making and little or no meaningful institutional capacity to mediate disputes or resolve conflict among armed power brokers, the internal balance of power is fluid and unstable; governing coalitions form among powerful individuals, but defection is common and commonly leads to violence. The insurgent ELF, for example, was riven with infighting between its Muslim leadership and a disenfranchised Christian faction. This internal power struggle produced open civil warfare within the movement between 1972 and 1974 and again in 1980–81, after the plenary leadership sought peace with the ruling Ethiopian regime.[40] In fact the potential resort to armed force is a normal background condition of internal decision making for fragile natural order actors.[41]

Basic natural order actors such as the RCD in Congo have regularized the unstable patterns of elite interaction typical of fragile natural orders. Like them, they have potentially elaborate named organizations of only limited independent capacity; decision making and implementation remains personalized and responsive to the balance of power among armed elites. Economic activity is still subject to extensive rents. Unlike fragile natural orders, however, elites under basic natural order have developed stable coalitions with recognized, if often unwritten, rules of the road to shape their interaction. Formal offices and organizations lack the power to overrule elites who choose to disobey them, but durable organizations often serve as venues for rivals to work out voluntary resolutions to disputes without resort to arms. Such organizations thus extend the shadow of the future, promote reciprocity, and serve much of the cooperation-enhancing functions of institutions in the theoretical literature—though they do so only with the continuing voluntary participation of elites whose independent violence potential enables them to overrule any decision they see as contrary to their self-interest. That conception of self-interest is typically longer term under such conditions, however, with factional defections less common and internecine violence possible but infrequent.

Mature natural order actors such as the LTTE, by contrast, have developed impersonal, hierarchical, perpetually lived organizations that exert authority by office rather than by individual, with the organizations and their authority able to survive leadership transition. These organizations serve as checks and balances on individuals' power and are capable of binding enforcement in conflict resolution. Procedures are explicit, communications are regularized, and there is a meaningful public/private distinction in commercial activity with only parts of the economy subject to significant rent seeking by officials. Politics is still normally the preserve of elites with limited participation by outsiders, but there is a clear distinction between civil authority and armed forces, with the latter ordinarily subordinate to the former; elite status is no longer coterminous with personal access to armed followers.

Of course there are many ways one could categorize internal political variation. But this taxonomy frames variance around the features most important for the control of violence—hence there is good reason to expect these categories to affect military behavior, and especially a military's ability to overcome the collective action dilemmas of midspectrum warfare.[42]

In particular, mature natural order institutions are most conducive to successful midspectrum war fighting. Their stable coalitional structure and perpetually lived organizations afford a basis for trust that extends beyond small personal affinity groups, as midspectrum combined arms, fire-and-movement actions, and logistics all require. Such institutions' acceptance of a separate economic sphere limits rent seeking and encourages military technical expertise. Their regularization of procedure facilitates coordination among complex military subspecialties. And their relative stability encourages all actors to adopt longer planning horizons, extending the shadow of the future and discouraging short-term exploitation of cobelligerents for personal gain. Collective action dilemmas are challenging for any combatant, but the unique features of mature natural order institutions provide critical assets that properly motivated actors can use to overcome them.[43]

The further from this model one gets, the harder it becomes for even highly motivated actors to overcome midspectrum collective action dilemmas. Basic natural order institutions enjoy stable internal political coalitions, which mitigates the threat of factional violence. But they require economic rents to maintain those coalitions, discouraging costly investments in technical expertise and promoting the corruption that often inhibits fighters' trust in their leaders and saps their combat motivation. Personalized internal politics promote cronyism, with further disincentives to technical expertise. In such environments, logistical capability is especially challenging: the fuel, food, clothing, spareparts, and even ammunition flows that any modern midspectrum logistical system must manage are all easy, natural targets for black marketeering. Hence the corruption needed to keep internal factions in balance under basic natural order will often systematically undermine the military's ability to sustain intense combat for the control of ground. Without reliable sustainment, many local commanders at the front will rationally opt out of decisive engagement against superior forces in settings where a midbattle shortage of ammunition or fuel could leave them dangerously exposed. The result can often be a relatively Napoleonic articulation of the theater of war, differentiated dispositions of uniformed combatants, and some effort at brute force contestation of ground—but unwillingness to accept decisive engagement, as midspectrum methods require, and a default to more-Fabian methods less reliant on complex logistical cooperation and the collective action this requires.

Fragile natural order institutions are still less able to overcome midspectrum collective action dilemmas. With volatile factional dynamics and an unstable, shifting internal balance of power, cooperation between members of potentially rival factions is dangerous, and military functions that require this become very risky. Under fragile natural order, reliance on others for logistical support is perilous, but so are combined-arms cooperation, fire-and-movement tactics, and any other method aimed at holding ground when positions could be undermined by the defection of a neighboring unit with unreliable loyalties. Under such conditions, Fabian small-unit raiding is much safer, with territorial defense limited to critical terrain housing leadership hideouts or critical supplies in an otherwise largely undifferentiated theater. Rational combatants in such political settings will rarely attempt midspectrum methods and will default instead to simpler, lower-risk, highly Fabian war making.

Informal natural order institutions are the least conducive to midspectrum methods and promote the most-Fabian military styles of all. With no

TABLE 4.1. Taxonomy of Nonstate Institutional Makeup

Informal	• No named suborganizations; no written or regularized specialization of labor • Limited hierarchical command and direction • Personalized decision making • No enforceable legal checks on elite action • Elite control of economic activity • Extensive rent extraction • Fluid internal balance of power
Fragile natural order	• Named suborganizations with written or regularized specialization of labor—but limited capacity • Limited hierarchical command and direction • Personalized decision making • No enforceable legal checks on elite action • Extensive rent extraction • Fluid internal balance of power
Basic natural order	• Named suborganizations with written or regularized specialization of labor and moderate capacity • Limited hierarchical command and direction • Personalized decision making • No enforceable legal checks on elite action • Extensive rent extraction • Stable internal coalitions
Mature natural order	• Named suborganizations with written or regularized specialization of labor and substantial capacity • Significant hierarchical command and direction • Impersonal decision making • Enforceable legal checks on elite action • Moderate rent extraction • Stable internal coalitions

meaningful institutional role specialization, cooperation is limited to very small groups of individuals whose basis of trust is personal rather than official. With such limited spans of cooperation, no ground can be held—hence even leadership hideouts must be temporary and moveable, supply caches must be small and expendable, and fighters' personal security can be assured only through intermingling with an indistinguishable civilian population. Rational combatants under informal natural order have little choice but to adopt very simple methods lying as close to the Fabian extreme as real warfare gets.

These institutional variations are summarized in table 4.1.

Stakes and Proficiency in Complex Military Methods

Mature institutions are necessary for complex midspectrum warfare, but they are not sufficient. Such methods also demand high levels of technical proficiency that can be obtained only via expensive training and preparation. Even institutionally mature actors will not always be willing to spend the money and resources needed for such training: the United States, an institutionally very mature state actor, failed to do this before its entry into World War II and the Korean War and consequently fell well short of effective midspectrum war fighting early in both conflicts.[44] The difference between institutionally mature actors who make this expenditure and those who do not is often the stakes they perceive in expected warfare.

Intuitively, a war's stakes are the importance or gravity of its prospective outcomes. Specifically, I define "stakes" as the absolute value of the perceived expected utility for the actor's senior leadership group of the war's potential outcomes.[45]

There are several meaningful elements to this definition. First, it is the leadership's *perception* that matters, not the objective or observed outcome of the conflict. These will often coincide, but where they do not it is the perception that motivates behavior, which is the dependent variable the theory seeks to explain. Hence it is the perceived stakes that matter for the theory.

Second, the actor whose perceptions matter is the combatant group's *senior leadership*, defined as the members of the selectorate's winning coalition.[46] The perceptions of the individual at the top of the group hierarchy are often a good proxy for those of the selectorate's winning coalition—in a matter as important as war and peace, serious disagreements between the chief and the winning coalition would typically topple the chief—but the theory formally defines stakes in terms of the majority perception of the selectorate's winning coalition.

Third, it is *expected* outcomes, not merely possible outcomes, that matter. Hence the prospective result and its perceived probability are both important. Defeat is almost always possible for almost any actor given the uncertainty of war; it matters for the severity of the stakes whether this possibility is considered likely or remote.

Fourth, the expected outcome that matters is the postwar *fate of the selectorate's winning coalition*. A war where defeat would likely kill or imprison the majority of the selectorate's winning coalition is existential for that combatant actor even if the general public would likely prosper afterward, and vice versa. For most actors, to suffer conquest, annexation, or other forms of extinction as an independent political entity creates existential stakes for the leadership elite given their inability to ensure their own freedom or physical safety under such conditions. Of course any war poses some risk of death for any individual participant; individuals among the elite may die even in a successful war effort, or even in a stalemated contest with little danger of conquest. I thus frame stakes around the expected *group* consequences for the critical elite group at the heart of decision making.

Finally, it is the perceived *utility* of that outcome that matters, not merely the outcome per se. Cognitive psychologists tell us that utility perceptions vary for prospective gains and prospective losses.[47] For most actors, fear of defeat weighs more heavily in perceived utility than hope of gain, hence aggressive wars in pursuit of gain with limited downside risk in the event of defeat will typically represent only low-to-moderate stakes for the theory even if the likely gains are large. By contrast, wars with a significant risk of defeat and ensuing death or imprisonment for the leadership will typically represent high stakes for the theory whether victory would yield gain or merely the status quo ante bellum.

Expected utility can be difficult to observe; in practical terms, however, the key observable issue for stakes in the theory is whether the actor's senior leadership believes the war poses a meaningful risk of their death or imprisonment if they fail militarily. If so, the case presents an existential stake for that actor. Conversely, wars in which the senior leadership believes defeat would forfeit potential gain but without their collective death or imprisonment would be coded as limited stakes, as would wars whose likely outcome is compromise partition of divisible financial or other aims, or stalemated conflicts where outright defeat is unlikely.[48]

War aims are related to, but distinct from, the war's stakes. Whereas *stakes* involve the consequences of a war's likely outcome for its combatants, *war aims* are the outcome a combatant will accept as a condition for ending the war. An enemy with modest war aims thus tends to reduce one's own stakes: in a war between A and B, if A will accept a compromise peace offer from B with small concessions from B rather than holding out for B's annihilation, then this reduces the disutility to B of the war's plausible worst-case outcome, yielding modest stakes for B. By contrast, an enemy with ambitious war aims can increase one's stakes: if A will accept only B's annihilation and will reject all compromise offers short of this, then the disutility to B of the war's plausible worst-case outcome could be very great (as long as A is strong enough for the threat of annihilation to be plausible). One's own war aims can likewise influence the war's stakes, but usually with smaller effects. A very ambitious war aim can increase the utility of the plausible best-case outcome to that actor (if the actor is strong enough for this aim to be plausibly achievable). But since the prospect of gain typically counts for less in utility perceptions than the fear of loss, ambitious aims of one's own usually have smaller effects on stakes than ambitious aims by one's enemy.

Geographic or other physical variables can also shape the stakes in a conflict. Indivisible territorial goals, for example (such as control of a holy city), tend to increase stakes by excluding compromise settlements that would moderate the difference between defeat and victory.

The new theory here does not, however, seek to explain in any systematic way the *sources* of stakes or the details of their causal interconnection with war aims; it is enough to note that stakes, not war aims, are an exogenous independent variable for the new theory, and to establish that stakes vary from actor to actor (if not why they vary).

In fact this variance in actors' stakes, like their institutional makeups, is substantial. At one extreme, some combatants fight for indivisible, existential stakes where victory means leadership survival, defeat means collective annihilation for the elite, and compromise settlement is difficult. World War II approximates this extremum for interstate warfare. Nazi Germany's war aims of an expansionist Aryan racial supremacy under Hitler's authority threatened non-Aryans with genocide and consigned even Aryan neighbors to extinction as independent polities.[49] Such aims made compromise all but impossible, as Nazi ideology offered no logical basis for coexistence, and hence no potential partner could be confident that Hitler would respect the terms of any compromise settlement they might reach. Hitler's ideological aims thus implied effectively indivisible stakes and created credible commitment problems that together made Germany's conflict with its neighbors existential for all: either Germany would prevail and conquer its neighbors, or it would be defeated and conquered by them, and for both sides, conquest would pose grave consequences for the leadership elite of the conquered.[50] The Chinese civil war offers a similar situation for nonstate actors. Mao's universalist Marxism posed an inherent threat to Chiang's government that Mao could not credibly commit to settle short of one side's subjugation by the other—any compromise division of the country would be seen by both parties as a mere lull in an inevitably existential struggle that threatened the entire elite of both sides.[51]

At the opposite extreme, some combatants fight for limited, divisible stakes where warfare threatens the distribution of spoils but not the existence of either combatant or its leadership group. In the interstate 1982 Falklands War, for example, Great Britain fought to overturn an Argentine invasion of the disputed Falkland Islands. While both sides saw the islands as worth fighting for, neither feared conquest of its homeland by the other, Britain's recapture of the islands did not lead to an invasion of the Argentine mainland, and the Argentines did not mobilize for total warfare even after being ejected from the islands.[52] The Angolan civil war offers a similar case for nonstate actors. For most of its course, the conflict between Savimbi's UNITA and the Angolan government turned chiefly on the control of lucrative diamond mines that each side sought for chiefly economic reasons. Angolan geography made it hard for the government to project enough force into the interior to crush Savimbi and repossess the mines, but also for Savimbi to project enough force to the regime's coastal political base to topple the government.[53] The mines were valuable enough for either side to fight for an expanded share, but for decades neither side found it worth the expense to wholly dispossess the other, and neither expected the other to annihilate it or imprison its leadership elite. In fact, many nonstate actors—and their state opponents—wage war subject to tacit bargains in which neither side truly accepts the other's viability yet in which neither really seeks or expects to annihilate the other; such conflicts can grind on for decades in a relatively stable wartime order in which both sides find the war worth waging but neither faces an existential threat from the other.[54]

These varying stakes affect a rational actor's willingness to accept risk and incur cost in military preparation. Existential stakes encourage actors to do whatever it takes to prevent death or imprisonment of the leadership elite by an opponent who intends this. This in turn makes it worth the cost to provide the expensive, burdensome training needed to master complex midspectrum methods. And if the alternative is defeat and annihilation, this makes it worth the risk to attempt the high-payoff but high-risk interdependencies of midspectrum warfare. By contrast, limited stakes allow rational actors to accept lower levels of preparedness, and they encourage actors to avoid the high risk of midspectrum interdependency when the high payoff of such methods is not necessary for survival. If the war's stakes concern the division of spoils rather than the existence or liberty of the respective leadership groups, then there are limits on the expenditures that it makes sense to incur: two actors fighting over the revenue stream from a diamond field would be crazy to spend more on the fighters needed to win the diamonds than the net present value of the diamonds themselves. Inasmuch as complex midspectrum war fighting both demands much greater (and more expensive) training and involves greater risk if poorly implemented than simpler, lower-risk, more Fabian methods, this implies:

(1) the more existential and less divisible the political stakes in the war, the greater the actors' incentives to incur the cost and accept the risk needed to field forces with the skills and tactics to realize the military potential of midspectrum methods; and

(2) conversely, the less existential and the more divisible the stakes, the lower the incentives to incur the needed cost and accept the needed risk of midspectrum methods.

Central Theoretical Predictions

These claims imply a series of observable implications for the behavior of historical nonstate actors, and predictions for their behavior in the future. The theory above is specified in mostly continuous variables—the dependent variable of military behavior is specified as a continuum between Fabian and Napoleonic extrema; technology is specified as a continuous variable reflecting progressive increases in lethality over time; and numerical imbalance is specified as a continuous variable reflecting the relative numerical disadvantage of nonstate actors versus their opponents. Internal politics is specified as a categorical variable (institutions can be informal, fragile natural order, basic natural order, or mature natural order; stakes can be high or low), but the logic of the argument presents a theory that is deliberately framed to explain incremental changes over time in actors' position on a behavioral continuum.

The appendix specifies this continuous-variable theory formally, presents explicit coding rules for mapping empirical observations into the formalization, and illustrates some of the resulting comparative statics. For a complete exposition, the reader should consult the appendix.

Here, I summarize the central predictions of this theory using natural language. This creates several challenges of presentation. To describe exhaustively the predictions of a theory with a continuous, real-valued dependent variable and four independent variables (technology, numerical imbalance, stakes, and institutions), two of which are themselves continuous and real-valued, would require plotting multiple three-dimensional surfaces. This would be analytically complete, but at the cost of a very abstract representation that would arguably add little in transparency to the formal description in the appendix.[55]

In the interest of conveying the theory's central intuitive claims for the non-technical reader, I instead present in table 4.2 a simplified categorical approximation of the theory's continua. This should not be read to imply a discrete categorical theory—on the contrary, my central claim in chapter 2 is that categorical treatments of nonstate war making misrepresent the phenomenon. Rather, table 4.2 is a summary presentational shorthand for the full theory as articulated in the appendix.

The simplification of table 4.2 assumes numerically inferior nonstate actors fighting state armies at a constant numerical disadvantage of 1:4, for four different technological moments (1960, 1990, 2020, and 2050), broken out for the theory's four variations in the nonstate actor's institutions (informal, fragile natural order, basic natural order, and mature natural order) and two variations in the nonstate actor's stakes ("low" and "high," for limited and existential). For each cell in the resulting matrix, a natural-language categorical approximation of the theory's predicted nonstate behavior is given: "very Fabian," "mostly Fabian," "slightly Fabian," and "midspectrum," reflecting values on the Fabian-Napoleonic spectrum of 0–1, 1–2, 2–3, and 3–4, respectively.[56]

For nonstate actors with technology no more lethal than that available in the mid-20th century, the theory expects that numerically superior state rivals should be able to crush such forces regardless of the nonstate actor's internal politics, and over a wide range of specific imbalances in troop strength. Rational nonstate combatants under such conditions face a choice between substantially Fabian military methods or annihilation if they attempt more-Napoleonic tactics and strategy; the theory predicts that most such actors will choose very to mostly Fabian methods.

Late 20th-century technology is more lethal and compels rational state combatants with large, numerically preponderant armies to spread out in order to survive. Late 20th-century weapons are not yet lethal enough, however, to require dispersion sufficient to make many nonstate actors fully competitive with state rivals given the former's typical overall inferiority in numbers. But such weapons *are* lethal enough to make some nonstate actors competitive enough to motivate meaningful movement toward less Fabian methods: in particular, nonstate actors with late 20th-century weapons, existential stakes, and basic or mature natural order institutions can profitably adopt somewhat more Napoleonic methods. The theory predicts that such actors will do so, but that others, comparably armed, will not.

Early 21st-century technology, by contrast, is lethal enough to compel rational state combatants to adopt very dispersed postures. To survive against

TABLE 4.2. Key Predictions—How Fabian?

					Stakes			
Institutions	Low	High	Low	High	Low	High	Low	High
Informal	Very	Mostly	Very	Mostly	Very	Mostly	Very	Mostly
Fragile NO	Very	Mostly	Very	Mostly	Very	Mostly	Mostly	**Slightly**
Basic NO	Very	Mostly	Mostly	**Slightly**	Mostly	**Slightly**	**Slightly**	**Slightly**
Mature NO	Very	Mostly	Mostly	**Slightly**	**Slightly**	**Midspectrum**	**Slightly**	**Midspectrum**
	1960		1990		2020		2050	

such modern weapons requires troop densities low enough that even numerically inferior nonstate actors can now compete with much larger, numerically preponderant state armies for control of territory—but only if their internal politics enable them to overcome the collective action dilemmas of midspectrum warfare and field fighters with the necessary skills and trust. This requires both stakes that warrant the expensive training needed to provide skill, and the institutions needed to provide trust. For nonstate actors without the stakes needed to motivate skill, trust has limited payoff: I might trust my comrades to do their best, but if their best isn't good enough to keep me alive in complex midspectrum war fighting then my optimum choice is still to default to safer, more Fabian methods. Nor is skill without trust sufficient: if I doubt a skilled comrade's motives, it will still be very risky for me to depend on him or her, and it is again safer to default toward Fabianism. Even in the 21st century, low stakes thus preclude midspectrum methods regardless of institutional maturity. High stakes, existentially motivated actors with weak institutions produce similar behavioral incentives: expensive training is now worthwhile, but without a reliable organizational framework to enable trust, cooperation and true interdependence is still very risky.

By the mid-21st century, existential stakes with fragile or basic natural order institutions will empower nonstate actors with potentially skilled fighters to expand the scope of cooperation somewhat, but the residual distrust endemic in unstable factionalized politics with systematic rent seeking by multiple armed elites will limit the span of safe cooperation; competent territorial defense of key locations can be provided by the better-trained small forces any given faction can field, but larger-scale cooperation will be too risky, so here, too, slightly Fabian methods are indicated. The incidence of slightly Fabian war making is likely to increase relative to the early 21st century, in that fragile natural order actors will be able to accomplish this against the more dispersed state enemies produced by 2050 technology. But true midspectrum war fighting will still require existential stakes to motivate expensive training, and mature natural order institutions to overcome collective action dilemmas and allow the necessary scale of cooperation among interdependent specialists. Actors with these traits can overcome even very adverse numerical imbalances and profitably adopt very state-like, midspectrum military methods even without state status—and in the 21st century, the theory here expects most such actors to do so.

5

Hezbollah in the 2006 Lebanon Campaign

HOW DO THE RESPECTIVE theories fare against the evidence? In this chapter I present the first of five case method tests. Hezbollah's behavior in its 2006 campaign against the Israel Defense Force (IDF) is a case with special leverage for the theories under study here. The results, which tend to corroborate the new theory but contradict the others, thus warrant a greater shift in confidence than would typically be possible from a single case study.

I develop this argument in seven steps. First, I discuss the problem of selection bias in case method research and the motivation for my selection of the 2006 case as one that mitigates the risk. Second, I outline briefly the main events of the case. Third, I develop values for the main independent variables associated with the competing theories. Fourth, I code the dependent variable: Hezbollah's observed military behavior. Fifth, I discuss Hezbollah's ability to execute its chosen methods proficiently, which provides an opportunity for process tracing on the causal mechanism in the theory above. Sixth, I consider several alternative accounts of the campaign whose details differ from the analysis I present. Finally, I compare Hezbollah's behavior to the respective theories' predictions given these values, assessing the relative fit between prediction and observation and the implications of this for the theories under study.

Why Hezbollah in 2006?

Case method poses an inherent danger of selection bias: a theory's success (or failure) in a small sample of cases might be an artifact of having chosen misleading or unrepresentative cases. Some act of selection is unavoidable in evaluating a continuous-valued theory; to minimize the danger and maximize the utility requires careful, theory-driven selection for the handful of cases to be studied. For the theories under study here, Hezbollah in 2006 offers two important advantages.

First, it approximates what Harry Eckstein termed a *critical case* for theories of military behavior. Eckstein argued that cases with extreme values on the main independent variables can create conditions where theories should be at their strongest (or weakest), making it unusually illuminating if a theory fails to perform as expected. A most-likely case is one where extreme values put a theory on its strongest possible ground—if it is going to be right anywhere, it should be right here. For such cases, a valid theory should fail very rarely; if we nevertheless observe failure, this surprising result warrants a greater loss of confidence in the theory than would a single disconfirmatory observation under less ideal conditions. Conversely, a least-likely case is one where extreme values make the theory unusually unlikely to succeed—even if the theory were generally valid, under such unfavorable conditions it might well fail anyway. For such cases, we would expect weak theories to be overwhelmed by confounding effects; if we nevertheless observe successful prediction, this surprise would warrant a greater gain of confidence than would a single confirmation under less extreme conditions.

Hezbollah in 2006 offers something approaching a most-likely critical case for tribal culture and materialist theories of military behavior, and a least-likely case for the new theory, making it an especially useful test. In particular, it provides a very close fit to the Arab tribal cultural model often cited as most conducive to low-exposure guerilla warfare, and to the asymmetric material disadvantage usually seen as mandating such methods. If tribal culture or inferior material really are the most important determinants of tactics and strategy, their mutual reinforcement here ought to produce highly Fabian methods for Hezbollah. If orthodox theories fail to predict the outcome under conditions so strongly matched to those they describe as the paradigm of guerilla warfare, then the case poses an unusually strong challenge to their validity.

The 2006 campaign also offers a particularly close fit with the materialist subvariant often described as "hybrid" or "fourth-generation warfare" theory. In fact, Hezbollah's methods in 2006 are largely responsible for popularizing these arguments, whose prominence rose substantially as a result of their apparent fit to the results of the 2006 fighting. As the flagship case for such theories, this case should prompt expectation that the details of its conduct will be especially consistent with the theories' provisions; important deviations would thus be unusually informative.

Conversely, the 2006 campaign provides a difficult hurdle for a theory emphasizing internal politics. The new theory predicts state-like, midspectrum methods for Hezbollah: as I will show, its internal politics were highly institutionalized, it saw Israel as an existential threat, and it had access to advanced, 21st-century technology (albeit in vastly lesser quantities than Israel had). Yet Hezbollah was a militia in a developing country facing the wherewithal of a modern, Westernized state with the world's 12th-largest defense budget at the time; notwithstanding Hezbollah's aid from its Iranian patron, its limited gross power resources in 2006 left it with the kind of massive resource disadvantage that orthodox materialists see as the wellspring of irregular war fighting.[1] And Hezbollah's power base in Shiite South Lebanon was a strongly tribal cultural community—in fact, it was a significantly more tribal society than the non-state Jaish al Mahdi's base in Shiite Baghdad from 2003 to 2008. It would not be surprising if these effects were to overwhelm the contrary influence of internal politics—even if the latter really were the single best explanation under ordinary circumstances. Hezbollah thus offers something close to a least-likely case for the new theory: for the theory to hold under conditions as apparently unfavorable as these provides a stronger corroboration than a single case study would otherwise provide. The fit between the case's specific characteristics and the nature of the theories under test thus enables a challenging test from a single case and helps mitigate the danger that selection bias will taint the results.

Finally, the 2006 campaign offers an opportunity for a controlled comparison with the Iraqi Jaish al Mahdi (JAM) case presented in chapter 6. No two cases are ever completely controlled, but the comparison of Hezbollah and the JAM offers a number of theoretically important similarities: both actors were Shiite Arab, both sprang from cultures with a strong tribal influence, both were at major material disadvantages relative to industrialized democratic opponents, and both had the same state sponsor in Iran. Their internal politics, however, were very different—and in particular, whereas Hezbollah was a strongly institutionalized actor with existential stakes, JAM politics were personalized and deeply factionalized with increasingly limited, distributional economic stakes. Hence the new theory predicts very different military behavior for the two cases under conditions where materialist or tribal culture explanations would not, and the difference in theoretical prediction under such similar conditions offers an opportunity for unusual leverage.

Overview of Events

The 2006 Lebanon campaign opened when Hezbollah ("The Party of God" in Arabic) ambushed an IDF patrol and captured two Israeli soldiers on July 12.[2] The Israeli Air Force (IAF) quickly retaliated against targets in Lebanon. Before dawn on July 13, the IAF executed Operation Specific Gravity, destroying more than 50 of Hezbollah's long-range rocket launchers in a preplanned, 34-minute strike.[3] Other early targets included Hezbollah observation posts along the border, Hezbollah compounds in the Dahyia section of Beirut, and roads and bridges that Israel believed might be used to exfiltrate the abducted soldiers. Over the course of the campaign, the IAF flew roughly 5,000 strike missions, primarily directed at the Dahyia, the Beqaa Valley near the Syrian border, and the region south of the Litani River.[4]

Meanwhile, despite losing many of its long-range launchers early in the war, Hezbollah began what would become a steady stream of rocket fire into Israel. In total, Hezbollah fired an estimated 4,000 rockets, the vast majority of which were 122-millimeter Katyushas stationed within 20 kilometers of the Israeli border.[5] Hezbollah launched 100 or more rockets on 22 of 34 days in the campaign, including 220 on the final day of the war. About 900 of these rockets landed in urban areas, causing 53 civilian deaths.[6]

Israel made its first major ground incursion into Lebanon on July 19. IDF units advanced from the Israeli village of Avivim toward Marun ar Ras, a Lebanese town on high ground controlling much of the border area as well as the approach to the larger town of Bint Jubayl. The IDF met heavier resistance than they expected, including a protracted firefight at the Shaked outpost overlooking Marun ar Ras on July 19 and another battle inside the town on July 20.[7] When the IDF moved into Bint Jubayl it encountered even tougher defenses, precipitating one of the largest firefights of the war on July 26.[8]

By the end of July, the IDF had conducted operations in several other towns close to the border, including Marwahin, Ayta ash Shab, Kafr Kila, and At Tayyibeh, but it had made no attempt to control territory systematically in southern Lebanon. This changed on July 31 when the Israeli Cabinet approved Operation Change of Direction 8, designed to take and hold a "security zone" several kilometers wide along the entire border. The operation involved roughly 10,000 soldiers from eight brigades including, for the first time in the campaign, the deployment of reserves into combat.[9] By August 9, IDF forces were operating in almost every town along the border, pushing as far as Dibil

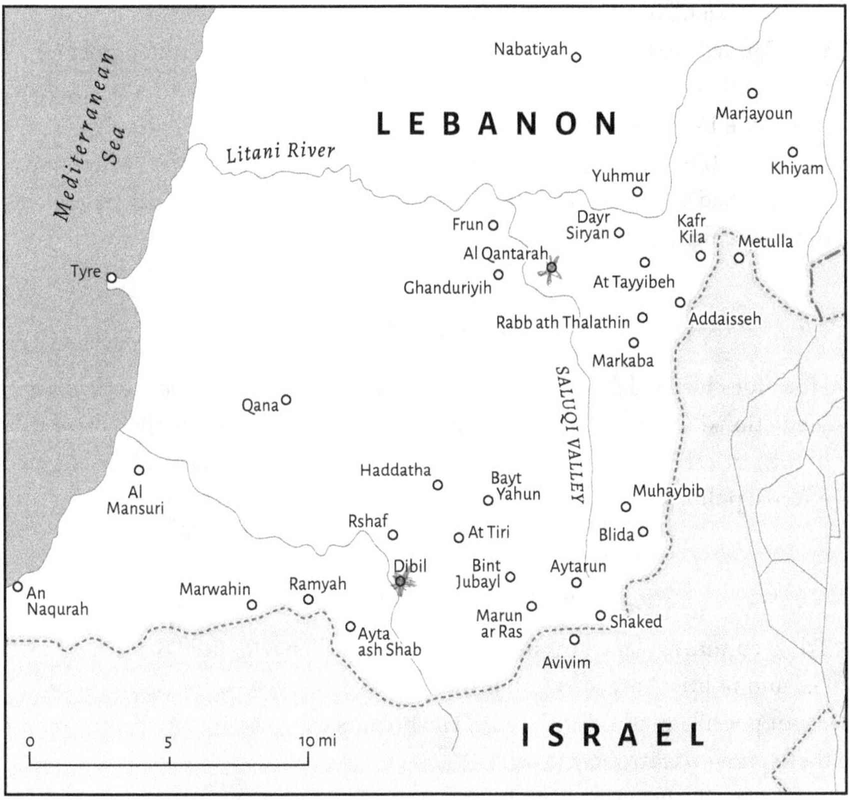

MAP 5.1. Southern Lebanon

in the south (4.5 kilometers from Israel) and Al Qantarah in the northeast (7 kilometers from Israel).[10]

On August 11, the IDF launched the final phase of the ground campaign, Operation Change of Direction 11.[11] Described as a "push to the Litani," the main effort was actually a westward advance parallel to the river: an armored column from the 401st Brigade moved from At Tayyibeh toward Frun and Ghanduriyih (about 12 kilometers west of Israel's northern tip) in order to link up with troops from the Nahal Brigade who had been airlifted into position.[12] As the 401st moved toward its objective through the Saluqi valley on August 12, it was ambushed with ATGM (antitank guided missile) fire; 11 tanks were hit and 12 soldiers killed.[13] Meanwhile, Hezbollah had regrouped in Ghanduriyih, leading to firefights in the town and its surrounding area throughout the final two days of the war.[14]

At 8:00 a.m. on August 14, Israel and Hezbollah implemented a UN Security Council cease-fire. By this time, the IDF had taken up ground positions in more than two dozen Lebanese towns, though a large portion of ground below the Litani—north of Al Mansuri and west of Ghanduriyih—had seen almost no IDF ground presence during the campaign.[15] In 34 days of fighting, the IDF had sustained 119 combat fatalities; Hezbollah had lost at estimated 650 to 750 fighters.[16]

Independent Variables

How does Hezbollah's 2006 behavior compare with the respective theories' predictions? To answer this question, I first characterize Hezbollah in terms of the critical independent variables of tribal culture, military materiel, and internal politics.

Hezbollah and Tribal Culture

Tribal culture explanations of nonstate military behavior hold that where social and political organization is ordered by familial descent, actors should adopt guerilla methods in war. In Hezbollah's case, the society from which they sprang was strongly tribal.[17]

In fact, tribalism is an important feature of social organization across much of the Arab Middle East; the struggle between tribal and statist forces for power and authority has shaped the region's politics for more than a century. Ottoman rulers sought to suppress the tribes in favor of imperial authority; European colonial powers sometimes suppressed and sometimes co-opted them, with varying success. Postcolonial Arab governments have generally sought to wrest power from the tribes, but rarely has this resulted in complete subjugation; in states such as Jordan, Saudi Arabia, and Ba'athist Iraq, for example, central governments combined repression with financial, political, and military concessions designed to buy off tribal leaders and enlist their voluntary cooperation with the regime.[18]

In Lebanon, a group of powerful land-holding families, the *zu'ama*, collectively dominated political life from the end of the Ottoman era through the civil war of 1975–90. Patriarchs of these families used their control of economic resources to enforce a classical tribal patronage system, and this patronage system in turn underwrote their control of the formal government. Throughout this period, parliamentary seats functioned as quasi-hereditary fiefdoms

by which powerful clans translated their wealth and status into political influence at the national level.[19] For the decade of the 1930s, for example, parliamentary representation in the Shiite Biq'a and South Lebanon regions was
effectively monopolized by the Haydar, Himadah, al-Zayn, al-Asad, Usayran,
and al-Fadl families, each of whom controlled seats via their ability to command votes for tribal patriarchs from extended client populations. The presidency of the Lebanese Chamber of Deputies was controlled by leaders of just
three clans (the Himadah, al-Asad, and Husayni) for all but seven years of the
half century from 1943 to 1992.[20]

Lebanese tribal influence extended far beyond just national politics. Marriage patterns, economic life, and social status were all shaped by family
identity and tribal position. Marriages, for example, were traditionally arranged within family lineages, with a preference for patrilineal first cousins
to keep property within the line; external unions were often designed to
cement interclan alliances. Economic activity was shaped by family identity,
with businesses forming along extended kinship lines and land controlled
by hereditary descent. Wealth, jobs, and resources were distributed within
tribes from prosperous to less affluent members, with the transfers acting
to solidify patronage relationships. Outside development aid was often allocated via clan leaders rather than through state agencies. Opportunities
for education and training were often allocated on the basis of birth order and
tribal status.[21]

Tribes frequently armed members for collective self-defense, and intertribe
conflicts over land, honor, or property were often violent and systematic, with
descent groups mobilizing for enforcement or revenge against comparable
opponents. As recently as the period from 2005 to 2011, armed tribal militia
engaged in pitched gunfights against one another and against state security
forces.[22] Given the constant danger of clan violence, elaborate systems of customary dispute resolution exist outside the formal Lebanese state legal apparatus to adjudicate tribal conflicts and reconcile aggrieved parties.[23] Well
into the 1990s, for example, the practice of vendetta, or th'ar, in the Biq'a Valley
required the male relatives of a murder victim to seek vengeance via the killing
of the perpetrator or senior members of the perpetrator's clan. Conversely, the
murderer was expected to seek, and be granted, protection with the tribal elders of an uninvolved clan pending the ruling of a tribal arbiter or al-a'rifah,
who was responsible for determining guilt, innocence, and compensation, or
diya, whose payment could warrant reconciliation of the aggrieved clan.[24] Recourse to the formal governmental legal system was uncommon in such cases,

with aggrieved parties often dropping charges once the tribal system had rendered a verdict, or with state judges adding only token punishment to that meted out under tribal arbitration.[25]

As in much of the Middle East, however, tribalism in Lebanon has been under pressure from modernizing forces in recent decades. Urbanization, for example, has weakened the traditional zu'ama's hold over rural client populations once dependent on them for land. The return of Lebanese diaspora populations in the 1960s and 1970s brought people with independent means acquired during life abroad into communities once dominated by the zu'ama's concentrated wealth. The growing influence of Islamist political ideology, especially following the Iranian Revolution of 1979, offered a competing model of authority and allegiance, diluting the influence of traditional patriarchs in favor of religious authorities and their political allies. These effects have varied in strength across Lebanon's confessional groups; for Lebanese Christians and Sunni Muslims, the traditional zu'ama have retained much of their former power and political influence. For the Shiite community from which Hezbollah sprang, however, the decay in the zu'ama's political power has been more pronounced: in 1992, the Shiite zu'ama's near-stranglehold on the presidency of the Chamber of Deputies, for example, was broken by Nabih Berri, a tribal outsider who was born in Sierra Leone, was educated in Detroit, and had been explicitly excluded from the al-Asad clan's electoral list in 1968 and 1972; none of the traditional clan leaders have held the office since. Shiite zu'ama parliamentary representation and influence have both declined; perhaps the most powerful Shiite clan of the pre-civil-war era, the al-Asads, have seen their current generation abandon the traditional route to office in favor of an effort to start a modern, nontribal political party (the Lubnan al-Kafa'at).[26]

But while the Shiite zu'ama's political influence has eroded, it has not disappeared. Some tribal patriarchs, such as Abdulatif al-Zayn and Ali Usayran, retain their parliamentary seats, even if their autonomy has been constrained by affiliation with an ideological party (Amal). The political role of the traditional zu'ama is now weaker in Biq'a, but it retains a stronger base in the south (both al-Zayn and Usayran, for example, represent southern constituencies).[27] And the dominant Shiite political institutions of today, Amal and especially Hezbollah, systematically exploit clan loyalties for political support; Hezbollah in particular has become a major element of traditional tribal dispute resolution as it has increasingly intervened as a mediator in conflicts between Shiite clans.[28]

And the role of tribal culture *outside* electoral politics per se remains strong throughout Shiite Lebanon. Political representation is only one of many dimensions of culture, and familial descent continues to exert an important influence on marital choice, business relationships, economic opportunity, interpersonal conflict, dispute resolution and adjudication, perceptions of loyalty and affiliation, and personal status.[29] And violence along tribal lines continues to be an important problem in Shiite Lebanon.[30] As Nizar Hamzeh put it, "Although the clans were not left untouched by the process of westernization especially in terms of life-style, tribal pre-national identities and tradition still persist. The Lebanese state has [not] been successful in eradicating tribal practices."[31]

Moreover, much of the change in the tribes' national political influence per se was a result, not a cause, of military phenomena. The civil war put a premium on political organizations that could generate military power. The Shiite zu'ama had traditionally fielded groups of armed tribesmen (*qabadayat*), but these were gradually eclipsed by the organized militias of two Shiite ideological parties whose superior combat effectiveness enhanced their national political clout: Amal and Hezbollah.[32] Tribal culture explanations of military behavior imply that tribalism trumps military exigency: if tribal cultures reshape themselves in response to battlefield requirements, then it is the latter, not the former, that is causal. Yet for the subset of tribal culture that involves national political influence, the Lebanese case shows two ideological actors who emerged with a superior military model during a time of tribal political ascendancy, and whose military superiority then contributed to the political decline of the tribes. National politics are but one dimension of tribalism as a cultural trait. But even here, the social context within which Hezbollah emerged as a military actor was clearly tribal—and the tribes' relative decline in the political arena since the civil war is more an effect than a cause of Hezbollah's military methods.

Hezbollah's Military Materiel

Unlike tribal culture, which is a strictly competing explanation of nonstate behavior, both the new theory and materialist views consider military materiel relevant. They differ, however, in the role they assign to material factors. In the new theory, materiel interacts with internal politics to explain behavior: increasingly lethal technology mutes the effect of numerical imbalance, giving actors with permissive internal politics the ability to employ midspectrum methods effectively.[33] In orthodox materialist accounts, by contrast, materiel per se is the central explanation of nonstate behavior, with material inferiority itself being a sufficient explanation for guerilla methods. In 2006, Hezbollah's military materiel was modern in important respects, but clearly inferior overall to the IDF's in quantity and quality.

Hezbollah's exact numerical strength in 2006 is unknown, but credible estimates range from a low of around 2,000 fighters to a high of around 7,000.[34] Not all these were regular, full-time combatants. Several thousand of their total strength were partially trained militia reservists with regular employment in the civil economy; a few hundred were elite "commandos."[35] These 2,000 to 7,000 fighters were equipped with a combination of light, unsophisticated infantry weapons, unguided short- and medium-range surface-to-surface missiles, and a smaller number of higher-technology antitank and communications systems.

The standard armament of most Hezbollah tactical units from the 1990s through 2006 consisted of small arms (overwhelmingly AK-47s), rocket-propelled grenades (mostly 1960s-era RPG-7s, with reports of some modern RPG-29s), some crew-served automatic weapons of DShK (12.7 millimeter) and PKM (7.62 millimeter) calibers, mortars, and a mix of antipersonnel and antitank landmines. Some units may have had access to a handful of M-113 armored personnel carriers.[36]

Hezbollah also deployed a variety of unguided surface-to-surface missiles with ranges sufficient to reach Israeli population centers from launch points in Lebanon. The great majority of these were variants of the 122-millimeter Katyusha, a technology introduced by the Soviets in World War II, with ranges of under 50 kilometers. Their small size made them easy to conceal and thus difficult for the IDF to destroy preemptively, but their short range limited practical deployment areas and feasible target sets. In addition to these short-range systems, Hezbollah had a smaller number of longer-range Fajr 3, Fajr 5, and Zelzal 1, 2, and 3 missiles of diameters from 220 to 610 millimeters and the ability to reach targets at distances of up to 220 kilometers; the Zelzal series were roughly comparable to the 1960s-era Soviet FROG-7. Their extended ranges required larger missiles and mostly truck-mounted launch systems, however, which made practical concealment harder and increased their vulnerability to IDF preemption. None, moreover, had effective mechanisms for terminal guidance, and their resulting inaccuracy left them unsuited for use against point military targets; all were essentially countervalue weapons usable only against Israeli cities and towns. Prewar Hezbollah inventories exceeded

10,000 such missiles overall, with IDF estimates of Katyusha holdings alone ranging from 10,000 to 16,000.[37]

Most of Hezbollah's weapons and equipment were thus fairly simple, mostly lightweight products of mid-20th-century technology. An important subset, however, were substantially more sophisticated. Hezbollah's communications and communications-intercept capabilities, for example, permitted mobile encrypted message transmission and enabled them to monitor Israeli radio transmissions.[38] They were reported to hold Russian-made SA-14, SA-16, and possibly SA-8 and SA-18 surface-to-air guided antiaircraft missiles, and they used the Chinese-designed CS-801 radar-guided antiship missile in an attack on an Israeli Navy corvette off the Lebanese coast.[39] They employed a small number of Iranian-made armed reconnaissance drones.[40]

Most important, they had access to tactically significant numbers of modern guided antitank missiles, including the Russian-made second-generation Kornet and Metis-M systems. The Kornet is a semiactive, command-to-line-of-sight, laser-beam-riding missile with a thermal sight capable of day/night operation and an effective range in excess of 5,000 meters. Its tandem shaped charge warhead is capable of penetrating over 1,000 millimeters of rolled homogeneous armor (RHA). Its overall performance is comparable to today's top-of-the-line US TOW-2 and Hellfire missiles.[41] The Metis-M is wire guided with a range of 1,500 meters and capabilities similar to the US M-47 Dragon.[42]

These forces were sustained on a base of military expenditure that has been estimated at anywhere from tens of millions to $1 billion per year. Most of this is believed to have been foreign direct military aid, chiefly from Iran; foreign assistance was supplemented with proceeds from private business ventures, taxation of civilians in Hezbollah-controlled areas, crime and money laundering, and Shiite religious contributions.[43]

The Israel Defense Force, by contrast, had at its disposal almost 170,000 full-time active-duty military personnel in 2006, with more than another 400,000 trained reservists available upon call-up. The Israeli Army alone comprised a force of 125,000 active and 380,000 reserve soldiers. Israeli ground forces were equipped with over 3,600 modern tanks, and more than 10,400 armored personnel carriers; over 5,400 heavy artillery pieces; and over 1,200 guided antitank missiles. The sophistication of this arsenal was designed to ensure decisive qualitative superiority over neighboring state militaries and included Israeli-made fourth-generation Merkava tanks not radically inferior to the US M-1 Abrams or the German Leopard II in protection; state-of-the-art American-made M-109A2 self-propelled 155-millimeter artillery; terminally guided artillery projectiles; and Western-style night vision, communications, and surveillance systems, including a suite of reconnaissance drones of varying size and range. The Israeli guided missile inventory included US-made Hellfires and TOW-2s of comparable performance to Hezbollah's Kornets, but in far greater numbers. Perhaps most important, Israel had an air force equipped with more than 400 modern high-performance fixed-wing combat aircraft and 90 attack helicopters; Israel's F-16s, F-15Es, and AH-64 Apaches were armed with thousands of current-generation precision-guided weapons and deployed advanced sensor suites for target acquisition. This force was sustained with almost $10 billion a year in defense expenditure.[44]

The net result of all this was a massive overall material superiority for the Israeli state military over Hezbollah. Israel's ground forces outnumbered Hezbollah's by a factor of at least 15:1 to as much as 65:1. Israel's defense expenditures exceeded Hezbollah's by a factor of 10:1 to perhaps 500:1. Israel had a fleet of modern tanks and armored vehicles with no meaningful equivalent for Hezbollah. Israel had a sophisticated modern air force with the latest ground-attack technology at its disposal; Hezbollah had none. Hezbollah could meet the IDF on equal technological ground in only a handful of categories, of which the most important was guided antitank missiles—this weapon class was important indeed, as will be discussed in detail below. But across the range of weapons actually employed by the two sides, the IDF enjoyed both generally superior technological sophistication and vastly larger potential numbers.

In fact, Israel's potential gross numerical superiority over Hezbollah was at least comparable to that of many historical state actors facing nonstate opponents. In 1964, for example, the South Vietnamese state opposed an estimated 106,000 Vietcong guerillas with a national military of 565,000, for a margin of about 5:1, or less than one-third of Israel's advantage over Hezbollah.[45] The Portuguese faced an Angolan FNLA, MPLA, and UNITA insurgency of perhaps 7,000 to 15,000 fighters with a national military of 123,000, yielding a ratio of between 8:1 and 18:1, or around one-half to one-third of Israel's relative preponderance.[46] Spain faced the Rif Rebellion in 1921 with a national military of 207,000 against some 3,000 to 6,000 rebels, for a ratio of between 35:1 and 70:1, roughly comparable to Israel's in 2006.[47]

Overall, then, in gross quantity of military material, the 2006 Lebanon campaign thus posed an asymmetry typical of wars between state and nonstate actors: Hezbollah was vastly outweighed by its state opponent in all meaningful categories. The picture is more complicated in qualitative terms, but here, too, Israel's state military likewise outclassed Hezbollah's in all but a few equipment classes where the latter could boast rough parity. Those few, however, combined to afford Hezbollah an important degree of modern firepower that it could use to threaten armored targets at substantial ranges, even if it still faced a tremendous asymmetry in the size and weight of the military forces at its disposal.

Hezbollah's Internal Politics

The new theory emphasizes two dimensions of an actor's internal politics: its stakes, and its institutions. Limited stakes and weak institutions are expected to discourage complex midspectrum methods; existential stakes and mature institutions enable such methods for nonstate actors with sophisticated weaponry.

HEZBOLLAH'S STAKES

For Hezbollah, the stakes in its conflict with Israel were high. The danger here was less that Israel would annihilate Hezbollah militarily—while Israel was committed publicly to Hezbollah's destruction, the latter had survived (and thrived) under Israeli occupation in the 1990s. The real risk for Hezbollah was political: military ineptitude against Israel would undermine the Party of God's raison d'être and its defining identity as the embodiment of effective resistance. While its social programming would probably keep it viable as a political party in some form, a Hezbollah that failed badly in a war with Israel would be a very different party thereafter; Hezbollah's very identity as an actor was at stake in its conflict with Israel.

Hezbollah began its existence as an offshoot of the preexisting Shiite ideological party Amal in the early 1980s. The reason for the split lay partly in Amal's comparatively secular outlook, but largely in its readiness to tolerate Israel and Israel's role in Lebanon. Amal had focused chiefly on asserting Shiite political rights in Lebanon's internal struggle among Shiites, Sunnis, Maronite Christians, and Palestinians; in Israel Amal saw, in part, a potential ally against a heavy-handed Palestinian presence in the Shiite heartland that many Shia resented. Hezbollah, by contrast, saw Israel and its backer the United States as the real enemy and regarded any collaboration with or tolerance of the Israeli presence as apostasy and treason.[48]

In its 1985 manifesto "An Open Letter to the Downtrodden of Lebanon and the World," for example, Hezbollah argued that

Israel must be wiped out of existence. . . . We do not recognize any cease-fire agreement, any truce or any separate or non-separate peace treaty with it. We condemn strongly all the plans for mediation between us and Israel and we consider the mediators a hostile party. . . . We cannot but stress that the policy of negotiating with the enemy is high treason.[49]

And while the 1985 "Open Letter" welcomes non-Muslim assistance in this war against Israel and its allies, the letter makes clear that Hezbollah regarded its resistance to these powers as a religious duty, not merely a strategic or tactical position of convenience or a means to other ends.[50]

This uncompromising stance vis-à-vis Israel and Islam was in fact the original reason for Hezbollah's existence: it was what motivated the split with Amal; it led to Hezbollah's original acts of violence against Israeli and Western targets beginning in 1982; and it gave rise to the civil war between Amal and Hezbollah that established the latter as the preeminent political force among Lebanese Shiites. Hostility between the two Shiite parties had grown steadily for years when in 1988 an Amal offshoot with Hezbollah connections kidnapped and killed US Marine lieutenant colonel William Higgins. This killing catalyzed rivalry into outright warfare between the two parties; in the subsequent two-year conflict from 1988 to 1990, Hezbollah's superior militia soundly defeated Amal's, and the Party of God emerged as the dominant Shiite political and military force.[51] The ideology that resulted fused Islamic universalism, opposition to Israel and the West, and the primacy of armed struggle as the means of advancing these goals.[52]

Hezbollah's subsequent political fortunes, moreover, were greatly enhanced by its military success against the Israeli occupation of South Lebanon in the 1990s. Its ability to inflict increasing casualties on IDF occupation forces garnered it widespread respect among Arabs in Lebanon and beyond, and its evident military proficiency contributed to growing political popularity among its Lebanese Shiite base. When the IDF then withdrew from its southern Lebanese security zone in 2000 this was widely seen as Israel's first major military defeat at the hands of Arab opponents, and Hezbollah was credited as the force that had driven Israel out. The Party of God consequently came to be seen as the embodiment of armed resistance against the hated Zionists, and its martial prowess as compared with the long record of Arab state futility in repeated wars against Israel gave it a unique status and political appeal.[53] By 1996, Hezbollah's political wing had won 7 of the 27 Shiite seats in the

Lebanese Parliament, with its longtime rival Amal reduced to 8; after its success in driving Israel from Lebanese soil, Hezbollah increased its strength to 9 seats with Amal falling to 6.[54]

Military symbolism has continued to play a central role in Hezbollah politics. Its party logo, emblazoned on its flag and repeated on thousands of posters and flyers and in party literature, depicts a fighter with raised fist clutching an AK-47. Hezbollah iconography emphasizes themes of military victory, martyrdom, and armed resistance; Hezbollah's "Information Unit" promotes public commemorations to celebrate "Victory Day," "Martyr's Day," and "Liberation Day." Public rallies and marches prominently feature uniformed fighters with assault rifles and heavy weapons.[55]

Hezbollah's military reputation and its ambitions for the destruction of Israel thus played a major role in the party's ideology, self-conception, and political program from its very birth. For this reason, one could expect its leaders to place a high value on military preparation and to see the stakes in its competition with Israel as very high.

By the same token, however, some have argued that by 2004 the radicalism of 1985 had tempered significantly under the pressure of Lebanese domestic electoral politics. In this view, Hezbollah's desire for political power and influence in Lebanon led it to accept a series of compromises with its original absolutism, including an increasing acceptance of a conservative and corrupt Lebanese state and, potentially, an increasing willingness to coexist with Israel.[56] Others see such compromises as tactical measures only—as cover for an underlying goal that had not changed since the 1985 manifesto.[57] But it is at least plausible that by 2004 Hezbollah had come to prioritize domestic political ambitions over the destruction of Israel.

Nor was Hezbollah exposed to a literally existential threat from Israel. In strictly military terms, Hezbollah could suffer any number of major reverses and still survive as an actor. The IDF is unlikely ever to exterminate the Party of God to the last member in combat; in practical terms, the most it could ever do would be to drive Hezbollah underground and reimpose a 1990s-style occupation. If done on a national basis this could leave Hezbollah weaker than in the original 1990s campaign (where they enjoyed sanctuaries outside Israel's security zone), but it would not literally destroy it, especially if its Iranian patrons continued their support.

Moreover, Hezbollah has important nonmilitary sources of political support in its remarkable program of social service provision. Hezbollah functions as an unusually effective cross between a local government and a religious charity, operating a system of schools and clinics, and performing conflict resolution, dispute adjudication, and mediation services. These functions have built it an impressive base of grassroots support among Lebanese Shia.[58]

Hezbollah is also an Iranian proxy with a strong connection to the Iranian state. Perhaps 70–80 percent of its annual revenues come from Iran, and it is possible that Iranian support could resuscitate Hezbollah even after a major defeat by the IDF.[59]

Neither its social service provisions nor its link to its outside patrons would necessarily be severed by even a severe military defeat in a war with Israel. But that does not mean Hezbollah's leadership could easily weather or tolerate such an outcome.

On the contrary, a Hezbollah that allowed itself to be beaten through a failure to perform effectively in a poorly waged campaign, or that proved unable to do a responsible job of defending the civilians who rely on it for protection, would lose a great deal indeed. Its martial reputation is at the heart of its self-conception and is central to the political system it has built among its supporters. It is difficult to imagine a Hezbollah leadership willing to risk this reputation and forfeit the advantages it has conveyed to the party both internally and among its base. Even if it survived a bungled war with Israel, the party to emerge from such an experience would probably have been very different from the one that entered it—quite possibly with a different leadership and a different appeal to its constituents, and exposed to a new source of potential vulnerability to domestic challengers. Whatever one's view of Hezbollah's commitment to Israel's destruction, its commitment to maintain its own martial reputation and self-conception as the embodiment of effective resistance to the Jewish state was a powerful motivator for military preparation and an important stake for its leadership.

Hezbollah's stakes in its conflict with Israel were thus not mere hopes of gain with little downside risk. Defeat in a prospective war with Israel would strike to its very identity and reason for being as a political entity, and a defeat would threaten serious losses to deeply held values. Military defeat might or might not threaten death or imprisonment for Hezbollah's senior leadership, but it would surely threaten their political careers—and assassination following defeat is a prospect that would be hard to rule out in a country where more than a dozen political assassinations were attempted between 2005 and 2008 alone.[60]

HEZBOLLAH'S INSTITUTIONS

In the new theory's terms, Hezbollah was a mature natural order actor in 2006. It had multiple suborganizations and a hierarchy of specialized entities with substantial capacity, impersonal decision making, moderate rent extraction, and stable internal coalitions. And by 2006, Hezbollah had demonstrated substantial ability to enforce plenary decisions on elites. The result was an institutional makeup of greater maturity than that of many states, notwithstanding its status as a nonstate actor.

By 2006, a seven-member Shura Council (Majlis al-Shura) sat atop a remarkably formal internal organizational hierarchy. Shura Council members were elected every two to three years, appointed the secretary general, and oversaw the work of five subcouncils (whose heads sat on the Shura Council): the Political Council, responsible for relations with Lebanese domestic political actors; the Jihad Council, responsible for resistance activity against Israel; the Parliamentary Council, which managed Hezbollah strategy in the Lebanese national legislature and provided constituent services; the Judicial Council, which adjudicated religious disputes and performed conflict mediation; and the Executive Council, which oversaw a series of suboffices dedicated to functions including health, education, public information, finance, and external relations. Other Hezbollah subagencies included Al-Qard al-Hasan, a microfinance institute; the Jihad al-Bina Development Organization, a Hezbollah-run construction agency to build and rebuild homes; and the Islamic Health Committee, which ran hospitals, clinics, and pharmacies. A deputy secretary general (Naim Qassem in 2006) served as second in command to the secretary general. A 200-member Central Council (Majlis al-Markazi) screened nominees for the Shura Council and elected its members (see figure 5.1).[61]

By the time of the war, these agencies provided much of the health, education, and judicial services available to the civilian population of South Lebanon, and they did so with an efficiency that few states in the region could exceed. The reach and popularity of these social services was a major contributor to Hezbollah's political standing among Lebanese Shia, and an important factor in Hezbollah military recruitment; in 2006 Hezbollah's institutional structure had real capacity and delivered real services on a major scale.[62]

This sociopolitical wing was accompanied by a military wing, also under the direction of the Shura Council. The military wing was itself suborganized

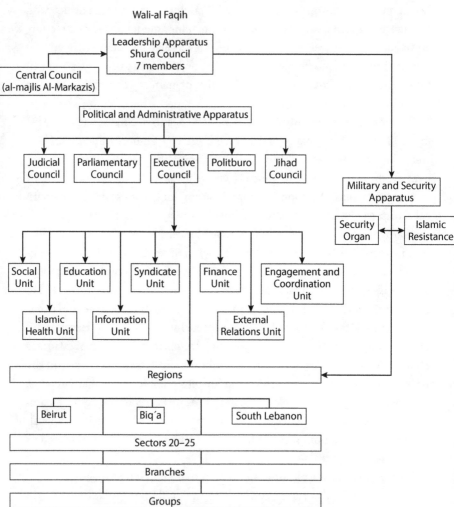

FIGURE 5.1. Hezbollah internal organization (from Hamzeh, *In the Path of Hizbullah*, 46)

into a security organization and the Islamic Resistance, or al-Muqawamah al-Islamiyyah. The security organization was in turn subdivided into an internal security agency, the Amn al-Hizb, and an external security branch, the Amn al-Khariji (or "Encounter Security," Amn al-Muddad), tasked with counterintelligence. The Islamic Resistance included separate organizations for recruitment and ideological indoctrination and combat operations, and it oversaw both the full-time military force and the paramilitary village guard units.[63]

Decision making in these institutions was shaped largely by the authority of office, and especially clerical office, rather than personality. Hezbollah's organizational structure afforded superior status to the Shiite world's senior clerics, with even the Shura Council serving under the *wali faqih*, or Shiite supreme jurist. While Hezbollah was not immune to the internal political horse trading typical of even highly institutionalized states, and while decision making could be contentious on controversial issues, decisions when reached were typically implemented even by those who opposed the outcome. In the early 1990s, for example, the question of Hezbollah participation in the Lebanese government was subject to contentious internal debate. But when the wali faqih, Ali Khamenei, announced his support, this resolved the debate and produced a stable decision for participation.[64]

Hezbollah played a meaningful role in the economy via direct service provision and business development activity. But corruption was relatively limited, and Hezbollah did not seek to control everyday commerce for rent extraction.[65]

Hezbollah's internal balance of power had stabilized by 2006 after an early period of factional strife centered on the question of participation in the Lebanese government. Beginning in 1989, pragmatists associated with Hassan Nasrallah and Abbas al-Musawi favored a combination of armed resistance to Israel via independent Hezbollah military action with participation in the Lebanese state via pursuit of elected office in Parliament. But others, and especially Subhi al Tufayli and Husayn al-Musawi, rejected compromise and political participation and insisted on continued radical opposition to the state from without.[66] Tufayli issued an open call for Shiites to boycott the 1992 election and attack the polling places, then launched an independent "revolution of the hungry" (*thawrat al-jiya'*) in 1997 without the support of the Shura Council in an implicit critique of what he saw as the party's failure to make good on its founding commitment to the Shiite poor. This in turn escalated to actual violence when Tufayli then ordered armed supporters to occupy a Hezbollah religious school in Ba'albeck, triggering a reaction by the Lebanese Army in which 8 were killed and 50 wounded. This proved the last straw, however, and the Shura Council finally voted to expel Tufayli from the party in January 1998 after Khamenei sided with Nasrallah and the pragmatists.[67] This 1998 purge removed the only serious threat to Hezbollah's internal unity. Since then, the party has been remarkably free of major dissension. There have been no further expulsions by the Shura Council, and no significant threats to Nasrallah's leadership as secretary general. By 2006 Hezbollah's internal balance of power had become remarkably stable, yielding a mature natural order actor by the criteria presented in chapter 4 and the appendix.

Dependent Variable: Hezbollah's Military Behavior

Given these characterizations, how does Hezbollah's military behavior correspond with the respective theories' predictions? Tribal culture and orthodox materialist explanations predict highly Fabian, classical guerilla methods for a tribal nonstate actor at an enormous material disadvantage relative to a powerful state opponent. "Hybrid" materialist theories predict a combination of classical guerilla tactics with terrorism and conventional methods, all in the same battle space, yielding methods intermediate to those of states and older nonstate actors. The new theory, by contrast, predicts state-like midspectrum war making for an actor with Hezbollah's high stakes, institutionalized internal politics, and access to 21st-century technology—notwithstanding its tribal culture or material disadvantage vis-à-vis Israel.

In fact, the 2006 campaign shows a nonstate actor with state-like midspectrum military behavior. Of course, Hezbollah was not radically massed and exposed—no one would confuse the 2006 fighting with Waterloo or Gettysburg. But no military has been able to fight that way and survive against a competent state foe since at least 1900. State practice for over a century has mandated greater levels of concealment—still well short of that of classical guerillas, but much more concealed than Pickett's Charge. Among the mostly intermediate behavior typical of modern states, Hezbollah falls well within the normal range.

To code behavior that thus falls between the popular stereotypes of state "conventional" and nonstate "irregular" methods requires a detailed treatment of subaspects that vary in their relative adherence to Fabian and Napoleonic principles. The combat behavior of real military organizations is always a complex story. To untangle the complexities and adjudicate the conflicting elements, I use the index method presented in the appendix and assess Hezbollah's methods against the specific traits enumerated in chapter 2 and the appendix. In particular, I consider, in turn: stealth; taking and holding ground; dispersion; coercion; distinguishability of combatants from noncombatant civilians; and functional differentiation within the theater of war.

1. Stealth

Stealthiness is a critical distinction between the Fabian archetype, with its emphasis on cover and concealment, and its Napoleonic opposite, which accepts exposure to maximize firepower. In 2006, Hezbollah's prepared fighting positions were remarkably well covered and concealed. When forced to maneuver, however, Hezbollah had systematic difficulty using the midspectrum techniques of fire and movement to avoid exposure.

IDF attackers were rarely able to identify Hezbollah combat positions prior to drawing fire from them, even from very short ranges. In Dayr Siryan, Israeli infantry approached to within 50 to 100 meters of Hezbollah fighters without spotting them; in Aytarun, tanks passed directly beneath the windows used to fire on them without seeing the defenders first; in Bint Jubayl, defensive positions in buildings were still invisible to infantry advancing up directly adjoining streets; in At Tayyibeh, Hezbollah defenders opened fire undetected from a range of 50 meters.[68] Repositioning within buildings often enabled urban defenders to remain concealed even after extended firing; especially in villages near the Israeli border, tunnels were dug between buildings to facilitate concealed movement within the prepared defensive system.[69] In the border area, combat preparations initiated years before the war resulted in civilian homes whose very construction was influenced by military tactical considerations: buildings in key locations were discovered with thicker, reinforced walls on the sides facing likely approach routes from Israel.[70] Other indoor combat positions near the border had sandbags or other reinforcements hidden in the interior to strengthen walls facing intended engagement areas.[71] Outdoor and rural positions were sometimes very elaborately prepared, with concrete dugouts, multiple chambers, concealed entry and exit points, and carefully camouflaged firing positions.[72] Antitank missile positions were especially difficult to locate, given the often extended range of ATGM engagements and Hezbollah's success at concealing launchers and crews.[73] Terminal defenses for rural Katyusha rocket launch areas, dubbed "nature preserves" by the IDF, were especially intricate, well camouflaged, and carefully prepared— sometimes including hydraulically raised and lowered launch tubes, concrete-reinforced caches, showers for garrisons, multiple entrances and exits, and interconnected outworks to enable concealed movement within the system.[74]

Hezbollah's fire discipline was strong and consistent, enabling positions to remain concealed until the last minute. Engagements were typically initiated by Hezbollah with coordinated, concentrated fire from multiple locations.

Defenders routinely allowed lead echelons to pass, opening fire on follow-on elements once larger formations had advanced into kill zones; locations were rarely given away by premature firing from nervous individuals.[75]

When its fighters were required to leave prepared positions and maneuver above ground, however, Hezbollah had difficulty combining movement with suppressive fire to reduce exposure. They had some ability to combine arms: they frequently used ATGMs in concert with small arms and heavy machine guns in direct fire, and they made significant use of mortars. But rarely were direct and indirect fires coordinated with movement for suppression, and movements themselves were often exposed.[76] Reactive movement, as opposed to planned counterattacks, was especially exposed: moving units taken under fire from previously concealed IDF positions often halted and fell back in disorder rather than reorienting to the new threat, redirecting suppressive fire, seeking cover, and continuing an advance by bounds.[77] In general, Hezbollah fighters were typically covered and concealed when stationary in prepared positions, but exposed when moving above ground.[78]

2. Taking and Holding Ground

A central feature of the Fabian extremum is unwillingness to accept decisive engagement to take or hold ground; at the Napoleonic extremum, combatants never willingly yield positions.[79] In 2006, Hezbollah showed far more commitment to contest ground than an archetypical Fabian militia, but also far less than the Napoleonic archetype.

To assess Hezbollah's relative commitment to taking and holding ground I use four observable referents of this commitment, as justified in detail in the appendix: the duration of firefights; the proximity of attackers to defenders; the incidence of counterattack; and the incidence of harassing fires and unattended minefields.

THE DURATION OF FIREFIGHTS

Defenders who seek to hold ground must remain in position as long as they are under attack. Against a determined attacker, this can produce extended engagements or a series of renewed firefights in single locations. By contrast, classical guerillas who seek only to inflict casualties at minimum cost and risk to themselves rarely remain in place over extended durations, as this enables government forces to fix their locations and bring superior firepower to bear.

Instead, classical guerilla ambushes are brief, to enable the guerillas to escape after a one-sided surprise volley of fire at an unsuspecting target. Of course, state "conventional" defenders who are destroyed or broken quickly can fail to hold a position very long; conventional attackers who are destroyed or driven off quickly can terminate engagements early. Brief firefights can thus be observed in either the Napoleonic or the Fabian extreme. But extended fire-fights over individual positions are inconsistent with an extremum of guerilla tactics and suggest instead an attempt to hold ground. Hence the longer the observed duration of firefights, the less Fabian and the more Napoleonic the actor's methods.

In Lebanon in 2006, Hezbollah defenders often engaged in very extended firefights—certainly far longer in duration than one would expect from arche-typical guerillas with no intention of holding ground. At the Shaked outpost, for example, a dug-in Hezbollah defensive position remained in place on a critical hillcrest near the Israeli border between Avivim and Marun ar Ras exchanging fire with IDF tanks and infantry for more than 12 hours before fi-nally being destroyed in place by Israeli fire.[80] At Marun ar Ras, Hezbollah defenders held their positions through a 5-to-7-hour struggle with IDF attack-ers.[81] At Bint Jubayl, Hezbollah defenders fought a series of pitched battles over a period of more than 4 days, including individual firefights lasting as long as 8 hours, as on July 26, and 6 hours, as on July 28, and sporadic fighting con-tinued in the town until the end of the war on August 14.[82] At Ghanduriyih the fighting lasted for more than 2 days (August 12–14), including firefights of 7 to 8 hours at a time.[83] The battle for At Tayyibeh on July 29–30 lasted 24 hours, including 4 to 5 hours of especially heavy fighting at close quarters.[84] Al Qantarah saw a 4-hour-long engagement.[85] In the Saluqi valley, Hezbollah antitank guided missile (ATGM) teams occupying a series of positions in depth received return fire from Israeli Merkava tanks after their initial launches but stood their ground and continued to fire at least 10 additional missiles, ceasing fire and withdrawing only when IDF artillery was brought to bear.[86] Some engagements were shorter, but many were sustained over many hours' or many days' duration.[87]

THE PROXIMITY OF ATTACKERS TO DEFENDERS

Defenders who seek to hold ground against an advancing attacker must also stand that ground even as the attacker closes with, and potentially reaches, their positions. By contrast, archetypical Fabian guerillas who seek only to inflict casualties at minimum cost and risk to themselves rarely allow superior government forces to close with them over any extended advance under fire. The risk of decisive engagement grows as an attacker closes with a defender; to allow an attacker into close proximity is to risk being unable to break contact and escape. Ambushes with an overwhelming concentration of fire delivered suddenly against an exposed target will sometimes be triggered at close range to maximize surprise and accuracy, but such tactics are risky for guerillas and, when undertaken, must be concluded quickly. Frequent combat at close proximity, and especially, close proximity tolerated for more than a few minutes in a surprise ambush, thus tends to imply behavior closer to the Napoleonic end of the spectrum. Other things being equal, the greater the observed incidence of close-quarters fighting, the less Fabian the actor's methods.

In Lebanon in 2006, Hezbollah defenders frequently held their positions and continued to fire even after IDF attackers closed to very short ranges— often well within the bounds of decisive engagement for the defenders. The Hezbollah defensive position at Shaked, for example, was finally overrun in place by Israeli assault; the garrison's 20 fighters were all killed without any attempt at withdrawal or surrender over the course of a 12-hour battle.[88] Hezbollah defenses at Marun ar Ras and Bint Jubayl were similarly held until destroyed in close combat after extended advances to ranges of as little as 10 to 100 meters with no apparent attempt to break contact or withdraw.[89] At Marun ar Ras, Aytarun, and Markaba, Hezbollah defenders held their fire until advancing IDF infantry had passed their outlying posts and were within the defense system itself, making withdrawal impossible.[90] At Bayt Yahun, Hezbollah defenders allowed Israeli tanks to drive by windows on the street below, opening small-arms fire against IDF armored vehicle commanders standing in open hatches at ranges of under 20 meters.[91] At Marun ar Ras, Hezbollah defenders fought literally room to room within buildings after IDF attackers had entered the structures.[92] At Ghanduriyih, defenders whose positions had been flanked but who retained potential escape routes through the town nevertheless remained in position and were eventually destroyed in close combat; IDF attackers could make only 600 meters of progress in a day of hard fighting. Fifty-seven bodies of dead Hezbollah fighters were recovered from the town.[93] At At Tayyibeh, the Hezbollah garrison lost 20 of its 30 fighters in close combat before being ordered to withdraw.[94] At Aytarun the defenders were withdrawn only when it became apparent that their position had become tactically irrelevant—the IDF had bypassed them, reaching Marun ar Ras from the southwest and rendering the blocking position at Aytarun moot.[95] At

Haddatha, some 30 fighters remained in position in the village until the cease-fire, even after the IDF had nominally occupied the village.[96]

Of course, not all fighting was at point-blank range. Modern ATGMs are designed for long-range engagement, and Hezbollah often took advantage of that capability to open fire with large-caliber antitank missiles at extended ranges. In the Saluqi valley fighting, for example, Hezbollah ATGM crews engaged Israeli tanks from firing positions north of the Litani River at ranges of over three kilometers.[97] Hezbollah also made very extensive use of long-range rockets to target Israeli towns and cities at distances of over 30 kilometers.[98] Exploitation of heavy weapons' range to maximize their lethality is not inconsistent with an intent to hold ground, however, and these longer-range attacks were not conducted in a way that suggests an intent to break contact before accepting decisive engagement: Hezbollah rocket fire continued for most of the war, and, as noted above, Hezbollah ATGM fire in the Saluqi valley continued even after the launchers came under effective return fire from their targets.

There was thus a substantial volume of close-quarters combat in 2006; some of the defenders involved may have expected to annihilate the attackers by surprise safely at point-blank range, but in many of these cases the defenders were accepting decisive engagement in the context of protracted firefights that are more consistent with an intent to hold ground.[99]

THE INCIDENCE OF COUNTERATTACK

Defenders who seek to hold ground must counterattack periodically to retake lost positions. Deliberately closing with the enemy in a counterattack, however, usually involves a greater degree of exposure than does a well-prepared defense. Archetypical guerillas who seek one-sided attrition of the enemy but not the retention of ground thus make very sparing use of counterattack by maneuver. Hence the greater the observed incidence of counterattack, the less Fabian the actor's methods.

Hezbollah did not routinely or uniformly counterattack when driven from positions, as German defenders, for example, typically did in World War II.[100] But there are multiple documented examples nevertheless of Hezbollah counterattacks in 2006. At Marun ar Ras on July 20, 15 to 30 Hezbollah fighters advancing from the direction of Bint Jubayl conducted a deliberate assault on an Israeli company position occupying a group of buildings on the crest of Hill 951. The Hezbollah attackers divided into two elements, supported by fire from a school building in the town east of the hill, striking the Israeli company simultaneously and by surprise, opening fire from a range of 40 meters, mounting multiple attempts after being beaten back initially, and eventually reaching hand-to-hand combat with the defenders.[101] At Bint Jubayl, a detachment of 40 to 60 fighters attacked Israeli defenses on Hill 850. The attackers were again divided into a main and secondary effort, with supporting ATGM fire from two directions and at least sporadic indirect-fire support from remotely located mortar teams. The attack closed to within 10 meters of the Israeli positions before being driven off.[102] In the casbah at Ayta ash Shab, Hezbollah fighters assaulted, and succeeding in entering, a group of IDF-defended buildings.[103] At Muhaybib, 15 to 20 Hezbollah fighters assaulted IDF-defended buildings in groups of 3 to 4, operating on multiple axes, and supported by ATGM fire.[104] At Ghanduriyih, a single team of 3 to 5 fighters counterattacked the IDF after it had taken up positions in the casbah.[105] At Dayr Siryan, Hezbollah fighters assaulted Israeli positions from two directions with supporting fire from rocket-propelled grenades (RPGs).[106] At Tayyibeh on July 29, 10 Hezbollah fighters counterattacked after the IDF took the first in a line of Hezbollah-occupied houses, in an apparent attempt to retake the building.[107] In fact there are many accounts of apparent counterattacks from across the theater; not all of these, however, can be distinguished unambiguously from confused movement toward undetected Israeli positions, ambush attempts, or other actions that may not have involved the intention to regain lost ground.[108] None of these actions, moreover, was at anything larger than platoon scale, and none succeeded in securing its territorial objective. But the engagements noted above were all unambiguous, deliberate attempts to close with Israeli defenders in positions recently taken by the IDF in ways that imply an intent to regain lost ground.[109]

THE INCIDENCE OF HARASSING FIRES AND UNATTENDED MINEFIELDS

Defenders seeking to hold ground by halting a determined attacker's advance require aimed fire in heavy volume. Minefields and other barrier systems can be of great assistance to any defender, but their ability to halt attackers is much reduced if the barrier is not overwatched by direct fire to interfere with clearance or avoidance. Aimed direct fire, however, requires an exposure to return fire. Archetypical Fabians who do not seek to halt an advance outright but merely to inflict casualties can avoid return fire by striking from a safe distance with harassing indirect fires and unattended minefields, and they will often prefer this. Harassing fires and unattended minefields can occur in any kind of conflict, but massed indirect fire and minefields or barriers tied in with direct-fire overwatch are thus much more common in archetypically Napoleonic warfare. Hence the greater the observed incidence of massed indirect fires and overwatched minefields, the less Fabian the actor's methods.

Hezbollah in 2006 made considerable battlefield use of indirect fire, especially mortars, and had mined substantial stretches of southern Lebanon. But rarely was Hezbollah mortar fire concentrated or intense. There were exceptions: at Markaba, for example, one IDF unit received at least 120 mortar rounds in the course of the assault.[110] And of course Hezbollah's rocket fire on Israeli civilian targets was heavy and sustained. Most battlefield mortar use, however, was accurate but light in volume and variable in its targeting.[111] Hezbollah minefield employment was sometimes tied into direct-fire defensive systems in a systematic way and sometimes not. The defenses in Ghanduriyih, for example, included mines and obstacles overwatched by fires.[112] The main approach route up the Saluqi valley to the Litani River was mined and overwatched by well-concealed ATGM positions, requiring the IDF to undertake deliberate assault clearance by combined-arms teams of combat engineers, tanks, and artillery.[113] Hezbollah defenses at Marun ar Ras were coordinated with elaborate mining of the main roadway at Junction 8; detonation of these explosives triggered the direct-fire action in defense of the town on July 20.[114] Some minefields south of the Litani were organized to canalize IDF vehicles into open ground within range and in view of ATGM positions north of the river.[115] Yet the most extensive Hezbollah minefields could readily be bypassed, and Israeli combat engineers encountered relatively few integrated barrier defenses requiring deliberate combat clearance under fire.[116] Booby traps were common, especially in and around abandoned houses, but little of the actual combat action took place through defended barrier systems, and massed indirect fires on assault forces in breaching operations were infrequent.[117]

3. Dispersion

Fabian irregulars employ widely distributed forces at low and uniform densities; archetypically Napoleonic armies operate in greater density and concentrate differentially at particular points. Hence the greater the relative forward concentration of combatants at the fighting front, the less Fabian the actor's methods. Hezbollah deployed a troop density in the decisive region south of the Litani that was lower than many state armies in the world wars, and Hezbollah's forces were significantly more uniformly disposed than these. But as state troop densities have fallen over time, even state militaries now rarely concentrate to levels much in excess of Hezbollah's in 2006.

Hezbollah's exact strength in 2006 is unknown, but Western estimates vary from a low of around 2,000 to a high of around 7,000.[118] Assuming a midrange figure of 4,500, and assuming that the great bulk of these forces were forward deployed south of the Litani, this implies an average density of around six fighters per square kilometer in the critical sector; this local concentration would have been perhaps 10 times higher than an archetypically Fabian uniform territorial defense of Lebanon would have produced.[119]

Midcentury state militaries deployed at much higher local densities, and much less uniformly over the theater as a whole. The French in 1940 defended the Maginot Line with 75,000 troops over 1,260 square kilometers, for a local density 10 times that of Hezbollah; the 1944 British offensive in Operation Goodwood concentrated its assault force to a local density perhaps 30 to 50 times greater than that of their forces in the Normandy theater overall, or a ratio of local to theater density at least three times higher than Hezbollah's in 2006.[120] As figure 3.8 illustrates, however, the ongoing, progressive decline in typical state military force-to-space ratios over time since 1900 had reduced normal state "conventional" troop densities radically by the late 20th century. For example, the US defense of Saudi Arabia in 1990, as noted above, deployed a density of under three troops per square kilometer on the critical coastal sector, which was actually less than Hezbollah's likely density in the crucial sector south of the Litani in 2006, and the US distribution of forces within that defended zone was not radically less uniform than Hezbollah's.[121] In important respects, the ongoing reduction in state force-to-space ratios over time has resulted in a standard of state practice not significantly more concentrated or less uniform than Hezbollah's.

4. The Balance of Brute Force and Coercion

The Napoleonic extreme at the strategic level of war relies heavily on brute force to seize or protect the disputed stake in the conflict without any voluntary decision to concede on the opponent's part. The Fabian extreme, by contrast, is strictly coercive, manipulating the enemy's costs and benefits to induce the enemy to concede a stake that it could still seize or withhold if it chose. Coercion is widely employed, even by powerful state actors in world wars;

brute force, by contrast, is never encountered above the tactical level in the pure Fabian archetype. At the strategic level, an observation of coercive action per se is thus a relatively weak indicator of the difference between Napoleonic and Fabian methods, but the more extensive the role of brute force in conduct above the tactical level the less Fabian the actor's methods.

Hezbollah's military strategy in 2006 is disputed, and its representatives' stated views on this are insufficient to establish the intended role of coercion and brute force definitively. And unlike its tactics, Hezbollah's strategy cannot be determined unambiguously via primary-source IDF interviews. Its strategic intent thus cannot be observed directly. One can, however, deduce from Hezbollah's observed behavior at the tactical and operational levels a strategic logic consistent with that behavior, and exclude otherwise plausible alternative accounts, subject to the assumption that Hezbollah is an instrumentally rational actor (in the minimal, Clausewitzian sense that its actions are means to obtain political ends).

In particular, Hezbollah's observed behavior is consistent with a model in which a largely brute force pattern at the operational level is designed to serve largely coercive strategic ends—a combination that falls short of the pure Napoleonic archetype, but which is very common in interstate great power warfare all the same. As a much weaker actor, Hezbollah surely understood that it could not destroy Israel or the IDF by force of arms in 2006. It also surely realized that Israel was capable of invading Lebanon and reestablishing or expanding on its pre-2000 occupation. A preeminent requirement for any rational Hezbollah strategist would thus have been to design a means of deterring Israel from such a reoccupation, or coercing it into halting one should deterrence fail.[122] In principle a variety of means for coercive pain infliction were available to Hezbollah; several of these options, however—and especially the use of suicide bombers—had been undermined by Israel's internal and border security policies. But rockets, which overfly border defenses and checkpoints, remained a powerful threat to Israeli population centers. Ideally, long-range launchers deployed in central or northern Lebanon would provide the needed coercive threat from locations beyond the reach of any plausible Israeli invasion. Long-range launchers, however, are large, distinctive, and relatively few in number, leaving them vulnerable to preemptive destruction by Israeli air strikes.[123] Shorter range rockets are smaller, easier to conceal, vastly greater in number, and potentially much less vulnerable to aerial preemption—but their range limited them to deployment in close proximity to the Israeli border and hence left them vulnerable to destruction by a ground invasion. This left Hezbollah with a dilemma: if they removed their chief coercive weapons from the reach of the Israeli Army, they would be vulnerable to the Israeli Air Force; if they used weapons survivable against the Air Force, they would be within reach of the Army.

The apparent solution to this dilemma was to rely chiefly on short-range rockets that could be concealed from air attack, but to protect these from ground invasion via a Hezbollah ground defense that would have to adopt a brute force operational doctrine of denying the IDF access to the launch areas.[124] Complete brute force denial would be impossible—the IDF was, and is, too strong. But if a ground defense could hold long enough, it would enable ongoing rocket fire in the meantime to inflict mounting coercive pain on Israeli society. Retaliatory Israeli air strikes, moreover, could be expected to inflame regional and world opinion, placing international political pressure on Israel to relent.[125] Neither of these coercive mechanisms, however, is quick—it takes time for political pressure to build and for leverage on Israeli decision makers to mount; even a massive wave of rocket attacks would have little coercive effect if it were a short-term spasm with no prospect of longer-term continuation and escalation. The key operational-level requirement was thus to buy the time needed for the coercive campaign to succeed—to prevent the Israelis from getting quick access to the key launch areas on the scale needed to search the terrain exhaustively and uproot concealed rocket launchers before enough pressure could be built on the Israeli government to yield the issue at stake.

This operational requirement could not be met with highly Fabian tactics, which allow enemy forces into the country but gradually penalize them for their presence with hit-and-run casualty infliction. Hezbollah could not preserve a system of hidden rocket launchers long enough for what might have to be thousands of individually small warheads gradually to build coercive pain if the IDF had ready access to the terrain in southern Lebanon. A brief incursion by tens of thousands of IDF soldiers might suffer a handful of losses to guerilla ambushes, but in the meantime it could roll up the entirety of Hezbollah's primary rocket force, end the coercive campaign against Israeli cities, then withdraw before its own casualties became prohibitive either. So Hezbollah set about the construction of a brute force defensive capability in southern Lebanon that might be able to delay an Israeli invasion long enough to enable a coercive strategy to succeed.

This analysis is broadly consistent with some assessments of Hezbollah's strategy in 2006.[126] But many have argued that Hezbollah intended its ground forces, as well as its rocket forces, to function coercively—as a classical guerilla approach at both the strategic *and* the operational level in which the ground force role was to impose pain via IDF military casualties rather than to contest control of southern Lebanon.[127] And surely Hezbollah welcomed the coercive benefit of killing Israeli soldiers. But their observed behavior is inconsistent with a conclusion that this was the primary mission of Hezbollah's ground forces.

In particular, the tactics they actually employed in 2006 are much more consistent with an intention to hold ground than they are with an assumption that territorial control was unimportant and that their goal was the archetypical Fabian aim of attrition per se. As I argue above, Hezbollah fighters defended positions too long, at ranges too short, with counterattack too often, to square with a model of classical Fabian intent. Nor did they exploit the potential of civilian intermingling in nearly the degree one would normally expect from a purely Fabian force, as I argue below. This is not to say that Hezbollah's operational doctrine was one of Maginot Line static defense, either—they accepted decisive engagement at some times and places but not others, they counterattacked to regain some lost ground but not all, and they used mines and indirect fires to complement direct-fire territorial defenses in some places but as harassment tools in others. And their operational level intent appears to have been to delay rather than to hold indefinitely. Like most real militaries, Hezbollah's tactics were between the extremes. But their tactics were especially far from the Fabian guerilla extreme. If their intent had been merely to coerce Israel through the killing of IDF soldiers, they could have done so at much more advantageous loss-exchange ratios (and hence have continued such attrition longer, and killed more Israelis with the forces available to them) if they had *not* accepted decisive engagement by holding positions so long, or if they had *not* attempted counterattacks, or if they had persuaded civilians to remain under lower-intensity combat and intermingled their fighters with the population. The tactical choices they made in 2006 are difficult to reconcile with an assumed intent to forgo brute force on the ground in favor of a pure Fabian approach.

That said, one should be wary of attributing too much prescience or strategic foresight to Hezbollah in 2006. Hassan Nasrallah and the Hezbollah leadership were surprised by the severity of the Israeli response to the July 12 kidnapping; they had not anticipated this and clearly had not intended war on this scale in 2006.[128] Hezbollah's reaction to the Israeli invasion thus involved an important degree of improvisation following a kidnapping that was apparently not designed for the result it caused. Yet Hezbollah was not improvising from scratch. The 2006 campaign appears to have been the product of a fairly generic plan for the conduct of an unspecified future war with Israel, which may or may not have been well suited to the circumstances in which they found themselves, but was available on short notice at the time. Most state militaries develop a variety of contingency plans for possible future conflicts, which they work out in peacetime, well in advance of an actual crisis, then shelve for possible future use. Thus, such plans cannot anticipate the political particulars of the crisis that may bring war in any actual case. Ideally they are updated and adapted to the situation as it unfolds, but in Hezbollah's case, the 2006 war was a surprise, and Israel's quick escalation left them with little time for strategic adaptation. What they did have was a generic design and a series of elaborately prepared defensive works and rocket launch sites developed for that design. So they used what they had. The result was a coherent campaign at the tactical through theater level—and one that was in many respects more state-like and midspectrum than often expected from nonstate actors—but this campaign may or may not have ultimately served Hezbollah's larger grand strategic interests.[129]

5. Distinguishability of Combatants and Civilians

Classical guerillas obtain much of their cover and concealment via intermingling with innocent civilians with whom they seek to blend in; actors at the Fabian extremum thus wear versions of typical civilian clothing, operate among the civilian population, and avoid the use of large-caliber weapons that are difficult to conceal under civilian clothing even when such weaponry is available. By contrast, archetypically conventional armies at the Napoleonic extremum avoid civilians where possible, use uniforms or other distinguishing marks to differentiate combatants from noncombatants, obtain cover and concealment via terrain rather than civilian intermingling, and exploit the heaviest weapons available to maximize their firepower. Hence the greater the incidence of uniformed combatants, the greater the physical separation of combatants from civilians, and the more extensive the use of available heavy weapons, the less Fabian the actor's methods.

Hezbollah's forces were largely segregated from the civilian population in the 2006 campaign. Hezbollah is often described as having used civilians as shields in 2006, and in fact they made extensive use of civilian homes as direct-fire combat positions, and to conceal launchers for rocket fire into Israel.[130] Yet the villages Hezbollah used to anchor its defensive system in southern Lebanon were largely evacuated by the time Israeli ground forces crossed the border on July 18. As a result, the key battlefields in the land campaign south of the Litani River were mostly devoid of civilians, and IDF participants consistently report little or no meaningful intermingling of Hezbollah fighters and noncombatants. Nor is there any systematic reporting of Hezbollah using civilians in the combat zone as shields. The fighting in southern Lebanon was mostly urban, in the built-up areas of the small to medium-size villages and towns typical of the region. But it was not significantly intermingled with a civilian population, which had largely fled by the time the ground fighting began. Hezbollah made very effective use of local cover and concealment, but this was obtained almost entirely from the terrain—both natural and man-made.[131]

As for distinguishing markings, in 2006, the great majority of Hezbollah's fighters wore uniforms. In fact, their equipment and clothing were remarkably similar to those of many state militaries—desert or green fatigues, helmets, web vests, body armor, dog tags, and rank insignia.[132] On occasion, IDF units hesitated to open fire on Hezbollah parties in the open because their kit, from a distance, looked so much like that of IDF infantry: at Addaisseh, seven Hezbollah fighters were mistaken for Israelis until an IDF soldier noticed that one of them was wearing track shoes.[133] Again there were exceptions: at Marun ar Ras, most fighters were seen in uniform, but some armed combatants were also observed in civilian clothes; 2 of 20 bodies of dead Hezbollah fighters at At Tayyibeh were found in civilian clothing; 2 fighters in civilian clothes were observed at Frun, and a few more at Al Qantarah; at At Tiri, combatants were observed in uniform pants but not tops.[134] But the great majority of Hezbollah fighters in 2006 were uniformed and visually distinguishable from civilians.[135]

Hezbollah also made extensive use of the heavy weapons at its disposal. From long-range surface-to-surface missiles, to heavy ATGMs such as the Kornet, to radar-guided antiship missiles, to heavy versions of crew-served machine guns such as the 12.7-millimeter DShK, Hezbollah did not restrict itself to light weapons that could be concealed in civilian garb—it used what it had in an effort to maximize its firepower against the Israelis.[136]

6. The Military Organization of the Theater of War

Archetypically Fabian warfare is a relatively uniform, undifferentiated territorial defense, without a distinguishable front or rear, waged by guerillas fighting largely where they live; archetypically Napoleonic armies differentiate the theater into distinct covering-force zones, main battle areas, rear areas, and communication zones, and sectors of main effort as opposed to supporting or economy-of-force areas. Hence the more uniform or undifferentiated the military organization of the theater of war, the greater the degree to which the actor's methods approach the Fabian extreme.

Our ability to distinguish the theater-level military organization of southern Lebanon is limited by our lack of access to senior Hezbollah sources. We do know, however, that IDF ground forces entered some areas without resistance, whereas other locations were heavily—and apparently preferentially—defended. Rabb ath Thalathin, for example, was entered on July 30 without opposition.[137] Blida, Rshaf, Marjayoun, Marwahin, and Kafr Kila were all entered without receiving fire.[138] By contrast, villages such as Bint Jubayl, Marun ar Ras, Ghanduriyih, At Tayyibeh, Muhaybib, Dayr Siryan, Aytarun, Bayt Yahun, Al Qantarah, and Markaba were all stoutly defended; the natural approach route through the Saluqi valley was manned and contested.[139] Villages commanding key road junctions in the central part of the theater such as Bint Jubayl and Marun ar Ras were especially heavily defended, and key terrain commanding the approaches to these junctions, such as the Shaked outpost overlooking Marun ar Ras, was garrisoned and fortified.[140] The southwestern sector (An Naqurah to Ramyah), by contrast, offered less-defensible terrain and appears to have been only lightly held.[141] Villages near the border with Israel were systematically better prepared for defense and more strongly manned than those in the interior.[142] Supplies and ammunition were stockpiled in locations commanding key terrain; other positions appear to have received little logistical prepositioning.[143]

Perhaps most important, Hezbollah exercised a degree of hierarchical, differentiated command and control over subunits operating in key areas during the campaign, making apparent decisions to favor some sectors over others, hold in some places but yield in others, counterattack in some locations but withdraw elsewhere. A formal chain of command operated from designated and well-equipped command posts; used real-time communications systems including landline cables and encrypted radio; issued orders; changed plans; and moved some elite units over considerable distances from rearward reserve areas to reinforce the key battle for the communications network in the central sector.[144]

The scale of differentiation and articulation should not be exaggerated—much of the Hezbollah defense was static; reserve movements were very small scale; Hezbollah commanders rarely succeeded in adapting to changing conditions quickly or responsively; and Hezbollah's limited freedom to maneuver under Israeli air supremacy made any large-scale integration for mobile defense at the theater level impossible even if Hezbollah would have attempted this otherwise. But neither were their dispositions in southern Lebanon an undifferentiated territorial defense without distinctions between front and rear, or main effort and economy of force; the theater of war was clearly articulated for military purposes into differentiated sectors of operations with distinctions in emphasis and role.[145]

Hezbollah Proficiency of Execution in Lebanon, 2006

A final important distinction concerns Hezbollah's proficiency of execution, which offers an opportunity for process tracing. The causal logic of the new theory turns on the unusual complexity of midspectrum as opposed to purely Napoleonic or Fabian war fighting, and the claim that mature institutions and existential stakes are required for military actors to field forces with the specialized skills and interpersonal trust needed to cope with this complexity under fire. Of course, inept performance is possible whether one attempts Napoleonic, midspectrum, or Fabian methods, and as Clausewitz's concept of friction implies, perfect military execution is impossible for real militaries in the fog, fear, and fatigue of battle. But variations of degree can be observed in the proficiency of different military organizations, and the new theory's causal logic implies that institutionalized, high-stakes actors should display reasonably competent execution of midspectrum methods in combat. Did Hezbollah?

Hezbollah's proficiency of execution in 2006 was imperfect, but well within the experience of many states—and especially, Arab states waging war against the IDF. Hezbollah did some things very well. As noted above, their fighting position siting and preparation were very effective, affording consistently strong cover, concealment, and fields of fire. As noted above, their fire discipline was excellent.

Hezbollah effectively coordinated direct fires in support of its counterattacks, often from multiple directions.[146] Barriers and overwatching ATGM positions were sometimes integrated with considerable skill over multikilometer distances: east of Ghanduriyih, for example, a series of minefields were placed in locations that canalized Israeli columns into engagement areas exposed to ATGM fire from concealed launchers located north of the Litani River some five kilometers away.[147] And Hezbollah mortar fire was consistently accurate and responsive.[148]

Other things were done much less well. As noted above, Hezbollah demonstrated reasonably effective combined-arms cooperation when operating from static positions, especially in direct fire, but had much more difficulty coordinating suppressive indirect fire in support of moving elements. Their adaptation to unexpected developments was often limited: where Hezbollah organized linear defenses, these were often flanked by Israeli attackers; the defenders, however, typically either fought on in the same positions or simply withdrew, rather than forming a new front to meet the assault. Although Hezbollah made apparent attempts to monitor Israeli communications networks, some of which (such as medical evacuation nets) operated in the clear, there is no evidence they were able to exploit any information gained.[149]

Hezbollah demonstrated little ability to control or coordinate the maneuver of large formations. Counterattacks, for example, never exceeded platoon strength, and many were considerably smaller, with individual maneuver elements sometimes as small as 3 to 5 soldiers; deliberate retrograde movements were normally limited to handfuls of combatants at a time; small detachments often fought isolated actions; and whereas perhaps 60 to 100 commandos were moved over great distances, no large reserve was withheld or maneuvered to counterconcentrate against IDF movements, and movements of Hezbollah forces within their forward defenses were small scale and over short distances.[150] This should be kept in context: the entire size of the Hezbollah combatant force in southern Lebanon was probably well under 7,000, or less than the strength of two US Army brigades—hence battalion- or brigade-size maneuver would be unrealistic. But the scale of maneuver attempted by Hezbollah in Lebanon was nonetheless very small by Western standards.[151]

Hezbollah direct-fire marksmanship was mixed. Small-arms fire, for example, was systematically inaccurate and caused few casualties.[152] Hezbollah ATGM crews, by contrast, could strike targets from extraordinary ranges: Israeli armored vehicles were regularly hit by missiles fired from four to five kilometers away. Hezbollah frequently fired such missiles in salvos at single targets, however, and IDF armored vehicles normally maneuvered evasively and used smoke for obscuration once under attack. The result of this combination was that the ratio of ATGM hits to total launches could be very low. In the Saluqi valley fighting, missiles were fired in volleys of perhaps a dozen rounds at a time, of which one to two would hit their targets; an IDF combat engineering battalion in Ghanduriyih received six to eight ATGM launches while maneuvering at night with no hits; on the night of August 12 outside At Tayyibeh a formation of more than 15 tanks received over a dozen Kornets fired from the village of Yuhmur, north of the Litani River roughly five kilometers away, suffering three hits, all of them against stationary vehicles—no moving targets were hit; in another engagement at At Tayyibeh, one of a volley of four Saggers hit an IDF D9 armored bulldozer; the survivors popped smoke, but Hezbollah continued firing without further success.[153] The net result was a potentially lethal threat, but a very large expenditure of missiles per target struck.[154]

On balance, this yields a mixed picture of Hezbollah proficiency: it did some things very well, such as its use of cover and concealment, its preparation of fighting positions, its fire discipline and mortar marksmanship, or its coordination of direct-fire support. But it also fell far short of contemporary Western standards in small-arms marksmanship and in controlling large-scale maneuver, integrating movement, using direct fire support, combining multiple combat arms, and reacting flexibly to changing conditions. Hezbollah appears to have *attempted* a remarkably state-like midspectrum system of tactics and theater operational art, but there is a difference between trying and achieving, and in 2006 at least, Hezbollah's reach in some ways exceeded its grasp.

Yet Hezbollah is hardly alone in this. Many state actors have fallen far short of today's Western standards of military proficiency, both in today's world and historically. Saddam's "elite" Iraqi state Republican Guard, for example, proved systematically incapable of integrating movement and indirect fire support, combining multiple combat arms, reacting flexibly to changing conditions, or consistently hitting targets with either small- *or* large-caliber weapons; in two wars with the United States, the Iraqi state military's use of cover and concealment, combat position preparation, and fire discipline were consistently far *less* proficient than Hezbollah's.[155] The Italian state military in 1941 proved much less proficient in conventional warfare than did Hezbollah in 2006; French defenses on the critical Sedan front in 1940 were more exposed and no more able to react to changing conditions than those of Hezbollah.[156] The Egyptian state military proved systematically less adept than Hezbollah in cover and concealment and little better than Hezbollah in coordinating large-scale maneuver with combined arms or in flexibly responding to changing conditions in 1956 or 1967; the Syrian state military did no better in 1967, 1973, or 1982.[157] In fact, Hezbollah inflicted more Israeli casualties per Arab fighter in 2006 than did any of Israel's state opponents in the 1956, 1967, 1973, or 1982 Arab-Israeli interstate wars.[158] Hezbollah's skills in conventional war fighting were clearly imperfect in 2006. But they were also well within the observed bounds of other state military actors in the Middle East and elsewhere, and significantly superior to those of many such states—as the new theory's causal logic anticipates for actors with Hezbollah's internal political makeup.

Alternative Accounts

The analysis above is broadly consistent with some prominent accounts of the 2006 campaign.[159] Others, however, are more substantially at odds with the analysis here.

Some, for example, have characterized Hezbollah in 2006 as an essentially terrorist organization using an information-age version of the asymmetric military methods seen as typical of nonstate actors historically. In this view, Hezbollah's goal was to win an information war for public opinion within and beyond Lebanon, solidifying its political position as the standard-bearer for Arab resistance to Israel by drawing Israel into a guerilla war it could not win while publicizing the inevitable Israeli miscues and civilian fatalities. The tactics to implement this strategy are seen as a higher-tech version of standard guerilla warfare: sniping, albeit with modern antitank missiles; hit-and-run ambushes; roadside bombs; harassing mortar and rocket fire, often against civilian targets in Israel; the use of Lebanese civilians as human shields to protect guerillas against Israeli firepower; and efforts to goad a state military into overuse of violence and widespread killings of innocents. What was new, in this account, was mainly Hezbollah's use of the internet and sympathetic cable news networks to publicize its military actions, which are held to have been intended chiefly as spectacles to attract this publicity.[160] A closer analysis, however, shows little correspondence between the actual evidence of Hezbollah's military behavior and the intuition behind such characterizations. Hezbollah in 2006 was indeed higher tech than many earlier nonstate actors, but its use of that technology was closer to that of traditional state militaries in "conventional" wars than to the model of nonstate guerilla warfare assumed in such accounts.

Others see the truly distinctive feature of Hezbollah's method and strategy as their integration of military, political, and social action. Certainly Hezbollah's combination of building grassroots domestic support and using military resistance against a hated foreign opponent has been highly distinctive and successful for them.[161] And it may well account for their unusual internal cohesion, their high degree of support from their Shiite base, their influence in Lebanese politics, and even some aspects of their relative proficiency in combat (such as their ability to conceal prewar military preparations from

Israeli intelligence, or their ability to recruit talented human capital for service). None of this, however, is actually at odds with anything in the new theory or the account above. This theory seeks to explain one aspect of nonstate behavior: their choice of concealment and exposure in combat as embodied in the distinction between Fabian and Napoleonic tactics and operations. This is an important aspect, inasmuch as it underlies the commonplace distinction between state and nonstate status in the making of war. But it is not everything. And in particular, it treats the deeper causes of its central explanatory variables as exogenous: if the actor is institutionally mature and motivated by existential stakes, the theory makes the same predictions regardless of how or why they came to be this way. Hezbollah's Lebanese domestic politics are thus neither confirmatory nor disconfirmatory evidence for the theory.

Still others see Hezbollah essentially as an Iranian puppet, waging a proxy war with Israel on behalf of its patron and thus to be properly viewed more as an arm of Iranian state policy than as an independent actor, state or not.[162] Certainly Hezbollah has always had an extremely close relationship with Tehran, and surely much of Iran's reason for its support was Hezbollah's utility to them in their conflict with Israel. Yet almost all nonstate military actors have outside patrons, even actors whose military methods are very different from Hezbollah's—the fact that Hezbollah often acts as a proxy for Iran does not explain why its methods are so different from those of many other nonstate actors, who also act as proxies for state patrons. Ceteris paribus, most patrons would prefer lethal, effective proxies, yet many fail to get them. Of course, Iran invested very heavily in Hezbollah. Yet this did not produce a material balance vis-à-vis Israel that was significantly better than in most wars between nonstate actors and state opponents—even with Iranian assistance, Hezbollah still faced massive material inferiority against Israel (as noted above). For the new theory, the crucial challenge is to explain variance in the behavior of nonstate actors who almost all have state patrons; the existence of a close relationship between Hezbollah and Iran does not in itself distinguish this from other cases, nor does it explain Hezbollah's particular choice between lethality and concealment.

Theoretical Implications

How do these observations square with the predictions of the respective theories? There are significant discrepancies between the details of the case and the expectations of tribal culture or materialist theories. Hezbollah in 2006 was a nonstate actor from a tribal culture at a major material disadvantage vis-à-vis a powerful state opponent. The commonplace expectation for such actors would be Fabian guerilla warfare at high levels of concealment and modest lethality. Yet their actual behavior was far more "conventional" than this. Nor did Hezbollah combine conventional *weapons* with irregular *tactics*, as hybrid warfare theorists expect: Hezbollah's tactics were no more "irregular" than those of most states. The Party of God's military behavior in 2006 was thus at odds with the expectations of both cultural and materialist theories.

In the new theory's terms, Hezbollah's military behavior was neither Fabian nor Napoleonic but well to the interior, midspectrum region of the range depicted in figure 2.1: the net of the behavioral traits described above yields a coded dependent variable value for the index measure presented in chapter 2 and the appendix of 3.50 on the theory's six-point scale.[163] This is as the new theory would expect for a nonstate actor with mature natural order institutions, existential stakes, and 2006-era weapon technology. In fact, the functional form presented in the appendix predicts a dependent-variable behavioral score of 3.497 for Hezbollah in 2006,[164] a remarkably close fit to the observed value of 3.50. And Hezbollah's proficiency of execution was well within the bounds of many states in interstate conflict, which is consistent with the causal mechanism from which the theory derives its prediction for the case. Neither the observation nor the formal prediction resembles the orthodox "guerilla" model of nonstate warfare in much of the literature; nor are the details of Hezbollah's conduct as consistent with the "hybrid" materialist variant as they are with the expectations of the new theory. No theory fits observed data perfectly, but the new theory thus offers a stronger fit than either culturalist or materialist alternatives.

On balance, the new theory thus outperforms the orthodox alternatives in a case where one would reasonably have expected the opposite. While no single case can ever validate any theory, much less one specified on a continuum, this does establish a degree of correspondence between the new theory and an important example of real warfare; it shows a closer correspondence for the new theory than the alternatives in a critical case; and it thus offers grounds for shifting our confidence in the respective theories accordingly.

6

The Jaish al Mahdi in Iraq, 2003–8

IN THIS CHAPTER I present the second of five case method tests. Muqtada al Sadr's Jaish al Mahdi (JAM) militia was among the more prominent non-state opponents in recent US military history. They were responsible for a major fraction of US combat casualties in Iraq; they played an important role in the sectarian warfare that was so central to the overall violence in the country in 2006–7; and their role in that sectarian struggle reshaped the demographic makeup of Baghdad, with the Shiite JAM driving their Sunni rivals from much of the city by mid-2007.

Of special importance for my purposes, the case also offers an unusual opportunity for theoretical leverage, as it approximates a controlled comparison with Hezbollah in 2006. Both were Shiite Arab actors in tribal societies. Both were confronted with materially superior Westernized state militaries. Both had at-risk populations of supporters to protect. And both had external support from the same Iranian patron. Tribal culture and materialist theories would thus expect both militaries to adopt similar, classically guerilla methods; if anything, tribalism was probably stronger in 2006 Lebanon than in 2003 Iraq, which would imply more-Fabian methods for Hezbollah than for the JAM if a tribal culture explanation were the strongest account of nonstate behavior. By contrast, their internal politics were very different: the JAM was riven by personalized factionalism and motivated increasingly by profit and political opportunism, whereas Hezbollah was institutionally mature with high stakes in its conflict with Israel. The new theory thus predicts very different behavior for the two actors, with Hezbollah's internal politics encouraging midspectrum methods and the JAM's institutions and stakes preventing this. In fact the case largely corroborates the new theory and contradicts the others, under conditions that warrant a greater shift in confidence than would typically be possible from a single case study.

I develop this argument in five steps. First, I outline briefly the main events of the case. Second, I develop values for the main independent variables associated with the competing theories. Third, I treat the theory's dependent variable of observed military behavior. Fourth, I process-trace the relationship between the theory's causal logic and the events of the case through a discussion of the JAM's proficiency of execution. I conclude by assessing the relative fit between prediction and observation given this analysis, and the case's implications for the theories under study.

Overview of Events

The Jaish al Mahdi (sometimes called the "Mahdi Army" in the West) was created by the upstart Shiite cleric Muqtada al Sadr in 2003, shortly after the US invasion toppled Saddam Hussein's Ba'athist government in Iraq. Saddam had ruled with an iron fist for almost a quarter century, and his sudden removal created a military and political vacuum. This vacuum brought a security dilemma in which Iraq's Sunni and Shiite sectarian communities (and Arab and Kurdish ethnic groups) each feared that others would settle old scores, restore lost privileges, or prey on rivals. The new American-led administration was slow to establish real control, allowing looting and general disorder that heightened fears and encouraged disempowered former Ba'athists to organize for revanchist insurgency. Saddam's regime had been dominated by Sunnis and had brutally repressed Shiite and Kurdish insurrections; growing signs of Sunni Ba'athist insurgency by mid-2003 thus created strong incentives for Shiites to mobilize in self-defense given the authorities' apparent inability to restore order. Among the most threatened of Iraq's Shiites were those of the massive Shiite slum in northeast Baghdad, Sadr City, whose poverty and proximity to wealthier Sunni neighborhoods unnerved both communities: Sunnis feared the loss of their property and privileges to newly empowered Shiite slum dwellers; Sadr City residents worried that Sunni death squads would kill to prevent this.[1]

Such conditions were ripe for sectarian political entrepreneurship. Among the most successful such entrepreneurs was Muqtada al Sadr. The son-in-law of a prominent Shiite dissident of the Saddam era, Sadr seized the opportunity to position himself as the defender of the downtrodden Shiite masses, juxtaposing himself simultaneously against revanchist Sunnis, American occupiers, and a wealthier Shiite establishment that he framed as distant and out of touch. From his base in Sadr City, he organized both a political movement, the Office of the Martyr Sadr (OMS, named for his revered father-in-law, who had been killed by Saddam), and an armed militia, the Jaish al Mahdi.[2]

The JAM's initial purpose was Shiite self-defense, and especially the protection of Sadr City slum dwellers from Sunni death squads. But Sadr's aspirations were broader, both politically and militarily. The traditional Shiite establishment had adopted a tolerant stance toward the American military presence, which they saw as a bulwark against Ba'athist revanchism. Sadr, by contrast, lacking traditional religious credentials or social stature, saw an opportunity to outflank the Shiite establishment politically by appealing directly to popular frustration with foreign military occupation. He thus adopted a public stance of fiery opposition to the United States and its troop presence. Together with his enthusiastic acceptance of Iranian assistance, this led to increasing tensions with the American-led Coalition.[3]

These tensions led to a series of military confrontations with Coalition forces. The first followed the US Army's March 2004 shutdown of the OMS-run newspaper *al-Hawza*, which the Coalition believed had been inciting violence against Coalition forces. The JAM responded with a wave of violence, storming police stations and government offices across much of central and southern Iraq. Coalition forces then counterattacked to restore control. The result was several months of sustained combat between JAM militiamen and US troops in Karbala, Najaf, Kufa, Baghdad, Basra, and elsewhere. After his militia suffered heavy losses, and with Coalition forces in control of almost all the contested areas, Sadr ordered a cease-fire in June.[4]

The JAM then attacked an Iraqi police station in Najaf on August 5, spurring another battle when American soldiers and Marines intervened. For the next three weeks, fighting raged across Najaf's seven-square-mile Wadi as-Salaam cemetery and surrounding city streets. Sadr then negotiated another cease-fire, with the JAM's fighters surrendering their weapons before being allowed to leave and with Coalition forces then reoccupying the battlefield.[5]

The JAM's next major action followed the Al Qaeda in Iraq (AQI) bombing of the Shiite Golden Dome mosque in Samarra in February 2006. The destruction of the mosque, a major Shiite shrine, led Sadr and other Shiite militia leaders to conclude that the government had failed in its duty to protect the Shiite community at large from Sunni insurgent depredations. Until then, the JAM's stance against Sunnis had been mostly defensive; after Samarra, however, Sadr ordered a broad offensive against Sunni insurgents and civilians in Baghdad. This offensive moved outward from Sadr City, with the JAM first establishing beachheads west of the Tigris in the Shiite enclaves of Kadhimiya in the north and West Rashid in the south. From there the JAM began infiltrating the accessible mixed districts of Shula, Huriya, and Washash adjoining

MAP 6.1. Iraq

Kadhimiya, and Jihad, Bayaa, and Abu T'Shir in the south. Conquests in these areas were used to establish forward bases and lines of communication for further drives into the heart of Sunni central Baghdad; by early 2007 the JAM had driven the Sunnis from much of Mansoor, Karkh, Adel, Ghazaliyah, Doura-Mekanik, Ferat, Aamel, and Saydiyah.[6]

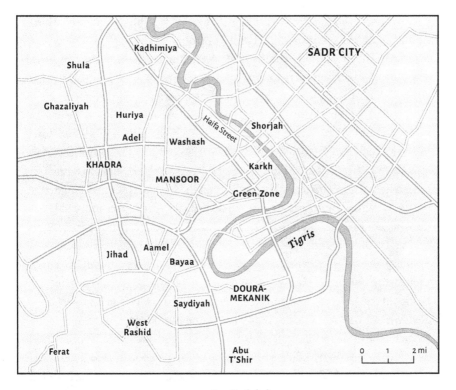

MAP 6.2. Baghdad

Coalition forces responded to this violence by reinforcing Baghdad in an attempt to stabilize the capital. Two successive operations were launched to halt the sectarian bloodshed and establish control, Operation Together Forward in June, and Operation Together Forward II in August. Unlike the earlier US counterattacks, however, these moves faced a much larger opponent: the JAM had grown in the interim and now fielded a force of multiple thousands in the capital, and the Coalition was now caught in the middle between the JAM and its Sunni insurgent enemies, both of whom targeted Coalition forces. To cope with opposition on this scale (and to further what was then the overall US strategy of rapid transition to Iraqi security responsibility), Operations Together Forward and Together Forward II were designed to rely heavily on Iraqi government soldiers and police. Yet the Iraqi Army (IA) and National Police (INP) proved slow to respond and ineffective in combat, leaving US forces without the strength needed to suppress the violence, which escalated rapidly.[7]

This crisis eventually led to a major change in US strategy, with a combination of significant reinforcements for US troops in the capital, a new commander in General David Petraeus, and new methods emphasizing distributed dispositions, dismounted patrolling, and direct provision of population security by US, not Iraqi, forces. This "Surge," or Operation Fard al-Khanoon, as its Baghdad component was known, was accompanied by a large-scale realignment of the JAM's primary Sunni opposition, which increasingly stood down in a series of negotiated settlements with US commanders. With this reinforced US presence increasingly freed of the need to fight Sunni insurgents, it turned its attention increasingly on the Shiite JAM. Sadr fought on for a time, but faced with an increasingly one-sided struggle against a reinforced Coalition that could focus its efforts on his militia, he announced another cease-fire on August 29, 2007, effectively ending his third major battle of the war.[8]

The JAM's final campaign began with the Iraqi government's offensive against the Sadrist presence in Basra in Operation Sawlat al-Forsan ("the charge of the knights") beginning on March 25, 2008. Designed to establish government control of a city that Iraqi prime minister Nouri al-Maliki had judged to be under militia rule, the offensive bogged down against heavy JAM resistance. Iraqi Army officers had been planning a coordinated action with US support, but Maliki short-circuited this and launched the attack prematurely without meaningful Coalition involvement; without this, the IA proved unable to make headway. A surprised Coalition command rushed an ad hoc combination of US reinforcements and supporting air strikes into the battle, which quickly turned the tide. With Iranian mediation, Sadr then negotiated yet another cease-fire, ending combat in Basra on March 30.[9]

Maliki then sought to exploit his apparent victory in Basra by expanding the offensive to al-Amara, where the IA advanced into JAM-held areas to assert government control. Sadr responded to these moves with a counteroffensive in Baghdad. His political and military base in Sadr City was still mostly free of US or government forces; he thus ordered JAM militia based there to attack government troops and facilities in retaliation for the government offensive in Basra, including a wave of rocket attacks against the Coalition nerve center in the "Green Zone" across the Tigris River. The United States responded with a counteroffensive into Sadr City itself, with the intention of clearing the neighborhoods from which the rockets were being launched. The result was a final sustained battle between the JAM and US forces, as the combined US-Iraqi assault moved directly into Sadr's base. In more than six weeks of fighting, the JAM failed to drive out the Coalition forces, and Sadr declared a final cease-fire on May 10, after which he formally disbanded the JAM on June 13, 2008.[10]

Sadr's formal announcement notwithstanding, his followers remain armed, and it is widely understood that Sadr retains the ability to renew hostilities should he find this in his interest. As of early 2012 he claimed the existence of a new, "Muqawimun" militia to defend the interests of Iraqi Shia by force if necessary. But the formal existence of the Jaish al Mahdi had thus come to an end as of June 2008—and its combat record as an explicit militia organization ended with the conclusion of open hostilities in Sadr City in May.[11]

Independent Variables

How does the JAM's behavior compare with the respective theories' predictions? As with Hezbollah, I first characterize the JAM in terms of the critical independent variables of tribal culture, military materiel, and internal politics.

The Jaish al Mahdi and Tribal Culture

As in much of the Arab world, Iraqi culture has important tribal elements. Loyalty to family, clan, and tribe influenced economic behavior, marriage choices, and social status in 2003–8 Iraq, as they did in Lebanon before 2006. And as it has in Lebanon, in Iraqi society conflict between tradition and modernizing forces has tended to reduce the net effect of tribalism over time. But this tendency has been neither uniform nor monotonic; national politics and military exigency have reinvigorated tribalism in Iraq since the late 1980s, but more strongly for rural Sunnis than for urban Shiites. For the JAM, the result was a cultural context that was certainly more tribal than, say, that of its US military opponents, but which was significantly less tribal than that of their Sunni rivals in Iraq or even the Shiite Hezbollah of Lebanon in 2006.

Iraqi tribal culture had been under pressure from a combination of Ottoman land reforms, British colonial repression, and gradual urbanization beginning as early as the mid-19th century. The traditional tribal hierarchy was built on inherited family ownership of agricultural land; as these patterns of dynastic wealth concentration were disrupted, the patriarchs' (or *sheiks'*) influence diminished relative to governmental or religious authority figures.[12] This process accelerated after the "14 July Revolution," which replaced Iraq's Hashemite monarchy with the Ba'ath Party's pan-Arab nationalism in 1958: the

Ba'athists' commitment to a self-conscious modernism put a premium on state institutions and further marginalized the clan and tribe as political actors.[13]

But the sheiks' authority was never completely erased. As in Lebanon, tribal influence in the social and economic spheres proved more resilient than it was in politics per se.[14] And tribalism in Iraqi politics saw a major revival with the series of national crises beginning in the 1980s.

In 1980 Saddam Hussein invaded neighboring Iran. After initial successes, his offensive bogged down, saddling Iraq with a long war of attrition against a larger, wealthier, and more populous opponent. To survive, Saddam turned to any source of support he could—including Iraq's tribes. Once a bitter opponent of tribalism as a throwback to a primitive past, Saddam now courted the sheiks, using them as vehicles for recruitment of tribesmen into the Iraqi Army.[15]

After a long, bitter war and compromise settlement with Iran, Saddam then invaded Kuwait in 1990. Western intervention on behalf of the Kuwaiti monarchy expelled Iraqi forces, imposed a humiliating defeat on the Iraqi military, and spurred uprisings among Iraq's restive southern Shia and northern Kurds. This was accompanied by harsh UN economic sanctions that crippled the Iraqi economy and isolated the Ba'athist regime in the international system. These developments posed an existential threat to the Iraqi regime. Saddam responded by grasping for any source of legitimization and authority within reach; this included a reversal of the Ba'ath Party's prior secularism and a deliberate turn to Islamist rhetoric as a means of rallying support against the West.[16] But it also included a redoubled outreach to Iraqi tribal leadership.

Saddam now tried to frame tribal culture as a cornerstone of Iraqi national identity. He courted the sheiks as grassroots leadership figures, promoting them as authentic representations of traditional authority, publicizing his own tribal background, and referring to himself as the Iraqi "sheik of sheiks." He armed and funded supportive tribal leaders to co-opt them as allies against the Kurdish and southern Shia uprisings, deputizing them to perform security duties and thus freeing state soldiers for action against the rebels. He revitalized traditional tribal dispute resolution mechanisms, empowering western Sunni sheiks with authority to settle even murder cases outside the state judicial system, and allowing others increased powers in civil and lesser criminal cases. In the process, a tribal system that had been in decline for generations found a new lease on life under the deliberate sponsorship of Saddam and the Iraqi state.[17]

This process of retribalization, however, was not uniform in its effects. The tribal system had always been stronger in rural areas than in cities, so its revitalization had less effect on urban populations.[18] Tribal organization had also traditionally been less cohesive among Iraqi Shiites than for Sunnis, with smaller, splintered clans and subclans.[19] Together these contributed to a weaker traditional role for the tribe relative to the mosque among Iraqi Shia, and thus a weaker social foundation for tribal regeneration.[20] And Saddam's tribal outreach was deliberately designed to strengthen his hand against insurrections in the Kurdish north and Shiite south; hence its benefits were directed disproportionately toward Arab Sunnis who could be relied on to back the regime against the rebels.[21] Shia tribes were thus less favored than others, and urban Shiites least of all. The net result of this was both to further the social and economic marginalization of Muqtada al Sadr's future political base, and to leave poor urban Shiites less connected to or influenced by traditional tribal mores than many other Iraqis—and especially the rural Sunnis so favored by Saddam.

As a whole, Iraqi society had thus been subject to more than a decade of deliberate state cultivation of tribal values by the time of the US invasion in 2003, and this policy had reversed at least some of the general decline in Iraqi tribalism over the preceding generations. But this trend has largely bypassed the poor urban Shiite population from which the Jaish al Mahdi drew its support and recruited its fighters. This is not to say that the JAM's culture was free of tribal influence or that it was somehow insulated from the norms and values of the surrounding society.[22] But it is fair to say that tribal norms probably played a less salient cultural role for the urban JAM between 2004 and 2008 than they did for Hezbollah's more rural southern Lebanese population base in the years leading up to the 2006 campaign. Both were clearly more tribal than the Israeli or American state militaries; but the JAM was probably less so than Hezbollah.

The Jaish al Mahdi's Military Materiel

Materialist theories expect materially inferior nonstate actors to resort to Fabian military methods. The new theory posits an interaction effect between materiel and internal politics wherein advanced technology can enable midspectrum methods for outnumbered nonstate actors with mature institutions and existential stakes. The JAM had some access to modern weaponry, but was at a major disadvantage in both quantity and quality of materiel relative to the US military.

Estimates of the JAM's numerical strength are uncertain at best. But official US assessments reportedly ranged from 6,000 to 10,000 fighters in Baghdad in 2006. By 2007–8, intelligence estimates put the JAM's overall strength at 25,000 to 40,000 active combatants (including their Iranian-trained "Special Groups"), with a large body of tacit sympathizers providing logistical, intelligence, or other support.[23]

These fighters were armed with a variety of mostly light weapons, including the ubiquitous AK-47 assault rifle, hand grenades, RPG-29 rocket-propelled grenade launchers, sniper rifles, and light crew-served machine guns. Some JAM elements, and especially the Special Groups, had access to simple indirect-fire systems, including 60-millimeter and 81-millimeter mortars and 107-millimeter Hesab, 122-millimeter Grad, and 240-millimeter Fajr rockets. The JAM also modified standard mortar shells to increase their range by adding field-expedient rocket motors (creating "IRAMs," or Improvised Rocket Assisted Mortars), and they are rumored to have had access to at least some SA-14 Strela handheld guided antiaircraft missiles.[24]

The JAM's most effective weapons, however, were improvised explosive devices, or IEDs. At their simplest these could be nothing more than scavenged artillery shells concealed under roadside debris with basic detonators and trip wires to trigger the explosives when contacted by a passing soldier. These simple early designs were quickly augmented with more elaborate devices using pressure plates to trigger buried explosives constructed with minimum metal content to thwart metal-sensing mine detectors; other designs relied on radio controls from garage door openers or communications transmitters to trigger explosives remotely upon command from hidden observers. Explosive charges grew from single shells to "daisy-chains" of multiple rounds wired together to respond to a single trigger, or multiple antipersonnel or antitank land mines buried one atop the other to increase blast yield. By 2007, massive charges buried under roadways were capable of destroying US M-1 Abrams tanks and overturning M-2 Bradley armored infantry fighting vehicles.[25]

Perhaps the best known, and certainly the most dangerous, of these were the EFPs, or Explosively Formed Projectiles, in widespread use by 2007 in Baghdad and elsewhere. EFPs used a modern, specially engineered shaped charge to project a slug of metal at near-hypersonic speeds over distances of up to 30 meters. Designed to penetrate the weaker flank and rear plates of passing armored vehicles, these weapons were often emplaced in arrays of a half dozen or more charges aimed at stretches of roadway along which Coalition convoys were expected. Their range enabled them to be concealed at a distance from the roadside, making early detection harder; remote detonation techniques allowed hidden observers to trigger an attack from still further away. Simultaneous detonation of multi-EFP arrays increased hit probabilities and created a chance of multiple strikes against a given vehicle or convoy. Multiple strikes, however, were not necessary for lethal effects—the EFPs in use by the JAM by 2007 could penetrate in a single shot any Coalition armored vehicle deployed in Iraq through the end of the conflict, and the projectiles' size made penetration very likely to kill or injure multiple crewmembers or to destroy the vehicle outright if the round struck fuel or ammunition within.[26] These EFPs were the most effective—and the most advanced—weapons in the JAM arsenal.

Little is known about the revenue stream supporting these forces. The JAM derived significant income from taxation, control of staple commodities such as gasoline and cooking oil needed by Shiite communities, diversion of revenue from the tourist trade to Shiite shrines in Karbala, patronage deriving from OMS parliamentary representation and control of the Ministries of Health, Transportation, and Agriculture, and other sources; the scale of these revenues, however, is unknown.[27] Iran clearly provided substantial financial aid to the JAM; Iranian assistance to the JAM Special Groups has been estimated at anywhere from $9 to $36 million a year by the US military, and Iranian support for the mainstream JAM militia reportedly approached $1 billion a year in 2004.[28] But the ultimate scale of Iranian funding remains unknown.

The JAM's Coalition opponents, by contrast, had much greater resources at their disposal. At the time of the Samarra Mosque bombing that spurred the JAM's 2006 offensive in Baghdad, the United States deployed a force of about 130,000 troops in Iraq, together with another 20,000 foreign allies and 230,000 Iraqi government soldiers and police. By mid-2007, the Bush administration's "Surge" had increased these figures to over 160,000 US and over 350,000 allied and Iraqi personnel.[29] These forces were but a portion of global US military power, moreover; though it could not have sustained in steady state a force any larger than the 160,000 troops deployed in mid-2007, the United States in principle had at its disposal a force of over 1.4 million personnel under arms overall, constituting the world's second-largest military in 2007. Even the Iraqi contribution alone made up the world's 10th-largest military in itself.[30]

These government forces varied in their equipment. Iraqi local police in particular were very lightly armed, traveling mostly in unarmored pickup trucks and carrying little more than the AK-47s used by their JAM opponents. Iraqi Army and National Police units were better armed, with access to armored Humvees and some wheeled armored cars, body armor, crew-served automatic weapons, and at least some basic night vision and communications equipment. But they had no meaningful heavy weapons and limited recon-naissance, surveillance, logistical, or aviation support. Non-US foreign troops were generally better armed, with British forces approaching US standards, especially in armor and armaments if not in surveillance and information pro-cessing. US forces, by contrast, defined the global state of the art in military materiel, with thousands of M-1 Abrams tanks; M-2 Bradley infantry fighting vehicles; MRAP (Mine Resistant Armor Protected) vehicles; specialized route clearance vehicles; AH-64 Apache attack and UH-60 Blackhawk air assault helicopters; AC-130 Spectre gunships; B-1B, F-15E, F-16, and A-10 strike air-craft; Predator, Reaper, and Scout drones; and a full panoply of sophisticated soldier-level equipment, electronics, sensors, and data processing systems. While Iraqi forces were poorly armed, US troops were unquestionably the best-equipped counterinsurgents in history.[31]

The funds devoted to operating and maintaining these forces were vastly greater than those available to the JAM. By mid-2007 the United States alone was spending some $131 billion a year in Iraq, with perhaps $126 billion of that underwriting US operations and $5.5 billion devoted to assistance for Iraqi forces.[32] The forces deployed in Iraq were also benefitting from research and development, training, mobilization, and other institutional capabilities whose budgets were not normally counted in standard assessments of spend-ing for Iraq; hence some additional fraction of the over $436 billion a year the United States spent on defense overall in 2007 could also be credited to sup-port for the war effort in the Gulf.[33]

Yet even so, this enormous force was widely considered undersized for the job. US military doctrine of the time called for a ratio of roughly one capable security force provider per 50 civilians in a country to be stabilized in coun-terinsurgency.[34] For a country of Iraq's population, this standard implies a requirement of about 600,000 capable counterinsurgents to succeed.[35] It is far from clear that the Iraqi security forces of 2007 met this standard; depending on how they are counted, Coalition forces in Iraq may have fallen short by as much as a factor of three or more even at their peak numerical strength.[36]

Of course, this apparent shortfall is not attributable strictly to the JAM. The US military worldwide had important commitments to meet in Afghanistan and elsewhere. And Coalition forces in Iraq per se were fighting a combination of opponents including multiple Sunni insurgent factions; the bin Laden–affiliated Al Qaeda in Iraq (AQI); and other Shiite militias, some of which, such as the ISCI (Islamic Supreme Council of Iraq) or Fadhila forces, were nominally integrated into the official Iraqi police. Some of these enemies fielded substantial forces: US intelligence reportedly estimated secular Sunni insurgent strength at perhaps 8,000 to 20,000 or more fighters in 2007, with AQI fielding another 5,000 in early 2008.[37] Coalition efforts were thus spread over a wider range of enemies than just the JAM.

The same could be said for the JAM itself, however: it was founded in the first place to defend Shiites from Sunni insurgents, and throughout 2007 in particular it fought a continuous battle against a variety of Sunni factions in the streets of Baghdad. Like the Coalition, the JAM faced multiple opponents. The Iraq War involved a complex web of fault lines; most combatants were forced to split their attention across multiple enemies.

As with Hezbollah, the net result was thus a material balance that strongly favored the Coalition of state militaries over their nonstate Jaish al Mahdi opponent (or, for that matter, over all Iraqi nonstate actors collectively). Counting just the active-duty US, UK, and Iraqi government ground forces, the state militaries outnumbered the JAM by a factor of 31 to as much as 41 (depending on how one counts the ISF and assuming that the JAM numbered about 33,000). The Western members of the Coalition fielded weapons and equipment far superior to the JAM's in all categories but perhaps one (the JAM's EFPs had no Coalition equivalent but were certainly very effective); Iraqi forces were far less capable, but even so their materiel was generally no worse than the JAM's.

The magnitude of this material asymmetry, however, was probably not radically different from that facing Hezbollah against the Israeli state in 2006. Whereas the Hezbollah/IDF troop ratio was perhaps 15 to 65:1, the Coalition/JAM ratio was around 31 to 41:1. Neither Hezbollah nor the JAM could match the armor, aviation, or surveillance capabilities of their state opponents. For both Hezbollah and the JAM, their one area of meaningful technological competitiveness was in antiarmor capability: guided antitank missiles for Hezbollah, and EFPs for the JAM. And whereas Hezbollah's Kornet and Metis-M missiles were nominally more sophisticated than the JAM's EFPs, the urban battlefields on which the JAM fought made the theoretical range advantage conveyed by the Kornet and Metis-M irrelevant for the battles the JAM would have to fight.

In practical terms, both Hezbollah and the JAM thus fought at major overall material disadvantages typical of most wars between state and nonstate combatants, albeit with an ability to compensate technologically in the crucial category of antiarmor weapons.

JAM Internal Politics

The new theory emphasizes two dimensions of an actor's internal politics: its stakes, and its institutions. Limited stakes and weak institutions are expected to discourage complex midconcealment methods; existential stakes and mature institutions permit such methods for actors with advanced weapons.

THE JAM'S STAKES

The external stakes for the JAM were never existential. Muqtada al Sadr is widely viewed as an opportunist, who saw the JAM as a vehicle for advancing his personal political ambitions. To do this, he positioned the JAM variously as a defender of Shiite civilians from Sunni death squads, as an armed nationalist resistance against foreign occupation, as a force for the poor over the rich, and as a less constrained alternative to Prime Minister Nouri al Maliki's state security forces. Meanwhile much of the militia's leadership saw the JAM chiefly as a means of extracting rents from a dependent population or from Iranian patrons. Iraqi Shiites, as a whole, faced serious threats in an intense, potentially zero-sum war of identity with Sunni insurgents. And Sadr, like other Shiite elites, faced potentially lethal internal threats from rival politicians seeking to monopolize the state's coercive power in an intra-Shiite contest for political power. But Sadr never faced an existential threat from his external foes—that is, the US military or Sunni insurgents outside the Shiite Iraqi regime. In the complex ecology of Iraq's combatant parties between 2004 and 2008, the JAM could safely assume that others would prevent its actual annihilation or that of its Shiite base, enabling it to pursue narrower and more limited ends at others' expense.

Sadr's stated aim in establishing the JAM was to resist foreign occupation. His initial manifestos called for a joint Sunni-Shia nationalist front to compel the US-led Coalition to withdraw, and he maintained a consistently antioccupation stance after that.[38] He withdrew his participation from Maliki's coalition government in November 2006 after Maliki declined to establish a timetable for American withdrawal, and his opposition to the foreign presence played an important role in blocking its continuation in the Status of Forces negotiations of 2008 and 2011.[39] Much of the JAM's early combat experience came in its two confrontations with American troops in 2004, the first of which resulted directly from US concern with Sadr's encouragement of violence against occupation forces.[40]

Nationalist resistance to hostile occupation can often create existential stakes and zero-sum war aims as foreign powers seek to annihilate the threat and nationalists struggle for survival. The JAM, however, faced no such threat from the Coalition in Iraq. This was because the Coalition was effectively aligned with the Shiite majority, and the Shiite mainstream political establishment was unwilling to risk alienating Sadr's urban base with an all-out crackdown on his movement. The Shiite establishment thus shielded Sadr from the Coalition, who could constrain but not eliminate the JAM, and Sadr surely knew this.

The Shiite political establishment of the period 2004–8 centered on a clerical and economic elite, much of which had opposed Saddam Hussein from exile in Iran and elsewhere during the 1980s and 1990s. When the Americans deposed Saddam, this group sought to stage-manage a transition to a government dominated by Iraq's Shiite majority and led by themselves. Their status as elites and former exiles, however, left them vulnerable to charges that they were out of touch with the growing urban masses of disenfranchised Shiite poor whose fortunes had deteriorated under Saddam. Sadr, excluded from the traditional elite by his youth and inexperience, had astutely exploited this weakness by positioning himself as a populist voice of the Shiite downtrodden; as such he posed an important political threat to the Shiite establishment. Under the influence of Grand Ayatollah Ali Sistani, the establishment saw Ba'athist restoration as the primary threat and sought Shiite unity as a means of preventing this: Shiites constituted a clear majority of the Iraqi population, and Sistani's circle understood that a majoritarian government would serve Shiite interests if Shiites could vote as a block and exploit their numbers. Moreover, they saw the American presence in mostly benign terms: the Americans supported a majoritarian democratic system that would ultimately empower a unified Shiite community, and the American military could serve as a bulwark against Sunni revanchist insurgency.[41]

The Sadrist movement, however, imperiled all this: Sadr threatened to split the Shiite vote, enabling the Sunni minority to reclaim power, and his opposition to the American presence would expose an immature government to attack from Sunni revanchists if he actually succeeded in compelling a US withdrawal. In principle, the Shiite establishment could have responded to this threat by trying to crush Sadr outright. But this would have been an extremely dangerous strategy, risking a fundamental fracture of the Shiite community— and one that could easily leave the establishment on the losing side if Sadr succeeded in painting them as defenders of privilege and puppets of foreign interests. Instead, they chose appeasement and sought to co-opt Sadr by trying to accommodate him within a big-tent model of Shiite politics, while constraining his more extreme tendencies to prevent him from undermining Shiite unity or alienating the Americans to the point of withdrawal. At the same time, the Shiite establishment worked to prevent the Americans from forcing a showdown that would compel them to take sides and risk a permanent rupture with the Sadrists.[42]

The result was repeated intervention by Sistani and his allies to broker cease-fires between Sadr and the Americans that left the JAM short of victory but kept the United States from destroying his militia.[43] The implications for Sadr were obvious: he could safely provoke the foreigners for political gain with little risk that state forces would annihilate him, as long as he stayed within the establishment's limits and did not himself compel a final showdown. An all-out campaign to evict the occupiers would raise the stakes and risk an otherwise unnecessary existential struggle with the combined forces of the Shiite establishment, its government security forces, and its American allies; by contrast, a limited military campaign was safe and survivable and would provide a national stage for political self-promotion. Sadr chose the latter. Unlike many nationalist resistance forces, the JAM could thus wage a limited war against the occupiers with little fear that the occupation army would crush them.

A second important objective for the JAM was sectarian. Sadr's nationalist platform called for Sunni-Shiite unity to evict the foreigners, but his political base in Sadr City was exposed to violence from Sunni insurgents, and Sadr used the JAM to defend them. This initially defensive aim expanded, however, after the Samarra Mosque bombing in February 2006. Grassroots Shiite anger at their government for failing to protect the shrine offered Sadr an opportunity, and he exploited it by launching an offensive designed to drive wealthier Sunni populations from Baghdad and thereby clear residential blocks for occupation by poor Sadrist Shiites. The ensuing sectarian offensive became one of the largest contributors to aggregate violence in Iraq in 2006–7.[44]

Sectarian identity conflicts often pose existential threats to the combatant parties, who commonly fear genocide from their rivals and mobilize accordingly. Here, too, though, the JAM faced lesser risks. Sadr's offensive quickly demonstrated that the JAM was militarily superior to its Sunni opponents in Baghdad—the JAM made continuous progress and by mid-2007 had pushed the Sunnis from much of the city. If it ever came down to a sectarian fight to the finish between substate Sunni insurgents and JAM militiamen, all indications were that the JAM would win: battlefield results gave Sadr little reason to fear annihilation by Sunni militants. The only combatant with the military capacity to destroy the JAM was the US-led coalition of state armies, but these were constrained by Shiite politics to limited warfare and containment only. For Sadr, sectarian warfare thus offered a prospect for gain at Sunni expense with limited downside perils.[45]

An increasingly important aspiration for the JAM was economic profit. The Shiite government's deference to Sadr left the JAM as the primary armed force in Sadr City. With Sunni death squads as an ever-present threat that only the JAM could thus counter, the militia found itself with great power over a Shiite population who were dependent on it for their very lives. Some commanders exploited this dependency to wrest gangland control over staple commodities such as rice, fuel, and cooking oil, and to extort protection payments from Shiite merchants and businessmen. As the JAM expanded its zone of control in 2006, the scope for economic predation increased, as did the scale of potential profit. Sectarian cleansing enabled looting in the wealthier Sunni neighborhoods of central Baghdad, while the JAM's increasing strength and influence increased the Sadrists' ability to land government ministries and the lucrative patronage opportunities these offered. Without a militia, Sadr would still have been an influential politician with the ability to command patronage—but with a powerful army at his disposal his ability to extract rents soared, and this opportunity for profit was an important motivation for many of Sadr's commanders.[46] In the new theory's terms, the JAM's stakes were thus distinctly limited.

JAM INSTITUTIONS

In the new theory's terms, the Jaish al Mahdi was a fragile natural order actor. It had multiple suborganizations and a nominal hierarchy of specialized entities, but real decision-making power was personalized rather than institutional, with multiple charismatic leaders relying on an internal balance of power among their armed followers to adjudicate conflict in the absence of meaningful procedural checks on elite action. Economic activity was tightly controlled by militia leaders for the enrichment of themselves and their fighters. And the internal balance of power itself was fluid and unstable, yielding repeated factional struggles that produced extensive intra-JAM violence and a progressive decay in Sadr's ability to exercise plenary control over his lieutenants' fighters.

Sadr's organization was modeled loosely on the Lebanese Hezbollah, and like Hezbollah it had a political wing, the OMS (Office of the Martyr Sadr), and a military wing, the JAM militia. The OMS maintained political cells and physical offices in multiple Iraqi cities, and it successfully fielded parliamentary candidates in multiple national elections. Like Hezbollah, the OMS ran an extragovernmental court system, it did voter outreach, and it organized committees on education, media, social health, religious affairs, and Friday prayers.[47]

Unlike Hezbollah, however, the OMS was never able to deliver real services through these civil suborganizations. Sadr's leadership style was chaotic, and the OMS lacked a clear internal hierarchy, a formal policy-making process, or any designated senior advisory or deliberative bodies—there was no OMS Politburo to adjudicate decisions, which instead were products of an opaque process of informal consensus building among Sadr and his chief lieutenants. And its original revenue base was limited to a modest religious tax (the *khum*) exacted from an impoverished population, which left it without the resources to accomplish extensive civil functions directly. Instead, Sadr opted for an indirect approach, using his influence in Parliament to secure appointments for his allies to head formal state ministries of health, transportation, and agriculture. This allowed the administrative apparatus of the official Iraqi state to provide services while enabling Sadr to claim credit through the ministers' affiliation with the OMS, without requiring Sadr's own organization to deliver benefits directly.[48]

The JAM militia was organized into often floridly named *squadrons* (one was called the al-'Amr bil Ma'ruf wa al-Nahi 'an al-Munkar squadron, or "prescribing good and prohibiting transgression") raised from given neighborhoods under the command of leaders drawn from the same population. Squadron commanders were expected to lead their fighters in combat, but formal rank structure was limited. Members carried identity cards unique to their squadron but were not regularly paid by the organization and were expected to provide their own personal weapons and equipment.[49] In addition to its fighting strength in the squadrons, the JAM maintained separate intelligence and internal surveillance organizations with separate identity cards and membership. After 2005 the JAM was supported by the "Mahdist Institute" (al-Ma'had al-Mahdawi), a propaganda office created "to teach Sadrists the basics of Shiite faith and the purpose of the al-Mahdi army."[50]

Like the OMS, however, leadership in the JAM militia was personalized, with authority flowing more directly from the individual commander than from the office he held and with haphazard procedures for coordination and

control. Sadr tried repeatedly to reign in JAM commanders who ignored plenary guidance, and the JAM's internal policing organization was created to
enable this, yet he was never able to impose his orders on unwilling subordinates, and his authority over the squadrons grew increasingly tenuous over time.
Among the reasons for his 2007 cease-fire was his recognition that he had lost
control over JAM commanders in Karbala, who had ignored his calls for calm,
and it is widely believed that Sadr cooperated with Coalition efforts to arrest
wayward lieutenants, handing them over to the Iraqi Ministry of Interior for
prosecution as a substitute for a functioning internal control system or an ability
to enforce compliance with his orders. As an Iraqi interviewed by the International Crisis Group put it: "One [JAM] gang has nothing to do with another. If
one Mahdi Army group arrests your brother and you appeal to another group
for help, you won't get anywhere. They can't do anything."[51] On paper, the JAM
had multiple suborganizations and a lean but hierarchical command system; in
practice, these organizations functioned more as independent tools of their own
commanders than as a centrally coordinated whole.[52]

The JAM was deeply involved in the economy, with extensive rent extraction for the benefit of militia leaders and their followers. Sadr's licit revenues
from khum payments were too small to support a movement of the size he
intended. Iranian support for Sadr's military wing funded a significant scale of
militia operations, but JAM commanders quickly took advantage of their positions to extract additional revenue directly from the population in the areas
they controlled. In fact, much of the economy in Sadr City and JAM-occupied
Baghdad came to be dominated by the militia, which imposed surcharges on
essential commodities. Crude oil moving from the southern oil fields to the
port at Um Qasr was routinely redirected into the black market for the benefit
of JAM cadres in Basra; the refinery at Baiji, the largest in Iraq, was controlled
by the militia and used to fund the leadership. Some JAM commanders ran
kidnapping and extortion rings; others operated protection rackets in which
businessmen were required to pay them a fee for protection mostly against the
JAM itself, whose fighters would attack any who declined participation. By
2007 the militia had established gangster-like control of most commerce in the
areas under their control; the rents extracted thereby had become a major
source of independent income for many JAM commanders, a major motivation for many JAM combatants, and an important contributor to Sadr's difficulty in extending his control over subordinates who enjoyed significant local
revenue streams as a result of their own arms rather than the organization's
formal budget or directives.[53]

This combination of weak formal hierarchy with limited capacity to adjudicate internal disputes and an increasing capacity for local commanders to raise their own revenue via control of local commerce created an unstable internal balance of power in which factional disputes were frequent, deep, and often violent.

These surfaced as early as the Battle of Najaf in August 2004. In the midst of the fighting, Qais Khazali, one of Sadr's top lieutenants and a prominent spokesman for the Sadrist movement, broke with Sadr and began issuing battlefield orders to his supporters without the approval of Sadr or the JAM plenary leadership. Together with Abd al-Hadi al-Darraji, Khazali's faction then rejected Sadr's cease-fire deal and continued its attacks on Coalition forces in Baghdad in violation of the pact reached between Sadr, Sistani, and the Coalition. Notwithstanding this insubordination, Sadr was unwilling to hazard a total breach with Khazali's supporters, and the two negotiated an uneasy reconciliation in which Khazali and two confederates were named to supervise the OMS' political offices in March 2005.[54] This reconciliation was never complete, however, and Khazali's "Special Groups" faction gradually moved away from Sadr's direct control and into closer alignment with its Iranian backers in Tehran's Revolutionary Guard Quds Force.[55]

As the Najaf fighting concluded, Ayatollah Kazem al-Haeri, an early Sadrist ally and major financial conduit for the movement, publicly disassociated himself from Sadr and issued a fatwa instructing his followers to cease the religious tax payments to the OMS that had made up much of Sadr's domestic revenue to that time. Al-Haeri was reportedly alienated by Sadr's military adventurism in Najaf, and its failure was the last straw for him and his supporters. This caused an immediate financial crisis for the JAM, which was then struggling to replace its losses from the fighting in Najaf and to compensate the families of the militiamen killed there; the loss of funds controlled by Haeri accelerated the JAM's search for other revenue and its increasing turn toward criminality. Like Khazali, however, Haeri was not simply ousted, as Hezbollah had done with Subhi al Tufayli and his faction; instead an ambiguous relationship continued until the two formally reconciled in 2007, when Haeri agreed to supervise Sadr's religious studies in Iran.[56]

In Basra in 2005, Sheik Ahmed al-Fartousi, the JAM's chief commander in the city, led an increasingly independent program of attacks on British occupation forces in the city. This produced tension with the JAM plenary leadership that culminated in an unsuccessful attempt by Sadr to relieve Fartousi of his command; Fartousi, however, ignored the edict and continued operations until he was arrested by the British in September 2005.[57]

By 2007 such internal dissension had produced at least four separate splinter groups with ongoing ties to the OMS that were conducting ongoing operations alongside the mainstream JAM but largely beyond the direct control of Muqtada al Sadr. The "Noble JAM" sought reconciliation with the Coalition, cooperating covertly with American forces in the Shula and Huriya neighborhoods of northwest Baghdad and informing on their nominal comrades. Khazali's Special Groups, conversely, wanted more aggressive action against occupation forces than the mainstream JAM did, emplacing sophisticated EFP arrays and mounting frequent rocket and mortar attacks against the foreign presence in the Green Zone. The al-Araji faction operated under the brothers Hazem and Bahaa al-Araji and competed with mainstream JAM and the Khazali Special Groups to control the Kadhimiyah shrine just west of the Tigris River. And a variety of criminal gangs operating under the JAM aegis fought over smuggling routes and economic access.[58]

Other factions active at various times included the Sayyid ash-Shuhada Movement, the Defense of the Holy Shrines Brigade, the Dhi Qar Organization, and the Karbala Brigade, all operating as cells of the JAM but with relative independence from Sadr, and sometimes in opposition to one another. Some were opposed to Sadr's repeated cease-fires and compromises with the Americans and with the Shiite clerical establishment; some rejected his willingness to participate in the Maliki government; some wanted more aggressive attacks on Sunni civilians; some chafed against attempted restrictions on profiteering, kidnapping, and corruption; some proved more responsive to Iranian wishes than to Sadr's.[59]

Faced with this increasing fragmentation, Sadr tried to reestablish control. Beginning in February 2007, he established the Thahabiya or "Golden Brigade" cell, with the mission of identifying and purging rogue elements operating outside his direction. Operating covertly under Sadr's guidance, cell members were empowered to imprison or assassinate nominal comrades as a means of enforcing loyalty to the plenary leadership. As many as several hundred JAM leaders and faction members were eventually killed, jailed, or expelled by Golden Brigade operatives.[60]

Nor was internecine violence limited to the Golden Brigade's operations. In fact, firefights between neighboring squadron leaders were common. As an Iraqi resident of the Shula neighborhood in Baghdad reported in 2007: "A fratricidal war within the Mahdi Army has been raging. The other day, Mahdi Army members hit one of my friends in the Hurriya neighbourhood. He lodged a complaint with the Maktab al-Sayyid al-Shahid in Shu'la. The office then dispatched four Mahdi Army men to summon the suspects to Hurriya. In response,

Mahdi Army members from Hurriya attacked the Shu'la envoys. To this day, Mahdi Army members are killing each other in Hurriya over this incident."[61]

The net result was a deeply divided organization where internal loyalties were never clear. Unlike Hezbollah, where an early schism yielded decisive, permanent expulsion of a discrete and overt dissident element, the JAM suffered a continuous, ambiguous, internal struggle in which sometimes covert sub-elements with access to their own funding (whether via crime, corruption, or Iranian connections) pursued their own agendas regardless of plenary direction but without a clear, public break with the plenary leadership. This factional insubordination, moreover, could have lethal consequences for nominal cobelligerents, as Noble JAM dissidents exposed mainstream JAM to Coalition attack; al-Araji, Khazali network, and mainstream JAM contended over religious sites; criminal gangs fought over turf; and Golden Brigade enforcers hunted down dissidents for expulsion or assassination. The combination of ambiguity and danger this produced made trust within the military organization extremely risky for all concerned.

Dependent Variable: JAM Military Behavior

Given these characterizations, how does the JAM's military behavior correspond with the respective theories' predictions? On balance, JAM methods, though not purely Fabian, were closer to the Fabian extremum than to Hezbollah's midspectrum behavior. To adjudicate this complex, interpenetrated admixture of behaviors that do not conform in any simple, uniform way to either of the popular stereotypes of state "conventional" or nonstate "irregular" methods, I again use the detailed criteria presented in chapter 2 and the appendix, coding the JAM's behavior in terms of its stealthiness; its commitment to taking and holding ground; its dispersion; coercion; the distinguishability of its combatants from noncombatant civilians; and its functional differentiation within the theater of war.

1. Stealth

Cover and concealment are the heart of Fabian war fighting. While individual militiamen varied in their skills, JAM positions were mostly well concealed prior to the initiation of fire.

In combat with Americans, the JAM fought mostly from within buildings in dense urban areas. In such settings, it was typically very difficult to locate shooters before they opened fire, and JAM fighters typically got the first shot in engagements with US forces. Militiamen were particularly adept at hiding IEDs among trash and other detritus along roadsides until detonation against passing US columns. But while JAM fighters were typically covered and concealed until firing, they often found it difficult to sustain fire without detection. JAM fighters were also systematically unable to master movement techniques for secure maneuver outside buildings, and militiamen were often casual in their dispositions when they believed they were not under observation, simplifying detection from overhead systems such as drones or helicopters. In static indoor positions prior to contact, JAM concealment was typically sufficient to prevent detection—but the JAM found concealed maneuver in the open systematically challenging.[62]

2. Taking and Holding Ground

Archetypically Fabian forces do not take and hold ground; archetypically Napoleonic ones never voluntarily relinquish it. The JAM clearly sought to cleanse urban neighborhoods of Sunni civilians to clear these for occupation by Shiite squatters. But they rarely contested ground when challenged by US military forces.

To assess the JAM's relative commitment to taking and holding ground I use the four observable referents of this commitment presented in the appendix: the duration of firefights; the proximity of attackers to defenders; the incidence of counterattack; and the incidence of harassing fires and unattended minefields.

THE DURATION OF FIREFIGHTS

Extended firefights in place are characteristic of Napoleonic methods, whereas Fabian tactics encourage brief ambushes that allow fighters to escape without risking decisive engagement. In Iraq, JAM fighters rarely stood their ground for sustained engagements.

Modal firefight duration for the JAM was very brief—often just a few minutes. Contact was commonly initiated by the JAM, via ambush (often in conjunction with an IED detonation), by sniper fire, or by harassing mortar or rocket fire. This fire could be intense, but rarely did it continue very long after US forces opened sustained counterfire. Rather than remaining in place or maneuvering to alternate or supplementary firing positions to sustain pressure on US forces, JAM fighters typically broke contact and withdrew upon receiving meaningful fire against their original locations.[63] Of course there were exceptions—on at least one occasion a JAM detachment of 35 fighters sustained an eight-hour-long night engagement against US forces; a 30-fighter detachment remained in contact for a four-to-six-hour firefight against an entire US infantry company.[64] But such exceptions were rare. Battles such as Najaf in 2004 and Sadr City in 2008 could continue for days or even weeks but consisted of an often-disjointed collection of brief local firefights rather than sustained combat to contest particular fighting positions.[65]

PROXIMITY OF ATTACKERS TO DEFENDERS

Napoleonic control of terrain often requires fighters to accept decisive engagement on the defense and to seek it on the attack; this requires Napoleonic fighters to accept close contact with the enemy in ways that Fabian self-preservation need not. In Iraq, the JAM sometimes fought at safe distances via unattended IEDs, sniping, or indirect fire from rockets or mortars. But the JAM's preference for urban terrain made long-range direct fire very difficult—lines of sight in built-up areas are rarely long enough to enable shooting from distances in excess of a couple of hundred meters, regardless of one's commitment to taking or holding ground. If the JAM had *sustained* close contact at such ranges, this would be consistent with acceptance of decisive engagement for Napoleonic control of territory—but in conjunction with the brief duration of the modal firefight, the JAM's frequency of close-range engagement is more suggestive of Fabian ambushes and raids under the geographic constraints of urban warfare than of Napoleonic willingness to accept decisive engagement in defense of ground.

In fact, most JAM direct-fire engagements took place at very short range—typically shorter than 300 meters and often less than 100. In fact, some fire was exchanged at ranges of 50 meters or less: in the Battle of Sadr City in 2008, for example, US armored vehicle crewmembers in open hatches killed multiple JAM fighters on rooftops using M-4 carbine fire from as little as 20 meters away.[66] Yet the dense urban terrain could still allow militiamen who wished to break contact to open fire from windows or sometimes rooftops at nearly point-blank range then escape from counterfire by quickly exiting the building through rear doors, tunnels, and alleys. This method was not always successful. Rapid counterfire could sometimes kill the shooter before he could flee, and US commanders learned to use staggered, parallel columns and overwatch from attack helicopters or drones to increase the odds of intercepting fleeing gunmen as they exited the scene of an ambush via alleyways.[67] But the nature of the terrain in urban battlefields such as Sadr City, Kadhimiyah, West Rashid, Najaf, or Basra meant that most direct-fire actions would be at very short ranges—even when a Fabian defender sought to avoid decisive engagement.[68]

INCIDENCE OF COUNTERATTACK

Napoleonic control of terrain often requires counterattack to regain lost ground; pure Fabian concern with limiting exposure precludes costly counterattacks and instead bids fighters to melt away once dislodged. In Iraq, the JAM sometimes sought to regain key locations once lost but did not routinely counterattack when driven from its positions. And even when the JAM did seek to regain key terrain, this was normally attempted via an increased tempo of raids and harassment rather than a systematic effort to overrun positions.

JAM militiamen normally broke contact and withdrew once taken under effective fire. US forces would sometimes then encounter new positions as they advanced, but subsequent engagements would more commonly involve US forces on the move encountering stationary JAM fighters disposed to the rear of the initial contact, rather than stationary US forces struck by moving JAM elements advancing on their former locations. Where militiamen did approach US forces, moreover, this was typically in very small formations (often as small as three to five fighters) and sometimes involved ill-considered tactics such as frontal assaults by militiamen in civilian cars and pickup trucks, firing from open car windows and truck beds. It is difficult to know whether such counterproductive efforts were the result of deliberate command decisions or idiosyncratic impulses from enthusiastic but untrained local elements.[69]

When US forces threatened key locations, JAM resistance often stiffened, as was the case during the 2008 Battle of Sadr City when US troops cleared JAM rocket launch locations within range of the Green Zone and erected 12-foot-tall concrete barriers to restrict JAM reentry. The JAM clearly hoped to drive American troops back out before US control could be consolidated. And JAM units sometimes launched set-piece assaults on Iraqi Army checkpoints and other static positions. The latter, however, were normally closer to raids in force than to attempts to seize and hold lost ground. And JAM counterpressure against American forces in Sadr City mainly took the form of an increased frequency of raids and sniper attacks (especially against US engineering elements engaged in wall construction), coupled with more-frequent ambushes against moving US forces—rarely did JAM counterpressure take the form of a sustained advance by significant forces to recapture lost ground by driving US forces out.[70] The JAM rarely displayed a Napoleonic willingness to accept exposure and decisive engagement in order to recapture positions once lost.[71]

THE INCIDENCE OF HARASSING FIRES AND UNATTENDED MINEFIELDS

Fabian methods rely heavily on harassing fires and unattended minefields. In Iraq, the JAM made extensive use of harassing indirect fires from rockets and mortars. Minefields (in the form of IED emplacements) were the JAM's single most common—and most lethal—weapon, but many were overwatched by militiamen in direct-fire positions rather than being left wholly unattended.

Through much of the 2006–8 period, the Green Zone in Baghdad was subject to regular, sometimes daily, fire from JAM rocket and mortar teams located in Sadr City and adjoining areas. These attacks rarely involved more than a half dozen rounds at a time, hastily fired from expedient mobile launchers, which then moved to restore concealment. In the spring of 2007 in particular, a pattern could be observed in which JAM indirect-fire attacks against Green Zone targets would gradually improve in accuracy over a period of days or weeks while US attack helicopter crews hunted the firing teams; when the helicopters eventually succeeded, indirect-fire accuracy would drop with the arrival of new, unseasoned JAM crews to replace those killed, and the process would repeat. This indirect fire was never massed in sufficient concentration to pose a threat of destroying major headquarters facilities or inflicting mass casualties. But it killed and wounded some headquarters personnel, it complicated movement with periodic lockdowns of the complex during attacks, and it compelled the construction of bunkers for protection and the deployment of expensive C-RAM close-in weapons systems to intercept as many incoming rounds as possible.[72] The JAM displayed similar methods in southern Iraq, particularly against British bases around Basra.[73]

Whereas harassing indirect fire inflicted relatively few Coalition casualties, JAM IEDs were extremely lethal. Overall, IEDs in Iraq killed almost 2,200 soldiers, or about 45 percent of all Coalition fatalities in the war.[74] Not all these weapons were emplaced by the JAM, but the IED was the JAM's signature weapon and easily its most effective capability. Thousands of them were emplaced throughout the JAM's operating areas between 2004 and 2008.

Relatively few of these were unattended, however. In fact the JAM commonly used IEDs to trigger ambushes in which Coalition vehicles struck by the mines were then attacked with concentrated small arms fire and RPGs; JAM IEDs were intended not merely for harassment but as their primary means of inflicting casualties and restricting Coalition freedom of movement. Of course, IEDs emplaced by militiamen who later withdrew or were driven from their positions then became unattended if not previously detonated or cleared by Coalition forces; JAM-occupied positions could thus remain dangerous long after the fighters departed, until Coalition clearance efforts removed the ordnance. And some IED emplacements were never designed to be overwatched and were indeed intended merely to harass. But most field reports suggest that most IED detonations in actively contested territory were tied into defended positions for use as the centerpiece of ambushes and were thus intended for more than simply harassment.[75]

3. Dispersion

Pure Fabian methods mandate dispersed postures that produce low, uniform troop densities. In Iraq, the Jaish al Mahdi deployed an unusually high density of fighters theaterwide by 2007 but disposed them relatively uniformly in their primary operating areas.

By 2007 the JAM probably deployed somewhere between 25,000 and 40,000 fighters and was active in several of Iraq's largest cities—especially Baghdad, Basra, Karbala, and Najaf.[76] If we combine the area of these cities as the JAM's effective theater of operations, this implies a theaterwide density of about 60 to 90 fighters per square kilometer in 2007. This is a very high troop density for a nonstate actor—the JAM lower bound is still more than six standard deviations above the mean troop density for the 41 nonstate actors in figure 3.9. In fact, the JAM's lower bound is actually higher than the median *state* value for World War II cases in figure 3.8 and is more than 25 times higher than the US troop density in Operation Desert Shield in 1990.

The JAM's disposition of these troops, however, was much more uniform than most state actors' disposition of troops. The Jaish al Mahdi did not literally distribute its fighters evenly across the territory in which it operated—it reinforced areas of active combat at the expense of others. In the 2008 Battle of Sadr City, for example, the JAM deployed a local density of about 100 fighters per square kilometer in the two neighborhoods the United States had targeted for clearance, yielding a maximum concentration of around 1.1 to 1.7 times their theaterwide average density.[77] By contrast, state militaries in mid-to-late 20th-century interstate warfare often deployed local concentrations at densities more than 20 times greater than their theaterwide values.[78] The nonstate Fabian extremum would be uniform dispositions with a local-to-theaterwide ratio of 1.0; JAM concentration was between the two—but much closer to the latter than the former.

4. The Balance of Brute Force and Coercion

Most warfare involves some mix of brute force and coercion; even very Napoleonic methods include coercing some enemy survivors to surrender or withdraw. But whereas Napoleonic methods do this by threatening brute force annihilation if survivors fight on, pure Fabian methods rely on gradual attrition that coerces by threatening not annihilation but cumulative costs that will eventually exceed stakes even if most enemies survive. In Iraq, the JAM's methods relied mostly on gradual coercive attrition—both against rival Sunni nonstate forces and against the US state military.

The JAM's 2006–7 battle with Sunni insurgents in Baghdad was clearly designed to drive Sunni civilians and insurgents from city neighborhoods. But little of this involved true brute force in Schelling's terms: taking an objective with no decision on the enemy's part to cede it. In this context, true brute force at the tactical level would require outright destruction of defending forces who remained in contested territory, enabling JAM fighters to occupy city blocks over the dead bodies of their defenders. (This is what "decisive engagement" means: a willingness to contest ground to the death if the enemy refuses to withdraw.) In 2006–7, JAM fighters rarely pressed the issue to this point. More commonly, the JAM relied on sniping, raids, ambushes on moving rival groups caught outdoors, mortar and rocket fire, and, especially, death squad activity in which civilians were abducted and murdered under the cover of darkness to intimidate Sunnis and encourage living civilians and fighters to leave. At that point, the JAM would advance to occupy the abandoned buildings, and Sadrist Shiite civilians would follow in their wake. This resulted in a systematic advance that extended JAM control over large parts of metropolitan Baghdad by mid-2007—but much of this advance was accomplished by coercing Sunnis to leave by threatening chronic violence on an intolerable scale if they stayed, resulting in a decision by the Sunnis themselves to vacate the contested ground. It was not a large-scale effort to overrun actively defended urban positions by annihilating their defenders.[79]

When US forces entered Sadr City in 2008, the frequency of JAM attacks went up, the size of militia elements committed to individual firefights went up, and Americans entering the JAM stronghold were particularly targeted. But here, too, militiamen rarely accepted decisive engagement in the defense of ground. And no specific location was ever contested by more than a small fraction of the estimated 2,000 to 4,000 militiamen available to the JAM in Sadr City—Sadr does not appear to have been willing to risk a fight to the finish by committing all his available forces to drive the Americans out by destroying those who tried to stay. To the extent that the JAM response was centrally coordinated, the logic appears to have been to inflict over time enough cumulative losses on US invaders to persuade them to leave Sadr City rather than suffer chronic casualties at this rate if they stayed.[80] Sadr was willing to dial upward at the margin the intensity of this coercive attrition when US forces entered the politically sensitive terrain of Sadr City, but his methods amounted to a willingness to allow US troops to enter (he did not fight to the finish at the frontier) followed by a more intensive program of coercive attrition afterward to persuade them to leave. Napoleonic combatants rely heavily on brute force and accept decisive engagement frequently to seize and hold broad swaths of terrain; midspectrum armies use brute force selectively and fight to the finish only for control of key locations. Sadr's JAM, by contrast, rarely if ever accepted brute force decisive engagement—even when the United States invaded the heart of his political base in Sadr City. Sadr's strategy was much more reliant on coercion.[81]

5. Distinguishability of Combatants and Civilians

Combatant intermingling with civilians, use of civilian clothing, and avoidance of heavy weapons are closely associated with Fabian methods. In Iraq, JAM militiamen fought among dense concentrations of civilians, systematically avoided military clothing, and had few heavy weapons at its disposal.

Almost all the JAM's combat activity was in urban environments, and many of these were among the most densely populated urban areas in Iraq. The teeming slum of Sadr City, for example, held a population of about 2.4 million in an area of just 35 square kilometers, for a density in 2008 more than twice that of Manhattan.[82] And unlike with Hezbollah's campaign in 2006, in the Iraq War these civilians were not evacuated—the JAM relied on them to restrain Coalition firepower, and JAM militiamen typically fought from within occupied buildings in densely occupied neighborhoods.[83]

Nor did the JAM wear distinguishing clothing. Militiamen carried identification cards; OMS noncombatant officials sometimes wore armbands, pins,
or other insignia on special occasions; and propaganda pictures often show
Mahdi Army militiamen in military formations with black clothing and sometimes camouflaged fatigues.[84] But in fact the Sadrist organization provided no
uniforms or other military equipment to its recruits, and there is no evidence
of any systematic use of clothing to identify them as combatants. Field reporting from US combatants indicates that few if any of the fighters they encountered wore distinguishing military clothing.[85]

Napoleonic war fighters use all firepower at their disposal; classical Fabian
insurgents eschew heavy weapons even when available in favor of smaller,
easier-to-conceal light arms. In Iraq, the JAM had few heavy weapons available
to it—unlike Hezbollah, it owned neither long-range missiles nor crew-served
guided antitank weapons, and it had access to no tanks and no heavy artillery.
It is believed to have had access to some SA-14 man-portable infrared antiaircraft missiles, but there is no evidence of JAM fighters using them against
Coalition aircraft.[86] Their heaviest weapons in regular use were their
107-millimeter Hesab, 122-millimeter Grad, and 240-millimeter Fajr rockets;
all, however, were fired from simple launch rails, often carried in civilian flat-
bed or pickup trucks, and could be easily concealed prior to use.[87] It is unclear
how the JAM would have used heavier weapons if available—they had few
such systems at their disposal.[88]

6. The Military Organization of the Theater of War

State armies typically break combat theaters down into multiple distinct spatial zones with different military functions. Pure Fabian nonstate warfare, by
contrast, lacks clear distinctions between front and rear, or forward and reserve, or logistical and combat zones. In Iraq, the Jaish al Mahdi's behavior lay
between these two models.

In 2006–7, for example, JAM operations in Baghdad displayed a clear distinction between a moving front, where the bulk of combat activity occurred,
and a relatively quiet rear. Much of the fighting in Baghdad in this period took
the form of JAM offensives against Sunni civilians and insurgent cells, aimed
at cleansing Sunni neighborhoods for resettlement by OMS-sympathetic Shiite families from Sadr City (until late 2007, US forces were not central to most
of this combat; Iraqi state army and police were either on the sidelines or
complicit with the JAM). At any given time, the JAM focused on Sunni

neighborhoods adjoining Shiite areas; once the next-nearest Sunni neighbor-hood was cleansed, the JAM moved on to the next, where the fighting continued—yielding a moving sectarian frontline at the sectarian boundary, along which most of the city's violence was concentrated.

In early-to-mid-2006, for example, the primary sectarian battlefields in the capital were in the neighborhoods bordering Kadhimiya, just west of the Tigris River to the city's north, and around West Rashid in southern Baghdad. The city's pre-2006 sectarian demography was something of a patchwork quilt, but west of the Tigris, central Baghdad was generally Sunni with intermingled neighborhoods north and south of this and two predominantly Shiite enclaves beyond these: Kadhimiya in the north and West Rashid in the south. After the Samarra Mosque bombing in February, JAM militiamen established lines of communication from their primary base in Sadr City into beachheads west of the Tigris in these two Shiite quarters. In the north, the JAM then began in-filtrating the accessible mixed districts to the south and west of Kadhimiya. The result was a sharp increase in fighting in Shula, Huriya, and Washash. By October 2006 these cleansing efforts had succeeded, much of northern Baghdad had become homogeneously Shiite, and violence there diminished. But sectar-ian fighting did not then stop—it simply moved. The JAM then drove south into Sunni Mansoor, southeast into predominantly Sunni Karkh along Haifa Street, south into Adel, and southwest into Ghazaliyah. In southern Baghdad, the JAM moved outward from its base in West Rashid, clearing areas with large Shiite populations such as Jihad, Bayaa, and Abu T'Shir and into the predominantly Sunni neighborhoods of Dora and Mechanic to the east, Ferat to the west, and both Aamel and Saydiyah to the north. In the process they extended their line of communications from Sadr City to enable further ad-vances south and southeast into the heart of Sunni central Baghdad.[89] At no point, moreover, was the violence uniformly distributed over the intermingled sections of the city. Even during the fighting for intermingled Shula, Huriya, Washash, Saydiyah, and Aamel, bloodshed was concentrated at the frontlines of the JAM advance through these districts from their bases in Kadhimiya and West Rashid, with localities off these frontiers relatively quiet.[90]

But while there was an identifiable distinction between front and rear, there was nothing resembling a true communications zone with a dedicated sup-porting infrastructure. There were IED workshops hidden in sheds and ga-rages, and weapons caches hidden throughout the JAM's area of control, but no orthodox logistical depots or maintenance facilities. The civilian OMS maintained fixed administrative and political offices, and the JAM militia leadership used specific buildings, often mosques, as military headquarters and adapted others for use as interrogation or torture facilities. But the leadership also moved irregularly among safehouses in unspecialized buildings, and it is unclear how reliant the JAM was on specific structures for command and control. Fighters often used known routes to reinforce combat sectors, or to move weapons and ammunition, and occasionally used mosques as staging grounds for raids, but there were no apparent persistent reserve assembly areas. The JAM thus did not operate a uniform, undifferentiated theater of war, but neither did they maintain the degree of spatial articulation of function typical among great power state militaries.[91]

JAM Proficiency of Execution

The JAM's proficiency of execution offers an opportunity for process tracing. The causal logic of the new theory implies that weakly institutionalized, limited-stakes actors should display limitations of skill and military coordination that would render complex, midspectrum warfare impractical if attempted. In Iraq, the JAM chose methods whose technical demands were modest. Their skills in executing even these undemanding methods varied, however—both across tasks and across suborganizations within the JAM—suggesting a very limited potential to master the much more complex techniques of modern midspectrum war fighting had these been attempted.

In general, the Iranian-trained Special Groups were the most proficient JAM fighters. They were particularly adept at placement of IEDs, and especially the more sophisticated Explosively Formed Projectiles (EFPs) that proved so lethal to US forces; almost half the casualties suffered by US forces in Iraq were attributable to IEDs, the great majority of which were hidden effectively enough to remain undetected prior to detonation. Special Group mortar and rocket crews also displayed decent marksmanship; especially against fixed targets, they proved able to hit with modest needs for registration fire, and they were adept at concealing launch platforms and moving quickly after firing.[92]

By contrast, JAM small-arms marksmanship and fire discipline were systematically poor. While some snipers could hit individual targets at nontrivial ranges, most JAM militiamen tended to spray ammunition rather than firing aimed shots. Combined-arms integration was extremely limited: the JAM could coordinate IEDs and direct-fire small arms on a small scale in local ambushes, and they could sometimes support these with mortar fire against fixed preregistration points, but they had great difficulty coordinating action by multiple units to block US reinforcements, they were rarely able to adjust mortar fire against moving targets to sustain suppression during an engagement, and they could not coordinate movement with suppressive fire to advance in contact. Maneuver of any kind on a scale larger than dozen-fighter detachments was very rare. Firing positions rarely provided overlapping fields of fire, and it was uncommon for JAM militiamen to move between supplementary or alternate firing positions to sustain contact as Americans returned fire. Individual fighters sometimes dashed suicidally into the open to fire on US troops, and militiamen displayed poor camouflage discipline when not in direct contact. Many US participants described mainstream JAM tactical execution as amateurish—even for the simple tactics they were attempting.[93] These shortcomings in proficiency are consistent with the new theory's causal logic for weakly institutionalized, limited-stakes actors such as the Jaish al Mahdi.

Theoretical Implications

Given the codings above, what do the respective theories predict for the JAM's military behavior? And in particular, how would their expectations for the JAM from 2004 to 2008 compare with those for Hezbollah in 2006?

Tribal culture theories would expect substantially Fabian behavior from both actors, given their tribal social structures. But whereas the JAM's urban base in Sadr City had seen a significant decay in tribal norms in the decades prior to 2003, rural southern Lebanon, from which Hezbollah drew much of its strength, was still a more traditional society with stronger tribal norms in 2006. Tribal culture explanations would thus predict at least fairly Fabian methods from both, but with Hezbollah closer to the Fabian extremum than the JAM.

Orthodox materialist theory would expect strongly Fabian methods from both actors, but to an even greater degree for the JAM than for Hezbollah.[94] Both were overmatched by materially superior developed-world state militaries. Both militias did have nontrivial access to high-lethality weapons—but whereas Hezbollah deployed long-range antitank missiles capable of killing Israeli tanks at distances of over five kilometers, the JAM's most lethal antiarmor system was the EFP, whose range was limited to roadside employment against passing armored vehicles. Given the urban terrain in which the JAM operated, this range restriction was less consequential than it would have been in the more open terrain of South Lebanon, but the EFP was clearly less versatile than Hezbollah's Kornet and Metis-M antitank missile systems. Neither nonstate actor deployed materiel comparable to their state opponent, but Hezbollah's deficit was smaller at the margin than the JAM's.[95]

The new theory, by contrast, predicts much more Fabian methods for the JAM than for Hezbollah. In the new theory's terms, both actors deployed enough modern weapons to penalize hostile concentration if employed properly, but the two actors' internal politics were very different. Hezbollah was a mature natural order actor with existential stakes; the JAM had fragile natural order institutions with limited stakes. This internal political difference should have made it virtually impossible for the JAM to overcome the collective action dilemmas of midspectrum warfare, whereas Hezbollah should have been able to adopt much of the midspectrum approach.

The observed outcome is strongly at odds with tribal culture theory, somewhat at odds with materialist theory, and strongly consistent with the new formulation. By the coding in the appendix, the JAM's score on the Fabian-Napoleonic spectrum of figure 2.1 is 1.3.[96] Hezbollah's is 3.6. In the categorical simplification of table 4.1, this makes the JAM a "mostly Fabian" actor, whereas Hezbollah is "midspectrum." The rank ordering of these two Shiite tribal organizations is thus the opposite of tribal culture theory's prediction. And the more tribal Hezbollah actually displays remarkably "conventional" state-like military behavior for a nonstate actor with the kind of tribal social organization often associated with "irregular" Fabian war fighting. Materialist theory gets the rank ordering of the two actors right and correctly anticipates the JAM's strongly Fabian methods—but as noted in chapter 5 above, it underpredicts the scale of Hezbollah's departure from irregular Fabianism.

The new theory thus displays the most consistency with the case. With a weak institutional foundation, a shifting internal balance of power among armed elites, frequent factional struggles, and periodic internal violence, the JAM created an environment in which cooperation among interdependent specialists would have been extremely risky for its fighters. Nor did it make sense for Sadr to accept the internal political risks of military professionalization—or to spend the resources needed for expensive training—in a setting where the downside risk of failure for him was limited. The result was a military force that was systematically unable to overcome the collective action dilemmas or meet the skill requirements of complex midspectrum warfare—and which therefore defaulted to simpler, lower-risk, less interdependent, much more Fabian methods. Whereas Hezbollah's stakes and institutions enabled it to exploit the military advantages of midspectrum warfare, the JAM's internal politics did not. And the result was midspectrum behavior for Hezbollah but much more Fabian behavior for the JAM—as the new theory expects.

That said, the case is not a perfect fit with the new theory, either. The functional form presented in the appendix predicts a "very Fabian" score of 0.9 for the JAM, given its institutions, stakes, technology, and material imbalance with the United States.[97] The JAM was a mostly Fabian actor in Iraq, with a score of 1.3 on the six-point scale presented in the appendix, but this is a somewhat higher (less Fabian) score than the formalization predicts. What explains the divergence? I would argue that in this case, the theory is actually a better guide to optimal military behavior than the actor's practice. Recall that the theory presented here is a rationalist conception: it assumes that actors will generally adopt methods well suited to their circumstances, and it seeks to identify what these optimal methods will be. In Iraq, the JAM suffered debilitating losses in its periodic battles with American forces. These losses, combined with the increasingly predatory economic behavior resulting from its internal political weaknesses, left Sadr with little choice but to declare a cease-fire in 2007 and disband the militia altogether in 2008. The theory here would explain this result as the consequence of an actor who attempted methods that were more Napoleonic than its politics could sustain. The JAM in Iraq was hardly a highly Napoleonic, state-like actor. But military methods exist on a continuum, and one of the benefits of acknowledging this is to clarify the consequences of differences in degree: the JAM was very Fabian, but its military fortunes would probably have improved if it had been even more so.

7

The Somali National Alliance
in Somalia, 1992–94

IN THIS CHAPTER I present the third of five case method tests: Mohammed Farah Aideed's Somali National Alliance (SNA) militia, from its founding in 1992 through the withdrawal of its American opponents in 1994. Somalia's warlords are often seen as a defining example of nonstate irregular military methods. This prominence is due largely to the SNA's startling ability to inflict 76 casualties, including 19 deaths, on a highly trained, heavily equipped force of 160 US Rangers, Delta Force commandos, and Navy SEALs in the October 1993 engagement made famous by the 2001 film and 1999 book *Blackhawk Down*.[1] The SNA's salience in the popular understanding of nonstate warfare makes it an important case for any theory of nonstate warfare. But for tribal culture theorists it is especially significant. Somali culture was as strongly tribal as anywhere in the modern world, making it an especially important case for those who see tribalism as an important determinant of nonstate war making. Somalia thus approximates an Ecksteinian critical case for such theories: if they are to succeed anywhere, they should succeed here.

I will argue, however, that the fit between SNA methods and tribal culture expectations is at best imperfect. Certainly the SNA was not the Wehrmacht, and its behavior was far from the popular conception of conventional warfare. But neither did it match the popular conception of irregular guerilla warfare. Even in Somalia, warlords sought to take and hold ground. Their battles had clear front lines, and Aideed's militia was willing to accept decisive engagement and conduct sustained close combat over a 15-hour battle against elite, heavily armed state soldiers who had adopted a positional defense in favorable urban terrain with extensive air cover. This was not a hit-and-run ambush by furtive guerilla raiders unwilling to close with a prepared enemy. The net result was still much closer to the Fabian extreme than its Napoleonic alternative—in the new theory's terms, SNA methods were much more Fabian than Hezbollah's in 2006, for example. But the SNA demonstrates that even a radically tribal organization at a major material disadvantage will still display an interior choice of military methods that includes important elements of intuitively "conventional" war fighting.

As with other cases, I develop this argument in five steps. First, I outline briefly the main events of the case. Second, I develop values for the main independent variables associated with the competing theories. Third, I discuss the new theory's dependent variable of observed SNA military behavior. Fourth, I process-trace the fit between the theory's causal logic and the proficiency of the SNA's execution of its chosen methods. Finally, I compare the SNA's behavior to the respective theories' predictions given these values, assess the relative fit between prediction and observation, and evaluate the case's implications for the theories under study.

Overview of Events

The Somali National Alliance was an outgrowth of the insurgency that toppled Siad Barre's socialist government in 1991. Barre's invasion of neighboring Ethiopia in the Ogaden War of 1977–78 had gone badly for Somalia. With defeat came the loss of all territory taken in the war's early offensives, economic crisis stemming from the war's high cost, and Ethiopian support for anti-Barre resistance forces within Somalia. Barre responded with repressive measures designed to limit internal threats to his regime—imprisoning suspected coup plotters, launching reprisals against communities thought to support dissidents, and eventually killing more than 120 people in Galcayo and Belet Weyn. This crackdown led to the withdrawal of most foreign aid by 1990, further crippling an already deteriorating economy, and stimulating popular resistance to the regime.[2]

Insurgent activity was initially concentrated among clansmen from the Majertain Darod and Isaq tribes, who had suffered disproportionately in the war (the Ogaden battlefields spanned traditional Isaq grazing lands). With Barre's Galcayo and Belet Weyn massacres, however, the insurgency expanded to the Hawiye clan, which formed the United Somali Congress (USC) and its associated militia and began active combat operations against the regime.[3]

The USC military campaign was led by Mohammed Farah Aideed. Aideed was an Italian- and Soviet-educated officer in the Somali state security forces

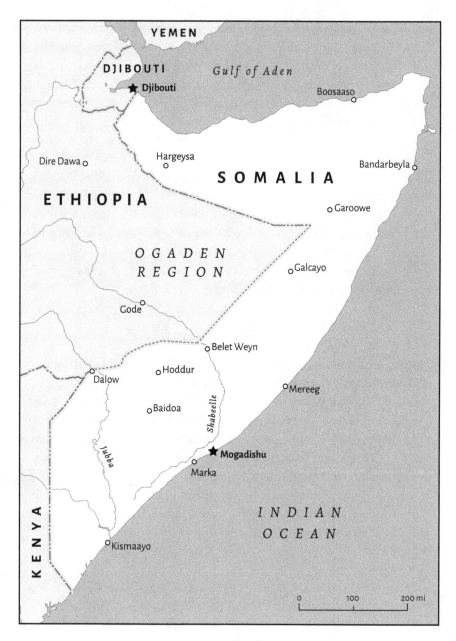

MAP 7.1. Somalia

who rose to service as intelligence minister following the coup that brought Siad Barre to power in 1969. Barre shortly thereafter had Aideed arrested as a suspected coup plotter; after five years in prison, Aideed was then rehabili-tated, serving as an aide-de-camp for Barre before the president named him Somali ambassador to India to remove him from Mogadishu. Aideed used the time abroad to plot his return, however. As a Habr Gidr Hawiye, a senior gov-ernment official, and an experienced soldier, he had a background that made him a natural choice for the USC, which persuaded him to leave New Delhi and return to Somalia as the USC's "father of war" in 1990.[4]

In the meantime, Barre's repression encouraged other opposition groups to organize and join the insurgency, which rapidly grew in strength. With the USC in a leading role, this mounting resistance drove Barre's forces from the capital in Mogadishu in January 1991, and the regime fell.[5]

As Aideed and his forces pursued Barre south, the USC established a new government in Mogadishu under Ali Mahdi Mohammed, a leader of the urban Abgal subclan of the Hawiye. Aideed, of the rural Habr Gidr Hawiye subclan, saw this as usurpation of his right to rule by virtue of his military role in Barre's ouster. This combination of personal and subclan rivalry split the USC into factions, with Aideed's Habr Gidr forming the Somali National Alliance (USC/SNA) and Ali Mahdi's Abgal creating the Somali Salvation Alliance (USC/SSA). The SSA quickly mobilized its own military wing from Abgal clansmen, yielding two armed Hawiye militias.[6]

The result was a civil war in which the respective USC militias fought for control of the capital and what remained of the central government. In the meantime, the other opposition groups that had been active against Barre commenced operations of their own against one another and the self-proclaimed USC government, beginning an era of chronic internecine warfare that continues today.[7]

This conflict tipped an already perilous economy into a condition of mass starvation. Facing a humanitarian crisis, the United Nations Security Council intervened. On April 24, 1992, it established the United Nations Operation in Somalia (UNOSOM I), which dispatched a team of 50 unarmed UN observ-ers to monitor an ostensible cease-fire between Aideed and Ali Mahdi. This was followed on July 26 with an emergency airlift of food and medicine to-gether with a force of 500 UN peacekeepers to oversee its distribution. This Pakistani peacekeeping contingent proved ineffective, however, as its limited strength and restrictive rules of engagement left it mostly confined to its base at the Mogadishu airport. In the meantime, Somali militias systematically commandeered aid deliveries, which they used to pay their own fighters and to control civilian populations. With the crisis worsening, the Security Council thus moved on December 3 to implement a Chapter VII humanitarian operation via Resolution 794, which authorized member nations to use "all necessary means," without the consent of the local parties to the conflict, to ensure the delivery of humanitarian supplies. The UN then dispatched a US-led multinational force of 33,000 (of whom 28,000 were Americans under Operation Restore Hope) as the "Unified Task Force" or UNITAF, which deployed to Somalia beginning on December 9.[8]

UNITAF proved more effective, and the threat of starvation receded as UNITAF's security umbrella enabled aid delivery and relief work. But UNITAF was meant only as a transitional effort pending a transfer of responsibility from American to other international forces, preferably with a permanent cease-fire among the warring Somali factions. Efforts to broker this cease-fire failed, however, and militia fighting resumed even as aid distribution continued. As UNITAF reached the end of its mandate, the Security Council thus authorized a follow-on mission, UNOSOM II, to be undertaken under UN command (though with an American admiral, Jonathan Howe, as the UN commander), and with a much smaller US contingent, beginning on May 1.[9]

On June 5, a Pakistani column dispatched to inspect an SNA weapons storage site was ambushed by Aideed's forces, which killed 24 UN soldiers. The following day, the Security Council passed Resolution 837, authorizing action against those responsible for the deaths and specifically naming the SNA. Violence against UNOSOM II components continued, however. In August a remote-controlled bomb killed four US soldiers, and a landmine wounded six. By this time, Admiral Howe had concluded that the reason the cease-fires had failed was the intransigence of Somali warlords, and especially Aideed. Together with UN secretary general Boutros Boutros-Ghali, who had developed an intense dislike for Aideed in previous interactions, Howe decided that a stable Somalia required the elimination of Aideed and his fellow militia leaders. To this end, Howe arranged for an American contingent of special forces to be deployed to Somalia and tasked with killing or capturing these leaders. US Task Force Ranger, consisting of a reinforced company of Army Rangers, a squadron of Delta Force commandos, and elements of the 160th Special Operations Aviation Regiment, was thus deployed to Mogadishu in August 1993.[10]

Task Force Ranger began a series of operations designed to kill or capture senior leaders of the SNA. One of these, on October 3, resulted in the loss of

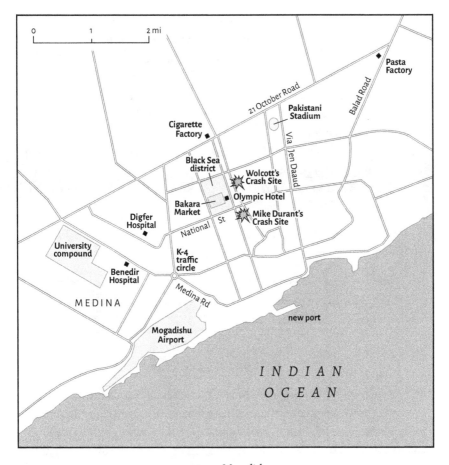

MAP 7.2. Mogadishu

two American Blackhawk helicopters. The ensuing battle to secure the crash sites and evacuate their casualties ultimately resulted in the 19 dead and 57 wounded Americans that seared "Blackhawk Down" into US popular awareness. The Clinton administration responded with a short-lived reinforcement meant to facilitate recovery of the captured pilot of one of the downed helicopters, but it soon withdrew all US forces from Somalia, with the last US troops departing on March 3, 1994. UNOSOM II continued for a time without its US contingent, but on March 28, 1995, the remaining international forces withdrew, and the UN mission ended.[11]

In the meantime, the Somali civil war continued. Fighting between the SNA and SSA intensified, with Aideed's forces pushing outward and capturing

Baidoa, Hoddur, and Dalow, and with sharp fighting along the contested frontier in Mogadishu. On the strength of SNA battlefield advances, Aideed declared himself president of Somalia in June 1995, but this neither ended the
fighting nor attracted foreign recognition. And in a fierce firefight between
SNA and SSA militiamen in Mogadishu on July 24, 1996, Aideed was fatally
wounded and died a few days later on August 1. Leadership of the SNA passed
briefly into the hands of his son, Hussein Mohamed Farrah, a US citizen and
former Marine infantryman. But with the elder Aideed's passing the SNA was
soon disbanded, merging instead into the new organization of the Somalia
Reconciliation and Restoration Council (SRRC). Somalia's civil war raged on
even so, but without the Somali National Alliance.[12]

Independent Variables

How does the SNA's behavior compare with the respective theories' predictions? I begin with the theories' independent variables of tribal culture, military materiel, and internal politics.

The SNA and Tribal Culture

Somali culture in the 1990s was strongly tribal. Siad Barre, like Saddam Hussein, had come into office with a modernizing agenda that sought to replace
traditional Somali tribalism with a combination of socialist political ideology
and nationalism. But like Saddam, he reverted to a deliberate revival of tribalism when military defeat and economic crisis threatened his regime; this reversal both reflected and reinforced the persistent power of tribal allegiance
in Somali culture.[13]

For centuries, family lineage and descent have shaped much of Somali society, from national politics to commerce and economic relationships, dispute
resolution and adjudication, marriage patterns, and social status. Somali clan
structure in the 1990s was dominated by six confederations: the Digil and
Rahanweyn of southern Somalia, the Dir in the northwest, the Isaq in the
north, the Darod of central and southern Somalia, and the Hawiye of central
Somalia and Mogadishu. Each in turn comprised multiple clans with member-
ships of under 100,000: the Darod, for example, was made up of the Dulbahante, Majertain, Warsangali, Ogadeni, and Marehan clans; the Hawiye sub-
sumed the Gurreh, Ajuran, Mobilen, Habr Gedir, Sheikkel, and Abgal. Clans
were further subdivided, down to the *diya*, or the kin group of as few as 100

male relatives responsible for paying blood money in the event that a member committed a capital crime against someone outside the group.[14]

This clan structure was so omnipresent in Somali life that the standard first question when Somalis met in the 1960s was to ask not "what do you do?" or "where are you from?" but "what is your clan?"[15] Unsurprisingly, such a ubiquitous institution had important influence on national politics. In colonial times, the Hawiye and Isaq tended to dominate civil administration given their predominance in and around Mogadishu, whereas the Somali military was disproportionately drawn from the rural Darod; British and Italian authorities manipulated the traditional rivalries among these groups to maintain control.[16]

Siad Barre's government, though nominally opposed to tribalism, was in fact disproportionately stocked with members of Barre's own Marehan clan: whereas the Marehan had been mostly excluded from the colonial administration, they secured 3 of the 25 seats in Barre's new Supreme Revolutionary Council (SRC), with 7 of the rest going to other Darods. Barre's nephew was made commandant of the Air Force; his son-in-law became director of the National Security Service; his son Abdurahman Siad "Maslah" was named commander of the critical military district of Mogadishu. Conversely, the once-influential Habr Gidr was reduced to just one of the seven SRC seats allocated to the Hawiye. The military was similarly dominated by Barre's Marehan: by 1987 perhaps 50 percent of the entire senior command was drawn from this single clan, as were most artillery and armor officers in Mogadishu. Somalis widely believed that the Barre government amounted to a tribal alliance between the three major clans of the Darod confederacy: Barre's Marehan, his mother's Ogadeni, and his son-in-law's Dulbahante.[17]

The insurrection that toppled the Barre regime was in turn fueled by clan resentment. The Hawiye and Isaq, in particular, were frustrated with their loss of status and influence under Barre. As tensions mounted in the aftermath of the Ogaden War and Barre's security services grew increasingly repressive, both confederations formed militias, which became the core of the subsequent insurgency.[18]

The post-Barre civil war similarly organized itself along tribal lines. Each of the major combatant forces was built around a clan. The Somali National Front (SNF) was Marehan. The Somali National Movement (SNM) was chiefly Isaq, with some participation by Hawiye subclans. The Somali Patriotic Movement (SPM) was mainly Ogandenis. The Somali Salvation Democratic Front (SSDF) was dominated by the Majertain. The United Somali Congress (USC) was Hawiye. A series of fluid alliances and realignments formed among these parties as battlefield fortunes shifted, and parties themselves periodically divided and recombined: the USC, for example, fractured into Aideed's Somali National Alliance (SNA) and Ali Mahdi's competing Somali Salvation Alliance (SSA); Aideed's SNA then formed a loose alliance with the Ogadeni SPM under Colonel Omar Jess. Throughout, however, the basic alignments were shaped by tribal identity: the USC, for example, split along clan lines, with the rural Habr Gidr Hawiye forming the SNA and the rival urban Abgal Hawiye forming the SSA.[19]

Economic life, like politics, was shaped by tribal identity. Access to agricultural and pastoral land, for example, was associated with clan and diya membership. Livestock were often owned by tribal groups rather than individuals, and members were obligated to defend tribal herds and grazing lands from rivals when necessary. Urban merchants and bureaucrats arranged jobs and patronage for rural kin and provided capital for pastoral clansmen to buy and maintain animals. Urban tradesmen and businesses were often associated with particular clans; the Herti of the Majeerteen clan, for example, controlled much of the business activity in Kismaayo. Basic financial services were often provided along kinship lines: without a meaningful insurance industry, life insurance for traffic accidents was provided via the blood payments of the traditional diya.[20]

Dispute resolution had powerful tribal elements. Informal tribal courts, or *guddi*, settled many intraclan conflicts via arbitration; the *shir*, or tribal assembly of all adult males, could be used to debate issues of disagreement within the group. Where the dispute was between members of a diya-paying group, its elders would enforce settlement terms; resolution of disputes between members of different diya-paying groups was subject to elaborate negotiation and could easily lead to violence if these negotiations failed. Crimes of murder, assault, and "insult" were commonly resolved by tribal guddi or shir; if the parties were unsatisfied, resort could be made to state courts, but the government recognized informal resolutions as legal if the parties agreed. At times state courts would enforce informal resolutions reached by guddi or shir. Nevertheless, and notwithstanding the existence of an unusually well-trained police force in the Barre era, informal tribal dispute resolution led to frequent interclan violence and sometimes extended internecine fighting between heavily armed tribesmen.[21]

Social life and marriage patterns were also strongly tribal. Cousin marriage, for example, was widespread as a means of keeping property within lineage groups. Cross-clan unions were common but were typically structured for political purposes as means of building alliances or resolving conflicts between clans. In fact, unmarried women were regarded as an important currency in interclan negotiations over conflict resolution; an exchange of brides was a commonplace means of sealing an agreement. In such cases, the partners were expected to owe mutual allegiance to both clans (children were expected to align chiefly with the matrilineal line).[22]

In fact, the ubiquity of clan and tribe in Somalia trumped most other sources of identity and social organization—including religion. Whereas Somalia had been Muslim since perhaps the 11th century, religious authorities played limited roles in Somali society in the 1990s. Imams were expected to assist in conflict mediation where tribal elders proved unable to resolve disputes between diya-paying groups; religious learning and piety were valued and afforded a degree of social status to individuals. But rarely did religious authorities play a central role in political or economic life.[23] As Clint Watts, Jacob Shapiro, and Vahid Brown put it: "Somali political culture is exceptionally pragmatic.... Related to this is a culture of negotiation that permeates Somali society and encourages Somalis to recalculate their bargaining position in partnerships on a daily basis. This aspect of Somali political culture provides little traction for movements based on sustained commitment to an abstract cause."[24] Tribalism was as important a feature of Somali culture in the 1990s as in any society of its time.

The SNA's Military Materiel

Both the new theory and prior materialist views see materiel as important, but with different implications—orthodox materialists see inferior materiel as a sufficient cause of nonstate Fabianism; the new theory does not, and it emphasizes the interaction of technological sophistication and internal politics. The SNA in Somalia, like many nonstate militias, employed mostly light weapons. But its material holdings depart from commonplace images of ragtag guerilla militias in two important respects: it had access to some surprisingly sophisticated guided weapons, and its gross balance of material strength varied enormously over time as a result of changing opposition. In 1991–2, when the SNA was at war chiefly with comparable nonstate rivals, the material balance between the primary combatants was not grossly asymmetric. Some were stronger than others, but none dominated in the way a state often outweighs a nonstate enemy. This changed dramatically in 1993 with the two major UN interventions of UNITAF and UNOSOM II. The international forces deployed by the UN, and especially their American components, were vastly superior to the SNA in firepower and in numbers of trained, professional combatants. The 1993 fighting in which these foreign forces were active combatants was thus highly asymmetric in physical military wherewithal. When this foreign presence withdrew, the material balance returned to its earlier condition of relative symmetry.

As with most nonstate actors, the SNA's order of battle can only be approximated. Estimates of their numerical strength range from 5,000 to 10,000, with perhaps 1,500 deployed in Mogadishu.[25] But these estimates are complicated by the Somali practice, common among nonstate militias, of complementing a smaller force of full-time professional fighters with much larger numbers of part-time combatants of varying commitment and military obligation. Americans in TF Ranger reported large numbers of apparently civilian sympathizers, including women and children, carrying arms and firing on US and UN soldiers but without evident skill or military training. As a function of whom one chooses to count, SNA combatant strength in 1993 was probably thus either less than 5,000 (in full-time fighters) or more than 10,000 (in total individuals under arms), but the upper bound includes large numbers of amateurs whose primary occupation was not warfare.[26]

Their equipment was primarily light infantry weaponry. The great majority of SNA combatants were armed with AK-47 assault rifles. Full-time fighters complemented these with RPG-7 rocket-propelled grenade launchers, hand grenades, sniper rifles, mortars, command-detonated mines, crew-served machine guns, and 106-millimeter recoilless rifles. Available crew-served weapons were often mounted on unarmored pickup trucks or jeeps called "technicals," affording a degree of mobility albeit without protection.[27]

But heavier weapons were available. The Barre regime deployed a well-equipped state military with almost 300 main battle tanks (including 123 US-made M-47s and 110 Soviet-made T-54/55s), over 450 Soviet- and Italian-made armored personnel carriers, over 200 towed artillery pieces, 100 Milan and TOW antitank guided weapons, 70 SA-2, SA-3, and SA-7 antiaircraft guided missiles, and an air force with 50 MiG17, MiG21, and J-6 fighters.[28] When the regime fell, some of this arsenal devolved to the remnant fighting on behalf of the SNF in southern Somalia, some left the country, but much remained behind in ill-defended depots.[29] Various militias, including the SNA, claimed parts of it: the SNA, for example, eventually acquired at least one SA-7 "Grail," 86 TOW missiles, 34 artillery pieces, a handful of tanks, and a variety of mortars and 106-millimeter recoilless rifles.[30] Beyond the mortars and recoilless rifles, little of this was ever used in combat. Many of the heavier weapons, and especially the armored vehicles, were inoperable owing to faulty maintenance; others presumably lacked trained crews and operators.[31]

But in practical terms, there was far more—and better—weaponry available to the SNA and its rivals than they actually employed in combat: in fact, the precision-guided TOWs in SNA stockpiles were broadly comparable in technological terms to the Kornet and Metis-M antitank missiles Hezbollah wielded so effectively against the IDF in Lebanon 13 years later.[32] Had the SNA used just the TOW missiles they owned against UNITAF and UNOSOM II forces with anything like Hezbollah's skill, the results could have been much heavier UN casualties: the relief column that ultimately fought its way through heavy SNA resistance to reach the TF Ranger perimeter on October 4 was heavily dependent on tanks and armored personnel carriers for protection; these vehicles would have been extremely vulnerable to well-directed TOW missile fire. None was received, but this was not because the weapons were unavailable to the SNA's nonstate militia.

It is impossible to know what financial resources Aideed had at his disposal for operating and equipping this force. The Barre regime had been the recipient of substantial military aid before its collapse: from FY 1982 through FY 1986, for example, the United States provided over $266 million in security assistance and sold $172 million in weapons to the government; some estimates place total Somali arms imports at $580 million between 1979 and 1983.[33] In 1988, however, the United States cut off military aid, and the regime's mounting economic difficulties contributed to systematic shortages of parts and ammunition.[34] Once the regime fell, nonstate militias had access to far smaller revenue streams. Ethiopia had supported several insurgent factions during the resistance to Barre, but it is unclear how much of this continued after Barre fell.[35] Al Qaeda is reported to have sent technical advisors to assist the SNA once it became engaged with Americans in UNITAF and UNOSOM II, but there are no reports of meaningful financial transfers.[36] Somali militias preyed systematically on international aid flows, which constituted a meaningful fraction of their overall revenue; such aid totaled almost $900 million in 1993 alone, but it is impossible to know how much of this was diverted, or how much of the diversion went to military purposes.[37] By comparison with Hezbollah or the Iraqi Jaish al Mahdi, the SNA almost surely had less revenue at its disposal, but how much less is unknown.

The SNA's indigenous rivals were similarly sized, equipped, and funded. Ali Mahdi's SSA was Aideed's principal Somali opponent; the SSA was probably somewhat smaller and less well equipped than the SNA, but the material difference was not overwhelming in itself: estimates of SSA combatant strength range from 5,000 to somewhat under 10,000.[38] As the descendant of the Barre regime's military, the SNF in southern Somalia probably inherited more than its share of Barre's equipment, but there is little evidence that the SNF proved much better than the SNA at sustaining it in the field, and estimates of SNF combatant strength range from 1,000 to 3,000, or perhaps a fifth to a half of Aideed's.[39] The Isaq Somali National Movement was estimated to field perhaps 5,000 to 6,000 fighters in 1993; the Majertain Somalia Salvation Democratic Front was thought to have around 3,000; the Ogadeni Somali Patriotic Movement had perhaps 2,000 to 3,000.[40] None were radically stronger than the SNA.

International forces, by contrast, were. The UN's member states could in principle have deployed almost unlimited forces to Somalia; the United States alone had more than two million personnel under arms in 1993, an annual defense budget of over $270 billion, and a sophisticated, diversified arsenal of cutting-edge weaponry.[41] Obviously no UN member sent more than a minute fraction of its national military to either mission, but even so the forces sent were large and capable by the standards of the respective Somali militias they were opposing.

UN forces in UNITAF numbered 37,000, of which the majority (21,000) were American. UNOSOM II was smaller, with about 30,000 troops, and the American contingent of 4,200 was much smaller. But these Americans included the 450 special operations forces of TF Ranger and were heavily supported from the air. Aircraft available to the task force included MH-60 Blackhawks, MH-6 assault helicopters, AC-130 gunships with 105-millimeter and 40-millimeter cannons, AH-1 Cobra attack helicopters with TOW missiles and 20-millimeter cannons, AH-6 attack helicopters with 2.75-inch rockets and 7.62-millimeter miniguns, and OH-58A helicopters for reconnaissance. The firepower inherent in these aircraft dwarfed anything actually fielded by Somali militiamen. A single AH-6 could saturate a football-field-sized target with minigun fire in five seconds; in the October "Battle of Mogadishu" repeated strafing runs by such weapons held forces of perhaps hundreds of Somalis at bay throughout the evening of October 3–4. US ground soldiers were equipped with state-of-the-art body armor, communications, and night vision equipment; M-16 and CAR-15 assault rifles; .50 caliber M-2, 7.62-millimeter M-60, and 5.56-millimeter M-249 machine guns; and M-203 rifle-mounted and MK-19 automatic grenade launchers. The MK-19 could project 40-millimeter explosive grenades to ranges of over 1,500 yards at a cyclic rate of over 300 rounds a minute; each grenade could kill anyone in a 15-foot radius. The M-2 could penetrate the frontal protection of Soviet-made armored personnel carriers at ranges in excess of 600 meters at a rate of up to 550 rounds a minute; American special forces' body armor could stop a Somali AK-47 round at all practical ranges. Allied Malaysian and Pakistani elements added German-made Condor armored personnel carriers and US-made M-48 tanks.[42] Numerically, these forces were sizeable but not vastly superior to those of their Somali opponents. The UN participants in UNOSOM II fielded more troops than any one militia taken alone, and about three times as many as Aideed's SNA, but the UN was responsible for territory that put it in potential conflict with multiple militias who could, in principle, have equaled or exceeded the UN's numbers if they had cooperated against it. And the 160 soldiers of TF Ranger were greatly outnumbered by the SNA fighters committed in Mogadishu on October 3. But the firepower at the disposal of these foreign troops was vastly superior in weight and accuracy, giving a significant material edge to the UN. The magnitude of this edge was thus important—but probably no greater than that enjoyed by the Israelis over Hezbollah in 2006 or by the United States over the JAM in 2007.

SNA Internal Politics

The new theory emphasizes two dimensions of an actor's internal politics: its stakes, and its institutional development. Existential stakes and formal institutions permit complex midspectrum methods for nonstate actors if their technology is lethal enough; limited stakes and institutions are expected to encourage simpler, more Fabian war fighting.

THE SNA'S STAKES

Until the deployment of TF Ranger in August 1993, the combatants in post-Barre Somalia were fighting mainly over the distribution of economic gain derived from international aid flows. While a few actors—notably Mohammed Farah Aideed—clearly harbored fond hopes of political power and had developed at least some rudimentary ideology to support that ambition, few of their followers shared this. Whatever Aideed's personal hopes, his organization waged war to affect the marginal distribution of economic spoils, as did its rival militias. When Admiral Howe decided that Aideed would have to be eliminated, however, and deployed TF Ranger to this end, the SNA's stakes escalated to self-preservation, and the war politicized, with Aideed's Habr Gidr clan unifying behind him and broad popular opposition to the UN presence mobilizing quickly. When the United States then withdrew in 1994, this existential threat was removed and the SNA's stakes returned to the profiteering of the pre-Ranger period.

Before 1993, fighting focused chiefly on critical income-producing assets such as aid distribution centers, ports, other transportation junctions, and productive agricultural areas. The port of Kismaayo, for example, was a major point of entry for international aid and thus offered the opportunity to extract transit payments, divert shipments, or extort protection money. Kismaayo was consequently a major battleground where General Mohammed Said Hersi Morgan and Jess's forces contested each other's access to this aid flow. In Mogadishu, commercial sites were fought over for their value in looted machinery, copper, or other materials; aid distribution centers and the associated food transportation and storage infrastructure were hotly contested; residential areas taken by militias were then rented back to the UN, foreign NGOs, or even their former owners at extortionate rates. "Cleansing" offensives to push rival populations from their homes for replacement with squatters, as was seen in Iraq, were less common than struggles to exclude rival clans from lootable economic assets.[43] As Ken Menkhaus put it: "the wars of 1991–92 morphed into a classic example of 'greed-based' warfare; militiamen mainly fought in order to loot civilians."[44]

Those militiamen displayed little fealty to causes beyond profiteering. Somali fighters were notorious for switching sides in response to offers of superior pay. The UN and private NGOs, for example, had to hire security forces to protect their aid shipments and staff; these security forces were drawn from the same clan groups that preyed on the aid. Individual gunmen could work for the SNA stealing UN food aid one week, then take their guns and supporters into UN employ protecting that aid from their own Habr Gidr clansmen the next, switching roles yet again later if offered more money by others.[45]

In fact few Somali warlords even bothered to issue ideological manifestos or to make any explicit appeals for others to join them on policy grounds; recruitment was overwhelmingly based on the prospect of looting organized along clan lines.[46] In this, Aideed was a partial exception: though they were little noticed, he published a series of rambling disquisitions laying out a nationalist political program for Somalia.[47] These proclamations are noteworthy chiefly for their rarity among Somali combatants. Nor is there much evidence that Aideed's own followers shared his vision: the SNA made no systematic effort to proselytize or mobilize political support among civilians outside Aideed's Habr Gidr subclan prior to 1993; nor did Aideed's survivors in the SNA leadership seek to advance his published program after his death.[48] The SNA was clearly interested in advancing the Habr Gidr's power, influence, and wealth at the expense of rival clans, but this was a matter of economic self-interest for a kin group, not an expression of ideological ambitions meant for all Somalis.

But whereas the war was essentially a contest for the division of economic spoils prior to 1993, the arrival of TF Ranger in August of that year changed its complexion and altered the stakes for Aideed and the SNA. Admiral Howe announced his aim of Aideed's death or capture publicly in June, even posting "wanted" signs around the capital offering a reward for Somalis to turn him in or provide information. (Aideed responded with his own posters, offering a much larger reward for *Howe's* death or capture.) Given the military wherewithal at Howe's disposal, his threat was taken very seriously by the SNA. In fact the Habr Gidr's elders gave extended consideration to turning over Aideed to the UN for prosecution; internal deliberations over Aideed's disposition continued for weeks even as Howe began using his reinforcements to conduct raids and air strikes aimed at achieving his objective unilaterally.[49] One such air strike resulted in two American helicopters firing 16 TOW missiles into a home where Habr Gidr elders were meeting to discuss Aideed's fate. The missiles failed to kill Aideed, but they did destroy the building and kill more than a dozen other elders, radicalizing the survivors and ending any prospect of cooperation.[50]

The heavy-handed methods used in the air strike and in ongoing Ranger and Delta raids alienated the general public as well. Whereas earlier UN military action had been apparently linked with humanitarian aid provision in the face of famine and with nonpartisan suppression of violence, the new manhunt and its associated collateral fatalities, break-ins, abductions, and low-altitude helicopter overflights (whose rotor wash could knock down pedestrians, blow down market stall tables, and raise suffocating clouds of dust) looked more like an aggressive effort to disempower the Somali Habr Gidr in favor of a foreign overlord (Howe). Popular passions had been muted in an interclan struggle for spoils going chiefly to wealthy warlords, but the public were now easily mobilized in opposition to an apparent power grab by a foreign occupier.[51]

The net result was to change the stakes for Aideed and the SNA. Whereas in 1992 the war was mainly a contest over prospective economic gain for

Somali warlords, many of whom had already grown wealthy from such looting, by mid-1993 the war had transformed into a life-and-death struggle for personal survival for the SNA's leadership, and a popular war of resistance to hostile occupation for many of their followers. The SNA's leaders had now been named by a superpower's local viceroy as targets to be killed or captured, and that superpower had demonstrated its bona fides by killing over a dozen of them while clearly intending to remove the rest as quickly as possible. Somali noncombatants who may once have seen foreign troops as protectors now increasingly resented them as an arrogant foreign army willing to kill some civilians and humiliate others to get its own way on who should be ruling over Somalis. This unified Somali civilians against TF Ranger and would have convinced any rational Habr Gidr elder to set aside internal differences and do whatever was necessary to defend their lives and freedom against a highly credible threat from Admiral Howe.

Yet this threat proved short-lived. From Howe's 1993 announcement through the end of 1994, Aideed and his colleagues faced a serious prospect of death or imprisonment if they failed on the battlefield. But their performance against TF Ranger in the Battle of Mogadishu led to a Western withdrawal that removed this threat and returned the war to the chiefly economic stakes it had posed before 1993. The war continued long after TF Ranger left, but with the departure of Howe and the Americans its nature reverted to a contest over the distribution of spoils without a meaningful ideological component and with limited downside risk of annihilation or imprisonment for the warlords who waged it.[52] The SNA thus waged war for interests that were existential for its leadership, but only briefly. For most of its existence, the SNA and its militia were fighting for much lesser stakes.

THE SNA'S INSTITUTIONS

The SNA was a prototypically informal, tribal organization without any meaningful formal or de jure institutional structure. A council of elders held real decision-making power for major issues, such as the disposition of Aideed following Admiral Howe's edict. Its membership comprised the senior figures in the Habr Gidr's main subclans and could trace lineage relationships (real or asserted) to one another by birth or marriage. As president of the SNA, Aideed was its nominal leader and held primus inter pares status, but Aideed's actual ability to impose decisions on other elders was limited. Instead, as in most tribal systems, the council operated under a norm of decision by consensus following extensive discussion; disagreement could produce extended periods of internal bargaining, as in the deliberations prior to the Abdi House raid of July 12, 1993. Specialized functions could be delegated to particular individuals: Osman Atto, for example, served as the SNA's chief financier; Aideed led the clan's military forces. But these grants of authority were personal, not institutional: when Aideed was killed in 1996, the military leadership succession went not to a lieutenant or unrelated second in command, but to Aideed's son Hussein Mohamed Farrah, who returned from the United States to take the reins in his father's place.[53]

Nor was there any meaningful structure of agencies, offices, staffs, or other persistent, impersonal, hierarchically organized division of labor. Subclans and factions instead operated with a great deal of autonomy under limited formal coordination or direction, with most retaining their own military forces capable of independent action against rivals from without or within. There was no formal system of legal or administrative sanction to enforce collectively reached decisions; alliances of elders could threaten ostracism or violence in the event of noncompliance with collective decisions, but it was the balance of power within the leadership ranks that determined enforcement, and enforcement was a product of elders' choices not a constraint on them. Economic activity in areas under SNA control was effectively monopolized by the Habr Gidr clan and its leadership; there was little or no meaningful independent commercial activity outside the control of tribal strongmen or independent of their influence.[54]

This tribal organization was subject to major factional tensions both before and after the struggle with Howe. The SNA was born as the product of an internal fissure between the Habr Gidr and Abgal clans of the Hawiye confederation, and factionalism continued within the SNA even as it waged war with its erstwhile confederates. Osman Atto, for example, maintained a sizeable private militia largely outside Aideed's authority and sought to supplant Aideed in his leadership role. Tensions between their respective camps subsided for a time following Atto's capture by the UN and Aideed's subsequent role in negotiating his release, but the rivalry rekindled after TF Ranger's withdrawal, with Atto and his fighters publicly defecting from the SNA in 1994 to ally instead with Ali Mahdi and the SSA.[55] In fact when Aideed was killed in factional fighting in 1996, it was believed by many to be at the hands of Atto's militiamen.[56] Atto subsequently changed sides again, as the fighting increasingly devolved to rival subclans within the Habr Gidr and Abgal; by 1995, conflict within these clans had largely supplanted warfare between them.[57]

This is not to say that the SNA's prototypically informal institutional structure was invariant. Though never highly bureaucratized, its degree of internal coordination and hierarchical direction increased meaningfully (if briefly) during TF Ranger's deployment in 1993. Aideed and Atto, for example, set their differences aside in the face of an existential common threat from the UN. A potentially fractious internal debate over Aideed's future following Howe's June pronouncement was ended with the Abdi House raid, after which the Habr Gidr unified around Aideed. Formerly freelancing subclan militias followed centralized leadership direction during the October battle against the Americans in Mogadishu. All this represents movement toward a minimal version of fragile natural order institutionalization. Its fragility was clear, however: with the withdrawal of TF Ranger in 1994 the SNA quickly lost any semblance of such coordination and reverted to its earlier condition of fluid, violent, internal realignment and unconstrained warlordism, marked by Atto's defection in 1994 and continuing through the SNA's final disestablishment in 2002.

Dependent Variable: SNA Military Behavior

Somali warlords' military behavior is often seen as a defining example of "irregular" or "guerilla" methods. Yet on close examination even the SNA fails to live up to the popular stereotype in important respects—few would mistake the SNA for a great power army, but to pin down its actual relationship to the Fabian ideal requires a detailed treatment of each observable referent of its position on the Fabian-Napoleonic spectrum as presented in chapter 2 and the appendix: stealth; commitment to taking and holding ground; dispersion; coercion; distinguishability of combatants from noncombatant civilians; and functional differentiation within the theater of war.

1. Stealth

At the Fabian extremum, actors sacrifice lethality for maximum cover and concealment; the Napoleonic archetype sacrifices stealth for maximum lethality. The SNA's full-time professional militiamen systematically adopted covered firing positions when stationary. Their part-time amateur fighters sometimes sought expedient cover but without apparent systematic selection of fighting positions for stealthiness. Neither group, however, adopted techniques that would allow systematic exploitation of cover on the move.

The armed civilians who converged on TF Ranger's positions on October 3 displayed little apparent concern with selecting or occupying covered or concealed fighting positions; movement toward the objective dominated stealth as an apparent goal, and these fighters typically fired on the move or from short halts behind, at most, expedient obstacles in the urban detritus of the streets. Movement itself was largely exposed with little apparent effort at suppressive fires to support maneuver by short rushes.[58]

The SNA's full-time professionals, by contrast, appear to have sought out windowed building interiors and defilade positions at constructed roadblocks that would provide cover and concealment with a field of fire toward enemy positions.[59] As one US participant put it: "They used concealment very well. Usually all you saw of a shooter was the barrel of his weapon and his head."[60] Most of the fire received by the US relief convoy as it drove through the SNA defenses around the Bakara Market was from building interiors or concealed rooftops in locations difficult to locate before firing activity.[61] It is unclear how extensively prepared or reconnoitered these positions were, and positions for weapons larger than personal small arms were typically exposed.[62] And there is no evidence that any of the Somali fighters, full-time or amateur, attempted to combine short rushes with systematic suppressive fire to enable covered maneuver. But the full-time subset of the SNA's fighting force appears to have sought out firing positions that afforded at least basic cover and concealment.[63]

2. Taking and Holding Ground

At the Fabian extremum, combatants never accept decisive engagement to contest ground; at the Napoleonic extremum, fighters always do. The SNA's behavior reflected neither of these extrema.

To assess the SNA's relative commitment to taking and holding ground I use the four observable referents of this commitment presented in the appendix: the duration of firefights; the proximity of attackers to defenders; the incidence of counterattack; and the incidence of harassing fires and unattended minefields.

THE DURATION OF FIREFIGHTS

Archetypically Napoleonic tactics are associated with extended firefights where defenders remain in position and under fire, whereas pure Fabian methods are associated with short-duration, hit-and-run ambushes or raids. In

Somalia, the SNA did indeed engage in short-duration ambushes, but they also conducted multiple sustained engagements with UN forces, including a 14-hour-long battle with TF Ranger in Mogadishu.

All militaries sometimes conduct short-duration ambushes and raids. And certainly the SNA did, too. The August 8 roadside bombing that killed four US soldiers was a hit-and-run action that lasted only minutes before the SNA fighters who triggered it disappeared, as were similar actions on August 19 and 22.[64] On June 12 an infantry company from the US 10th Mountain Division was ambushed by the SNA in a "brief but intense" action on the 21 October Road.[65] Through July and August SNA militiamen regularly harassed UN bases with mortar and RPG rounds fired by crews who immediately fled the scene before air strikes or counterfire could be brought to bear.[66]

The important distinction, however, is whether such short-duration actions are accompanied by sustained firefights: for conventional armies, sustained firefights are expected; for guerillas, they are not. Yet the SNA did sustain such firefights. The October 3 Battle of Mogadishu was an intense, close-quarters struggle that began shortly after 3:30 p.m. on the afternoon of the third and did not end until after 5:45 a.m. the following day—more than 14 hours later. In fact the battle would have continued even longer if the SNA had had its way: it was the UN, not the SNA, that disengaged to end the fighting. The relief column that ultimately extracted TF Ranger had to fight its way into and out of the Bakara Market; SNA fighters were resisting fiercely until UN forces crossed out of Aideed's zone of control and withdrew to their bases.[67]

Nor was the October 3–4 battle the only such sustained action. On June 17, Moroccan forces fought a four-hour-long battle with SNA militia near the Digfer Hospital in Mogadishu; it was the Moroccans, not the Somalis, who broke contact and withdrew. On September 6, Nigerian forces that had just relieved an Italian garrison in downtown Mogadishu were attacked and pinned down for three hours of continuous combat; again it was the UN forces that disengaged. On September 9, US and Pakistani troops clearing roadblocks near the Cigarette Factory were attacked by a mixed force of perhaps 1,000 SNA fighters and armed civilians; the ensuing battle lasted over two hours before US helicopter gunships drove away the attackers. On September 13 a US Quick Reaction Force (QRF) from the 10th Mountain Division was ambushed southeast of Benedir Hospital in the Mogadishu Medina; the ensuing firefight lasted two hours and ended only when US forces fought their way out of the engagement area. On July 2, SNA fighters ambushed an Italian detachment along Balad Road near the Pasta Factory in Mogadishu; after nearly four hours of continuous combat the Italian commander negotiated a cease-fire to permit the withdrawal of his forces. The June 5 SNA ambush of the Pakistanis that killed 24 UN soldiers and triggered UNSC Resolution 837 was a three-and-a-half-hour fight in which the Pakistanis were ultimately extracted from an ongoing battle by multiple UN relief columns.[68]

Certainly the SNA did its share of hit-and-run fighting. But it was also prepared to accept sustained combat in place and did so, occasionally before the passage of UN Resolution 837 in June and Admiral Howe's decision to kill or capture the SNA senior leadership, but increasingly so thereafter.[69]

PROXIMITY OF ATTACKERS TO DEFENDERS

Archetypically Napoleonic armies accept decisive engagement as attackers close with their positions, and they seek decisive engagement when on the offensive; pure Fabian guerillas break contact while distant enough to enable safe withdrawal. In Somalia the SNA certainly did some of its fighting at safe distances via unattended landmines, remotely detonated roadside bombs, sniping, and mortar or rocket fire.[70] But state militaries sometimes do the same. As with battle duration, the real question is whether nonstate fighters complement this with close-quarters fighting at greater risk to themselves. And the SNA certainly did.

In fact, the October Battle of Mogadishu was fought at remarkably short ranges. American participants commonly report Somali militiamen exchanging fire with US Rangers and Delta Force soldiers at distances of under 50 meters. Urban terrain can sometimes enable relatively safe sniping from even very short ranges if the shooter has arranged for hidden withdrawal routes through building interiors or narrow alleys. But the fighting in Mogadishu was often so close that disengagement would have been dangerous even in the urban environment. Americans and militiamen fought as close together as opposite sides of low mud walls less than a couple of feet thick; at such distances, simple hand grenades could easily kill or disable anyone unable to kill the enemy first. Fire was regularly exchanged across distances as short as the width of a city street between fully exposed shooters who could not reasonably have expected to survive and withdraw if they missed their target.[71] Journalist Mark Bowden reports accounts of Somali civilians trying to discourage others from approaching the downed Blackhawks given the obvious danger of closing with US combat troops, yet mobs continued to do so even in face of withering American fire; by late afternoon on the opening day of the battle it was clear that US troops were fighting for their lives, and many of the earlier strictures on harming noncombatants had melted away in the heat of battle with the result being prodigious volumes of American fire. Yet thousands of Somalis—civilians as well as militiamen—pressed onward into close contact at ranges of as little as 10 to 15 feet.[72] The brigade commander of the 10th Mountain Division relief force characterized typical firefight ranges during their rescue mission as "a matter of feet."[73]

Elsewhere SNA fighters closed to similarly short ranges in firefights with UN forces. In the June 14 battle between the SNA and the Moroccans, militiamen using women and children as shields advanced to within 35 meters of UN positions. In a June 17 firefight with a joint Italian-Moroccan force, SNA fighters again closed to ranges of 30 to 40 meters. In the September 13 action between the SNA and elements of the US 10th Mountain Division, the SNA ambush elements engaged at ranges of 30 to 200 meters.[74] Then-major Martin Stanton of the 10th Mountain Division's Task Force 2–87 Infantry estimates that the average engagement range for combat with militiamen in his area of operations was less than 25 meters.[75] The SNA did sometimes fight from safe distances, but it was also prepared to close with the enemy and did so regularly.[76]

INCIDENCE OF COUNTERATTACK

Archetypically Napoleonic defenders counterattack at the cost of greater exposure; pure Fabian guerillas avoid costly counterattacks and instead melt away once dislodged. The issue underlying the distinction is territorial control: it is because Napoleonic defenders are expected to hold ground that they must counterattack to regain it; Fabian fighters with less commitment to holding ground are not expected to risk the exposure this requires. In Somalia, fighting between rival warlords involved frequent counterattacks to regain control of economically valuable locations. This internecine warfare was thus highly territorial, though ground per se was important only when it offered specific commercial value. Against foreign enemies who posed an existential threat, this territoriality became more pronounced and less economically focused. In particular, by fall 1993 the SNA was mounting increasingly violent counterattacks against UN forces that entered territory the SNA was using to shield Aideed and his lieutenants from Admiral Howe's counterleadership campaign; these counterattacks climaxed in the Battle of Mogadishu in response to UN penetration of the SNA's critical Bakara Market stronghold.

Combat between rival Somali militias was frequently a seesaw affair in which commercially lucrative assets changed hands repeatedly; such repossessions represent territorial counterattacks to regain lost ground.[77] Beginning in 1991, for example, hundreds of kilometers of southern agricultural land between Mogadishu and the Kenyan border came under control of successive warlords in a series of freewheeling offensives and counteroffensives using mostly jury-rigged technicals to move fighters and project force.[78] The port of Kismaayo was subject to repeated attacks and counterattacks by militias trying to control its commerce; the UN's unwillingness to prevent Morgan's militia from driving Aideed's ally Jess from the city in February 1993 contributed to Aideed's growing disaffection with the UN and led Jess to mount a major counteroffensive there in May.[79] Mogadishu neighborhoods with lootable assets were hotly contested, and the city itself was the target of a major counteroffensive by former Barre regime elements allied with the SNF in 1991, which reached the capital's outskirts in April before being driven back in turn by the SNA.[80]

The UN intervention initially muted, but ultimately reinforced, the SNA's willingness to counterattack for control of territory. The UN presence threatened warlord interests from the very beginning—after all, its purpose was to protect aid shipments that the SNA and others had been looting. But an outright war against the UN would clearly have been costly to the militias, and in a war for profit cost is taken seriously. Hence the militias mostly tolerated the foreign troops initially, allowing them considerable freedom of movement through formerly militia-controlled areas while gradually testing the UN's limits to see how much theft could be accommodated without triggering open warfare.

Had this process continued, it is possible that a stable equilibrium could have emerged in which the warlords and the UN arrived at a mutually tolerable rate of theft. Such equilibria are common in weak states, wherein struggles between state authority and nonstate militias sometimes yield mutual coexistence between forces that cannot monopolize power but can prevent the other from doing so. In such cases, territorial "control" is often incomplete and permeable, with overlapping spheres of partial influence, and with multiple actors able to move through the same areas, sometimes triggering combat but other times not.[81] In the Somali context, this could have produced a UN-enforced ban on major offensives or outright interdiction of aid, but with substantial latitude allowed for warlords to profiteer short of inducing famine, and with UN troops enjoying significant freedom to patrol in enforcement of the implicit deal as long as they looked the other way while warlords took a partial cut from international aid flows. Such equilibria are imperfect, and periodic bloodshed is commonplace in a form of violent tacit bargaining over terms and limits. But the very persistence of such equilibriums suggests that the violence can remain within mutually tolerable limits for extended periods. In such a scenario, true territorial control would have been limited; fighting would have been mostly hit-and-run harassment at the margins of the SNA's allowable scope of looting; and "counterattacks" in the normal sense would have been very rare.

For Admiral Howe, however, it was an intolerable affront to decency to allow warlords to loot international aid meant for starving Somalis; Howe would not accept theft on anything like a scale sufficient to satisfy the SNA. Nor was Howe (or the UN General Assembly) willing to tolerate the SNA's gradually escalating attacks on UN forces. Howe and the UN responded by escalating the conflict into a zero-sum struggle for exclusive control, with a particular emphasis on eliminating Aideed and the others he saw as responsible for militia predation. This changed the stakes for the SNA in a way that also changed the meaning of terrain and its control, and changed significantly the SNA's incentives for counterattack.

Before this, critical terrain was certainly lucrative, but no single piece of ground was decisive, and none truly had to be held. For highly valuable assets like Kismaayo, aid distribution points, or productive agricultural centers, fighting was worth the cost, but control could be relatively fluid, and actors could lose and then regain it over and over. Now, however, SNA leaders' personal survival turned on their ability to hide themselves from UN raids—and this required meaningful, persistent control of a large, contiguous territory in which to hide. If UN forces were free to move about Mogadishu, conduct searches, man checkpoints, observe traffic, and arrest and interrogate suspects or potential informants, they would eventually find any SNA leader who tried to remain viable as a militia commander. To survive against such a manhunt would have required Aideed and his lieutenants to lie so low as to lose their ability to command their organization, which would have withered in the meantime without leadership. This degree of UN access and freedom of movement would also have starved the SNA of its chief revenue source in diverted aid. For the SNA to survive as a combatant militia (and for Aideed to have retained his freedom), it now needed to exclude UN forces from critical terrain wherein the leadership could carry out its essential command functions without capture by the UN.

The result was an increasingly territorial conflict. Militia arms caches and cantonment points had long been flashpoints, but much of the violence had previously occurred at random points along UN patrol routes; now there were increasingly clear frontiers delineating areas of more-or-less contiguous SNA control within which an intense firefight was a near certainty for UN convoys. In Mogadishu, for example, the K-4 traffic circle was understood to be the southwestern boundary of Aideed's territory; a Pakistani checkpoint there constituted the limit of safe movement for the UN by October 1993.[82] In the October 3–4 battle, relief columns passing this checkpoint into the Black Sea/ Bakara Market neighborhood immediately began to receive fire; convoys crossing it in the opposite direction reached sanctuary and were not fired on even though surrounded by crowds of Somalis.[83] On the eastern side, Via Jen Daaud served as a frontier; the multinational relief force that eventually fought its way to the crash sites was able to drive north along the road without incident, but as soon as it turned west into Bakara Market along National Street it immediately encountered a fusillade of small arms and RPG fire. From that point to the crash sites the column had to fight its way "literally one building and one block at a time" as the convoy commander, Lieutenant Colonel William David, later put it.[84] Upon exit, UN forces again reached sanctuary and drove on to the Pakistani Stadium on safe ground.[85]

This does not mean there was a continuously manned front line in Mogadishu of the kind seen in many interstate wars. In the October 3 battle, for example, the original air assault was accompanied by a ground movement to the Olympic Hotel in the heart of Bakara Market by a column of vehicles who were to remove the prisoners taken and extract the raiders; this initial ground penetration arrived mostly without incident. Subsequent movements on essentially the same route, by contrast, drew intense fire, and the original convoy had to fight its way *out* of Bakara Market against stiff opposition.[86] This suggests that the SNA did not maintain a standing defense of a perimeter, but instead relied on an alert system to mobilize forces quickly once an incursion was detected and to route fighters to the threatened area thereafter. In fact SNA spotters did observe both the air and the ground elements of the UN raid as they left their bases at the airport.[87] Shortly thereafter, US aircrews noted that Somalis had started to light burning tires around the city, a device the SNA had previously used to signal incursions and initiate counteractions. From previous engagements, US staff officers had estimated a typical response time of 20 to 40 minutes from such signals to the arrival of SNA fighters on the scene, and airborne observers on October 3 quickly detected large movements of armed Somalis toward the US objective area (and toward the crash sites of the downed helicopters after these were shot down).[88] These Somalis then closed with TF Ranger on the ground, as noted above, and tried to overrun the US positions (succeeding in the case of their assault on the second crash site), sustaining close contact and heavy fire until US forces withdrew.

The result did not much resemble the German defense of the Normandy beaches in 1944: whereas the Allied invaders on D-Day took heavy fire from the time they were spotted, TF Ranger reached its initial objective before the SNA rallied. But the SNA *was* trying to control the area, and it was, effectively, conducting a major counterattack to destroy or repel an incursion into that area once it was detected. Even in interstate warfare, defenders rarely control ground so absolutely that attackers cannot penetrate meaningful distances before being stopped. Napoleonic defense of ground normally works, effectively, by killing enough of the attackers who enter it as to convince the survivors or their leadership to withdraw and not return. And this often involves the use of a lightly manned outpost zone whose role is not to halt the attack but simply to detect it, localize it, and facilitate reaction by defenders elsewhere who will move to the threatened point once alerted. In fact this concept is the very heart of modern defense in depth. As noted above, the Germans, who first implemented modern-system methods, even coined their defensive concept the *An-sich-herankommen-lassen,* or "invitation-to-walk-right-in," system.[89] State defenses vary widely in the density or porousness of their forward garrisons: some contest every inch of ground from the outset, others are much more yielding, and the latter often rely much more heavily on counterattack to expel attackers after they enter the defended area rather than killing them as they enter. The SNA was certainly not expecting to kill any UN soldier who entered the Bakara Market the moment they entered. But they were trying to detect entry, localize it, mass forces against it, and destroy it or drive it out thereafter. The contrast between this behavior when UN forces entered critical terrain like the Bakara Market and other UN movements elsewhere is instructive: UN movements outside the SNA's controlled territory would often be harassed by random mine attacks or hit-and-run ambushes, but movements that breached the boundaries of critical terrain could expect a much more coordinated, concentrated, systematic reaction. The latter amounted to a porous but nonetheless territorial defense of ground via an extremely elastic, yielding resistance with a heavy emphasis on counterattack after penetration.[90]

THE INCIDENCE OF HARASSING FIRES AND
UNATTENDED MINEFIELDS

Another indicator of actors' relative emphasis on holding ground is the incidence of harassing fires and unattended minefields. Any combatant will employ such tactics at times. Archetypically Fabian guerillas, however, rely on them to a much more extensive degree given the Fabian unwillingness to risk exposure and its focus on gradual attrition rather than retention of ground per se. In Somalia, the SNA followed this Fabian expectation closely: they made extensive use of mortars, rockets, and mines as stand-alone tools of low-exposure harassment but rarely as integrated components of a combined-arms team even after June 1993.

For interclan warfare among Somali militias, much of the fighting took the form of artillery duels using rocket and mortar fire.[91] The targets were often in populated areas, and such exchanges produced mounting casualty tolls among civilians on both sides. In the three months between November 1991 and February 1992, for example, perhaps 14,000 were killed and 27,000 wounded in Mogadishu.[92] Yet this was hardly a case of concentrated fire for decisive military effect. Little of this fire was combined in any meaningful way with ground maneuver, and its intensity, while high enough to kill thousands of civilians over time, was nevertheless far lower than the weapons' material potential: if fired at their maximum sustained rate for three months, even a handful of 81-millimeter mortars could have covered the entire land area of Mogadishu with fragmentation more than 20 times over, killing vastly larger numbers.[93] These artillery duels were a form of intimidation and harassment, not mass destruction.

The SNA's battle with UNOSOM likewise involved extensive mortar and rocket fire, but this, too, was mostly harassment. By midsummer, UN bases were frequently attacked with indirect fire. The TF Ranger garrison at the airport, for example, was struck so regularly that the troops eventually started a betting pool with 10-minute time slots; if a mortar round landed during a better's slot he would win the money wagered on that day's pool. As the base was hit daily, there were ample opportunities to gamble.[94] The 10th Mountain Division QRF (Quick Reaction Force) base at the university compound in Mogadishu received almost nightly mortar and RPG attacks after June 12, typically beginning at 10 p.m. and lasting until 1 a.m.[95] Other UNOSOM facilities were similarly receiving near-nightly mortar and rocket fire by late June.[96]

None of these attacks, however, concentrated sustained fire on a given target—SNA mortar crews would normally fire a handful of rounds then quickly evacuate the position, ending the fire mission before air strikes or counterfire could be brought to bear. These attacks did occasionally kill or injure UNOSOM troops, but casualties were generally light on both sides; the chief effect was harassment, not destruction.[97]

The SNA also made extensive use of landmines against UN forces beginning in mid-July. By August, mine incidents were becoming increasingly frequent, and deadly: on August 8, four US Marines were killed when their vehicle hit an SNA mine on Jialle Siad Street in Mogadishu during a routine patrol. As the density of SNA minelaying increased, UNOSOM began a series of countermine sweeps to clear major roadways and ordered the construction of a bypass route around the heavily mined and barricaded 21 October Road. These sweeps found and destroyed mines on August 12, 13, 15, and 17 but were unable to prevent US vehicles from striking others on the 19th and 22nd. Many of these attacks were surely intended as harassment to wear down UN forces without really denying them access—the early clearance operations, for example, were frequently able to clear mines without being fired on in the process, indicating that the cleared mines were unattended or disconnected from any systematic defensive system for holding ground. Some SNA mining was actively overwatched: the mine that killed the Marines on August 8 was command detonated, with nearby militiamen triggering it only when they saw the US vehicle enter the kill zone; the attacks on August 19 and 22 were also command detonated. And by September, the obstacle systems on 21 October Road were routinely defended by militiamen who fired on UNOSOM clearance teams; two of these engagements, on September 9 and 16, yielded multihour firefights. An ambush the morning of October 3 near the new port in Mogadishu was initiated with a command-detonated mine attack on a Marine Humvee that was followed up with small arms and RPG fire on the helicopters brought in to evacuate the wounded. Yet the SNA's most sustained engagement with UNOSOM, the October 3–4 Battle of Mogadishu, was waged overwhelmingly with small arms and RPGs without any systematic use of minefields; ad hoc barriers were widespread on October 3–4, but few of these were supported with mines (or indirect fire).[98] On balance, the SNA's use of mine warfare was much closer to guerilla harassment than it was to an integral component of a defensive system for holding ground.[99]

3. Dispersion

Archetypically Napoleonic state armies concentrate their forces at a chosen point of attack; pure Fabian nonstate irregulars disperse and operate at low, uniform densities across the theater of war. The SNA in Somalia deployed a large combatant force for the size of its primary theater of operations in Mogadishu and made a clear, if incomplete, effort to concentrate forces into the critical combat zone in the Bakara Market on October 3–4. It thus did not undertake a pure Fabian uniform territorial defense. Yet neither did it concentrate as aggressively as many state militaries—or even as aggressively as midspectrum nonstate actors such as Hezbollah.

Estimates of SNA troop density are necessarily imprecise given the softness of available figures on SNA combatant strength, but if one assumes 1,500 fighters in Mogadishu this would imply a substantial density of about 24 combatants per square kilometer in the SNA's primary theater.[100] By the time of TF Ranger's assault on October 3, moreover, much of the local population had grown disaffected with the US mission, and there is evidence to suggest that large numbers of armed civilians who were not normally part of Aideed's militia joined in the fight spontaneously.[101] Small arms were widely distributed in Mogadishu for civilian self-defense amid the city's chaos; this spontaneous mobilization could thus easily have doubled or tripled the armed opposition, and thus the available combatant density, in the Mogadishu theater during the battle.[102] This theaterwide density was unusually high for a nonstate militia. It exceeded Hezbollah's troop density in Lebanon by at least a factor of four; it was higher than all but 3 of the 42 nonstate examples in figure 3.9; and it approached the JAM's figure of 60 to 90 fighters per square kilometer in 2007. In fact, the SNA deployed more fighters per square kilometer theaterwide than the US state military did in its 1990 defense of Saudi Arabia.[103]

Once the battle with TF Ranger began, the SNA made a systematic effort to concentrate these forces from across the city to the critical Black Sea district, where Aideed was hiding out. Once initiated, this movement was poorly directed and coordinated, and it produced sometimes extremely dense concentrations of fighters on some particular streets and alleys leading to the two downed Blackhawks but little or no strength on others; averaged across the zone of active combat, however, this movement is likely to have increased the local force-to-space ratio in the Black Sea district per se to a figure of perhaps

60 to 180 fighters per square kilometer, or about two to three times the density of a prototypically Fabian uniform area defense of the theater.[104]

The SNA's dispositions for combat were thus not a pure Fabian uniform area defense. But neither was this the kind of state-like concentration Hezbollah adopted in 2006, which produced local densities in the critical sector that exceeded its theaterwide figure by about a factor of 10. In 1993, SNA dispersion was thus less Napoleonic than Hezbollah's—but neither did it display a true Fabian extremum.

4. The Balance of Brute Force and Coercion

At the tactical and operational levels of war, archetypically Napoleonic war fighting relies on brute force seizure of objectives whereas Fabian warfare depends on coercive pain imposition to persuade enemies who could remain to select withdrawal instead. At the strategic level, even states in world wars must rely on coercion if they are smaller or weaker than their rivals, but archetypically Napoleonic tactics and operations emphasize brute force. In Somalia, Aideed's strategy was indeed chiefly coercive. But his tactics and operations combined elements of both coercion and brute force, especially in his struggle with UNOSOM after June 1993.

The SNA's operations against other warlord militias were clearly intended to seize or retain critical terrain, and especially economically productive assets. Its campaigns to realize these ends, however, were often more coercive than in many interstate conventional wars. In Mogadishu, for example, much of the SNA's campaign against the USC took the form of extended, moderate-intensity artillery fire with limited follow-up in direct-fire ground assaults against defended positions. Each side defended its territory against the other with militia infantry that could resist such assaults if mounted. But sustained ground assaults were rare. Instead, each used artillery fired from safe distances to wear the other down gradually over time by imposing cumulative casualties and property damage. When withdrawals or advances took place, these rarely resulted from the annihilation of the defender and a consequent inability to prevent the attacker from taking the position; nor were commanders pulling out of positions *threatened* with imminent destruction if they had remained. Instead, withdrawals more often represented decisions made by commanders who chose to reduce casualties but whose forces could still have repelled an actual ground attack if the defenders had chosen to remain in place. These decisions were coerced, not imposed through brute force: an advance required a decision by the defender that the cost of staying exceeded the value of the ground; if the defender had chosen otherwise, the attacker would have found it impractical to destroy the defender in place.[105]

The SNA's initial strategy vis-à-vis UNOSOM was at least as coercive in nature. Aideed had no meaningful prospect of destroying the foreign presence. In fact he did not even try: there were no serious efforts to overrun UN bases or even to cut their supply lines. UN bases were regularly attacked, but only with desultory mortar or rocket fire meant to harass and not to annihilate. Especially after Howe's escalation of the war to a manhunt aimed at Aideed, the SNA clearly sought to engineer a UN withdrawal. But the mechanism for bringing this about was coercive pain infliction: by killing UN soldiers, the SNA would impose cumulative costs on the UN that would eventually persuade the foreigners to opt for departure.

Yet there was an important element of brute force in this basically coercive strategy. In particular, the SNA clearly felt it needed to defend critical terrain by threatening annihilation of intruders. Against rival warlords, this is what bought the SNA the time it needed to expand via coercive artillery fire. At this campaign's modest intensity, weeks of firing was needed to impose enough cost to induce an enemy pullback. If a USC ground offensive could sweep the SNA's firing locations and destroy SNA ammunition stocks in the meantime, the SNA would lose its primary offensive capability; worse, the SNA would be unable to protect the economic assets it depended on to fund its operations, threatening its very viability as a combatant. The SNA did not necessarily need to drive USC militiamen out of their strongholds—coercive fire would gradually persuade enemy fighters to pull themselves back—but the SNA did require the ability to prevent the USC from driving *SNA* fighters out, or penetrating SNA territory at will.

This requirement for brute force in the defense of critical terrain became much more salient in the SNA response to the October 3 TF Ranger raid on the Bakara Market, which was clearly an attempt to destroy an intruding force that threatened the leadership cadre's survival. UNOSOM movements elsewhere were subject to harassment, but not to the kind of all-out counterattack the SNA mounted against the UN's effort to penetrate the sanctuary Aideed had established to protect himself and his lieutenants. Aideed appears to have committed almost the entirety of his available forces (including large numbers of sympathetic armed civilians) in a committed effort to close with American forces in Bakara Market and destroy them—and in fact this succeeded in overrunning the US defense of *Super 64*, the second Blackhawk shot down in the battle. SNA attempts to overrun this and other US positions on October 3 resulted in as many as 2,000 Somali casualties, a toll vastly higher than in comparable periods of fighting before this, and much higher than a purely Fabian ambush of a patrol would normally tolerate to inflict gradual coercive pain on an occupation force.[106] If the UN had free rein to manhunt aggressively throughout Mogadishu it would eventually kill or capture the SNA leadership; Aideed could afford to be patient and allow gradually cumulative UN losses to coerce a UN withdrawal from Somalia, but he could not afford to allow the UN to search anywhere for him in the meantime. By October, for the SNA's coercive strategy to get the time it needed to succeed, brute force territorial defense of at least a critical territorial subset of Mogadishu had become necessary.[107]

5. Distinguishability of Combatants and Civilians

Combatant intermingling with civilians, use of civilian clothing, and avoidance of heavy weapons are closely associated with Fabian methods. In Somalia, SNA militiamen wore civilian clothing and were heavily and systematically intermingled with the civilian population, which was routinely used to shield fighters from attack by UNOSOM forces; heavy weapons were available, but the SNA made no apparent effort to use them.

SNA intermingling of combatants with civilians is one of the most widely reported features of the October 3–4 battle among US participants. Once the TF Ranger penetration was detected, the SNA deliberately encouraged civilians to leave their homes and approach US positions: Mark Bowden reports that militia operatives with megaphones called out "*Kasoobaxa guryaha oo iska celsa cadowga* (come out and defend your homes)," and in fact large crowds comprising thousands of civilian men, women, and children filled the streets and pressed forward into close proximity with TF Ranger positions.[108] Militiamen mingled with the crowds, firing at Rangers from within the throngs of civilians and making it all but impossible to return fire without killing innocents.[109]

Not all the apparent innocents were actually noncombatants. Multiple US participants report active participation in the October 3–4 fighting by Somali women and children. Somali children pointed out Ranger positions for engagement by militiamen or recovered weapons from fallen gunmen. Others sprayed automatic rifle fire from AK-47s; a woman holding a baby in one arm aimed a pistol at Rangers with the other; still others carried RPG rounds or rifle ammunition for fighters.[110]

The fighters themselves wore no distinctive uniforms or systematic identification as combatants. As Bowden put it: "all the Somali fighters looked the same, skinny black guys with dusty bushes of hair, long baggy pants and loose, oversized shirts."[111] Even full-time militiamen wore civilian clothing into battle; only the visible employment of weapons distinguished fighters from noncombatants.[112]

In fact none of this was unique to the Battle of Mogadishu in October. Militia intermingling with civilians, absence of uniforms, and deliberate use of civilians as human shields was widely reported by UNOSOM participants in actions as early as June in locations around the country.[113]

The SNA made occasional use of its "technicals" and regularly used rockets and light mortars to harass UNOSOM bases but made no apparent use of a substantial array of heavier weapons in its stockpiles. As noted above, by 1993 the SNA had acquired a handful of tanks, at least one infrared-guided antiaircraft missile, and, especially, some 86 US-made TOW wire-guided precision antitank missiles.[114] Little of this, however, was ever used in combat, and none was in action during the critical October 3–4 fighting.[115]

6. The Military Organization of the Theater of War

Archetypically Napoleonic state armies break combat theaters down into multiple distinct spatial zones with different military functions. Pure Fabian irregulars, by contrast, avoid functional distinction between front and rear, or forward and reserve, or logistical and combat zones. In Somalia, the SNA organized territory it controlled into different districts under command of subordinate officers who acted as components of a loose command hierarchy, and there was some distinction between front and rear. Differentiation of function was modest, however, with limited interdependence among the parts.

In Mogadishu, for example, the SNA deployed scouts and informants around major UN bases outside Aideed's stronghold of the Bakara Market/ Black Sea district. These forward elements monitored UN activity, provided early warning of raids and patrols, launched periodic harassing fire with mortars and rockets, and occasionally mined exit roads from bases. But they did not normally sustain close combat or seek to halt or destroy UN columns as they left their bases; their role approximated the function of a lightly manned outpost zone in a conventional defense.[116]

The bulk of the SNA's capital-area combatant strength was distributed among Habr Gidr neighborhoods at greater distance from foreign bases. A disproportionate fraction were billeted in Aideed's Bakara Market/Black Sea stronghold, whose perimeter amounted to a front line demarking territory the SNA would actively defend from meaningful foreign penetration. But militia were also held in other districts of Mogadishu and in surrounding villages, and SNA forces outside the Bakara Market/Black Sea concentration mounted periodic disruptive ambushes against UN patrols elsewhere.

SNA militia appear to have maintained themselves in a normal condition of low-to-moderate readiness, with arms and ammunition distributed and fighters reachable by radio, but with little or no ongoing manning of combat positions. Upon warning of UN penetration of the defended zone, SNA fighters would be mobilized quickly to occupy fighting positions or assault UN intruders, but until mobilized the SNA could generate only limited combat power, as noted above. The bulk of the fighters were thus dependent on warning from scouts to reach fighting positions and resist attacks.

A rudimentary command system was used to coordinate activities of the various local units and to orchestrate their response to warning of attack. In the Battle of Mogadishu, local commanders began receiving radioed movement orders from superiors by midafternoon, and the TF Ranger command group soon detected militia subunits moving on foot and via a motley collection of vehicles toward the locations of the downed US helicopters. Later commands arrived directly from Aideed and his senior lieutenants, who communicated by courier using written orders to avoid US electronic eavesdropping. Over the course of October 3, the SNA moved thousands of fighters from other districts of the city and from outlying villages into the Bakara Market/Black Sea stronghold after the TF Ranger intrusion was detected.[117]

This command system was only loosely organized, however. Subordinate leaders could not be relied on to follow orders: Aideed, for example, claimed downed US helicopter pilot Michael Durant as his property (the other pilots were killed), but the local SNA commander whose fighters captured Durant refused to hand him over to Aideed's representatives; Aideed ultimately had to pay his own nominal subordinates to gain control of the hostage. Many of the fighters engaged on October 3–4 were not full-time soldiers but part-time gunmen and even armed civilians; some answered to no one, and few of the part-timers were under complete control by the SNA leadership.[118]

The component elements of this system were also largely self-sufficient. Aideed and his immediate lieutenants, to be sure, needed the cooperation of enough fighters to sustain a stronghold in which to hide from UNOSOM. And certainly his plans for expansion required support from as many militiamen as possible. But the individual subunits that made up the SNA militia could survive for extended periods with little or no support from other SNA elements. Many had their own sources of income—often from employment in protection rackets or other forms of grassroots extortion—and all could simply melt into the population if challenged by superior Western forces. There is no evidence of a meaningful SNA logistical system, and neither the forward scouts near UNOSOM bases nor the mainstream militiamen in SNA strongholds truly depended on the other for survival in the short run. If the scouts failed, a UNOSOM or TF Ranger raid would escape with limited losses, but beyond the elders captured by the raiders, the rest of the SNA force structure would survive. If the militia in the stronghold failed, the scouts would similarly survive. In a conventional defense, failure by either the covering force or the main line of resistance could lead to breakthrough and the collapse of the theater defense, threatening all; the component parts are mutually interdependent for survival. In Aideed's SNA, there was indeed a degree of spatial articulation to the combat theater, but its parts were much less interdependent.[119]

SNA Proficiency of Execution

As before, proficiency of execution offers an opportunity for process tracing. The new theory's causal logic implies that informally institutionalized, limited-stakes actors should display limitations of skill and military coordination that would render complex, midspectrum warfare impractical. In Somalia, the SNA displayed surprising proficiency in some key areas—especially in its tactics for attacking US helicopters. For the SNA, however, real skill was limited chiefly to areas where small teams of experienced fighters could operate independently. Tasks requiring the cooperation of teams larger than a half dozen or a dozen individuals were performed only in the simplest possible ways. And even some critical individual skills—especially small-arms marksmanship—were notably absent from the SNA rank and file.

The SNA's most impressive feat was its ability to shoot down multiple US helicopters without the use of any modern antiaircraft weapon. Aideed's forces owned at least one SA-7 Grail infrared-guided shoulder-fired antiaircraft missile, but there is no evidence of its employment against Western aircraft.[120] Instead, the SNA modified the ubiquitous RPG-7 rocket-propelled antitank grenade to accommodate an airburst fuze that could detonate the warhead in the vicinity of an airborne target. They further understood that a helicopter's tail rotor assembly was the most effective aim point: a fragile, complex subsystem, the tail rotor could be disabled with a single hit, and if it was disabled and unable to offset the rotational force created by the helicopter's main rotor, the result would be an unrecoverable spin that would cause the aircraft to crash. Damage elsewhere on the fuselage could often be overcome, but a hit to the tail rotor was typically fatal, and SNA antiaircraft gunners knew this and aimed accordingly. They also developed a novel firing posture in which pits were dug in dirt streets to enable a long weapon normally fired horizontally to be aimed upward by a prone shooter, accommodating the RPG's considerable back-blast and allowing the shooter to conceal himself under camouflage as long as possible. The SNA apparently did not devise these methods itself—it has been reported that Al Qaeda advisors who had fought Soviet helicopters in Afghanistan traveled to Somalia to train Aideed's antiaircraft gunners and teach them how to modify the RPG for airburst detonation. The militiamen they trained proved capable of absorbing the instruction and using it to good effect in Mogadishu.[121]

Individual fighting positions selected by the SNA's more capable gunmen were often well concealed, with little more than the shooter's head and gun barrel visible over a windowsill or pile of rubble. Some appear to have understood the function of American infrared strobes, which were used to track US soldiers—downed pilot Michael Durant's strobe was stripped from him after his capture and driven around Mogadishu in an apparent effort to confuse US searchers.[122] American Delta Force soldier Paul Howe, not easily impressed, nevertheless offered grudging praise for some SNA fighters' discipline and determination in a subsequent interview with journalist Mark Bowden.[123]

Finally, the SNA was quite adept at massing large numbers of militiamen quickly against specific points whose locations they would not have been able to anticipate. Aideed proved able to direct nearly overwhelming numbers of fighters against the TF Ranger positions around the downed helicopters in the Battle of Mogadishu, for example, and to do so within minutes to hours of the helicopters going down. The SNA also quickly established roadblocks across the main routes that any UN reaction force would have to use to reach the TF Ranger perimeters.[124]

The SNA also had many profound shortcomings, however. Among the most widely noted were systematically poor small-arms marksmanship, weak fire discipline, and substandard maintenance of weapons and equipment. AK-47 fire in the Battle of Mogadishu was typically of the "spray and pray" variety, in which shooters emptied magazines on full automatic with no apparent attempt to aim shots at individual targets. SNA ambushes were frequently launched with premature fire at the lead UN vehicle, alerting the rest of the column to the attack and enabling countermeasures before entering the kill zone. Many of the SNA heavy weapons and armored vehicles the UN eventually collected in cantonment sites were inoperable or less than mission capable for mechanical reasons, and SNA weapons were frequently rusted or dirty.[125]

Crew-served weapon positions were often exposed. Attacks on TF Ranger positions were often simple mass frontal assaults in the open down exposed city streets. Mortar and rocket fire was rarely adjusted (even though SNA observers could in principle have seen the fall of shot within UN base complexes) and typically inaccurate. Mortars were not combined with direct fire, and crew-served weapons were rarely supported in any systematic way with small arms. There was no apparent effort to combine movement with suppressive fire, to maneuver against flanks or other vulnerable points of UNOSOM positions, or to coordinate the movement of multiple formations.[126]

This pattern of strengths and weaknesses is strongly suggestive of an organization that could field some small teams of competent individuals but which could not orchestrate complex activity over any formation larger than a handful of fighters. The SNA fielded a mix of full-time, dedicated combatants and a much larger number of part-timers; some estimated a ratio of perhaps one full-time fighter for every four or five part-timers. The full-time combatants were far from elite soldiers, but at least some had mastered basic individual skills and with proper instruction could be taught to employ novel methods such as RPG fire against moving helicopters. What they could not do was to cooperate closely with other teams, especially over distances at which they could not see one another. Where the SNA was able to direct action over distance these actions were simple and could be carried out with minimal direction. Their system for alerting forces and concentrating them against the crash sites in the Battle of Mogadishu, for example, required only brief radio or courier messages instructing subordinate leaders to converge on the smoke columns created by burning tires or downed helicopters. Barriers to block UN reaction forces could be placed in preplanned locations given the known positions of static UN bases and the available route structure into the Black Sea/ Bakara Market neighborhood; here, too, simple execution orders could trigger local militia cells to carry out prearranged actions on cue. And the subordinates could carry out such instructions with little reliance on others to provide supplies, intelligence, supporting or suppressive fires, flank protection, or route security. All they needed to do was move local debris into the road at the agreed locations and light the pile on fire, or to move toward the apparent scene of battle on order and execute individual-level or small-team techniques (such as RPG antiaircraft fire) when they got there.

None of this is to suggest that Aideed was not a talented officer or that individual SNA militiamen could not be adaptive or resourceful. By observing TF Ranger and UNOSOM and analyzing their methods, Aideed and his lieutenants devised a simple but effective plan that inflicted considerable losses on a technically far superior force. But the SNA fell far short of the maximum lethality potentially available to them. If their fighters had been able to hit targets consistently, combine suppressive fire with movement, maintain and employ heavy weapons, or integrate direct and indirect fire, to suggest just a few possibilities, it is entirely plausible that their numerical strength could have overwhelmed an isolated force of American light infantry and prevented its extraction. The SNA in 1993 could not.

Theoretical Implications

Given the codings above, what do the respective theories predict for the SNA's military behavior? Tribal culture theories would predict behavior at or very near the Fabian extreme for the SNA. Somali society in 1993 was as deeply tribal as any in the modern world; if any military actor were to be constrained to Fabian methods by tribalism it should be the SNA.

The material imbalance here, by contrast, was more modest than in many cases of nonstate warfare. For over a year and a half, the war pitted rival militias against one another, with no state military engaged; neither the SNA nor its enemies enjoyed a decisive material edge. Only when American forces arrived after December 1992 did the SNA face a material disadvantage, and even here the material balance was less favorable to the Western forces than in cases such as Iraq: the SNA had access to a substantial arsenal of sophisticated weapons inherited from the Siad Barre state military, and the SNA fielded an unusually large combatant force for the size of its operating area. Materialist theories would thus expect Aideed's methods to change over time, with little need for the SNA to adopt highly Fabian irregular methods prior to 1993, but with increasingly Fabian "asymmetric" war fighting after that; neither period, however, should display a historical extremum of the kind that tribalist arguments would expect.

The new theory, by contrast, predicts change in SNA behavior over time, but in the opposite direction. The SNA's political organization was always personalized and highly informal; if the new theory is correct, this should constrain the SNA to significantly Fabian behavior throughout the period of study. The SNA's stakes, however, changed dramatically by mid-1993. Before that, SNA stakes were limited and economic, but when American admiral Jonathan Howe declared in August 1993 that his goal would be Aideed's capture and imprisonment and began targeting Aideed and his chief lieutenants, the war suddenly took on existential stakes for the SNA's leadership. For the new theory, the SNA's weak institutionalization would preclude highly complex midspectrum warfare even so, but the radical change in stakes should motivate movement in that direction even for a nonstate militia—hence the new theory would predict *less* Fabian war fighting after the American intervention, not more (as materialists would expect), and not stasis (as tribal culture would predict).

How do these predictions compare with the SNA's observed behavior? In fact the case shows change, and change in the direction of an increasing effort by the SNA to hold key territory after August 1993. At no point did this amount to truly state-like midspectrum warfare, but neither was it the extremum of irregular methods predicted by tribal culture, and the direction of change was toward the Napoleonic end of the spectrum after the United States intervened and the material balance worsened for the SNA—not the opposite, as materialist logic would imply. More specifically, the combat behavior described above yields a computed index value of 1.2 for SNA methods prior to August 1993, and 2.5 after this, which would be described as mostly, and slightly, Fabian, respectively, by the framework in chapter 4.[127]

This creates significant tensions with tribal culture explanations. While the SNA was hardly a state-like, midspectrum military organization, neither was it a classically irregular Fabian extremum. In fact, the SNA's duration of engagements, typical engagement ranges, troop concentration, and reliance on counterattack were all roughly as "conventional" as Hezbollah's—SNA engagement ranges were typically shorter, in fact; its force-to-space ratio was much higher; and the SNA's entire concept for defense of its Black Sea/Bakara Market stronghold was heavily dependent on counterattack to expel intruders from a territorial sanctuary. These are not the hallmarks of a tribalist pure Fabian irregular archetype—the SNA's actual behavior shares too many features of archetypically "conventional" war fighting.

Materialist theory also has trouble with the SNA. Materialist approaches, for example, would predict an increasingly Fabian fighting style for Aideed's militia as its material military balance decayed with the American reinforcements after August 1993; in fact, the SNA's behavior did change, but in precisely the opposite direction: the SNA became *less* Fabian, not more, after August.

The hybrid materialist subschool also faces important challenges in explaining the SNA. Aideed's militia had significant access to the modern, precision weapons that hybrid materialists see as the central driver behind Hezbollah-like midspectrum warfare. The key technology underlying the hybrid thesis is precision-guided antitank weaponry (ATGW). The SNA was not as well equipped as Hezbollah, but they did inherit a meaningful arsenal of heavy weapons from the Barre regime, and among these were at least 86 US-made TOW missiles.[128] The BGM-71 TOW (tube-launched, optically tracked, wire-guided) is a terminally guided large-caliber antitank weapon able to penetrate over 760 millimeters of armor at ranges in excess of three kilometers. In 1993 it was the primary first-line Western ATGW and was in wide use among NATO state armies. In physical size, logistical requirements, technical sophistication, and potential lethality it was in the same general family as Hezbollah's Russian-made Kornets. Of course the Kornet in 2006 was a more modern weapon than the SNA's TOWs, but it is far from clear that the difference was militarily meaningful in the 1993 context: in skilled hands either weapon could be expected to achieve hit probabilities as high as 0.9 against armored targets at extended ranges, and to penetrate any armored target they were likely to encounter. In principle the SNA's TOW holdings were more than sufficient to have wiped out the entire armored column that eventually relieved TF Ranger on October 3–4, and to have held off any UNOSOM reinforcements sent from elsewhere in the theater.[129] The SNA, however, made no recorded use of these missiles, which were found by UNOSOM among the heavy weapons Aideed voluntarily cached at secured weapon cantonment sites in Mogadishu.[130] But the difference between Hezbollah's antiarmor performance in 2006 and the SNA's in 1993 was not due to any lack of weaponry on the SNA's part—if Aideed had chosen to use his missiles rather than storing them, then his fielded technology and Hezbollah's would not have been radically different. Of course, Aideed's ability to *employ* those missiles would probably have been very different (his willingness to store the missiles under UNOSOM surveillance probably reflected doubt that his gunners could operate them effectively, combined with the SNA's limited stakes in the conflict prior to Howe's escalation). But this is not attributable to the materiel itself; as a materialist theory predicting nonstate military behavior from actors' technology, the hybrid warfare thesis would thus predict comparable behavior for actors with comparable technology and would thus imply similar methods for Hezbollah and the SNA.

The new theory, by contrast, correctly anticipates the SNA's failure to reach the purely Fabian extremum, which the new theory sees as vanishingly rare. The SNA's mostly-to-slightly Fabian behavior is consistent with its informal institutional structure, as the new theory expects. And the new theory, unlike materialist approaches, can accommodate the SNA's shift away from the Fabian extremum after August 1993, when its altered stakes altered its incentive structure for defending ground. This behavior is a stronger fit to the new theory's expectations than to those of its orthodox competitors.

This is not to claim a perfect fit. As with the JAM, the SNA's observed behavior is more Napoleonic than the functional form in the appendix anticipates: for the conditions here, the functional form predicts a very Fabian behavioral score of just 0.1 before August 1993, and 1.1 afterward.[131] The direction of change is indeed as predicted, but both predictions are significantly more Fabian than the SNA's actual choices. As with the JAM, however, there may be reasons to think that the SNA would have been better served with more-Fabian behavior than they actually displayed in 1993. The SNA took very heavy casualties in the Battle of Mogadishu; although estimates vary, some put the figure as high as 2,000 and even the SNA's own leadership placed its militia losses at 312 fighters killed and 814 wounded (or at least 17 times UNOSOM's losses), many of whom were surely disabled before firing a shot given their often-exposed postures (whereas TF Ranger began the battle with strict restrictions on collateral damage, the desperation of the unfolding battle led to less and less reticence on firing into crowds of noncombatants, hence the SNA's reliance on intermingling alone for cover probably afforded them little advantage by the end of the engagement).[132] A stealthier posture with fewer frontal assaults and more use of building interiors for cover, for example, might have inflicted similar losses on TF Ranger with fewer SNA casualties while remaining well within the capacity of an informally institutionalized actor. But the scale of divergence between prediction and observation for the new theory, while nonzero, is nevertheless smaller than for its competing explanations—and for a case where culturalist theory, in particular, should be on its strongest possible ground.

8

The ZNG, HV, and SVK in the Croatian Wars of Independence, 1991–95

IN THIS CHAPTER I present the fourth of five case method tests: the Croatian National Guard (ZNG), Croatian Army (HV), and Krajina Serb Army (SVK) in the Croatian Wars of Independence, from the initial fighting of 1991 through the 1995 Dayton Accords that ended Croatia's active participation in the Balkan Wars. Croatia became a state in 1992, whereupon the nonstate ZNG transformed into a state actor (the HV) in the new theory's terms. But the Republic of Serbian Krajina, whose various militias and eventual army, the SVK, was the ZNG/HV's longtime opponent, never achieved international recognition or state status and thus remained a separatist nonstate actor until its formal reintegration with Croatia in 1998, three years after its military dissolved.[1]

The case offers a theoretically illuminating combination of a largely shared, nontribal culture; material asymmetries (especially between the separatist ZNG and the Jugoslav state military); and wide variance in internal politics. It also presents a different class of nonstate actor: a private military firm, Military Professional Resources Incorporated (MPRI), which the new Croatian state hired to advise and train its fledgling military.

I will argue that the case contradicts materialist expectations for military behavior while supporting those of the new theory—and that MPRI's role illustrates how military privatization can interact with internal politics to reshape military behavior and capability. In particular, I will show that by hiring outsiders with no local constituency or power base, divided Croatian elites could improve capability against an external enemy (the SVK) without undermining the internal balance of political power among themselves. This in turn allowed an imperfectly institutionalized emergent Croatian state to overcome the effects of internal division and circumvent the constraints that factionalized internal politics normally impose on complex military methods. The result was a Croatian military that effectively annihilated its SVK opposition in a four-day blitzkrieg in 1995. The Croatian case shows that internal politics are indeed a critical determinant of military behavior and capability—and that among the most important functions of nonstate private military firms can be their potential to end-run otherwise restrictive politics within and among the actors that hire them.

As before, I develop this argument in five steps. First, I outline briefly the main events of the case. Second, I develop values for the main independent variables associated with the competing theories. Third, I code the dependent variable of military behavior for the respective actors. Fourth, I trace the causal processes in the case by assessing the actors' proficiency in executing their chosen methods and how this does or does not conform to the new theory's logic of explanation. Finally, I compare the ZNG/HV's and SVK's observed behavior to the respective theories' predictions given these values, assessing the relative fit between prediction and observation and discussing the case's net implications for the theories under study.

Overview of Events

With the death of longtime Jugoslav strongman Josef Brozip Tito in 1980, the Federation of Jugoslavia began a long side toward dissolution in a series of ethnic civil wars. By early 1990, separatist political parties had been established in the Jugoslav republics of Slovenia, Croatia, and Bosnia, and in spring 1990 the Croatian nationalist HDZ (Hrvatska demokratska zajednica, or Croatian Democratic Union) won the republic's first multiparty elections. The Serb-dominated federal government in Belgrade, fearing possible secession, then ordered the Jugoslav National Army (JNA) to disarm the Croatian Territorial Defense force (TO), a home guard of trained reservists whose mission had been to defend Croatian territory from foreign invasion. Croatia responded by expanding its Ministry of Interior police force (MUP), triggering debate in Belgrade over continued suppression.[2]

In the midst of this uncertainty, the Serbian minority within Croatia took matters into its own hands. Threatened by the prospect of minority status within a new state dominated by ethnic Croats, Croatian Serbs thus declared the Serbian Autonomous Region of Krajina (SAOK) on February 28, 1991, and announced their intention to secede from Croatia if Croatia itself separated from Jugoslavia. This led to sporadic violence between the MUP and Croatian Serbs as the latter sought to consolidate control over Serb-populated localities within Croatia, and especially along the Serbian border and the Krajina region along the Bosnian border. In May the HDZ created a new National Guard Corps, the ZNG, from paramilitary elements of the MUP and the remnants of the disarmed TO. Caught in the middle, the JNA was ordered by Belgrade to act as a buffer to separate armed Croatian Serbs from Croatian police and the new ZNG National Guards, but in fact the Serb-heavy JNA tended to side with their ethnic brethren at the expense of the Croatian nationalists.

As low-level violence continued through the spring, neighboring Slovenia declared its own independence from the Jugoslav Federation on June 25, 1991. The JNA launched an immediate offensive against the Slovenians but was defeated in a brief, 10-day campaign as a combination of defections by ethnic Slovene troops, political divisions in Belgrade over appropriate responses, and morale problems in the JNA's ranks hamstrung efforts to suppress secessionist forces.

The Slovenian declaration forced the HDZ's hand, and Croatia quickly issued its own formal declaration of independence, also on June 25. Yet there was no immediate JNA offensive in Croatia. The JNA maintained substantial garrisons in the republic, and its troops had been conducting operations to suppress internal violence for months. But the JNA was initially preoccupied with the campaign in Slovenia, and the federal government in Belgrade was divided over its policy toward secession. In particular, the JNA command and some hardline politicians wanted aggressive action to crush secessionists and preserve the unified Jugoslav state. But Jugoslav president Slobodan Milosevic was more concerned with advancing the secular interests of his own, Serbian ethnic group than in reconstructing a multiethnic federal union. Milosevic and his allies were thus willing to let non-Serb territories go as long as areas with mixed populations including Serb minorities were cleansed of non-Serbs and united in a greater Serbia centered on Belgrade and the rump of the old Jugoslav state. As this debate unfolded in Belgrade, the JNA carried on in Croatia but did not move to destroy the new Croatian National Guard, to unseat the HDZ, or to seal Croatia's borders.

Instead, the Croatian nationalists moved first. On September 14, 1991, the ZNG attacked JNA garrisons across Croatia, initiating large-scale hostilities. In the process they seized valuable arms and ammunition and overran enough of the JNA's base structure to establish a tenuous but contiguous zone of control across central Croatia.

The JNA responded with a large-scale counterattack, in combination with Croatian Serb militias backed by the SAOK. This Jugoslav government offensive gradually drove the Croatian ZNG from the Krajina, consolidating Serbian/JNA control of central Croatia, eastern Slavonia, and northern Dalmatia.

As the JNA advanced, however, ZNG resistance stiffened. Croatian nationalist counterattacks regained control of most of western Slavonia, and eventually the front stabilized with perhaps 70 percent of the republic's territory under nationalist control and the remainder in the hands of the Croatian Serb SAOK and its JNA allies.

A cease-fire brokered by UN special envoy Cyrus Vance was then signed on January 2, 1992, ending the initial phase of the war. The Vance plan brought UN peacekeepers under the UN Protection Force (UNPROFOR), and the establishment of UN-protected areas in Croatia and neighboring Bosnia, where a civil war of its own had broken out in April 1992.

In the meantime, the European Community had requested formal applications from Jugoslav republics seeking recognition as independent states, and Germany formally recognized the new Croatian government on December 24, 1991. The EC followed in January; the United States in April; and by May the UN followed suit, establishing an unambiguously independent Croatian state. With independence, the new Croat state formed the HV, or Croatian national army, to replace the nonstate ZNG. The Serbian Croat SAOK, by contrast, united with the neighboring Croatian Serb enclaves of Western Slavonia and Eastern Slavonia-Baranja-Western Srem to form the Republic of Serbian Krajina (RSK), which then petitioned the EC and the UN for recognition as an independent state on December 23, 1991, but was denied; in fact no state or major international organization ever recognized the SAOK or RSK as independent.[3]

The Vance cease-fire was imperfect, with occasional outbreaks of fighting and a major violation in January 1993 in which the HV sought to clear lines of communication between southern Dalmatia and central Croatia. The HV was also deeply involved with efforts by the Croatian minority in neighboring Bosnia to cleanse rivals and gain territory at the expense of ethnic Serbs and Bosnian Muslims there. But within the boundaries of the old Jugoslav Croatian republic the war was largely in remission between 1992 and 1995.

During this time, the Croatian government sought to build its new state institutions while developing its military capabilities. To this end it hired an American private firm, Military Professional Resources Incorporated (MPRI) to assist in developing and improving the HV.

MAP 8.1. Croatia

On August 4, 1995, the improved Croatian HV used its new capabilities to launch a major offensive, Operation Storm, on multiple simultaneous fronts against the Serbian Autonomous Region of Krajina and its SVK militia. This offensive was coordinated closely with a Bosnian government army assault on Bosnian Serb positions, and it coincided with a program of NATO air strikes against Serbian targets in Bosnia under Operation Deliberate Force. Operation Storm crushed the SVK as a military force in just four days of fighting, sweeping the Krajina of Serbian forces and leaving the Croatian Serb authorities with no choice but to accede to the Erdut agreement, which liquidated most of the Republic of Serbian Krajina, leaving only a small demilitarized rump in eastern Slavonia under UN protection. This remnant was itself absorbed into Croatia on the government's terms in 1998, but the 1995 Erdut agreement effectively ended the Serbian nonstate military presence in Croatia and, in the process, ended the Croatian Wars of Independence.

Independent Variables

How does the military behavior of the ZNG, HV, and SVK compare with the respective theories' predictions? I begin with the theories' independent variables of tribal culture, military materiel, and internal politics.

Tribal Culture in Croatia

Culture, in the sense of ethnic self-identity, was a major theme in all the Balkan Wars of the 1990s. Croatian nationalists promoted a conception of Croatian cultural distinctiveness based on its Catholic religion, its history, and its Western-leaning values by contrast with the Orthodox and Eastern-oriented Serbs or the Muslim Bosnians. Tension between these ethnocultural groups became the rallying point for a decade of warfare in the region. This does not mean that ethnic tension caused the wars: "ancient hatreds" between Balkan ethnic groups had rarely yielded war in centuries of mostly peaceful coexistence prior to the 1990s. Without Milosevic and others' deliberate promotion of ethnic rivalry there would probably have been no warfare in the 1990s, either, and the salience of ethnicity among competing sources of identity was a social construction of relatively recent provenance.[4] Yet there was nevertheless a cultural distinction that was widely perceived in the region and that played a role—whether as cause or effect—in the region's warfare.

Croatian as opposed to Serbian national culture is not, however, the distinction that matters for the nonstate military behavior debate. Familist tribalism is. It is the unique features of tribal social organization based on family relationships that this literature sees as conducive to guerilla warfare. And in these terms, neither Croatian nor Serbian society was notably tribal in the 1990s.[5]

Before the mid-19th century, patrilineal agricultural kinship groups called *zadrugas* had played a major role in Balkan Slavic society. A zadruga comprised several interrelated families living communally and sharing property; though zadrugas of 80 or more members have been documented, groups of 10 to 20 individuals were more common. The head of the kin group coordinated its economic activity, consumption, and social interactions with outsiders; marriage patterns and dispute resolution were commonly mediated by the zadruga head in a classically tribalist manner.[6]

This system began to break down, however, with industrialization and urbanization after the 1860s. Zadruga tribal organization was anchored in a quasi-feudal peasant agricultural economy in which land ownership and tenure shaped social standing and community life. As opportunities grew for nonfarm employment away from ancestral lands, the strength of the old ties weakened, and the influence of zadruga familial structure atrophied. When changes to the legal system abolished the vestiges of feudalism, this process accelerated: in 1870, a law was passed in Croatia allowing formerly integral zadruga land to be divided among individual owners; the result was a rush to break up the old holdings. By the early 20th century, little of the old economic foundation of Balkan familial tribalism was left, and what did remain was stronger in eastern Slavic lands—Croatia in the west was among the first to transform.[7]

This is not to say that family relationships had become irrelevant in Croatia or the larger Balkans by the 1990s. As recently as the late 1960s, anthropologist Lorraine Baric reports that urban migrants used kin relationships with landholding farmers to maintain claims on the property and its use, and that "kin rights and duties frequently override political and economic considerations."[8] Olivera Buric reports that "sentiments . . . of kinship solidarity" survived well into the 1970s and were manifested in the form of material aid to farming communities by urban relatives, and shared agricultural labor during harvests and other critical times.[9] And of course the family unit has remained an integral element of most industrialized Western societies to this day. But by the 1990s, the role family relationships played in Balkan conflict resolution, economic activity, politics, and social standing was not substantially different from that in other Western societies—and was radically different, and smaller, than the role played by tribe and family in 1990s Somalia, or even early 21st-century Lebanon or Iraq.

By contrast with this decline in zadruga familism, the rise of ethnic self-awareness in the late 20th century played an increasing role in Balkan politics and public life. But this ethnic identification spanned populations of far greater size than traditional tribes or clans. Self-described ethnic Croatians in 1990 numbered some 4.5 million individuals; Jugoslav Serbs accounted for a population of more than 8.5 million.[10] Collectives of this size constituted economically—and militarily—viable states. And whereas classical tribal systems are subject to fluid in-group/out-group definition ("me against my brother, my brother and I against my cousin, and all of us against the stranger"), Balkan ethnic groups, once mobilized, constituted much more fixed communities with stable membership. Of course Balkan ethnic parties could shift interethnic alliances for strategic purposes (Bosnian Croats, for example, alternately fought Bosnian Muslims then supported them against a common Serb enemy), but so do states in the international system. And Balkan ethnic parties could certainly divide into factional disputes over policy, strategy, or the division of spoils (much more on this below), as do many state governments. Classical tribal systems, however, recognize multiple identity subgroups with no fixed loyalty claims; alignment is transient and ephemeral, and real trust thus inheres in very localized small-scale kinship groups. Balkan nationalist politics could be as factionalized or strategic as that of any state, but its *identity* component spanned much larger groups with much less fluid membership than in traditional tribal systems.

Military Materiel

Materiel is important both for the new theory and in prior materialist accounts. The new theory sees materiel's role in interaction with internal politics, and it emphasizes technological sophistication as the material variable with greatest leverage. Orthodox materialist theories see materiel itself as the primary determinant of nonstate war fighting, with the material inferiority of most nonstate actors in both quality and quantity condemning them to irregular methods for lack of a viable alternative. In Croatia, the material military balance varied over time as nationalists mobilized resources while Serbia gradually withdrew support from its Croatian Serb ally. In the initial campaigns of 1991, the Croatian nationalist MUP and then the ZNG were both outnumbered and outgunned by a better-equipped and better-trained state army in the JNA. This material disadvantage had diminished somewhat by 1992, and the new Croatian state used the cease-fire years to further expand its military establishment. Meanwhile the JNA was mostly withdrawn from Croatia between 1992 and 1995, leaving its nonstate Serbian SVK ally to fend increasingly for itself. By the time of Operation Storm in 1995 the material tables had turned, with the Croatian state HV enjoying a substantial material advantage over the SVK. From almost the beginning of this process, however, both sides had obtained significant arsenals of modern weapons, which played a significant role throughout.

In July 1991, the Croatian ZNG fielded a total of only 8,000 active-duty soldiers, with perhaps another 40,000 reservists available. Fewer than half of the reservists were armed, however, and neither group had access to heavy weapons; when the JNA disarmed the Croatian territorial TO in 1990, this left nothing more than small arms and light equipment in police hands.[11] This small, lightly armed force was distributed over a Croatian republic of some 56,600 square kilometers, yielding a force-to-space ratio of 0.8 fighters per square kilometer—or less than 5 percent of the SNA's in Mogadishu in 1993.

Arrayed against this nationalist protoarmy were nearly 100,000 heavily armed JNA regulars plus 16,000 Serbian militiamen drawn from territorial forces located in the Serb-majority Krajina, supported by an annual Jugoslav state military budget of over $3.5 billion.[12] The result was a numerical advantage in armed combatants of more than 4:1 for the JNA and its allies in the summer of 1991, to say nothing of the JNA's enormous advantages in firepower, mobility, and armor protection.

The material balance began to change with the ZNG's September offensive against the JNA's garrisons in Croatia. Almost overnight the ZNG acquired the beginnings of a modern arsenal, capturing perhaps 200 T-55 tanks, 100 M-80 infantry fighting vehicles, over 300 artillery pieces, over 600 120-millimeter heavy mortars, and a variety of wire-guided antitank missiles from Jugoslav government armories.[13] In the meantime, recruitment and mobilization increased the numerical strength of nationalist forces—by the end of 1991, HDZ defense minister Anton Tus claimed to have as many as 250,000 men under arms.[14]

This is not to say the ZNG could actually operate all this equipment or utilize anything like its nominal strength. Many of the new recruits had little or no training: as one soldier who had enlisted in fall 1991 put it: "I tried to find someone to tell me which end of the RPG to point at the enemy"; the trained and combat-capable force was considerably smaller than the ZNG's nominal strength in 1991.[15] Maintenance and sustainment for the equipment captured from the JNA posed organizational challenges that took time to meet: many ZNG soldiers were familiar with the hardware from their time in Jugoslav government service, but the ZNG still had no logistical, repair, or maintenance infrastructure, nor was there yet any organizational framework for operating or sustaining this capital stock. And of course the state JNA they faced was large, fully trained, and much better armed—not only did its surviving armor and artillery far outnumber the ZNG's, but the JNA enjoyed a modern air force with over 280 high-performance combat aircraft, 165 helicopters, and a navy (which was used to augment JNA firepower with shore bombardment during the 1991 campaign).[16] The net result was a ZNG with nominal access to late 20th-century weapon technology from almost the earliest days of the conflict, but which faced a major, ongoing firepower imbalance in the JNA's favor that continued through the 1992 cease-fire.

By 1995, the JNA withdrawal from Croatia and the continued mobilization of the new Croatian state military had created a different picture. Notwithstanding UN sanctions designed to preclude arms shipments to warring parties in the Balkans, the new Croatian state military proved able to expand its arsenal as well as its personnel strength. On the eve of Operation Storm, the Croatian HV deployed over 200,000 well-equipped troops, supported by a fledgling air force with 28 MiG21 fighter-bombers, some 31 Mi-8 transport helicopters, and 8 Mi-24 helicopter gunships.[17] Croatian state military expenditures exceeded $1 billion in 1994.[18]

Their Croatian Serb SVK opponents were well equipped but fielded a much smaller force. The JNA left behind ample supplies of arms and equipment (including some 400 armored vehicles and 350 large-caliber artillery pieces), and Croatian Serbs, like their nationalist rivals, had used the intervening years to increase their personnel strength. Yet this mobilization yielded only about 50,000 soldiers by 1995, or about the same raw troop strength as the ZNG fielded ab initio in the summer of 1991.[19] The SVK's territory was smaller, and its armament was more lethal; its force-to-space ratio was higher than the ZNG's in 1991, and the SVK was certainly better equipped than the ZNG. But their numerical disadvantage relative to their state opponent was similar: whereas nonstate Croatian nationalists had waged war in 1991 at a numerical disadvantage of over 4:1, the Croatian state HV thus enjoyed a numerical advantage of about 4:1 over the nonstate Serbian SVK by 1995.

Internal Politics

The new theory emphasizes two dimensions of an actor's internal politics: its stakes, and its institutional development. Limited stakes and informal institutions are expected to discourage complex midconcealment methods;

existential stakes and formal institutions permit such methods for nonstate actors with at least late 20th-century technology.

STAKES

By contrast with the SNA's economic war aims in Somalia, in Croatia both the ZNG/HV and the SVK were fighting for ideological and political stakes tied to ethnonational ruling programs. One might expect this to produce a zero-sum struggle with uniform, existential incentives for all sides to develop proficient militaries as quickly as possible. Yet the picture in Croatia was more complex.

In principle, all sides in the Balkan Wars faced existential stakes: each had legitimate fears of oppression and ethnic cleansing at the others' hands if defeated. In practice, however, different actors had very different assessments of the real risk they faced. For most of the conflict, Croatian Serbs believed (albeit incorrectly) that the Serbian state under Milosevic would protect them; for them, the war looked like a limited conflict over the scale of their power and influence. By the time their error became clear in 1995 it was too late, and they were overrun in Operation Storm. Croatian nationalists, by contrast, realized by mid-1991 that they were on their own, with no state backer to save them from the Jugoslav Army; the HDZ quickly assessed the stakes as existential. Their actual risk of annihilation eased once the JNA withdrew in 1992. But for most of the 1991 campaign the nationalist leadership believed they were fighting a war of survival, whereas Croatian Serbs believed almost until the end that they were fighting for limited stakes in a war where the downside risks were bounded.

Croatian Serbs had ample reason to expect protection from Belgrade. From the beginning of the conflict, the JNA had consistently protected Serbian interests at nationalists' expense. As early as August 1990, Jugoslav Air Force MIGs had intercepted Croatian MUP helicopters en route to the Krajina, forcing them back to base.[20] At the Battle of Plitvice in March–April 1991, the JNA's nominal interposition actually protected Serbs from nationalist incursion, in the process creating a defensible western border for the threatened Serb enclave.[21] In August 1991 the JNA Ninth Corps attacked and seized the strategic nationalist-controlled town of Kijevo and the Maslenica bridge that connected the Dalmatian coast with Serbian holdings in northern Croatia.[22] By the fall of 1991 the JNA had abandoned even the pretense of neutrality and was waging open war against the ZNG.[23]

In fact, Belgrade had played an instrumental role in creating the Croatian Serb protostate and its militia in the first place, and in sustaining them thereafter. The Jugoslav government provided covert arms and technical assistance to the Krajina Serbs even before their sovereignty referendum in August 1990, and Belgrade played a crucial role in organizing the Krajina Serbian Democratic Party (SDS), which became the political core of the SAOK. And this assistance continued long after the Vance cease-fire. When the JNA withdrew from Croatia in 1992 it left behind more than just arms: JNA officers raised in the Krajina remained, joining the Serb SVK as trained leadership cadre. Though they were nominally in SVK service, their salaries were paid by Belgrade. Jugoslav government military aid and logistical assistance to the SVK continued throughout the war, and JNA officer and NCO transfers continued to stiffen the SVK ranks. In fact, the Jugoslav Army assistant chief of staff, General Mile Mrksic, left his position after the fall of Slavonia to take command of the SVK in Croatia. Belgrade even returned nearly 5,000 Croatian Serb draft dodgers to the Krajina for induction into SVK service and occasionally reintroduced JNA combat units to augment SVK formations in 1993 and 1994.[24]

This assistance persuaded many Croatian Serbs that Belgrade was behind them, and would recommit the JNA as necessary to prevent the Croatian state military from overrunning the RSK. Milosevic's whole political program, after all, was centered on the creation of a "greater Serbia" that would unify the Serb populations in each of the former Jugoslav republics; it was hardly delusional for Croatian Serbs to expect him to protect them from absorption into a Croatian state. And Milosevic offered just such assurances directly and explicitly in 1991 as part of Belgrade's efforts to persuade SDS leader Milan Babic to accept the Vance cease-fire plan: Babic had voiced concern that a JNA withdrawal would leave Serbs exposed, whereupon Belgrade assured him that the JNA would intervene as necessary to defend them; Babic accepted the plan.[25] As David Rohde reported in 1995, Krajina Serbs "have long assumed that military support from their 'homeland' would come—if they are severely threatened by the Croatian or Bosnian governments."[26] Of course no diplomatic assurance is ever ironclad, and prudent Serbs should have harbored some degree of doubt. But until Belgrade actually broke its promises in 1995, the available indications had given the Croatian Serb leadership a reasonable expectation that their state ally would defend them in extremis. And this meant that for the Krajina Serbs, the conflict with Croatia looked in important respects like a limited war: the fighting would surely shape the size and influence of the

Croatian Serb political entity, but there was ample reason to expect the JNA to step in and save them well short of communal extinction if that war went badly.[27]

Croatian nationalists, by contrast, quickly recognized they faced existential stakes in the 1991 campaign. Initially, HDZ leader Franjo Tudjman harbored fond hopes of Western backing in the event of war. As late as August he expressed a belief to US ambassador Walter Zimmerman that the United States would come to Croatia's aid in a fight with the JNA, and he sought diplomatic pressure from the West to dissuade Belgrade from the use of force.[28] By the fall, however, it was clear that the Serbs would fight—and that Croatia was on its own. Not only was Western military intervention not forthcoming, but Western-backed UN sanctions established an arms embargo that denied Croatian nationalists licit access to foreign weapons or equipment to compete with a heavily armed state opponent in the JNA. Western diplomacy sought a cease-fire but showed no evidence of any willingness to use force to bring Serbs to the table, and with an ongoing JNA offensive driving deep into Croatian territory there would be little reason to expect the Serbs to halt simply because Cyrus Vance asked them to.

And if the JNA did not halt, the consequences for Croatian nationalists could be severe. The Balkan Wars became notorious for their cruelty and mass violence, and the beginnings of later ethnic cleansing campaigns were already evident in the 1991 fighting. Croatian nationalists could expect a harsh occupation under a conqueror's rule if the JNA won.

The Croatian politico-military elite could expect especially harsh treatment. In February 1991, the Jugoslav government indicted General Martin Spegelj, Croatia's new defense minister, for "organizing and coordinating 'the criminal act of armed rebellion'"—Spegelj faced prison if his ministry's armed forces failed in battle.[29] In fact, the JNA High Command issued a secret report in January 1991 in which it indicated its readiness to arrest the Croatian government and impose martial law; the threat of imprisonment faced the entire ruling elite.[30] Even the fighting itself posed serious risks for Croat elites: the JNA Air Force controlled the air space over Croatia, and in October 1991 it bombed the presidential palace in Zagreb while Tudjman was inside.[31] As early as January 1991 Croatian parliamentarians voiced concerns that Tudjman "would not come back alive" from an official trip to Belgrade.[32] For the Croatian nationalists, preventing the JNA from overrunning Croatia in 1991 was thus literally a matter of freedom versus prison or life versus death. And unlike the Croatian Serbs, HDZ nationalists could not assume that a state ally would save them from this fate if they failed to do so themselves.

The existential stakes of 1991 eased, however, after the JNA offensive stalled and the Serbs accepted the Vance cease-fire. Once the JNA withdrew from Croatia, the risk of national extinction diminished for Tudjman and his government: while it was reasonable to expect the JNA to defend their allies if the HV invaded the Krajina, the JNA was unlikely to start a new war itself by invading metropolitan Croatia. Of course war is always a possibility, and prudent Croatian statesmen would surely protect against such a threat; it is not uncommon for wars to rekindle, and the JNA remained a potentially dangerous opponent. But the HV's primary rival after the cease-fire was not the state JNA but the nonstate SVK—and the latter posed no meaningful threat to conquer Croatia. While the stakes confronting the ZNG in 1991 were unlimited, the war after that posed more limited downside consequences for Croatia.

INSTITUTIONS IN THE CROATIAN WARS OF INDEPENDENCE

Political development varied widely in this period. At its outset, the Croatian war pitted nonstate actors on both sides; each needed to create new institutions quickly to resolve internal conflicts and wage war against outsiders. In the 1991 campaign, Croatian nationalists met this challenge more successfully than their Croatian Serb rivals: by the time of the Vance cease-fire, the HDZ government had achieved roughly the status of a basic natural regime in the terms used here, whereas the Croatian Serb protostate was at best a fragile natural regime. Although gradual political development on both sides continued during the 1991–95 lull, little real change resulted, and each side plateaued with the same basic institutional dynamics they had lived through in 1991. The most important post-1991 change, in fact, was the HV's ability to escape the limitations of its indigenous institutions via a different, transnational, nonstate actor: Military Professional Resources Incorporated (MPRI), an American private business hired by the Croatian state to train and prepare its military for renewed war with the SVK.

Croatian nationalist institutions. For the nonstate HDZ in 1991, political development was jump-started by its control of a preexisting, if subnational, government. The 1974 Jugoslav constitution had granted the republics extensive local autonomy, and the Croatian Jugoslav republic in 1991 had a functioning court system; an elected, bicameral legislature; and an established array of functioning administrative agencies, including an Interior Ministry that managed a significant police force. It even issued its own passports. To paraphrase

M. Cherif Bassiouni, by 1991 the Jugoslav substate republics had the *institutions* of states but without the legal status—or the armies—of states.[33] When the Croatian republic seceded, the HDZ inherited this system essentially intact, and thus began the war with a state-like structure of preexisting checks and balances, administrative accountability, and bureaucratic organization.

This inheritance provided a tremendous head start in administration. Yet it fell short of mature natural order status in several important respects—and especially in civil-military relations and in economic rent seeking.

As for the latter, the international arms embargo promoted a culture of corruption and state control over the economy that encouraged rent seeking at the highest levels in the new government. When the UN denied Croatia access to legal arms imports the new government resorted to smuggling and illicit arms transfers to equip its forces; this gave entre to underworld elements with the necessary skills and networks in the black-market arms trade and tended to legitimize a sub-rosa economy that grew well beyond the limits of military spending per se. As recently as 1999, Transparency International ranked Croatia the 25th most corrupt among 99 world countries surveyed.[34] The result was a scale of often-opaque government involvement in commerce and trade that muddied the boundary between public and private domains and promoted conflict of interest in the conduct of official duties.[35]

Perhaps more important was the new state's politicized civil-military relations. Relative to the other agencies of the new Croatian state, the armed forces were less institutionally mature: whereas there were preexisting republican courts, economic regulatory agencies, and legislative bodies, there was no official republican military prior to 1991; when Croatia declared its independence it instead had multiple police, militia, and territorial defense forces operating under separate chains of command and oversight. Some of the larger paramilitaries, and especially the Croatian Party of the Right's HOS militia, were significant military forces with up to 15,000 fighters under arms and equipment that sometimes outstripped the ZNG's.[36] Consolidation of these potentially competing actors posed important political challenges—armed internal rivalry in fluid institutional settings is a major barrier to military cooperation and can easily yield internecine warfare.[37]

In 1991, Tudjman responded to this challenge with a strategy of politicization and gradual consolidation, installing trusted loyalists in the key security institutions while tolerating substantial militia independence in the near term and testing the political waters for a more forceful unification of rival paramilitaries later. By fall 1991, the new Defense Ministry, for example, was in the hands of Gojko Susak, a prominent HDZ party fundraiser and close personal friend of Tudjman's. The Interior Ministry was led by Ivan Vekic, a founding member of the HDZ and a longtime ally of Tudjman's. The ZNG military staff was headed by General Anton Tus, who then became Tudjman's personal military advisor and was replaced by General Janko Bobetko, who stood for election following his military retirement as an HDZ candidate for Parliament. The intelligence services were led by Josip Manolic, the cofounder of the HDZ and a personal confidant of Tudjman's. And in 1993 Tudjman placed his son, Miroslav, in control of the National Security Office, a new agency to oversee and coordinate the intelligence and security apparatus, reporting directly to President Tudjman.[38] Elements of the military police and Army guards formations also reported directly to Tudjman and were not under the control of the military staff.[39]

As Tudjman solidified his hold over the new security bureaucracy he sought to marginalize rival nationalists such as the Party of the Right (HSP). As early as fall 1991, Tudjman arrested and briefly held HSP party leader Dobroslav Paraga on sedition charges; in the face of press opposition Paraga was released, but the HOS was placed under nominal command of the ZNG. After the Party of the Right polled only 5 percent of the vote in the August 1992 elections, and with HDZ control of all key security agencies assured, Tudjman moved more forcefully, rearresting Paraga in 1993, this time on weapons charges, disbanding the HOS, absorbing its members into the state military, and eliminating the HSP as a serious political rival.[40] By 1995, the net result was a consolidated and stable but politicized security sector in which a unified national military was overseen by senior officials whose reliability was established not by de jure position but by personal connections, and where talent, while preferred, was not the foremost requirement for high office.[41]

Yet this politicization at the senior levels was tempered by the ever-present awareness of existential threat from the JNA. In practice this produced contrasting tendencies at the lower and higher ranks: whereas senior officials were politicized and cronyism was commonplace, military officers through brigade command were promoted on the basis of demonstrated merit and subject to harsh selection effects based on combat performance in the field. It was not uncommon for lower-ranking officers who displayed incompetence or cowardice or otherwise failed in their duties to be removed on the spot: the commander of the ZNG 137th Brigade, for example, was relieved after failing to prevent the JNA breakout from the Logoriste barracks in November 1991; a battalion commander in the HV 102nd Brigade was sacked in the middle of

Operation Storm in 1995; and the commander of the ZNG Ninth Motorized Brigade was relieved following unsuccessful attacks on Tulove Grede, Velike, Mala Bobija, and Obrovac in 1991, to cite but a few examples.[42] Conversely, junior officers who displayed talent in the field could advance rapidly: at least one officer rose from leading a company to commanding a brigade in a span of just six weeks in fall 1991.[43] Over time, this produced a younger generation of battle-tested officers whose influence grew as they rose through the ranks, but their influence over ministerial politics and supreme command functions was still limited by the time Operation Storm ended in 1995.

The net result was a rapid transition from fragile to basic natural order by fall of 1991, but a system that remained short of mature natural order status through the end of the 1995 campaign: ministerial and senior military leadership was personalized rather than fully institutionalized; political patronage played a significant role; and personal economic gain intertwined with security policy making for key elites—yet the relationships among key elites were stable and regularized, with no meaningful threat of internecine violence, with an important role for formal institutions with extensive division of labor and systematized responsibilities, and with a court system and legislature that acted as a meaningful if imperfect check on elite preferences.

In Croatia, however, there was also an important role for a different class of nonstate actor: the American private company Military Professional Resources Incorporated (MPRI). MPRI was a private firm comprising chiefly retired US military commissioned and senior noncommissioned officers, which provided advisory and training services to a wide range of clients. In 1994 the Croatian government contracted with MPRI to design and implement a series of training courses for the new national army. MPRI dispatched a team of 10 retired US Army colonels, 3 retired command sergeant majors, and 1 retired major general, who arrived in October 1994 and developed four instructional programs. One was modeled after the US Army Command and General Staff College course and was aimed at HV majors and lieutenant colonels; another mirrored the US Officers Advanced Course and was for HV lieutenants and captains; one was the equivalent of the US Noncommissioned Officers (NCO) Academy and was for HV sergeants; another comprised a series of seminars for senior managers in the Croatian Ministry of Defense. These courses included some instruction on civil-military relations and the laws of war, but their primary focus was on weapons employment, military tactics, operational art, campaign planning, logistics, and combat staff procedures and organization. In fact the curriculum was nearly identical to that at the corresponding US military schools, albeit on a compressed timeline to enable rapid completion. These courses enrolled a total of 200 to 300 HV officers, NCOs, and officials at a time and lasted four months, with immediate transition to a new class as soon as the previous one finished; the first cohort graduated in April 1995 and provided a substantial number of field commanders and staff for Operation Storm in August.[44]

Many have speculated that MPRI provided more than just instruction. Multiple NATO officers, for example, have argued that the design and conduct of Operation Storm was eerily similar to US methods and doctrine, and that the proficiency with which the operation was conducted could not have been achieved by such a new organization; they believe MPRI personnel actively participated in the planning, if not the command, of the operation itself.[45] MPRI has consistently denied this, and in fact the head of their delegation, Major General Richard Griffitts (USA retired), was on vacation in the Mediterranean and was not in Croatia at the time of the offensive.[46] Croatian authorities similarly deny that MPRI played any active role, and there is no actual evidence to suggest otherwise.[47]

What MPRI clearly did contribute, however, was technical knowledge on the conduct of war—and especially on the coordination and support of large formations in mobile operations. The HV's field-grade and senior officers either had been trained by the JNA in Soviet-style methods before the war or had learned as much of their craft as they could via trial and error during combat. There had been some out-of-country training in Germany and the Netherlands, but on a limited scale. The result was a largely informal and inconsistent approach to the technical side of war at the operational level. Some units had formal paper-based logistical systems; others operated on word of mouth and handshakes. Some staffs could do route planning and convoy administration; others could not. Some headquarters could coordinate fire support and arrange for its sustainment on the move; others could not. And some approached these tasks in the rigid, centralized system taught in the JNA, whereas others wanted to adopt a more flexible, decentralized style in keeping with Western doctrines.[48] What MPRI offered was a consistent, systematic, technically sophisticated method for planning and conducting coordinated operations across the HV.

Perhaps most important, they provided these skills in a way that did not threaten the internal balance of power within the Tudjman government. In a basic natural order regime, personal reliability trumps technical expertise; whereas talent is not necessarily precluded, political reliability is paramount.

Some of Tudjman's confidants were also capable officials, but others were not, and to replace the senior command echelon with disinterested military technocrats would risk undermining the political alliances that underwrote Tudjman's control of the security sector. MPRI, by contrast, had no constituency in Croatian politics and could be relied on to leave the scene when their contract ended—they could provide military technical skills without empowering any faction save Tudjman himself.[49]

Croatian Serb institutions. The Croatian Serbs faced a similar problem of creating institutions on the fly. Unlike the nationalists, however, they did not inherit an intact republican government on which to build. Their population, moreover, was divided among three noncontiguous territorial enclaves. A major objective of the JNA's 1991 offensive had been to interconnect these, but the Vance cease-fire left this goal unachieved. The new leadership tried to assemble a new governing infrastructure in the face of these challenges, but the result was a combination of inexperience, redundancy, and rivalry that left the Republic of Serbian Krajina in the status of a fragile natural order actor through its defeat in Operation Storm.

For most of the 1991 campaign, Croatian Serbs maintained three separate, noncontiguous governing entities, the Serbian Autonomous Oblasts, or Regions (SAOs), of Krajina, Western Slavonia, and Eastern Slavonia-Baranja-Western Srem, each representing its respective population. The SAOK (Krajina) was the largest and most militarily active, but each developed a separate judicial, administrative, and legislative apparatus. Much of the prewar republican government had been based in Zagreb, the capital of the new nationalist proto-state, and staffed with ethnic Croats who now overwhelmingly supported Croatian independence. The new Croatian Serb entities thus had to start nearly from scratch, and their staffing requirements greatly exceeded the availability of trained, experienced officials. Village and local functions could be performed by the same people as before, but the crucial state and especially security sector agencies were formed as pick-up teams in which new institutions were created and staffed largely by collections of amateurs with little experience or technical training. As US ambassador to Bosnia Victor Jackovich put it, a man could "milk cows in the morning, and be a judge in the afternoon," and there was little or no professional civil or military administration.[50]

Nor was it clear what the relationship would be among the respective SAOs' new agencies or leaderships. In part this was due to uncertainty over the future direction of Serbian Croatia.

Would the SAOs be absorbed into the Serbian Republic, as Jugoslav president Milosevic clearly preferred? Or would they become independent states of their own, either separately or as a unified Croatian Serb nation? And if so, which SAO's officials would take the senior positions in such a unified entity? The noncontiguous nature of Croatian Serb territory contributed to duplication of functions and redundancy, as each SAO built its own courts, legislatures, intelligence operations, and protoministries of the interior; the pervasive uncertainty contributed to rivalry among these duplicative agencies, as each tried to position itself for primacy in the event of future amalgamation.[51]

Consolidation into a unified security sector was further hindered by distrust and policy disagreement between Milan Babic, the founder of the Croatian Serb SDS and leader of the Krajina SAO, and Slobodan Milosevic in Belgrade, and between Babic and internal rivals aligned with Milosevic. Though confident that Milosevic would not allow Croatian Serbs to be overrun, Babic was less convinced that Milosevic had Babic's (or the SAOK's) political best interests at heart. The two leaders' relationship, always complex, became openly conflictual during the negotiations over the Vance cease-fire proposal, when Milosevic sought Croatian Serb approval but Babic wanted to fight on in the interest of connecting the noncontiguous Croatian Serb territories. Frustrated, Milosevic formed an anti-Babic political party in the Krajina and set up a new Krajina Serb Assembly to end-run Babic. The new assembly appointed Goran Hadzic president and voted to accept the Vance plan. In response, Babic formed his own assembly, which voted to reinstall him as president. Subsequent elections held in December 1993 pitted the respective factions against one another in a campaign subject to extensive interference from Belgrade; eventually Milosevic's protégé Milan Martic emerged from a runoff and replaced Hadzic as president.[52] Hadzic, meanwhile, hinted loudly that he was prepared to secede from the new Republic of Serbian Krajina with his own Slavonian SAO, eventually forming a "coordinating board" of five Slavonian mayors to explore options for independence from the RSK.[53] In the process, Croatian Serb politics became deeply factionalized with bitter, shifting alignments under extensive manipulation from Milosevic.

The security sector leadership that emerged from this cauldron was similarly divided. The Jugoslav state intelligence service quickly organized a nascent Croatian Serb military around a collection of local police and territorial defense units in the Serbian enclaves. These were eventually formalized as the SVK in March 1992, and placed under a staff in Knin composed of an amalgamation of former JNA officers (often detailed to this duty under Jugoslav state direction) and territorial commanders. During the 1991 campaign, however, much of the non-JNA Croatian Serb combat strength operated as semi-independent militias under individual organizers such as Vojislav Seselj, Dragoslav Bokan, and especially the infamous Zeljko Raznjatovic (or "Arkan"). Even after the formation of the official SVK in 1992, several of the militia leaders kept their organizations and continued to operate under their own leadership—neither Arkan's Tigers nor Bokan's White Eagles, for example, were ever integrated into the SVK. Discipline in these paramilitaries was notoriously poor, and their fighters were responsible for many of the worst atrocities in a war marked by widespread cruelty. Military coordination of their operations was haphazard at best, and the existence of multiple armed power centers led to factional disputes both between militia leaders, many of whom harbored political ambitions, and between them and the nominal SVK/RSK leadership.[54]

Nor were relationships between the leaders of the official security sector agencies stable or hierarchical. Jugoslav intelligence installed former police officer Milan Martic as head of the new SAOK Interior Ministry in 1991. When the SVK staff was created in 1992, Martic saw this as a threat to his position; feuding between the heads of the police and the army continued and came to a head after Martic assumed the presidency in 1993, whereupon he fired the SVK operational commander, former JNA general Mile Novakovic, and replaced him in 1994 with an officer Martic believed would be more malleable. Tensions, however, continued through the conclusion of Operation Storm in 1995, and the RSK security sector leadership remained deeply factionalized.[55]

Finally, there is evidence to suggest that economic corruption was a problem among the Croatian Serb leadership as it was among their nationalist rivals. Hadzic in particular has been accused of collaborating with Arkan in profiteering from illegal oil sales, and former Croatian Serb military leaders have bemoaned the RSK's poverty and corruption as a barrier to success as an independent state. The private and public sectors were no more separated in the RSK than they were in nationalist Croatia.[56]

While the Croatian Serb protostate thus did have an array of nominal governing agencies with specialization and a division of labor—it was not informal in the terms used here—these were highly personalized institutions with ill-trained and often rudimentary staffing and deep factional rivalries that were never resolved in any stable or persistent way. Multiple armed elites operated independently, pursuing often conflicting political agendas with limited integration into the official command hierarchy. Political penetration into commerce was probably about as widespread as among the nationalists. Political order required a delicate balancing of power among elite factions with limited mediation by perpetually lived bureaucracies. On balance, then, the Croatian Serb RSK is best coded as a fragile natural order regime.

Dependent Variable: Military Behavior in the Croatian War of Independence

Croatian nonstate actors attempted remarkably state-like military methods in the War of Independence. In the terms here, the nationalist ZNG and the Croatian Serb SVK both adopted midspectrum tactics and operations within weeks to months of their founding as military organizations—neither adopted the archetypically Fabian irregular methods often associated with nonstate actors. Their proficiency in executing midspectrum techniques varied widely, both in cross section and over time, an issue I address in more detail below. And proficiency aside, the methods attempted by both sides, as in the Hezbollah, JAM, and SNA cases above, represent varying admixtures of Fabian and Napoleonic elements rather than a simple uniform categorical style. To adjudicate this complex picture, I thus again use the index measure presented in the appendix and again code its elements in sequence: stealth; commitment to taking and holding ground; dispersion; coercion; distinguishability of combatants from noncombatant civilians; and functional differentiation within the theater of war.

1. Stealth

At the Fabian extremum, actors sacrifice lethality for maximum cover and concealment; the Napoleonic archetype sacrifices stealth for maximum lethality. While their proficiency of execution varied (more on this below), both the ZNG and the SVK actively sought a balance between cover, concealment, and effective fields of fire.

The nationalist ZNG began the war with radically exposed positions but quickly adopted more covered and concealed dispositions. In the war's opening actions, ZNG militiamen failed to dig in, movements were attempted without covering or suppressive fire, and some fighters even viewed cover and concealment as a sign of cowardice: as late as September 1991, inexperienced soldiers in Samobor refused to dig or to wear helmets until they observed comrades get killed in JNA artillery barrages.[57]

Such mistakes were costly, however, and nationalist units quickly sought cover and concealment. By October they had discovered that ad hoc positions in homes or basements offered inadequate protection from intense JNA artillery bombardments, and they increasingly moved combat positions away from village centers and into the outskirts of towns in carefully dug interconnected entrenchments with heavy overhead cover, camouflage, deep dugouts, and interlocking fields of fire with range stakes for small arms and preregistered aim points for mortar fire. Such positions were often fronted with landmines and barriers. As time permitted, these were often extended into multiple bands of defenses prepared in depth with lightly manned forward observation posts serving to alert the garrisons of deep dugouts to move into firing positions only once Serb-JNA ground assaults began. Aggressive security patrolling limited Serb infiltration to preserve concealment, and it provided intelligence on Serb dispositions.[58]

Low-exposure offensive movement came slower. In the ZNG's 1991 fall and winter offensives only a handful of elite units sought to integrate movement and suppressive fire; none could exploit limited visibility effectively or employ smoke or obscurants for concealed movement.[59] Only after acceding to state status in the 1995 campaign did most, now-HV, units execute effective fire-and-movement techniques for reduced-exposure movement under fire; the HV's nonstate ZNG predecessor's modal methods were covered and concealed when stationary but largely exposed when moving.[60]

The Serbian Croat SVK sought similarly covered and concealed fighting positions, albeit with substantially less proficient execution (see below). Entrenchment was extensive, with interconnected trenches that resembled the ZNG's in design, lending the battlefield a visual quality resembling the World War I western front and affording ample cover to SVK defenders. Sentries, observation posts, minefields, and wire barriers were deployed to thwart ZNG reconnaissance patrols and preserve concealment.[61]

SVK movement outside its trenches, however, embraced even less of the midspectrum exposure-reduction tool kit than did the ZNG's. Serb militiamen on the attack simply walked forward in the open, during daylight, without smoke or obscurants, in a rough skirmish line or bunched up behind JNA tanks—they rarely sought concealment in darkness or low-visibility conditions, or used local terrain for cover, or attempted to coordinate suppressive fire and movement by successive bounds to continue an advance under fire.[62]

2. Taking and Holding Ground

Pure Fabian irregular warfare is associated with an unwillingness to accept decisive engagement to take and hold ground. Both the ZNG and the SVK displayed a substantial willingness to contest ground and to accept decisive engagement to this end.

To assess the ZNG's and SVK's relative commitment to taking and holding ground I use the four observable referents of this commitment presented in the appendix: the duration of firefights; the proximity of attackers to defenders; the incidence of counterattack; and the incidence of harassing fires and unattended minefields.

THE DURATION OF FIREFIGHTS

Archetypically Napoleonic tactics are associated with extended firefights where defenders remain in position and accept decisive engagement as attackers close with their positions; classical guerillas are conversely expected to break contact while distant enough to enable safe withdrawal and to prefer short-duration, hit-and-run ambushes or raids. In Croatia, the ZNG sustained continuous engagements with JNA and SVK opponents that often lasted for weeks or months of close-quarters combat.

As early as August 1991, for example, ZNG forces that had retaken the town of Kostajnica subsequently dug in and resisted a multiweek counteroffensive from Croatian Serb militia before being overrun on September 13.[63] A combination of ZNG troops and Croatian police defended Vukovar against a combined Serb militia and JNA siege for more than two months between September 14 and November 18, when the battered survivors surrendered.[64] The ZNG defended Dubrovnik under continuous JNA attack from October 27 through December 7, when a local cease-fire was declared.[65] At Nova Gradiska in Western Slavonia in October the ZNG 121st Brigade held defensive positions under daily shelling for a month.[66]

As for the SVK, their assaults could likewise be protracted engagements. Typical JNA-Serb militia offensive tactics called for a preparatory artillery barrage of 30 to 90 minutes, often beginning at dawn, followed by a deliberately paced advance by JNA tanks with Serb militia infantry in support; unless the initial assault was successful, successive attempts could be sustained for hours before halting to regroup and resupply.[67]

Contributing to the extended duration of these actions was the SVK's tendency to fall back quickly when fired on, regroup behind artillery fire on ZNG positions, then renew the attack on the weakened defenders rather than pressing the assault home the first time. With sufficient artillery support, an extended succession of such desultory advances could eventually grind down the defense to the point where advancing armor and infantry could occupy abandoned ground rather than overrunning occupied positions directly, but this often caused prolonged battering for days or weeks at a time before defenses yielded.[68]

In the 1995 campaign between the HV and the SVK, by contrast, the HV effectively destroyed the SVK in a 10-day mobile offensive. The fighting was not prolonged, but this was hardly due to any unwillingness to sustain battle on the HV's part, and the combat involved direct overrun of substantial SVK positional defenses.[69] Whether in 1991 or 1995, the fighting thus did not conform to a guerilla-like pattern of quick hit-and-run actions without decisive engagement—even where Serbs proved unwilling to drive infantry assaults home, the result was instead a long-duration program of artillery attrition against dug-in ZNG targets deployed in sustained contact with JNA-SVK ground forces.[70]

PROXIMITY OF ATTACKERS TO DEFENDERS

Archetypically Napoleonic armies accept decisive engagement as attackers close with their positions, and they seek decisive engagement when on the offensive; pure Fabian guerillas break contact while distant enough to enable safe withdrawal. In Croatia, engagement ranges were often very short, owing to the extensive entrenchments often employed and the tendency for the trench lines to be dug at close proximity to enemy positions. At Gospice in August–September 1991, for example, the trench systems lay mostly within 500 to 600 meters of one another, with some stretches only 50 meters apart.[71] At Tenjski in December 1991, ZNG defenders occupied foxholes as close as 50 to 100 meters from the Serbs, whom the defenders could hear talking between assaults.[72] At Nova Gradiska in October 1991 the two sides' trench lines lay about 100 meters apart.[73] ZNG patrols and counterattacks could sometimes get very close to Serbian positions undetected: at Farkasic on October 19, for example, a ZNG patrol closed to within 2 meters of Serb troops, and a ZNG counterattack crept within 30 to 50 meters of Serbian trenches before being noticed; at Nova Gradiska, ZNG raids often approached to within 10 to 15 meters of Serb positions.[74]

INCIDENCE OF COUNTERATTACK

Napoleonic defenders, who cannot yield ground voluntarily, must counterattack to regain it even at the cost of exposure; pure Fabian defenders melt away rather than risk casualties to retake ground. In Croatia, counterattack was frequent on both sides, and especially for the nationalists, whose defensive posture in 1991 posed more need for the recovery of lost ground.

As early as June 26, Croatian Special Police and ZNG infantry battalions counterattacked Serbian militia forces that had overrun the Glina police station, driving the Serbs from the facility and reestablishing nationalist control over most of the town. On July 13–14 Serb militia that had captured police substations in Kraljevcani and Dragotinci were driven out by Special Police and ZNG counterattackers, who were then evicted in turn by JNA armored units. The 45-day Battle of Kostajnica opened with a nationalist counterattack to regain control of a series of police stations between Kostajnica and Dvor that had been lost to the Serbs; the subsequent fighting consisted of a Serbian counteroffensive to retake the town.[75] This pattern continued through the summer and fall, and the central purpose of the ZNG's November–December 1991 campaign was to reverse Serb gains of the summer and fall and retake lost ground. The result was a series of major counteroffensives in Western Slavonia and central Croatia.[76] And of course Operation Storm in 1995 was a theater-level counterstroke designed to retake the entirety of the ground nationalists lost to the Serbs in 1991.

In addition to these larger-scale counteroffensives, smaller local counterattacks were commonplace throughout the war. At Vukovar, ZNG defenders counterattacked nightly to retake any ground lost during the day.[77] The village of Medari in Western Slavonia changed hands at least 10 times in a seesaw series of attacks and counterattacks in November.[78] Nationalist Interior Ministry Special Police units were used almost exclusively for counterattack; as much as 80 percent of their combat experience in 1991 was on the tactical offensive.[79] In nationalist HOS militia battalions a platoon was normally held in reserve with a standing mission of counterattack to retake ground; many retook the same positions multiple times.[80] In Croatia's struggle to take and hold ground, counterattack was a commonplace feature of the fighting on all sides.[81]

THE INCIDENCE OF HARASSING FIRES AND
UNATTENDED MINEFIELDS

Another indicator of actors' relative emphasis on holding ground is the incidence of harassing fires and unattended minefields, whose use is associated
with archetypical Fabians, who seek to inflict attrition per se rather than to
control territory. In Croatia, indirect fire and minefields were both extremely
common—but each was employed chiefly to take or hold ground rather than
to harass.

The Serbs' normal offensive tactics in 1991 called for heavy JNA artillery
barrages on nationalist positions, sometimes sustained for days or weeks;
there was thus a tremendous volume of indirect fire in the War of Independence. But this was intended to destroy defensive positions outright, not to
harass them. By contrast with, say, Somali SNA use of mortars and rockets, the
JNA typically fired intense barrages of sometimes thousands of rounds an
hour on narrow frontages. Artillery fire this heavy routinely leveled entire villages; as one veteran on the receiving end of such bombardments put it, "you
cry for the earth to open so you could hide."[82] Much of the Serbian ground
gain in 1991 was accomplished by pulverizing defenses with such fires then
walking forward to occupy the vacated position.

Minefields were also very common, on both sides. But as with artillery,
their purpose was to control ground, not to harass, and they were typically tied
into defensive systems with direct overwatch by supporting infantry. Minefields could end up unattended after the garrison they were meant to protect
moved on, and this could cause civilian or military casualties; systems for
marking and recording minefield locations were often haphazard, especially
in the war's early months. But their primary purpose was to protect defending
infantry from direct assault, not to inflict incidental casualties on noncombatants or to harass forces on random patrols or administrative movements.[83]

3. Dispersion

Archetypically Napoleonic state armies concentrate their forces at a chosen
point of attack; pure Fabian nonstate irregulars disperse and operate at low,
uniform, densities. In Croatia, the theaterwide density of forces was initially
low and not unlike many nonstate actors'—as noted above, the ZNG's theaterwide force-to-space ratio in summer 1991 was only around 0.8 fighters per
square kilometer, which was actually lower than the Vietcong's in 1965.[84] The

fully mobilized ZNG of December was larger, yielding a theaterwide troop density of around four fighters per square kilometer, which was still far lower than, say, the Somali SNA's in Mogadishu.[85] The local troop density at key points, however, was often much higher, reflecting the nonuniform distribution of forces typical of the fighting in Croatia. The ZNG defenders of Vukovar, for example, deployed over 2,000 troops in a roughly 10-square-kilometer zone, for a local density of around 200 troops per square kilometer, or about 50 times the theaterwide figure; for its October offensive in Western Slavonia the ZNG concentrated 7,000 troops on a 20-kilometer front, for a local density of about 175 troops per square kilometer (assuming a depth of 2 kilometers for the concentration), or more than 40 times the theaterwide density; SVK concentrations in support of JNA offensives were broadly similar.[86]

4. The Balance of Brute Force and Coercion

Pure Fabian irregulars rely heavily on coercion. In Croatia, both the ZNG and the SVK relied heavily on brute force. As noted above, both the 1991 and the 1995 campaigns were centrally concerned with brute force seizure of ground or denial thereof. The Battle of the Barracks from September to November 1991 was a nonstate offensive to seize JNA armories by brute force and capture the weapons and equipment held there. The JNA-Serb militia offensives in the fall of 1991 were designed to connect isolated Serbian enclaves into a contiguous territory by taking nationalist-held ground. The nonstate ZNG's winter 1991 counteroffensive was intended to roll back the Serbians' territorial gains by brute force. And the HV's 1995 offensive in Operation Storm was a successful effort to destroy the nonstate SVK's positional defenses outright and recapture the ground they held without relying on coercive concession by the Serbs.[87] Few wars are purely brute force with no coercive element, but for both sides in the Croatian Wars of Independence the fighting involved a very extensive brute force component.

5. Distinguishability of Combatants and Civilians

Pure Fabian combatants intermingle with innocent civilians for concealment; actors at the Fabian extremum thus wear versions of typical civilian clothing, operate among the civilian population, and avoid the use of large-caliber weapons that are difficult to conceal under civilian clothing even when such weaponry is available. By contrast, archetypically Napoleonic armies avoid civilians where possible, use uniforms or other distinguishing marks to differentiate combatants from noncombatants, obtain cover and concealment via terrain rather than civilian intermingling, and exploit the heaviest weapons available to maximize their firepower. Hence the greater the incidence of uniformed combatants, the greater the physical separation of combatants from civilians, and the more extensive the use of available heavy weapons, the less Fabian the actor's methods.

In Croatia, most combatants sought cover chiefly via the terrain, wore uniforms, and used the heaviest weapons available to them. Civilians suffered desperately in the War of Independence, and a series of war crimes prosecutions have sought to punish combatants on both sides for atrocities against the civilian population. Yet neither side adopted the common guerilla tactic of seeking indistinguishability from noncombatants as a means of cover while fighting.

The ZNG, for example, adopted a conscious policy of moving defensive positions out of villages and other populated areas as the 1991 campaign unfolded. In the initial battles some units chose positions in and around civilian buildings, as at Vukovar in August or at Pisarovina along the Kupa River in October.[88] By November, however, it had become standard practice to dig entrenchments outside the built-up area wherever possible, often with overhead cover and concealed communications trenches back to the village and with rotation policies wherein units would be billeted in civilian homes but would fight from positions outside the town. This did not prevent JNA artillery from leveling the villages themselves, but it tended to reduce ZNG casualties from such barrages; some units reported suffering heavier losses among troops in their billets in the nominal rear than among those in the forward trenches.[89] SVK defenses in the 1995 campaign were similarly disposed mainly in rural entrenchments rather than the interior of towns and villages.[90]

Nor did the respective forces make any systematic effort to conceal their identity as combatants by wearing civilian clothing. When Croatia declared independence, neither the nationalists nor the Serbs could equip all their recruits with weapons, much less uniforms. Prewar police had their service uniforms, as did many former JNA soldiers; others had only civilian clothing, and none had systematic identifying insignia to distinguish them from the enemy. Rather than exploiting this for cover, however, both sides quickly moved to provide military clothing. In fact, individuals frequently purchased this on their own or obtained military-style clothing and accoutrements in any way they could. This was widely considered a sign of status and political

commitment: as one former ZNG officer put it: "People wanted to look serious and important, so they sought uniforms as fast as they could. Anything of
military origin was interesting. . . . Anyone with access to military surplus
made a killing."[91] Even militias that operated outside the official chain of command typically wore military-style uniforms, usually with distinctive organizational insignia identifying them as members of a specific militia: the HOS,
for example, created a circular patch with an embroidered red-and-white
checkerboard shield in the center, to be worn on the left shoulder of military
camouflage fatigues obtained from abroad; the Serbian White Eagles used a
shoulder patch with a white eagle on a red shield.[92] The variety of patterns and
inconsistent standards could make it hard to distinguish friend from foe on
the battlefield—some ZNG units resorted to colored ribbons tied around
sleeves to prevent misidentification in combat[93]—but both sides sought military clothing that made combatants relatively easily distinguished from civilians.[94] And as the ZNG assault on JNA barracks in 1991 and the SVK's preferred cooperation with JNA armor indicated, both forces actively sought and
used the heaviest weapons they could obtain.[95]

6. The Military Organization of the Theater of War

Archetypically Fabian warfare is a uniform, undifferentiated territorial defense
without a distinguishable front or rear waged by guerillas fighting largely
where they live; pure Napoleonic armies differentiate the theater into distinct
covering force zones, main battle areas, rear areas and communication zones,
and sectors of main effort as opposed to supporting or economy-of-force
areas. Hence the more uniform or undifferentiated the military organization
of the theater of war, the greater the degree to which the actor's methods approach the Fabian extreme.

In Croatia, both nonstate actors maintained clear distinctions between
fronts and rear areas and main and supporting efforts. In October 1991, for
example, the Pakrac-Novska front in Western Slavonia was a sector of main
effort for the ZNG whereas the Ogulin-Otocac front was not; whereas the
ZNG deployed almost four brigades on a 12-mile front for the former, it left a
single brigade to man a 17-mile front for the latter.[96] Zagreb and Knin were rear
areas for most of the war and were largely untouched by the fighting whereas
Vukovar and Dubrovnik were on the front lines; Vukovar was virtually destroyed, and Dubrovnik was heavily damaged.[97] Both armies, moreover,
quickly developed rearward logistical systems that were designed to provide

food, water, ammunition, and supplies without requiring fighters to extract these goods directly from the local population. Soldiers always welcome popular support, and it was not uncommon for sympathetic civilians to provide food or shelter to coethnic combatants in their midst, but the forces' military needs were met chiefly through dedicated, spatially distinct military channels.[98] None of the fighting in Croatia took the form of a geographically uniform, undifferentiated territorial defense.[99]

Proficiency of Execution

The respective actors' proficiency of execution offers an opportunity for process tracing. The causal logic of the new theory implies that weakly institutionalized, limited-stakes actors should display limitations of skill and military coordination that would render complex, midspectrum warfare impractical if attempted, but that strongly institutionalized actors with high stakes should be able to master the complexities of midspectrum war fighting. In Croatia, proficiency varied widely. Serb militias attempted demanding military tasks but never progressed beyond rudimentary small-unit defensive skills in executing them. The nationalist ZNG began the war with no greater proficiency than the Serbs but made faster progress in a similarly demanding agenda until hitting a ceiling in late 1991: by then, the ZNG could execute consistent basic defensive tactics, and some brigades could handle small-scale offensive actions, but the institution could not coordinate operations above the brigade level. These problems were not overcome until the relative lull between the 1991 and 1995 campaigns; by 1995, the new Croatian state HV proved capable of proficient midspectrum methods through the theater-strategic level of war.

Unlike the nationalist ZNG, the main Serbian militias in 1991 operated in conjunction with a state military, the JNA. The militias' chief role in this partnership was to provide infantry for a heavily armed but undermanned state army: a combination of ethnic defections and a halting mobilization process had left the JNA badly understrength in 1991, and its commanders looked to the allied Serb militias to redress the resulting infantry shortage. The militias, however, lacked the skills needed to support armor and exploit artillery. With little formal training and a notorious lack of military discipline, the militias were incapable of performing the military functions of infantry in modern combined-arms tactics. As noted above, on the offensive, SVK infantry mostly just walked forward in a rough skirmish line or bunched up behind JNA tanks—they were rarely able to operate under concealment in darkness or low-visibility conditions, to use local terrain for cover, or to coordinate suppressive fire and movement by successive bounds to continue an advance under fire. And their tendency to go to ground or flee when fired on left them unable to observe ZNG antitank positions for buttoned-up JNA tank crews, to direct the tanks' fire, or sometimes even to alert the tanks to the fact that the infantry was pinned down; JNA tanks would frequently continue to advance after their infantry had halted, leaving an unsupported pure tank force to be cut up once it encountered dug-in antitank positions too well camouflaged for the crews of buttoned-up armored vehicles to see. Nor could the militiamen coordinate their movements closely enough with supporting JNA artillery to cover much of their advance before receiving fire from ZNG defenders. Modern combined-arms tactics require infantry to advance while their own artillery is still firing, keeping defenders' heads down until the last minute and thus limiting attackers' exposure to a short sprint after the artillery finally lifts from the objective; this requires the infantry to work in very close to an ongoing barrage so as to shorten the period of exposure. Serbian militia, however, were rarely willing to approach an active barrage zone; JNA-Serb assaults typically began their advance only after their artillery had ceased firing. This delay gave ZNG defenders time to emerge from cover and man their firing parapets long before the assault reached them, confronting exposed Serb militiamen with unsuppressed small-arms fire that the militia could rarely counter. The Serb-JNA combination could take ground by destroying defenses outright with massed artillery without exposing attackers to fire, but only at the cost of a ponderously slow advance while waiting for prolonged barrages to destroy increasingly deep ZNG entrenchments; nothing faster was possible given the attackers' systematically poor combined-arms cooperation.[100]

Nor were Serb militias much more proficient on the tactical defense in 1991. Entrenchment was often casual, and militia infantry did little security patrolling forward of their prepared positions. Sentries and observation posts were deployed but often failed to detect ZNG patrols; minefields and barrier systems were plentiful but inconsistently placed; and security perimeters were often porous. Small-arms marksmanship was adequate for the JNA but poor for Serb militia infantry, while noise and light discipline were systematically weak: ZNG defenders could frequently see and hear Serbian militiamen moving and speaking casually in their trenches, facilitating targeting for the limited mortar fire at the ZNG's disposal, and enabling raiding parties to penetrate Serbian front lines to gather intelligence or take prisoners.[101]

With the Vance cease-fire the tempo of operations diminished, much of the JNA withdrew, and the Serbs consequently devoted considerable time to preparing stronger defensive fortifications to protect their territorial gains against an expected HV counteroffensive. The cumulative effect of several years of such efforts was an extensively prepared system of positions, with interconnected trenches, overhead cover, concrete bunkers, and extensive camouflage. Yet these positions often had very little tactical depth—sometimes a kilometer or less—and the troops occupying them displayed a number of systematic shortcomings even as late as Operation Storm in 1995. In particular, the garrisons fought a mostly static defense, with little maneuver to react to HV penetrations, to shift between supplementary and alternate firing positions, or to counterconcentrate rearward reserves. Combined-arms integration remained problematic, with HV attackers commonly reporting incoming direct or indirect SVK fire but rarely both together. SVK artillery was plentiful but inaccurate, with no ability to hit moving targets and only limited capacity to strike fixed prearranged impact points. Perhaps the SVK's greatest shortcoming in 1995, however, was its inability to coordinate operations at brigade level and above. As early as 1991, joint JNA-militia operations were plagued by poor interbrigade communications between militia commanders and JNA officers; in actions such as the siege of Vukovar this lack of coordination resulted in the ZNG's ability to keep supply lines into the city open for weeks owing to their enemies' inability to seal a perimeter. By 1995, the SVK had in principle established unity of command with formal staff organizations at corps and theater levels. Brigade commanders, however, appear often to have ignored them, and independent action by uncoordinated brigades frequently left neighboring formations exposed and compelled to retreat to avoid encirclement. Some corps commanders had to assign critical staff officers to take over battle groups directly as a means of getting their orders followed by their subordinates; others, conversely, refused to grant access to their corps headquarters for their own higher command in the SVK theater staff at Knin. Some of these problems may have been aggravated by HV efforts at disrupting SVK communications, but much of the difficulty reflected a basic failure of operational-level coordination on a fluid battlefield.[102]

On the nationalist side, the ZNG began the war with little better skills than the Serbian militias. Like the Serbs, many nationalist recruits had some prior military service with the JNA, but only the police had any unit training or experience, and the police had not been trained for modern combat. While most fighters thus understood basic individual weapon employment, they often lacked even rudimentary small-unit tactical skills: troops failed to dig in, movements were attempted without covering or suppressive fire, combat arms were used independently rather than combined, and fighting positions lacked depth or adequate fields of fire.[103] As noted above, however, nationalist units quickly learned basic defensive tactics. By October they had prepared systematic defensive trench systems fronted with overwatched landmines and wire barriers, and as time permitted, these positions were expanded into depth, coupled with forward outpost zones to provide early warning of Serb-JNA ground attacks, and screened with aggressive patrolling.[104]

Offensive tactics, as noted above, came more slowly, and operational-level coordination remained elusive through the end of the 1991 campaign. In the ZNG's 1991 fall and winter offensives multibrigade operations were infrequent, and badly coordinated when attempted. Operation Whirlwind in December, for example, involved an effort to cross the Kupa River and break through Serbian positions near Popusko; the plan required the ZNG 102nd Novi Zagreb Brigade to execute a 40-to-60-kilometer approach march at night, followed by an in-stride river crossing with support from the 10th Brigade and elements of the Second Guards and 144th Brigades. The supporting brigades failed to arrive, however. Elements of the 102nd reached the far riverbank just before dawn but were isolated there; artillery support was requested, but never provided. Under heavy fire, the assault force was forced back across the river, abandoning 9 of the 10 tanks committed on the far bank (the 10th vehicle was destroyed by enemy fire).[105]

By 1995, however, performance was much improved, and especially so at the operational and theater-strategic levels of war. In Operation Storm a high-tempo, multibrigade offensive essentially destroyed a 40,000-man Serbian defense and seized over 10,000 square kilometers of defended ground in just three days. In the process they sustained an opposed advance to a depth of over 60 kilometers without significant logistical or command problems and successfully coordinated an array of specialized arms including infantry, armor, artillery, close air support, signals, and electronic warfare. UN and NATO observers were so impressed with the HV's performance that many of them doubted that Croatian officers could have been in charge; although there is no evidence to support the conjecture, a number of Western officers speculated that MPRI must have been responsible given the sophistication of theater-level coordination displayed. The HV's 1995 offensive was not perfect—a number of reserve brigades in particular displayed important shortcomings—but on balance it presented not just state-level proficiency but the performance of an unusually accomplished state military in complex conventional operations.[106]

Theoretical Implications

Given the codings above, what do the respective theories predict for military behavior in Croatia? As for tribal culture explanations, neither the nationalist ZNG nor the Croatian Serb militias of 1991 nor the SVK of 1995 sprang from a familist tribal culture. A tribal culture perspective would thus expect both the nationalists and the Serbs to adopt the proficient state-like methods it associates with nontribal cultures.

Orthodox materialism expects outnumbered, outgunned nonstate actors to adopt irregular methods; each of Croatia's nonstate actors faced forbidding material imbalances. The nationalist ZNG fought the JNA-Serb alliance in mid-1991 at a numerical disadvantage of perhaps 4:1 and a disadvantage in gross firepower that may have been even greater. The Serbian SVK was well equipped, but outnumbered by the then-state Croatian HV by around the same 4:1 margin the ZNG had faced. Orthodox materialists would thus expect both the ZNG and the SVK to adopt high-concealment classically Fabian war fighting.

Hybrid warfare materialists expect nonstate actors with access to modern weapons to wage proficient midspectrum warfare along the lines of Hezbollah in 2006. The Serbian SVK was lavishly equipped with such weaponry by their allies in Belgrade. But even the ZNG had substantial access to advanced weapons once the Battle of the Barracks provided them with captured JNA stocks, which included AT-3 Sagger wire-guided precision antitank weapons, T-55 tanks, M-80 infantry fighting vehicles, and hundreds of tubes of modern artillery. In fact, the ZNG had access to more firepower than Hezbollah did; hybrid warfare theory would thus expect both the ZNG and the SVK to adopt Hezbollah-like proficient midspectrum methods.

The new theory, by contrast, predicts different behavior for the two different Croatian nonstate actors: proficient midspectrum tactics for the ZNG in 1991 albeit with problematic operational-level coordination; and inability to implement proficient midspectrum tactics or operations for the SVK. The Croatian nationalist leadership faced an existential threat, which motivated them to sacrifice as necessary to field capable forces; they also inherited a substantial institutional infrastructure, which provided a foundation for the large-scale coordination that proficient midspectrum operations require. Croatian *security* institutions, however, were less developed than the civil agencies of the new regime and took longer to professionalize—by the end of the 1991 campaign they were still substantially personalized at the senior leadership echelons. The new theory would predict proficient tactics from such a combination, but problematic coordination of higher-level formations. The Croatian Serbs, by contrast, believed they had a state ally whose army, the JNA, would protect them from annihilation, and their institutions were much less mature, less professionalized, and more riven by factional strife. This sapped their motivation to sacrifice for military capability and diminished the span of trust available for coordinated action at all levels of war. The new theory would predict high-concealment Fabian methods as the optimal choice for such an actor.

In fact, the military behavior of Croatian nationalists and Serbs was not the same. They *attempted* similar methods—by the index measure presented in chapter 2 and the appendix, both actors' behavior corresponded to a value of 4.9, a value that is in the middle range of the Fabian-Napoleonic spectrum but is actually more Napoleonic and ostensibly "state-like" than some state militaries, such as the United States in Operation Desert Storm or the German defenses at Operation Goodwood in 1944.[107] But their proficiency of execution varied widely in ways that materialist theory cannot account for. By the end of 1991, only the ZNG had developed the skills to execute the attempted methods competently, and only at the small-unit tactical level. The coordination necessary for proficient execution of such methods at the theater level was beyond any of the nonstate actors in 1991 and was grasped only by the new Croatian state's army in 1995. None of the Serbian nonstate actors ever developed proficiency in any significant part of this agenda, whether in 1991 or afterward.

This pattern is inconsistent with orthodox materialism, which predicts similar and irregular methods for both the nationalists and the Serbs, yet military behavior in Croatia was neither irregular nor uniform.

Tribal culture and hybrid warfare theories are consistent with the midspectrum agenda Croatian actors sought. But these theories do not explain why nonstate actors who were all nontribal and who all had access to modern weapons would vary so widely in their proficiency with these methods.

The new theory, by contrast, can account for wide variance in proficiency: the actor's differing stakes and institutional development are consistent with the observed differences in skill. Yet the new theory would expect an actor with the Serbs' limited perceived stakes and weak institutionalization to avoid midspectrum methods whose complexity was beyond their capacity. The rationalist logic in the new theory would predict that an actor like the Serbs would choose less complex, higher-concealment methods closer to the Fabian end of the behavioral spectrum than the highly complex midspectrum methods the Serbs tried to implement. (In fact, the functional form in the appendix identifies a very Fabian index score of 0.72 as the optimal Serbian SVK choice,[108] as opposed to their observed score of 4.9.)

Perhaps the Serbs should have followed the theory's prescription—if they had, the results may well have been more favorable to them. In particular, a more Fabian approach in 1995 would probably have increased the HV's costs, and lengthened the duration of the conflict considerably. The Serbs had potential access to mountainous terrain near Knin, and sanctuary across the border on their Jugoslav state patron's territory. Conditions for a Fabian insurgency would not have been ideal: the Croatian-Jugoslav border area is separated from the rugged terrain of the Denaric Alps and their foothills; an insurgency based in the latter would be hard to supply from the former. And any insurgency of this kind imposes heavy costs on the insurgents and their supporters—it is far from clear that a long, grinding insurgency that ceded initial control of the population to the enemy would have been judged worth it by the Croatian Serb leadership (or their patrons in Belgrade). But the general approach would have been far from crazy—in fact the prewar Jugoslav defense strategy had rested on exactly this kind of distributed resistance from territorial defense units using largely hit-and-run methods to bleed larger state militaries who could not be excluded absolutely from friendly terrain.[109] A more Fabian approach for Croatian Serbs in 1995 would have represented a return to a familiar strategy rather than a radical departure.

In effect, what the Serbs in the Croatia case demonstrate is the costs and consequences of failing to follow the new theory's logic. The heart of the new theory is a claim that actors who lack the institutional infrastructure that is needed to master complex military behaviors will suffer gravely if they try to use such methods anyway. This is precisely what happened to the Croatian Serbs in 1995. As a rationalist "as if" argument, the new theory assumes that actors who ignore the logic of war will be removed for their errors, hence in steady state the international system as a whole will be characterized mostly by actors who either internalize such logic or behave as if they have. What the Croatian case does is to demonstrate this logic via an example of the consequences to be suffered in ignoring it, and in the process to suggest counterfactual implications for other actors—such as the Somali SNA—who did not overreach to the degree that the Serbs did.

A final important theoretical implication concerns the role of MPRI. The new theory argues that actors whose stakes and institutions permit proficient midspectrum warfare will acquire the skills needed—the limiting constraint is the actor's politics, not the availability of skill. Yet the skills required can be very demanding. Where do new actors get them? For many, a state sponsor is the natural source for the needed training and expertise. But while most non-state actors have such sponsors, some do not—nationalist Croatians, for example, sought Western state support but were denied it. If military skill (and forces) were the exclusive province of states, then actors like the Croatian ZNG without a state sponsor would be unable to develop midspectrum military proficiency and would be consigned to simpler, more Fabian methods. In fact, however, neither military skills nor military forces are confined to states or even would-be states such as insurgents or secessionists. The private military industry is now capable of providing these goods and services directly. MPRI in Croatia provided neither forces nor direct military leadership, but it did provide skills via intensive military training that covered the entire range of command levels from noncommissioned officers through brigade and corps commanders and staffs. Croatian nationalist politics enabled the new state to exploit these skills and use them to their fullest—but to an important degree the source of the skill was the private military marketplace.

This role for private military actors also helped overcome some of the remaining internal political constraints that could otherwise have hamstrung HV performance in 1995. Tudjman had bought stability in the Croatian security sector by personalizing the senior leadership functions. While some of these loyalist appointees proved quite able, others were not. To dismiss political allies in favor of military technocrats would have risked the balance among elites that Tudjman depended on for order in a still maturing government. What MPRI offered in this setting was a source of technocratic expertise, extending to the most senior levels, that did not require Tudjman to upset the elite balance of power by reshuffling security sector leadership appointments or empowering some at the expense of others. MPRI's American contractors had no Croatian constituency and presented no meaningful threat to the political position of any of Tudjman's senior appointees. In a fragile or informal political order, even nominally disinterested military contractors—whether in the form of trainers or actual forces—would still be dangerous: how could a potentially threatened member of the elite be sure that this new power would not be captured by one of their rivals and used against them? In a basic or mature natural order, however, the greater role of formal offices and the established norms of interaction among elite officeholders offer a degree of protection against the more egregious forms of internal aggression—and this enables such regimes to take advantage of outside skills (or even forces, in the right setting) because these will not constitute clear and imminent threats to the established order. The result in Croatia was a significant improvement in a new military's proficiency in the very demanding skills of theater-level mid-spectrum military cooperation.

On balance, then, the case is more consistent with the new theory—and especially the new theory's causal logic—than its competitors are. And while the new theory does not fit the case perfectly—it implies that the SVK should have adopted simpler, more Fabian methods than those it actually employed—it is wrong for the right reasons.[110] That is, it explains the SVK's inability to execute the methods it chose given its internal politics, and in the process sheds light on the incentive structures faced by all nonstate actors: while most will choose more astutely than the Croatian Serbs, the new theory explains what will happen to those who do not.

9

The Vietcong in the Second Indochina War, 1965–68

IN THIS CHAPTER I present the book's final case method test: the Vietcong (VC) in the Second Indochina War, from the introduction of American combat troops in 1965 through the virtual destruction of the VC as a major combatant in the Tet Offensive of 1968. The Vietcong are perhaps the paradigmatic nonstate irregular force in the eyes of most Americans, and their methods had a profound influence on subsequent policy and scholarship; any theory of nonstate warfare must account for the Vietcong. The case also offers a theoretically important opportunity to observe nonstate warfare prior to the advent of precision firepower—in fact, the 1965–68 era in Vietnam offers one of the last examples of warfare before the dawn of modern precision weaponry, which was introduced in the war's latter campaigns. As such, the case offers an important opportunity to assess the importance of technological change by exploring a region of the theoretical space unobserved in the other four cases above.

The chief finding from the case is to corroborate the new theory's account of technology's role in nonstate war fighting. The Vietcong faced existential stakes and had remarkably formal, mature institutions. There is good reason to believe they could have mastered the complexity of modern midspectrum warfare. Yet they chose mostly Fabian methods instead—and suffered gravely when they departed from this pattern as in Tet. I argue that their inability to succeed militarily with less Fabian methods is attributable to their low-lethality weapon technology, which combined with the difficult jungle terrain of their primary operating areas to leave them unable to control territory on the necessary scale even though they deployed a large combatant force. With only light, low-firepower weapons at their disposal, the VC could not prevent their

American, and to some extent South Vietnamese, state opponents from massing overwhelming combat power at chosen points. The problem here was not numerical imbalance per se, or even technological asymmetry—Hezbollah and the Croatian ZNG both proved able to control ground with midspectrum methods under comparable numerical and technical inferiority. But whereas Hezbollah and the ZNG had modern weapons lethal enough to force better-equipped state enemies to disperse, yielding manageable local imbalances at the critical points, the VC did not. The Vietcong's 1960s-era light weapons and small arms could cause gradual attrition over time, but they could not stop a massed state offensive from crushing their defenses at any given point. Nor could the Vietcong take ground against state armies' positional defenses with such arms. Their only option was thus to resort to the high-concealment methods of Fabian irregular warfare, notwithstanding their existential motivation and mature institutions. Later nonstate actors with more advanced weapons were able to make different choices even when faced with materially superior state opponents.

As before, I develop this argument in five steps. First, I outline briefly the main events of the case. Second, I develop values for the key independent variables associated with the competing theories. Third, I code the dependent variable of VC military behavior. Fourth, I process-trace the relationship between the theory's causal logic and the events of the case through a discussion of the VC's proficiency of execution. I conclude by assessing the relative fit between prediction and observation in light of this, and the case's net implications for the theories under study.

Overview of Events

French defeat at the hands of the Vietminh in the First Indochina War of 1946–54 left Vietnam partitioned between a northern Communist state controlled by the Vietminh and a southern republic under the US-allied emperor Bao Dai and prime minister Ngo Dihn Diem. The Vietminh had operated in the south as well as the north during the first war, however, and never fully withdrew from southern Vietnam; cadres remained who eventually renewed insurgent activity against the non-Communist Diem government. Beginning with an assassination campaign in 1957, these cadres, together with reinforcements infiltrated from the North, mounted a gradually escalating series of attacks on southern government forces and officials. These attacks eventually consolidated a series of "liberated zones" that enabled the announcement of a National Liberation Front (NLF) to constitute the political wing of the insurgency in December 1960 in Tay Ninh.[1]

The insurgents' armed wing, known to the southern government as the "Vietcong," a contraction of *Việt Nam Cộng-sản* (Vietnamese Communist), continued to grow. By early 1963 they had strengthened to the point where they could inflict serious casualties on the southern government Army of the Republic of Vietnam (ARVN), as they demonstrated at Ap Bac in January when they mauled elements of two South Vietnamese Civil Guard battalions and three battalions of ARVN regulars, shooting down five government helicopters in the process before slipping away after nightfall.[2]

With the Diem government clearly unable to control the insurgency, the increasingly dissatisfied Americans sought his ouster. On November 2, 1963, he was assassinated in an American-supported coup d'état, producing an extended period of instability until the eventual installation of ARVN general Nguyen Van Thieu as president in June 1965.[3]

In the meantime, infiltration of Vietcong cadres from the north had been augmented with the introduction of elements of a northern state army, the Communist People's Army of Vietnam (PAVN, or NVA for "North Vietnamese Army") into the south, and its resupply and reinforcement via the Ho Chi Minh Trail in neutral Cambodia and Laos.[4] With the state NVA fighting largely in the northern and central parts of South Vietnam and the VC operating primarily in the south and the Mekong delta, the insurgency continued to expand its influence. Faced with a problem clearly beyond the capacity of its Vietnamese allies to contain, the Johnson administration in Washington decided to escalate American involvement from providing aid and advisors to waging a bombing campaign against North Vietnam, then to the deployment of 3,500 US ground combat troops beginning in March 1965. By the end of the year the US presence had grown to 185,000, and the United States had become the Vietcong's primary opponent, with the ARVN playing mostly a supporting role.[5]

From 1965 to 1967 much of the fighting revolved around a series of major American offensives against VC and NVA base camps and operating areas as in Operations Attleboro, Cedar Falls, and Junction City, September to November 1966, January 1967, and February to May 1967. A system of fortified garrisons and firebases was also established in the country's interior, but US offensives rarely sought to consolidate sustained control over territory, resulting in reinfiltration by insurgents after American assault forces moved on.[6]

This pattern of US sweeps followed by departure and insurgent reinfiltration was broken, however, by the Communist Tet Offensive of 1968. Beginning

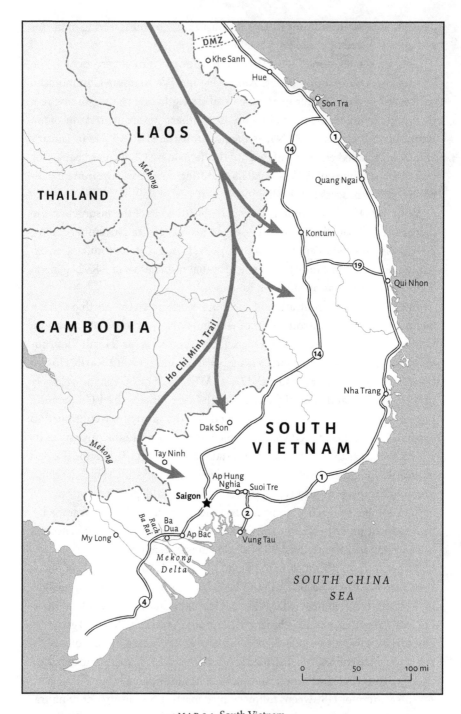

MAP 9.1. South Vietnam

on January 30, the VC and NVA launched a coordinated series of set-piece attacks on US and allied bases, garrisons, and cities across South Vietnam. In the process they briefly seized control of the provincial capital of Hue, breached the US Embassy perimeter in Saigon, and besieged the US Marine base at Khe Sanh. Most of the offensive's hundreds of attacks failed outright, however, and even the partial successes at Hue and Khe Sanh were soon reversed: Hue was retaken in late February, and the siege of Khe Sanh was lifted in early April. The offensive's main goal, to trigger a general popular uprising against the Thieu government, went unrealized, and in the process the VC and NVA suffered heavily. Communist casualties have been estimated at 40,000, and VC losses in particular were so heavy that it became necessary to rebuild Vietcong units with NVA regulars. The offensive's *political* effect was very different, however: the offensive's intensity shocked Americans, who had been told the war was being won, and its effect on public opinion was an important contribution to the eventual US withdrawal and defeat. But in military terms the offensive failed to meet its aims and cost the Communists dearly. In fact, it essentially destroyed the Vietcong as a meaningful military organization—after Tet it was the NVA, and not the VC, that carried the war for the Communists. With the end of the Tet Offensive the role of the Vietcong as a major nonstate military actor thus effectively came to an end as well.[7]

Independent Variables

How does the military behavior of the Vietcong compare with the respective theories' predictions? I begin with the theories' independent variables of tribal culture, military materiel, and internal politics.

The Vietcong and Tribal Culture

Vietnamese society in the 1960s was relatively homogeneous, with a population that mostly shared a common language and ethnic background. In this shared culture, family played an important role and served as the most important single social unit—yet the cultural role of descent was on balance less pervasive and influential than in 1990s Somalia or southern Lebanon in 2006.

There were some areas where kin and clan mattered centrally, especially in the Vietnamese practice of ancestor worship and in the geographic distribution of rural households. Patrilineal ancestors were subjects of veneration, with altars and land reserved for the practice among those wealthy enough to afford it, and with the eldest male family member responsible for the cult.[8] Kin groups, moreover, lived in close proximity, and villages normally comprised a handful of subgroups who shared some degree of patrilineal consanguinity. Brides were expected to emigrate to the husband's village, reinforcing the concentration of patrilineal kin in localities over time.[9] This proximity inevitably influenced behavior and surely shaped local decision making to favor kin groups over outsiders.

In other respects, tribal influences were real but weaker. Marriage choices, for example, were sometimes arranged by kin, but the spouses chosen were almost always from outside the kin group. In fact, cousin marriage or other in-group pairings were culturally taboo, and spouses were sought from outside the village community and the immediate family line.[10]

Economic activity was influenced by kin relationships, but this influence was attenuated by land ownership patterns. Especially in rural areas, the family was the essential economic unit, and family lineage often shaped employment, credit, and purchasing choices. The importance of kin was summed up in a popular saying: "a drop of blood is deeper than a pond of water."[11] Yet absentee landlords owned much of the arable farmland, especially in the south, which limited the potential role of inheritance through descent for wealth accumulation in the countryside. Whereas small businesses or local construction activity often relied on kin for labor, in an agricultural economy there were limits to the cultural importance of such links. And even in commerce and construction, friends and neighbors often loomed as large as family connections as organizing principles for cooperation.[12]

Nor was dispute resolution or political leadership shaped primarily by family descent; wealth, religion, ideology, and social class played larger roles than family lineage per se. Under Diem, for example, Catholic religious affiliation was widely considered important for political advancement, with ambitious individuals such as Thieu converting for reasons that many saw as careerist rather than theological; family connections, by contrast, played a more muted role. In the north, Communist Party membership and ideological affiliation played more consequential roles, and kin relationships were again less salient.[13]

Moreover, the influence of kin and clan tended to be weakest in the south and Mekong delta regions—where the VC was most active—and stronger in the central and northern parts of South Vietnam, where the NVA was the predominant Communist combatant. Kin influence also tended to be stronger among the middle-class and wealthier families whose land and business ownership made inheritance more consequential and who enjoyed some control over hiring and employment; the NLF tended to be weaker among such populations. And as in many societies, in Vietnam the social influence of descent weakened in general after the 1950s, as shifting patterns of production, land ownership, and settlement tended to segment clan groups and diminish their size and prominence.[14]

On balance, then, South Vietnam in the 1960s was a society in which tribalism did matter, and was more influential than it was in, say, 1990s Croatia. But Vietnamese tribalism was *less* influential than in societies like Shiite southern Lebanon in 2006—and much less influential than in 1990s Somalia, where almost every social transaction of any consequence was shaped by family descent and clan membership.

Military Materiel

Orthodox materialism sees nonstate actors through a dyadic lens—it emphasizes nonstate material inferiority to larger, richer, state enemies, and it expects nonstate actors to resort to Fabian irregular warfare in response. Material variables matter for the new theory, too, but the new theory emphasizes the systemic technological state of the art as much as the dyadic balance of forces, and it treats technology in interaction with internal politics. In particular, it argues that nonstate actors with at least late 20th-century technology will be able to implement midspectrum methods if their internal politics are permissive—but that technological eras prior to the late 20th century preclude survivable midspectrum war fighting regardless of internal politics. In the 1960s, Vietcong materiel was certainly inferior to that of their South Vietnamese and especially American state opponents. But also important was the absolute lethality of that materiel: the VC's 1960s-era weaponry was much less lethal than that of later nonstate actors with access to more sophisticated weapons.

Vietcong forces comprised several different subcomponents of very different makeup. "Main force" VC units deployed full-time soldiers who were often native southerners but had usually been trained in the north and reinfiltrated; these units were better equipped, could conduct battalion- or even regimental-scale operations, served under direct theater command, and could in principle operate anywhere. "Provincial" and "district" units also deployed full-time soldiers but were less well equipped, less likely to have been trained outside the south, were capable only of platoon- or company-level operations, and rarely fought outside their home provinces or districts. "Village militia" were the least capable component, comprising part-time fighters with limited formal training who conducted a restricted range of missions locally in the vicinity of their homes.[15]

The numerical strength of these forces is difficult to establish definitively. Credible US estimates for VC fighters in 1965 usually range from 55,000 to 80,000 main force combatants and 85,000 to 120,000 others, for a total strength of perhaps 140,000 to 200,000. North Vietnamese sources cite higher numbers: their official history reports 92,000 main force VC; 80,000 provincial and district fighters; and 174,000 village militia for the end of the year, or 346,000 total combatants.[16] The nonstate VC combatants were augmented by the state NVA; northern state soldiers fighting in the south numbered perhaps another 58,000 by 1966, of whom around 10 percent served as replacements in VC formations.[17] The Communists disposed these forces with the VC operating chiefly in the southern third of the theater; this implies a force density for the VC of roughly two to six combatants per square kilometer in its primary operating area—or more than three times the Croatian ZNG's in July 1991 and perhaps 50 percent more than the ZNG's at the time of the Vance cease-fire.[18]

The firepower available to the VC, however, was very limited. The heaviest weapons available to most VC main force battalions were 81-millimeter and 82-millimeter mortars. A few other crew-served weapons such as 75-millimeter recoilless rifles, 12.7-millimeter machine guns, and light 107-to-140-millimeter rockets were also available at the main force battalion level. Most units, however, were equipped only with AK-47 and SKS rifles, RPG-7 rocket-propelled grenades, hand grenades, and a variety of improvised mines and booby traps. NVA regulars in the south were somewhat better equipped than the VC in 1965—and by the 1972 Easter Offensive the northern state army were deploying an impressive arsenal including a large fleet of T-55 tanks, a sizeable air force, and heavy artillery; the VC, however, remained lightly armed through the end of the Tet Offensive.[19]

The VC's two state opponents, the ARVN and the United States military, deployed larger and far more heavily equipped forces. The ARVN in 1965 fielded some 245,000 regulars, supported by 256,000 Regional Force and Popular Force militia.[20] US forces were just beginning a buildup that would eventually see a half million troops in South Vietnam; by the end of 1965 about 184,000 of that total had arrived.[21] The ARVN, too, expanded over the course of the war, reaching a strength of 400,000 by 1972 with another 500,000 militia under arms.[22]

These forces were equipped with the full panoply of mid-20th-century military technology, from third-generation jet fighters and nuclear aircraft carriers to 45-ton main battle tanks and armored, self-propelled artillery, to a fleet of more than 450 transport and gunship helicopters.[23] In 1965 alone, US air strikes in Operation Rolling Thunder dropped 33,000 tons of bombs on North Vietnam at a cost of almost $500 million; American forces sustained firepower on a vast scale in Vietnam.[24] ARVN forces were somewhat less lavishly equipped than their American allies but still had access to much heavier weaponry than the Vietcong. ARVN equipment in 1965 included M-24 light tanks and M-113 armored personnel carriers, A-1 Skyraider attack aircraft, and US-operated UH-1 Iroquois helicopters in addition to standard infantry mortars and small arms; later they were upgraded to M-41 and M-48 tanks, F-5 jet fighters, and 105-millimeter tube artillery.[25]

The result was a substantial material asymmetry: theaterwide in 1965, US/ARVN forces outnumbered the VC/NVA by perhaps 2:1 to 3.5:1 in total combatants and around three or four to one in full-time soldiers, with a vast advantage in firepower. Yet this gross asymmetry was probably not radically greater than that faced by the ZNG in Croatia (which was outnumbered 4:1 by the JNA) or Hezbollah in Lebanon (which faced an IDF with at least 15 times their numbers), both of whose state opponents deployed much heavier firepower than they did. The biggest difference between the VC and the ZNG or Hezbollah was instead the absolute, not the relative, scale of firepower available to them. The Vietcong's light weapons were simply unable to project enough firepower to compel their enemies to disperse and seek cover: if confronted by a determined attack, mortar fire and small arms could cause casualties but not halt a concentrated assault. By contrast, the ZNG's captured artillery and guided antitank weapons could in principle have devastated a concentrated JNA offensive launched over open ground; Hezbollah's Kornet and Metis-M precision missiles could (and did) punish massed attacks in the open severely, forcing the IDF to spread out and seek cover. The Vietcong had no similar capability. All three were outnumbered—but only the VC was handicapped by technology that left them potentially exposed to the full mass of a concentrated enemy if they tried to stand their ground.

Internal Politics

The new theory emphasizes two internal political characteristics: actors' stakes in the conflict, and their institutional development. Limited stakes and informal institutions are expected to discourage complex midspectrum methods; existential stakes and formal institutions permit such methods even for non-state actors if their technology is sufficiently advanced.

STAKES

The Vietcong fought for high stakes. By contrast with the Somali SNA's essentially commercial, readily divisible war aims of the pre- and post-Howe era, the Vietcong's aims were indivisible ideological goals of long standing, creating much higher stakes for the VC leadership.

As early as 1946, the Vietcong's Vietminh predecessors had waged war to create an independent Vietnam governed under Communist principles. The First Indochina War had achieved part of that goal: it had expelled the French colonialists and established a Communist government in Hanoi. But the Geneva settlement, which ended the first war, had partitioned the country and left perhaps half of what the Vietminh had regarded as the Vietnamese nation under an inimical Western-allied regime. The Vietcong's primary aim in the Second War was to reunite the country, creating an integral nation state under a Communist government.[26]

This aim was partly partisan in its preference for Communist over democratic free-market governance, and it was partly nationalist in its preference for self-government in a state that unified the ethnic Vietnamese population of Indochina. The relative salience of Communism and nationalism in Vietcong motivation has been debated; for my purposes, however, both motives are ideological as distinct from commercial or economic. And neither Communist nor nationalist goals imply readily divisible war aims: either way, VC purposes could not readily be achieved without the complete overthrow of the Bao Dai/Diem regime and its successors, and the absorption of the southern republic under Hanoi.[27]

These indivisible, ideological aims created a high-stakes conflict. Even without full mobilization, the Americans deployed enough force in Vietnam to pose an existential threat to the Vietcong: it is estimated that the war eventually cost the VC at least 500,000 fatalities, and by as early as 1966 it was clear that US/ARVN military pressure was potentially lethal to much of the VC military and civilian leadership structure.[28] In the late 1950s an anti-Communist crackdown under Diem had threatened the survival of the entire Communist cadre in the south; the combined US/ARVN forces of the post-1965 period posed a far greater peril.[29] And whereas some nonstate actors, such as the Croatian Serbs, felt they could rely on state patrons to bail them out if their own efforts proved insufficient, the VC had much less basis for such expectations in 1965. Their primary state patron, the Hanoi government, was already fully committed to the war and suffering heavily for that commitment: by 1965 the US Rolling Thunder bombing campaign had already dropped approximately 33,000 to 34,000 tons of explosives on North Vietnam and showed few signs of relenting any time soon.[30] The Vietcong would have had little reason to expect that Hanoi would mobilize even greater efforts to compensate for a VC failure to exert itself. Nor could the VC reasonably expect Hanoi's patrons in Beijing or Moscow to provide a safety net: the Chinese and Soviets provided important aid and assistance, but with an American superpower committed on the ground in South Vietnam, neither the Chinese nor the Soviets were willing to risk World War III by sending major ground forces to rescue a Vietcong client whose own efforts fell short and thus faced annihilation. Of course, the VC's ideological commitment to their aims was clear and comparable in its ardor to Hanoi's; there is no reason to suppose that free-riding on Hanoi was ever seriously considered in the south. But their strategic circumstances would have precluded this even if they had wanted it: unlike the Croatian Serbs, reasonable VC decision makers in 1965 would have had every reason to conclude that their fate was tied closely to the scale of their own efforts, and that their downside risk in the event of failure was large.[31] To an important degree, the Vietcong thus faced unlimited liability in the war; steady-state limited-liability coexistence was not a meaningful prospect given their war aims.

VIETCONG INSTITUTIONS

The Vietcong and the NLF were remarkably institutionalized. In the terms used here, they had attained mature natural order status by 1965, with a role-specialized bureaucracy of perpetually lived offices staffed meritocratically, extensive checks and balances, very limited factional infighting, and a limited role for economic rent seeking in governance.

The Vietcong served as the military wing of an NLF civil governing body, which was itself under the direction of a political party, the People's Revolutionary Party (PRP). Each of these institutions comprised a hierarchically organized bureaucracy of subagencies with specialized functions. For the VC, this hierarchy started at the Central Office for South Vietnam (COSVN), a combined politico-military theaterwide headquarters that integrated both VC and NVA operations across the country. The COSVN's Military Affairs Committee (MAC) exercised this control via four successive levels of subordinate commands: the regional, provincial, district, and village "committees" or headquarters. These headquarters controlled combat units organized at levels from 3-man guerilla cells to 12-man squads, 3-to-4-squad platoons, 3-to-4-platoon companies, 3-company battalions, 3-battalion regiments, and 3-regiment divisions. Main force units at battalion level and above controlled their own logistical, signal, reconnaissance, and sapper elements; main force divisions included artillery, medical, and rear services specialists (the typical Vietcong infantry division of 7,000 to 12,000 men had a medical element of up to 800 people).[32]

The NLF and PRP maintained parallel organizations, with "committees" at the regional, provincial, district, and village level that operated under their own vertical chains of command. Through these committees the NLF maintained a fully functioning quasi-state administrative organization, running schools, hospitals, and agricultural advisory teams, overseeing taxation, administering budgets, and managing clothing factories and crude arsenals for the production of rudimentary munitions. It even operated internationally, sending delegates to the Afro-Asian conference, participating in meetings of the World Peace Council and international student organizations, and establishing permanent offices abroad.[33]

The PRP exercised political oversight over both the NLF and especially the VC military. Party elements were colocated with VC military headquarters at each echelon and acted as political commissars to monitor and cross-check commanders to ensure that party policies and directives were followed. These commissars typically outranked their associated military commander, reinforcing the subordination of military to political considerations. Decision making at each level was normally by consensus, however, with collaborative exchange between PRP, VC, and NLF leadership the norm, rather than unilateral imposition of party preference per se. To facilitate cooperation in the face of such systematic oversight, Army officers sat as de jure members of NLF committees at all levels, and cross-assignment was frequent, in which officers were periodically given duties in nominally civilian party or NLF jobs and party commissars were periodically given military command.[34]

The leadership that staffed these organizations was selected and promoted chiefly on the basis of merit. Officers or officials would normally enter at the village or squad level and move up the ranks as their experience, training, and performance indicated. Of course nepotism was not unknown, and promotion beyond the squad level normally required party membership and political orthodoxy. But by contrast with, for example, the Somali SNA or the Croatian Serb SVK, the Vietcong and the NLF were substantially more meritocratic and less personalized. In fact, personnel turnover could be significant, especially where casualties were heavy, and the Vietcong expected new leaders to function as their predecessors had; it was the office that held responsibilities, not just the individual holding it.[35]

Decision making in this system could be contentious, with extensive and sometimes extended debate between advocates of differing policies, and commonplace disagreements between NVA and VC commands over strategy. These disagreements were adjudicated by the pertinent institutions, however, and there was little or no real factionalism of the kind seen in the JAM, the pre- or post-Howe SNA, or the SAOK. No disaffected actors ever left the VC/NLF to found rival organizations, insubordination was rare, and there is no evidence of meaningful internecine violence between armed Communist subgroups. Decisions by the COSVN, once reached, were typically followed by subordinate agencies to the best of their ability.[36]

The result was a system that met all the criteria established above for mature natural order status. It fell short of open-access status as North, Wallis, and Weingast define this for states:[37] real power was limited to Communist Party members; political competition with the party was suppressed; and although there was little overt rent seeking, the economy was nevertheless controlled by the party and the regime in typical Communist fashion. But relative to the JAM, the SNA, or the SAOK, the VC/NLF had a much more stable and systematic institutional infrastructure.

Dependent Variable: Vietcong Military Behavior

The Vietcong displayed very Fabian military methods for most of the period of interest. This was not because they lacked the ability to conduct skilled, disciplined operations; in fact, their proficiency as a fighting organization was remarkably high. But their weapon technology lacked the firepower needed to succeed in midspectrum warfare against numerically superior state foes, and the VC suffered badly when they tried to employ midspectrum methods against skilled state opponents.

Not even the Vietcong, however, fit the Fabian archetype in all its particulars. To adjudicate the admixture of observed VC behaviors I again use the detailed criteria presented in chapter 2 and the appendix, coding the VC's behavior in terms of its stealthiness; its commitment to taking and holding ground; its dispersion; its use of coercion; the distinguishability of combatants from noncombatant civilians; and functional differentiation within the theater of war. This discussion will focus on VC methods prior to the 1968 Tet Offensive. I then treat Tet—an operation with dramatically different methods, and one that cost the Vietcong heavily—separately in a contiguous discussion to help clarify the distinction with what came before.

1. Stealth

Cover and concealment are among the traits most commonly associated with "irregular" Fabian war fighting. VC tactics displayed a systematic emphasis on stealth.

Defensive positions were carefully prepared, with often-extraordinary attention to cover and concealment. Vietcong fighting positions often remained invisible to American attackers at ranges of just a couple of feet; in fact, VC defenders commonly emerged from undetected "spider holes" after the first wave of attackers had already passed through the position, engaging the attackers from behind. Logistics bases and command posts were often protected with elaborate systems of interconnected trenches, dugouts, and underground tunnels, which the VC would use to enable covered movement from location to location; such tunnels were so common, in fact, that US units began to rely on "tunnel rats," or soldiers of slight stature who specialized in dropping into and clearing the dark, winding, often booby-trapped underground networks. In a single search-and-destroy mission in fall 1967, the First Brigade of the US First Infantry Division discovered over 100 VC bunkers, many with overhead cover, 198 prepared fighting positions, 61 foxholes, 96 prone shelters, 27 tunnels, and over 3,600 meters of camouflaged trenches.[38] Sympathetic civilians were relied on to provide warning of hostile forces' approach, enabling fighters to reach such positions before being overtaken; civilian warning networks were augmented with forward observation and listening posts to enable combat units to occupy concealed fighting positions in time. Dummy positions were used to distract American attention from real defenses, and real defense lines were rarely laid out in any predictable or regular geometric pattern. Elaborate as they were, such defensive works would commonly be sacrificed and reconstructed as necessary if attacked by superior allied forces; the Vietcong would prepare positions extensively to enable maximum attrition of the enemy before breaking contact, but they would not allow defensive preparations to pin them to a location and would simply rebuild elsewhere or reoccupy later as needed to maintain concealment.[39]

Vietcong movement techniques were disciplined, carefully planned, and articulated to minimize exposure. Rather than simple unitary columns, VC march formations were typically broken down into multiple elements including advance guards, flank guards, and rear security detachments to reduce the number of fighters subject to detection if encountered unexpectedly by the enemy. Routes were carefully reconnoitered in advance, often in cooperation with local political cadre. Fighters on the move routinely took cover when they heard American aircraft overhead, and movements were planned to ensure ready availability of trailside cover to protect against air attack or aerial observation, often at night.[40]

2. Taking and Holding Ground

Archetypically Fabian forces do not take and hold ground; archetypically Napoleonic ones do. The Vietcong rarely contested terrain against superior state forces.

To assess the VC's relative commitment to taking and holding ground I again use the four observable referents of this commitment presented in the appendix: the duration of firefights; the proximity of attackers to defenders; the incidence of counterattack; and the incidence of harassing fires and unattended minefields.

THE DURATION OF FIREFIGHTS AND THE
PROXIMITY OF ATTACKERS TO DEFENDERS

Archetypically Napoleonic tactics often involve protracted combat wherein defenders accept decisive engagement as attackers close progressively with their positions; by contrast, pure Fabian tactics call for short-duration, hit-and-run ambushes or raids at safe distances without extended, methodical advances under fire. The Vietcong were perhaps the paradigmatic example of the latter.

In fact, VC command guidance instructed local commanders specifically to avoid sustained combat and extended firefights in place. Where possible, engagements were to be limited to durations of as little as 20 minutes or less, and great efforts were to be taken to reconnoiter concealed withdrawal routes to enable VC fighters to break contact safely and melt away after a brief, intense firefight initiated if at all possible by the VC themselves with the benefit of surprise. Engagement ranges could often be very short—in fact, the VC preferred to open actions at point-blank range to maximize shock effect and the lethality of an initial burst of fire; it was not unusual for concealed VC fighters to open fire on advancing Americans from the rear after US troops had passed over their spider holes or tunnel entrances. This was facilitated by the heavily forested terrain of the VC's primary operating area, which offered an atypical availability of close-in ambush positions with concealed withdrawal opportunities. But the VC rarely pressed an advance under fire to close with an enemy they had not surprised at close quarters, and they often broke contact and withdrew before US forces could fix them in place for decisive engagement. The result was a strong preference for ambush over set-piece attacks, a great reluctance to remain in position against superior forces, and a pattern of often very short engagement durations.[41]

On November 21, 1966, for example, fighters from the Vietcong 274th Regiment remained concealed along Route 1 near Ap Hung Nghia until a convoy from the US 11th Armored Cavalry Regiment entered a prepared engagement zone, triggering an ambush. In just eight minutes of intense firing at ranges of 20 meters and less, the VC destroyed two armored personnel carriers and four trucks, killed or wounded 15 American soldiers, then broke contact and withdrew through banana groves and dense jungle when US Air Force F-100s and F-5s appeared and began bombing and strafing runs. An American relief force arrived on the scene just 35 minutes after the ambush was triggered yet met only light resistance in a sweep through the original VC positions because their primary combat elements had already left the battlefield; US mop-up operations continued for another five hours, but the great bulk of the combat activity occurred in a period of less than 10 minutes' duration. The VC withdrew even though the initial firefight had inflicted only moderate damage on the American convoy of more than 80 vehicles and their crews. The 274th could have inflicted considerable additional casualties on the then-stationary US column in continued fighting, but only at the risk of decisive engagement; they broke contact and retired instead.[42]

On the night of December 31, 1967, two platoons of the US Ninth Infantry Division were en route to rendezvous with a convoy in support of Operation Kitty Hawk when they were struck by a Vietcong ambush on Route 2 north of Vung Tau. Shortly after 4:00 a.m., the lead vehicle in the column, a tank, was struck by an RPG that killed its driver and immobilized the vehicle, blocking the road. The entire column was then taken under concentrated fire at point-blank ranges of under 20 meters by concealed assailants hidden along the roadside. After quickly destroying 5 of the column's 11 armored vehicles, damaging 4, and killing or wounding 42 US soldiers, the VC then withdrew unharmed before the Americans could organize a counterattack. The entire engagement lasted less than 10 minutes.[43]

In January 1965 the Vietcong 514th Battalion ambushed an ARVN battalion column on the road between My Long and Ba Dua. The extended ARVN formation was cut in half, with the rear element retreating toward its line of departure while the forward elements were encircled by two companies of Vietcong; the ARVN lead company was destroyed, whereas the VC lost only one dead and five wounded in a firefight of only 45 minutes' duration.[44]

Of course, there are also exceptions. At Rach Ba Rai on September 15, 1967, for example, Vietcong defenders from the 514th Local Force and 263rd Main Force Vietcong battalions resisted all day before retiring after nightfall.[45] During Phase II of Operation Junction City on March 21, 1967, two battalions of the Vietcong 272nd Regiment attacked US Firebase Gold near Suoi Tre. After breaching the firebase perimeter, the VC assault stalled under heavy US ground fire and air strikes by American F-5 fighters; when the assault force tried to break contact and withdraw they were struck in the flank by a counterattack from a US armored column dispatched to support the Firebase defenders. The VC resisted for four hours but were overrun, suffering almost 650 fatalities in the process.[46]

Even in cases such as these, however, the actual exchange of fire was often brief, concentrated, and intermittent: at Rach Ba Rai, for example, the initial ambush lasted just 20 minutes before US elements broke contact and regrouped; much of the battle was a series of such sharp, brief, local engagements.[47] Where actual firefights persisted over more than brief intervals, it was often either because the Vietcong had atypically become trapped and pinned down without viable escape routes, or because critical VC infrastructure was under threat in ways that made its simple abandonment impossible, or because VC commanders felt they had trapped isolated US or ARVN small units under conditions so favorable that the VC expected to be able to annihilate them altogether if they pressed the fight.[48] Such cases were the exception rather than the norm, however. In general, engagements with the Vietcong could be very intense but were unusually brief.[49]

INCIDENCE OF COUNTERATTACK

Counterattack to regain lost ground is associated with Napoleonic defenders; pure Fabians neither hold ground nor counterattack to regain it. The Vietcong occasionally counterattacked, but typically as a way to enable heavily engaged units to break contact and withdraw—rarely did VC counterattacks retain seized ground, and counterattacks for any purpose were relatively infrequent.[50]

THE INCIDENCE OF HARASSING FIRES AND UNATTENDED MINEFIELDS

Another indicator of actors' relative emphasis on holding ground is the incidence of harassing fires and unattended minefields. These are particularly suited to pure Fabians, who seek to inflict attrition per se rather than to control ground. The Vietcong made heavy use of both and were especially reliant on unattended booby traps and minefields.

Many US installations were regularly rocketed by Vietcong gunners using simple unguided 122-millimeter rockets fired from isolated launch rails in concealed locations. Such attacks were typically sporadic, enabling the small teams of gunners to flee before the Americans could locate their firing positions for counterfire. As such they had no ability to destroy a large US facility or cause heavy casualties in any one barrage; instead, they were meant to inflict attrition over time and to disrupt operations on the targeted base.[51]

The Vietcong also used a wide variety of landmines. Soviet and Chinese patrons provided larger antitank and dual-purpose antitank/antipersonnel mines, while the Vietcong themselves produced simpler antipersonnel mines in small village workshops.[52] The VC also made very heavy use of captured or salvaged US mines; in fact, the chief of staff of the US First Marine Division estimated in 1967 that some 90 percent of all Vietcong mine components were of US origin.[53] The salvage operations that provided this captured materiel were so effective that some allied troops became reluctant to lay mines themselves for fear that VC sappers would remove so many of them and turn them to use against their former owners: in one particularly infamous incident, the VC lifted 10,000 of the 30,000 M-16 antipersonnel mines laid in an Australian minefield in Phuoc Tuy Province and then used them against the Australians before the latter cleared their own minefield to avoid further pilferage.[54]

Plentiful as manufactured mines could be, the VC made even more extensive use of field-expedient booby traps created by the fighters in the field from often ad hoc combinations of available materials, discarded ordnance, and camouflage of various types. These ranged from "toe-poppers" made of spent cartridge cases filled with black powder, fragments, and a simple fuze; to hand grenades attached to trip wires and covered with forest litter; to punji sticks (sharpened bamboo spikes hidden upright in pits and covered with brush to impale soldiers who fell through the brush covering); to explosives wired to left-behind property of ostensible intelligence value such as maps and records or hidden in corpses.[55]

The scale of VC minelaying was enormous. In fact, mines and booby traps were the largest single cause of US casualties in the war, accounting for fully one-third of all fatalities and serious wounds. Several divisions reported over 50 percent of all losses were due to mines and booby traps.[56]

Sometimes these minefields were overwatched by VC fighters, usually as part of an ambush. Often, however, mines and booby traps were left, unattended, across trails known to be used by US troops or in areas where US forces were expected to operate. In fact, many booby traps were set up in areas deliberately abandoned by the Vietcong, with the expectation that the traps would kill or injure Americans securing the area or inspecting vacated positions for intelligence leads.[57] Used thus, they had little ability to bring an American advance to a halt; their purpose was to inflict casualties per se and progressively erode American morale.[58]

3. Dispersion

Fabian methods mandate dispersed postures that produce low, relatively uniform troop densities with minimal massing at critical points. The Vietcong were more uniformly disposed than were, for example, the Croatian ZNG or SVK in 1991, or Hezbollah in 2006. But even the Vietcong did not conduct a literally uniform area defense: they concentrated fighters locally when necessary to attack US forces or when Americans struck particularly important VC supply or command infrastructure.

VC dispositions certainly did not conform to a Napoleonic linear frontier in contact with the enemy, and the Vietcong did not conduct concentrated breakthrough operations of the kind one might expect on an interstate battle-field. District and village Vietcong, especially, were disposed among the people where the people lived, whether those villages were in immediate proximity to US or ARVN forces or not. This produced a more uniform spatial distribution than is common in interstate warfare.

That said, Vietcong deployments were never literally uniform over their operating area in South Vietnam. As noted above, VC troop density averaged perhaps 2 to 6 fighters per square kilometer across the theater as a whole. But local troop densities in prepared base camp areas were typically closer to 10 or 15 fighters per square kilometer.[59] And at the point of attack in the Vietcong's occasional pre-Tet assaults on US or ARVN firebases and perimeters, the local VC troop density could reach 60 or more. At the Battle of Suoi Tre on March 21, 1967, for example, two main force Vietcong battalions from the 272nd Regiment massed to a local density of more than 60 troops per square kilometer in their assault on Firebase Gold; at the Battle of Ap Bau Bang the previous day, the VC 273rd Regiment concentrated more than 75 fighters per square kilometer in their attack on Fire Support Base 14.[60] Such local massing was brief and unusual—and the units involved often suffered heavily for such choices: at Firebase Gold, VC casualties probably exceeded 50 percent of the committed assault force.[61] But even the Vietcong did not conduct a uniformly distributed area defense.[62]

4. The Balance of Brute Force and Coercion

Pure Fabian warfare avoids brute force battles of annihilation and relies on gradual attrition to coerce an enemy by imposing costs that exceed their stakes. Vietcong strategy in the Second Indochina War was centrally coercive in nature.

Communist strategy for the war was a subject of intense debate in Hanoi. "North Firsters" under Ho Chi Minh and General Vo Nguyen Giap argued for a slower-paced campaign in South Vietnam to enable faster economic development in the north; a more powerful north would then be in a stronger position to compel unification. "South Firsters" under Communist Party chief Le Duan and General Nguyen Chi Thanh argued for a faster campaign in the south to catalyze a general uprising that would topple a weak regime in Saigon without requiring economic development of the north as a prerequisite. Though US intervention posed an important setback for Duan and Thanh by backstopping Saigon and precluding a quick collapse, debate continued, and Duan and Thanh ultimately prevailed, instituting a policy that eventually produced the Tet Offensive in 1968.[63]

Both sides in this strategy debate, however, were advocating coercive strategies. Neither Ho and Giap nor Duan and Thanh had any expectation of destroying the American military and the ARVN and seizing Saigon and the south by brute force in 1968. By the early 1970s, following US withdrawal from the conflict, northern strategy began to contemplate seriously a shift to Mao's "third phase" of conventional warfare. But the entire debate in the years before Tet revolved around different approaches to coercive action—one that sought faster coercion, and another approach that was more patient. The vast majority of Vietcong violence throughout this period, moreover, was inflicted on civilian, not brute force military, targets: Guenter Lewy estimates that 80 percent of VC violence was directed at noncombatant civilians.[64] Throughout the period of study, the Vietcong engaged in a systematic program of political assassination and intimidation, aimed at coercion of civilians and government officials alike. While VC attacks on US and ARVN positions were certainly designed to overwhelm and destroy isolated garrisons if possible, under normal circumstances expectations were that these would inflict casualties and weaken the opponents' resolve, not annihilate opposing positions outright.[65] Even Tet itself was designed to catalyze an uprising that would render the Thieu government's political position untenable and persuade them to cede power; neither Duan nor Thanh expected Tet to annihilate the opposing military or push them into the sea so terms could be dictated.[66]

5. Distinguishability of Combatants and Civilians

Combatant intermingling with civilians, use of civilian clothing, and avoidance of heavy weapons are closely associated with Fabian methods. The Vietcong certainly used the forests of the Mekong delta for natural cover, especially when preparing ambushes. And their main force units wore military uniforms. But most VC combatants wore civilian clothing and often operated in close proximity to civilians in rural village environments where it was often impossible to distinguish them from noncombatants.

After 1965, main force VC fighters adopted essentially the same khaki-and-green uniforms and personal equipment worn by NVA state soldiers. Other Vietcong, however, wore the loose-fitting, often-black pants and jackets favored by rural villagers, together with sandals and the conical hat commonly seen on peasant farmers in the fields. Neither main force nor other VC wore rank insignia, and clothing other than main force was essentially indistinguishable from that of the civilians among whom they lived and fought.[67]

Proximity to civilians was among the basic principles of Vietcong tactics. Following Mao, VC fighters sought to be fish among the sea of the people and systematically intermingled with village populations in ways that made it difficult to avoid collateral damage to civilian targets when firing on VC combat positions. Sympathetic civilians were also recruited to provide intelligence and support for VC fighters in combat, blurring the line between combatant and noncombatant personnel even when individuals were isolated in custody.[68] In fact, the psychological stress of being unable to distinguish the enemy from innocent civilians was one of the defining characteristics of the Vietnam experience for many US combatants and is one of the most discussed of the war's features in its historiography.[69]

6. The Military Organization of the Theater of War

Fabian nonstate warfare lacks clear distinctions between front and rear, or forward and reserve, or logistical and combat zones. In this the VC were notably Fabian. This is not to say that there was no meaningful theater design or geographic articulation of forces in South Vietnam: the northern part of the country was generally allocated to the NVA and the south to the VC; supply bases and headquarters were in areas expected to be relatively secure; the Ho Chi Minh Trail in Cambodia and Laos was hardly randomly located or positioned. But VC dispositions in the Mekong delta did not concentrate forces on a front line that separated a quiet rear area from a linear frontier in contact with the enemy. Rather than as an orthodox front line trace, the war in South Vietnam was characterized as a shifting patchwork of noncontiguous zones controlled by one side or the other and large areas of contested control where neither side could deny the other freedom of movement. In fact, Stathis Kalyvas and Matthew Kocher have calculated that of the districts covered by the US Hamlet Evaluation System from July to December 1969, less than 22 percent were clearly controlled by either the government or the VC; the rest were in various stages of contestation in which neither side could be denied access.[70]

Together with the difficulty of distinguishing fighters from noncombatants, this absence of an apparent front and rear is one of the most commonly noted features of the war in the Vietnam historiography.[71]

The Tet Offensive

This pattern of highly Fabian war fighting was starkly reversed in the 1968 Tet Offensive. In Tet, the VC and NVA sought to take and hold a series of critical territorial objectives—and especially a series of provincial capitals—as a means of inspiring a general uprising that would topple the Thieu regime. The result was a systematic reversal of the methods employed in the previous three years of warfare.

In place of brief raids and ambushes designed to avoid decisive engagement, the VC and their NVA allies now laid siege to the Marine base at Khe Sanh and maintained their positions under heavy US air and ground attack for more than six months. The VC and NVA took Hue City by storm, and rather than melting away afterward they instead dug in and sought to hold the city against a sustained monthlong counterattack that eventually overran their defenses. They waged a 14-day battle for the provincial capital of Kontum. The VC and NVA launched a concerted attack on a variety of objectives within Saigon itself, maintaining offensive pressure for more than a month. In the process, VC/NVA attackers sustained advances over considerable distances in the course of wresting control over urban areas in Hue and elsewhere.[72]

To regain lost ground, the VC and the NVA launched local counterattacks in Hue and Saigon. They concentrated forces against territorial objectives in an attempt to create local numerical advantages: against Hue they massed a division-size force of 10 battalions; against Khe Sanh they deployed over two divisions and 20,000 troops with 2 battalions of light tanks and more than 3 battalions of tube and rocket artillery; for their Saigon assault they concentrated 35 battalions from three different divisions. And many of these actions were conducted against cities whose populations were aligned with the government: while there were sympathizers, fifth columnists, and sleeper cells in many major southern cities, the Vietcong's political base was in outlying rural districts, not large urban areas.[73]

This shift from highly Fabian methods to a much more Napoleonic offensive cost the Vietcong dearly. Their ability to concentrate locally, combined with a degree of tactical surprise (especially against less alert ARVN defenses), enabled them to seize some of their initial objectives. But their lack of heavy artillery or other mass suppressive firepower made these initial assaults very expensive for the VC light infantry that typically led these attacks. And neither the VC nor the NVA had the kind of long-range precision firepower needed to compel their much better equipped state enemies to disperse in self-defense when those enemies counterattacked to retake the ground they had lost. The United States and its ARVN allies were thus able to counterconcentrate overwhelming force against overextended VC/NVA positions that were now pinned to relatively static positional defenses of terrain. The United States and ARVN eventually cleared Hue with a massed force of more than eight battalions; the siege of Khe Sanh was broken by a relief force of over 6,000 troops operating on a frontage of less than seven kilometers, combined with an air campaign of more than 24,000 sorties; the United States and the ARVN eventually committed fully 24 battalions to the battle in Saigon.[74]

The result of such massed conventional counteroffensives was not just that the VC and NVA were driven from the ground they tried to hold—their forces were decimated in the process. VC/NVA casualty figures are notoriously unreliable, but some estimates suggest that by the time Tet ended in September their fatalities may have made up fully half of the entire force they committed to the offensive, let alone the additional toll in wounded or missing fighters.[75] Losses on this scale are unsustainable for any military, state or nonstate. And in fact, Tet essentially destroyed the Vietcong as a fighting force. Wrecked VC main force regiments were nominally restored afterward, but only by replacing losses with NVA regulars from the north.[76] And the VC attempted no further major combat action in the war—the later offensives that toppled the Saigon government following the US withdrawal were conducted by the NVA, not the Vietcong.[77] For all intents and purposes, the VC's massive losses in a conventional offensive in Tet destroyed them as a nonstate actor.

Vietcong Proficiency of Execution and the Role of Technology, 1965–68

As before, proficiency of execution offers an opportunity for process tracing, given the salience of skill and complexity in the new theory's causal mechanism. The Vietcong case also offers an important opportunity to explore the role of technology for that mechanism: the new theory holds that without the lethality of modern weapon technology, even institutionally mature actors with the stakes needed to master complex midspectrum methods will be

unable to prevent massed state opponents from overwhelming them numerically and will be compelled to default to more-Fabian methods as a result. In
fact, the Vietcong were highly proficient combatants capable of unusually
complex operations. Of course, they were not perfect—like many state militaries, they often found it difficult to coordinate large-unit operations involving
multiple formations maneuvering over large areas in difficult terrain. But their
skills were not the chief constraint on their ability to conduct effective midconcealment warfare—their technology was.

Vietcong tactics prior to Tet were high concealment but not low complexity. A typical VC ambush, for example, could consist of as many as five separate, interdependent components: a network of observation posts, a command
post, a forward blocking detachment, an assault force, and a rearward blocking
element. Each had a different mission, each was located separately in noncontiguous positions, and each element's role could change on the fly in the course
of the engagement as a function of unfolding events. If the lead element halted
the enemy column, the assault force would engage while the rear element maneuvered to block enemy reinforcements and prevent the column from escap-
ing. If the entire enemy column was caught in the engagement area simultaneously, however, the rear element would assault directly into the engagement
area from behind the column. If enemy forces were too strong to be destroyed
in the engagement area, one element would be designated as a rear guard to
protect the withdrawal of the others while the remainder of the ambush force
retired via predesignated exfiltration routes. This degree of coordination
greatly enhanced the lethality of each element. But each element required the
others; if any one failed in its mission, all would be threatened, and if any element failed to react promptly to changing orders in a fluid situation all could
be cut off and destroyed in detail. A typical VC ambush involved high levels
of interdependence among subunits with specialized functions.[78]

Planning for VC ambushes was often very extensive. Intelligence on the
target unit could be compiled for weeks in advance of the action, integrating
leaks from allied soldiers, reports from covert agents within the ARVN, and
intercepts of US or ARVN radio traffic. VC reconnaissance elements would
often monitor target units or outposts for weeks to determine the enemy's
patrol patterns and habits, times when guard shifts changed, troop strength,
weapon and vehicle availability, or other operational details. Ambush trigger
points were carefully scouted and often prepared with command-detonated
mines or obstacles. Concealed exfiltration routes were typically reconnoitered
in advance, carefully mapped, and prepared in advance with foxholes, bunkers,

or supply caches along their course for protection against US air strikes or ad hoc local defense if overtaken during retirement.[79]

Sapper raids on US and ARVN bases were likewise carefully prepared and conducted. As with ambushes, raids typically involved multiple independently operating elements, in this case including an assault force to breach the allied perimeter, indirect fire support elements with light and medium mortars, a blocking team to interdict reinforcements, and sometimes a reserve. Reconnaissance and planning were similar to that for ambushes, and similarly extensive. Preassault rehearsals were customary and often involved sand-table mockups of the defenses to be attacked. Logistical planning received as much attention as operations planning, and stocks of food, water, and ammunition would be cached forward near the intended battle area; VC commanders referred to this practice as "feathering the nest in advance"; US officers likened it to a logistical "nose" in contrast to the typical Western logistical "tail." When the attackers disengaged, rear guard elements would remain in contact to screen a staged withdrawal of the main body subunit by subunit.[80]

Taken together, this suggests an organization that carried out its tactics with considerable proficiency and was capable of sophisticated, complex operations. Prior to Tet, the Vietcong did not choose to employ these skills in mid-spectrum conventional warfare. But this does not mean they lacked the expertise to do so. What they lacked was the technology: they lacked the firepower needed to prevent massed US forces from overwhelming them if the VC accepted decisive engagement and tried to contest ground.

From 1965 to 1968, US ground offensives routinely massed forces in concentrations that the Vietcong simply lacked the resources to counter. In so-called search-and-destroy missions as in Operations Attleboro, Cedar Falls, or Junction City, the US Army concentrated division-sized assault forces against particular fronts while maintaining sufficient forces elsewhere in the theater to defend US and ARVN base structures and urban centers. In Operation Attleboro, for example, the United States swept through a corridor about five kilometers wide with roughly a division of infantry and armor supported lavishly with artillery and airpower.[81] In Operation Cedar Falls, an assault force of two US divisions swept through the roughly 40-square-kilometer "Iron Triangle" northwest of Saigon; in Operation Junction City, more than two divisions of infantry again swept a corridor less than 30 kilometers wide.[82] The VC's ability to counter these local concentrations by moving reserves from elsewhere in the theater was constrained partly by their limited mobility—whereas the United States could exploit air mobility via helicopter to move large forces rapidly over dense forest, the VC was limited to foot mobility in country that made rapid ground movement difficult. But even if the VC had had American-style air mobility, they simply lacked the needed theaterwide troop strength to match such local preponderance without leaving themselves too vulnerable elsewhere. While the numerical strength of the VC and NVA between 1965 and 1968 is hard to establish with precision, it is likely that the United States and the ARVN enjoyed a raw numerical superiority of perhaps 2:1 to 3.5:1 in total combatants and around three or four to one in full-time soldiers, with a vast advantage in firepower. Even if the VC had enjoyed mobility comparable to that of the Americans, their raw numerical inferiority would have made it very difficult to prevent allied forces from concentrating differentially to produce crushing local advantages at chosen points. To survive and hold ground under such conditions requires an ability to punish high-density troop concentrations with precision firepower, compelling enemies to disperse and capping a superior opponent's usable local preponderance—but the VC lacked this capacity. Instead, the concentrated attackers in Attleboro, Cedar Falls, or Junction City simply steamrollered any opposition that failed to get out of the way in time. If the VC had tried to resist such offensives with Napoleonic positional defenses they would simply have been destroyed.

Indeed this is essentially what happened when the VC did attempt a more Napoleonic military style in the Tet Offensive. With the advantage of surprise they managed to manufacture local numerical advantages at key points and were thus able to take initial objectives in some places. But when their state enemies responded by counterconcentrating conventional forces to regain the lost ground, VC and even NVA defenders who tried to hold that ground were simply crushed. This process took longer in some places than in others, but in no case were the VC or the NVA able to retain any of the objectives they took in the offensive's initial phases. The results were politically powerful owing to their effects on American public opinion, but the military losses they suffered in the process essentially destroyed the Vietcong as a combatant force.

The Vietcong had the institutional and political wherewithal to master the complexity of midspectrum methods—but they lacked the sheer material mass of a state military, and without modern technology to make state enemies spread out they simply could not survive the more Napoleonic fight that they tried to wage in 1968. As the new theory implies, the Vietcong case shows that permissive internal politics and modern technology are *both* important prerequisites for effective midspectrum warfare.

Theoretical Implications

Given the codings above, what do the respective theories predict for Vietcong military behavior? Tribal culture theory would expect a fairly conventional style for the VC—while the family was an important social unit in midcentury South Vietnam, the role of tribalist familism was substantially less prominent than in the southern Lebanese culture that produced Hezbollah, and far less prominent than the Somali culture that produced Aideed's SNA. Hence an explanation of military methods based on tribal culture would expect the Vietcong to be far more conventional than the SNA, and at least as conventional as Hezbollah.

Both materialism and the new theory presented here, by contrast, would expect irregular methods for the Vietcong, albeit for somewhat different reasons. Orthodox materialism emphasizes the relative, dyadic balance of firepower between the VC and its US/ARVN foes; the new theory emphasizes the limited absolute lethality of midcentury technology as a systemic, rather than dyadic, variable.

In fact, the pre-Tet Vietcong displayed the most Fabian methods of the five nonstate actors studied here. On the six-point Fabian-Napoleonic spectrum presented in chapter 2 and the appendix, the Vietcong score a value of 0.2—substantially more Fabian than even Mohammed Farah Aideed's Somali National Alliance.[83] Even the Vietcong do not represent a true, pure Fabian extremum, and of course they departed radically from this archetype in Tet. But they represent an unusually Fabian actor all the same.

Is this relative Fabianism attributable to the dyadic imbalance of firepower in Vietnam, as orthodox materialism would suggest, or to the VC's monadic lack of modern weaponry, as the new theory claims? Both are relevant, but the analysis above highlights the problem of inadequate midcentury weapon technology in particular. Other, more recent nonstate armies have faced dyadic imbalances as great or greater than that in Vietnam yet have employed far less Fabian methods without suffering annihilation: Hezbollah in 2006 and the Croatian ZNG in 1991 both faced state enemies whose dyadic material superiority was at least comparable to that enjoyed by US forces in Vietnam. Yet Hezbollah and the ZNG adopted midspectrum methods without suffering the fate of Vietcong attackers in the Tet Offensive, and with much greater stopping power than Vietcong defenders could muster against Operations Attleboro, Cedar Falls, and Junction City. With modern high-firepower weapons at their disposal, Hezbollah and the ZNG could make massed state offensives prohibitively costly to their state foes; when the latter spread out in response, nonstate armies with smaller forces in the theater as a whole found they could deploy forces at the front large enough to compete with state armies for the control of ground. The Vietcong had the skills to do so, too. What they lacked was the technology, as the new theory claims.

10

Conclusion and Implications

FOR GENERATIONS, most analysts have expected state and nonstate actors to fight very differently. States fighting other states have been expected to wage high-intensity "conventional" warfare wherein large, uniformed, heavily armed formations would maneuver in the open on mostly rural battlefields away from large civilian populations, using massed firepower to destroy one another as a means to take and hold ground. Nonstate actors have been expected to intermingle indistinguishably with civilians, using roadside bombs, snipers, ambushes, assassinations, and suicide vests to coerce state rivals rather than taking and holding ground or seeking decisive battle. More recently, some analysts have posited a new "hybrid warfare" model, wherein nonstate actors add precision weapons and information warfare to irregular battlefield tactics. These expectations have usually derived from assumptions about nonstate material inferiority or tribal culture; some now see new technology as the underpinning of nonstate hybrid war fighting.

I have argued, however, that there are no conceptually important military distinctions of kind between state and nonstate actors as combatants, or between conventional, hybrid, and irregular war fighting as methods. All combatants must respond to a common set of incentives created ultimately by the nature of weapon technology. And since at least 1900, all sound war-fighting systems, whoever adopts them, have had to blend features commonly associated with both "conventional" *and* "irregular" warfare—the very categories themselves are artificial heuristics that appear in their pure form only as rare extrema on a continuous spectrum in which almost all real actors occupy points somewhere in the middle. This does not mean the resulting differences of degree are unimportant—in fact they have major policy implications, to which I return below. But the range of typical variance is narrower, the differences that matter are subtler, and the underlying similarities are more important than commonly supposed. To treat state and nonstate actors—or conventional, irregular, and hybrid methods—as categorical distinctions of kind is an oversimplification with potentially serious consequences for policy and scholarship.

The causes of this subtler variance are also different. Although materiel, in particular, does matter, I have argued that nonstate actors' internal politics play a far more important role than typically recognized, and that nonstate war fighting cannot be properly understood without a systematic treatment of how materiel (and especially technology) interacts with institutions and stakes.

The importance of institutions and stakes in this political theory of nonstate war fighting arises from the military demands of surviving modern firepower. All warfare poses a trade-off between lethality and concealment; the most effective resolution of this tension requires militaries to role specialize internally and rely on complex cooperation among the resulting interdependent specialists. Yet this specialization heightens collective action challenges that are inherent in all warfare: how does one fighter know that others on whom he or she depends will risk their lives on his or her behalf rather than fleeing instead? The greater a military's reliance on interdependent specialists, the greater the risk if collective action fails. The result is a central role for the traits that shape cooperation in the presence of collective action dilemmas—and, especially, an actor's institutional structure and stakes.

In particular, nonstate actors with mature institutions and existential stakes can master the complexity of interdependent midspectrum warfare. If their weapon technology can compel numerically preponderant enemies to disperse, then nonstate actors with mature institutions and existential stakes can exploit midspectrum war fighting and have strong incentives to do so. By contrast, nonstate actors with weak institutions and limited stakes face major barriers to internal cooperation that often prevent them from mastering interdependent military complexity regardless of their equipment; their best choices given the political constraints they face resemble the more Fabian "irregular" warfare often associated with guerillas.[1]

Nonstate actors vary widely along these dimensions. Some, such as Hezbollah, the Croatian ZNG, or the Sri Lankan LTTE, have had elaborate, mature institutions that rival those of many states. Others, such as Mohammed Farah Aideed's SNA in Somalia, the Jaish al Mahdi in Iraq, or the RUF in Sierra Leone, have been ruled by loose coalitions of armed elites whose wary personal interactions shape decisions. Stakes are similarly variable. In 2006, Hezbollah's existence turned on its narrative of existential zero-sum conflict with

Israel; in 1991 the Croatian separatist leadership faced death or imprisonment if their military failed. UNITA in the Angolan civil war, by contrast, fought for years over limited economic stakes with little fear of government conquest; prior to US intervention, Aideed's SNA was similarly waging a limited war for limited economic aims.

This variance in internal politics implies important variance in nonstate actors' likely ability to use modern weapons to their full potential. As technology proliferates, some will be able to exploit new weapons to wage state-like midspectrum warfare—but others, faced with the same technological opportunities, will not. And for any given actor, this means that the best way to anticipate their methods is not to focus on their technology alone; this does matter, but only in interaction with their internal politics. Without a sound analysis of their institutional structure and stakes, intelligence reporting on their technology alone is a very poor predictor of actors' military behavior.

I assess this theory in a series of case studies of nonstate warfare conducted under conditions of special importance for the theory's validity: Hezbollah in the 2006 Lebanon campaign; the Jaish al Mahdi (JAM) in Operation Iraqi Freedom from 2003 to 2008; Mohammed Farah Aideed's Habr Gedir militia in Somalia from 1992 to 1994; the Croatian nationalist ZNG and Croatian Serb SVK in the Croatian Wars of Independence of 1991–95; and the Vietcong in the American phase of the Second Indochina War from 1965 to 1968. The results are summarized in table 10.1.[2]

As table 10.1 indicates, although no theory offers a perfect correlation between prediction and observation, the new theory outperforms materialist and tribal culture views under conditions that might have been expected to provide easy confirmations for these other views if sound. The most significant predictive failure for the new theory involves the Croatian Serb SVK, whose combination of fragile natural order institutions and low stakes suggests very Fabian behavior as its best choice. Yet the SVK actually chose midspectrum methods. The new theory predicts otherwise because it assumes that actors will adopt the methods best suited to their actual ability to perform militarily. As the SVK's military performance in 1995 demonstrates, this would indeed have been a far more Fabian approach than they adopted. When the SVK attempted midspectrum methods ill suited to their institutions and stakes, the result was disaster: annihilation in a brief, five-day campaign in Operation Storm. Though the new theory gets the prediction wrong, it thus gets the underlying military logic right.

TABLE 10.1. Case Study Results

	Independent Variable Values			Theoretical Predictions			
	Materiel	Tribal Culture	Internal Politics	Orthodox Materialist	Tribalist	New Theory	Observed Outcome
Lebanese Hezbollah, 2006	21st c., inferior to IDF foe	Tribal	Mature natural order, high stakes	Fabian	Fabian	Midspectrum	Midspectrum
Iraqi JAM, 2003–8	21st c., inferior to US foe	Less tribal than Hezbollah	Fragile natural order, low stakes	Fabian, similar to Hezbollah	Less Fabian than Hezbollah	Much more Fabian than Hezbollah	Much more Fabian than Hezbollah
Somali SNA, 1992–94	Late 20th c., initial parity, later inferiority	Tribal	Informal institutions; low stakes initially, higher later	Increasingly Fabian over time	Fabian extremum	Less Fabian over time, nonextremum	Less Fabian over time, nonextremum
Croatian ZNG and SVK, 1991–95	Late 20th c., inferior to state foes	Nontribal	ZNG: basic natural order, high stakes SVK: fragile natural order, low stakes	Fabian	Midspectrum	ZNG: nearly midspectrum SVK: very Fabian optimum, catastrophe if midspectrum	ZNG: midspectrum SVK: midspectrum, with catastrophic results
Vietnamese Vietcong, 1965–68	Mid-20th c., inferior to state foes	Nontribal	Mature natural order, high stakes	Fabian	Midspectrum	More Fabian than Hezbollah	More Fabian than Hezbollah

By contrast, an orthodox materialist account that frames nonstate methods as a chiefly Fabian response to material inferiority would fail to explain Hezbollah in 2006, the Croatian ZNG in 1991, or the Croatian SVK in 1995, each of whom used far less Fabian methods than their material inferiority would suggest. Orthodox materialism would also have difficulty with the Somali National Alliance between 1992 and 1994: the SNA's material circumstances declined dramatically when the United States intervened in 1993, yet the SNA's behavior became less, not more, Fabian as a result. A tribal culture account that frames nonstate methods as a Fabian response to tribalism would fail to explain Hezbollah in 2006 (a midspectrum military force drawn from a tribal culture) or the Vietcong from 1965 to 1972 (a highly Fabian military force drawn from a nontribal culture). A tribalist account would also have difficulty with the Iraqi JAM, which was drawn from a less tribal urban culture than Hezbollah's mostly rural population in South Lebanon, yet whose methods were much more Fabian than Hezbollah's. And a tribalist account would even have difficulty with the Somali National Alliance: Somali culture in the 1990s was as tribal as any in the modern world, yet even the SNA's military methods failed to meet the orthodox description of irregular "guerilla" methods in important ways.

In fact, none of these cases' outcomes display paradigmatically "irregular" methods at the pure, Fabian extreme—not even the SNA fits this description well. But neither do any of these cases present some kind of canonically "conventional" Battle of Waterloo in which a linear defense is rigidly defended to the death by massed formations of exposed soldiers. All fall well to the middle of the spectrum, and all display elements commonly associated with both "conventional" and "irregular" war fighting. None fits neatly into any of the categories commonly used to discuss nonstate military methods. Nor does the variance actually observed correlate well with either tribal culture or military materiel as prospective causes; differences in institutions and stakes in interaction with technology are more closely related to the observed variance in warfighting style—as the new theory would expect, but the alternative views would not.

Of course, superior performance in a small sample of cases does not establish a theory's validity, especially for a theory specified on a continuum. But it should shift our confidence in the relative strength of the competing views. And it does suggest a degree of initial plausibility sufficient to warrant considering the new theory's implications for policy and scholarship.

Implications for Policy: Future Opponents' Military Methods

This new theory has very different policy implications than those that are suggested by the alternative views. It implies, for example, faster change in military methods for many actors than tribal culture theorists would expect, but it does not predict the scale of convergence that many fourth-generation or hybrid warfare theorists anticipate. Technology is spreading rapidly, but actors' internal politics vary and will continue to do so. Because politics are an important constraint on actors' military methods, this means that war-fighting methods are unlikely to converge as fast as technology does, and that technology will be a weak predictor of nonstate actors' behavior. Nonstate combatants with permissive internal politics will be able to exploit modern weapons to wage increasingly state-like midspectrum warfare as their technology grows more lethal—but others will not, regardless of how modern or lethal their equipment becomes. The net result is thus likely to be increased variance, as some nonstate actors' war fighting comes increasingly to resemble that of states, but others retain older, more Fabian styles even as they acquire modern weapons. And where change can be expected, this is not toward any new or alien method of war—what 21st-century technological change is actually doing is changing the distribution of actors across preexisting methods.

This argument is illustrated graphically in figure 10.1, which depicts the theory's implied frequencies for different styles of warfare and how these are changing over time. (Available data sets do not enable observed values for these frequencies, hence the figure depicts the theory's ex ante predictions for unobserved values, rather than an ex post presentation of observational data.) Per the theory presented here, the figure characterizes war-fighting methods in terms of their respective positions on the Fabian-Napoleonic spectrum presented in chapter 2. The figure presents the expected frequency of each style for a given class of actor in a given historical era. Expected frequency distributions are presented for five historical classes of actor: states in the mid-20th century; states in the early 21st century; nonstate actors in the mid-20th century; nonstate actors in the early 21st century; and an aggregate distribution over all actors in the early 21st century that represents the sum of the state and nonstate predictions for each point on the war-fighting choice spectrum.[3]

In this view, state and nonstate warfare tended to be very different in the mid-20th century; while individual actors varied from one another even

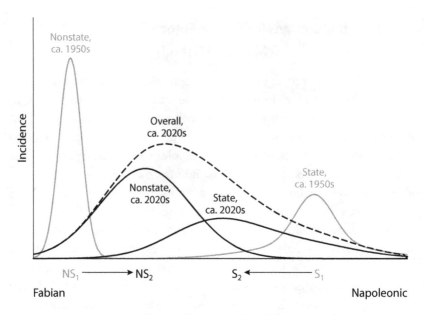

FIGURE 10.1. Expected frequency of war-fighting methods

within these categories, the difference in the two categories' modal methods was large relative to the difference between actors within each category. By the early 21st century, however, technological change has both increased the spread in behavior within each category and moved the modal choices closer together.

This is because the increasing firepower of advanced technology gives all actors incentives to move toward the middle of the war-fighting spectrum— but persistent variation in internal politics will allow only some to act on that incentive. Midcentury technology permitted states to concentrate forces at levels that smaller nonstate actors could not counter; a midcentury nonstate actor who tried to take and hold ground against a state opponent would typically have been crushed by weight of numbers. States fighting other states, moreover, required an important degree of exposure to concentrate sufficient forces to cope with peer rivals. States could thus operate in relatively more exposed, concentrated formations toward the right-hand, Napoleonic side of the spectrum depicted (S_1), but nonstate actors were compelled to disperse and conceal their forces more thoroughly, resorting to more-Fabian methods closer to the left-hand side of the scale (NS_1). Because states and nonstate actors all vary in their internal politics there was thus always variance within categories (this is clearly true for nonstate actors but is probably true for states as well to at least some degree),[4] but the within-category variance induced by political variation among nonstate actors was small relative to the across-category variance induced by the large difference in material endowments between states and nonstate actors as classes.

By the early 21st century, however, increasing firepower had made midcentury states' degree of relative concentration less tenable. Such postures were now suicidal in the face of even small numbers of highly lethal precision weapons, compelling even large state armies to disperse more aggressively in search of adequate concealment (S_2). This in turn gave some nonstate actors an opportunity to contest ground against increasingly dispersed state militaries who can no longer bring their full numerical advantages to bear: technological change thus gives some nonstate forces an incentive to move rightward on figure 10.1 and adopt more state-like methods (NS_2). But taking and holding ground in dispersed, concealed postures poses major collective action challenges for nonstate actors. Some, with mature institutions and existential stakes, can meet this challenge and exploit the potential new weapons offer to contest ground effectively well to the right of NS_1. Others, with only moderately mature institutions or more limited stakes, can control only essential ground and must resort to coercive irregular methods elsewhere, moving less to the right of NS_1. Still others, with more limited institutions and stakes, cannot make good on the promise of new firepower and must retain NS_1's midcentury, more Fabian military methods in spite of new technology. So as technological incentives encourage nonstate actors to move to the right, more and more nonstate actors hit the limits of their internal politics and can safely move no further—hence the variance in the nonstate distribution grows as their modal choice moves to the right but exposes more and more groups as unable to cope with the internal political demands of holding ground in such dispersed, concealed postures, thus defaulting to more-Fabian methods instead.

In fact, these trends are likely to create a meaningful degree of overlap in future state and nonstate military methods. Differences in states' unit-level traits are likely to create variance in their behavior; some of these traits are likely to constrain their ability to implement complex midspectrum methods, hence variance in state methods, like nonstate methods, is likely to grow over time.[5] Two unimodal distributions with significant tails whose modes are moving together are likely to present an increasing overlap over time. While the modal state choice is likely to remain more Napoleonic than the modal nonstate choice $(S_2 > NS_2)$, the changes presented in figure 10.1 are likely to produce an increasing number of nonstate actors whose methods could well be more "conventional" than those of some states. In fact this is already discernible in early 21st-century warfare: in 2003, the Iraqi state military deployed tens of thousands of irregular Saddam Fedayeen militia who often wore civilian clothing and relied on hit-and-run attacks with light weapons to inflict coercive attrition on Coalition forces; the Iraqi Fedayeen state military forces were far less Napoleonic in their methods than the nonstate combatants fielded by Hezbollah three years later in South Lebanon.[6] In fact, such state-fielded irregular militias are now extremely common: nearly two-thirds of all states involved in civil warfare since 1989 have been supported by such irregulars; any of these cases present states whose military methods were less Napoleonic overall than Hezbollah's in 2006.[7]

And this implies that for nonstate actors in particular, the salience of politics for predicting military methods is growing relative to their weapon holdings, numerical strength, and the scale of assistance they receive from allies or state patrons. The job of anticipating such actors' methods is thus increasingly the social science challenge of understanding actors' internal political dynamics rather than the traditional military task of counting weapons or assessing technology per se.

Across all actors, the net trends are likely to produce a systemic distribution of military methods like that depicted in the "overall" curve in figure 10.1. The sharply bimodal midcentury distribution of military methods is thus likely to moderate with some degree of convergence over time—but with very large tails to the distribution. Many actors, both states and not, will adopt methods that contest ground as midcentury states sought to do, but with postures whose dispersal and concealment leave them more Fabian than those of midcentury states.[8] But this does not mean that all actors will adopt a common military style in the future—varying internal politics create limits on convergence and will cause older styles to persist even as modal methods grow more similar. The net result is thus likely to be a wider range of possibilities. As the "overall" curve in figure 10.1 suggests, the aggregate incidence of military methods across all actors will likely involve many whose postures will lie between those of midcentury state and nonstate combatants, but with tails to the distribution that encompass much of the range of the last century's military experience.

Implications for Policy: Force Structure and Modernization

If the distribution of military methods across potential future opponents looks something like that depicted in figure 10.1, what does this imply for the kind of military the United States should build? A complete answer to this question requires analysis beyond my scope—including prescriptions for US grand strategy as a whole and an assessment of the relative importance of the scenarios in which particular opponents might threaten US interests. But if we accept something like current US grand strategy as a point of departure and focus mostly on a series of arguments others have advanced that are based on claims about the nature of future opponents, then some initial observations are possible.

In particular, it is worth evaluating in this light two recent arguments for transformational change in the US military: the high-tech revolution school that became popular beginning with the 1991 Gulf War, and the low-tech revolution school that gained currency with the advent of large-scale insurgency in Iraq by 2006.

The high-tech "revolution in military affairs," or RMA, transformation school held that future warfare would be dominated by new standoff firepower and networked information technologies in the hands of sophisticated state opponents. To cope with such enemies, it sought to transform a legacy US military weighed down with large, heavy, labor-intensive ground forces into one in which long-range precision weapons did most of the killing and in which a much smaller, faster, leaner ground component served mainly to acquire targets for air or missile attack from standoff ranges.[9]

Conversely, the low-tech or counterinsurgency revolution argument held that future warfare would be dominated not by new technology but by new opponents—and specifically, by nonstate actors who would use irregular methods to hamstring a musclebound US military that had been designed to fight other states in massed conventional warfare. To cope with the low-intensity "war among the people" expected from such nonstate enemies, this school advocated a transformation agenda precisely the opposite of the RMA camp's: it sought a reduced emphasis on speed and standoff weaponry, a larger number of more lightly equipped ground forces, and methods that would minimize their use of firepower while providing persistent population security in areas they would not leave once occupied.[10]

The RMA view had achieved a status close to orthodoxy in the US policy community by 2004. It then suffered a period of decline as the Iraq insurgency came to dominate the debate and as contrary evidence drawn from recent combat experience began to accumulate; the low-tech revolution school had largely supplanted it by 2007. But then the intellectual tide turned again. With the 2014 collapse of the Iraqi Army in Mosul and the Afghan Security Forces' inability to defeat the Taliban after 2014, the low-tech revolution camp entered a period of decline, and the fortunes of higher-tech advocates for standoff airpower and small special forces teams are now once again ascendant. A future failure of limited-liability standoff warfare, however, could lead to yet another reversal of fortunes—to date neither argument has been banished, and advocates of each remain vocal in their support.[11]

Neither, however, is a natural fit to the distribution of future opponents implied by figure 10.1. In fact, both transformation schools represent efforts to redesign the US military around the demands of a kind of opposition that is likely to become less common in the future.

This argument is illustrated in figure 10.2. Here the x-axis is the same as before: a continuum of war fighting methods from most Fabian on the left, to most Napoleonic on the right. But whereas figure 10.1 plotted the expected frequency of such methods' use by different classes of actors, figure 10.2 plots the US military's capability to oppose such methods, with five curves presenting different US postures that differ in their ability to meet the challenges of different kinds of foe.

The untransformed "legacy" US military of 2001 was a lineal descendant of a Cold War force designed to defeat the midcentury Soviet state foe in central Europe and was best suited to such opponents. It fielded a mix of forces including light infantry, special forces, and standoff precision firepower, but much of its total troop strength was devoted to heavy tank and mechanized units intended to destroy comparably organized land forces in close combat: 32 brigade-strength formations in the active US Army in 2001, 20 were armored or mechanized.[12] The Army and Marines together fielded an end strength of 659,375 people whereas the Air Force had only 363,692.[13] This force mix was very effective against exposed, massed opponents of the kind represented by the far-right end of the spectrum in figure 10.2, but it was also highly effective against more-concealed state forces closer to the middle of the spectrum, and in particular against state foes with methods equivalent to S_1 in figure 10.1: its heavy ground forces enabled it to close with and destroy enemies whose concealment made them difficult targets for standoff airpower but whose relative concentration required a significant weight of close combat capability to overcome. The 2001 force mix also afforded some residual capability against

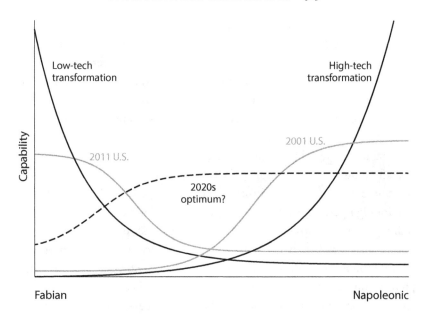

FIGURE 10.2. Distribution of US capability across enemy war-fighting methods

nonstate foes further to the left in figure 10.2—its light infantry and special operations forces (SOF), in particular, were theoretically well suited to such opposition, and its heavy ground forces could (and were) pressed into service in counterinsurgency in Iraq. But its armored vehicles, artillery, and precision antitank weapons imposed important opportunity costs on the kind of persistent, large-scale light infantry presence that US doctrine came to emphasize for counterinsurgency (COIN), and the mechanized, high-firepower training this force emphasized was ill suited to COIN. The capability embodied by the 2001 force mix thus fell off rapidly against enemies at the Fabian end of the war fighting spectrum in figure 10.2.

The hard experience of counterinsurgency in Iraq and Afghanistan, however, led to a significant reorientation of the US military after about 2006. Army and Marine end strength grew considerably, from a combined 659,375 in 2001 to 766,489 by 2011. Much of the expansion went into light infantry, Stryker infantry, and special forces, whose brigade equivalents grew from 12 to more than 20 by 2017.[14] And even nominally heavy tank, artillery, and mechanized infantry formations were commonly *employed* as light infantry, with howitzer crews retrained as foot soldiers and with armored vehicle crews operating dismounted much of the time.[15] Modernization, moreover, increasingly emphasized systems designed to support counterinsurgency against irregular opposition: the Army cancelled the Future Combat System (FCS) program designed to replace Army and Marine Corps tanks and infantry fighting vehicles and instead invested nearly $50 billion in a new family of Mine-Resistant Armor Protected (MRAP) vehicles whose vee-shaped hulls and high ground clearance offered superior protection against insurgents' improvised landmines but whose light armor and high profiles would leave them extremely vulnerable to large-caliber antitank fires.[16] COIN-oriented programs for drone aircraft, improved body armor, and electronic countermeasures against roadside bomb detonators similarly prospered at the expense of slower modernization for high-performance fixed-wing aircraft and long-range bombers.[17] And training for mechanized interstate warfare all but stopped in the Army and Marine Corps, with existing maneuver facilities reconfiguring themselves for COIN training and with stateside training syllabi shifting overwhelmingly to preparation for the ongoing nonstate COIN fight rather than a potential interstate war sometime in the unspecified future.[18] These adaptations created a US military whose proficiency against irregular foes improved dramatically, contributing both to a major reduction in violence in Iraq by 2008 and to a reversal in previously negative trends in Afghanistan by 2012; the 2011 US military was far more capable than its 2001 predecessor against nonstate opponents operating near the Fabian end of the spectrum in figure 10.2.[19] But these adaptations had major opportunity costs of their own. Slower modernization of heavy ground force equipment and standoff airpower meant less capability than would otherwise have been available against 21st-century state foes operating in the vicinity of S_1 or S_2 in figure 10.1. And more importantly, the lack of training time devoted to heavy mechanized operations led to a significant atrophy in skills for the extremely complex and demanding methods embodied in war fighting styles closer to S_2 than to S_1. Of course, the United States retained considerable capability for interstate warfare all the same—the 2011 military would probably have been more effective in mechanized combat than the 2001–5 US military proved to be in counterinsurgency. But by 2011, the net result was nevertheless a very different posture now oriented to fighting nonstate opponents near the Fabian end of figure 10.2 and less effective than 2001's against state foes waging midspectrum warfare.

Transformation advocates saw neither of these postures as adequate. The high-tech transformation agenda's emphasis on standoff precision firepower and small, fast-moving ground forces would, if implemented, produce a military very different from the 2001 legacy force—but it would be even more different from the COIN-oriented military the United States had developed by 2011. An RMA-model high-tech transformation would yield less light infantry for persistent population security, not more; fewer MRAPs, not more; and more emphasis on speed and standoff firepower, not less. And these changes would yield a US military that would be less effective than either the 2011 or the 2001 US postures against a highly Fabian enemy operating toward the left-hand end of the spectrum in figure 10.2. After all, the whole point of irregulars' high-concealment methods is to protect themselves from state firepower; while 21st-century US airpower is now somewhat more effective against concealed targets than in previous decades, it is still radically less lethal against dismounted fighters in civilian clothing operating in populated areas than it is against massed armor in the open.[20] The net result is that figure 10.2 plots an expected capability for an RMA-transformed US military that is lower than any of the alternatives against highly Fabian enemies.

In exchange, the RMA high-tech transformation agenda would yield a US military far more effective than even the 2001 legacy force against massed, exposed enemies operating near the Napoleonic extremum in figure 10.2. Modern precision firepower can annihilate such formations at standoff distances with very little risk to the air and missile forces carrying out the strikes. And an RMA-transformed force would maximize US capability for such strikes by retiring much of the heavy, slow-moving legacy ground forces of 2001 and reinvesting those resources in standoff firepower and the networked information infrastructure needed to enable it. Against an exposed enemy most vulnerable to this kind of firepower, an RMA-transformed force would be radically effective.

This radical effectiveness against very exposed enemies comes at a price, however. Not only would an RMA military be less effective than the 2011 force against Fabian enemies; it would also be less effective than the 2001 legacy force against moderately concealed foes, such as those operating in the neighborhood of S_2 in figure 10.1. Just as the point of Fabian methods is to shield irregulars from state firepower, so the whole point of midspectrum methods like those at S_2 is to shield state soldiers from precision standoff weapons—it is precisely the advent of such weapons that gives state forces an incentive to move leftward from S_1 to S_2. And as I argued in chapter 3, recent combat experience shows that militaries with the ability to overcome collective action challenges and master the complexity of midconcealment warfare can reduce their vulnerability to standoff fires dramatically. Of course, this does not mean that 21st-century precision firepower is unimportant or unhelpful. But its greatest value against midspectrum enemies is in combination with ground forces capable of effective close combat in the complex terrain that such foes will increasingly seek out. Yet the RMA-transformed force depicted in figure 10.2 would reduce just such close-combat ground forces in order to maximize standoff weapon delivery. Against midspectrum enemies operating near S_2, this would produce a US military that would be less effective than the legacy force of 2001.

The low-tech transformation force would produce the opposite result. With it, US capability would improve against highly Fabian enemies operating near NS_1 in figure 10.1: the low-tech, COIN-transformed military would enjoy even larger light infantry end strength than the 2011 military's, with even better COIN equipment and organization and a continued training emphasis that would further ingrain the population security measures stressed in modern US COIN doctrine. Hence at the left-hand side of the figure, a COIN-transformed military would be even more capable than the 2011 force. But this COIN transformation would pose large opportunity costs in heavy ground force modernization, tank and mechanized force structure, standoff weapon acquisition, and training for complex midspectrum operations. In fact, it would pose larger trade-offs in all these dimensions than even the COIN-oriented 2011 force does—the whole point of the COIN transformation thesis is that the 2011 force had not yet liquidated these holdover capabilities as completely as COIN advocates want.[21] Hence a COIN-transformed military would be less effective than either the 2011 or the 2001 force against state foes operating in the vicinity of S_2 or even S_1, against whom the kinds of heavier, higher-firepower forces sacrificed in this model are most needed.

Each transformation agenda thus has some real strengths—but also some grave weaknesses against some kinds of opponents. Neither agenda is robust against all possible future enemies. In fact, neither agenda offers as much residual capability against unexpected foes as the preexisting US postures the transformations would replace: the 2001 legacy military was hardly optimized against Fabian enemies but was more capable against them than an RMA alternative would be; the 2011 military was hardly optimized against midspectrum state militaries but would be more effective against them than the COIN-transformed alternative would be.

In an important sense, the entire transformation debate thus amounts to a call for taking a relatively balanced preexisting military and specializing it against one kind of possible foe. High-tech transformation would specialize the US military for exposed, Napoleonic enemies at the cost of greater vulnerability against more Fabian, more concealed foes. Low-tech transformation would do the opposite. In the process, each would increase US capability against one kind of enemy while creating weaknesses that would not otherwise exist against other kinds of threats.

Yet the theory presented here suggests that such approaches pose major risks. The predicted distribution of military methods across the international system in figure 10.1 shows not a single future threat but a wide range of them. Persistent variation in internal politics combined with ongoing proliferation of advanced weapons is likely to create a future distribution of enemy methods spanning the entire range from NS_1 to S_1 and beyond. To optimize the US military narrowly against any one subset of this range is to increase substantially the odds that the United States will find itself with a military radically ill adapted to the war it is eventually asked to fight—whichever kind of war the United States optimizes for.

Worse, the specific kinds of enemies around which the transformation debate revolves are both becoming *less*, not more, common over time. While figure 10.1 suggests a future distribution that will encompass both highly exposed and highly concealed enemies, it also shows a systematic shift in *modal* methods away from either of these extremes and toward the middle of the spectrum. The center of mass in the distribution of future war-fighting styles is thus moving away from the kinds of foe that either transformation school presupposes, and toward one that would pose serious challenges to any "transformed" US force.

In fact, the kind of US military best suited to the modal opposition of the future would actually look more like the 2001 legacy force than any of the alternatives depicted. If a future opponent chooses methods like NS_2, S_2, or points in between, that foe will be combining a heavy emphasis on complex terrain for cover and concealment with a capacity to take and hold ground using traditional fire-and-movement methods with sustained logistical support. As Hezbollah's 2006 version of such methods suggests, much of such warfare will occur in forested, built-up, or rough terrain precisely because such environments limit exposure to modern standoff firepower—very little of the 2006 campaign involved empty rural areas or massed Hezbollah fighters moving or standing in the open. (In fact, the IDF's occasional exposure in the open led to heavy losses and the quick resort to cover, as in the Saluqi valley fighting on August 12.)[22] To operate effectively against such opposition requires both ample close-combat ground forces capable of penetrating cover and exploiting it themselves, and just enough standoff precision firepower to punish harshly any enemy failure to remain under cover and impose the challenges of complex, concealed, midspectrum methods on the enemy over the deepest possible area.[23] And the ground forces that will be tasked with close combat in complex terrain will need armored vehicles to do this and survive: recent experience with sustained urban warfare strongly suggests that mobile protected firepower (i.e., something like a modern tank) is a crucial advantage with the ability to reduce casualties significantly.[24] This mix of close combat ground forces with access to armored vehicles and supporting standoff fires is not a bad approximation to the military the United States fielded in 2001.

This is not to say that one would want literally the same military—or the same mix of forces—as the US posture in 2001. A military optimized for midspectrum enemies of the (N_2, S_2) variety would ideally deploy somewhat more infantry, less armor, and less artillery than the 2001 force did. In effect, it would approximate a "medium-weight" version of the heavy legacy force of 2001. The kind of urban and complex-terrain combat to be expected from (N_2, S_2) type opponents requires combined arms that include heavy armor and artillery—but the ideal balance would involve a greater proportion of dismountable infantry and a relatively smaller proportion of tanks and artillery than a mix designed for a more open, rural warfare of the S_1 kind anticipated in the Cold War. And a lighter, medium-weight force would enjoy other advantages as well, especially an improvement in strategic mobility and an enhanced ability to respond quickly to distant contingencies. But this does not mean that every vehicle in such a medium-weight force should itself be medium weight—this is not necessarily a call for something like Army general Eric Shinseki's proposed "Objective Force" of the early George W. Bush administration, in which weight reductions were to be obtained by trading heavy M-1 Abrams tanks and M-2 Bradley infantry fighting vehicles for wheeled Stryker light armored vehicles.[25] To be effective in close combat against (N_2, S_2) type opponents in complex terrain requires better protection for the needed tanks than a light Stryker provides. For this kind of warfare, weight reduction is largely a consequence of an infantry-heavier combined-arms mix, not necessarily lighter tanks where tanks are needed. But overall, even a new posture with a more infantry-heavy force structure will be closer in makeup and design to the 2001 military than it would be to either transformation design—or even to the 2011 military forged in Iraq and Afghanistan.

A medium-weight version of the 2001 legacy force would create a somewhat different capability distribution than the 2001 force—and a very different distribution than any of the others. With more dismountable infantry than the

legacy force, it would be somewhat more capable against highly Fabian opponents operating near the left end of the figure 10.1 spectrum, though less so
than the 2011 force with its COIN-oriented equipment and training focus, and
much less so than the low-tech transformation model. Conversely, its realloca-
tion of forces away from standoff fires and toward infantry would leave it somewhat less capable than the 2001 force against massed opponents fighting in the
open near the right end of the figure 10.1 spectrum, and much less capable than
the RMA transformation model against such exposed enemies. Here, though,
the difference is smaller than on the left side of the spectrum: modern weapon
technology is so lethal against massed targets in the open that even a small
standoff precision arsenal, properly employed to conceal its shooters and sustain their fires, can be very effective if its enemies oblige by operating in the
kind of exposed postures implied by the Napoleonic side of the spectrum here.
Even a force that is not optimized for such opposition can thus be substantially
effective anyway if it finds itself fighting enemies as exposed as S_1 or more so.

The chief advantage of the medium-weight force is its performance against
opponents closer to the middle of the behavioral spectrum, and in particular,
against foes whose methods fall in the (N_2, S_2) range from figure 10.1. The
legacy force is too infantry light to be as effective as a medium-weight posture
against midspectrum opponents in complex and urban terrain; conversely, the
2011 force's training and modernization emphasis put too little stress on con-
testing the control of ground in midspectrum combat. The two transformation
alternatives are even worse on these scores. And the medium-weight force's
advantages in this domain are likely to be increasingly important as the distribution of military methods among potential rivals in the international system
shifts toward exactly this part of the spectrum.

Of course, none of these postures can convey very high effectiveness against
all possible future opponents at the same time—each sacrifices something in
order to enable its strengths in other respects. In fact, the sacrifices posed by
the medium-weight posture actually yield a lower peak capability than any of
the other alternatives considered: the 2001 legacy force, the 2011 force, the
high-tech transformation model and the low-tech transformation option all
outperform the medium-weight force against some opponent. But they also
radically *underperform* the medium-weight option against the others. And the
medium-weight option outperforms all the alternatives against the kind of
midspectrum enemies that the theory above sees as the likely modal opposition of the future—a particularly important point on the spectrum. The
medium-weight force also offers more residual capability against other

possibilities than does any alternative posture not specifically optimized for that kind of enemy per se.[26] It may look too much like the Cold War legacy force to satisfy many transformation advocates on either side of the debate, but a medium-weight version of the legacy force is actually a stronger fit to the likely future of warfare than either radical transformation school's agenda.

Perhaps ironically, the most ostensibly visionary, radical proposals in the current debate are thus actually the most reactionary and backward looking in important respects: each would redesign the US military to specialize around a kind of threat whose incidence in the international system is in relative decline, and each would leave the United States less well adapted to the kind of warfare that is likely to become more common in the future. If the theory above is correct, the most truly visionary design for the future US military may well be among the least radical.

Implications for Scholarship

The new theory also has important implications for scholars, including a number of promising directions for new research and new insights from existing scholarship. One such direction involves the determinants of state, as well as nonstate, behavior. The new theory argues that institutions and stakes shape nonstate actors' military methods in important ways; do similar effects obtain for state war making? Recent work on state military behavior has highlighted the role of a number of internal political variables such as regime type or civil-military relations, but the theory above identifies several additional possibilities.[27] Do the extent of specialization of labor, legal checks and balances on elites, the government's role in the economy, official rent seeking, or internal coalitional structure affect state military choices in the way they do for those of nonstate actors? War aims and stakes have attracted attention as a cause of victory and defeat in interstate war; do they also affect states' tactics and strategies for conducting those wars, as I argue they do for nonstate actors?[28]

More broadly, the new theory suggests the possibility of a unified theory of state and nonstate war making. Above I argue that all actors face the same military material reality of an increasingly lethal modern battlefield, and that nonstate actors' responses to this reality are shaped by their institutions and stakes. But states also vary in their institutions and stakes. Is there a similar causal relationship among these variables in state war making? If so, does the deductive logic of material-political interactions presented above offer the basis for a unified explanation of military choices that treats states and non-state actors as special cases of a more general relationship?

To answer these questions is beyond my scope in this book—it would require, inter alia, a major expansion of case evidence to consider state as well as nonstate behavior over an appropriate range of conditions. But the analysis presented here suggests, though it does not establish, the possibility of a broader theory that would cover all actors, state and nonstate alike.

This in turn suggests an important challenge to the widespread tendency to isolate studies of civil war from research on interstate war and to assume unique dynamics for each. Civil war has attracted a large and growing literature, which has made important contributions to our understanding of internal conflict.[29] This literature's defining feature, however, is a putative category distinction from interstate warfare, which is assumed to operate according to different rules and to follow different causal relationships. Few studies of civil war are informed by any explicit analysis of interstate combat, or place civil and interstate war on any common or unified theoretical framework. Instead they are viewed as separate phenomena and typically analyzed in isolation.

This has tended to focus attention on features of civil warfare that seem most distinct from interstate war, such as atrocities, civilian targeting, relative incidence of discriminate as opposed to indiscriminate violence, the use of child soldiers, or sexual violence.[30] By contrast, military strategy and tactics for use of combatant forces against other combatants have received much less attention in the civil war literature and are often treated by assumption rather than interrogated—the civil war literature often simply assumes that nonstate actors will use irregular methods, especially when fighting state enemies. Even where "conventional" nonstate behavior is treated, this is almost always presented as an autonomous, categorical alternative to "irregular," or "symmetric nonconventional" alternatives rather than as an interpenetrated difference of degree along a continuum.[31] And even the counterinsurgency subset of the civil war literature, which emphasizes the conduct of war and military technique, tends to assume irregular methods by insurgents and often highlights the difference between appropriate state methods in COIN and those suited for conventional warfare; in fact, the 2006 edition of the US counterinsurgency manual *FM 3–24* has an entire section on "Paradoxes of Counterinsurgency Operations" whose central point is that the assumptions soldiers bring to COIN from conventional war fighting are often wrong.[32]

Of course few of the traits often associated with civil warfare are actually unique to wars within states. Certainly atrocities, civilian targeting, indiscriminate violence, the use of child soldiers, and sexual violence have all been features of conventional interstate war for centuries.[33]

But in fact, very few features literally distinguish all state from all nonstate warfare. There are important differences of degree, but very few clear categorical distinctions of kind. In the conduct of war, there is actually nothing intrinsic to state or nonstate status in the methods actors adopt to wage war. Some nonstate actors with weak institutions and low stakes will adopt methods well toward the Fabian end of the continuous spectrum of warfare. But others will not. Even numerically inferior nonstate actors can increasingly use modern weapons to enable very effective midspectrum, state-like, war-fighting methods if their institutions are mature and their stakes are existential. In fact, some nonstate actors have already adopted more intuitively "state-like" military methods than some states, and their incidence is likely to grow over time.

And this in turn suggests that a more unified view of state and nonstate warfare could enrich the study of both. The academic tendency to pigeonhole civil and interstate warfare as noncomparable phenomena to be studied mostly by scholars in different subfields leads to an impoverished understanding of each. I have argued that neither class of actor's military methods can be properly explained in isolation—the result is an exaggerated treatment of differences, a tendency to mask gradual change and to misrepresent continuous incremental adaptation as a series of discontinuous jumps, and a multiplication of explanatory categories over time that risks theoretical degeneracy. Studies of civil war risk error if they assume nonstate actors unconcerned with taking or holding ground, unable to conduct combined-arms operations, or whose behavior is predetermined by their equipment. Studies of interstate war risk error when they assume state actors who concentrate uniformed, heavily armored formations in the open on substantially rural battle spaces away from large populations of innocent civilians whose behavior and political alignment is largely irrelevant to the outcome. None of these are safe assumptions today—nor have they been for decades. A more integrated study of warfare that treats state and nonstate actors on a continuum, as special cases of more general phenomena, could avoid these pathologies and set either subfield's work on a fruitful trajectory with the potential for novel insight through cross-fertilization.

Generations ago the study of conflict resolution began as an explicitly interdisciplinary enterprise that viewed phenomena as disparate as interstate war, civil war, crime, labor strife, and domestic violence as interrelated special cases of the more general underlying problem of human conflict. Over time, separate disciplines gravitated toward separate analyses of pieces of this broader agenda, with international relations theory tending to focus on inter-state war, comparative politics on civil war, and economics, psychology, and sociology on criminality or labor unrest.[34] This specialization yielded impor-tant insight. But it also gradually obscured some of the underlying commonali-ties that inspired early students of conflict resolution, and it has promoted an artificially stove-piped understanding of human conflict. With an increasingly interrelated conduct of state and nonstate war on the horizon, now would be an excellent time to return to that earlier vision and realize more of its poten-tial to fuel real understanding on topics of the greatest importance both for scholars and for citizens.

APPENDIX

THIS APPENDIX PRESENTS a more precise operational definition of the theory's dependent and independent variables and a more precise statement of the functional form that interrelates them. I do this in four steps. First I operationalize the dependent variable and identify the domain limits within which I will explain its variance. Next I operationalize the independent variables. I then present the functional form for their interaction. Finally I provide a series of illustrative comparative statics derived from this functional form.

Operationalizing the Dependent Variable: Military Behavior

The theory's dependent variable is the military behavior of a given nonstate actor in conflicts involving numerically superior state opponents.[1] While the theory has implications for the behavior of nonstate militaries in warfare against other nonstate actors without active state involvement, this is not its focus, and the analysis is not meant to be dispositive for such cases. My explanation does not address weapons of mass destruction (nuclear, chemical, and biological) or their use by or against nonstate actors. It includes the use of air or naval assets to influence conflicts on major land masses, but it does not address conflicts waged entirely at sea by nonstate actors (e.g., piracy), nor does it address independent strategic bombing by future nonstate air forces conducted without simultaneous land warfare. The theory's temporal domain for dispositive explanation begins with the advent of mature industrialized warfare; I will take 1900 as a start point.[2] Its temporal domain extends into the future until such time as cover and concealment via terrain become irrelevant for survival; in other work I have argued that this domain will extend well into the mid-21st-century or beyond.[3]

Chapter 2 above argues that orthodox characterizations of nonstate military behavior artificially bifurcate a continuum into dichotomous (or sometimes trichotomous) categories. Orthodox characterizations also suffer from ambiguity in coding rules, such that the same actor's methods—for example Hezbollah's in 2006—can be described by some as terrorism, others as irregular, others as conventional, and still others as "hybrid."[4] An important contributor to this ambiguity is the lack of clear, operational criteria for classifying cases. To do better than the common Potter Stewart-esque stance of knowing "irregular" when one sees it, it is thus essential to operationalize the Fabian-Napoleonic spectrum defined above in the most objective, measurable terms possible.

To do this, note that the definitions in chapter 2 above for the Fabian and Napoleonic extrema comprise six distinct dimensions of military behavior:

1. Stealth: how covered and concealed are the actor's forces?
2. Holding ground: how often does the actor accept decisive engagement to contest territory?
3. Dispersion: how dispersed are the actor's forces?
4. Coercion: how coercive is the actor's strategy?
5. "Asymmetry": how distinguishable are the actor's forces from civilian noncombatants?
6. "Asymmetry": how uniform and functionally undifferentiated is the theater of war?

Each of these implies observable referents that can be objectively coded for any wartime actor given sufficient observational evidence. Taken together, they imply a rough scale that can be used to position nonstate actors on the spectrum between Fabian and Napoleonic extrema on the basis of that actor's observed behavior: if each dimension is scored on a $(0, 1)$ range, the result is a continuous, real-valued $(0, 6)$ scale with zero corresponding to purely Fabian war making, six corresponding to purely Napoleonic war making, values below three leaning Fabian, values above three leaning Napoleonic, and higher values denoting relatively more Napoleonic behavior than lower values.

Of course any linear index of this kind suffers some inherent shortcomings. In particular, any linear index implies equal weight for each component element: acceptance of decisive engagement, for example, is accorded neither more nor less importance than concentration of forces, or spatial differentiation of the theater of war, and so on. While there is no prima facia reason to assume greater or lesser weight for any given element in the list here, it is unlikely that all are literally equal in importance.[5] Especially when used as an independent variable, it will thus often be better to theorize the elements separately as distinct variables rather than aggregating them in an opaque index, or to estimate a latent variables model empirically.[6] For my purposes, however, the index serves as a dependent, not independent, variable. A theory with separate causal mechanisms to account for each of six different dependent variables would incur a heavy burden of increased complexity. As a point of departure, I thus rely here on a linear index of military behavior, but its shortcomings should be kept in mind nevertheless.

1. Stealth: Relative Acceptance of Exposure to Maximize Firepower

What observable referents can be used to code an actor's emphasis on stealth? The key issue here is the actor's willingness to accept exposure to maximize firepower: the intuitive conception of guerilla warriors is that they will not do so; the intuitive conception of conventional soldiers is that they will. To this end, I distinguish four degrees of stealthiness: fully exposed forces, which I code as strongly Napoleonic (1.0); forces that are exposed when moving but covered when stationary, which I code as moderately Napoleonic (0.7); forces that are exposed when moving but are both covered and concealed when stationary, which I code as weakly Napoleonic (0.5); and forces whose movements are covered, concealed, and/or protected by friendly suppressive fire and which are both covered and concealed when stationary, which I code as Fabian (0.0).[7] For each, I code combatants based on the majority of observed behavior; if sub-elements differ systematically (as with, for example, elite formations of superior skill, or reserve or auxiliary formations of inferior skill) I code a rough mean of observed behavior weighted by the proportion of total forces represented by the modal and atypical sub-elements' relative numerical strength.

2. Holding Ground: Acceptance of Decisive Engagement to Contest Territory

What observable referents can be used to code an actor's willingness to hold ground? To hold ground requires an actor to accept decisive engagement when needed. This can be observed in the field via at least four denotata:

- the duration of firefights;
- the proximity of attackers to defenders;
- the incidence of counterattack;
- the incidence of harassing fires and unattended minefields.

The duration of firefights. At the tactical level, defenders who seek to hold their ground must remain in position as long as they are under attack. Against a determined attacker, this can produce extended engagements or a series of renewed firefights in single locations. By contrast, Fabian combatants who seek only to inflict casualties at minimum cost and risk to themselves need not remain in place over extended durations and have an incentive to avoid such protracted positional firefights, as these enable locally superior opponents to fix their locations and bring superior firepower to bear. A pure Fabian ambush with no intention to hold ground can thus be very brief—as little as a single, one-sided surprise volley of fire executed in minutes against an unsuspecting target followed by the shooters' escape. Fabian defenders taken by surprise by superior attackers have an incentive to disengage rather than standing their ground, breaking contact and exfiltrating as quickly as possible. Of course, Napoleonic defenders who are destroyed or broken quickly can fail to hold a position very long; Napoleonic attackers who are destroyed or driven off quickly can terminate engagements early. Fabian ambushers who see an opportunity to finish off a crippled target may sometimes persist until all targets are destroyed. And panicked forces can flee the battlefield in disorder regardless of any intended tactics. Unambiguous coding thus requires observation under conditions where an orderly combatant plausibly had the freedom to persist or break off the engagement if they had so chosen. Given this, I code voluntary persistence in sustained firefights of durations in excess of eight hours as strongly Napoleonic (1.0); voluntary persistence of durations between one and eight hours I code as weakly Napoleonic (0.5). Durations under one hour I code as Fabian (0.0) as long as neither side is annihilated. Cases where either side is annihilated, and/or where the coded combatant lacked the freedom to persist or disengage are coded as ambiguous. Coding is assessed on the basis of the median duration of the engagements observed.[8]

The proximity of attackers to defenders. At the tactical level, defenders who seek to hold ground against an advancing attacker must also stand that ground even as the attacker closes with, and potentially reaches, their positions. By contrast, Fabian combatants who seek only to inflict casualties at minimum cost and risk to themselves rarely allow superior forces to close with them over any extended advance under fire. The risk of decisive engagement grows as an attacker closes with a defender; to allow an attacker into close proximity is to risk being unable to break contact and escape. Ambushes with an overwhelming concentration of fire delivered suddenly against an exposed target will sometimes be triggered at close range to maximize surprise and accuracy, but

such tactics are risky for inferior forces and, when undertaken, must be concluded quickly. Frequent combat at close proximity, and, especially, close
proximity tolerated for more than a few minutes in a surprise ambush, thus
tends to imply behavior closer to the Napoleonic end of the spectrum. Other
things being equal, the greater the observed incidence of sustained close-
quarters fighting, the greater the degree to which the actor's methods approximate the Napoleonic extreme. For combat actions of duration longer than
one hour, I thus code proximity of under one kilometer as strongly Napoleonic
(1.0); proximity at ranges of between one and two kilometers as weakly
Napoleonic (0.5); and combat only at ranges in excess of two kilometers as
Fabian (0.0). Coding is assessed on the basis of the median proximity of engagements with durations of greater than one hour. Where there is insufficient
evidence of engagements with duration of greater than one hour, the subcategory is dropped.[9]

The incidence of counterattack. At the tactical or operational level, defenders
who seek to hold ground must counterattack periodically to retake lost positions. Deliberately closing with the enemy in a counterattack, however, usually
involves a greater degree of exposure than does a well-prepared defense. Fabian combatants who seek one-sided attrition of the enemy but not the retention of ground thus make very sparing use of counterattack by maneuver.
Hence the greater the observed incidence of counterattack, the greater the
degree to which the actor's methods approach the Napoleonic extreme. Of
course, not all movements toward the enemy in combat represent intentional
attempts to regain lost ground; units sometimes lose their orientation and
unknowingly approach the enemy, or encounter unexpected enemy units they
did not intend to assault. I thus code as an observed counterattack only actions
in which defenders continue to advance on the enemy after taking fire, indicating a deliberate effort to take the position under assault and not simply error
or surprise. In particular, I code an incidence of more than two observed counterattacks by detachments of platoon size (roughly 40 fighters) or larger from
units of brigade size or smaller (roughly 3,000 to 5,000 fighters) in less than
one week of fighting as strongly Napoleonic (1.0); an incidence of one or two
such observed counterattacks as weakly Napoleonic (0.5); and the absence of
observed counterattacks as Fabian (0.0).[10]

The incidence of harassing fires and unattended minefields. At the tactical level,
defenders seeking to hold ground by halting a determined attacker's advance
require aimed fire in heavy volume. Minefields and other barrier systems can
be of great assistance to any defender, but their ability to halt attackers is much

reduced if the barrier is not overwatched by direct fire to interfere with clearance or avoidance. Aimed direct fire, however, requires an exposure to return fire. Fabian combatants who do not seek to halt an advance outright but merely to inflict casualties can avoid return fire by striking from a safe distance with harassing indirect fires and unattended minefields and will often prefer this. Harassing fires and unattended minefields can occur in any kind of conflict, but massed indirect fire and minefields or barriers tied in with direct-fire overwatch are thus much more common in Napoleonic than classical Fabian warfare. Hence the greater the observed incidence of massed indirect fires and overwatched minefields, the greater the degree to which the actor's methods approximate the Napoleonic extreme. I thus code an absence of unattended minefields and unaimed harassing indirect fire as strongly Napoleonic (1.0); an incidence of more than zero but fewer than two such observations per brigade-size formation over at least a week of combat as weakly Napoleonic (0.5); and an incidence greater than that as Fabian (0.0).

I code a combatant's overall acceptance of decisive engagement to contest territory as the arithmetic mean of its four component scores.[11]

3. Concentration of Forces as Opposed to Dispersal

What observable referents can be used to code relative concentration of forces? I use the relationship between the density of forces at a local point of attack and the overall density of forces in the theater as a whole. Classical intuitively guerilla forces employ widely distributed forces at low, relatively uniform, densities; classical intuitively conventional armies operate in greater density and concentrate differentially at particular points. Hence the greater the relative concentration of combatants, the greater the degree to which the actor's methods approximate the Napoleonic extreme. To reflect this, I code the following expression:

$$C = \min\left\{ \frac{\left(\frac{\rho_{loc}}{\rho_{thw}}\right)-1}{100}, 1 \right\} \qquad [A1]$$

where:

$C \equiv$ concentration score (dimensionless)
$\rho_{loc} \equiv$ fighters per square kilometer at threatened locality
$\rho_{thw} \equiv$ fighters per square kilometer in the theater of war

This expression reflects the difference, if any, between the density of forces at points of particular concentration—typically opposite an enemy attack or at a chosen point of one's own attack—and the density of forces overall.[12] An archetypically guerilla force with uniform density and no local concentrations of forces (i.e., $\rho_{loc} = \rho_{thw}$) will return a value of 0.0. Conversely, Bonaparte's French Grande Armee at the Battle of Austerlitz in 1805 would return a value of 1.0: with 74,000 French soldiers on a battlefield of roughly 100 square kilometers, the local force density was about 740 fighters per square kilometer at the threatened point in the theater; the Austrian theater as a whole was about 620,000 square kilometers; the first argument in the minimization function would thus yield a value of 62, returning a value of 1.0 for C.[13] A more dispersed but still state "conventional" force, such as the German defenses at Caen opposite Operation Goodwood in July 1944, would yield values of 629 for ρ_{loc}, 29.4 for ρ_{thw}, and thus 0.2 for C.[14]

4. Reliance on Brute Force as Opposed to Coercion

Unlike some of the operationalizations above, to code reliance on brute force as opposed to coercion requires a synthetic assessment of an actor's strategic logic for the conduct of the war, rather than direct observation of physical behavior alone. In common intuition, the conventional extreme at the strategic level of war relies heavily on brute force to seize or protect the disputed stake in the conflict without any voluntary decision to concede on the opponent's part. The guerilla extreme, by contrast, is overwhelmingly coercive, manipulating the enemy's costs and benefits to induce the enemy to concede a stake that it could still seize or withhold if it chose. Coercion is widely employed, even by powerful actors in chiefly conventional wars; brute force, by contrast, is rarely encountered above the tactical level in classical guerilla warfare. At the strategic level, an observation of coercive action per se is thus a relatively weak indicator of the difference between conventional and guerilla methods, but the more extensive the role of brute force in conduct above the tactical level the greater the degree to which the actor's methods approximate the conventional extreme. Actors whose strategic plan for the conduct of the war is purely brute force in that it requires no voluntary concession by the enemy I thus code as strongly Napoleonic (1.0). Actors whose strategic logic includes explicit countervalue cost imposition but does not rest solely on this I code as weakly Napoleonic (0.5). Actors whose strategic logic rests chiefly on explicit countervalue cost imposition I code as Fabian (0.0).

5. Distinguishability from Civilian Noncombatants

To code distinguishability from civilian noncombatants I rely on three observable referents:

- intermingling of combatants and noncombatant civilians;
- use of distinguishing clothing or markings by combatants; and
- reliance on heavy weapons and equipment when available.

In common intuition, classical guerillas obtain much of their cover and concealment via intermingling with innocent civilians; classical conventional armies, by contrast, avoid civilians where possible and tend to obtain cover and concealment via terrain rather than civilian intermingling. Hence the greater the proximity of combatants to civilians, the greater the degree to which the actor's methods approximate the Fabian extreme. Of course, even conventional armies are sometimes driven into or trapped in cities (Union forces at Gettysburg, for example, conducted a fighting withdrawal through the still-inhabited town after being dislodged from defensive positions to the north and west on the first day of the battle; in 1945, German defenders fought in the streets of Berlin after the advancing Red Army overran positions on the city outskirts).[15] Other conventional armies choose to fight in cities for the defensive advantages of their terrain, or to protect important economic or political assets located there. But most intuitively conventional armies do much of their fighting on rural battlefields. By contrast, classical Maoist guerillas who seek to be "fish among the sea of the people" require inhabited population centers to provide concealment. I thus code combatants for whom the majority of forces are deployed in rural areas outside towns, villages, or cities as strongly Napoleonic (1.0). Combatants for whom more than one-fourth of fighters are deployed in such rural areas I code as weakly Napoleonic (0.5). Combatants for whom less than one-fourth of fighters are deployed in such rural areas I code as Fabian (0.0).

Similarly, intuitively conventional state militaries use uniforms or other distinguishing marks to differentiate combatants from noncombatants; classical nonstate guerillas, by contrast, who seek to blend in with intermingled civilians rather than to distinguish themselves from them, often wear versions of typical civilian clothing. Hence the greater the incidence of uniformed combatants, the greater the degree to which the actor's methods approximate the Napoleonic extreme. I thus code use of distinguishing clothing via the fraction of total combatants wearing uniforms, with a 0 value being purely Fabian, a value of 1.0 being purely Napoleonic, and intermediate values representing increasingly Napoleonic behavior as the proportion increases.[16]

And just as uniforms make soldiers visibly different from civilian noncombatants, so does the use of heavy weapons and military equipment. In many world conflict zones, assault rifles and other light small arms are ubiquitous even among wary civilians; archetypical guerillas can possess such light arms for personal use without necessarily revealing themselves as combatants, especially given the ease of concealing such small weapons on their persons or in homes or other buildings. Tanks, howitzers, or high-performance jet fighter aircraft, by contrast, are unambiguously military, and their size makes them harder to conceal amid a civilian population. I thus code a combatant's reliance on available heavy weapons and equipment using a distinction between small arms and light crew-served weapons, and all other armament. "Small arms" are weapons that can be carried and fired by a single individual without assistance; these include pistols, assault rifles, light machine guns, hand grenades, light rocket-propelled grenades (RPGs) such as the Russian-made RPG-7 or RPG-29, landmines, booby traps, improvised explosive devices (IEDs), and light "man-portable air defense systems" (MANPADs) such as the American-made Stinger or the Russian-made SA-7 or SA-18. Light crew-served weapons require more than one but no more than two people to operate, are not armor protected, normally weigh under 40 kilograms, and include light mortars or ballistic rockets, crew-served machine guns, and some recoilless rifles. All are easily concealed amid a civilian population until actual use. Of course, state conventional armies use all these weapons, too—the difference is that intuitively "conventional" state armies also employ much heavier equipment such as tanks, large-caliber artillery, or aircraft. The *availability* of such heavier equipment, however, is a material variable; the dependent variable for the theory below is the military behavior of nonstate actors, not their materiel. For my purposes, the useful distinction is thus the behavioral choice of combatants who have access to heavy equipment: where a combatant has access to heavy weapons and equipment but makes no observable use of it in combat, I thus code this as Fabian (0.0); where a combatant has access to heavy weapons and equipment but is observed to employ it in combat inconsistently, I thus code this as weakly Napoleonic (0.5); where a combatant has access and uses such equipment consistently, I code this as strongly Napoleonic (1.0).[17]

I code a combatant's overall distinguishability from civilian noncombatants as a weighted mean of its three component scores. Inasmuch as physical proximity to civilians is required for either civilian clothing or avoidance of available heavy weapons to provide actual protection, the "intermingling" score receives a weight of 0.5; the "distinguishing markings" and "reliance on heavy weapons when available" subscores each receive weights of 0.25.[18]

6. Functional Spatial Differentiation of a Theater of War

Classical intuitively guerilla warfare is a relatively uniform, undifferentiated territorial defense without a distinguishable front or rear, waged by guerillas fighting largely where they live; classical intuitively conventional armies differentiate the theater into distinct covering force zones, main battle areas, rear areas and communication zones, and sectors of main effort as opposed to supporting or economy-of-force areas. Hence the more uniform or undifferentiated the military organization of the theater of war, the greater the degree to which the actor's methods approximate the Fabian extreme. I thus code an additional distinction based on the *posture* of the forces at different locations, and the degree to which an articulated theater with a functionally differentiated spatial distribution of forces can be distinguished: dispositions without a discernible difference between a "front" where forces are prepared for imminent direct-fire combat and a "rear" where forces are not I code as Fabian (0.0); dispositions where there is an discernible difference between "front" and "rear" but where no further differentiation is observable I code as weakly Napoleonic (0.5); dispositions with internally differentiated covering force zones and main battle areas within a forward area of troops postured for direct-fire combat, and/or internally differentiated assembly areas within a rear area of troops not postured for direct-fire combat, I code as strongly Napoleonic (1.0).[19]

The resulting scoring system is summarized in table A.1.

Note that occasional appearance of Fabian methods by mostly Napoleonic combatants, or vice versa, will shift the coding overall in that direction, but only to a degree commensurate with the scale of observed behavior: a single unattended harassing minefield in the Maginot Line would not yield a Fabian extremum for the French in 1940. My central claim is that almost all real warfare involves elements of both paradigms—the whole challenge in coding is to resolve such mixed cases by assessing the preponderance of methods used. The index presented here is designed to structure and facilitate such coding of cases that will almost all display a combination of techniques.

TABLE A.1. Coding Rules

	Scoring Criterion			Weighting
	0	0.5	1	
Stealth: acceptance of exposure to maximize firepower	Covered, concealed when moving and stationary	Exposed when moving, covered when stationary (.7); covered and concealed when stationary (.5)	Fully exposed	1
Holding ground: acceptance of decisive engagement to contest territory				
• duration of firefights	< 1 hr.	1–8 hrs.	> 8 hrs.	0.25
• proximity of attackers to defenders	> 2 km	1–2 km	< 1 km	0.25
• incidence of counterattack	1 brigade, 1 week: 0 platoons	1 brigade, 1 week: 1–2 platoons	1 brigade, 1 week: > 2 platoons	0.25
• incidence of harassing fires, unattended minefields	1 brigade, 1 week: > 2	1 brigade, 1 week: 0–2	1 brigade, 1 week: 0	0.25
Concentration as opposed to dispersal		$\min\left\{ \dfrac{\left(\dfrac{\rho_{\text{loc}}}{\rho_{\text{thw}}}\right)-1}{100}, 1 \right\}$		1
Reliance on brute force as opposed to coercion	No brute force; voluntary concession required	Brute force vs. key locations only; voluntary concession required	Brute force common; voluntary concession not required	1

(continued)

TABLE A.1. Continued

| | Scoring Criterion | | | Weighting |
	0	0.5	1	
Distinguishability from civilian noncombatants				
• Combatant/civilian intermingling	<25 percent outside cities, towns, villages	25–50 percent outside cities, towns, villages	>50 percent outside cities, towns, villages	0.5
• Distinguishing markings		Fraction of combatants wearing uniforms		0.25
• Reliance on heavy weapons and equipment when available	No use of available heavy materiel	Inconsistent use of available heavy materiel	Consistent use of available heavy materiel	0.25
Articulated theater, functionally differentiated spatial distribution	No front-rear distinction	Front-rear; no distinct battle zones; and/or no distinct assembly areas	Front-rear; distinct battle zones; distinct assembly areas	1

Operationalizing the Independent Variables

The theory is specified with four independent variables: technology, numerical imbalance, institutions, and stakes. Technology and numerical imbalance are material variables; institutions and stakes are nonmaterial political variables. Institutions and stakes are monadic qualities of the actor whose behavior is to be explained. Numerical imbalance is a dyadic quality of the relationship between that actor's numerical strength and its opponent's. Technology is a systemic quality of the state of the art at the time of the coded military campaign.

Technology

The theory treats technology, *t*, as a systemic variable reflecting the progressive increase in net lethality of firepower over time, per the discussion in chapter 3. Specifically, technology is coded as the year of the military action under study.

Of course actors vary cross-sectionally in their weapon holdings at any given time; a systemic treatment is a simplification. This simplification elides the utility of dyadic technological advantages enjoyed by one actor relative to another. In other work, I have operationalized *state* military technology as a weighted mean year of introduction for a given state's major weapons, enabling treatment both of progressive changes in the state of the art and of dyadic advantage or disadvantage relative to an enemy.[20] For nonstate actors, however, it is much more difficult to document with confidence all actors' specific holdings by weapon type and number; systemic treatment is straightforward, but monadic or dyadic specification would pose probably insurmountable empirical challenges. It is also worth noting that diffusion of weapon technology has produced more widespread holdings of modern technology among both states and nonstate actors than sometimes assumed. Elsewhere I have argued that the actual magnitude of technological asymmetries between state combatants in post-1900 interstate war has been surprisingly small—diffusion does not eliminate all differences between combatants, but decisive technological edges are rare.[21] This diffusion affects nonstate actors, too: the proliferation of advanced weapons has put perhaps surprisingly advanced weapons in the hands of perhaps surprisingly diverse actors in recent decades. The case studies above provide detailed treatments for the nonstate actors considered here; for now, it will suffice to note that even Mohammed Farah Aideed's Somali tribal militia had access to American-made wire-guided TOW antitank missiles in 1993, for example (see chapter 7). In the 19th century, it may sometimes have been possible for state armies armed with machine guns to slaughter nonstate rivals armed only with spears; this is not a realistic prospect in the modern world.

The causal logic in chapter 3, moreover, centers not on dyadic relative technological advantage but around the absolute level of sophistication in the systemic technological state of the art at any given time. In particular, chapter 3 argues that (a) even very superior militaries have had great difficulty annihilating opponents through preemptive firepower even as recently as 2001, (b) even small numbers of surviving modern weapons can compel opponents to disperse, (c) the scale of the needed dispersion has grown over time as weapon lethality has grown, (d) this dispersion has profound consequences for the military utility of mass, and (e) this decline in the utility of mass has had important consequences for the military viability of numerically inferior nonstate actors. Hence it is the absolute, not relative, lethality of weapon technology that is central to the theory's causal claim. Given the empirical challenges facing the study of nonstate actors per se, the theory thus simplifies its treatment of technology to consider only its absolute, and not relative lethality, and to treat this as a simple, systemic variable coded as the year of the military action under study.

Numerical Imbalance

I operationalize "numerical imbalance," or force-to-force ratio, f, as the ratio of the coded nonstate actor's combatant troop strength to its opponent's. I define "combatant troop strength" as fighters under arms and available for combat on short notice (with less than a month of advance warning). This includes part-time fighters, armed child soldiers, and armed civilians temporarily under military command, mobilized and readily mobilizable state reserves, and active regular soldiers, but it excludes unarmed auxiliaries, and seasonal levies when not activated for duty at the time of dependent variable observation. For the coded nonstate actor, all its fighters in the afflicted or contiguous states are included. For coded states, all troops in the afflicted state under the command of that state or its combatant allies are included, together with any troops under the command of the afflicted state or its combatant allies in any adjoining contiguous states. (For example, Israel Defense Force soldiers on Israeli soil are included as "opponent" forces for Hezbollah in southern Lebanon, as are IDF soldiers on Lebanese soil. For the Afghan Taliban, all

Taliban fighters in Afghanistan, Pakistan, Uzbekistan, Tajikistan, Turkmeni-
stan, China, and Iran would be included as the nonstate actor's active combatant troop strength.)

Internal Politics

I operationalize two dimensions of nonstate actors' internal politics: their institutions, and their stakes in the conflict.

A nonstate actor's institutional makeup, i, is coded as a four-valued categorical variable, as shown in table A.2.

A nonstate actor's stakes are coded as a binary categorical variable s. Stakes
are either high or low. "High" stakes refer to existential conflicts with outsiders
in which defeat could plausibly yield destruction of the actor as an organized
political entity and significant risk of death or imprisonment for the actor's
leadership and component elites. "Low" stakes refer to all other conflict types
(and particularly to limited-aims conflicts over the division of economic spoils
with limited risk of overthrow by outside actors).

Interrelating the Dependent and Independent Variables

The text in chapters 3 and 4 presents in natural language the deductive logic
by which the theory interrelates technology, numerical imbalance, and internal politics to explain military behavior. Chapter 4 summarizes this theory's
key predictions via a categorical, natural-language tabulation (table 4.1). The
categorical treatment in table 4.1 is a simplification, however. As chapter 2 argues, nonstate military behavior is properly understood as a continuum—not
as a discrete set of two or three autonomous, mutually exclusive categories. A
continuum can be summarized with a series of categories in the interest of
compact presentation in natural language, but natural language is impractical
for complete specification of a multivariate theory of continuous variation. I
thus present here a formal specification consistent with the logic in chapters 3
and 4 to enable a more precise articulation of the theory's expectations for
individual cases and to identify a specific form by which the theory can predict
incremental change along a continuum of military behavior. The causal argument is the same; the language, however, is different in a way that enables a
more complete articulation of the argument in chapters 3 and 4. My aim here
is not to present a mathematical proof—rather, my goal is simply to describe
how I claim the theory's variables interrelate in a more complete and specific

TABLE A.2. Institutional Makeup Coding Rules

i:

0	Informal	• No named suborganizations; no written or regularized specialization of labor • Limited hierarchical command and direction • Personalized decision making • No enforceable legal checks on elite action • Elite control of economic activity • Extensive rent extraction • Fluid internal balance of power
1	Fragile natural order	• Named suborganizations with written or regularized specialization of labor—but limited capacity • Limited hierarchical command and direction • Personalized decision making • No enforceable legal checks on elite action • Extensive rent extraction • Fluid internal balance of power
2	Basic natural order	• Named suborganizations with written or regularized specialization of labor and moderate capacity • Limited hierarchical command and direction • Personalized decision making • No enforceable legal checks on elite action • Extensive rent extraction • Stable internal coalitions
3	Mature natural order	• Named suborganizations with written or regularized specialization of labor and substantial capacity • Significant hierarchical command and direction • Impersonal decision making • Enforceable legal checks on elite action • Moderate rent extraction • Stable internal coalitions

way than natural language permits for complicated multivariate interactions of the kind I posit above.

More specifically, a continuous-variable functional form consistent with the claims presented above for φ, the value of an actor's military behavior score on the Fabian-Napoleonic spectrum as presented in chapter 2 and table A.1, would be:

$$\varphi = s + \frac{f}{1+e^{\alpha}} + \frac{i}{1+e^{-\alpha}} \qquad [A2]$$

Where:

$$\alpha = \frac{k_1(t - k_2)}{k_3} \qquad \text{[A3]}$$

and where f is the force-to-force ratio (the actors' combatant strength divided by its opponent's), i is the actor's institutional maturity (a categorical variable with values of 0, 1, 2, or 3 corresponding to informal, fragile, basic, and mature natural order, respectively), s is the actor's stakes (a categorical variable with values of 0 for limited stakes and 1 for existential), t is the sophistication of available technology (coded as the year of combat), and k_1, k_2, and k_3 are constants equal to 0.5, 1990 and 5, respectively.

Comparative Statics

Table 4.1 presents a categorical, natural-language summary of the theory's comparative statics; using the formal-language articulation in equation [A2] I now present a series of continuous-variable illustrations that enable a more complete treatment of the theory's predictions.

Figure A.1 presents the predicted effect of institutional variation, i, on military behavior, φ, operationalized as a nonstate actor's position on the Fabian-Napoleonic spectrum (per table A.1), for technology values, t, ranging from 1940 to 2030, holding constant the actor's stakes, s (at 1.0, or "high") and the actor-to-opponent force-to-force ratio, f (at 0.25). As noted in the categorical summary of the theory in table 4.1, for early 20th-century technology, a nonstate actor's institutional makeup makes little difference: in figure A.1, 1940-era weapons, for example, imply a predicted φ of 1.25 for a nonstate actor with informal institutions ($i = 0$) and only 1.27 for one with mature natural order institutions ($i = 3$). Even here, a mature natural order nonstate actor is expected to adopt slightly more Napoleonic methods than an informal actor, but the difference is small, and both scores are well toward the Fabian end of the $(0, 6)$ range of behavioral variation. With only midcentury weapons, no nonstate actor can safely adopt midspectrum methods to contest ground—numerically superior state opponents will concentrate to overwhelm any such attempt, and the nonstate actors' less lethal early weapons will not suffice to prevent such concentration. Rational nonstate actors under such conditions will instead adopt substantially more coercive, more intermingled, less exposed, intuitively "guerilla"-like methods almost regardless of their institutional makeup.

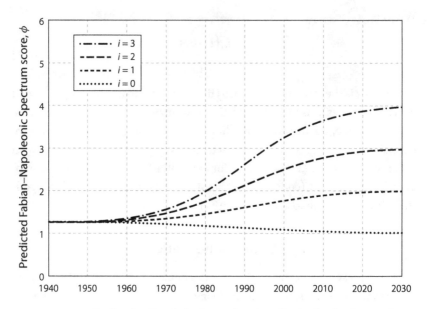

FIGURE A.1. Predicted military behavior as a function of institutional makeup and technology, assuming high stakes ($s = 1, f = 0.25$)

By the time nonstate actors acquire early precision-era weapons, institutional makeup begins to matter more. For $t = 1980$, for example, predicted military behavior, φ, for mature natural order nonstate actors ($i = 3$) has shifted from the mostly Fabian value of 1.27 with 1940-era technology to the somewhat higher but still mostly Fabian value of 1.99. Basic and fragile natural order nonstate actors' predicted behavior also becomes slightly less Fabian (at $\varphi = 1.72$ and 1.45, respectively), but the difference is smaller for them. For informally institutionalized nonstate actors, by contrast, predicted behavior is actually slightly more Fabian ($\varphi = 1.18$ as opposed to 1.25) for the more lethal weapons of midcentury technology—with little or no ability to overcome collective action dilemmas and coordinate activity among interdependent specialists, informally institutionalized actors are merely exposed to more-lethal firepower as technology changes and must adopt increasingly intermingled, concealed methods to survive (though still well within the same "mostly Fabian" category of the simplified presentation in table 4.1).

The effects of institutional variation become ever more important as increasingly lethal technology creates increasing opportunities for institutionally mature nonstate actors to take and hold ground. With 2000-era weapons, predicted φ is now 3.26 for nonstate actors with mature natural order institutions ($i=3$), 2.53 for those with basic natural order institutions ($i=2$), 1.80 for those with fragile natural order institutions ($i=1$), and 1.07 for those with informal institutions ($i=0$). And by the time nonstate actors gain 2030-era weapons, predicted φ grows to 3.95, 2.97, and 1.99, respectively, for mature, basic, and fragile natural order nonstate actors (corresponding to the "midspectrum," "slightly Fabian," and "mostly Fabian" categories in the table 4.1 simplification). The behavioral consequences of institutional variation, small with early-century weapons, are now much more substantial: whereas different institutions yield a predicted φ difference of no more than 0.02 for with 1940-era weapons, this grows to as much as 2.94 with 75 years of improvements in weapon technology. And whereas more-lethal technology can be expected to shift institutionally mature nonstate actors toward less Fabian methods, for informally institutionalized nonstate actors it has the opposite effect: predicted behavior becomes more, not less, Fabian for informal actors (φ falls from 1.25 with 1940-era weapons to 1.00 with 2030-era technology) as weapons grow more lethal (though both values are well within the bounds of the same "mostly Fabian" category in the table 4.1 simplification).

For weapon technology at or beyond mid-1990s sophistication, predicted mature natural order war fighting becomes consistently midspectrum in table 4.1's terms (i.e., φ values consistently exceed 3.0)—predicted φ rises monotonically with respect to t, and exceeds 3.0 for all t values in excess of 1995, but never exceeds table 4.1's "midspectrum" band of 3.0 to 4.0. In fact, the infinite limit of φ with respect to t in equation [A2] is 4.0 on the (0, 6) conceptual range for φ presented in table A.1. Hence no amount of technological progress implies highly Napoleonic methods for rational nonstate actors in the theory here. And this limiting value presupposes mature natural order institutions (and high stakes)—less mature institutions are subject to lower ceilings on φ as t increases to infinity. For basic natural order actors, this limiting value is 3.0; for fragile natural order actors it is 2.0; and for informally institutionalized actors it is 1.0. *State* actors can rationally adopt more Napoleonic behaviors than these, as a function of technology, numerical imbalance, and presumably other influences. But the theory here implies a midspectrum limit on the degree to which a numerically inferior nonstate actor can rationally adopt Napoleonic military styles.

Figure A.2 replaces the assumption of "high," or existential, stakes ($s=1$) in figure A.1 with the converse condition of "low," or limited stakes ($s=0$), again holding the actor-to-opponent force-to-force ratio, f, constant at 0.25. As noted

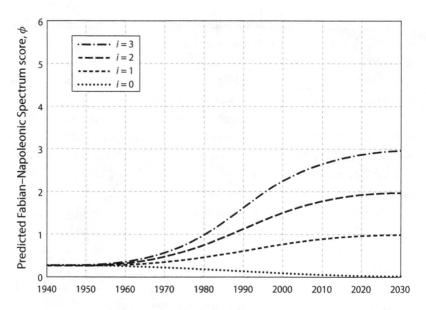

FIGURE A.2. Predicted military behavior as a function of institutional makeup and technology, assuming low stakes $(s=0, f=0.25)$

in the categorical summary of the theory in table 4.1, low stakes undermine the case for expensive training of the kind needed to make less-Fabian war fighting viable and preclude midspectrum methods $(3 < \varphi < 4)$ regardless of technology and regardless of a nonstate actor's institutions. Simply owning advanced weapons does not imply an ability to use them to take and hold ground with the midspectrum methods needed to survive against modern weapons—this requires both mature institutions *and* an incentive to train with the needed intensity. More-mature institutions always imply less Fabian methods: predicted $\varphi|_{(i=3)} > \varphi|_{(i=2)} > \varphi|_{(i=1)} > \varphi|_{(i=0)}$ for all t. But for no institutional makeup does predicted φ rise above table 4.1's "slightly Fabian" range when stakes are low.

Figure A.3 completes the analysis by presenting the theory's predictions for military behavior φ as a function of variations in the actor-to-opponent force-to-force ratio, f, and technology, t, for constant mature natural order institutions $(i=3)$ and high stakes $(s=1)$. The theory in chapters 3 and 4 argues that increasingly lethal weapon technology has rendered numerical superiority progressively less important over time. And the domain over which numerical superiority is most important (i.e., low weapon lethality) is also the domain in which nonstate actors are least competitive with state actors and least able

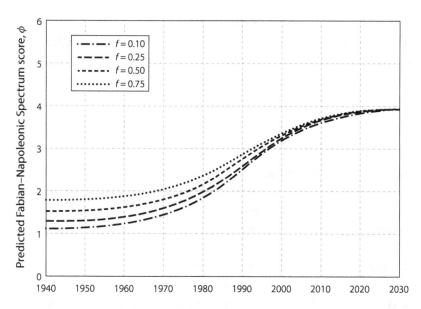

FIGURE A.3. Predicted military behavior as a function of actor-to-opponent numerical imbalance and technology, assuming high stakes and mature natural order institutions $(s=1, i=3)$

to survive less-Fabian war fighting. Taken together, these claims imply the summary view presented in table 4.1: predicted nonstate behavior is largely insensitive to numerical imbalance. Figure A.3 illustrates and qualifies this argument in continuous-variable terms via equation [A2]. Over most of the 1940–2030 range shown for technology (t), the effect of numerical imbalance, f, is insufficient to change predicted military behavior (φ) enough to push the value across any of table 4.1's categories. For all t values between 1940 and 1970, predicted behavior is within table 4.1's "mostly Fabian" category ($1<\varphi<2$) regardless of f. For all t values between 1985 and 1992, predicted behavior is within table 4.1's "slightly Fabian" category ($2<\varphi<3$) regardless of f. And for all t values greater than 1996, predicted behavior is within table 4.1's "midspectrum" category ($\varphi>3$) regardless of f. For 70 years of the 90-year span for t in figure A.3, the table 4.1 categorical coding is thus insensitive to f.

Yet there are some exceptions: for t values between 1970 and 1982, for example, predicted φ varies between table 4.1's "slightly Fabian" ($3<\varphi<2$) and "mostly Fabian" ($2<\varphi<1$) range, depending on f. For t values between 1992 and 1996, predicted φ varies between table 4.1's "slightly Fabian" ($3<\varphi<2$) and "midspectrum" ($4<\varphi<3$) range, depending on f. In all, about 18 percent of the t values considered in figure A.3 present predicted φ results that fall outside the simplified categories in table 4.1. Categorical simplifications such as table 4.1 enable more-compact natural-language summaries of complex, multivariate continuous relationships, but they also have important limitations—including a tendency to mask change and differences of degree, as illustrated here, and to obscure exceptions to more-typical outcomes.

Such exceptions are uncommon, and one might defensibly exclude f from the theory altogether in the interest of parsimony given this. I include it largely because numerical imbalance plays such an important role in the theory's underlying causal logic: it is the inability of outnumbered nonstate actors to cope with superior state forces in the era before high-lethality weapons that explains the infrequency of less Fabian nonstate methods until recently. Variance in numerical imbalance within any given technological era rarely suffices to change nonstate behavior in an important way, but numerical imbalance thus plays an important, if implicit, role in explaining the effects of technological change on nonstate behavior, which *is* important. And f can, under some special conditions, affect predicted φ enough to push it across a categorical threshold. I thus include it in the theory—notwithstanding its modest contribution to the theory's comparative statics.

NOTES

Chapter One: Introduction

1. See, e.g., David Martin Jones, Celeste Ward Gventer, and M.L.R. Smith, eds., *The New Counter-insurgency Era in Critical Perspective* (New York: Palgrave Macmillan, 2014), 1–8; David Ucko, *The New Counterinsurgency Era: Transforming the U.S. Military for Modern Wars* (Washington, DC: Georgetown University Press, 2009); James Russell, *Innovation, Transformation, and War: Counterinsurgency Operations in Anbar and Ninewa Provinces, Iraq, 2005–2007* (Palo Alto, CA: Stanford University Press, 2010); Christopher Chivvis et al., *Initial Thoughts on the Impact of the Iraq War on U.S. National Security Structures* (Santa Monica, CA: RAND, 2019); Eric Edelman et al., *Providing for the Common Defense: The Assessment and Recommendations of the National Defense Strategy Commission* (Washington, DC: US Institute of Peace, 2018), vii, 25; Col. Sean MacFarland, Col. Michael Shields, and Col. Jeffrey Snow, "The King and I: The Impending Crisis in Field Artillery's Ability to Provide Fire Support to Maneuver Commanders," 2007, White Paper, https://www.npr.org/documents/2008/may/artillerywhitepaper.pdf; Chivvis et al., *Initial Thoughts on the Impact of the Iraq War*, 1–7.

2. See, esp., Department of Defense, *Summary of the 2018 National Defense Strategy of the United States of America: Sharpening the American Military's Competitive Edge* (Washington, DC: Government Printing Office, 2018), https://www.defense.gov/Portals/1/Documents/pubs/2018-National-Defense-Strategy-Summary.pdf, 1. This argument predates the Trump administration: see, e.g., Zbigniew Brzezinski, *The Grand Chessboard: American Primacy and Its Geostrategic Imperatives*, 2nd ed. (New York: Basic Books, 2016); US Department of Defense, *Sustaining U.S. Global Leadership: Priorities for 21st Century Defense*, January 2012; Colin Clark, "U.S. Military to Scrap COIN, Focus on Pacific, Says Vice Chairman," *Breaking Defense*, November 17, 2011, http://breakingdefense.com/2011/11/17/u-s-military-is-scrapping-coin-focusing-on-pacific-says-vice/; "Remarks by President Obama to the Australian Parliament," November 17, 2011, https://obamawhitehouse.archives.gov/the-press-office/2011/11/17/remarks-president-obama-australian-parliament.

3. See, e.g., M.L.R. Smith and David Martin Jones, *The Political Impossibility of Modern Counterinsurgency* (New York: Columbia University Press, 2015); Daniel Bolger, *Why We Lost: A General's Inside Account of the Iraq and Afghanistan Wars* (New York: Houghton Mifflin Harcourt, 2014); Gian Gentile, *Wrong Turn: America's Deadly Embrace of Counterinsurgency* (New York: New Press, 2013); Douglas Porch, *Counterinsurgency: Exposing the Myths of the New Way of War* (New York: Cambridge University Press, 2013); Edward Luttwak, "Dead End: Counterinsurgency Warfare as Military Malpractice," *Harper's*, February 2007, 33–42.

4. See, e.g., Seth Jones, "The Future of Warfare Is Irregular," *National Interest*, August 26, 2018, https://nationalinterest.org/print/feature/future-warfare-irregular-29672; Daniel Byman, "Why States Are Turning to Proxy War," *National Interest*, August 26, 2018, https://nationalinterest.org/print/feature/why-states-are-turning-proxy-war-29677; Kenneth Pollack, "To Minimize the Mullahs: An American Strategy for the Middle East," *National Review*, May 24, 2018, https://www.nationalreview.com/magazine/2018/06/11/middle-east-foreign-policy-us-strategy-minimizing-iran/; David Ucko, "Critics Gone Wild: Counterinsurgency as the Root of all Evil," *Small Wars and Insurgencies* 25, no. 1 (May 28, 2014): 161–79; Octavian Manatea, "Reflections on the 'Counterinsurgency Decade': *Small Wars Journal* Interview with General David H. Petraeus," *Small Wars Journal*, September 1, 2013, http://smallwarsjournal.com/jrnl/art/reflections-on-the-counterinsurgency-decade-small-wars-journal-interview-with-general-david; Frank Sobchak, "The Army Is Trying to Bury the Lessons of the Iraq War," *Defense One*, March 8, 2019, https://www.defenseone.com/ideas/2019/03/us-army-trying-bury-lessons-iraq-war/155403/; Thomas R. Mockaitis, *The COIN Conundrum: The Future of Counterinsurgency and U.S. Land Power* (Carlisle, PA: US Army War College Strategic Studies Institute, 2016); Max Boot, *The Savage Wars of Peace: Small Wars and the Rise of American Power* (New York: Basic Books, 2014), 353–72.

5. See, e.g., Ryan Evans, "COIN Is Dead, Long Live the COIN," *Foreign Policy*, December 16, 2011, https://foreignpolicy.com/2011/12/16/coin-is-dead-long-live-the-coin/; Crispin Burke, "Like It or Not, Small Wars Will Always Be Around," *World Politics Review*, January 24, 2012, https://www.worldpoliticsreview.com/articles/11238/like-it-or-not-small-wars-will-always-be-around; Andrew Exum, "Amid COIN Debate, U.S. Army Struggles to Find Its Way," *World Politics Review*, January 24, 2012, https://www.worldpoliticsreview.com/articles/11271/amid-coin-debate-u-s-army-struggles-to-find-its-way; Eli Berman, Jacob Shapiro, and Joseph Felter, "Can Hearts and Minds Be Bought? The Economics of Counterinsurgency in Iraq," *Journal of Political Economy* 119, no. 4 (2011): 766–819; Eli Berman, Michael Callen, Joseph H. Felter, and Jacob Shapiro, "Do Working Men Rebel? Insurgency and Unemployment in Afghanistan, Iraq, and the Philippines," *Journal of Conflict Resolution* 55, no. 4 (2011): 496–528.

6. See, e.g., Michael O'Hanlon, *The Future of Land Warfare* (Washington, DC: Brookings, 2015), 135–67; Sally Donnelly and Douglas Waller, "Ten Questions for General Schoomaker," *Time*, April 22, 2005; Lieutenant Colonel Michael Negard, "Schoomaker: Army Must Fight in 4 Quadrants," *Army News Service*, November 22, 2005.

7. Christoph Mikulaschek and Jacob Shapiro, "Lessons on Political Violence from America's Post–9/11 Wars," *Journal of Conflict Resolution* 62, no. 1:174–202; Martha Crenshaw et al., *APSA Task Force on Political Violence and Terrorism Report*, https://www.apsanet.org/politicalviolence. For reviews of the civil war literature, see, e.g., Stathis Kalyvas and Paul Kenny, "Civil Wars," in Robert A. Denemark, ed., *The International Study Association Compendium Project* (Oxford: Blackwell, 2009); Barbara F. Walter, "The New New Civil Wars," *Annual Review of Political Science* 20 (May 2017): 469–86; Nicholas Sambanis, "Terrorism and Civil War," in Phillip Keefer and Norman Loayza, eds., *Terrorism and Economic Development* (Cambridge: Cambridge University Press, 2008); Corinna Jentzsch, Stathis N. Kalyvas, and Livia Isabella Schubiger, "Militias in Civil Wars," *Journal of Conflict Resolution* 59, no. 5 (2015): 755–69.

8. See, e.g., Ucko, *New Counterinsurgency Era*; Jones, "Future of Warfare"; Boot, *Savage Wars of Peace*; Gentile, *Wrong Turn*; Porch, *Counterinsurgency*; Luttwak, "Dead End"; O'Hanlon,

Future of Land Warfare. See also Rupert Smith, *The Utility of Force: The Art of War in the Modern World* (New York: Vintage, 2008); Richard Betts, *American Force: Dangers, Delusions, and Dilemmas in National Security* (New York: Columbia University Press, 2013), e.g., 149; Audrey Kurth Cronin, *Power to the People: How Open Technological Innovation Is Arming Tomorrow's Terrorists* (New York: Oxford University Press, 2019), 40, 263; James Fearon and David Laitin, "Ethnicity, Insurgency, and Civil War," *American Political Science Review* 97, no. 1 (February 2003): 75–90 at 75; Jeremy Weinstein, *Inside Rebellion: The Politics of Insurgent Violence* (New York: Cambridge University Press, 2006), 203; Benjamin Valentino, Paul Huth, and Dylan Balch-Lindsay, "'Draining the Sea': Mass Killing and Guerrilla Warfare," *International Organization* 58, no. 2 (Spring, 2004): 375–407 at 383–85; Lisa Hultman, "Battle Losses and Rebel Violence: Raising the Costs for Fighting," *Terrorism and Political Violence* 19, no. 2 (2007): 205–22 at 208; I. William Zartman, "Dynamics and Constraints in Negotiation in Internal Conflict," in I. W. Zartman, ed., *Elusive Peace: Negotiating an End to Civil Wars* (Washington, DC: Brookings, 1995), 7; Anna Simons, "War: Back to the Future Author," *Annual Review of Anthropology* 28 (1999): 73–108 at 84–85; Mary Kaldor, *New and Old Wars: Organized Violence in a Global Era* (Cambridge, UK: Polity, 1999); Kalevi J. Holsti, *The State, War, and the State of War* (New York: Cambridge University Press, 1996); Eliot Cohen, Conrad Crane, Jan Horvath, and John Nagl, "Principles, Imperatives, and Paradoxes of Counterinsurgency," *Military Review*, March–April 2006, 49–53; Martin van Creveld, *The Transformation of War* (New York: Free Press, 2009); T. X. Hammes, *The Sling and the Stone: On War in the 21st Century* (St. Paul, MN: Zenith, 2004); Bing West, *The Wrong War: Grit, Strategy, and the Way Out of Afghanistan* (New York: Random House, 2011); Chairman of the Joint Chiefs of Staff, *Joint Publication 3-24: Counterinsurgency* (Washington, DC: Government Printing Office, November 22, 2013), esp. II-1 to II-2; John Nagl, *Learning to Eat Soup with a Knife: Counterinsurgency Lessons from Malaya and Vietnam* (Chicago: University of Chicago Press, 2005); Andrew Krepinevich, *The Army and Vietnam* (Baltimore: Johns Hopkins University Press, 1986); and the more detailed description and documentation in chap. 2 below.

9. David E. Cunningham and Douglas Lemke argue, in fact, that civil and interstate warfare are too similar to justify the commonplace separation of the two domains in the political science literature: Cunningham and Lemke, "Combining Civil and Interstate Wars," *International Organization* 67, no. 3 (2013): 609–27. Cunningham and Lemke focus on the causes, duration, and outcome of wars; I focus here on their military conduct. But I argue below for a similar synthesis in the study of civil and interstate war.

10. Greg Myre, "Israeli General Resigns over War with Hezbollah," *New York Times*, January 17, 2007, https://www.nytimes.com/2007/01/17/world/middleeast/17israel.html; Amos Harel and Avi Issacharoff, *34 Days: Israel, Hezbollah, and the War in Lebanon* (New York: Palgrave Macmillan, 2008); Avi Kober, "The Israel Defense Forces and the Second Lebanon War: Why the Poor Performance?," *Journal of Strategic Studies* 31, no. 1 (February 2008): 3–40.

11. See, e.g., Stephen Biddle, *Afghanistan and the Future of Warfare: Implications for Army and Defense Policy* (Carlisle, PA: US Army War College Strategic Studies Institute, 2002); Olga Oliker, *Russia's Chechen Wars, 1994–2000* (Santa Monica, CA: RAND, 2001); *Balkan Battlegrounds: A Military History of the Yugoslav Conflict, 1990–1995*, 2 vols. (Washington, DC: Central Intelligence Agency, 2002–3); Defense Intelligence Agency Report, "Rwanda: The Rwandan Patriotic Front's Offensive," May 9, 1994, www.gwu.edu/~nsarchiv/NSAEBB/NSAEBB53/rw050994.pdf, accessed May 8, 2008; Donald Jameson, "Missing Pieces of the Rwanda Puzzle,"

Washington Times, May 23, 1994, A20; Donatella Lorch, "Rwanda Rebels: Army of Exiles Fights for a Home," *New York Times*, June 9, 1994, A10.

12. See, e.g., Michael Gordon and Bernard Trainor, *Cobra II: The Inside Story of the Invasion and Occupation of Iraq* (New York: Vintage, 2007), 164, 235–38, 321–45; Stephen Biddle, "Speed Kills: Reevaluating the Role of Speed, Precision, and Situation Awareness in the Fall of Saddam," *Journal of Strategic Studies* 30, no. 1 (February 2007): 3–46.

13. Christopher Chivvis, *Toppling Qaddafi: Libya and the Limits of Liberal Intervention* (New York: Cambridge University Press, 2014), 109–10; Kareem Fahim and David Kirkpatrick, "Qaddafi Massing Forces in Tripoli as Rebellion Spreads," *New York Times*, February 23, 2011, https://www.nytimes.com/2011/02/24/world/africa/24libya.html.

14. Vitaly Shevchenko, "'Little Green Men' or 'Russian Invaders'?," BBC, March 11, 2014, https://www.bbc.com/news/world-europe-26532154; Christopher S. Chivvis, *Understanding Russian "Hybrid Warfare"* (Santa Monica, CA: RAND, 2017).

15. Anthony Cordesman, *Iran's Revolutionary Guards, the Al Quds Force, and Other Intelligence and Paramilitary Forces* (Washington, DC: CSIS, 2007); Ali Alfoneh, *Iran Primer: The Basij Resistance Force* (Washington, DC: US Institute for Peace, 2013), http://iranprimer.usip.org/resource/basij-resistance-force. On state-sponsored militias more broadly, see, esp., Ariel Ahram, *Proxy Warriors: The Rise and Fall of State-Sponsored Militias* (Palo Alto, CA: Stanford University Press, 2011).

16. See, e.g., Chairman of the Joint Chiefs of Staff, *Joint Publication 3–24*, esp. II-1 to II-2; David Galula, *Counterinsurgency Warfare: Theory and Practice* (Westport, CT: Praeger, [1964] 2006); Roger Trinquier, *Modern Warfare: A French View of Counterinsurgency* (Westport, CT: Praeger, [1961] 2006); Robert Thompson, *Defeating Communist Insurgency* (New York: Praeger, 1966); Robert Taber, *War of the Flea: A Study of Guerrilla Warfare Theory and Practice* (New York: Lyle Stewart, 1965); Nagl, *Learning to Eat Soup with a Knife*; E. Cohen, Crane, Horvath, and Nagl, "Principles, Imperatives, and Paradoxes of Counterinsurgency"; Boot, *Savage Wars of Peace*; David Kilcullen, *Out of the Mountains: The Coming Age of the Urban Guerrilla* (New York: Oxford University Press, 2013), e.g., 102–5. Note that much counterinsurgency analysis assumes an insurgent progression from irregular to conventional methods as the insurgency strengthens, but such analyses rarely consider cross-sectional variation in methods, or nonstate actors who begin conflicts with other than irregular methods. For a partial but important exception, see Seth Jones, *Waging Insurgent Warfare: Lessons from the Vietcong to the Islamic State* (New York: Oxford University Press, 2017), which is more descriptive than theoretical but which explicitly distinguishes "conventional" from "guerilla" insurgent methods and evaluates the former.

17. See, e.g., Paul Collier and Anke Hoeffler, "Greed and Grievance in Civil War," *Oxford Economic Papers* 56 (2004): 563–95; Stathis Kalyvas, *The Logic of Violence in Civil War* (New York: Cambridge University Press, 2006); Weinstein, *Inside Rebellion*; Fearon and Laitin, "Ethnicity, Insurgency, and Civil War"; Michael Doyle and Nicholas Sambanis, "International Peacebuilding: A Theoretical and Quantitative Analysis," *American Political Science Review* 94, no. 4 (2000): 779–801; Nicholas Sambanis, 'Do Ethnic and Non-ethnic Civil Wars Have the Same Causes? A Theoretical and Empirical Inquiry (Part 1)," *Journal of Conflict Resolution* 45, no. 3 (2001): 259–82; Michael L. Ross, "What Do We Know about Natural Resources and Civil War?," *Journal of Peace Research* 41, no. 3 (May 2004): 337–56; Dara Cohen, *Rape during Civil War*

(Ithaca, NY: Cornell University Press, 2016); Elisabeth Jean Wood, "Variation in Sexual Vio-lence during War," *Politics and Society* 34, no. 3 (September 2006): 307–42; Amelia Hoover Green, *The Commander's Dilemma: Violence and Restraint in Wartime* (Ithaca, NY: Cornell Uni-versity Press, 2018); James D. Fearon, "Why Do Some Civil Wars Last So Much Longer Than Others?," *Journal of Peace Research* 41, no. 3 (2004): 275–301; Sarah Zukerman Daly, *Organized Violence after Civil War* (New York: Cambridge University Press, 2016); Page Fortna, *Peace Time: Cease-Fire Agreements and the Durability of Peace* (Princeton, NJ: Princeton University Press, 2004); Jessica Stanton, *Violence and Restraint in Civil War: Civilian Targeting in the Shadow of International Law* (New York: Cambridge University Press, 2016).

18. "Symmetric nonconventional" civil wars involve states using low-firepower counterin-surgency approaches against irregular nonstate foes: see, esp., Stathis Kalyvas and Laia Balcells, "International System and Technologies of Rebellion: How the End of the Cold War Shaped Internal Conflict," *American Political Science Review* 104, no. 3 (August 2010): 415–29, which explains nonstate actors' choices between "conventional," "symmetric nonconventional," and "irregular" methods by reference to international system polarity and the end of the Cold War, but which codes actors' choices by their equipment rather than their behavior; Laia Balcells, *Rivalry and Revenge: The Politics Of Violence During Civil War* (New York: Cambridge University Press, 2017); Adam Lockyer, "The Dynamics of Warfare in Civil War," *Civil Wars* 12, nos. 1–2 (2010): 91–116. Work that observes, but does not explain, conventional behavior by nonstate actors includes S. Jones, *Waging Insurgent Warfare*; J. Stanton, *Violence and Restraint in Civil War*, 27, 226, 241; M.L.R. Smith, "Guerillas in the Mist: Reassessing Strategy and Low Intensity War-fare," *Review of International Studies* 29, no. 1 (January 2003): 19–37. Many also note that in classical Maoist theory a nonstate insurgent force will transition from irregular to conventional methods in its final stage of maturation before unseating an incumbent government: see, e.g., Kalyvas and Balcells, "International System and Technologies of Rebellion"; Isabelle Duyvesteyn, "Conventional War and Collapsed States," in Isabelle Duyvesteyn and Jan Ang-strom, eds., *Rethinking the Nature of War* (Abingdon: Routledge, 2004), 65–87. My concern here is more general and is explanatory as well as descriptive.

19. See, e.g., Oliker, *Russia's Chechen Wars*; Timothy L. Thomas, "The Battle for Grozny: Deadly Classroom for Urban Combat," *Parameters* 29 (Summer 2003): 87–102; *Balkan Battle-grounds*; David Makovsky and Jeffrey White, *Lessons and Implications of the Israel-Hizballah War* (Washington Institute Policy Focus no. 60, 2006); Andrew Exum, *Hizballah at War: A Military Assessment* (Washington Institute Policy Focus no. 63, 2006); S. Biddle, *Afghanistan and the Future of Warfare*; Michael Eisenstadt and Jeffrey White, *Assessing Iraq's Sunni Arab Insurgency* (Washington Institute Policy Focus no. 50, 2005).

20. See, e.g., Robert Keohane, "The Globalization of Informal Violence, Theories of World Politics, and the 'Liberalism of Fear,'" *International Organization* 1 (Spring 2002), https://pdfs .semanticscholar.org/4616/85a2958fcf5b613d37e5617398858f321d14.pdf?_ga=2.111542029 .827134347.1599707639-1806323161.1599707639; Stephen D. Krasner, *Sovereignty: Organized Hy-pocrisy* (Princeton, NJ: Princeton University Press, 1999); Stephen Brooks, *Producing Security: Multinational Corporations, Globalization, and the Changing Calculus of Conflict* (Princeton, NJ: Princeton University Press, 2005); P. W. Singer, *Corporate Warriors: The Rise of the Privatized Military Industry* (Ithaca, NY: Cornell University Press, [2003] 2007); Deborah Avant, *The Market for Force: The Consequences of Privatizing Security* (Cambridge: Cambridge University

Press, 2005); Michael Barnett and Martha Finnemore, *Rules for the World: International Organizations in Global Politics* (Ithaca, NY: Cornell University Press, 2004); Susan Strange, *The Retreat of the State: The Diffusion of Power in the World Economy* (Cambridge: Cambridge University Press, 1996). See also Martin van Creveld, *The Rise and Decline of the State* (Cambridge: Cambridge University Press, 1999); Jessica Matthews, "Power Shift," *Foreign Affairs*, January/February 1997, 50–66; Thomas L. Friedman, *The Lexus and the Olive Tree* (New York: Farrar, Straus, and Giroux, 1999); Thomas L. Friedman, *The World Is Flat* (New York: Farrar, Straus, and Giroux, 2005); Rodney Bruce Hall and Thomas J. Biersteker, eds., *The Emergence of Private Authority in Global Governance* (Cambridge: Cambridge University Press, 2002); Abram Chayes and Antonia Chayes, *The New Sovereignty: Compliance with International Regulatory Agreements* (Cambridge, MA: Harvard University Press, 1995); Neil Walker, *Sovereignty in Transition* (Oxford: Hart, 2004); Paul Verkuil, *Outsourcing Sovereignty: Why Privatization of Government Functions Threatens Democracy and What We Can Do about It* (Cambridge: Cambridge University Press, 2007); John Boli and George Thomas, *Constructing World Culture: International Nongovernmental Organizations since 1875* (Stanford: CA: Stanford University Press, 1999); Ann Florini, *The Third Force: The Rise of Transnational Civil Society* (Washington, DC: Carnegie Endowment for International Peace, 2000); Thomas Risse, Steve Ropp, and Kathryn Sikkink, *The Power of Human Rights: International Norms and Domestic Change* (Cambridge: Cambridge University Press, 1999); van Creveld, *Transformation of War* (New York: Free Press, 1991); Robert Kaplan, *The Coming Anarchy* (New York: Vintage, 2001). For counterarguments, see, e.g., T. V. Paul, John Ikenberry, and John Hall, *The Nation-State in Question* (Princeton, NJ: Princeton University Press, 2003).

21. See, e.g., Anne-Marie Slaughter, *A New World Order* (Princeton, NJ: Princeton University Press, 2004); John Arquilla and David Ronfeldt, eds., *Networks and Netwars: The Future of Terror, Crime, and Militancy* (Santa Monica, CA: RAND, 2001); Newt Gingrich and Nancy Desmond, *The Art of Transformation* (Washington, DC: CHT, 2006); Michele Flournoy, Clark Murdock, Christopher Williams, and Kurt Campbell, *Beyond Goldwater-Nichols: Defense Reform for a New Strategic Era* (Washington, DC: CSIS, 2004); Henry Carey and Oliver Richmond, *Mitigating Conflict: The Role of NGOs* (Hove, East Sussex, England: Frank Cass, 2003); Chester Crocker, Fen Osler Hampson, and Pamela Aall, *Leashing the Dogs of War: Conflict Management in a Divided World* (Washington, DC: USIP, 2007).

22. See, e.g., Chairman of the Joint Chiefs of Staff, *Joint Publication 3–24*, II-1; van Creveld, *Transformation of War*; van Creveld, *Rise and Decline of the State*; R. Smith, *Utility of Force*, e.g., 374–76; Ucko, *New Counterinsurgency Era*; Holsti, *State, War, and the State of War*; Fearon and Laitin, "Ethnicity, Insurgency, and Civil War," 79–80; Weinstein, *Inside Rebellion*, 203; Hammes, *Sling and the Stone*, e.g., 40–41; Kaldor, *New and Old Wars*; Lockyer, "Dynamics of Warfare in Civil War"; Thomas P. M. Barnett, *The Pentagon's New Map: War and Peace in the Twenty-First Century* (New York: Berkley Books, 2004); Thomas K. Adams, "Private Military Companies: Mercenaries for the 21st Century," in *Non-state Threats and Future Wars*, ed. Robert J. Bunker (Portland, OR: Frank Cass, 2003), 54–67; Robert J. Bunker, "Battlespace Dynamics, Information Warfare to Netwar, and Bond-Relationship Targeting," in in Bunker, *Non-state Threats and Future Wars*, 97–108. Michael C. Fowler, *Amateur Soldiers, Global Wars: Insurgency and Modern Conflict* (Westport, CT: Praeger Security International, 2005); Frank Hoffman, *Conflict in the 21st Century: The Rise of Hybrid Wars* (Arlington, VA: Potomac Institute for Policy Studies,

2007); John Arquilla, *Worst Enemy: The Reluctant Transformation of the American Military* (Chicago: Ivan R. Dee, 2008); Frank G. Hoffman, "Complex Irregular Warfare: The Next Revolution in Military Affairs," *Orbis* 50, no. 3 (Summer 2006): 395–411; Bruce Berkowitz, *The New Face of War: How War Will Be Fought in the 21st Century* (New York: Free Press, 2003); Her Majesty's Government, *Securing Britain in an Age of Uncertainty: The Strategic Defense and Security Review* (London: Stationary Office, 2010); Sean J. A. Edwards, *Swarming and the Future of Warfare* (Santa Monica, CA: RAND, 2005); John Arquilla and David Ronfeldt, "The Advent of Netwar (Revisited)," in Arquilla and Ronfeldt, *Networks and Netwars*, 1–25.

23. See, e.g., Richard Shultz and Andrea Dew, *Insurgents, Terrorists and Militias: The Warriors of Contemporary Combat* (New York: Columbia University Press, 2009), 13, 43–44, 114, 139, 252, 262; Ada Bozeman, *Conflict in Africa: Concepts and Realities* (Princeton, NJ: Princeton University Press, 1971), 208, 214; T. E. Lawrence, *Seven Pillars of Wisdom* (London: Jonathan Cape, 1935), e.g., 224; T. E. Lawrence, "Twenty-Seven Articles," *Arab Bulletin*, August 20, 1917, https://wwi.lib.byu.edu/index.php/The_27_Articles_of_T.E._Lawrence; John Walter Jandora, *Militarism in Arab History* (Westport, CT: Greenwood, 1997), 4, 8–9, 123–24; Montgomery McFate, "The 'Memory of War': Tribes and the Legitimate Use of Force in Iraq," in Jeffery Norwich, ed., *Armed Groups: Studies in National Security, Counterterrorism, and Counterinsurgency* (Newport, RI: Naval Institute Press, 2008), 187–202; Jeffrey B. White, "Some Thoughts on Irregular Warfare," *Studies in Intelligence* 39, no. 5 (1996), https://pdfs.semanticscholar.org/f002/9c82e20597 594bccc14df36c16ff9f252681.pdf; Francis Fukuyama, *The Origins of Political Order* (New York: Farrar, Straus and Giroux, 2011), 72–79.

24. See, e.g., van Creveld, *Transformation of War*; R. Smith, *Utility of Force*; Ucko, *New Counterinsurgency Era*; T. Barnett, *Pentagon's New Map*; Fowler, *Amateur Soldiers, Global Wars*.

25. See, e.g., F. Hoffman, *Conflict in the 21st Century*; Hammes, *Sling and the Stone*; Arquilla, *Worst Enemy*; Berkowitz, *New Face of War*. Note that the term "hybrid warfare" has been used in multiple, very different ways in the defense debate. In particular, in the aftermath of the 2014–18 Russian campaigns in the Crimea and Ukraine, some have come to use the term to refer to methods that cross the boundary between peace and war; see, e.g., Chivvis, *Understanding Russian "Hybrid Warfare."* For yet a different usage, see Josef Schroefl and Stuart J. Kaufman, "Hybrid Actors, Tactical Variety: Rethinking Asymmetric and Hybrid War," *Studies in Conflict and Terrorism* 37 (2014): 862–80. In this book, I refer to its earlier use as a description of military methods that blend "conventional" and "irregular" or "guerilla" strategies and tactics, per the sources cited above. David Kilcullen also emphasizes "hybrid" warfare in which irregular methods are combined with high-tech weapons, and in which states and nonstate actors are converging on a common praxis. Kilcullen, however, as I do here, sees this as movement on a continuum rather than between categories; we differ on the causes of this expected movement, but we agree on its description. See David Kilcullen, *The Accidental Guerrilla: Fighting Small Wars in the Midst of a Big One* (New York: Oxford University Press, 2011), 1–38; David Kilcullen, *The Dragons and the Snakes: How the Rest Learned to Fight the West* (New York" Oxford University Press, 2020), e.g., 1–6.

26. S. Jones, *Waging Insurgent Warfare*, presents "conventional," "guerilla," and "punishment" as alternative but not mutually exclusive categories of insurgent strategy (11), though much of the discussion presents them as discrete alternatives, and it codes actors as one or the other at any given time and place (see, e.g., fig. 3.1 on p. 54). I treat the distinction as a true continuum

here, in which almost all actors (state as well as nonstate) employ features of Jones's "conventional" and "guerilla" categories simultaneously, albeit in varying proportion. (I treat the methods Jones frames as "punishment" as elements of Fabianism rather than as a discrete or orthogonal category.) By contrast, most recent work in the civil war literature treats "conventional" and "irregular" (or "guerilla") methods as mutually exclusive categories even when it allows for nonstate use of the former: see, e.g., Kalyvas and Balcells, "International System and Technologies of Rebellion." Lockyer, "Dynamics of Warfare in Civil War," allows nonstate actors to wage conventional war in one location and irregular war in another, but he still treats the two as categorically distinct. For a treatment closer to the stance I adopt here, see M.L.R. Smith, "Guerillas in the Mist."

27. See, e.g., Andrew Krepinevich, "Cavalry to Computer: The Pattern of Military Revolutions," *National Interest*, no. 37 (Fall 1994): 30–42; Vice Admiral Arthur Cebrowski and John Garstka, "Network-Centric Warfare," *U.S. Naval Institute Proceedings*, January 1998, https://www.usni.org/magazines/proceedings/1998/january/network-centric-warfare-its-origin-and-future; Eliot Cohen, "A Revolution in Warfare," *Foreign Affairs*, March/April 1996, https://www.foreignaffairs.com/articles/united-states/1996-03-01/revolution-warfare#:~:text=For%20almost%20a%20decade%20American,as%20the%20military%2Dtechnical%20revolution.&text=Observers%20constantly%20describe%20the%20warfare,progress%20of%20methods%20of%20warfare; Norman C. Davis, "An Information-Based Revolution in Military Affairs," *Strategic Review* 24, no. 1 (Winter 1996): 43–53; Stephen J. Blank, "Prepping for the Next War: Reflections on the Revolution in Military Affairs," *Strategic Review* 24, no. 2 (Spring 1996): 17–25; John Arquilla, "The 'Velvet' Revolution in Military Affairs," *World Policy Journal* 14, no. 4 (Winter 1997/1998): 32–43; Williamson Murray and MacGregor Knox, "Thinking about Revolutions in Warfare," in Murray and Knox, eds., *The Dynamics of Military Revolution, 1300–2050* (Cambridge: Cambridge University Press, 2001); Brigadier General David A. Deptula, *Effects-Based Operations: Change in the Nature of Warfare* (Aerospace Education Foundation, 2001).

28. See, e.g., R. Smith, *Utility of Force*; Ucko, *New Counterinsurgency Era*; Alan J. Vick, Adam Grissom, William Rosenau, Beth Grill, and Karl P. Muller, "Grand Strategy and Counterinsurgency," in *Air Power in the New Counterinsurgency* (Santa Monica, CA: RAND, 2006), 53–80; Stephen T. Hosmer, *The Army's Role in Counterinsurgency and Insurgency*, report prepared for the US Army (Santa Monica, CA: RAND, 1990); Steven Metz, "Learning from Iraq: Counterinsurgency in American Strategy," Strategic Studies Institute, January 2007; Steven Metz and Raymond Millen, "Insurgency and Counterinsurgency in the 21st Century: Reconceptualizing Threat and Response," Strategic Studies Institute, November 2004.

29. See, e.g., John T. Bennett, "Obama Follows in Rumsfeld's Footprints," *Hill*, January 7, 2012, https://thehill.com/policy/defense/202867-obama-follows-in-rumsfelds-footprints; Robert Martinage, *Toward a New Offset Strategy: Exploiting U.S. Long-Term Advantages to Restore U.S. Global Power Projection Capability* (Washington, DC: Center for Strategic and Budgetary Assessments, 2014); Larry O. Spencer, "US Air Force Key to Third Offset Strategy," *Defense News*, November 7, 2016, https://www.defensenews.com/opinion/commentary/2016/11/07/us-air-force-key-to-third-offset-strategy/; Department of Defense, *Summary of the 2018 National Defense Strategy of the United States of America*, 6–7.

30. Note that this finding pertains to the mid-to-high-intensity continental warfare that is the new theory's empirical domain (see the discussion of domain limits below). Maritime

warfare in theaters such as the western Pacific is a different undertaking with different military requirements; for a more detailed discussion, see Stephen Biddle and Ivan Oelrich, "Future Warfare in the Western Pacific: Chinese Antiaccess/Area Denial, U.S. Air Sea Battle, and Command of the Commons in East Asia," *International Security* 41, no. 1 (Summer 2016): 7–48.

31. Malcolm Shaw, *International Law* (New York: Cambridge University Press, 2003), 178. (For a critique of this definition, see Carmel Davis, "Agent-States: The Quetta Shura Taliban," paper presented to the 2013 ISAC/ISSS annual meeting, Washington DC, October 6, 2013.) As an operational proxy I use the Correlates of War project's list of international system membership to identify the list of sovereign states at any given time: Meredith Reid Sarkees and Frank Wayman, *Resort to War: 1816—2007* (Washington, DC: CQ Press, 2010). Note that I assess nonstate status at the outset of a war—I treat separatist movements that begin as nonstate actors but who gain recognition by some UN members as sovereign states during the course of their war of independence as "nonstate actors" until that war reaches a conclusion.

32. This definition thus follows the Correlates of War project's identification of "war": Sarkees and Wayman, *Resort to War*. Note also that I do not restrict "war" to the pursuit of political aims as opposed to profit, hatred, self-expression, or other nonpolitical purposes. I treat the purposes of armed violence in war in greater detail below in chap. 2, but for now suffice to say that given the range of motives often ascribed to nonstate actors I have chosen to define the phenomenon per se via its *scale* as opposed to its *purpose*, and thus the book's scope extends to any of the prospective motives advanced in the literature.

33. The account below is drawn from Shultz and Dew, *Insurgents, Terrorists and Militias*; Lawrence, *Seven Pillars of Wisdom*; Lawrence, "Twenty-Seven Articles"; Bozeman, *Conflict in Africa*; Fukuyama, *Origins of Political Order*, 72–79; McFate, "'Memory of War'"; White, "Some Thoughts on Irregular Warfare"; and Jandora, *Militarism in Arab History*; also Thomas H. Johnson and M. Chris Mason, "No Sign until the Burst of Fire: Understanding the Pakistan-Afghanistan Frontier," *International Security* 32, no. 4 (Spring 2008): 41–77 at 61–63; and Reed Wadley, "Treachery and Deceit: Parallels in Tribal and Terrorist Warfare?," *Studies in Conflict and Terrorism* 26, no. 5 (2003): 331–45; and it also draws on the broader causal logic in Francis Fukuyama, *Trust: The Social Virtues and the Creation of Prosperity* (New York: Free Press), 23–32; and Lucian Pye, "Introduction: Political Culture and Political Development," in Lucian Pye and Sidney Verba, eds., *Political Culture and Political Development* (Princeton, NJ: Princeton University Press, 1965), 3–26.

34. See, e.g., Donald P. Cole, "Alliance and Descent in the Middle East," in Akbar S. Ahmed and David M. Hart, eds., *Islam in Tribal Societies* (London: Routledge and Kegan Paul, 2007), 169–86 at 81.

35. Shultz and Dew, *Insurgents, Terrorists and Militias*, 262.

36. See, e.g., Alastair Iain Johnston, "Thinking about Strategic Culture," *International Security* 19, no. 4 (Spring 1995): 32–64; Elizabeth Kier, *Imagining War: French and British Military Doctrine between the Wars* (Princeton, NJ: Princeton University Press, 1997); Carl Builder, *The Masks of War: American Military Styles in Strategy and Analysis* (Baltimore: Johns Hopkins University Press, 1989); Russell Weigley, *The American Way of War: A History of United States Military Strategy and Policy* (Bloomington: Indiana University Press, 1977); Peter J. Katzenstein, ed., *The Culture of National Security* (New York: Columbia University Press, 1996); Dima Adamsky, *The Culture of Military Innovation* (Palo Alto, CA: Stanford University Press, 2010); Theo Farrell,

The Norms of War: Cultural Beliefs and Modern Conflict (Boulder, CO: Lynne Rienner, 2005); Thomas Berger, "From Sword to Chrysanthemum: Japan's Culture of Anti-militarism," *International Security* 17, no. 4 (Spring 1993): 119–50; Jeffrey Legro, "Military Culture and Inadvertent Escalation in World War II," *International Security* 18, no. 4 (1994): 108–42; Brian McAllister Linn, *The Echo of Battle: The Army's Way of War* (Cambridge, MA: Harvard University Press, 2007); John Keegan, *A History of Warfare* (New York: Alfred A. Knopf, 1994); Victor Davis Hanson, *Carnage and Culture: Landmark Battles in the Rise of Western Power* (New York: Anchor Books, 2001).

37. The theory below is thus an example of "as if" theorizing: I do not claim that actors solve equations, but I assume that one can approximate their choices by assuming that they behave *as if* they had, using a selection mechanism as the causal logic by which the "as if" assumption is viable. On "as if" theorizing, see, e.g., Milton Friedman, *Essays in Positive Economics* (Chicago: University of Chicago Press, 1953), 41; cf. Timothy McKeown, "The Limitations of 'Structural' Theories of Commercial Policy," *International Organization* 40, no. 1 (Winter 1986): 43–64. Note also that I assume only a very weak version of rationality. Among the more important constraints I impose on behavioral choice are several that relate to limited skill as a consequence of organizational failure to train or educate or motivate their members. I do not assume clairvoyant or boundlessly energetic leaders or fighters. The theory below is thus within the intellectual traditions of rational choice theory broadly defined, but only with a very "thin" definition of rationality that amounts to a minimalist assumption that actors behave purposefully: their actions are intended to produce outcomes beneficial to the actors (given a variety of constraints on actors' knowledge and abilities). On thin or "procedural" definitions of rationality, see, e.g., Herbert Simon, *Models of Bounded Rationality* (Cambridge, MA.: MIT Press, 1982).

38. These interviews were conducted under ground rules that permitted interviewees to be identified only to the degree that they preauthorized. Some are thus cited below by full name and rank, some by rank and initials, some by rank and only first initial, and some only by interview number. All interviews were audiotaped; audio files have been deposited with the US Army Military History Institute archive in Carlisle, Pennsylvania, where preauthorization so permitted. The Somalia case benefited from an extensive interview with former US ambassador Robert Oakley but did not receive the scale of participant interaction that the Lebanon, Iraq, and Croatia cases did. The politico-military conduct of the Vietnam War is unusually well documented; interview access was unnecessary to code the key variables for this case. In addition to these 137 interviews on the Iraq, Croatia, Lebanon, and Somalia cases, the work documented here was also informed by the results of an additional 46 interviews conducted with US participants in the post-2001 Afghan war against the Taliban, and an additional 176 interviews with US participants in the 2003 campaign against the Iraqi state military: see S. Biddle, *Afghanistan and the Future of Warfare*; S. Biddle, "Speed Kills." On the issue of bias in field research and its minimization, see, esp., Romain Malejacq and Dipali Mukhopadhyay, "The 'Tribal Politics' of Field Research: A Reflection on Power and Partiality in 21st-Century Warzones," *Perspectives on Politics* 14, no. 4 (December 2016): 1011–28.

39. On the requirements of sound case selection more broadly, see, e.g., Alexander George and Andrew Bennett, *Case Studies and Theory Development in the Social Sciences* (Cambridge, MA: MIT Press, 2005); Andrew Bennett and Colin Elman, "Case Study Methods in the

International Relations Subfield," *Comparative Political Studies* 40, no. 2 (February 2007): 170–95; Robert Yin, *Case Study Research: Design and Methods* (Thousand Oaks, CA: Sage, 2009); Harry Eckstein, "Case Study and Theory in Political Science," in Fred Greenstein and Nelson Polsby, eds. *Strategies of Inquiry*, vol. 7 of *The Handbook of Political Science* (Menlo Park, CA: Addison-Wesley, 1975), 79–137; Alexander George, "Case Studies and Theory Development: The Method of Structured, Focused Comparison," in Paul G. Lauren, ed., *Diplomacy: New Approaches in History, Theory, and Policy* (New York: Free Press, 1979), 43–68; Arend Lijphart, "Comparative Politics and the Comparative Method," *American Political Science Review* 65 (September 1971): 682–93; Arend Lijphart, "The Comparable-Cases Strategy in Comparative Research," *Comparative Political Studies* 8, no. 2 (July 1975): 158–77.

Chapter Two: The Fallacy of Guerilla Warfare

1. See, e.g., Guenter Lewy, *America in Vietnam* (New York: Oxford University Press, 1978), 44, 114, 136, 437–41; Krepinevich, *Army and Vietnam*; Nagl, *Learning to Eat Soup with a Knife*; Ucko, *New Counterinsurgency Era*, e.g., 28–29, 43; Max Boot, *The Road Not Taken: Edward Lansdale and the American Tragedy in Vietnam* (New York: Liveright, 2019); Thomas Ricks, *Fiasco: The American Military Adventure in Iraq* (New York: Penguin, 2007); Linda Robinson, *Tell Me How This Ends: General David Petraeus and the Search for a Way Out of Iraq* (New York: Public Affairs, 2008).

2. Carl von Clausewitz, *On War*, trans. Michael Howard and Peter Paret (Princeton, NJ: Princeton University Press, [1832] 1989), e.g., 88.

3. See, e.g., Shultz and Dew, *Insurgents, Terrorists and Militias*, 1–7; van Creveld, *Transformation of War*; Philip Meilinger, "Busting the Icon: Restoring Balance to the Influence of Clausewitz," *Strategic Studies Quarterly* 1 (Fall 2007): 116–45; Steven Metz, "A Wake for Clausewitz: Toward a Philosophy of 21st-Century Warfare," *Parameters* 24 (Winter 1994–95), https://www.clausewitz.com/readings/Metz.htm; Keegan, *History of Warfare*; Ralph Peters, "The Warrior Class," *Parameters* 24 (Summer 1994): 16–24.

4. On lootable resources and their role in indiscriminate violence, see, e.g., Weinstein, *Inside Rebellion*; Paul Collier and Anke Hoeffler, "Resource Rents, Governance, and Conflict," *Journal of Conflict Resolution* 49, no. 4 (2005): 625–33; Paul Staniland, "Organizing Insurgency: Networks, Resources, and Rebellion in South Asia," *International Security* 37, no. 1 (Summer 2012): 142–77; M. Ross, "What Do We Know about Natural Resources and Civil War?"

5. David Kilcullen, "Countering Global Insurgency," *Journal of Strategic Studies* 28, no. 4 (2005): 597–617; Sergei Boeke, "Al Qaeda in the Islamic Maghreb: Terrorism, Insurgency, or Organized Crime?," *Small Wars and Insurgencies* 27, no. 5 (2016): 914–30; Michael F. Morris, "Al Qaeda as Insurgency," *Joint Force Quarterly*, no. 39 (Winter 2005): 41–49. Cf. Thomas Rid and Marc Hecker, *War 2.0: Irregular Warfare in the Information Age* (Westport, CT: Praeger, 2009), which argues that *insurgents* seek to control populations, whereas internet-age *terrorists* increasingly seek only nihilist violence (e.g., 220). Yet Rid and Hecker see the latter as a self-defeating artifact of internet terrorism's inability to control its own radically decentralized adherents—in fact, this is not an *aim*; it is an unintended consequence of failure in the pursuit of aims that are actually not meaningfully different from those of classical insurgents, i.e., the control of populations.

6. Stephen Biddle, Jeffrey A. Friedman, and Jacob N. Shapiro, "Testing the Surge: Why Did Violence Decline in Iraq in 2007?," *International Security* 37, no. 1 (Summer 2012): 7–40 at 13–18; Silva Meznaric and Jelena Zlatkovic Winter, "Forced Migration and Refugee Flows in Croatia, Slovenia and Bosnia-Herzegovina: Early Warning, Beginning and Current State of Flows," *Refuge* 12, no. 7 (February 1993): 3–5. Nor is this unique to modern religious warfare, or to nonstate actors in irregular conflicts. The Old Testament motivates Moses's destruction of the Canaanite kingdoms of Sihon and Og as efforts to prevent sin among living Israelites: Deuteronomy 20:16–18. Perhaps the closest recent approximation of a true extermination campaign, the Nazi Holocaust, occurred in the context of a major interstate conventional world war. Religious motivations can affect the intensity or duration of the fighting—see, e.g., Michael Horowitz, "Long Time Going: Religion and the Duration of Crusading," *International Security* 34, no. 2 (Fall 2009): 180–87—or the methods used (see below). But the aim is still normally to control the choices and behavior of living human populations, not simply to slaughter in God's name for its own sake.

7. Human Rights Watch, *Q&A on Joseph Kony and the Lord's Resistance Army*, March 21, 2012, https://www.hrw.org/news/2012/03/21/qa-joseph-kony-and-lords-resistance-army.

8. T. Johnson and Mason, "No Sign"; Peter Tomsen, *The Wars of Afghanistan: Messianic Terrorism, Tribal Conflicts, and the Failures of the Great Powers* (New York: Public Affairs, 2011), 45–62; James W. Spain, *The Way of the Pathans* (Oxford: Oxford University Press, 1972).

9. Omar Bortolazzi, "Hezbollah: Between Islam and Political Society Popular Mobilization and Social Entrepreneurship in Lebanon," paper presented at Takaful 2011: The First Annual Conference on Arab Philanthropy and Engagement, American University in Cairo, April 16–17, 2011, 26–36; Krista E. Wiegand, "Reformation of a Terrorist Group: Hezbollah as Lebanese Political Party," *Studies in Conflict and Terrorism* 32, no. 8 (2009): 669–80; cf. Brynjar Lia and Thomas Hegghammer, "Jihadi Strategic Studies: The Alleged Al Qaida Policy Study Preceding the Madrid Bombings," *Studies in Conflict and Terrorism* 27, no. 5 (September 2004): 355–75.

10. Andrew Kydd and Barbara Walter, for example, enumerate the goals of terrorism as "regime change, territorial change, policy change, social control, and status quo maintenance"; all involve the use of violence to control the decisions of civilian governments or populations: Kydd and Walter, "The Strategies of Terrorism," *International Security* 31, no. 1 (Summer 2006): 49–79 at 52.

11. *Jacobellis v. Ohio*, 378 U.S. 184 (1964). On the difficulty of defining "guerilla" or "irregular" warfare, see M.L.R. Smith, "Guerillas in the Mist"; also Duyvesteyn, "Conventional War and Collapsed States."

12. See, e.g., Mao Tse-Tung, *On Guerilla Warfare*, trans. Samuel B. Griffith (Mineola, NY: Dover, 2005), 97; Ernesto Guevara, *Guerilla Warfare* (Old Chelsea, NY: Ocean, 2006), 22; Bard E. O'Neill, *Insurgency and Terrorism: Inside Modern Revolutionary Warfare* (Dulles, VA: Brassey's, 1990), 53–57.

13. For a more detailed discussion, see Stephen Biddle, *Military Power: Explaining Victory and Defeat in Modern Battle* (Princeton, NJ: Princeton University Press, 2004), chaps. 3 and 4.

14. See, e.g., Richard Holmes, *Acts of War: The Behavior of Men in Battle* (New York: Free Press, 1986); Christopher Hamner, "Enduring Danger, Surviving Fear: Combat Experience and American Infantrymen in the War for Independence, the Civil War, and the Second World War"

(PhD diss., Department of History, University of North Carolina, 2004), e.g., 11, 29, 36, 54, 109, 141, 185–86, 198–99.

15. See, e.g., Mao, *On Guerilla Warfare*, 92–93; Guevara, *Guerilla Warfare*, 19–20, 26; S. Jones, *Waging Insurgent Warfare*, 35–43, 57–82; R. Smith, *Utility of Force*, 280–86; Ian F. W. Beckett, *Modern Insurgencies and Counter-insurgencies* (New York: Routledge, 2001), 2; Anthony James Joes, *Resisting Rebellion: The History and Politics of Counterinsurgency* (Lexington: University Press of Kentucky, 2004), 13; Richard Clutterbuck, *Guerillas and Terrorists* (Athens: Ohio University Press, 1980), 26; David Kilcullen, "Counterinsurgency Redux," *Survival* 48, no. 4 (December 2006): 119.

16. On urban combat in conventional warfare, see Michael C. Desch, ed., *Soldiers in Cities: Military Operations on Urban Terrain* (Carlisle, PA: Strategic Studies Institute, 2001); William G. Robertson and Lawrence A. Yates, eds., *Block by Block: The Challenges of Urban Operations* (Fort Leavenworth, KS: US Army Command and General Staff College Press, 2003); *FM 90-10: Military Operations on Urban Terrain* (Washington, DC: Headquarters, US Department of the Army, 1979); *Handbook for Joint Urban Operations* (Washington, DC: Joint Staff, 2000); John A. English, *On Infantry* (New York: Praeger, 1984), 185–216.

17. Another form of "stealth" in interstate war is deception, which has played a major role in a wide range of conventional interstate wars including the World War II Normandy invasion and the 1973 Egyptian invasion of the Sinai. On deception in interstate war, see, e.g., Richard Betts, *Surprise Attack: Lessons for Defense Planning* (Washington, DC: Brookings, 1982); Ephraim Kam, *Surprise Attack: The Victim's Perspective* (Cambridge, MA: Harvard University Press, 2004); Barton Whaley, *Turnabout and Deception: Crafting the Double-Cross and the Theory of Outs* (Annapolis, MD: US Naval Institute Press, 2016).

18. "Decisive engagement" is a condition wherein defenders remain in position under assault even after the attackers have gotten close enough that the defenders cannot readily withdraw without being overrun. As the Defense Department defines it, "in land and naval warfare, an engagement in which a unit is considered fully committed and cannot maneuver or extricate itself. In the absence of outside assistance, the action must be fought to a conclusion and either won or lost with the forces at hand" (http://www.js.pentagon.mil/doctrine/jel/doddict/data /d/01536.html). On the unwillingness of classical guerillas to accept decisive engagement for the defense of ground, see, e.g., Mao, *On Guerilla Warfare*, 52, 97, 102; Guevara, *Guerilla Warfare*, 20, 22, 26; Beckett, *Modern Insurgencies and Counter-insurgencies*, 2; O'Neill, *Insurgency and Terrorism*, 25–26; Joes, *Resisting Rebellion*, 18; Walter Laqueur, *Guerrilla: A Historical and Critical Study* (Boston: Little, Brown, 1976), viii, 3; Robert B. Asprey, *War in the Shadows: The Guerilla in History* (Garden City, NY: Doubleday, 1975), 1:xi; S. Metz and Millen, "Insurgency and Counterinsurgency in the 21st Century," 2; Harel and Issacharoff, *34 Days*, 129.

19. See, e.g., *FM 3.0: Operations* (Washington, DC: Headquarters, Department of the Army, 2001), paras. 8–28 through 8–31; *FM 71-1, Tank and Mechanized Infantry Company Team* (Washington, DC: Headquarters, Department of the Army, 1998), chap. 4, sec. 6.

20. See, e.g., *FM 3.0: Operations*, paras. 8–14 through 8–19.

21. See, e.g., *FM 71-1, Tank and Mechanized Infantry Company Team*, chap. 3, sec. 6; chap. 4.

22. See, e.g., *FM 5-102, Countermobility* (Washington, DC: Headquarters, Department of the Army, 1985), chap. 2; *FM 6-20-30, Tactics, Techniques, and Procedures for Fire Support for Corps*

and Division Operations (Washington, DC: Headquarters, Department of the Army, 1989), appendix B, secs. I and II.

23. During the Chinese civil war from 1945 to 1949, for instance, Communist forces attempted to hold several cities in the face of nationalist offensives: In 1945, 110,000 Communist troops suffered 40,000 casualties in a failed defense of Szeping; in 1946, 20,000 of 70,000 Communists were killed trying to defend Jukao; in 1947, 20,000 of 60,000 Communists were killed when nationalist forces relieved the siege of Tehwei (figures from Michael Clodfelter, *Warfare and Armed Conflicts: A Statistical Reference to Casualty and Other Figures, 1500–2000*, 2nd ed. [Jefferson, NC: McFarland, 2002], 695–96). Greek insurgents concentrated 12,000 fighters in the Grammos Mountain region in 1949; they suffered large numbers of casualties attempting to protect the area and could no longer continue significant resistance (Joes, *Resisting Rebellion*, 185–86). FARC guerillas in Colombia have demonstrated the willingness and capability to resist combined ground-air attacks from government forces (David Spencer, "Bogota Continues to Bleed as FARC Find Their Military Feet," *Jane's Intelligence Review*, November 1, 1998, 35; Jeremy McDermott, "Colombian Insurgency Escalates as Guerillas Go Back on Offensive," *Jane's Intelligence Review*, July 1, 2005). Guerilla groups have conducted numerous offensives and sieges against important strategic locations: prominent examples include the 1968 Tet Offensive in Vietnam, the 1975 Khmer Rouge offensive against Phnom Penh, the 1989 FMLN offensive against San Salvador, and the Chinese Communist attack on Suchow in 1948 (see, e.g., Clodfelter, *Warfare and Armed Conflicts*, 689–90, 696, 712, 757–59).

24. See, e.g., Mao, *On Guerilla Warfare*, 52, 97–98, 102–4; S. Jones, *Waging Insurgent Warfare*, 40–41; O'Neill, *Insurgency and Terrorism*, 25–26, 37; Joes, *Resisting Rebellion*, 12–13, 19; Laqueur, *Guerilla*, viii, 124–25; Asprey, *War in the Shadows*, 1:xi; Kilcullen, "Counterinsurgency Redux," 117–18, 120; S. Metz and Millen, "Insurgency and Counterinsurgency in the 21st Century," 6.

25. See, e.g., *FM 71-1, Tank and Mechanized Infantry Company Team*, chap. 3, sec. 2; on "infiltration tactics" in World War I, see, e.g., Timothy Lupfer, *The Dynamics of Doctrine: Changes in German Tactical Doctrine during the First World War*, Leavenworth Paper 4 (Fort Leavenworth, KS: US Army Combat Studies Institute, 1981), 43–46; Shelford Bidwell and Dominick Graham, *Firepower: British Army Weapons and Theories of War, 1904–1945* (London: Allen and Unwin, 1985), 94–130, 139–46; Paddy Griffith, *Battle Tactics of the Western Front* (New Haven, CT: Yale University Press, 1994), 93–100, 120–58; Bruce Gudmundsson, *Stormtroop Tactics: Innovation in the German Army, 1914–1918* (New York: Praeger, 1989); English, *On Infantry*, 17–26; J.B.A. Bailey, *Field Artillery and Firepower* (Oxford: Military Press, 1989), 141–52; Robin Prior and Trevor Wilson, *Command on the Western Front* (Oxford: Blackwell, 1992), 311–15, 362–66; G. C. Wynne, *If Germany Attacks: The Battle in Depth in the West* ([London: Faber and Faber, 1940] Westport, CT: Greenwood, 1976), 327.

26. Jeffrey Jukes, *Kursk: The Clash of Armor* (New York: Ballantine, 1968), 54.

27. Max Hastings, *Overlord* (New York: Simon and Schuster, 1984), 176.

28. Rick Atkinson, *Crusade: The Untold Story of the Persian Gulf War* (New York: Mariner, 1993), 418–21; Steven Lee Myers, "Iraqi Missile Hits Army Base," *New York Times*, April 7, 2003, https://www.nytimes.com/2003/04/07/international/worldspecial/iraqi-missile-hits-army -base.html.

29. M. Gordon and Trainor, *Cobra II*, 648.

30. Thomas Schelling, *Arms and Influence* (New Haven, CT: Yale University Press, 1966), esp. 2–6.

31. See, e.g., Ivan Arreguin-Toft, *How the Weak Win Wars: A Theory of Asymmetric Conflict* (Cambridge: Cambridge University Press, 2005); S. Jones, *Waging Insurgent Warfare*, 41–43; Hammes, *Sling and the Stone*; Roger W. Barnett, *Asymmetrical Warfare: Today's Challenge to U.S. Military Power* (Washington, DC: Brassey's, 2003); H. John Poole, *Tactics of the Crescent Moon: Militant Muslim Combat Methods* (Emerald Isle, NC: Posterity), 2004; R. Smith, *Utility of Force*; Frank Kitson, *Low Intensity Operations: Subversion, Insurgency, Peace-Keeping* (Harrisburg, PA: Stackpole), 1971; Gil Merom, *How Democracies Lose Small Wars: State, Society, and the Failures of France in Algeria, Israel, and Lebanon, and the United States in Vietnam* (New York: Cambridge University Press), 2003; O'Neill, *Insurgency and Terrorism*; Joes, *Resisting Rebellion*; Shultz and Dew, *Insurgents, Terrorists, and Militias*, 18–54; S. Metz and Millen, "Insurgency and Counterinsurgency in the 21st Century," 2, 6; Andrew J. R. Mack, "Why Big Nations Lose Small Wars: The Politics of Asymmetric Conflict," *World Politics* 27, no. 2 (January 1975): 175–200; Stephen P. Rosen, "War and the Willingness to Suffer," in Bruce M. Russett, ed., *Peace, War and Numbers* (Beverly Hills, CA: Sage, 1972), 167–83.

32. Schelling, *Arms and Influence*, 2–6.

33. Schelling, *Arms and Influence*, 22–24, 32, 176–84.

34. This is consistent with the understanding of conventional interstate war termination as coercive bargaining inherent in the bargaining model of war: see, esp., Dan Reiter, *How Wars End* (Princeton, NJ: Princeton University Press, 2009); Paul Pillar, *Negotiating Peace: War Termination as a Bargaining Process* (Princeton, NJ: Princeton University Press, 2009).

35. Charles Webster and Noble Frankland, *The Strategic Air Offensive against Germany, 1939–1945* (London: HMSO, 1961); Tami Davis Biddle, *Rhetoric and Reality in Air Warfare: The Evolution of British and American Ideas about Strategic Bombing, 1914–1945* (Princeton, NJ: Princeton University Press, 2002), 214–88; Robert A. Pape, *Bombing to Win: Air Power and Coercion in War* (Ithaca, NY: Cornell University Press, 1996), 87–136, 254–313.

36. On the coercive nature of the Gulf War air campaign, see Eliot A. Cohen, Director, *Gulf War Airpower Survey*, vol. 1, part 1, *Planning* (Washington, DC: Government Printing Office, 1993), 123, 130–31, 163; Pape, *Bombing to Win*, esp. 214–19.

37. See, e.g., Ivo H. Daalder and Michael E. O'Hanlon, *Winning Ugly: NATO's War to Save Kosovo* (Washington, DC: Brookings Institution Press, 2000), esp. 91–96, 101, 208–10.

38. James B. Wood, *Japanese Military Strategy in the Pacific War* (Lanham, MD: Rowman and Littlefield, 2007), 23; Gerhard L. Weinberg, *A World at Arms: A Global History of World War II* (New York: Cambridge University Press, 1994), 190–91; Woodburn Kirby, *The War against Japan* (London, HMSO, 1969), 5:96, 149, 393–406; Robert J. C. Butow, *Japan's Decision to Surrender* (Stanford, CA: Stanford University Press, 1954), 43, reference 1; Pape, *Bombing to Win*, 110–13.

39. See, e.g., Gunther Rothenberg, "Moltke, Schlieffen, and the Problem of Strategic Envelopment," in Peter Paret, ed., *Makers of Modern Strategy* (Princeton, NJ: Princeton University Press, 1986), 296–325; Jehuda Wallach, *The Dogma of the Battle of Annihilation* (Westport, CT: Greenwood, 1986); J. P. Harris, "The Myth of Blitzkrieg," *War in History* 2, no. 3 (November 1995): 335–52.

40. Erich von Falkenhayn, *General Headquarters and Its Critical Decisions* (London: Hutchinson, 1919), 216; Ottokar Czernin, *In the World War* (New York: Cassell, 1919), 116; Hein

Goemans, *War and Punishment: The Causes of War Termination and the First World War* (Princeton, NJ: Princeton University Press, 2000), 88, 97.

41. Weinberg, *World at Arms*, 587–88; John Keegan, *The Second World War* (New York: Penguin, 1990): 209–10; B. H. Liddell Hart, *History of the Second World War* (New York: Putnam's, 1970), 169, 485, 493; Pape, *Bombing to Win*, 288–89.

42. Clausewitz, *On War*, 90–99.

43. US military doctrine defines "asymmetric warfare" as warfare involving "dissimilarities in organization, equipment, doctrine, capabilities, and values between other armed forces (formally organized or not) and US forces. . . . Engagements are symmetric if forces, technologies, and weapons are similar; they are asymmetric if forces, technologies, and weapons are different, or if a resort to terrorism and rejection of more conventional rules of engagement are the norm." Department of the Army, *Field Manual 3–0, Operations* (Washington, DC: Government Printing Office, 2001), 4–31. On US military usage, see also Joint Chiefs of Staff, *Joint Publication 1–02, Department of Defense Dictionary of Military and Associated Terms* (Washington, DC: Government Printing Office, 2016), 17; Steven Metz and Douglas Johnson, *Asymmetry and U.S. Military Strategy: Definition, Background, and Strategic Concepts* (Carlisle, PA: US Army War College Strategic Studies Institute, 2001); R. Barnett, *Asymmetrical Warfare*; Clinton J. Ancker and Michael D. Burke, "Doctrine for Asymmetric Warfare," *Military Review* 83, no. 4 (July–August 2003): 18–25; Stephen Pomper, *Principles of Asymmetry* (Fort Leavenworth, KS: US Army Command and General Staff College, 2005).

44. In fact some see suicide bombing, in particular, as a distinctively nonstate tactic of sufficient importance to warrant extended analysis of its effectiveness per se: see, e.g., Robert Pape, *Dying to Win: The Strategic Logic of Suicide Terrorism* (New York: Random House, 2006); Mia Bloom, *Dying to Kill: The Allure of Suicide Terror* (New York: Columbia University Press, 2007); Martha Crenshaw, "Explaining Suicide Terrorism: A Review Essay," *Security Studies* 16, no. 1 (2007): 133–62. Of course, suicide attacks are not unique to nonstate actors, either, as illustrated by the Japanese kamikazes of World War II; on the history of suicide warfare by state and nonstate actors, see, e.g., M. Bloom, *Dying to Kill*, 1–18; Pape, *Dying to Win*, 11–15, 35–37. On the effectiveness of suicide bombing by nonstate actors in particular, see, esp., S. Jones, *Waging Insurgent Warfare*, 59, 72–75. Below I treat suicide bombing not as a sui generis phenomenon, but as one element of the larger system of Fabian war making.

45. Stephen Biddle, "The Past as Prologue: Assessing Theories of Future Warfare," *Security Studies* 8, no. 1 (Autumn 1998): 1–74 at 45–51; Jonathan House, *Toward Combined Arms Warfare: A Survey of 20th Century Tactics, Doctrine and Organization* (Fort Leavenworth, KS: US Army Combat Studies Institute, 1984), 123; Robert Citino, *Armored Forces: History and Sourcebook* (Westport, CT: Greenwood, 1994), 49–50.

46. Robert A. Pape, "Why Japan Surrendered," *International Security* 18, no. 2 (Fall 1993): 154–201; Jeffrey Record, *Japan's Decision for War in 1941: Some Enduring Lessons* (Carlisle, PA: Strategic Studies Institute, 2009), 24–47; John Ellis, *Brute Force: Allied Strategy and Tactics in the Second World War* (New York: Viking, 1990), 537. There was eventually a major US strategic bombing campaign directed against the Japanese homeland for a combination of purposes— some of them coercive (to break Japanese will to fight by imposing pain), and some much closer to brute force (to destroy Japanese war-supporting industry and thereby undermine Japanese military forces' effectiveness in the field). The war ended with an essentially coercive atomic

bombing of Hiroshima and Nagasaki, but planning was already well under way for a brute force invasion of the Japanese home islands (Operation Olympic) in the event that the Japanese fought on: D. M. Giangreco, "Operation Downfall: The Devil War in the Details," *Joint Force Quarterly* (Autumn 1995): 86–94. US strategy thus involved a much larger element of brute force than did Japan's, which was almost entirely coercive in its logic throughout the war.

47. Jeffrey Hughes, "The Origins of World War II in Europe: British Deterrence Failure and German Expansionism," *Journal of Interdisciplinary History* 18, no. 4 (Spring 1988): 851–91; Alex Weisiger, *Logics of War: Explanations for Limited and Unlimited Conflicts* (Ithaca, NY: Cornell University Press, 2013), 105–40; Randall Schweller, "Tripolarity and the Second World War," *International Studies Quarterly* 37, no. 1 (March 1993): 73–103.

48. On the ubiquity of asymmetry in warfare, see, e.g., S. Metz and Johnson, *Asymmetry and U.S. Military Strategy*; Edward Luttwak, *Strategy: The Logic of War and Peace* (Cambridge, MA: Belknap Press of Harvard University Press, 2002), 2–5; Basil Liddell Hart, *Strategy: The Indirect Approach* (London: Faber and Faber, 1954). In fact, the concept has been central to warfare for over a millennium; see Sun Tzu, *The Art of War*, trans. Samuel B. Griffith (New York: Oxford University Press, 1963), e.g., 67, 69, 89, 101.

49. Other common uses of the term "asymmetric warfare" include the use of ballistic missiles, cyberattacks, naval mines, or propaganda to offset American advantages in weight or precision of firepower: see, e.g., S. Metz and Johnson, *Asymmetry and U.S. Military Strategy*, 14.

50. International law adds the criterion of not fighting under the command of a recognized state authority to the definition of "irregular," but this, too, makes the formulation circular for my purposes by treating the distinctive quality of nonstate warfare as whatever nonstate actors do in war: Michael Skerker, "The Rights of Irregular Combatants," *International Journal of Intelligence Ethics* 2, no. 1 (2011): 36.

51. Michael Lee Lanning and Dan Cragg, *Inside the VC and the NVA: The Real Story of North Vietnam's Armed Forces* (New York: Ivy Books, 1992), 117–18, 203; James W. Trullinger, *Village at War: An Account of Conflict in Vietnam* (Stanford, CA: Stanford University Press, 1994), 83; George K. Tanham, *Communist Revolutionary Warfare: From the Vietminh to the Viet Cong* (Westport, CT: Praeger, 2006), 88; Warren Wilkins, *Grab Their Belts: The Viet Cong's Big-Unit War against the U.S., 1965–66* (Annapolis, MD: Naval Institute Press, 2011), 18, 35–36.

52. US Department of Defense Dictionary of Military and Associated Terms, http://www .dtic.mil/doctrine/dod_dictionary/.

53. See, e.g., *Joint Publication 3–05, Special Operations* (Washington, DC: US Department of Defense, 2014), x, II-3, GL-12.

54. Note that this framing posits a more extreme version of Fabian strategy than even Fabius himself was willing to adopt: the soldiers under his command in the Second Punic War wore uniforms, fought in rural areas without civilian intermingling, concentrated for local attacks on Carthaginian foraging parties, and were armed and equipped in ways broadly similar to the Carthaginian infantry (though without the elephants Hannibal used as shock forces): see, e.g., John Francis Lazenby, *Hannibal's War: A Military History of the Second Punic War* (Norman: University of Oklahoma Press, 1998), 13–16, 68; Dexter Hoyos, *A Companion to the Punic Wars* (Oxford, UK: Wiley-Blackwell, 2011), 285; the Fabian archetype described here is rare enough that not even its namesake embraced it fully.

55. Note that even Napoleonic state armies employed skirmishers and light cavalry whose mission was to harass and delay massed hostile infantry, inflict gradual attrition, and raid enemy communications: see, e.g., David Chandler, *The Campaigns of Napoleon* (New York: Scribner, 1973), 345; Rory Muir, *Tactics and the Experience of Battle in the Age of Napoleon* (New Haven, CT: Yale University Press, 2000), 105–9. Like the Fabian extreme, the "Napoleonic" archetype above is rare enough that not even Bonaparte embraced it fully in its pure form.

56. On this central problem of modern tactics—surviving what Ernst Junger termed the modern battlefield's "storm of steel"—see S. Biddle, *Military Power*, chap. 3; Ernst Junger, *The Storm of Steel*, translated by Basil Creighton (London: Chatto and Windus, 1929).

57. On the UVF, see, e.g., Office of the Chief of the General Staff, *Operation Banner: An Analysis of Military Operations in Northern Ireland* (London: Her Majesty's Stationery Office, 2006); Jacob Shapiro, *The Terrorist's Dilemma* (Princeton, NJ: Princeton University Press, 2013), 192–96; Aaron Edwards, *UVF: Behind the Mask* (County Kildare, Ireland: Merrion, 2017), chap. 9; Steve Bruce, "Terrorism and Politics: The Case of Northern Ireland's Loyalist Paramilitaries," *Terrorism and Political Violence* 13, no. 2 (2001): 27–48.

58. Specifically, a coding of (0, 0, na, 0, 0, 0, 0, 0, 1, na, 0) by the scoring system described in the appendix and tabulated in table A-1, yielding a weighted overall value of 0.3. (Note that without full case studies it is difficult to code nonstate actors rigorously. The illustrative codings in this chapter thus make conservative assumptions with respect to the conventional wisdom of nonstate "guerilla" behavior where evidence is lacking: in such cases, the illustrative codings here assume, for example, perfectly uniform distribution of entirely civilian-clothed fighters in the absence of secondary-source documentation to the contrary. The nonstate values here are thus lower bounds on the values that would emerge from a more detailed, case-length analysis, which would produce equal or higher index scores for these actors. For a more detailed discussion of coding criteria, see the appendix.)

59. On the RUF, see, e.g., Ibrahim Abdullah, "Bush Path to Destruction: The Origin and Character of the Revolutionary United Front/Sierra Leone," *Journal of Modern African Studies* 36, no. 2 (June 1998): 203–35; "The Revolutionary United Front," Globalsecurity.org, http://www.globalsecurity.org/military/world/para/ruf.htm; Larry J. Woods, *Military Interventions in Sierra Leone: Lessons from a Failed State* (Darby, PA: Diane, 2010), 27–31.

60. Specifically, a coding of (0.5, 0.5, 0.5, 0, 0, 0, 0.5, 0.5, 1, na, 0.5), yielding a value of 2.4 by the index described in the appendix.

61. See, e.g., Nasreen Ghufran, "The Taliban and the Civil War Entanglement in Afghanistan," *Asian Survey* 41, no. 3 (May/June 2001): 462–72; David Rohde and Dexter Filkins, "Taliban Troops Abandon Capital without a Fight," *New York Times*, November 14, 2001, https://www.nytimes.com/2001/11/13/international/asia/taliban-troops-abandon-capital-without-a-fight.html. By the index described in the appendix, the Northern Alliance would be coded as (0.7, 1, 0.5, 0.5, 0, 1, 1, 1, 0.5, 1, 0.5), yielding the value of 4.575 presented in fig. 2.1.

62. Kenneth Slepyan, *Stalin's Guerrillas: Soviet Partisans in World War II* (Lawrence: University Press of Kansas, 2006); Alexander Hill, *The War behind the Eastern Front: The Soviet Partisan Movement in North-West Russia, 1941–1944* (London: Frank Cass, 2005); Leonid D. Grenkevich, *The Soviet Partisan Movement, 1941–1944: A Critical Historiographical Analysis* (London: Frank Cass, 1999), 223–72. By the index described in the appendix, Soviet partisans in Operation

Concerto would be coded as (0, 0, 0.5, 0, 0.5, 0, 1, 0.5, 0, na, 0), yielding the value of 1.6 presented in fig. 2.1.

63. J. E. Kaufmann, *The Maginot Line: None Shall Pass* (Westport, CT: Praeger, 1997), 57–58, 67, 85, 88; Vivian Rowe, *Great Wall of France: The Triumph of the Maginot Line* (New York: Putnam, 1959), 86; Jean-Yves Mary, Alain Hohnadel, and Jacques Sicard, *Hommes et Ouvrages de la Ligne Maginot* (Paris: Histoire et Collections, 2001), 1:13–14; J. E. Kaufmann and H. W. Kaufmann, *Fortress France: The Maginot Line and French Defenses in World War II* (Mechanicsburg, PA: Stackpole Books, 2006), 11; Nick Smart, "The Maginot Line: An Indestructible Inheritance," *International Journal of Heritage Studies* 2, no. 4 (April 2007): 229; Marc Romanych and Martin Rupp, *Maginot Line 1940: Battles on the French Frontier* (Westminster, MD: Osprey, 2010), 16–19; J. E. Kaufmann, H. W. Kaufmann, A. Jancovič-Potočnik, and P. Lang, *The Maginot Line: History and Guide* (Barnsley: Pen and Sword, 2011), chap. 2. By the index described in the appendix, the Maginot Line would be coded as (0.7, 1, 0.5, 1, 1, 1, 1, 1, 1, 1, 1), yielding the value of 5.575 presented in fig. 2.1.

64. S. Biddle, *Military Power*, 30. On the eve of the battle, British general Hubert Plumer is said to have observed to his staff: "Gentlemen, we may not make history tomorrow, but we shall certainly change the geography." Ian Hogg, *The Guns, 1914–1918* (New York: Ballantine, 1971), 131. On the artillery program at Messines, see John Terraine, "Indirect Fire as a Battle Winner/Loser," in Corelli Barnett et al., *Old Battles and New Defenses: Can We Learn from Military History?* (London: Brassey's, 1986), 7–32 at 11; weight of explosive per shell is computed from John Keegan, *The Face of Battle* (New York: Random House, 1977), 235; and Prior and Wilson, *Command on the Western Front*, 363. For W48 yield, see Thomas Cochran et al., *Nuclear Weapons Databook*, vol. 1, *U.S. Nuclear Forces and Capabilities* (Cambridge: Ballinger, 1984), 54.

65. See, e.g., Wynne, *If Germany Attacks*, 191–318; Lupfer, *Dynamics of Doctrine*, 1–36; Wilhelm Balck, *Development of Tactics, World War*, trans. Harry Bell (Fort Leavenworth, KS: General Service Schools Press, 1922, trans. of 1920 orig.), 151–68; Ritter von Leeb, *Defense*, trans. Stefan Possony and Daniel Vilfroy (Harrisburg, PA: Military Service, 1943, trans. of 1938 orig.), 77–99. By the index described in the appendix, the Elastic Defense would be coded as (0, 1, 1, 1, 0.5, 0.5, 0.5, 1, 1, 1, 1), yielding the value of 3.875 presented in fig. 2.1.

66. S. Biddle, *Military Power*, chap. 6. By the index described in the appendix, German defenses at Goodwood would be coded as (0, 1, 0.5, 1, 0.5, 0.2, 0.5, 1, 1, 1, 1), yielding the value of 3.45 presented in fig. 2.1.

67. Troop counts are taken from Eliot A. Cohen, Director, *Gulf War Air Power Survey*, vol. 5, *Statistical Compendium* (Washington, DC: Government Printing Office, 1993), 51, for the week ending October 31, 1990; dispositions are taken from US Department of Defense, *Conduct of the Persian Gulf War*, Final Report to Congress Pursuant to Title V of Public Law 102–25 (Washington, DC: Government Printing Office, April 1992), 40, and represent deployments as of "October 1990." The troop count in Cohen is for US Army and Marine contributions; dispositions in the coastal sector include one Saudi Arabian infantry brigade and two Saudi mechanized battalions in the covering force zone; I assume a total of 7,000 soldiers for these, which is almost certainly an overestimate. I also assume an entire division personnel slice for each US division shown in the sector, which is also an upper bound on actual strength in the defended zone. The troop density figures in the text above are thus highly conservative. By the index

described in the appendix, the US defenses in Desert Shield would be coded as (0, 1, 0.5, 1, 0.5, 0.06, 0.5, 1, 1, 1, 1), yielding the value of 3.31 presented in fig. 2.1.

68. S. Biddle, *Military Power*.

69. That is, *Military Power* presents a more detailed breakout of the specific techniques that constitute the choices in the two-to-five middle range in fig. 2.1 and the theory presented in chap. 3. The appendix discusses the relationship between these related taxonomies in greater detail.

Chapter Three: Materially Optimal Behavior

1. Max Weber, *The Theory of Social and Economic Organization*, trans. A. M. Henderson and Talcott Parsons (New York: Free Press, 1947), 156.

2. These data are drawn from Jeffrey A. Friedman, "Manpower and Counterinsurgency," *Security Studies* 20, no. 4:1–36, and were provided by Professor Friedman.

3. On Hezbollah defense expenditure and revenue, see, e.g., Martin Rudner, "Hizbullah Terrorism Finance: Fund-Raising and Money-Laundering," *Studies in Conflict and Terrorism* 33, no. 8 (2010), https://www.tandfonline.com/doi/abs/10.1080/1057610X.2010.494169; Judith Palmer Harik, *Hezbollah: The Changing Face of Terrorism* (London: I. B. Tauris, 2004), 86–87, 93; Ahmad Nizar Hamzeh, *In the Path of Hizbullah* (Syracuse, NY: Syracuse University Press, 2004), 63; Scott Wilson, "Lebanese Wary of a Rising Hezbollah," *Washington Post*, December 20, 2004, https://www.washingtonpost.com/archive/politics/2004/12/20/lebanese-wary-of-a-rising-hezbollah/a09fad05-e608-4b58-97da-fcb0971bcda3/; Magnus Ranstorp, *Hizballah in Lebanon: The Politics of the Western Hostage Crisis* (New York: Macmillan, 1997), 82–84; Jo Becker, "Beirut Bank Seen as Hub of Hezbollah's Financing," *New York Times*, December 14, 2011, A1. For the ZNG, note that the Croatian state spent only $1 billion on its military in 1994: Ozren Zunec, "Democracy and the 'Fog of War': Civil-Military Relations in Croatia," in Constantine P. Danopoulos and Daniel Zirker, eds., *Civil-Military Relations in the Soviet and Yugoslav Successor States* (Boulder, CO: Westview, 1996), 213–22 at 220. The Jugoslav state military of 1991 had an annual military budget of at least $3.5 billion: *Balkan Battlegrounds*, 2:45–46, 178; International Institute for Strategic Studies, *The Military Balance, 1991–1992* (London: Brassey's, 1991), 96.

4. Anthony Cordesman, *Preliminary "Lessons" of the Israeli-Hezbollah War* (Washington DC: Center for Strategic and International Studies, August 17, 2006), 16–19; Dan Byman, *A High Price: The Triumphs and Failures of Israeli Counterterrorism* (New York: Oxford University Press, 2011), 248.

5. *Balkan Battlegrounds* 2:108, 178.

6. Thomas Grove and Warren Strobel, "Special Report: Where Ukraine's Separatists Get Their Weapons," Reuters, July 29, 2014, http://www.reuters.com/article/us-ukraine-crisis-arms-specialreport-idUSKBN0FY0UA20140729; Oren Dorell, "Analysis: Ukraine Forces Outmanned, Outgunned by Rebels," *USA Today*, February 23, 2015, http://www.usatoday.com/story/news/world/2015/02/23/ukraine-military-hard-pressed-by-russian-backed-rebels/23883435/.

7. Lanning and Cragg, *Inside the VC and the NVA*, 96, 122–28, 140; Truong Nhu Tang, *A Viet Cong Memoir: An Inside Account of the Vietnam War and Its Aftermath* (New York: First Vintage

Books, 1986), 159–60; Department of Defense, *Know Your Enemy: The Viet Cong*, DoD Gen-20 (Washington, DC: Government Printing Office, 1966), 4. On the importance and distribution of the AK-47 automatic assault rifle, see, esp., C. J. Chivers, *The Gun* (New York: Simon and Schuster, 2011).

8. Some analysts emphasize the role of outside material support for insurgent success: see, e.g., the review in Austin Long, *On "Other War": Lessons from Five Decades of RAND Counterinsurgency Research* (Santa Monica, CA: RAND, 2006). Below I discuss the quantity and quality of outside support available to the nonstate actors in the case studies in chaps. 5 through 9, but I do not theorize outside support as an explicit independent variable here. This is because of its near ubiquity in nonstate warfare. Seth Jones, for example, concludes that more than 80 percent of all insurgencies worldwide since 1946 have enjoyed meaningful outside support: S. Jones, *Waging Insurgent Warfare*, 136. In fact most of the nonstate actors studied in detail below had at least some external state support, including some of the most Fabian (the Jaish al Mahdi or the Vietcong) and least Fabian (Hezbollah or the SVK) of those studied here. As a contributor to an actor's material wherewithal, outside support is not irrelevant (this is why I discuss it in the case studies). But in the interest of theoretical parsimony I thus focus here on the variables I believe have the greatest explanatory leverage.

9. See, e.g., Anthony Tucker-Jones, *The Iraq War: Operation Iraqi Freedom 2003* (Barnsely, South Yorkshire: Pen and Sword, 2014), 82.

10. Unmanned or robotic weapons obviously pose no meaningful risk of human casualties when used alone without flesh-and-blood combatants in direct support. But the trade-off between survivability and lethality is just as sharp for survival of the weapon system itself. If anything, there is reason to suppose that for the foreseeable future, unmanned weapons are likely to be more vulnerable to return fire, other things being equal. And adding robotic combatants to mixed forces including human frontline troops can increase, rather than reduce, human casualty rates as a function of the robots' own vulnerability: see, e.g., John Matsumura et al., *Exploring Advanced Technologies for the Future Combat Systems Program* (Santa Monica, CA: RAND, 2002), RAND MR-1332.

11. Bidwell and Graham, *Firepower*, 137–38; on tank vulnerability in 1918, see also John Terraine, *The Smoke and the Fire* (London: Sidgwick and Jackson, 1980), 154.

12. See, e.g., Headquarters, Department of the Army, *FM 3–90.1: Tank and Mechanized Infantry Company Team* (Washington, DC: Government Printing Office, 2002). This is a central finding of S. Biddle, *Military Power*; and Stephen Biddle, "Theory and Practice of Continental Warfare," in John Baylis, James J. Wirtz, and Colin S. Gray, eds., *Strategy in the Contemporary World*, 5th ed. (London: Oxford University Press, 2016), 247–64.

13. S. Biddle and Oelrich, "Future Warfare in the Western Pacific."

14. On the lethality-survivability trade-off for terrorists in particular, see Shapiro, *Terrorist's Dilemma*.

15. S. Biddle, *Military Power*, 29–30.

16. Hew Strachan, *European Armies and the Conduct of War* (Abingdon-on-Thames, UK: Routledge, 2005), 117; Larry H. Addington, *The Patterns of War since the Eighteenth Century*, 2nd ed. (Bloomington: Indiana University Press, 1994), 104; B. P. Hughes, *Firepower: Weapons Effectiveness on the Battlefield, 1630–1850* (New York: Chas. Scribner's Sons, 1974).

17. Addington, *Patterns of War*, 3, assuming a closing speed of six kilometers per hour.

18. Addington, *Patterns of War*, 103; Prior and Wilson, *Command on the Western Front*, 311.

19. The Correlates of War data set: Meredith Reid Sarkees and Frank Wayman, *Resort to War: 1816–2007* (Washington, DC: CQ Press, 2010); Steven Ross, *From Flintlock to Rifle: Infantry Tactics, 1740–1866* (Madison, NJ: Fairleigh Dickinson University Press, 1979), 89; Bailey, *Field Artillery and Firepower*, 127, and conservatively assuming a ratio of at least one crew-served machine gun per artillery piece.

20. Data were drawn from I. Hogg, *Guns, 1914–18*; David Isby, *Weapons and Tactics of the Soviet Army* (New York: Jane's, 1988); T. Nicholas and R. Rossi, *U.S. Missile Data Book, 1996* (Fountain Valley, CA: Data Search, 1995).

21. Data were drawn from Headquarters, Department of the Army, *FM 7–90, Tactical Employment of Mortars* (Washington, DC: Government Printing Office, 1992); and I. Hogg, *Guns, 1914–18*; Isby, *Weapons and Tactics of the Soviet Army*; Nicholas and Rossi, *U.S. Missile Data Book, 1996*; using areas estimated for systems not in *FM 7–90* according to the regression equation $L = .82C—34.9$, where L is the diameter of the lethal area (in meters) and C is the caliber of the round (in millimeters).

22. Data were drawn from Gordon Swanborough and Peter M. Bowers, *United States Military Aircraft since 1909* (London: Putnam Aeronautical, 1989).

23. Representative opposing weapons are the US M-4A3E8 tank and the German PzKw IVh for 1945, the US M-60A1 tank and BGM-71 TOW missile and the Soviet T-55 tank for 1975; the US M-60A3 tank and BGM-71 TOW missile and the Soviet T-62 tank for 1985; the US M-1A1 tank, BGM-71F TOW-2B and AGM-114 Hellfire missiles and the Russian T-72 tank for 1995; and the US M-1A1 tank, BGM-71F TOW-2B, AGM-114 Hellfire, and ATACMS/BAT missiles and the Russian T-80 tank for 2005. Data are drawn from F. M. Von Senger und Etterlin, *German Tanks of World War II*, trans. of *Die deutschen Panzer 1926–45* (Munich: J. F. Lehmans Verlag, 1968), trans. J. Lucas, 21–28, 34–74, 194–210; J. Ellis, *Brute Force*, table 62; Richard Ogorkiewicz, *Technology of Tanks* (Coulsden, Surrey: Jane's, 1991), 1:111; *Jane's All the World's Weapon Systems, 1985* (Coulsden, Surrey: Jane's, 1985), 65, 67; and House, *Toward Combined Arms Warfare*, 109; penetration ranges for US weapons versus the T-72 are inferred from Gulf War experience: e.g., Atkinson, *Crusade*, 447, 466; Robert Scales et al., *Certain Victory: The U.S. Army in the Gulf War* (Washington, DC: Office of the Chief of Staff, 1993), 267, 293; and missile ranges per Nicholas and Rossi, *U.S. Missile Data Book, 1996*.

24. An automatic weapon's cyclic rate is always much higher than its sustained rate of fire, which is reduced by the need to change magazines and to dissipate heat buildup in the barrel between rounds in continuous firing. It does, however, provide a valid measure of a weapon's ability to produce peak firepower in a critical moment. On the operation of automatic weapons, see, e.g., Chivers, *Gun*.

25. Standard issue for machine guns in the German army in 1914, for example, was only 24 per division of 17,000 troops: Clodfelter, *Warfare and Armed Conflicts*, 387.

26. Kalyvas and Balcells, "International System and Technologies of Rebellion." Kalyvas and Balcells's data cover 101 civil wars prior to 1991, and 46 civil wars from 1991 to 2004.

27. Kalyvas and Balcells, "International System and Technologies of Rebellion," 419.

28. Lon O. Nordeen, *Air Warfare in the Missile Age* (Washington, DC: Smithsonian Books, 2010), 21; United States Forces, Somalia, *After Action Report and Historical Overview: The United States Army in Somalia, 1992–1994* (Washington, DC: Center of Military History, 2003), 95;

William J. Martinez, "Somalia: A Lesson in Peace-Enforcement," *Personal Experience Monograph: Somalia* (Carlisle, PA: US Army War College, 1994), 43.

29. F. Stephen Larrabee, Peter A. Wilson, and John Gordon IV, *The Ukranian Crisis and European Security: Implications for the United States and U.S. Army* (Santa Monica, CA: RAND, 2015), 8.

30. Anthony H. Cordesman, George Sullivan, and William D. Sullivan, *Lessons of the 2006 Israeli-Hezbollah War* (Washington, DC: Center for Strategic and International Studies, 2007), 12–14; Exum, *Hizballah at War*, 5–7; Iver Gabrielsen, "The Evolution of Hezbollah's Strategy and Military Performance, 1982–2006," *Small Wars and Insurgencies* 25, no. 2 (2014): 257–83; Gao, "Russia Has a Missile to Kill NATO Tanks If War Ever Comes"; Michel Fiszer and Jerzy Gruszczynski, "On Arrows and Needles," *Journal of Electronic Defense*, December 2002, http://www.jedonline.com/; Sarah Chankin-Gould and Matt Schroeder, "MANPADS Proliferation," Federation of American Scientists Issue Brief no. 1, January 2004, https://fas.org/asmp/campaigns/MANPADS/MANPADS.html; Globalsecurity.org, http://www.globalsecurity.org/military/world/russia/sa-16.htm.

31. *Balkan Battlegrounds*, 2:108, 178.

32. On Israeli, French, and German antitank guided weapon holdings in 1994, see International Institute for Strategic Studies, *The Military Balance, 1993–1994* (London: Brassey's, 1993), 42, 46, 118. For a related argument on the importance of technological change and increasing lethality on nonstate actors' ability to contend with state foes, see Cronin, *Power to the People*, which sees an increasing success rate for nonstate irregulars against state enemies, but not a more conventional nonstate military style.

33. *Tactical Employment of Field Artillery*, TR 430–105 (Washington, DC: US War Department, September 5, 1924), 92; Bidwell and Graham, *Firepower*, 8–9. Note that this figure, and those below, give the weapons' maximum rate of fire, which a single gun can sustain only for short periods lest the barrel overheat. Sustained rates of fire are lower, but still high enough to slaughter exposed infantry massed in the open.

34. Keegan, *Face of Battle*, 234.

35. Keegan, *Face of Battle*, 311.

36. W. J. Schultis et al., *Comparison of Military Potential: NATO and Warsaw Pact* (Alexandria, VA: Weapon System Evaluation Group, June 1974), WSEG Report 238, declassified December 31, 1982, 105; *Jane's Armour and Artillery 1981–1982* (London: Jane's, 1982); *The BMP: Capabilities and Limitations*, TRADOC Bulletin no. 7 (Fort Monroe, VA: US Army Training and Doctrine Command, June 30, 1977), 11–12.

37. Simon Dunstan, *Yom Kippur War 1973: The Sinai* (Oxford: Osprey, 2003), 14.

38. Jesse Orlansky and Col. Jack Thorpe, eds., *73 Easting: Lessons Learned from Desert Storm via Advanced Distributed Simulation Technology* (Alexandria, VA: Institute for Defense Analyses, 1992), IDA D-1110, I-114, I-121 to 125.

39. Alexander McKee, *Caen: Anvil of Victory* (London: Souvenir, 1964), chap. 17. On British armor losses, see Carlo D'Este, *Decision in Normandy* (New York: HarperCollins, 1983), 385–56; Martin Blumenson, *Breakout and Pursuit* (Washington, DC: Office of the Chief of Military History, 1961), 193. On Operation Goodwood, see also S. Biddle, *Military Power*, chap. 6.

40. Nor are even very sophisticated tanks invulnerable to modern firepower. Advanced armor can be a cost-effective buy, but it does not purchase immunity to fire: the US M-1 Abrams tank is remarkably well protected and has sometimes been described as "the king of the killing

zone," but it can still be penetrated and destroyed by well-directed antitank fire. Even the Iraqi Army, notable for its poor marksmanship and limited skills, was able to knock out at least 4 US M-1s in the 1991 Battle of Wadi al-Batin (18 Abrams were lost in the war as a whole), and the United States lost more than 80 M-1s between 2003 and 2005 in Iraq: see Scales et al., *Certain Victory*, 267–70; Steven Komarow, "Tanks Take a Beating in Iraq," *USA Today*, March 29, 2005, https://usatoday30.usatoday.com/news/world/iraq/2005-03-29-abrams-tank-a_x.htm. According to US officials, the nonstate ISIS militia damaged at least 28 Iraqi government M-1s in 2014: Jeremy Binnie, "Iraqi Abrams Losses Revealed," *Jane's 360*, June 20, 2014, http://www.janes.com/article/39550/iraqi-abrams-losses-revealed. The Abrams is a fine tank—but no armored vehicle is immune to modern antitank weapons, and M-1 losses would surely be much higher against enemies more skilled than Saddam's army: Stephen Biddle, "Victory Misunderstood: What the Gulf War Tells Us about the Future of Conflict," *International Security* 21, no. 2 (Fall 1996): 139–79; S. Biddle, *Military Power*, chap. 7.

41. On tactical adaptations in 1915, see S. Biddle, *Military Power*, chap. 3; also Bidwell and Graham, *Firepower*, chap. 5.

42. C.R.M.F. Cruttwell, *A History of the Great War, 1914–1918* (Chicago: Academy, [1934] 1991), 245; weight of explosive per shell inferred from Keegan, *Face of Battle*, 235. For W48 yield, see Cochran et al., *Nuclear Weapons Databook*, 1:54.

43. On the artillery program at Messines, see Terraine, "Indirect Fire as a Battle Winner/Loser," 11; explosive weight per shell is computed from Keegan, *Face of Battle*, 235; and Prior and Wilson, *Command on the Western Front*, 363. For W48 yield, see Cochran et al., *Nuclear Weapons Databook*, 1:54.

44. Martin Blumenson, *Salerno to Cassino* (Washington, DC: Office of the Chief of Military History, 1969), 433–48.

45. Department of the Scientific Advisor to the Army Council, *Military Operational Research Unit Report No. 23: Battle Study, Operation "Goodwood,"* October 1946, declassified January 16, 1984, 13–20; L. F. Ellis, *Victory in the West*, vol. 1, *The Battle of Normandy* (London: Her Majesty's Stationery Office, 1962), 337–40.

46. S. Biddle, *Afghanistan and the Future of Warfare*, 34–35; Col. Andrew N. Milani, *The Pitfalls of Technology: A Case Study of the Battle on Takur Ghar Mountain, Afghanistan* (Carlisle, PA: US Army War College Strategic Research Project, 2003).

47. Junger, *Storm of Steel*.

48. S. Biddle, *Military Power*, esp. chap. 3.

49. For a colorful account, see E. D. Swinton, *The Defence of Duffer's Drift* (Wayne, NJ: Avery, [1907] 1986), 53–54.

50. L. G. Starkey et al., *Capabilities of Selected U.S. and Allied Antiarmor Weapon Systems* (Alexandria, VA: Weapon System Evaluation Group, May 1975), WSEG Report 263, declassified December 31, 1983, 35–36; Warren Olson, *A Terrain Analysis of Four Tactical Situations* (Aberdeen, MD: US Army Materiel Systems Analysis Agency, 1972), AMSAA Technical Memorandum no. 158; Richard Simpkin, *Race to the Swift: Thoughts on Twenty-First Century Warfare* (New York: Brassey's, 1985), 69.

51. Chandler, *Campaigns of Napoleon*, 1118.

52. Assuming accurate enfilading fire for the 75-millimeter guns; an average frontage for an 8,000-soldier division of 1,500 yards in three ranks' depth, per Paddy Griffith, *French Napoleonic*

Infantry Tactics 1792–1815 (Oxford: Osprey, 2007), 4–8; and 75-millimeter field gun effectiveness per *Tactical Employment of Field Artillery,* TR 430–105, 92.

53. Assuming a roughly two-foot-square area physically occupied per standing soldier with kit and weapon; standing posture for all soldiers; the distribution of forested and built-up cover on the Austerlitz battlefield as derived from the Google Maps representation of the same area as of January 2017; and an occupation of 1 percent of the physically available cover to ensure location uncertainty and deter the opponent from simply area-barraging covered terrain in the absence of targeting information. Note that today's Austerlitz battlefield is much more covered than it was in 1805, given the expansion of towns and villages in the area; to obtain this much cover and concealment with the 1805 topography would have required a much greater area than assumed above.

54. Sources for these data are S. Biddle, *Military Power,* 92, 119 (assuming 14,000 troops per World War I division); US Army CDB-90 data set: Robert Helmbold, *Personnel Attrition Rates in Historical Land Combat Operations* (Bethesda, MD: US Army Concepts Analysis Agency, 1995), CAA-RP-95–1; Chandler, *Campaigns of Napoleon;* Trevor Roy, *Crimea: The Great Crimean War, 1854–1856* (New York: St. Martin's, 2000); Vincent J. Esposito, *The West Point Atlas of American Wars* (New York: Praeger, 1959); Gordon Craig, *The Battle of Koeniggratz* (Philadelphia: University of Pennsylvania Press, 2003); George Hooper, *The Campaign of Sedan: The Downfall of the Second Empire* (London: G. Bell and Sons, 1887).

55. Of course this does not mean that 19th-century insurgents never achieved temporary local numerical advantages against elements of overstretched state armies. In the Peninsular War of 1807–14, for example, Spanish insurgents at the First Battle of El Bruch on June 6, 1808, converged on an isolated French march column caught in a ravine, ambushed it with a superior number of fighters, and imposed heavy losses on it in a running firefight as the French sought to extract themselves: see, e.g., David Gates, *The Spanish Ulcer: A History of the Peninsular War* (Boston: Da Capo, 2001), 59; Adolpho Carrasco, "La Accion del Bruch en 1808," *Boletín de la Real Academia de la Historia* 44 (1904): 333–51; Antoni Moliner Prada, "Popular Resistance in Catalonia: Somatenes and Migueletes in the French War," *Revista d'Història Moderna i Contemporànea,* no. 1 (2003): 35–56. Classical guerilla tactics seek out such isolated targets for ambush or defeat in detail and will often concentrate briefly at such points, as noted in chap. 2 above. But such tactics were possible only against isolated elements of state occupation forces. A massed French force in 1808 could easily annihilate insurgent opponents, as demonstrated at the Battle of Evora in July, where roughly 8,000 French state soldiers slaughtered a mixed force of Spanish and Portuguese nonstate militia and reassembled regulars: see, e.g., Charles Oman, *A History of the Peninsular War* (Oxford: Clarendon, 1902), 1:217–19.

56. On the survival incentives of civilians in wartime and their influence on political alignment, see, esp., Kalyvas, *Logic of Violence in Civil War,* e.g., 4.

57. These problems are why counterinsurgency theory emphasizes the importance of insurgent safe havens outside the combat zone—guerillas with sanctuaries in nearby countries whose state militaries can protect the insurgents' bases from hostile government attack allow insurgents to overcome at least some of these military drawbacks. See, e.g., Seth Jones, "Counterinsurgency in Afghanistan," *RAND Counterinsurgency Study* 4 (2008): 37–67.

58. On the unattractiveness of Fabian methods for combatants who have other options, see, e.g., Laqueur, *Guerrilla,* vii–xi, 382–409.

59. Mao Tse-tung, *Selected Works* (London: Lawrence and Wishart, 1955), 1:203–48; Tang Tsou and Morton H. Halperin, "Mao Tse-Tung's Revolutionary Strategy and Peking's International Behavior," *American Political Science Review* 59, no. 1 (March 1965): 88–89.

60. These values are derived from the Cunningham, Gleditsch, and Salehyan's Non-state Actors in Armed Conflict Dataset (NSA), version 3.3 (January 24, 2012): David Cunningham, Kristian Gelditsch, and Idean Salehyan, "Non-state Actors in Civil Wars: A New Dataset," *Conflict Management and Peace Science* 30, no. 5 (2013): 516–31. Values shown are for cases where the data set identifies actors' operating areas and combat strength, and where operating areas are described as all or "much of" an identifiable standard geographical area. (Where the data set uses the phrase "much of," I assume a value of 60 percent of the identified area; dates are the end points for the given entries.)

61. See, e.g., S. Biddle, *Military Power*, 40–42, 210–11.

62. Of the 230 battles in the US Army's CDB-90 data set in which defenders were outnumbered at least 2:1, 56 are coded as defender victories: CDB-90: Helmbold, *Personnel Attrition Rates*.

63. Casualty rates are also strongly sensitive to the instantaneous local force ratio; a reduction in the attacker's numerical advantage in each wave of a multiwave attack will cause a disproportionate increase in attacker losses relative to a single-wave attack with all available forces massed against the same defense: see, e.g., Stephen Biddle, "The European Conventional Balance: A Reinterpretation of the Debate," *Survival*, March–April 1988, 99–121; James G. Taylor, "Attrition Modeling," in Reiner K. Huber et al., eds., *Operational Research Games for Defense* (Munich: R. Olden-bourg, 1979), 139–89; F. W. Lanchester, *Aircraft in Warfare: The Dawn of the Fourth Arm* (London: Constable, 1916), 39–66.

64. Michael Miller, *Hybrid Warfare: Preparing for Future Conflict* (Montgomery, AL: Air War College, 2015), 20; Gjorgji Veljovski, Nenad Taneski, and Metodija Dojchinovski, "The Danger of 'Hybrid Warfare' from a Sophisticated Adversary: The Russian 'Hybridity' in the Ukranian Conflict," *Defense and Security Analysis* 33, no. 4 (2017): 292–307; Frank G. Hoffman, "Hybrid Warfare and Challenges," *Joint Force Quarterly*, no. 52 (2009): 34–47.

65. As the poet Hilaire Belloc colorfully assessed colonial warfare in 1898: "whatever happens we have got, the Maxim gun and they have not." Hilaire Belloc and Basil Temple Blackwood, *The Modern Traveller* (London: Edward Arnold, 1898), 41.

66. Chivers, *Gun*.

Chapter Four: Politically Achievable Behavior

1. Colonel Michael D. Krause, *The Battle of 73 Easting, 26 February 1991: A Historical Introduction to a Simulation* (Washington, DC: US Army Center of Military History and the Defense Advanced Research Projects Agency, August 27, 1991); J. R. Crooks et al., *73 Easting Re-creation Data Book* (Westlake, CA: IEI, 1992), IEI Report no. DA-MDA972-1-92, appendix, shoot history by vehicle for Eagle Troop, 4.

2. Author's inspection based on observed spent shell casings, Objective Montgomery battlefield Iraq, May 4, 2003; US Army Strategic Studies Institute OIF Research Collection, US Army Military History Institute: Stephen Biddle, Memo for the Record, Objective "Montgomery" Battlefield Inspection, May 4, 2003; Tape 050303p2sb Lt. Col. Ferrell et al. interview;

S. Biddle, "Speed Kills," 30, 34–35. Such performance is hardly unique to the Iraqi military in 2003; in the American Civil War, for example, 500-soldier infantry regiments firing rifled muskets nominally capable of a 50 percent hit probability at 100 to 200 yards regularly exhausted entire regimental basic loads of around 30,000 rounds in hours-long, fully exposed firefights at such ranges while hitting fewer than their own number of enemy troops: Paddy Griffith, *Battle Tactics of the Civil War* (New Haven, CT: Yale University Press, 2001), 29–52, 73–90, 137–64.

3. In fact Bonaparte's successes were sometimes achieved with armies raised quickly and trained hastily: Chandler, *Campaigns of Napoleon*, 865–98. Early 19th-century armies differed in their training intensity and tactical proficiency, but diminishing returns to effort set in at relatively low levels of training, and Clausewitz, for example, was less impressed with the utility of technical proficiency at the tactical level than he was with judgment at higher levels of command: Clausewitz, *On War*, 122–23. On the training of Napoleonic militaries, see, e.g., Terry Crowdy, *Napoleon's Infantry Handbook* (Barnsley, UK: Pen and Sword, 2015), 161–200; Chandler *Campaigns of Napoleon*, 332–67. Of course this does not mean that skill or ability were irrelevant in the Napoleonic Wars—Bonaparte's talent inspired Clausewitz's fascination with the notion of military genius. Nor does it mean that Napoleonic warfare was simple or easy to execute—on the contrary, it inspired Clausewitz's concept of friction and its account of the intrinsic difficulty of even apparently simple things on the battlefield. At the tactical level, however, high-firepower low-concealment methods are relatively simpler to execute than midspectrum methods that require a combination of both firepower and concealment.

4. On the general problem of trade-offs in engineering design, see, e.g., Terry Bahill and Azad Madni, *Tradeoff Decisions in System Design* (Berlin: Springer Verlag, 2017); Gregory Parnell, *Tradeoff Analytics: Creating and Explaining the System Tradespace* (New York: Wiley, 2016).

5. See, e.g., Bailey, *Field Artillery and Firepower*; Bidwell and Graham, *Firepower*, 21, 253–57.

6. Headquarters, Department of the Army, *FM 3–90.1: Tank and Mechanized Infantry Company Team*, chap. 2; English, *On Infantry*; Anthony Farrar-Hockley, *Infantry Tactics* (London: Almark, 1976).

7. Richard Simpkin, *Tank Warfare: An Analysis of Soviet and NATO Tank Philosophy* (New York: Crane Russak, 1979); Richard Simpkin, *Antitank* (Amsterdam: Elsevier, 1982); Rolf Hilmes, *Main Battle Tanks: Developments in Design since 1945* (London: Brassey's, 1987); Headquarters, Department of the Army, *FM 3–90.1: Tank and Mechanized Infantry Company Team*, chap. 2.

8. On combined-arms methods and theory, see, e.g., House, *Toward Combined Arms Warfare*; Bidwell and Graham, *Firepower*; S. Biddle, *Military Power*, chap. 3.

9. As seen in the techniques for tank-infantry intercommunication improvised in World War II: Michael D. Doubler, *Closing with the Enemy* (Lawrence: University Press of Kansas, 1994), e.g., 16–17, 47–51. On the requirements of successful combined-arms implementation, see, e.g., Doubler, *Closing with the Enemy*; House, *Toward Combined Arms Warfare*; US Army Center for Army Lessons Learned, *Small-Unit Operations in Afghanistan: Tactics, Techniques and Procedures* (Fort Leavenworth, KS: US Army Combined Arms Center, 2009).

10. Ivan Oelrich et al., *Who Goes There: Friend or Foe?* (Washington, DC: Office of Technology Assessment, 1993), OTA-ISC-537, 37; Paul E. Snyder, "Revolution or Evolution? Combined Arms Warfare in the Twenty-First Century," a thesis presented to the faculty of the US Army Command and General Staff College, June 4, 1999, 1–15.

11. See, e.g., Bailey, *Field Artillery and Firepower*, 132–34, 169–71, 184–86; Bidwell and Graham, *Firepower*, 21, 253–57; English, *On Infantry*, chap. 1.

12. On the logistic demands of modern warfare, see, e.g., Martin van Creveld, *Supplying War: Logistics from Wallenstein to Patton* (New York: Cambridge University Press, 2004); Michael O'Hanlon, *The Science of War* (Princeton, NJ: Princeton University Press, 2013) 141–69; William G. T. Tuttle, *Defense Logistics for the 21st Century* (Annapolis, MD: US Naval Institute Press, 2013); Moshe Kress, *Operational Logistics: The Art and Science of Sustaining Military Operations* (New York: Springer, 2015).

13. For high lethality–low survivability behavior choices, campaigns will be intense but very short: fighters will quickly kill the enemy or be killed themselves. Hence at any given moment, the sensitivity of short-term firepower to logistical capacity will be modest: few shooters will ever expend more than their initial basic load of ammunition before winning or dying. For intermediate choices of concealment, by contrast, campaigns will be much longer as more-survivable fighters continue to expend ammunition and fuel over longer durations of sustained combat. At any given random time within such extended campaigns, some shooters will not yet have expended their initial basic loads, but others will have done so multiple times. For the latter, their ability to project firepower in the short-term future will be highly sensitive to their logistical system's ability to resupply them under fire.

14. International Institute for Strategic Studies, *The Military Balance, 2001–2002* (London: Oxford University Press, 2001), 18–19. Note that US Defense Department "Operations and Maintenance" expenditures include some costs other than those enumerated above; total "O&M" expenditures for FY 2000 were $108.1 billion: International Institute for Strategic Studies, *Military Balance, 2001–2002*.

15. See, e.g., Anne W. Chapman, *The Origins and Development of the National Training Center, 1976–1984* (Washington, DC: Office of the Command Historian, US Army Training and Doctrine Command, 1992), 81–110, 145–48; Kenneth W. Drylie, *The National Training Center and Fort Irwin* (Mount Pleasant, SC: Arcadia, 2016), 39–66; Erica Felci, "Troops Get Urban Combat Training in Massive Mock City," *Palm Springs Desert Sun*, January 26, 2011, A1; US Marine Corps, *Twentynine Palms Fact Sheet*, https://www.repi.mil/Portals/44/Documents/Current%20 Year%20Fact%20Sheets/AllMarineCorps.pdf; Kelly O'Sullivan and Emily Dugo, *Community Impact Report, 2016, Marine Air Ground Task Force Training Command, Marine Corps Air Ground Combat Center Twentynine Palms, California*, https://www.29palms.marines.mil/Portals/56 /Docs/G5/book.community_impact_report_2016.pdf, 3.

16. Note that this is inherent in the role specialization represented by tanks and infantry—it is not an ephemeral feature of changing technology. Robert Cameron, "Armored Operations in Urban Environments: Anomaly or Natural Condition," *Armor*, June 2006, 8; John M. Hutcheson, "Of Tank and Infantry: Lessons of Heavy-Light Integration Learned, Forgotten, and Relearned," an individual study project, US Army War College, April 5, 1991, 29–52.

17. S. Biddle, *Military Power*, chap. 6.

18. Martin Blumenson, *Breakout and Pursuit*, 236.

19. Charles R. Shrader, *Amicide: The Problem of Friendly Fire in Modern War* (Fort Leavenworth, KS: US Army Combat Studies Institute, 1982), 22–23, 88–89. See also Oelrich et al., *Who Goes There*, 7–48.

20. On this trade-off and its resolution in modern state militaries, see, esp. Ryan T. Baker, "Logistics and Military Power: Tooth, Tail, and Territory in Conventional Military Conflict" (PhD diss., George Washington University, 2020).

21. In game theoretic terms, this situation constitutes a Stag Hunt game: mutual cooperation yields a higher payoff than unilateral defection for both players, but if cooperation is not mutual (if the other player defects) then defection pays better than cooperation. (That is, CC > DC ≥ DD > CD, where C denotes cooperation and D denotes defection.) The result is two potentially stable equilibriums: mutual cooperation (CC), but also mutual defection (DD)—with the latter the more likely if either doubts the other's willingness to cooperate. On the Stag Hunt game and its properties, see, e.g., Robert Jervis, "Cooperation under the Security Dilemma," *World Politics* 30, no. 2 (January 1978): 167–214; Kenneth A. Oye, "Explaining Cooperation under Anarchy: Hypotheses and Strategies," in Kenneth Oye, ed., *Cooperation under Anarchy* (Princeton, NJ: Princeton University Press, 1986), 1–24; Richard H. McAdams, "Beyond the Prisoners' Dilemma: Coordination, Game Theory, and Law," *Southern California Law Review* 82 (2009): 220–22.

22. For the effects of partial combinations of these traits, see the discussion of comparative statics in the appendix.

23. Foundational works in this literature include Elinor Ostrom, *Governing the Commons: The Evolution of Institutions for Collective Action* (New York: Cambridge University Press, 1990); Elinor Ostrom, *Understanding Institutional Diversity* (Princeton, NJ: Princeton University Press, 2005); Oye, *Cooperation under Anarchy*; Robert Axelrod and Robert Keohane, "Achieving Cooperation under Anarchy: Strategies and Institutions," *World Politics* 38, no. 1 (October 1985): 226–54; Terry Moe, "The New Economics of Organization," *American Journal of Political Science* 28 (1984): 739–77; Mancur Olsen, *The Logic of Collective Action: Public Goods and the Theory of Groups* (Cambridge, MA: Harvard University Press, 1971). For applications and reviews, see, e.g., Henry Farrell, *The Political Economy of Trust: Institutions, Interests and Interfirm Cooperation in Italy and Germany* (New York: Cambridge University Press, 2009); Peter Hall and Rosemary Taylor, "Political Science and the Three New Institutionalisms," *Political Studies* 44 (1996): 936–57; B. Guy Peters, *Institutional Theory in Political Science* (New York: Continuum, 2005).

24. Weber, *Theory of Social and Economic Organizations*; James March and Herbert Simon, *Organizations* (New York: Wiley, 1958); Douglass C. North, "Institutions," *Journal of Economic Perspectives* 5, no. 1 (Winter 1991): 97–112; Kenneth A. Shepsle, "Rational Choice Institutionalism," in Sarah A. Binder, R.A.W. Rhodes, and Bert A. Rockman, eds., *The Oxford Handbook of Political Institutions* (New York: Oxford University Press, 2006), 23–38; James G. March and Johan P. Olsen, *Rediscovering Institutions* (New York: Free Press, 1989).

25. Note that I make no claims on the origins of these institutions or the causes of the political variance I observe—I treat nonstate institutions and stakes as exogenous independent variables. I argue here that they vary, but I do not seek to explain why. For a functionalist theory that explains military behavior as the politically constrained pursuit of military effectiveness, if the politics are militarily predetermined this would create a risk of endogeneity. There is little evidence of this, however, in the cases below: for the Somali SNA, weak institutions did not become strong as the threat grew after December 1992; strong institutions largely predated

military threat for the Croatian nationalist ZNG (see chaps. 7 and 8 below). More broadly, while military factors play an important role in the political development literature for modern states, they have been less salient in the emerging literature on theories of rebel governance, which has tended to emphasize rebel-civilian relationships, preconflict social networks, and variations in revenue sources: see, e.g., Zachariah Mampilly, *Rebel Rulers: Insurgent Governance and Civilian Life during War* (Ithaca, NY: Cornell University Press, 2011); Paul Staniland, *Networks of Rebellion: Explaining Insurgent Cohesion and Collapse* (Ithaca, NY: Cornell University Press, 2014); Weinstein, *Inside Rebellion*; Sarah Elizabeth Parkinson, "Rethinking High-Risk Mobilization and Social Networks in War," *American Political Science Review* 107, no. 3 (August 2013): 418–32. Ana Arjona, *Rebelocracy: Social Order in the Colombian Civil War* (New York: Cambridge University Press, 2016), sees a greater role for military threat but argues that more-threatened groups will be less institutionalized, contra the functionalist logic presented here; Michael Woldemariam, *Insurgent Fragmentation in the Horn of Africa: Rebellion and its Discontents* (New York: Cambridge University Press, 2018), sees military stability as conducive to rebel political cohesion, which would similarly not suggest that threat yields institutionalization in any straightforward way. The sources of nonstate internal politics are certainly an important opportunity for research, but I limit myself here to their consequences for military behavior, which distinct enough concerning causality to warrant independent study.

26. Mampilly, *Rebel Rulers*, 110–11.

27. Mampilly, *Rebel Rulers*, 2; Ana Arjona, "Social Order in Civil War" (PhD diss., Yale University, 2010), 228–67, 309–87; Roman Ortiz, "Insurgent Strategies in the Post–Cold War: The Case of the Revolutionary Armed Forces of Colombia," *Studies in Conflict and Terrorism* 25 (2002): 127–43.

28. Shapiro, *Terrorist's Dilemma*, 89–98; Rukmini Callimachi, "Moktar Belmoktar, Terrorist, Clashed with Al Qaeda Leaders over Expense Reports," Associated Press, May 28, 2013.

29. Shapiro, *Terrorist's Dilemma*, 192–96; Bruce, "Terrorism and Politics," 46.

30. Mampilly, *Rebel Rulers*, 190–208; Gerard Prunier, "The Catholic Church and the Kivu Conflict," *Journal of Religion in Africa* 31 (2001): 139–62.

31. I. Abdullah, "Bush Path to Destruction," 224.

32. Eliot Cohen, "Distant Battles: Modern War in the Third World," *International Security* 10, no. 4 (Spring, 1986): 143–71; Stephen Biddle and Robert Zirkle, "Technology, Civil-Military Relations, and Warfare in the Developing World," *Journal of Strategic Studies* 19, no. 2 (June 1996): 171–212; James T. Quinlivan, "Coup-Proofing: Its Practice and Consequences in the Middle East," *International Security* 24, no. 2 (Fall 1999): 131–65; Risa Brooks, *Political-Military Relations and the Stability of Arab Regimes* (London: International Institute for Strategy Studies, 1999), Adelphi Paper no. 324; Ulrich Pilster and Tobias Bohmelt, "Coup-Proofing and Military Effectiveness in Interstate Wars, 1967–99," *Conflict Management and Peace Science* 28, no. 4 (2011): 331–50; Caitlin Talmadge, *The Dictator's Army: Battlefield Effectiveness in Authoritarian Regimes* (Ithaca, NY: Cornell University Press, 2015), 15–18; Erica DeBruin, "Preventing Coups d'Etat: How Counterbalancing Works," *Journal of Conflict Resolution* 62, no. 7 (2018): 1433–58; Cameron S. Brown, Christopher J. Fariss, and R. Blake McMahon, "Recouping after Coup-Proofing: Compromised Military Effectiveness and Strategic Substitution," *International Interactions* 42,

no. 1 (2016): 1–30; Andrew W. Bausch, "Coup-Proofing and Military Inefficiencies: An Experiment," *International Interactions* 44, no. 1 (2018): 1–31.

33. In Saddam's Iraqi state regime, for example, there were no fewer than six separate intelligence and internal security services, four of which were dedicated to spying on the military. Four different organizations controlled ground combat formations: in addition to the Regular Army, there was a separate Republican Guard, Special Republican Guard, and Saddam Fedayeen paramilitary. The Saddam Fedayeen, moreover, deployed members in and among Regular Army formations to act as a check on the loyalty of Army commanders and a form of political commissarship to oversee their decisions. The senior leadership was dominated by Saddam's Tikriti clan, horizontal communications within the military were routinely channeled through Baghdad for surveillance, and officers were rarely allowed to leave the country. On Ba'athist Iraq, see S. Biddle, "Speed Kills"; Stephen T. Hosmer, *Why the Iraqi Resistance to the Coalition Invasion Was so Weak* (Santa Monica, CA: RAND, 2007), https://www.rand.org/content /dam/rand/pubs/monographs/2007/RAND_MG544.pdf, 41–76; Talmadge, *Dictator's Army*, 162–63; S. Biddle and Zirkle, "Technology, Civil-Military Relations, and Warfare in the Developing World."

34. Douglass North, John Wallis, and Barry Weingast, *Violence and Social Orders: A Conceptual Framework for Interpreting Recorded Human History* (New York: Cambridge University Press, 2009).

35. On the ubiquity of controlling armed factions and internal power balancing for nonstate actors, see, e.g., Mampilly, *Rebel Rulers*, 48–92; Stacy E. Goddard and Daniel H. Nexon, "The Dynamics of Global Power Politics: A Framework for Analysis," *Journal of Global Security Studies* 1, no. 1 (2016): 4–18; Fotini Christia, *Alliance Formation in Civil Wars* (New York: Cambridge University Press, 2012); Staniland, *Networks of Rebellion*; Peter Krause, *Rebel Power: Why National Movements Compete, Fight, and Win* (Ithaca, NY: Cornell University Press, 2017); Dipali Mukhopdhyay, *Warlords, Strongman Governors, and the State in Afghanistan* (New York: Cambridge University Press, 2014); Arjona, *Rebelocracy*; Woldemariam, *Insurgent Fragmentation in the Horn of Africa*; Lee J. M. Seymour, "Why Factions Switch Sides in Civil Wars: Rivalry, Patronage, and Realignment in Sudan," *International Security* 39, no. 2 (Fall 2014): 92–131; Stathis Kalyvas, "Ethnic Defection in Civil War," *Comparative Political Studies* 41 no. 8 (August 2008): 1043–68; Lindsey L. Hager and Danielle F. Jung, "Negotiating with Rebels: The Effect of Rebel Service Provision on Conflict Negotiations," *Journal of Conflict Resolution* 61, no. 6 (2017): 1203–29; Thomas Risse, "Governance in Areas of Limited Statehood: Introduction and Overview," and Sven Chojnacki and Zeljko Branovich, "New Modes of Security: The Violent Making and Unmaking of Governance in War-Torn Areas of Limited Statehood," in Thomas Risse, ed., *Governance without a State: Policies and Politics in Areas of Limited Statehood* (New York: Columbia University Press, 2011), 1–35 and 89–114, respectively.

36. Note that the theory's institutional independent variable refers to organizational design and the interaction among elites. The theory's dependent variable refers to combat behavior, and in particular the realized balance of lethality and concealment on the battlefield. Cooperation in the presence of collective action dilemmas is an intervening variable facilitated by some kinds of institutions, which in turn facilitates effectiveness in midrange concealment choices and thus encourages these ceteris paribus. The independent variables, intervening variables,

and dependent variable thus all involve some dimensions of behavior inter alia—this is not a theory that explains behavior solely in structural material terms. But the theory uses different dimensions of behavior (e.g., political decision making as opposed to battlefield tactics) by different actors (e.g., elites as opposed to soldiers) in the independent and intervening as opposed to the dependent variables.

37. North, Wallis, and Weingast, *Violence and Social Orders*, 30–105. North, Wallis, and Weingast specify four categories of political development among states: fragile natural order, basic natural order, mature natural order, and "open access." Below I describe nonstate analogs to the first three, but the features of "open access" status restrict its application to modern industrial democratic states such as the United States and Great Britain. As such, this category excludes essentially all nonstate military actors, and I thus drop it from the taxonomy used below. S. Jones, *Waging Insurgent Warfare*, and Shapiro, *Terrorist's Dilemma*, characterize nonstate organization as "centralized" or "decentralized." I share their emphasis on nonstate actors' internal organization, but I frame the issue around actors' politics rather than their organization per se, and I frame internal politics around the power balancing dynamics underlying groups' ability to resolve collective action dilemmas, not a centralized-decentralized dichotomy. These distinctions do not necessarily correlate: informal chieftaincies, for example, can be highly centralized or the opposite, as can mature natural order quasi states. Jones, for example, also associates "guerilla" strategies with highly developed political institutions (*Waging Insurgent Warfare*, 39), whereas I argue the opposite.

38. I thus use an organizational definition of "institution" as opposed to alternative formulations based on norms or rules of behavior: John Duffield, "What are International Institutions," *International Studies Review* 9, no. 1 (Spring, 2007): 1–22.

39. On *personalized* regimes, see Barbara Geddes, "What Do We Know about Democratization after Twenty Years?," *Annual Review of Political Science* 2 (1999): 115–44; Jessica Weeks, "Autocratic Audience Costs: Regime Type and Signaling Resolve," *International Organization* 62, no. 1 (2008), 35–64.

40. David Pool, *From Guerrillas to Government: The Eritrean People's Liberation Front* (Athens: Ohio University Press, 2001); Haggai Ehrlich, *The Struggle over Eritrea, 1962–1978* (Stanford, CA: Hoover, 1983); Gebru Tareke, "From Lash to Red Star: The Pitfalls of Counter-insurgency in Ethiopia, 1980–1982," *Journal of Modern African Studies* 40, no. 3 (2002): 465–98; Roy Pateman, *Eritrea: Even the Stones Are Burning* (Trenton, NJ: Red Sea, 1990), 135–36.

41. This category thus corresponds directly to a nonstate version of North, Wallis, and Weingast's (*Violence and Social Orders*) characterization of "fragile natural order states"; the categories of basic and mature natural order below do likewise.

42. In fact, North Wallis, and Weingast see the control of internal political violence as the central issue for political development in general: North, Wallis, and Weingast, *Violence and Social Orders*, 13–18, 257–68. Their taxonomy is thus built around the considerations I argue matter most for actors' ability to manage organized violence more broadly.

43. Effective midspectrum warfare also requires existential stakes—see below. Mature natural order institutions and existential stakes are thus mutually necessary but insufficient conditions for proficient midconcealment military operations in the theory presented here.

44. See, e.g., Charles Heller and William Stofft, eds., *America's First Battles, 1776–1965* (Lawrence: University Press of Kansas, 1986).

45. More formally:

$$\aleph = \left| \int_{x=-1}^{x=1} p_x U_x \right| \qquad\qquad [4.1]$$

Where:

$\aleph \equiv$ the actor's stakes

$x \equiv$ the war's outcome, measured as the actor's share of the war's disputed assets minus the opponent's share (where 1.0 corresponds to the actor receiving the entirety of the disputed asset, with the opponent receiving none; -1.0 corresponds to the opponent receiving the entirety of the disputed asset, with the actor receiving none, and 0 corresponding to an equal division of the disputed asset between the two sides).

$p_x \equiv$ the actor's perceived probability of outcome x obtaining at the war's end

$U_x \equiv$ the actor's utility for outcome x

And where I assume a prospect theoretic functional form for U_x, and, in the interest of definitional parsimony, unidimensional and mutually exclusive war aims for the two combatants. (Note that the appendix and the cases below code stakes as a binary distinction between existential and not, which elides a variety of empirical exceptions to this assumption of unidimensional and mutually exclusive war aims; below I code as "existential" those wars in which the actor's leadership group perceives a significant risk of collective loss of life or liberty for the leadership, with "significant" lying intuitively somewhere above a one-in-four probability. The formalization in [4.1] is intended as a means of clarifying the logic of the qualitative, natural-language treatment in the text—it is not intended to enable quantitative measurement of actors' stakes.)

46. On the concepts of a selectorate and a winning coalition, see, esp., Bruce Bueno de Mesquita, Alastair Smith, Randolph Siverson, and James Morrow, *The Logic of Political Survival* (Cambridge, MA: MIT Press, 2003). For a critique, albeit one set in an explanatory context different from mine, see Mary E. Gallagher and Jonathan K. Hanson, "Power Tool or Dull Blade: Selectorate Theory for Autocracies," *Annual Review of Political Science* 18 (2015): 367–85.

47. See, e.g., Daniel Kahneman and Amos Tversky, "Prospect Theory: An Analysis of Decision under Risk," *Econometrica* 47, no. 2 (1979): 263–91; Rose McDermott, "Prospect Theory in Political Science: Gains and Losses from the First Decade," *Political Psychology* 25, no. 2 (April 2004): 289–312; Jonathan Mercer, "Prospect Theory and Political Science," *Annual Review of Political Science* 8 (2005): 1–21.

48. Cases where victory was seen as a forgone conclusion would also be coded here as limited stakes, though such cases will be uncommon for nonstate actors.

49. On Nazi war aims, see Norman Rich, *Hitler's War Aims: Ideology, the Nazi State, and the Course of Expansion* (New York: Norton, 1992).

50. The postwar Nuremberg Trials condemned to death 12 of the 22 surviving Nazi leadership defendants, with 7 of the others sentenced to prison terms of 10 years to life and with three Nazi political and military organizations declared criminal in nature. On the Nuremberg Trials, see, e.g., Whitney Harris, *Tyranny on Trial: The Trial of the Major German War Criminals at the End of the World War II at Nuremberg Germany 1945–1946* (College Station: Texas A&M University Press, 1999); Robert E. Conot, *Justice at Nuremberg* (New York: Basic Books, 1993). After World War I, the Versailles Treaty called for the imprisonment and trial of the defeated German Kaiser Wilhelm II, though the neutral Netherlands refused to extradite him following his exile

there: Nigel J. Ashton and Duco Hellema, "Hanging the Kaiser: Anglo-Dutch Relations and the Fate of Wilhelm II, 1918–20," *Diplomacy and Statecraft* 11, no. 2 (July 2000): 53–78. On the postwar fate of defeated leaders generally, see Bruce Bueno de Mesquita and Randolph M. Siverson, "War and the Survival of Political Leaders: A Comparative Study of Regime Types and Political Accountability," *American Political Science Review* 89, no. 4 (December 1995): 841–55; H. E. Goemans, "Fighting for Survival: The Fate of Leaders and the Duration of War," *Journal of Conflict Resolution* 44, no. 5 (October 2000): 555–79 (note that most nonstate actor leaderships approximate the "mixed regime" category that Goemans associates with the greatest postwar danger in defeat).

51. Note that neither Mao's successors in the PRC nor the descendants of Chiang's rump government on Taiwan have yet been able to negotiate a stable settlement that would enable disarmament, more than a half century later: Andrew J. Nathan and Andrew Scobell, *China's Search for Security* (New York: Columbia University Press, 2014), 193–240. On Mao's and Chiang's war aims and threat perceptions, see Odd Arne Westad, *Decisive Encounters: The Chinese Civil War, 1946–1950* (Palo Alto, CA: Stanford University Press, 2003); W.A.C. Adie, "Chinese Strategic Thinking under Mao Tse-tung," *Canberra Papers on Strategy and Defence*, no. 13 (1972): 1–26; Robert E. Bedeski, "Pre-Communist State-Building in Modern China: The Political Thought of Chiang Kai-Shek," *Asian Perspective* 4, no. 2 (Fall–Winter 1980): 149–70.

52. See, e.g., Lawrence Freedman, *The Official History of the Falklands Campaign*, 2 vols. (New York: Routledge, 2005).

53. Jeffrey Herbst, *States and Power in Africa* (Princeton, NJ: Princeton University Press, 2000), 150–51; Philippe le Billon, "Angola's Political Economy of War: The Role of Oil and Diamonds," *African Affairs* 100, no. 398 (2001): 67–72.

54. See, esp., Paul Staniland, "States, Insurgents, and Wartime Political Orders," *Perspectives on Politics* 10, no. 2 (June 2012): 243–64; also Paul Staniland, "Armed Politics and the Study of Intrastate Conflict," *Journal of Peace Research* 54, no. 4 (2017): 459–67.

55. The appendix presents the theory's predictions formally in equation A2 and illustrates graphically some of its more important particulars in the comparative statics of figures A.1, A.2, and A.3. Note that as a continuous, real-valued theory, it cannot be tested exhaustively by observing cases that fill all a discrete number of theoretical categories—this would require an infinite number of cases. The testing strategy below thus selects cases chosen to occupy a wide range of divergent points in the relevant theoretical space, and to offer cases where alternative explanations would predict different outcomes, but no case selection could exhaust the theoretical space of a continuous, real-valued theory.

56. More formally, table 4.1 assumes values of $f = 0.25$, $t = [1960, 1990, 2020, 2050]$, $i = [0, 1, 2, 3]$, and $s = [0, 1]$, for equation A2, with cell values of "very Fabian" corresponding to $(0 < \phi < 1)$, "mostly Fabian" corresponding to $(1 < \phi < 2)$, "slightly Fabian" corresponding to $(2 < \phi < 3)$, and "midspectrum" corresponding to $(3 < \phi < 4)$. For the variable values assumed here, no cell pre­sents predicted $\phi > 4$.

Chapter Five: Hezbollah in the 2006 Lebanon Campaign

1. For details on Hezbollah's and Israel's military wherewithal, see the discussion below; on Israel's ranking in world defense expenditure, see International Institute for Strategic Studies, *The Military Balance 2004–5* (London: Oxford University Press, 2004), 353–58.

2. Yaakov Katz, Herb Keinon, et al., "Eight IDF Soldiers Killed, 2 Kidnapped on Northern Frontier," *Jerusalem Post*, July 12, 2006, https://www.jpost.com/israel/eight-idf-soldiers-killed -2-kidnapped-on-northern-frontier; Harel and Issacharoff, *34 Days*, 3–5; Nicholas Blanford, "Deconstructing Hizbullah's Surprise Military Prowess," *Jane's Intelligence Review*, November 1, 2006, 20–27.

3. William M. Arkin, *Divining Victory: Airpower in the 2006 Israel-Hezbollah War* (Maxwell Air Force Base, AL: Air University Press, 2007), 170–71; Uzi Rubin, *The Rocket Campaign against Israel during the 2006 Lebanon War* (Ramat Gan: Begin-Sadat Center for Strategic Studies, 2007), 18; "Halutz: Mr. PM, We Won the War," YNetnews.com, August 27, 2006, https://www .ynetnews.com/articles/0,7340,L-3296031,00.html.

4. Arkin, *Divining Victory*, 63, 73, and appendix C.

5. Rubin, *Rocket Campaign*, 10–11; Arkin, *Divining Victory*, 55–56, 59.

6. Rubin, *Rocket Campaign*, 10–15.

7. Eliyahu Winograd et al., *Final Report* (Tel Aviv: Inquiry Commission to Examine the Events of the Military Campaign in Lebanon 2006, 2008) (in Hebrew), 87–89; Ofer Shelah and Yoav Limor, *Captives in Lebanon* (Tel Aviv: Yedioth Ahronoth, 2007) (in Hebrew), 161–65; Amir Rapaport, *Friendly Fire* (Tel Aviv: Ma'ariv, 2007) (in Hebrew), 145–47; Yaakov Katz, "Heavy IDF Casualties in Firefight at Border," *Jerusalem Post*, July 21, 2006, 1.

8. Winograd et al., *Final Report*, 111, 131; Shelah and Limor, *Captives in Lebanon*, 187–91; Rapaport, *Friendly Fire*, 198–99; Ed Blanche, "IDF Setback at Bint Jbeil," *Jane's Defence Weekly*, August 9, 2006, https://www.researchgate.net/publication/294236612_IDF_setback_at_Bint _Jbeil.

9. Winograd et al., *Final Report*, 140–41; Alon Ben-David, "Israel Re-establishes 'Security Zone' in Southern Lebanon," *Jane's Defence Weekly* August 9, 2006, https://www.researchgate .net/publication/295961109_Israel_re-establishes_%27security_zone%27_in_southern _Lebanon; Harel and Issacharoff, *34 Days*, 173; Makovsky and White, *Lessons and Implications of the Israel-Hezbollah War*, 41.

10. Arkin, *Divining Victory*, 51; Blanford, "Deconstructing Hizbullah's Surprise Military Prowess."

11. Winograd et al., *Final Report*, 201–5.

12. Alon Ben-David, "IDF Conducts Massive Airlift Operation into Lebanon," *Jane's Defence Weekly* August 23, 2006, https://www.researchgate.net/publication/295712149_IDF_conducts _massive_airlift_operation_into_Lebanon.

13. Winograd et al., *Final Report*, 212–13; Shelah and Limor, *Captives in Lebanon*, 395–96; Exum, *Hizballah at War*, 11; Harel and Issacharoff, *34 Days*, 221–24.

14. Winograd et al., *Final Report*, 212–13, 217–18, 224; Shelah and Limor, *Captives in Lebanon*, 395–96.

15. Arkin, *Divining Victory*, 51–52.

16. This range is given in Arkin, *Divining Victory*, 74.

17. Other noteworthy features of Shiite culture in Lebanon include its emphasis on martyrdom and usurpation; Middle Eastern Arab culture more broadly is often associated with egalitarianism and individualism. Tribalism is, of course, just one element of a rich cultural mosaic. On the Shiite culture of martyrdom and usurpation, see, e.g., Graham Fuller and Rend Francke, *The Arab Shi'a: The Forgotten Muslims* (New York: Macmillan, 1999); Seyyed Nasr, *The Shia*

Revival: How Conflicts within Islam Will Shape the Future (New York: Carnegie Council for Ethics in International Affairs, 2006); Fouad Ajami, *The Vanished Imam: Musa al-Sadr and the Shia of Lebanon* (Ithaca, NY: Cornell University Press, 1986); Daniel Bates and Amal Rassam, *People and Cultures of the Middle East* (Upper Saddle River, NJ: Prentice Hall, 2001); Gabriele Marranci, *The Anthropology of Islam* (Oxford: Berg, 2008). On the Arab values of egalitarianism and individualism, see, e.g., Charles Lindholm, "The New Middle Eastern Ethnography," *Journal of the Royal Anthropological Institute* 1, no. 4 (December 1995): 805–20; G. P. Makris, *Islam in the Middle East: A Living Tradition* (Malden, MA: Blackwell, 2007); Brinkley Messick, *The Calligraphic State: Textual Domination and History in a Muslim Society* (Berkeley: University of California Press, 1993); Bates and Rassam, *People and Cultures of the Middle East*; Charles Lindholm, *The Islamic Middle East: Tradition and Change* (Malden, MA: Blackwell, 2002).

18. See, e.g., Ibn Khaldun, *The Muqaddimah* (Princeton, NJ: Princeton University Press, 2004 [abridged ed. of 1377 orig.]), 123–263; Philip S. Khoury and Joseph Kostiner, eds., *Tribes and State Formation in the Middle East* (Berkeley: University of California Press, 1990); Steven Simon, "The Price of the Surge: How U.S. Strategy Is Hastening Iraq's Demise," *Foreign Affairs* 87, no. 3 (May/June 2008): 57–76; Hussein D. Hassan, *Iraq: Tribal Structure, Social, and Political Activities* (Washington, DC: Library of Congress, 2007), 3.

19. See, e.g., Rodger Shanahan, *The Shi'a of Lebanon: Clans, Parties and Clerics* (London: Tauris, 2005); Arnold Hottinger, "Zu'amā' and Parties in the Lebanese Crisis of 1958," *Middle East Journal* 15, no. 2 (Spring 1961): 127–40; Clyde G. Hess Jr. and Herbert L. Bodman Jr., "Confessionalism and Feudality in Lebanese Politics," *Middle East Journal* 8, no. 1 (Winter 1954): 10–26.

20. Arnold Hottinger, "Zu'ama in Historical Perspective," in Leonard Blinder, ed., *Politics in Lebanon* (New York: Wiley, 1966), 85–106; Shanahan, *Shi'a of Lebanon*, 56, 65.

21. Thomas Collelo, ed., *Lebanon: A Country Study* (Washington, DC: Government Printing Office for the Library of Congress, 1987), 72–73; Myriam Klat and Adele Khudr, "Cousin Marriages in Beirut, Lebanon: Is the Pattern Changing?," *Journal of Biosocial Science* 16, no. 3 (1984): 369–73; Shanahan, *Shi'a of Lebanon*, 39–44; A. Nizar Hamzeh, "Clan Conflicts, Hezbollah and the Lebanese State," *Journal of Social, Political, and Economic Studies* 19, no. 4 (Winter 1994): 433–46 at 336.

22. See, e.g., "Gunfight between Two Lebanese Tribes in Bekaa," Kuwait News Agency, June 3, 2005, http://www.kuna.net.kw/NewsAgenciesPublicSite/ArticleDetails.aspx?Language =en&id=1567426; Mitchell Prothro, "Baalbek Tribe Repels Botched Lebanon Army Raid," *National*, April 27, 2010, http://www.thenational.ae/news/worldwide/middle-east/baalbek-tribe -repels-botched-lebanon-army-raid; "Two People Killed in Baalbek Clash," *NOW Lebanon* (Beirut, Lebanon), October 13, 201, https://now.mmedia.me/lb/en/latestnews/two_people _killed_in_baalbek_clash; "Army Defuses Live Bombs Found in Bekaa Arms Cache," *Daily Star* (Beirut, Lebanon), October 27, 2010, https://www.dailystar.com.lb/News/Lebanon-News /2010/Oct-27/59768-army-defuses-live-bombs-found-in-bekaa-arms-cache.ashx; "Baalbek Security Calms Following Clashes between Army, Local Clan," *Daily Star* (Beirut, Lebanon), April 19, 2010, https://www.dailystar.com.lb//News/Lebanon-News/2010/Apr-19/56578 -baalbek-security-calms-following-clashes-between-army-local-clan.ashx; "Lebanese Army Arrests 11 over Tripoli, Hermel Clashes," *Daily Star* (Beirut, Lebanon), http://www.dailystar.com .lb/News/Lebanon-News/2009/Sep-07/55445-lebanese-army-arrests-11-over-tripoli-hermel

-clashes.ashx, September 7, 2009; "Family Feud, Ouzai Style," *NOW Lebanon* (Beirut, Lebanon), August 9, 2010.

23. Hamzeh, "Clan Conflicts, Hezbollah and the Lebanese State"; M.J.L. Hardy, *Blood Feuds and the Payment of Blood Money in the Middle East* (Beirut: Catholic Press, 1963).

24. Hamzeh, "Clan Conflicts, Hezbollah and the Lebanese State," 434; M.J.L. Hardy, *Blood Feuds*; Jocelyne Zablit, "'Gentleman's Agreement' Draws Bekaa Clans Closer to State," Agence France Presse (Beirut, Lebanon), October 27, 2009, http://www.dailystar.com.lb/News/Lebanon-News/2009/Oct-27/55818-gentlemans-agreement-draws-bekaa-clans-closer-to-state.ashx.

25. As Nizar Hamzeh put it: "The clans' leaders use the state and its legal system as an instrument in the service of tribal tradition": "Clan Conflicts, Hezbollah and the Lebanese State," 436.

26. On the decline of the Lebanese Shiite *zu'ama*, see, esp., Shanahan, *Shi'a of Lebanon*, chap. 2.

27. Shanahan, *Shi'a of Lebanon*, 83, 86; Kais M. Firro, "Ethnicizing the Shi'is in Mandatory Lebanon," *Middle Eastern Studies* 42, no. 5 (2007): 741–59.

28. Hamzeh, *In the Path of Hizbullah*, 102–8; Martin Kramer, "The Moral Logic of Hizballah," in Walter Reich, ed., *Origins of Terrorism: Psychologies, Ideologies, Theologies, States of Mind* (Washington, DC: Woodrow Wilson Center Press, 1990), 134; Hamzeh, "Clan Conflicts, Hezbollah and the Lebanese State"; Shanahan, *Shi'a of Lebanon*, 126–27; Zablit, "'Gentleman's Agreement' Draws Bekaa Clans Closer to State."

29. On the role of tribe in contemporary marriage patterns, for example, see Klat and Khudr, "Cousin Marriages in Beirut, Lebanon." Nor has tribal influence on electoral politics per se disappeared, especially at the local level: see, e.g., "Polls Deepen Sectarian Leaders' Hold on Fiefdoms," *Daily Star* (Beirut, Lebanon), May 6, 2010, https://www.dailystar.com.lb/News/Lebanon-News/2010/May-06/60796-polls-deepen-sectarian-leaders-hold-on-fiefdoms.ashx.

30. See, e.g., Karim Tellawini, "Lebanon: Shia Tribes Seek Highly Regarded Image," *Jarariya News*, http://www.jafariyanews.com/2k9_news/oct/26lebanon_shia_tribes.htm, updated October 26, 2009; Nedaa Syria, "Clashes between Lebanese Tribes on the Syrian Border," *Syria Call*, June 21, 2018, http://nedaa-sy.com/en/news/6812.

31. Hamzeh, "Clan Conflicts, Hezbollah and the Lebanese State," 436.

32. Shanahan, *Shi'a of Lebanon*, 77–80, 84.

33. For a formalization, see equations A2 and A3 in the appendix.

34. For various estimates of Hezbollah's troop strength, see "Hizbullah," *Jane's World Insurgency and Terrorism*, June 26, 2007; Steven Erlanger and Richard A. Oppel Jr., "A Disciplined Hezbollah Surprises Israel with Its Training, Tactics, and Weapons," *New York Times*, August 7, 2006, A8; "Hizbullah's Islamic Resistance," *Jane's Terrorism and Security Monitor*, September 13, 2006; Anthony H. Cordesman, "Lebanese Security and the Hezbollah," working draft, revised July 14, 2006, 25; International Crisis Group, "Hizbollah and the Lebanese Crisis," Middle East Report no. 69, October 2007; International Crisis Group, "Israel/Hizbollah/Lebanon: Avoiding Renewed Conflict," Middle East Report no. 59, November 2006.

35. Arkin, *Divining Victory*, 25.

36. Cordesman, *Preliminary "Lessons" of the Israeli-Hezbollah War*; Ranstorp, *Hizballah in Lebanon*, 67; David Hirst, "South Lebanon: The War That Never Ends?," *Journal of Palestine Studies* 28, no. 3 (1999): 5–18.

37. Around 4,000 Kayushas were fired during the campaign: Rubin, *Rocket Campaign*, 10–11; Arkin, *Divining Victory*, 55–56, 59. On Hezbollah missile stocks and capabilities, see, e.g., Cordesman, *Preliminary "Lessons" of the Israeli-Hezbollah War*, 4–5.

38. See, e.g., Byman, *High Price*, 248.

39. Cordesman, *Preliminary "Lessons" of the Israeli-Hezbollah War*, 17–19.

40. Cordesman, *Preliminary "Lessons" of the Israeli-Hezbollah War*, 16; Ash Rossiter, "Drone Usage by Militant Groups: Exploring Variation in Adoption," *Defense and Security Analysis* 34, no. 2 (2018): 113–26; Milton Hoenig, "Hezbollah and the Use of Drones as a Weapon of Terrorism," *Public Interest Report* 67, no. 2 (Spring 2014): 1–2.

41. Hezbollah also employed larger numbers of first-generation wire-guided AT-3 Sagger antitank missiles: Cordesman, *Preliminary "Lessons" of the Israeli-Hezbollah War*, 18; Nicholas Blanford, *Warriors of God: Inside Hezbollah's Thirty-Year Struggle against Israel* (New York: Random House, 2011), 132. On the Kornet and its use in Lebanon, see, e.g., Cordesman, *Preliminary "Lessons" of the Israeli-Hezbollah War*, 18; Jonathan Marcus, "Tough Lessons for Israeli Armour," BBC News, August 15, 2006, http://news.bbc.co.uk/2/hi/middle_east/4794829.stm.

42. Federation of American Scientists, "AT-7 Metis Saxhorn, AT-13 Metis-M," https://fas .org/man/dod-101/sys/land/row/at-7.htm, 2015; Scott Stewart, "Anti-tank Guided Missiles Pose a Serious Threat," *Security Weekly*, April 30, 2015, 1; Eliot A. Cohen, *The Big Stick: The Limits of Soft Power and the Necessity of Military Force* (New York: Basic Books, 2017), 79.

43. For estimates of Hezbollah defense expenditure and revenue sources, see, e.g., Rudner, "Hizbullah Terrorism Finance"; Harik, *Hezbollah*, 86–87, 93; Hamzeh, *In the Path of Hizbullah*, 63; Wilson, "Lebanese Wary of a Rising Hezbollah"; Ranstorp, *Hizballah in Lebanon*, 82–84; Becker, "Beirut Bank Seen as Hub of Hezbollah's Financing."

44. International Institute for Strategic Studies, *The Military Balance, 2007* (London: Oxford University Press, 2006), 227–29; Benjamin S. Lambeth, *Air Operations in Israel's War against Hezbollah: Learning from Lebanon and Getting It Right in Gaza* (Santa Monica, CA: RAND, 2011), 73–75; David E. Johnson, *Hard Fighting: Israel in Lebanon and Gaza* (Santa Monica, CA: RAND, 2011), 19.

45. Vietcong troop strength is taken from Clodfelter, *Warfare and Armed Conflicts*, 740; Republic of Vietnam military personnel figure is drawn from the Correlates of War data set, J. David Singer, Stuart Bremer, and John Stuckey, "Capability Distribution, Uncertainty, and Major Power War, 1820–1965," in Russett, *Peace, War and Numbers*, 19–48.

46. Portuguese national military strength is from the Correlates of War data set, Sarkees and Wayman, *Resort to War*. For Angolan insurgent troop strengths, see W. S. Van der Waals, *Portugal's War in Angola, 1961–1974* (Rivonia: Ashanti, 1993), 91, 141, 161, 173–74.

47. Rif troop strength is taken from David Woolman, *Rebels in the Rif: Abd el Krim and the Rif Rebellion* (Stanford, CA: Stanford University Press, 1986), 83, 88–91; Spanish strength is drawn from the Correlates of War data set: Sarkees and Wayman, *Resort to War*.

48. Rola El Husseini, "Hezbollah and the Axis of Refusal: Hamas, Iran, and Syria," *Third World Quarterly* 31, no. 5 (2010), 803–15.

49. "Open Letter to the Downtrodden of Lebanon and the World," English translation from the Arabic in *FBIS Near East/South Asia Report*, JPRS-NEA-85-056, April 19, 1985, 12, 14.

50. This duty, moreover, was seen as shared by all Muslims, not merely Hezbollah members: "Open Letter to the Downtrodden of Lebanon and the World," 14–19.

51. Hamzeh, *In the Path of Hizbullah*, 101–2; Augustus Richard Norton, *Hezbollah: A Short History* (Princeton, NJ: Princeton University Press, 2007), 43–44.

52. See, e.g., Amal Saad-Ghorayeb, *Hizbu'llah: Politics and Religion* (London: Pluto, 2002); Angel Rabasa and Peter Chalk, *Beyond al-Qaeda: Part 2, The Outer Rings of the Terrorist Universe* (Santa Monica, CA: RAND, 2002), 5–24.

53. See, e.g., Pete Ajemian, "Resistance beyond Time and Space: Hezbollah's Media Campaigns," *Arab Media and Society*, no. 5 (May 2008), http://www.arabmediasociety.com/?article =671.

54. Hamzeh, *In the Path of Hezbollah*, 112–22.

55. See, e.g., Zeina Maasri, *Off the Wall: Political Posters of the Lebanese Civil War* (London: I. B. Tauris, 2009), 96–99; Mona Harb, "On Religiosity and Spatiality: Lessons from Hezbollah in Beirut," in Nezar al Sayyad and Mejgan Massoumi, eds., *The Fundamentalist City? Religiosity and the Remaking of Urban Space* (London: Routledge, 2010), 125–54 at 144–48; Anthony Shadid, "Pessimism Deepens in Postwar Lebanon," *Washington Post*, November 21, 2006, https://www.washingtonpost.com/wp-dyn/content/article/2006/11/20/AR2006112001326 _pf.html; "Hezbollah Displays Military Might with Parade," Associated Press, October 28, 2005.

56. Wiegand, "Reformation of a Terrorist Group."

57. Shaw S. Pick, *Hezbollah: The Myth of Moderation* (Fort Leavenworth, KS: Command and General Staff College, 2010), 12–19.

58. Simon Haddad, "The Origins of Popular Support for Lebanon's Hezbollah," *Studies in Conflict and Terrorism* 29, no. 1 (2006): 21–34; James B. Love, *Hezbollah: Social Services as a Source of Power* (Hurlburt Field, FL: Joint Special Operations University, 2010), 1–36.

59. Ali Bakeer, "Hezbollah's Finances Are Its Achilles Heel," *National Interest*, January 27, 2019, https://nationalinterest.org/feature/hezbollahs-finances-are-its-achilles-heel-42462. For an account of the creation of Hezbollah and the role of Iran, see Ranstorp, *Hizbollah in Lebanon*, 30–40.

60. "Timeline: Lebanon Assassinations," *Al Jazeerah*, February 13, 2008, https://www .aljazeera.com/news/middleeast/2007/12/2008525172717634160.html.

61. Jonathan Masters and Zachary Laub, "Hezbollah," *Council on Foreign Relations*, January 3, 2014, https://www.cfr.org/backgrounder/hezbollah; Eitan Azani, *Hezbollah—a Global Terrorist Organization—Situational Report as of September 2006*, report prepared for the use of the House Committee on International Relations—Subcommittee on International Terrorism and Nonproliferation, September 28, 2006, 10, http://www.investigativeproject.org/documents /testimony/260.pdf; Casey L. Addis and Christopher M. Blanchard, *Hezbollah: Background and Issues for Congress* (Washington, DC.: Congressional Research Service, January 3, 2011), 10–11, https://fas.org/sgp/crs/mideast/R41446.pdf; Marc R. DeVore, "Exploring the Iran-Hezbollah Relationship: A Case Study of How State Sponsorship Affects Terrorist Group Decision-Making," *Perspectives of Terrorism* 6, nos. 4–5 (2012), http://www.terrorismanalysts .com/pt/index.php/pot/article/view/218/html; Robert G. Rabil, "Hezbollah, the Islamic Association and Lebanon's Confessional System" *Levantine Review* 1, no. 1 (Spring 2012): 49–67; Hamzeh, *In the Path of Hizbullah*, 46.

62. See Norton, *Hezbollah*, e.g., 76, 95, 107–12; Hamzeh, *In the Path of Hizbullah*, e.g., 52–53; Masters and Laub, "Hezbollah"; Andrew Exum, "Hizballah at War: Explaining Victory through the Comprehensive Approach to Conflict" (PhD diss., King's College, London, 2010), 91–133.

63. See, e.g., D. Johnson, *Hard Fighting*, 47–49; Hamzeh, *In the Path of Hezbollah*, 70–74.

64. Norton, *Hezbollah*, 100–101; Joseph Alagha, *The Shifts in Hizbullah's Ideology* (Amsterdam: Amsterdam University Press, 2006), 42–43.

65. Norton, *Hezbollah*, 101, 109–10.

66. Hamzeh, *In the Path of Hizbullah*, 109–10.

67. BBC, "Lebanese Army Hunts Down Radical Cleric," January 31, 1998, http://news.bbc .co.uk/2/hi/middle_east/52217.stm; Hamzeh, *In the Path of Hizbullah*, 111.

68. COL A int., US Army Military History Institute Archive Lebanon 2006 Collection, henceforth MHI:122007p; 1LT Y int., MHI:031308p1; MAJ S int., MHI:031708a3; LTC S int., MHI:031608a2. For other examples from Bint Jubayl, Marun ar Ras, Mays al Jabal, Aytarun, and elsewhere, see, e.g., COL H int., MHI:121817a; LTC R int., MHI:121807p4; 1LT T int., MHI:031308p2; 1LT O int., MHI:031308a1; MAJ Z int., MHI:031608p4; LTC A int., MHI:031608p3. Of course, there were exceptions. In Haddatha, IDF intelligence learned of a Hezbollah position and a ground unit then spotted them moving around in a building: 1LT T int., MHI:031308p2. In Bayt Yahun, IDF ground forces identified a Sagger position in a house, and one mobile Sagger outdoors, and killed both before the crews realized they had been seen: MAJ S int., MHI:031608p1. In Ghanduriyih, many positions were concealed, but some could be identified prior to contact: cf. LTC R int., MHI:121807p4, and LTC A int., MHI:031608p3. But these exceptions were unusual. In most engagements, Hezbollah defenders got the first shot from positions that had not been identified beforehand.

69. See, e.g., LTC A int., MHI:121607a; LTC R int., MHI:121807p4.

70. At Bint Jubayl, for example, reinforced walls facing the Israeli border remained standing after the rest of the structures had been destroyed: 1LT B int., MHI:031308a2.

71. See, e.g., COL H int., MHI:121817a; LTC A int., MHI:121607a; LTC R int., MHI:121807p4; LTC N int., MHI:031308p3. Note that while there is some evidence of similar preparations elsewhere (on Ghanduriyih, for example, see LTC R int., MHI:121807p4), interior positions in villages remote from the border were typically less extensively prepared: see, e.g., COL A int., MHI:122007p; MAJ K int., MHI:031608p2. Even some border area positions appear to have been more hastily prepared, as with some buildings at Marun ar Ras (1LT T int., MHI:031308p2; or Mays al Jabal, cf. LTC R int., MHI:121807p4 and MAJ E int., MHI:031708a1), and in few cases were even better prepared buildings fitted with loopholes, razor wire, or interior obstacles; Hezbollah urban defensive techniques were thus variable across the theater, and often not as extensive as in some other historical urban warfare—though the net results typically afforded Hezbollah defenders very effective concealment prior to, and often subsequent to, the exchange of fire.

72. See, e.g., 1LT O int., MHI:031308a1; LTC A int., MHI:121607a.

73. See, e.g., 1LT O int., MHI:031308a3; COL M int., MHI:031608a1; MAJ Z int., MHI:031608p4; 1LT Y int., MHI:031308p1; MAJ E int., MHI:031708a2.

74. LTC D int., MHI:121807p3.

75. See, e.g., LTC D int., MHI:121807p3; 1LT O int., MHI:031308a1; COL H int., MHI:121817a.

76. See, e.g., MAJ K int., MHI:031608p2; LTC N int., MHI:031308p3; LTC A int., MHI:121607p; 1LT B int., MHI:031308a2; MAJ E int., MHI:031708a2; 1LT O int., MHI:031308a3. There were exceptions: at Bint Jubayl, for example, a Hezbollah counterattack combined direct fire support with suppressive indirect fire from remotely located mortars, which continued as

Hezbollah ground forces advanced. Such exceptions were uncommon, however. In general, Hezbollah was more successful combining arms from static defensive positions against Israeli assaults than in support of their own movement: COL H int., MHI:121817a; LTC S int., MHI:031608a2; 1LT O int., MHI:031308a3; COL M int., MHI:031608a1.

77. See, e.g., 1LT B int., MHI:031308a2; LTC A int., MHI:121607a; COL H int., MHI:121817a.

78. Corresponding to a score of 0.5 on the (0, 1) scale for stealth in the coding system presented in the appendix.

79. As noted in chap. 2, "decisive engagement" is a condition wherein defenders remain in position under assault even after the attackers have gotten close enough that the defenders cannot readily withdraw without being overrun. As the Defense Department defines it: "In land and naval warfare, an engagement in which a unit is considered fully committed and cannot maneuver or extricate itself. In the absence of outside assistance, the action must be fought to a conclusion and either won or lost with the forces at hand" (http://www.js.pentagon.mil /doctrine/jel/doddict/data/d/01536.html).

80. 1LT O int., MHI:031308a1.

81. 1LT T int., MHI:031308p2; see also LTC N int., MHI:031308p3.

82. MAJ S int., MHI:031708a3; COL H int., MHI:121817a; 1LT B int., MHI:031318a2.

83. LTC R int., MHI:121807p4; LTC A int., MHI:031608p3; COL M int., MHI:031608a1.

84. LTC S int., MHI:031608a2.

85. LTC A int., MHI:031608p3.

86. 1LT O int., MHI:031308a3.

87. The firefight at Haddatha on August 12, for example, lasted under two hours: MAJ K int., MHI:031608p2; the action at Rabb ath Thalathin on July 30 lasted about an hour: MAJ E int., MHI:031708a2. Not all engagements were of extended duration, but many were—far more than one would expect of a combatant with no intention of holding ground. Overall, this pattern implies a score of 1.0 on the "duration of firefights" subscore for holding ground, contributing 0.25 points to the overall index score for Hezbollah in the coding system presented in the appendix.

88. 1LT O int., MHI:031308a1.

89. COL H int., MHI:121817a; MAJ S int., MHI:031708a3; LTC O int., MHI:121607p; 1LT O int., MHI:031308a1; 1LT T int., MHI:031308p2.

90. 1LT O int., MHI:031308a1; 1LT Y int., MHI:031308p1.

91. 1LT Y int., MHI:031308p1.

92. 1LT T int., MHI:031308p2.

93. LTC R int., MHI:121807p4; LTC A int., MHI:031608p3. Note that the survivors eventually withdrew in violation of orders to stand their ground: LTC A int., MHI:031608p3.

94. LTC S int., MHI:031608a2.

95. 1LT O int., MHI:031308a1. See also LTC D int., MHI:121807p3, on receiving fire from Hezbollah positions that had been previously bypassed throughout the theater.

96. MAJ K int., MHI:031608p2.

97. 1LT O int., MHI:031308a3.

98. Eric Goldstein and Bonnie Docherty, "Civilians under Assault: Hezbollah's Rocket Attacks on Israel in the 2006 War," *Human Rights Watch* 19, no. 3 (E) (August 2007): 1, https:// www.hrw.org/sites/default/files/reports/iopt0807.pdf.

99. Overall, the net of observed very-long- and very-short-range engagement implies a score of 0.5 on the "proximity of attackers to defenders" subscore for holding ground, contributing 0.125 points to the overall index score for Hezbollah in the coding system presented in the appendix.

100. See, e.g., Timothy A. Wray, *Standing Fast: German Defensive Doctrine on the Russian Front during World War II: Prewar to March 1943* (Fort Leavenworth, KS: US Army Command and General Staff College, 1986), 9–16; House, *Toward Combined Arms Warfare*, 163.

101. LTC N int., MHI:031308p3 and associated sketch map, MHI:031308p3m; COL H int., MHI:121817a. Note that COL H describes the school building as being to the north of Hill 951. For other instances of counterattacks at Marun ar Ras, see LTC A int., MHI:121608a.

102. On this and several other observed Hezbollah counterattacks in Bint Jubayl using multiple assault teams on multiple axes with supporting fire from ATGMs or mortars, see LTC N int., MHI:031308p3; COL H int., MHI:121817a; 1LT B int., MHI:031308a2. For a secondary account of this fighting, see Blanche, "IDF Setback at Bint Jbeil."

103. COL H int., MHI:121817a.

104. 1LT B int., MHI:031308a2.

105. LTC R int., MHI:121807p4. Hezbollah defenders at Ghanduriyih occupied a series of defensive lines disposed in depth; on several occasions when a line was taken, defenders would maneuver to the attackers' flanks in an apparent attempt to retake the positions: LTC A int., MHI:031608p3.

106. COL A int., MHI:122007p.

107. LTC S int., MHI:031608a2

108. See, for example, the accounts of actions at At Tayyibeh, Aytarun, Haddatha (in which a small team of about five fighters assaulted an IDF-occupied house on August 12, supported by fire from multiple directions; they successfully entered the building, killed an IDF soldier in an exchange of fire at very short range, and attempted to pull the body from the house before being driven off with the loss of at least four attackers), and Mays al Jabal in: COL A int., MHI:122007p; 1LT Y int., MHI:031308p1; MAJ K int., MHI:031608p2; LTC R int., MHI:121807p4.

109. Overall, this pattern implies a score of 0.5 on the "incidence of counterattack" subscore for holding ground, contributing 0.125 points to the overall index score for Hezbollah in the coding system presented in the appendix.

110. COL A int., MHI:122007p.

111. See, e.g., MAJ E int., MHI:031708a1; LTC A int., MHI:121607a; LTC R int., MHI:121807p4; 1LT O int., MHI:031308a1; LTC A int., MHI:031608p3; COL H int., MHI:121807a; LTC O int., MHI:121607a.

112. LTC R int., MHI:121807p4.

113. 1LT O int., MHI:031308a3.

114. LTC N int., MHI:031308p3.

115. COL M int., MHI:031608a1.

116. MAJ Z int., MHI:031608p4.

117. LTC R int., MHI:121807p4; COL M int., MHI:031608a1; MAJ E int., MHI:031708a1; LTC A int., MHI:121607p; 1LT B int., MHI:031308a2. Overall, this pattern implies a score of 0.5 on the "incidence of harassing fires, unattended minefields" subscore for holding ground, contributing 0.125 points to the overall index score for Hezbollah in the coding system presented

in the appendix, and yielding an overall "holding ground" score of 0.625 across its four subcomponents.

118. For various estimates of Hezbollah's troops strength, see "Hizbullah," *Jane's World Insurgency and Terrorism*; Erlanger and Oppel, "Disciplined Hezbollah Surprises Israel with Its Training, Tactics, and Weapons"; "Hizbullah's Islamic Resistance"; Cordesman, *Lebanese Security and the Hezbollah*, working draft, 25.

119. Corresponding to a score of 0.13 on the (0, 1) scale for dispersion in the coding system presented in the appendix (assuming an area of 10,450 square kilometers for Lebanon and 750 square kilometers for Lebanese territory south of the Litani River; see map 5.1).

120. The Maginot Line was 140 kilometers in length, and its fortifications were about 4 kilometers in depth on average. The line was also supported with artillery, including guns with a 27-kilometer maximum range. Assuming the standard rule of thumb that artillery is generally positioned one-third of its range behind the front, this implies that the average total depth of the Maginot Line defenses was 9 kilometers. In 1940, France deployed 25 regiments of fortress infantry to the line, at roughly 3,000 troops per regiment, for an estimated complement of 75,000. For these figures, see Kaufmann, *Maginot Line*, 57–58, 67, 85, 88; Rowe, *Great Wall of France*, 86. On British concentration at Goodwood, see S. Biddle, *Military Power*, chap. 6, and assuming a 3-kilometer assault frontage with the forward assault divisions concentrated within 10 kilometers of the line of contact.

121. As noted in chap. 2.

122. Note that a plan for coercive pain infliction would be necessary even if Hezbollah calculated that a reoccupation would serve its domestic political interests: if it ultimately failed to inflict significant coercive pain on an Israeli occupier, its legitimacy in the eyes of its Shiite constituency would eventually collapse.

123. As demonstrated in the 2006 campaign by Israel's air strike in Operation Specific Gravity.

124. Some have argued that Hezbollah could solve this problem not by defending the launchers, but simply by deploying so many of them that the IDF could not possibly destroy them all: see, e.g., Rubin, *Rocket Campaign*, 26–27. It is far from clear, however, that this offered a practical solution without a credible, brute force defense of southern Lebanon. To do this with long-range rockets fired from northern Lebanon, for example, would require saturating the Israeli Air Force's ability to destroy targets whose size makes them relatively easy for the IAF to find. Modern, high-technology air forces are very good at destroying exposed targets quickly and in large numbers; to acquire more targets than the IAF has munitions would be an extremely inefficient solution and would require Hezbollah to field an impractically large number of relatively scarce assets. To try this approach with short-range rockets, by contrast, is to assume that an unchallenged IDF ground invasion would not simply saturate the region with so many soldiers as to enable them to find even nominally hidden rockets quickly in large numbers. The IDF is large enough, and southern Lebanon is small enough, to have enabled Israel to do this if the cost of doing so were low; the whole logic of the analysis presented below is premised on the assumed need for Hezbollah to make this impossible by impeding the IDF's access to the launch areas.

125. Note that a short, intense air campaign of the kind needed to destroy Hezbollah long-range missile launchers could be concluded before such external political pressure would get

very far. For external pressure to develop much leverage on Israel, a sustained campaign of extended duration would be required. Hezbollah may well have expected to profit politically from the collateral damage inevitably associated with Israeli air operations, but if they based their strategy on long-range missiles alone this profit would have been slight. An ability to protract the campaign was essential for the success of any strategy involving external political pressure on Israel.

126. In particular, Exum, *Hizballah at War*, 8; Giora Romm, "A Test of Rival Strategies," in Meir Elran and Shlomo Brom, eds., *The Second Lebanon War* (Tel Aviv: Yediot Aharonot Books and Chemed Books, 2007) (in Hebrew), 49–60 at 58–59; Blanford, "Deconstructing Hizbullah's Surprise Military Prowess."

127. See, e.g., Avi Kober, "The Second Lebanon War," Begin-Sadat Center for Strategic Studies, Perspectives Paper no. 22, September 2006; Kober, "Israel Defense Forces in the Second Lebanon War," 3–4; Gabriel Siboni, "The Military Campaign in Lebanon," in Shlomo Brom and Meir Elan, eds., *The Second Lebanon War: Strategic Perspectives* (Tel Aviv: Institute for National Security Studies, 2007), 62–63; Rubin, *Rocket Campaign*, 26–27; Edward Cody and Molly Moore, "The Best Guerilla Force in the World," *Washington Post*, August 14 2006, A01.

128. See Herb Keinon, "No Second Round Looming," *Jerusalem Post*, August 28, 2006, 1; Matthew Schofield and Leila Fadel, "Regrets over Captures Aired," *Miami Herald*, August 28, 2006, A12.

129. For arguments that Hezbollah was not successful in the 2006 war, see Charles Krauthammer, "Hezbollah's 'Victory,'" *Washington Post*, September 1, 2006, A21; Edward N. Luttwak, "Misreading the Lebanon War," *Jerusalem Post*, August 21, 2006, 13; Asher Susser, "Lebanon: A Reassessment," *Jerusalem Post*, September 13, 2006, 15. Whatever one's view of the war's net utility for Hezbollah, the coding this strategic pattern implies would be a value of 0.5 on the (0, 1) scale for "reliance on brute force" in the coding system presented in the appendix.

130. See, e.g., Reuven Erlich, *The Use of Lebanese Civilians as Human Shields* (Gelilot: Center for Special Studies/Intelligence and Terrorism Information Center, 2006); Erlanger and Oppel, "Disciplined Hezbollah Surprises Israel with Its Training, Tactics and Weapons," A8; "Israel's Dilemma after Qana," *Jane's Intelligence Digest*, August 4, 2006; Blanford, "Deconstructing Hizbullah's Surprise Military Prowess."

131. See, e.g., LTC A int., MHI:121607a; COL H int., MHI:121817a; LTC R int., MHI:121807p4; COL A int., MHI:122007p; 1LT T int., MHI:031308p2; LTC N int., MHI:031308p3; MAJ S int., MHI:031608p1; MAJ E int., MHI:031708a1. There are reports of occasional exceptions. In Bint Jubayl, for example, a woman was seen waving a white flag from what was believed to be a Hezbollah-occupied house: LTC A int., MHI:121607a. "A few women" were spotted in At Tayyibeh: LTC R int., MHI:121807p4. Some civilians were seen in Aytarun in the early days of the war, but not later: 1LT O int., MHI:031308a1. Isolated movement by civilian vehicles was reported in Haddatha: MAJ K int., MHI:031608p2. We heard no accounts, however, of any significant civilian population on any battlefield south of the Litani, or any systematic effort by Hezbollah to exploit civilian intermingling as a shield. This pattern implies a score of 0.5 on the "intermingling" subscore for distinguishability, contributing 0.25 points to the overall index score for Hezbollah in the coding system presented in the appendix.

132. See, e.g., LTC A int., MHI:121607a; COL H int., MHI:121817a; LTC R int., MHI:121807p4; COL A int., MHI:122007p; 1LT B int., MHI:031308a2; MAJ K int., MHI:031608p2; LTC A int.,

MHI:031608p3. Some Hezbollah fighters wore face paint for camouflage, further differentiating themselves from civilians: LTC R int., MHI:121807p4.

133. COL A int., MHI:122007p. Similarly, at Hill 951 at Marun ar Ras some IDF units were hesitant to fire on Hezbollah counterattackers because the latter looked so much like Israeli infantry: LTC N int., MHI:031308p3.

134. 1LT T int., MHI:031308p2; LTC S int., MHI:031608a2; MAJ E int., MHI:031708a1; LTC A int., MHI:031608p3; LTC I int., MHI:031708p.

135. This pattern implies a score of 1.0 on the "distinguishing markings" subscore for distinguishability, contributing 0.25 points to the overall index score for Hezbollah in the coding system presented in the appendix.

136. Cordesman, *Preliminary "Lessons" of the Israeli-Hezbollah War*, 17–19; Marcus, "Tough Lessons for Israeli Armour"; Ranstorp, *Hizballah in Lebanon*, 67; Hirst, "South Lebanon"; Rubin, *Rocket Campaign*, 10–11; Arkin, *Divining Victory*, 55–56, 59; E. Goldstein and Docherty, "Civilians under Assault," 10, 30. This pattern implies a score of 1.0 on the "distinguishing markings" subscore for distinguishability, contributing 0.25 points to the overall index score for Hezbollah in the coding system presented in the appendix, and yielding an overall "distinguishability" score of 0.75 across its three subcomponents.

137. MAJ E int., MHI:031708a1.

138. 1LT T int., MHI:031308p2; LTC A int., MHI:121607a; MAJ J int., MHI:031508p; MAJ S int., MHI:031608p1; MAJ E int., MHI:031708a1.

139. See, e.g., 1LT T int., MHI:031308p2; LTC N int., MHI:031308p3; MAJ S int., MHI:031708a3; COL H int., MHI:121817a; LTC R int., MHI:121807p4; LTC S int., MHI:031608a2; LTC A int., MHI:031608p3.

140. See, e.g., 1LT O int., MHI:031308a1; COL H int., MHI:121817a; MAJ S int., MHI:031708a3; 1LT T int., MHI:031308p2; LTC N int., MHI:031308p3; 1LT B int., MHI:031308a2.

141. LTC D int., MHI:121807p3; LTC A int., MHI:121607a; MAJ S int., MHI:031608p1. Some, however, have attributed the lighter resistance encountered in the southwest to superior IDF tactics employed by the units operating there: MAJ J int., MHI:031508p.

142. LTC R int., MHI:121807p4.

143. In Bint Jubayl, Marun ar Ras, Muhaybib, and elsewhere, for example, extensive stocks of ammunition, weapons, food, and water were discovered, sufficient for weeks of combat without resupply: see, e.g., LTC A int., MHI:121607a; 1LT B int., MHI:031308a2; MAJ K int., MHI:031608p2. Bint Jubayl was contested through the end of the campaign with no apparent supply difficulties for the Hezbollah garrison. By contrast, Beit Yaroun was subject to much less extensive fighting, yet by the end of the campaign, Hezbollah fighters were observed moving from house to house searching for food; Hezbollah supplies had apparently run out, and no unconsumed prestocks of food or ammunition were observed in the village following its capture: MAJ S int., MHI:031608p1.

144. See, e.g., LTC N int., MHI:031308p3; MAJ J int., MHI:031508p; COL M int., MHI:031608a1; MAJ K int., MHI:031608p2; MAJ E int., MHI:031708a1; COL H int., MHI:121817a; LTC S int., MHI:031608a2; LTC A int., MHI:031608p. Hezbollah also appears to have devoted considerable effort to intercepting IDF communications, though it is unclear whether they proved able to exploit any such intercepts: MAJ S int., MHI:031608p1; COL M int., MHI:031608a1; MAJ K int., MHI:031608p2.

145. Taken together, this pattern implies a value of 1.0 on the (0, 1) scale for "articulated theater" in the coding system presented in the appendix.

146. See, e.g., COL H int., MHI:121817a; MAJ S int., MHI:031708a3; 1LT B int., MHI:031308a2; LTC N int., MHI:031308p3; MAJ K int., MHI:031608p2.

147. COL M int., MHI:031608a1.

148. See, e.g., LTC A int., MHI:121607a; LTC R int., MHI:121807p4; 1LT O int., MHI:031308a1; LTC A int., MHI:031608p3; MAJ E int., MHI:031708a1 (though some felt Hezbollah's mortar marksmanship, though good, was actually stronger in the 1990s: COL H int., MHI:121817a).

149. See, e.g., 1LT B int., MHI:031308a2; LTC A int., MHI:121607a; COL H int., MHI:121817a.

150. COL H int., MHI:121817a; COL M int., MHI:031608a1; 1LT B int., MHI:031308a2; LTC N int., MHI:031308p3; LTC S int., MHI:031608a2; MAJ K int., MHI:031608p2.

151. I am indebted to Yuri M. Zhukov for this observation. On Hezbollah troop strength in southern Lebanon, see "Hizbullah," *Jane's World Insurgency and Terrorism*, June 26, 2007; Steven Erlanger and Richard A. Oppel Jr., "A Disciplined Hezbollah Surprises Israel with Its Training, Tactics, and Weapons," *New York Times*, August 7, 2006, A8; "Hizbullah's Islamic Resistance," *Jane's Terrorism and Security Monitor*, September 13, 2006; Anthony H. Cordesman, "Lebanese Security and the Hezbollah," working draft, revised July 14, 2006, 25; International Crisis Group, "Hizbollah and the Lebanese Crisis," Middle East Report no. 69, October 2007; International Crisis Group, "Israel/Hizbollah/Lebanon: Avoiding Renewed Conflict," Middle East Report no. 59, November 2006.

152. See, e.g., MAJ J int., MHI:031508p; LTC R int., MHI:121807p4.

153. 1LT O int., MHI:031308a3; MAJ Z int., MHI:031608p4; MAJ E int., MHI:031708a2.

154. Some sources have estimated hit rates as low as 8 percent of all missiles fired for Hezbollah ATGMs: Alon Ben-David, "ATGM Threat Poses Quandary for IDF Armour," *Jane's Defence Weekly* August 16, 2006, https://www.researchgate.net/publication/294457003_ATGM _threat_poses_quandry_for_IDF_armour; Ed Blanche, "Hizbullah ATGMs Take Heavy Toll in Lebanon," *Jane's Missiles and Rockets*, September 1, 2006. Estimated penetration rates per hit as reported in public sources vary from 20 to 45 percent: Erlanger and Oppel, "Disciplined Hezbollah Surprises Israel with Its Training, Tactics and Weapons"; Alon Ben-David, "Israeli Armour Fails to Protect MBTs from ATGMs," *Jane's Defence Weekly* August 30, 2006, https:// www.researchgate.net/publication/294236910_Israeli_armour_fails_to_protect_MBTs_from _ATGMs. On balance, the result was low per-round efficiency, but high aggregate lethality, accounting for over 50 of the IDF's 119 fatalities: Blanford, "Deconstructing Hizbullah's Surprise Military Prowess."

155. See, esp., S. Biddle, "Speed Kills"; S. Biddle, "Victory Misunderstood."

156. See, e.g., ISO Playfair et al., *The Mediterranean and Middle East I: The Early Successes against Italy* (London: Her Majesty's Stationery Office, 1954); Allan R. Millet and Williamson Murray, *Military Effectiveness III: The Second World War* (London: Unwin Hyman, 1991), 136–79; Robert Doughty, *The Breaking Point: Sedan and the Fall of France, 1940* (Hamden, CT: Archon, 1990), 103–65; Florian Rothbrust, *Guderian's XIXth Panzer Corps and the Battle of France* (New York: Praeger, 1990).

157. See, e.g., Kenneth Pollack, *Arabs at War: Military Effectiveness, 1948–1991* (Lincoln: University of Nebraska Press, 2002); Anthony Cordesman and Abraham Wagner, *The Lessons of Modern War: The Arab-Israeli Conflicts, 1973–1989* (Boulder, CO: Westview, 1990).

158. Assuming 2006 Israeli casualty and Hezbollah strength figures documented above, with strength and casualty figures for 1956, 1967, 1973, and 1982 drawn from J. David Singer and Melvin Small, *Correlates of War Project: International and Civil War Data, 1816–1992* (computer file) (Ann Arbor, MI: Inter-university Consortium for Political and Social Research, 1994).

159. See, e.g., Exum, *Hizballah at War*; Makovsky and White, *Lessons and Implications of the Israel-Hezbollah War*; Erlanger and Oppel, "Disciplined Hezbollah Surprises Israel with Its Training, Tactics, and Weapons," A8; Jonathan D. Zagdanski, "Round 2 in Lebanon," *Infantry*, September/October 2007, 32–35.

160. See, e.g., Siboni, "Military Campaign in Lebanon," 62–63; Reuven Erlich and Yoram Kahati, *Hezbollah as a Case Study of the Battle for Hearts and Minds* (Gelilot: Center for Special Studies/Intelligence and Terrorism Information Center, 2007); Erlich, *Use of Lebanese Civilians as Human Shields*; Sarah E. Kreps, "The 2006 Lebanon War: Lessons Learned," *Parameters* 37, no. 1 (Spring 2007): 72–83; Cody and Moore, "Best Guerilla Force in the World"; Kober, "Second Lebanon War," 2.

161. See, e.g., Ernst Dijxhoorn, *Quasi-state Entities and International Criminal Justice: Legitimising Narratives and Counter-narratives* (Oxfordshire, UK: Taylor and Francis, 2017), 127; Shawn Teresa Flanigan and Mounah Abdel-Samad, "Hezbollah's Social Jihad: Nonprofits as Resistance Organizations," *Middle East Policy* 16, no. 2 (2009): 122–37.

162. See, e.g., Abbas William Samii, "A Stable Structure on Shifting Sands: Assessing the Hizbullah-Iran-Syria Relationship," *Middle East Journal* 62, no. 1 (Winter 2008): 32–53; Ante Lucic, "Hezbollah: An Iranian Project?," *National Security and the Future* 1, no. 10 (2009): 78–87; Zayn Knaub, "Why Is Hezbollah in Syria?," *Small Wars Journal*, November 19, 2013, https://smallwarsjournal.com/jrnl/art/why-is-hezbollah-in-syria.

163. Corresponding to a scoring of (0.5, 1, 0.5, 0.5, 0.5, 0.13, 0.5, 0.5, 1, 1, 1) on the criteria given in table A-1.

164. As implied by equation [A2], for values of $f = 0.008$, $i = 3$, $s = 1$, and $t = 2006$, per the discussion above.

Chapter Six: The Jaish al Mahdi in Iraq, 2003–8

1. M. Gordon and Trainor, *Cobra II*, 465–73; Daniel Byman, "An Autopsy of the Iraq Debacle: Policy Failure or Bridge Too Far?," *Security Studies* 17, no. 4 (2008): 603–8, 610–14; Patrick Cockburn, *Muqtada: Muqtada al-Sadr, the Shia Revival, and the Struggle for Iraq* (New York: Scribner, 2008), chap. 11; Michael R. Gordon and General Bernard E. Trainor, *The Endgame: The Inside Story of the Struggle for Iraq, from George W. Bush to Barack Obama* (New York: Vintage Books, 2013), 19–26; Geraint Hughes, "The Insurgencies in Iraq, 2003–2009: Origins, Developments and Prospects," *Defence Studies* 10, nos. 1–2 (March–June 2010): 155–64; Nicholas Krohley, *The Death of the Mehdi Army: The Rise, Fall, and Revival of Iraq's Most Powerful Militia* (Oxford: Oxford University Press, 2015), 32–34, chap. 3.

2. Cockburn, *Muqtada*, chap. 11; Krohley, *Death of the Mehdi Army*, chap. 3.

3. Anthony H. Cordesman and Jose Ramos, *Sadr and the Mahdi Army: Evolution, Capabilities, and a New Direction* (Washington, DC: CSIS, 2008), 8; Krohley, *Death of the Mehdi Army*, chap. 3.

4. Cockburn, *Muqtada*, chap. 12; M. Gordon and Trainor, *Endgame*, 67–73; Krohley, *Death of the Mehdi Army*, 65–67.

5. Cockburn, *Muqtada*, 148–52, 158–59, 161–62; Francis X. Kozlowski, *U.S. Marines in Battle: An-Najaf, August 2004* (Washington, DC: US Marine Corps History Division, 2009), 11–42; Mark D. Sherry, "Fighting in the Valley of Peace," chap. 3 in *Tip of the Spear: U.S. Army Small-Unit Action in Iraq, 2004–2007*, ed. Jon T. Hoffman (Washington, DC: US Army Center of Military History, 2009), 65–83; M. Gordon and Trainor, *Endgame*, 102–5.

6. US Army Military History Institute, Iraq Surge Collection (henceforth MHI/ISC), audio files 10, 11, 17, 18, 23, 26, 35, 36, 38, 55, and 61; M. Gordon and Trainor, *Endgame*, 192–95, 213–16, 224–25; Krohley, *Death of the Mehdi Army*, 72–76.

7. M. Gordon and Trainor, *Endgame*, 212, 218, 220–28; Kimberly Kagan, *The Surge: A Military History* (New York: Encounter Books, 2009), chap. 1, esp. 11–18; Thomas E. Ricks, *The Gamble: General Petraeus and the American Military Adventure in Iraq* (New York: Penguin Books, 2009), 49–51.

8. M. Gordon and Trainor, *Endgame*, 420–25; S. Biddle, Friedman, and Shapiro, "Testing the Surge"; Kagan, *Surge*, chap. 2.

9. M. Gordon and Trainor, *Endgame*, chap. 25; Marisa Cochrane, *The Battle for Basra*, Iraq Report 9 (Washington, DC: Institute for the Study of War, 2008).

10. Marisa Cochrane, *The Fragmentation of the Sadrist Movement*, Iraq Report 12 (Washington, DC: Institute for the Study of War, 2009), 34, 37; M. Gordon and Trainor, *Endgame*, 488–502.

11. M. Gordon and Trainor, *Endgame*, 501, 504.

12. Samira Haj, "The Problems of Tribalism: The Case of Nineteenth-Century Iraqi History," *Social History* 16, no. 1 (January 1991): 55–56; Faleh A. Jabar, "Shaykhs and Ideologues: Detribalization and Retribalization in Iraq, 1968–1998," *Middle East Report* 215 (Summer 2000): 28; Amal Vinogradov, "The 1920 Revolt in Iraq Reconsidered: The Role of Tribes in National Politics," *International Journal of Middle Eastern Studies* 3, no. 2 (April 1972): 128; Hanna Batatu, *The Old Social Classes and the Revolutionary Movements of Iraq: A Study of Iraq's Old Landed and Commercial Classes and Its Communists, Ba'thists, and Free Officers* (Princeton, NJ: Princeton University Press, 1978), 13, 22, 74, 90–91, 94, 95; Marion Farouk-Sluglett and Peter Sluglett, "The Transformation of Land Tenure and Rural Social Structure in Central and Southern Iraq, c. 1870–1958," *International Journal of Middle East Studies* 15, no. 4 (November 1983): 495; Michael Eisenstadt, "Tribal Engagement Lessons Learned," *Military Review* (September–October 2007): 21; Phebe Marr, *The Modern History of Iraq*, 3rd ed. (Boulder, CO: Westview, 2012), 20, 41; Orit Bashkin, "Iraqi Democracy and the Democratic Vision of 'Abd al-Fattah Ibrahim," in *Iraq between Occupations: Perspectives from 1920 to the Present*, ed. Amatzia Baram, Achim Rohde, and Ronen Zeidel (New York: Palgrave Macmillan, 2010), 118; Yitzhak Nakash, *The Shi'is of Iraq* (Princeton, NJ: Princeton University Press, 1994), 33–36, 46–47, 88–89, 92; McFate, "'Memory of War,'"; Charles Tripp, *A History of Iraq*, 3rd ed. (New York: Cambridge University Press, 2007), 18.

13. Amatzia Baram, "Neo-tribalism in Iraq: Saddam Hussein's Tribal Policies 1991–96," *International Journal of Middle East Studies* 29, no. 1 (February 1997): 3–4; Phebe Marr, "One Iraq or Many: What Has Happened to Iraqi Identity?," chap. 1 in Baram, Rohde, and Zeidel, *Iraq between the Occupations*, 26.

14. Marr, "One Iraq or Many," 16; Jabar, "Shaykhs and Ideologues," 28–31.

15. Amatzia Baram, *Building toward Crisis: Saddam Husayn's Strategy for Survival* (Washington, DC: Washington Institute for Near East Policy, 1998), 25.

16. See, e.g., Marr, *Modern History of Iraq*, 234–35, 241–44; Tripp, *History of Iraq*, 259–67.

17. Katherine Blue Carroll, "Tribal Law and Reconciliation in the New Iraq," *Middle East Journal* 65, no. 1 (Winter 2011): 18; Judith Yaphe, "Tribalism in Iraq: The Old and the New," *Middle East Policy* 7, no. 3 (June 2000): 52, 55, 56; Marr, *Modern History of Iraq*, 235; Jabar, "Shaykhs and Ideologues," 30–31; Hayder Al-Mohammad, "Relying on One's Tribe: A Snippet of Life in Basra since the 2003 Invasion," *Anthropology Today* 26, no. 6 (December 2010): 23–24; Tripp, *History of Iraq*, 260; Baram, *Building toward Crisis*, 25; Baram, "Neo-tribalism in Iraq," 9, 20.

18. Baram, *Building toward Crisis*, 25; Baram, "Neo-tribalism in Iraq," 3; Bashkin, "Iraqi Democracy and the Democratic Vision of 'Abd al-Fattah Ibrahim," 118; Marr, *Modern History of Iraq*, 20, 41.

19. Baram, "Neo-tribalism in Iraq," 3; Baram, *Building toward Crisis*, 30; Tripp, *History of Iraq*, 81.

20. Nakash, *Shi'is of Iraq*, 37–38; Tripp, *History of Iraq*, 12; Batatu, *Old Social Classes*, 82; Cockburn, *Muqtada*, 142.

21. Baram, "Neo-tribalism in Iraq," 9; Baram, *Building toward Crisis*, 25; Carroll, "Tribal Law and Reconciliation in the New Iraq," 18.

22. See, e.g., Marr, "One Iraq or Many," 16; Al-Mohammad, "Relying on One's Tribe," 23–24.

23. Anthony Cordesman, *Iraq's Insurgency and the Road to Civil Conflict* (Westport, CT: Praeder Security International, 2008), 1:345; Cordesman and Ramos, *Sadr and the Mahdi Army*, 14.

24. Cordesman and Ramos, *Sadr and the Mahdi Army*, 15–16; Anthony Cordesman, *Iraq's Sectarian and Ethnic Violence and the Evolving Insurgency* (Washington, DC: Center for Strategic and International Studies, 2007), 112–13; Ahmed S. Hashim, *Insurgency and Counter-insurgency in Iraq* (Ithaca, NY: Cornell University Press, 2006), 162; Cochrane, *Fragmentation of the Sadrist Movement*, 27; Farook Ahmed and Marisa Cochrane, "Recent Operations against Special Groups and JAM in Central and Southern Iraq," Institute for the Study of War Backgrounder, April 7, 2008, http://www.understandingwar.org/backgrounder/recent-operations-against -special-groups-and-jam-central-and-southern-iraq, 2; Michael Knights, "The Evolution of Iran's Special Groups in Iraq," *CTC Sentinel*, November 1, 2010, http://www.ctc.usma.edu/posts /the-evolution-of-iran%E2%80%99s-special-groups-in-iraq.

25. John Ismay, "The Most Lethal Weapon Americans Faced in Iraq," *At War* (blog), *New York Times*, October 18, 2013, https://atwar.blogs.nytimes.com/2013/10/18/the-most-lethal -weapon-americans-faced-in-iraq/; Adrian Wilkinson, James Bevan, and Ian Biddle, "Improvised Explosive Devices (IEDs): An Introduction," chap. 14 in *Conventional Ammunition in Surplus: A Reference Guide*, ed. James Bevan (Geneva: Small Arms Survey, 2008). See also Paul Gill, John Horgan, and Jeffrey Lovelace, "Improvised Explosive Device: The Problem of Definition," *Studies in Conflict and Terrorism* 34, no. 9 (2011): 732–48.

26. M. Gordon and Trainor, *Endgame*, 151–57; Noah Shachtman, "Superbombs 101" *Wired*, March 6, 2007, https://www.wired.com/2007/03/efp-101-the-sup/; "The Deadliest IEDs," *Washington Post* graphic, October 2, 2007, http://www.washingtonpost.com/wp-dyn/content /graphic/2007/10/01/GR2007100102020.html; Ismay, "Most Lethal Weapon Americans Faced in Iraq."

27. Amatzia Baram, "Sadr the Father, Sadr the Son, the "Revolution in Shi'ism," in Baram, Rohde, and Zeidel, *Iraq between the Occupations*, 154; Cochrane, *Fragmentation of the Sadrist Movement*, 18.

28. Nimrod Raphaeli, "Understanding Muqtada al-Sadr," *Middle East Quarterly* 11, no. 4 (Fall 2004): 33–42; Kimberly Kagan, *Iran's Proxy War against the United States and the Iraqi Government*, Iraq Report 6 (Washington, DC: Institute for the Study of War, 2007), http://www .understandingwar.org/report/irans-proxy-war-against-united-states-and-iraqi-government, 5.

29. International Institute for Strategic Studies, *The Military Balance* (London: Routledge, 2007), 226; International Institute for Strategic Studies, *The Military Balance* (London: Routledge, 2008), 244. See also Michael E. O'Hanlon and Jason H. Campbell, *Iraq Index: Tracking Variables of Reconstruction and Security in Post-Saddam Iraq* (Washington, DC: Brookings Institution, December 31, 2007), 25, 31. For a detailed breakdown of coalition forces in Iraq, see Stephen A. Carney, *Allied Participation in Operation Iraqi Freedom* (Washington, DC: US Army Center of Military History, 2011).

30. These totals reflect active forces only. See International Institute for Strategic Studies, *Military Balance* (2008), 29, 244. The world rankings were calculated using the "milper" variable in the Correlates of War National Military Capabilities data set (v5.0) for the year 2008, which is taken directly from *Military Balance* (2008) and reflects personnel estimates as of November 2007. The first version of this data set was published in J. Singer, Bremer, and Stuckey, "Capability Distribution."

31. For a relatively standardized comparison of equipment, see International Institute for Strategic Studies, *Military Balance* (2008), 13–24, 29–54, 157–63, 226–30, 244–46.

32. Amy Belasco, *The Cost of Iraq, Afghanistan, and Other Global War on Terror Operations since 9/11*, report RL33110 (Washington, DC: Congressional Research Service, December 8, 2014), 15, 62.

33. Pat Towell, Stephen Daggett, and Amy Belasco, *Defense: FY2008 Authorization and Appropriations*, report RL33999 (Washington, DC: Congressional Research Service, January 23, 2008), 9.

34. Headquarters, Department of the Army, *Field Manual 3-24 Counterinsurgency* (Washington, DC: Government Printing Office, 2006), para. 1–67.

35. Given an Iraqi population of 30,399,572 per Central Intelligence Agency, *The World Factbook: Iraq*, https://www.cia.gov/library/publications/the-world-factbook/geos/iz.html, accessed September 14, 2011.

36. On the Iraqi Security Forces' proficiency in mid-2007, see General James L. Jones, USMC (Ret.), Chairman, *The Report of the Independent Commission on the Security Forces of Iraq*, September 6, 2007, http://media.csis.org/isf.pdf, accessed September 14, 2011, 9, 10, which states: "The challenge for the [Iraqi] Army is its limited operational effectiveness, caused primarily by deficiencies in leadership, lack of disciplinary standards, and logistics shortfalls." The Iraqi local and national police rated even harsher assessments: "In general, the Iraqi Police

Service is incapable today of providing security at a level sufficient to protect Iraqi neighborhoods from insurgents and sectarian violence. . . . The National Police have proven operationally ineffective, and sectarianism in these units may fundamentally undermine their ability to provide security. The force is not viable in its current form." The commission saw the ISF as improving and regarded this as grounds for hope looking forward, but they saw the ISF that actually existed at the time as a far from effective partner.

37. Iraqi intelligence estimated a larger Sunni insurgency of 15,000–40,000 core fighters: Cordesman, *Iraq's Insurgency and the Road to Civil Conflict*, 1:167; Kimberly Kagan et al., *Iraq Situation Report: Backgrounder #22* (Washington, DC: Institute for the Study of War, February 2008), http://www.understandingwar.org/backgrounder/iraq-situation-report-2008.

38. Cochrane, *Fragmentation of the Sadrist Movement*, 12; Hashim, *Insurgency and Counterinsurgency in Iraq*, 251; Cordesman, *Iraq's Insurgency and the Road to Civil Conflict*, 1:58; Cockburn, *Muqtada*, 134.

39. Cochrane, *Fragmentation of the Sadrist Movement*, 22.

40. These confrontations are detailed in Cockburn, *Muqtada*, 144–52, 158–59, 161–62; M. Gordon and Trainor, *Endgame*, 67–73, 102–5; Krohley, *Death of the Mehdi Army*, 65–67; Kozlowski, *U.S. Marines in Battle*, 11–42; Sherry, "Fighting in the Valley of Peace."

41. Tripp, *History of Iraq*, 279–80; M. Gordon and Trainor, *Endgame*, 40–41; Cockburn, *Muqtada*, 134.

42. Marr, *Modern History of Iraq*, 277, 278, 285; Cockburn, *Muqtada*, 148–49, 159, 161; Baram, "Sadr the Father, Sadr the Son," 154; Cochrane, *Fragmentation of the Sadrist Movement*, 22.

43. Marr, *Modern History of Iraq*, 278, 285; Cockburn, *Muqtada*, 148–49, 159, 161; Baram, "Sadr the Father, Sadr the Son," 154.

44. Cordesman, *Iraq's Insurgency and the Road to Civil Conflict*, 1:297, 2:381; Cockburn, *Muqtada*, 136, 185; Cochrane, *Fragmentation of the Sadrist Movement*, 21, 22; Cordesman, *Iraq's Sectarian and Ethnic Violence*, 104; Kagan et al. *Iraq Situation Report*; S. Biddle, Friedman, and Shapiro, "Testing the Surge."

45. In many sectarian identity wars, a mutual fear of genocide drives mutual escalation to higher levels of violence as the weaker side mobilizes greater resources, spurring its rival to reciprocate and initiating a cyclic intensification with potentially existential consequences for both sides. Clausewitz analyzed wars of this kind, with unlimited political stakes of group survival, as approaching the theoretical limit of absolute war: Clausewitz, *On War*, e.g., 75–76, 77. In 2007, however, Iraqi Sunnis had an alternative option in the form of realignment with a nonsectarian third party, the Americans: see, e.g., S. Biddle, Friedman, and Shapiro, "Testing the Surge." Given the deep divisions among Sunni insurgent factions and the challenges this posed for cooperative escalation, realignment offered Sunnis a better chance for survival; this new Sunni-American alliance, however, posed little real threat to JAM survival given the JAM's ability to opt out of fighting by declaring a cease-fire with confidence that the Shiite political establishment would prevent the Americans from ignoring it and destroying them. The result was much lower escalatory incentives and the absence of existential threat for Sadr and the JAM.

46. Sabrina Tavernise, "A Shiite Militia in Baghdad Sees Its Power Wane," *New York Times*, July 27, 2008, https://www.nytimes.com/2008/07/27/world/middleeast/27mahdi.html; Sabrina Tavernise, "Cleric Said to Lose Reins of Parts of Iraqi Militia," *New York Times*, September 28, 2006, https://www.nytimes.com/2006/09/28/world/middleeast/28sadr.html; Lauren

Frayer, "U.S. Soldiers Find Tips Flowing from Rifts within Powerful Shiite Militia Run by Young Cleric," Associated Press, May 16, 2007; Baram, "Sadr the Father, Sadr the Son," 154; Cockburn, *Muqtada*, 196; Cochrane, *Fragmentation of the Sadrist Movement*, 21, 27.

47. International Crisis Group (ICG), *Iraq's Civil War, the Sadrists and the Surge,* ICG Middle East Report no. 72, February 7, 2008, 9; Cochrane, *Fragmentation of the Sadrist Movement*, 12.

48. International Crisis Group (ICG), *Iraq's Muqtada al-Sadr: Spoiler or Stabilizer?*, ICG Middle East Report no. 55, July 11, 2006, 8, 18–19; Cochrane, *Fragmentation of the Sadrist Movement*, 18. The OMS's inability to administer a detention system, for example, resulted in a policy whereby OMS courts could only impose fines rather than sentencing offenders to prison: ICG, *Iraq's Muqtada al-Sadr*, 20n152. As the ICG put it in 2006: "This semblance of organisation should not be exaggerated. Sadrists remain essentially undisciplined, and Muqtada's recurring reprimands or punishments do little to prevent a steady flow of dissent and disorder at all levels" (ICG, *Iraq's Muqtada al-Sadr*, 20–21).

49. ICG, *Iraq's Muqtada al-Sadr*, 19n140, 20; Andrea Plebani, "Muqtada al-Sadr and His February 2014 Declarations: Political Disengagement or Simple Repositioning?," ISPI Analysis no. 244, April 2014, 4, http://www.ispionline.it/sites/default/files/pubblicazioni/analysis_244 ___2014_0.pdf. Squadrons could be further subdivided into "companies" of 50–75 men: Lt. Col. William Zemp, Memorandum for the Record, "3–320th FAR 'Task Force Red Knight Valorous Unit Award Submission,'" Headquarters, Third Battalion, 320th Field Artillery Regiment, Third Brigade Combat Team, 101st Airborne Division (Air Assault), AFZB-KC-J-CO, September 8, 2008, 10.

50. ICG, *Iraq's Muqtada al-Sadr*, 13, 13n95; ICG, *Iraq's Civil War*, 8; Cochrane, *Fragmentation of the Sadrist Movement*, 16.

51. ICG, *Iraq's Civil War*, 9n56.

52. ICG, *Iraq's Civil War*, 8, 9n49, 16; ICG, *Iraq's Muqtada al-Sadr*, 18–21.

53. ICG, *Iraq's Muqtada al-Sadr*, 18–19; ICG, *Iraq's Civil War*, 2, 6; David E. Johnson, M. Wade Markel, and Brian Shannon, *The 2008 Battle of Sadr City: Reimagining Urban Combat*, report RR-160-A (Santa Monica, CA: RAND, 2013), 26–27; Krohley, *Death of the Medhi Army*, 99, 121, 138, 140.

54. Cochrane, *Fragmentation of the Sadrist Movement*, 15–17; Michael Harari, "Status Update: Shi'a Militias in Iraq," Institute for the Study of War Backgrounder, August 16, 2010, http://www .understandingwar.org/sites/default/files/Backgrounder_ShiaMilitias.pdf, 2; Kagan, *Iran's Proxy War against the United States and the Iraqi Government*, 10.

55. Knights, "Evolution of Iran's Special Groups in Iraq"; F. Ahmed and Cochrane, "Recent Operations," 1; Cochrane, *Fragmentation of the Sadrist Movement*, 26; Cochrane, *Fragmentation of the Sadrist Movement*, 32; Cordesman, *Iraq's Insurgency and the Road to Civil Conflict*, 2:602.

56. Nazila Fathi, "Ex-Mentor of Rebel Iraqi Cleric Breaks from His Protégé," *New York Times*, September 5, 2004, https://www.nytimes.com/2004/09/05/world/middleeast/exmentor-of -rebel-iraqi-cleric-breaks-from-his-protege.html#:~:text=QUM%2C%20Iran%20%2D%20 The%20Shiite%20cleric,encouraged%20armed%20opposition%20by%20Mr; Cochrane, *Fragmentation of the Sadrist Movement*, 11–12, 15, 21–22, 30; Joseph Felter and Brian Fishman, *Iranian Strategy in Iraq: Politics and "Other Means"* (West Point, NY: US Army Combating Terrorism Center, October 13, 2008), 29–30, 33, 39; Edward T. Pound, "Special Report: The Iran Connection," *U.S. News and World Report*, November 22, 2004, 32–48.

57. Anthony Lloyd, "Murder, Violence and Politics: How Rogue Police Can Live Outside Law," *Times* (London), September 22, 2005, 42; Cochrane, *Fragmentation of the Sadrist Movement*, 21; Toby Dodge, "If We Move In, We Have to Stay Committed," *Independent on Sunday* (UK), May 3, 2009, https://link.gale.com/apps/doc/FQ4201831249/INDA?u=nypl&sid=INDA&xid=6ff16cec.

58. Cochrane, *Fragmentation of the Sadrist Movement*, 25–27. See also Lauren Frayer, "U.S. Seeks Gains in Shiite Militia Rifts," Associated Press, May 15, 2007, https://oklahoman.com/article/3054496/us-seeks-gains-in-shiite-militia-rifts; Krohley, *Death of the Mehdi Army*, 68, 78–80, 166–67; Kagan, *Surge*, 54–59; Peter R. Mansoor, *Surge: My Journey with General David Petraeus and the Remaking of the Iraq War* (New Haven, CT: Yale University Press, 2013), 236.

59. Cordesman, *Iraq's Insurgency and the Road to Civil Conflict*, 2:602; Cochrane, *Fragmentation of the Sadrist Movement*, 25–27; Krohley, *Death of the Mehdi Army*, 68, 78–80, 166–67; Kagan, *Surge*, 54–59.

60. Amit R. Paley, "Sadr's Militia Enforces Cease-Fire with a Deadly Purge," *Washington Post*, February 21, 2008, https://www.washingtonpost.com/wp-dyn/content/article/2008/02/20/AR2008022000726.html?nav=E8; Babak Dehghanpisheh, "Iraq's New Guns for Hire," *Newsweek*, May 7, 2007, http://140.234.252.185/c/articles/24898836/iraqs-new-guns-hire; Cochrane, *Fragmentation of the Sadrist Movement*, 25–26; Kagan, *Iran's Proxy War against the United States and the Iraqi Government*, 21; Frayer, "U.S. Seeks Gains in Shiite Militia Rifts"; Kagan, *Surge*, 58.

61. Quoted in ICG, *Iraq's Civil War*, 9n55. For other examples, see D. Johnson, Markel, and Shannon, *2008 Battle of Sadr City*, 23; Krohley, *Death of the Mehdi Army*, 167.

62. US Army JAM interviews RS1, R2, R3, R4, R5; D. Johnson, Markel, and Shannon, *2008 Battle of Sadr City*, 41, 45, 102; Mansoor, *Surge*, 243–45; Captain John C. Moore, "Sadr City: The Armor Pure Assault in Urban Terrain," *Armor* 113, no. 6 (November–December 2004): 35–36; Robert Murdough, "METT-TC Dependent: Observations and Recommendations for Improving the Way We're Fighting the War in Iraq," *Infantry* (January–February 2007): 30; Peter R. Mansoor, *Baghdad at Sunrise: A Brigade Commander's War in Iraq* (New Haven, CT: Yale University Press, 2008), chap. 10; Cockburn, *Muqtada*, 148. This pattern implies a score of 0.5 on the (0, 1) scale for stealth in the coding system presented in the appendix.

63. US Army JAM interviews RS1, R2, R3, R4, R5; Moore, "Sadr City," 31–37; Murdough, "METT-TC Dependent," 30; Mansoor, *Baghdad at Sunrise*, 281–83; D. Johnson, Markel, and Shannon, *2008 Battle of Sadr City*, 45.

64. US Army JAM interviews R2, R3.

65. Overall, this pattern implies a score of 0.0 on the "duration of firefights" subscore for holding ground, contributing 0.0 points to the overall index score for the JAM in the coding system presented in the appendix.

66. US Army JAM interviews RS1, R2, R4, R5; Moore, "Sadr City," 34, 35; Mansoor, *Baghdad at Sunrise*, 281–83.

67. See, e.g., D. Johnson, Markel, and Shannon, *2008 Battle of Sadr City*, 48–60; Leigh Neville, *Modern Snipers* (New York: Osprey, 2016), chap. 4; US Marine Corps Warfighting Laboratory, *Urban Patrolling Tactics, Techniques, and Procedures* (Quantico, VA: Marine Corps Warfighting Laboratory, 1998), 11.

68. By the coding criteria in the appendix, this pattern means that the "proximity of attackers to defenders" subscore for holding ground cannot be coded for the JAM, as it did not sustain

contact long enough to meet the criterion. Instead, the weights for "duration of firefights," "incidence of counterattack," and "incidence of harassing fires and unattended minefields" are increased from 0.25 to 0.33 for the JAM when computing the overall index value.

69. US Army JAM interviews RS1, R4, R5 (for exceptions that prove the rule, see interviews R2 and R3); Moore, "Sadr City," 35; Murdough, "METT-TC Dependent," 30; D. Johnson, Markel, and Shannon, *2008 Battle of Sadr City*, 41, 45, 59, 68, 76.

70. See, e.g., D. Johnson, Markel, and Shannon, *2008 Battle of Sadr City*, xvii, 10n6, 39–64; Michael R. Gordon, "War over Wall Persists in Sadr City Despite Truce," *New York Times*, May 15, 2008, https://www.nytimes.com/2008/05/15/world/middleeast/15wall.html; M. Gordon and Trainor, *Endgame*, 494–95.

71. Overall, this pattern implies a score of 0.0 on the "incidence of counterattack" subscore for holding ground, contributing 0.0 points to the overall index score for the JAM in the coding system presented in the appendix.

72. Author's observation during service in Baghdad with the MNF-I Joint Strategic Assessment Team, March–April 2007. (A video of C-RAM engaging incoming mortar rounds in Baghdad can be found at https://www.youtube.com/watch?v=GAK22XkEa-0.) The US offensive into Sadr City in 2008 was designed in large part to end the JAM's indirect fire harassment of the Green Zone following an increase in the frequency of such fires in the aftermath of the Iraqi government's Charge of the Knights operation in March: D. Johnson, Markel, and Shannon, *2008 Battle of Sadr City*, chap. 4.

73. Author's observation during battlefield inspection, Basra Governate, Iraq, November 2007. See also Thomas Harding, "Rocket Attacks on Basra Airbase Increase," *Telegraph* (UK), August 20, 2007, http://www.telegraph.co.uk/news/1560822/Rocket-attacks-on-Basra-airbase-increase.html.

74. Anthony H. Cordesman, Charles Loi, and Vivek Kocharlakota, *IED Metrics for Iraq: June 2003–September 2010* (Washington, DC: Center for Strategic and International Studies, 2010); "Iraq Coalition Casualties Count," icasualties.org.

75. US Army JAM interviews RS1, R2, R3, R4, R5, R7. Overall, the net of an observed high frequency of harassing indirect fires but low frequency of unattended minefields implies a score of 0.5 on the "proximity of attackers to defenders" subscore for holding ground, contributing 0.165 points to the overall index score for the JAM in the coding system presented in the appendix, and yielding an overall "holding ground" score of 0.165 across its four subcomponents.

76. Cordesman, *Iraq's Insurgency and the Road to Civil Conflict*, 1:345; Cordesman and Ramos, *Sadr and the Mahdi Army*, 14.

77. D. Johnson, Markel, and Shannon, *2008 Battle of Sadr City*, fig. 4.5.

78. German defenses at Caen opposite Operation Goodwood in July 1944, for example, deployed a local troop density about 21 times greater than their theaterwide value: S. Biddle, *Military Power*, 114–20, and assuming an area of 11,500 square kilometers for Normandy. The pattern displayed by the JAM corresponds to a value of 0.004 on the (0, 1) scale for dispersion in the coding system presented in the appendix.

79. MHI/ISC: audio files 11, 18, 38, 51, 55.

80. D. Johnson, Markel, and Shannon, for example, are uncertain whether Sadr's methods constituted a coordinated "territorial defense" of Sadr City: D. Johnson, Markel, and Shannon, *2008 Battle of Sadr City*, 59.

81. This pattern implies a value of 0.0 on the (0, 1) scale for "reliance on brute force" in the coding system presented in the appendix.

82. D. Johnson, Markel, and Shannon, *2008 Battle of Sadr City*, 17.

83. This pattern implies a score of 0.0 on the "intermingling" subscore for distinguishability, contributing 0.0 points to the overall index score for the JAM in the coding system presented in the appendix.

84. US Army JAM interview R6; ICG, *Iraq's Muqtada al-Sadr*, 13n95, 20; Hoda Abdel Hamid, "Who Are the Mahdi Army?," Al Jazeera, August 30, 2007, http://www.aljazeera.com/news/middleeast/2007/01/2008525135739989284.html.

85. US Army JAM interviews RS1, R4, R5, R6, R7; ICG, *Iraq's Muqtada al-Sadr*, 19. This pattern implies a score of 0.0 on the "distinguishing markings" subscore for distinguishability, contributing 0.0 points to the overall index score for the JAM in the coding system presented in the appendix.

86. JAM militiamen sometimes fired RPGs or machine guns at US helicopters, and US aircraft carried flares and other countermeasures to defeat infrared antiaircraft missiles (the author observed flare release on multiple occasions during helicopter travel in Baghdad and central Iraq in March–April and November 2007), but there is no evidence of the JAM actually firing an infrared missile at a Coalition aircraft: US Army JAM interviews R2, R3, R4, R5, R6, R7.

87. This concealment was not always successful even so; see, e.g., D. Johnson, Markel, and Shannon, *2008 Battle of Sadr City*, fig. 4.11.

88. As the JAM lacked significant access to heavy weapons, no score can be computed for the "reliance on heavy weapons" subcomponent of distinguishability. Per the discussion in the appendix, the distinguishability score is thus computed on the basis of two, not three, subcomponents, reweighted per the discussion in the appendix.

89. MHI/ISC: audio files 10, 11, 17, 18, 23, 26, 35, 36, 38, 55, and 61.

90. MHI/ISC: audio files 11, 18, 38, and 55. Similar patterns characterized violence east of the Tigris. In Rusafa, for instance, Sunnis lived mostly in mahala-sized clusters like the roughly 3.5-square-kilometer Sheikh Omar neighborhood. This was divided from the Shia sections of Al-Fadl to the south by a market known as "Line Square." Sheikh Omar's perimeter was walled, Line Square was defended on both sides with barriers and snipers, and this is where the sectarian violence mainly occurred (audio file 14). In the Madain district south of Baghdad, the sects were also largely divided into homogeneous clusters, with Sunni living to the north and Shia to the south. Violence largely took place along this fault line, with JAM evicting Sunnis and emplacing squatters as they left (audio file 51).

91. US Army JAM interviews R6, R8; D. Johnson, Markel, and Shannon, *2008 Battle of Sadr City*, 46–47, 80; Zemp, Memorandum for the Record, 10, 11. Taken together, this pattern implies a value of 0.5 on the (0, 1) scale for "articulated theater" in the coding system presented in the appendix.

92. Mortar and rocket crews from other JAM factions, however, displayed very mixed marksmanship, as the author observed in Baghdad in March–April 2007. On JAM Special Group proficiency, see, e.g., US Army JAM interview R6; Kozlowski, *U.S. Marines in Battle*, 8, 14; Cordesman and Ramos, *Sadr and the Mahdi Army*, 17; M. Gordon and Trainor, *Endgame*, 476, 478; Mansoor, *Baghdad at Sunrise*, 319; D. Johnson, Markel, and Shannon, *2008 Battle of Sadr City*, 24, 25–26, 41.

93. See, e.g., US Army JAM interviews R6, RS1, R2, R3, R4, R5; Sherry, "Fighting in the Valley of Peace," 73; Cockburn, *Muqtada*, 135, 147; Moore, "Sadr City," 35–36; D. Johnson, Markel, and Shannon, *2008 Battle of Sadr City*, 24, 41, 68–69, 102.

94. The hybrid variant of materialist theory makes somewhat different predictions for different authors' interpretations of "hybrid." For those who interpret "hybrid" warfare as irregular tactics with precision weapons, the implied prediction would be similar—irregular—methods for both actors with respect to the tactics and operations of interest here. But those who interpret "hybrid" more broadly as an intermediate method with tactics between those of irregular nonstate actors and conventional state militaries would presumably expect less-Fabian "hybrid" behavior for Hezbollah (given its heavier equipment) but not for the JAM.

95. In principle, a materialist approach might predict different JAM behavior for Sadr's struggle with Sunni insurgents—a fellow nonstate actor with military material no better than the JAM's—than in combat with heavily armed US state soldiers. But the close proximity of presumptively hostile US forces would make materialist theories' predictions ambiguous in this scenario: even JAM fighters engaged with Sunni insurgents would have to be aware of, and prepared for, possible engagement with nearby Americans and their much heavier firepower. I thus evaluate materialist predictions for the case of JAM fighters against US forces without a separate consideration of JAM-Sunni combat.

96. Reflecting a scoring of (0.5, 0, na, 0, 0.5, 0.004, 0, 0, 0, na, 0.5) for the index measure presented in the appendix.

97. As implied by equation [A2], for values of $f = 0.07$, $i = 1$, $s = 0$, and $t = 2007$, per the discussion above.

Chapter Seven: The Somali National Alliance in Somalia, 1992–94

1. A relief column from the US 10th Mountain Division suffered an additional 29 wounded and 2 killed in fighting their way through to the Task Force Ranger position: US Army, 10th Mountain Division History, http://www.drum.army.mil/AboutFortDrum/Pages/hist_10thMountainHistory_lv3.aspx.

2. I. M. Lewis, *A Modern History of the Somali* (Athens: Ohio University Press, 2003), 252–59, 262–310; I. M. Lewis, *Understanding Somalia and Somaliland: Culture, History, Society* (New York: Columbia University Press, 2011), 9–10, 71–101; Kenneth R. Rutherford, *Humanitarianism under Fire: The US and UN Intervention in Somalia* (Sterling, VA: Kumarian, 2008), 1–8; Home Office, *Somalia: Country of Origin Information (COI) Report* (London, 2011), 23–24.

3. Rutherford, *Humanitarianism under Fire*, 7–8; Neil Henry, "Rebels, Rights Groups Attack Somalia," *Washington Post*, February 18, 1990, https://www.washingtonpost.com/archive/politics/1990/02/18/rebels-rights-groups-attack-somalia/2d7b0f91-be48-4c32-8a96-82a0e3358f08/.

4. John L. Hirsch and Robert B. Oakley, *Somalia and Operation Restore Hope: Reflections on Peacemaking and Peacekeeping* (Washington, DC: United Institute of Peace, 1995), 14; Scott Peterson, *Me against My Brother: At War in Somalia, Sudan and Rwanda* (New York: Routledge, 2000), 22; Lewis, *Modern History of the Somali*, 263; "Death of a Warlord," *Times*, August 3, 1996, http://rd8hp6du2b.search.serialssolutions.com/directLink?&atitle=SOMALIA%3A+Death+of+a+Warlord&author=&issn=0040781X&title=Time&volume=148&issue=7&date=1996-08

-12&spage=17&id=doi:&sid=ProQ_ss&genre=article; Gideon S. Hall, *Warlords of the Somali Civil War (1988–1995)* (Maxwell Air Force Base, AL: Air University Press, 2015), 8–10.

5. Glenn M. Harned, *Stability Operations in Somalia 1992–1993: A Case Study* (Carlisle, PA: US Army War College Press, 2016), 9–10.

6. Lewis, *Modern History of the Somali*, 263–64; Rutherford, *Humanitarianism under Fire*, 15.

7. Rutherford, *Humanitarianism under Fire*, 14–20; Robert F. Baumann and Lawrence A. Yates, *"My Clan against the World": US and Coalition Forces in Somalia 1992–1994* (Fort Leavenworth, Kansas: Combat Studies Institute Press, 2003), 17–18.

8. Lewis, *Modern History of the Somali*, 268–69; Hirsch and Oakley, *Somalia and Operation Restore Hope*, 21–27; Walter S. Poole, *The Effort to Save Somalia* (Washington, DC: Office of the Chairman of the Joint Chiefs of Staff, 2005), 2.

9. Lewis, *Modern History of the Somali*, 270–71; Baumann and Yates, *"My Clan against the World,"* 25–32.

10. Hirsch and Oakley, *Somalia and Operation Restore Hope*, 118–22; Baumann and Yates, *"My Clan against the World,"* 48.

11. Kenneth Allard, *Somalia Operations: Lessons Learned* (Columbus, OH: University Press of the Pacific, 2002), 17; Mark Bowden, *Blackhawk Down: A Story of Modern War* (New York: Penguin, 1999).

12. Lewis, *Modern History of the Somali*, 274–81; Rutherford, *Humanitarianism under Fire*, 185; Ron Kampeas, "From Marine to Warlord: The Strange Journey of Hussein Farrah Aidid," Associated Press, February 11, 2002; Annabel Lee Hogg, "Timeline: Somalia, 1991–2008," *Atlantic*, December 22, 2008, https://www.theatlantic.com/magazine/archive/2008/12/timeline-somalia-1991-2008/307190/.

13. Hirsch and Oakley, *Somalia and Operation Restore Hope*, 9; Ioan M. Lewis, *Blood and Bone: The Call of Kinship in Somali Society* (Lawrenceville, NJ: Red Sea, 1994), 156–57, 171, 223; Walter S. Clarke, *Somalia: Background Information for Operation Restore Hope, 1992–93* (Carlisle, PA: US Army War College Strategic Studies Institute, 1992), 9, 11–12; Rutherford, *Humanitarianism under Fire*, 5; Lewis, *Understanding Somalia and Somaliland*, 46; Mohamed Diriye Abdullahi, *Culture and Customs of Somalia* (Westport, CT: Greenwood, 2001), 31; Peterson, *Me against My Brother*, 13; Baumann and Yates, *"My Clan against the World,"* 14.

14. W. Clarke, *Somalia*, 6, 9; I. M. Lewis, "The Politics of the 1969 Somali Coup," *Journal of Modern African Studies* 10 (1972): 383–408; Paolo Contini, "The Evolution of Blood-Money for Homicide in Somalia," *Journal of African Law* 15, no. 1 (1971): 77–84.

15. David Laitin, "The Political Economy of Military Rule in Somalia," *Journal of Modern African Studies* 14, no. 3 (1976): 449–68 at 456.

16. W. Clarke, *Somalia*, 9–10; Stig J. Hansen, "Warlords and Peace Strategies: The Case of Somalia," *Journal of Conflict Studies* 23, no. 2 (2003): 68–70.

17. Rutherford, *Humanitarianism under Fire*, 5; W. Clarke, *Somalia*, 11–12; Lewis, *Understanding Somalia and Somaliland*, 46; Lewis, *Blood and Bone*, 223; Abdullahi, *Culture and Customs of Somalia*, 31; Peterson, *Me against My Brother*, 13; Baumann and Yates, *"My Clan against the World,"* 14.

18. W. Clarke, *Somalia*, 12; Rutherford, *Humanitarianism under Fire*, 7.

19. W. Clarke, *Somalia*, 13–15; Rakiya Omaar, "Somalia: At War with Itself," *Current History*, May 1992, 234; Terrence Lyons and Samatar, *Somalia: State Collapse, Multilateral Intervention,*

and Strategies for Political Reconstruction (Washington, DC: Brookings Institution, 1995), 19; Lewis, *Understanding Somalia and Somaliland*, 75; Lewis, *Modern History of the Somali*, 263; Marshall Ecklund, "Task Force Ranger vs. Urban Somali Guerillas in Mogadishu: An Analysis of Guerilla and Counterguerilla Tactics and Techniques Used during Operation Gothic Serpent," *Small Wars and Insurgencies* 15, no. 3 (2004): 55; John Drysdale, "Foreign Military Intervention in Somalia: The Root Cause of the Shift from UN Peacekeeping to Peacemaking and Its Consequences," in Walter Clarke and Jeffrey Herbst, eds., *Learning from Somalia: The Lessons of Armed Humanitarian Intervention* (Boulder, CO: Westview, 1997), 118–19.

20. Peter D. Little, "Rural Herders and Urban Merchants: The Cattle Trade in Southern Somalia," in Catherine Besteman and Lee V. Cassanelli, eds., *The Struggle for Land in Southern Somalia: The War behind the War* (Boulder, CO: Westview, 1996), 95; Lewis, *Modern History of the Somali*, 9, 14; Lewis, "Politics of the 1969 Somali Coup," 383–408; James Merryman, "The Economy of the Geedo Region and the Rise of Smallholder Irrigation," in Besteman and Cassanelli, *Struggle for Land in Southern Somalia*, 77.

21. Haji N. A. Noor Muhammad, "Civil Wrongs under Customary Law in the Northern Regions of the Somali Republic," *Journal of African Law* 11, no. 2 (Summer, 1967): 99–118; Contini, "Evolution of Blood-Money for Homicide in Somalia," 77–84; Helen Chapin Metz, *Somalia: A Country Study* (Washington, DC: Library of Congress, 1992), 145.

22. Jean Ensminger and Jack Knight, "Changing Social Norms: Common Property, Bridewealth, and Clan Exogamy," *Current Anthropology* 38, no. 1 (February 1997): 12–14; W. Clarke, *Somalia*, 13; Abdullahi, *Culture and Customs of Somalia*, 119–36; Lewis, *Understanding Somalia and Somaliland*, 9, 15, 50.

23. Lewis, *Understanding Somalia and Somaliland*, 1–3, 16–23, 85–90; Ken Menkhaus, "Political Islam in Somalia," *Middle East Policy* 9, no. 1 (March 2002): 110–18; Abdullahi, *Culture and Customs of Somalia*, 55–70; David Last and Anthony Seaboyer, *Clan and Islamic Identities in Somali Society* (Toronto: Defence R&D Canada, 2011), viii.

24. Clint Watts, Jacob Shapiro, and Vahid Brown, *Al-Qa'ida's (Mis)Adventures in the Horn of Africa* (West Point, NY: Combating Terrorism Center at West Point, 2007), 30.

25. United States Forces, Somalia, *After Action Report and Historical Overview*, 65; International Institute for Strategic Studies, *Military Balance, 1993–1994*, 128.

26. The UN estimated 950–1,000 SNA "militiamen"—probably a reasonable estimate of the number of full-time fighters—but also "thousands of Habr Gidr SNA sympathizers in southern Mogadishu who were organized by neighborhoods and city blocks to prevent any penetration of their safe haven." Lawrence E. Casper, *Falcon Brigade: Combat and Command in Somalia and Haiti* (Boulder, CO: Lynne Rienner, 2001), 45.

27. United States Forces, Somalia, *After Action Report and Historical Overview*, 10, 65, 105; Baumann and Yates, *"My Clan against the World,"* 37; Casper, *Falcon Brigade*, 18; John Allison, "Force Protection during Urban Operations Case Study: Mogadishu Urban Force Protection," in Russell W. Glenn, ed., *Capital Preservation: Preparing for Urban Operations in the Twenty-First Century* (Santa Monica, CA: RAND, 2000), 163–93 at 167; Robert Oakley, "The Urban Area during Support Missions Case Study: Mogadishu, the Strategic Level," in Glenn, *Capital Preservation*, 309–54 at 325.

28. International Institute for Strategic Studies, *The Military Balance, 1989–1990* (London: Brassey's, 1989), 113.

29. Robert M. Press, "Somali Civil War Is Fueled by Huge Stockpiles of Weapons," *Christian Science Monitor*, October 14, 1992, https://www.csmonitor.com/1992/1014/14012.html; Jane Perlez, "The World: Somalia, Abandoned to Its Own Civil War with Others' Weapons," *New York Times*, January 6, 1991, https://www.nytimes.com/1991/01/06/weekinreview/the-world-somalia-abandoned-to-its-own-civil-war-with-others-weapons.html.

30. United States Forces, Somalia, *After Action Report and Historical Overview*, 65; Martinez, "Somalia," 43.

31. International Institute for Strategic Studies, *Military Balance, 1991–1992*, 119.

32. Federation of American Scientists, "AT-7 Metis Saxhorn"; Charlie Gao, "Russia Has a Missile to Kill NATO Tanks If War Ever Comes," *National Interest*, December 23, 2017, https://nationalinterest.org/blog/russia-has-missile-kill-nato-tanks-if-war-ever-comes-23762.

33. Jeffrey A. Lefebvre, *Arms for the Horn: U.S. Security Policy in Ethiopia and Somalia 1953–1991* (Pittsburgh, PA: University of Pittsburgh Press, 1991), 202–41.

34. Lefebvre, *Arms for the Horn*, 252.

35. Lewis, *Modern History of the Somali*, 253–54; Hirsch and Oakley, *Somalia and Operation Restore Hope*, 10; Rutherford, *Humanitarianism under Fire*, 6.

36. Bowden, *Blackhawk Down*, 110.

37. *World Development Indicators and Global Development Finance* (Washington, DC: World Bank Group, 2011), http://databank.worldbank.org/ddp/home.do?Step=1&id=4.

38. United States Forces, Somalia, *After Action Report and Historical Overview*, 66; International Institute for Strategic Studies, *Military Balance, 1993–1994*, 128.

39. Lynn Thomas and Steve Spataro, "Peacekeeping and Policing in Somalia," in R. B. Oakley, M. J. Dziedzic, and E. M. Goldberg, eds., *Policing the New World Disorder: Peace Operations and Public Security* (Washington, DC: National Defense University Press, 1998), 175–214; International Institute for Strategic Studies, *Military Balance, 1993–1994*, 128; International Institute for Strategic Studies, *Military Balance, 1991–1992*, 119.

40. International Institute for Strategic Studies, *Military Balance, 1993–1994*, 128–29.

41. International Institute for Strategic Studies, *Military Balance, 1993–1994*, 19.

42. United States Forces, Somalia, *After Action Report and Historical Overview*, 10, 12, 61–62, 119, 138; Baumann and Yates, *"My Clan against the World,"* 118, 123, 146; Matt Eversmann, "Operation Gothic Serpent," in Matt Eversmann and Dan Schilling, eds., *The Battle of Mogadishu: Firsthand Accounts from the Men of Task Force Ranger* (New York: Ballantine Books), 10, 18, 20, 22; Dan Schilling, "On Friendship and Firefights," in Eversmann and Schilling, *Battle of Mogadishu*, 169; Casper, *Falcon Brigade*, 28, 40, 69; Martinez, "Somalia," 40; Bowden, *Blackhawk Down*, 95, 96; Headquarters, Department of the Army, *FM 23–65: Browning Machine Gun Caliber .50 HB, M2* (Washington, DC: Government Printing Office, 2002), table 1.5, pp. 1–19, table 1.1, pp. 1–7; Globalsecurity.org, http://www.globalsecurity.org/military/systems/aircraft/ac-47.htm; http://www.globalsecurity.org/military/systems/ground/mk19.htm; http://www.fas.org/man/dod-101/sys/land/row/btr-60.htm; all websites accessed June 30, 2012. Note that US body armor covered only the front of the torso in 1993; Rangers struck in other places could be killed or seriously wounded. Note also that body armor does not necessarily prevent *injury* regardless of the surface struck: the impact of a bullet strike that does not penetrate can still break ribs or cause other blunt force trauma that can remove soldiers from battle.

43. Andre Le Sage, *Stateless Justice in Somalia: Formal and Informal Rule of Law Initiatives* (Geneva: Centre for Humanitarian Dialogue, 2005), 1; Christian Webersik, "Mogadishu: An Economy without a State," *Third World Quarterly* 27, no. 8 (2006): 1464.

44. Ken Menkhaus, "Local Security Systems in Somali East Africa," in Louise Andersen, Bjorn Moller, and Finn Stepputat, eds., *Fragile States and Insecure People? Violence, Security, and Statehood in the Twenty-First Century* (New York: Palgrave Macmillan, 2007), 77. Also: "[Warlords] sought conflicts and conquest to provide war booty for their militiamen and provoked famine to attract relief agencies and food aid that had become a major source of revenue. Militiamen fed their families by pillaging occupied villages and government buildings." Ken Menkhaus, "State Collapse in Somalia: Second Thoughts," *Review of African Political Economy* 30, no. 97 (September 2003): 416.

45. Interview, Ambassador Robert B. Oakley, February 22, 2012.

46. See, e.g., "Somalia: Beyond the Warlords; The Need for a Verdict on Human Rights Abuses," *News from Africa Watch* 5, no. 2 (March 1993): 2, 5.

47. See Mohammed Farah Aidid, "Democracy in Somalia—Its Root and Its Future Scenario," in Mohammed Farah Aidid and Satya Pal Ruhela, eds., *The Preferred Future Development in Somalia* (New Delhi, India: Vikas, 1993); Mohammed Farah Aidid and S. P. Ruhela, "Opening a New Chapter in the Lives of the Somali Nomads and Minorities," in Aidid and Ruhela, *Preferred Future Development in Somalia*; and Mohammed Farah Aidid, "Foreign Aid for Somali Nation's Development: A Challenge to Our Integrity and Future," in Aidid and Ruhela, *Preferred Future Development in Somalia*.

48. The SNA did mount a propaganda campaign against the UN presence after June 17 (when UNSCR 837 committed the UN to removing Aideed) and held regular rallies to this effect, but these were aimed at removing a UN threat, not establishing domestic support for a governing agenda: see, e.g., Casper, *Falcon Brigade*, 133; Jeffrey Gettleman, "In Somalia, Those Who Feed Off Anarchy Fuel It," *New York Times*, April 25, 2007, https://www.nytimes.com/2007/04/25/world/africa/25somalia.html.

49. United States Forces, Somalia, *After Action Report and Historical Overview*, 132; Hirsch and Oakley, *Somalia and Operation Restore Hope*, 121; Peterson, *Me against My Brother*, 118.

50. Ken Menkhaus and Louis Ortmayer, *Key Decision in the Somalia Intervention* (Washington, DC: Institute for the Study of Diplomacy, 1995), 17; John Evans, "Task Force 1–22 Infantry from Homestead to Port-au-Prince" (MA thesis, US Army Command and General Staff College, Fort Leavenworth Kansas, 2000), 45–46; William Finnegan, "A Million Enemies," *New York Times*, March 14, 1999, https://www.nytimes.com/1999/03/14/books/a-million-enemies.html; Hirsch and Oakley, *Somalia and Operation Restore Hope*, 121–23. Cf. United States Forces, Somalia, *After Action Report and Historical Overview*, 132, which sees the Abdi House attack as creating opportunities for Aideed's rivals, though it is unclear whether these "opportunities" were ever acted on.

51. See, e.g., Bowden, *Blackhawk Down*, 74. This evolution may be inevitable when foreign powers intervene in civil wars: see, e.g., Richard Betts, "The Delusion of Impartial Intervention," *Foreign Affairs*, November/December 1994, https://www.foreignaffairs.com/articles/1994-11-01/delusion-impartial-intervention. Inevitable or not, however, it clearly contributed to a shift in the war's casus belli by mid-1993.

52. Alex de Waal, *The Prairie Fire That Burned Mogadishu: The Logic of Clan Formation in Somalia* (Somerville, MA: World Peace Foundation, 2018), 28–31. Note that Aideed himself was killed in battle in 1996; no war is ever completely without risk for its combatants, and Aideed accepted more such risk than most in his willingness to lead from the front after TF Ranger's departure. In a war of economic profit, however, Aideed's death posed no existential peril to the Habr Gidr clan and its SNA embodiment, and both carried on in his absence after his death.

53. Interview, Ambassador Robert B. Oakley, February 22, 2012.

54. Interview, Ambassador Robert B. Oakley, February 22, 2012; Jutta Bakonyi and Kirsti Stuvoy, "Violence and Social Order beyond the State: Somalia and Angola," *Review of African Political Economy* 32, nos. 1045 (June–September 2005): 366–68; Lyons and Samatar, *Somalia*, e.g., 46.

55. Peterson, *Me against My Brother*, 23, 102, 103, 147; Webersik, "Mogadishu," 1470; Ken Menkhaus, "Somalia: Political Order in a Stateless Society," *Current History* 97, no. 619 (May 1998): 222.

56. Lewis, *Modern History of the Somali*, 281.

57. Le Sage, *Stateless Justice in Somalia*, 23–24; Webersik, "Mogadishu," 1470–71; Menkhaus, "Somalia," 222–23; Menkhaus, "State Collapse in Somalia," 410–11.

58. See, e.g., Eversmann, "Operation Gothic Serpent," 18, 19, 28; Mike Kurth, "Through My Eyes," in Eversmann and Schilling, *Battle of Mogadishu*, 71; Bowden, *Blackhawk Down*, 31, 110.

59. Ecklund, "Task Force Ranger vs. Urban Somali Guerillas in Mogadishu," 55; Bowden, *Blackhawk Down*, 103, 110–11.

60. As quoted in Bowden, *Blackhawk Down*, 234.

61. Kent DeLong and Steven Tuckey, *Mogadishu! Heroism and Tragedy* (Westport, CT: Praeger, 1994), 5; Eversmann, "Operation Gothic Serpent," 25; Raleigh Cash, "Sua Sponte: Of Their Own Accord," in Eversmann and Schilling, *Battle of Mogadishu*, 43, 46.

62. See, e.g., Bowden, *Blackhawk Down*, 168.

63. For the pre-Howe period where SNA combatants were chiefly full-time militiamen, this pattern implies a score of 0.5 on the (0, 1) scale for stealth in the coding system presented in the appendix. For the October Battle of Mogadishu wherein perhaps half the fighters engaged were armed but untrained civilians who were fully exposed, this implies a score of 0.75 per the weighting system described in the appendix.

64. United States Forces, Somalia, *After Action Report and Historical Overview*, 98.

65. J. Evans, "Task Force 1–22 Infantry," 40.

66. United States Forces, Somalia, *After Action Report and Historical Overview*, 97; Casper, *Falcon Brigade*, 96; Martin Stanton, *Somalia on $5.00 a Day: A Soldier's Story* (Novato, CA: Presidio, 2001), 252.

67. Bowden, *Blackhawk Down*, 6, 286.

68. United States Forces, Somalia, *After Action Report and Historical Overview*, 94, 103, 104, 105, 132, and 127–28, respectively; Sebastian Kaempf, "US Warfare in Somalia and the Trade-Off between Casualty-Aversion and Civilian Protection," *Small Wars and Insurgencies* 23, no. 3 (2012): 388–413 at 394.

69. Overall, this pattern implies a score of 0.0 on the "duration of firefights" subscore for holding ground prior to June, contributing 0.0 points to the overall index score for the SNA in

the coding system presented in the appendix, but a score of 1.0 afterward (and especially for the critical October 3 Battle of Mogadishu), contributing 0.25 points to the SNA's overall index score after June.

70. See, e.g., Bowden, *Blackhawk Down*, 94; United States Forces, Somalia, *After Action Report and Historical Overview*, 95, 97, 102; Baumann and Yates, "My Clan against the World," 66; J. Evans, "Task Force 1–22 Infantry," 43.

71. See, e.g., Bowden, *Blackhawk Down*, 122, 162, 167, 170, 184, 231, 257.

72. Bowden, *Blackhawk Down*, 170.

73. Casper, *Falcon Brigade*, 68.

74. United States Forces, Somalia, *After Action Report and Historical Overview*, 94, 130–31; Baumann and Yates, "My Clan against the World," 128.

75. M. Stanton, *Somalia on $5.00 a Day*, 235.

76. By the coding criteria in the appendix, this pattern means that the "proximity of attackers to defenders" subscore for holding ground cannot be coded for the SNA prior to June, as it did not sustain contact long enough to meet the criterion. Instead, the weights for "duration of firefights," "incidence of counterattack," and "incidence of harassing fires and unattended mine-fields" are increased from 0.25 to 0.33 for the SNA when computing the overall index value for the pre-June period. For the period of June and afterward, the observed pattern implies a score of 1.0 on the "proximity of attackers to defenders" subscore for holding ground, contributing 0.25 points to the overall index score for the SNA in the coding system presented in the appendix.

77. See, e.g., Peterson, *Me against My Brother*, 23; Rutherford, *Humanitarianism under Fire*, 24.

78. Menkhaus, "State Collapse in Somalia," 410.

79. Baumann and Yates, "My Clan against the World," 107; United States Forces, Somalia, *After Action Report and Historical Overview*, 66; Rutherford, *Humanitarianism under Fire*, 133; Drysdale, "Foreign Military Intervention in Somalia," in W. Clarke and Herbst, *Learning from Somalia*, 130; Rick Lyman, "Torn between Clans, Somali Port Fears a Wave of Violence," *Philadelphia Inquirer*, April 11, 1994.

80. Lyons and Samatar, *Somalia*, 22.

81. See, e.g., Staniland, "States, Insurgents, and Wartime Political Orders"; Paul Staniland, "The Future of Violence in Afghanistan," *National Interest*, July 18, 2012, https://nationalinterest.org/commentary/the-future-violence-afghanistan-7207; Max G. Manwaring, *Insurgency, Terrorism and Crime* (Norman: University of Oklahoma Press, 2008).

82. Paul Watson, *Where War Lives* (Toronto: Rodale Books, 2008), 11–12, 25–26; Casper, *Falcon Brigade*, 28, 44; Bowden, *Blackhawk Down*, 271.

83. See, e.g., Eversmann, "Operation Gothic Serpent," 30; Daniel P. Bolger, *Death Ground: Today's American Infantry in Battle* (New York: Random House, 2007), 203–43.

84. DeLong and Tuckey, *Mogadishu!*, 68; Casper, *Falcon Brigade*, 54, 85–86. Note that critical terrain in Mogadishu had been spatially delimited both before and after the UN intervention: the "Green Line" long divided city districts controlled by the SNA from those held by Mahdi's forces: see, e.g., Susan Rosegrant, "A 'Seamless' Transition: United States and United Nations Operations in Somalia—1992–1993 (A)," Kennedy School of Government Case Program C09-96-1324.0 (1996), 20; John F. Antal and Robert L. Dunaway, *Peace-Making in Somalia: A*

Background Study for "Operation Restore Hope" (Carlisle, PA: US Army Military History Institute), 7; Ecklund, "Task Force Ranger vs. Urban Somali Guerillas in Mogadishu," 55; Hussein M. Adam, "Somalia: Militarism, Warlordism or Democracy?," *Review of African Political Economy* 19, no. 54 (July 1992): 21; Peterson, *Me against My Brother*, 20; United States Forces, Somalia, *After Action Report and Historical Overview*, 65; Casper, *Falcon Brigade*, 109; P. Watson, *Where War Lives*, 21. Kismaayo, too, had seen clearly demarked battle lines separating zones of rival militia control: Lyman, "Torn between Clans."

85. Casper, *Falcon Brigade*, 86; Eversmann, "Operation Gothic Serpent," 30.

86. Bowden, *Blackhawk Down*, 50–54.

87. Bowden, *Blackhawk Down*, 206.

88. Baumann and Yates, *"My Clan against the World,"* 126; Bowden, *Blackhawk Down*, 11, 18, 84.

89. Wynne, *If Germany Attacks*, 149.

90. Note the contrast with the JAM's response to US incursions into Sadr City in 2008: whereas the SNA sought to close with and overrun TF Ranger via decisive engagement in a single sustained battle after the Americans penetrated the Bakara Market in 1993, the JAM systematically avoided decisive engagement with American forces in 2008 and sought instead only to inflict gradual attrition over days and weeks via hit-and-run raids to persuade the Americans to withdraw of their own volition without any attempt to overrun US positions if the Americans declined to withdraw. The former is much more clearly characteristic of Napoleonic counterattack to regain lost ground than is the latter. Overall, this pattern of SNA behavior implies a score of 0.5 on the "incidence of counterattack" subscore for holding ground prior to June 1993, contributing 0.165 points to the weighted overall index score for the SNA in the coding system presented in the appendix, but a score of 1.0 afterward (and especially for the critical October 3 Battle of Mogadishu), contributing 0.25 points to the SNA's overall index score after June 1993.

91. See, e.g., Drysdale, "Foreign Military Intervention in Somalia," 118, 120, 130.

92. "Somalia: Beyond the Warlords," 5. See also Douglas C. Peifer, *Stopping Mass Killings in Africa: Genocide, Airpower, and Intervention* (Collingdale, PA: Diane, 2009), 23.

93. Assuming 50 tubes at a sustained firing rate of 18 rounds per minute, 12 hours of firing a day, ample ammunition, a lethal area per round of 700 square meters, and a land area of 1,660 square kilometers for the city of Mogadishu; on 81-millimeter mortar performance, see Headquarters, Department of the Army, *FM 7–90, Tactical Employment of Mortars*, esp. table B-1.

94. Bowden, *Blackhawk Down*, 154.

95. J. Evans, "Task Force 1–22 Infantry," 43.

96. United States Forces, Somalia, *After Action Report and Historical Overview*, 95.

97. Casper, *Falcon Brigade*, 17, 22, 96; J. Evans, "Task Force 1–22 Infantry," 43; United States Forces, Somalia, *After Action Report and Historical Overview*, 95, 97, 102; Martinez, "Somalia," 42; Peterson, *Me against My Brother*, 98; Baumann and Yates, *"My Clan against the World,"* 115.

98. United States Forces, Somalia, *After Action Report and Historical Overview*, 97, 98, 102, 104, 134; Baumann and Yates, *"My Clan against the World,"* 115; Casper, *Falcon Brigade*, 17, 45, 66; Bowden, *Blackhawk Down*, 18, 54, 84, 271, 281.

99. Overall, this pattern implies a score of 0.0 on the "incidence of harassing fires and unattended minefields" subscore for holding ground, contributing 0.0 points to the overall index score for the SNA in the coding system presented in the appendix, and yielding an overall

"holding ground" score of 0.165 across its four subcomponents for the SNA prior to June 1993, and 0.75 thereafter.

100. Assuming an area of 90 square kilometers for the city of Mogadishu, per Perry-Casteñeda Library map collection, https://legacy.lib.utexas.edu/maps/somalia.html; https://legacy.lib.utexas.edu/maps/africa/txu-pclmaps-oclc-795784383-somalia_2012_neighborhoods_of_mogadishu.jpg; and SNA control of 70 percent of the city, per United States Forces, Somalia, *After Action Report and Historical Overview*, 65.

101. Bowden, *Blackhawk Down*, e.g., 42, 106, 130, 141, 217, 364.

102. Some estimates of total Somali combatants opposing TF Ranger in Mogadishu on October 3–4 range as high as 8,000: Matthew Eversmann, "The Urban Area during Support Missions Case Study: Mogadishu, the Tactical Level I," in Glenn, *Capital Preservation*, 413–27 at 424. On the ubiquity of small arms in Mogadishu in 1993, see Allison, "Force Protection during Urban Operations," at 166; Oakley, "Urban Area during Support Missions," 311.

103. See the discussion in chaps. 2 and 5 above.

104. Taking the area between the K-4 traffic circle, Via Jen Daaud and the 21 October Road as the area of active combat (see map 7.2), and assuming that the SNA succeeded in concentrating a majority of its combatants in Mogadishu into this area. This pattern corresponds to a value of 0.015 on the (0, 1) scale for dispersion in the coding system presented in the appendix.

105. See, e.g., the accounts of intermilitia warfare in Mogadishu in Drysdale, "Foreign Military Intervention in Somalia," 118, 120, 130.

106. For Somali casualty estimates, see Rick Atkinson, "Firefight in Mogadishu: The Last Mission of Task Force Ranger 2/2," *Washington Post*, January 31, 1994, A1+; US ambassador Robert Oakley, as quoted on *Frontline*, WGBH, http://www.pbs.org/wgbh/pages/frontline/shows/ambush/interviews/oakley.html.

107. This pattern implies a value of 0.0 on the (0, 1) scale for "reliance on brute force" in the coding system presented in the appendix for the period before June 1993, and 0.5 thereafter.

108. Bowden, *Blackhawk Down*, 31; Casper, *Falcon Brigade*, 78.

109. Bowden, *Blackhawk Down*, 18, 38, 42, 43, 46, 49, 62, 63, 106, 111, 130, 141, 179, 364; Casper, *Falcon Brigade*, 78; DeLong and Tuckey, *Mogadishu!*, 11–12, 15; Ecklund, "Task Force Ranger vs. Urban Somali Guerillas in Mogadishu," 54, 56; Bradley T. Gericke, "Somalia 1993," in John Antal and Bradley T. Gericke, eds., *Forests of Steel: Modern City Combat from the War in Vietnam to the Battle for Iraq* (Fort Worth, TX: Historical Explorations, 2007), 132.

110. Bowden, *Blackhawk Down*, 42, 106, 130, 141, 217, 364; Casper, *Falcon Brigade*, 78; DeLong and Tuckey, *Mogadishu!*, 11–12. This pattern implies a score of 0.0 on the "intermingling" subscore for distinguishability, contributing 0.0 points to the overall index score for the SNA in the coding system presented in the appendix.

111. Bowden, *Blackhawk Down*, 103.

112. Bowden, *Blackhawk Down*, 103, 109, 145, 167, 215; Daniel Byman and Matthew Waxman, *The Dynamics of Coercion: American Foreign Policy and the Limits of Military Might* (Cambridge: Cambridge University Press, 2002), 196.

113. See, e.g., United States Forces, Somalia, *After Action Report and Historical Overview*, 94, 131; Baumann and Yates, "My Clan against the World," 123; Rutherford, *Humanitarianism under Fire*, 155; Jane Boulden, *Peace Enforcement: The United Nations Experience in Congo, Somalia, and Bosnia* (Westport, CT: Praeger, 2001), 68; M. Stanton, *Somalia on $5.00 a Day*, vii, 164, 222. This

pattern implies a score of 0.0 on the "distinguishing markings" subscore for distinguishability, contributing 0.0 points to the overall index score for the SNA in the coding system presented in the appendix.

114. United States Forces, Somalia, *After Action Report and Historical Overview*, 65; Martinez, "Somalia," 43.

115. This pattern implies a score of 0.0 on the "reliance on heavy weapons" subscore for distinguishability, contributing 0.0 points to the overall index score for the SNA in the coding system presented in the appendix, and yielding an overall "distinguishability" score of 0.0 across its three subcomponents.

116. See, e.g., Bowden, *Blackhawk Down*, 206.

117. See, e.g., Atkinson, "Firefight in Mogadishu"; Bowden, *Blackhawk Down*, 18; Casper, *Falcon Brigade*, 45.

118. Bowden, *Blackhawk Down*, 309, 312; Atkinson, "Firefight in Mogadishu."

119. Taken together, this pattern implies a value of 0.5 on the (0, 1) scale for "articulated theater" in the coding system presented in the appendix.

120. United States Forces, Somalia, *After Action Report and Historical Overview*, 90.

121. Bowden, *Blackhawk Down*, 110–11.

122. Bowden, *Blackhawk Down*, 163, 230, 234, 256.

123. Bowden, *Blackhawk Down*, 234.

124. Bowden, *Blackhawk Down*, 163; Donatella Lorch, "U.N. Says It Will Press Effort to Disarm Somalis," *New York Times*, July 14, 1993, https://www.nytimes.com/1993/07/14/world/un-says-it-will-press-effort-to-disarm-somalis.html.

125. Bowden, *Blackhawk Down*, 16, 31, 47, 49, 62, 103, 167, 216, 203, 262.

126. Bowden, *Blackhawk Down*, 110, 168.

127. Corresponding to codings of (0.5, 0, na, 0.5, 0, 0.015, 0, 0, 0, 0, 0.5) and (0.75, 1, 1, 1, 0, 0.015, 0.5, 0, 0, 0, 0.5), respectively.

128. United States Forces, Somalia, *After Action Report and Historical Overview*, 90; Martinez, "Somalia," 43.

129. The most important differences between the TOW in 1993 and the Kornet in 2006 involved weapon guidance and warhead design. Both the baseline BGM-71A version of the TOW that the SNA probably owned and the 9M133 Kornet are SACLOS (Semi-active Command to Line of Sight) missiles, but the TOW uses wire to communicate guidance commands from the launcher to the missile, whereas the Kornet is a beam rider with no wire; the warhead on the BGM-71A is a unitary shaped charge, whereas the Kornet mounts a two-stage shaped charge. Neither difference would have been consequential in Somalia. Beam riders are more effective in wooded areas and are not range restricted to the length of the guidance wire, but in urban Mogadishu neither advantage would be decisive. Two-stage shaped charges are designed to overcome explosive reactive armor (ERA), but none of UNOSOM's armored vehicles were so equipped, hence none required two-stage warheads to defeat. On TOW capabilities, see, e.g., John R. Angolia, "TOW Engagement in the Active Defense" (MA thesis, US Army Command and General Staff College, Fort Leavenworth KS, 1978), esp. 19, 22; on the Kornet, see, e.g., Gao, "Russia Has a Missile to Kill NATO Tanks If War Ever Comes"; Miguel Miranda, "Kornet: Anti-tank Guided Missiles," *Military Today*, http://www.military-today.com/missiles/kornet.htm.

130. United States Forces, Somalia, *After Action Report and Historical Overview*, 90. Nor was inheritance from Barre the only means by which Aideed could, in principle, have availed himself of this technology. While TOW missiles are more expensive than AK-47s (which could be purchased in Mogadishu for around $200 each in 1993), they are comparatively cheap all the same: in 1978, Hughes aircraft sold TOWs to the US government for around $3,000 per missile and $27,000 per launcher; even with a substantial black-market premium, ATGW are thus not prohibitively expensive for nonstate actors. On costs, see Bowden, *Blackhawk Down*, 109; and Angolia, "TOW Engagement," 25.

131. As implied by equation [A2], for early-case values of $f = 0.15$, $i = 0$, $s = 0$, and $t = 1993$; and late-case values of $f = 0.15$, $i = 0$, $s = 1$, and $t = 1993$, per the discussion above.

132. On SNA casualties, see Atkinson, "Firefight in Mogadishu"; US ambassador Robert Oakley, as quoted on *Frontline*, WGBH, http://www.pbs.org/wgbh/pages/frontline/shows/ambush/interviews/oakley.html. On TF Ranger's diminished restrictions on engaging intermingled targets, see Bowden, *Blackhawk Down*, 30, 127, 164, 225, 273, 288.

Chapter Eight: The ZNG, HV, and SVK in the Croatian Wars of Independence, 1991–95

1. Marcus Tanner, *Croatia: A Nation Forged in War* (New Haven, CT: Yale University Press, 2010), 305; Klejda Mulaj, "International Actions and the Making and Unmaking of Unrecognized States," in Nina Casperson and Gareth Stansfield, eds., *Unrecognized States in the International System* (New York: Routledge, 2011), 41–57 at 49; Chuck Sudetic, "Life Turns Bleak and Perilous in Serb-Held Area in Croatia," *New York Times*, October 14, 1992, https://www.nytimes.com/1992/10/14/world/life-turns-bleak-and-perilous-in-serb-held-area-in-croatia.html.

2. Unless otherwise noted, the discussion below is drawn from: Laura Silber and Allan Little, *Yugoslavia: Death of a Nation* (New York: Penguin, 1997), 82–204; R. Craig Nation, *War in the Balkans, 1991–2002* (Carlisle, PA: US Army War College Strategic Studies Institute, 2003), 91–148; Tanner, *Croatia*, 184–339.

3. Stephen Kinzer, "Slovenia and Croatia Get Berlin's Nod," *New York Times*, December 24, 1991; David Binder, "U.S. Recognizes Three Yugoslav Republics as Independent," *New York Times*, April 8, 1992, https://www.nytimes.com/1992/04/08/world/us-recognizes-3-yugoslav-republics-as-independent.html; "Three Ex-Yugoslav Republics Are Accepted into UN," *New York Times*, May 23, 1992, https://www.nytimes.com/1992/05/23/world/3-ex-yugoslav-republics-are-accepted-into-un.html; David Raic, *Statehood and the Law of Self-Determination* (The Hague: Kluwer Law International, 2002), 389.

4. See, e.g., Stuart J. Kaufman, *Modern Hatreds: The Symbolic Politics of Ethnic War* (Ithaca, NY: Cornell University Press, 2001); Donald Horowitz, *Ethnic Groups in Conflict* (Berkeley: University of California Press, 2000); V.P. Gagnon, *The Myth of Ethnic War: Serbia and Croatia in the 1990s* (Ithaca, NY: Cornell University Press, 2004); cf. Robert Kaplan, *Balkan Ghosts: A Journey through History* (New York: St. Martin's, 1993).

5. "Ethnic" and "tribal" are sometimes used interchangeably in accounts of the Balkan Wars. And the terms share an emphasis on perception of common descent and exclusion of outgroups as a motivator for behavior. Ethnicity, however, normally involves much larger population aggregates than tribe—in fact, the ethnic warfare literature emphasizes the commonplace

aspirations of warring ethnic groups for state status, an ambition rarely shared by tribes. Tribal elders often wish to *control* a state that includes many tribes, but rarely do tribal groups seek statehood with borders collinear to their unique tribal homeland in the way that many ethnic groups have. On the distinctions between tribe, ethnicity, and nation, see, e.g., Jack David Eller, *From Culture to Ethnicity to Conflict: An Anthropological Perspective on International Ethnic Conflict* (Ann Arbor: University of Michigan Press, 1999), chap. 1; Walker Connor, *Ethnonationalism* (Princeton, NJ: Princeton University Press, 1993), 44.

6. See, e.g., Lorraine Baric, "Levels of Change in Yugoslav Kinship," in Maurice Freedman, ed., *Social Organization: Essays Presented to Raymond Firth* (Chicago: Aldine, 1967), 4–5, 8, 23; Joel M. Halpern, "Peasant Culture and Urbanization in Yugoslavia," in J.-G. Peristiany, ed., *Contributions to Mediterranean Sociology: Mediterranean Rural Communities and Social Change* (Paris, France: Mouton, 1968), 295; Philip E. Mosely, "The Peasant Family: The Zadruga, or Communal Joint-Family in the Balkans, and Its Recent Evolution," in Robert F. Byrnes, ed., *Communal Families in the Balkans: The Zadruga* (Notre Dame, IN: University of Notre Dame Press, 1976), 19–30 at 19, 28.

7. George W. Hoffman, "Yugoslavia: Changing Character of Rural Life and Rural Economy," *American Slavic and East European Review* 18, no. 4 (December 1959): 568, 571; Olivera Buric, "The Zadruga and the Contemporary Family in Yugoslavia," in Byrnes, *Communal Families in the Balkans*, 117–38 at 125–26; Jozo Tomasevich, *Peasants, Politics, and Economic Change in Yugoslavia* (Stanford, CA: Stanford University Press, 1955), 184–89; Baric, "Levels of Change in Yugoslav Kinship," 5–6, 8–9; Halpern, "Peasant Culture and Urbanization in Yugoslavia," 295, 307–8, 310.

8. Baric, "Levels of Change in Yugoslav Kinship," 10–17.

9. Buric, "Zadruga and the Contemporary Family in Yugoslavia," 120–32.

10. Central Intelligence Agency, *CIA World Factbook, 1990* (Washington, DC: Government Printing Office, 1990).

11. *Balkan Battlegrounds*, 2:45–46, 178; Laura Silber, "Presidency Acts over Yugoslav Ethnic Clashes; Croatian Commandos Ordered to Withdraw from Serbian-Dominated Town," *Financial Times*, March 4, 1991.

12. *Balkan Battlegrounds*, 2:45–46, 178; International Institute for Strategic Studies, *Military Balance, 1991–1992*, 96.

13. *Balkan Battlegrounds*, 2:108, 178.

14. Silber and Little, *Yugoslavia*, 187; Biljana Vankovska and Haken Wiberg, *Between Past and Future: Civil-Military Relations in the Post-Communist Balkans* (New York: I. B. Tauris, 2003), 207.

15. Private VP int. Also BG Petar Bajan int.; BJ int.; CPT Tihomir Tolić int.; COL J. M. int.; LTC Alojzije Hren int.; Private Tomislav Galović int.; MAJ (retd) Krunoslav Samošćanec int.; Private TL int. Note, however, that some nationalist units had more extensive training and prior experience: see, e.g., LTC Valentino Rajkovic int.; DT, AV int. The ZNG in late 1991 was thus a heterogeneous force of mostly green and some better-trained troops.

16. *Balkan Battlegrounds*, 2:135, 141; International Institute for Strategic Studies, *Military Balance, 1991–1992*, 96.

17. *Balkan Battlegrounds*, 1:274, 276.

18. Zunec, "Democracy and the 'Fog of War,'" 220.

19. *Balkan Battlegrounds*, 1:270.

20. Lenard J. Cohen, *Broken Bonds: The Disintegration of Yugoslavia* (Boulder, CO: Westview, 1993), 133.

21. Tim Judah, *The Serbs: History, Myth, and the Destruction of Yugoslavia* (New Haven, CT: Yale University Press, 2010), 175–76.

22. Mile Bjelajac and Ozren Zunec, "The War in Croatia, 1991–1995," in Charles Ingrao and Thomas A. Emmert, eds., *Confronting the Yugoslav Controversies: A Scholars' Initiative* (West Lafayette, IN: Purdue University Press, 2009), 242.

23. Branka Magas and Ivo Zanic, *The War in Croatia and Bosnia-Herzegovina 1991–1995* (New York: Routledge, 2013), 28–36.

24. Silber and Little, *Yugoslavia*, 103, 347; Judah, *Serbs*, 170–71; L. Cohen, *Broken Bonds*, 225; *Balkan Battlegrounds*, 1:269–71, 361–62, 376; Roger Cohen, "Despite Vow, Serbia Is Said to Supply Serbs Fighting in Bosnia," *New York Times*, December 12, 1994, 11.

25. Jonathan S. Landay, "Serb-Croat Pact Puts Pressure on Bosnian Muslims," *Christian Science Monitor*, January 24, 1994, 1; Silber and Little, *Yugoslavia*, 202–4.

26. David Rohde, "Brotherhood of Serbs Falters for Croatia's Rebels," *Christian Science Monitor*, May 15, 1995, 6.

27. Croatian Serb leadership also had a reasonable expectation of comfortable exile across the border in Serbia proper if the worst did happen and Belgrade reneged on its pledge; in fact there is evidence that a number of SAOK civil and military elites owned property in Serbia and expected to be able to seek refuge there if necessary: Judah, *Serbs*, 255; Bjelajac and Zunec, "War in Croatia, 1991–1995," 254; Tanner, *Croatia*, 297.

28. Ivo Goldstein, *Croatia: A History* (Montreal: McGill-Queen's University Press, 1999), 215; *Balkan Battlegrounds*, 1:91, 94; Bjelajac and Zunec, "War in Croatia, 1991–1995," 243.

29. Marko Milivojevic, "The Armed Forces of Yugoslavia: Sliding into War," in Sabrina Petra Ramet and Ljubisa S. Adamovich, eds., *Beyond Yugoslavia: Politics, Economics, and Culture in a Shattered Community* (Boulder, CO: Westview, 1995), 67.

30. Silber and Little, *Yugoslavia*, 114–15.

31. L. Cohen, *Broken Bonds*, 227.

32. Silber and Little, *Yugoslavia*, 114–15.

33. M. Cherif Bassiouni, *Final Report of the United Nations Commission of Experts Established Pursuant to Security Council Resolution 780 (1992), Annex III: The Military Structure, Strategy, and Tactics of the Warring Factions* (UNSC S/1994/674/Annex III, 1994), 15. On Croatian federal institutions more broadly, see also Jovan Djordjevic, "Remarks on the Yugoslav Model of Federalism," *Publius* 5, no. 2 (Spring, 1975): 77–88 at 86, 87; Ivo Lapenna, "Main Features of the Yugoslav Constitution 1946–1971," *International and Comparative Law Quarterly* 21, no. 2 (April 1972): 209–29 at 221–22; Igor Štiks, *A Laboratory of Citizenship: Shifting Conceptions of Citizenship in Yugoslavia and Its Successor States* (Edinburgh: University of Edinburgh, School of Law, 2010), CITSEE Working Paper 2010/02, esp. 8; Gene S. Leonardson and Dimitar Mircev, "A Structure for Participatory Democracy in the Local Community: The Yugoslav Constitution of 1974," *Comparative Politics* 11, no. 2 (January 1979): 189–203.

34. That is, Croatia rated 74th out of 99 surveyed countries in order of increasing corruption: see Transparency International, 1999, http://archive.transparency.org/policy_research/surveys_indices/cpi/previous_cpi/1999. It subsequently, in 2011, improved to 66th of 182, http://www.transparency.org/cpi2011/results.

35. AMB Jackovich int.; Radovan Vukadinovich and Lidija Cehulik, "Development of Civil-Military Relations in Croatia," in Plamen Plantev, ed., *Civil-Military Relations in South Eastern Europe* (Vienna: National Defense Academy, 2000), 63–88 at 83; Dijana Plestina, "Democracy and Nationalism in Croatia: The First Three Years," in Ramet and Adamovich, *Beyond Yugoslavia*, 123–54 at 146–47; Lenard J. Cohen, "Embattled Democracy: Post-Communist Croatia in Transition," in Karen Dawisha and Bruce Parrott, *Politics, Power, and the Struggle for Democracy in South-East Europe* (New York: Cambridge University Press, 1997), 69–121.

36. LTC (retd) Rajkovic int.; COL J.M. int.; COL (retd) Benić int.; also Robert Hislope, "Intra-ethnic Conflict in Croatia and Serbia: Flanking and the Consequences for Democracy," *East European Quarterly* 30, no. 4 (January 1997): 471–94 at 478, 487.

37. See, e.g., John Gledhill, "Competing for Change: Regime Transition, Intrastate Competition, and Violence," *Security Studies* 21, no. 2 (2011): 43–82.

38. L. Cohen, "Embattled Democracy," 86–87; Stephen Engelberg, "Croatia Ousts Defense Chief as Serbs Outgun Its Forces," *New York Times*, August 2, 1991, A2; Charles T. Powers, "Croatia Agrees to Cease-Fire, Juggles Cabinet," *Los Angeles Times*, August 4, 1991, A1; Tanner, *Croatia*, 222, 253; *Balkan Battlegrounds*, 1:91, 267; Blaine Harden, "Another Croatian Cease-Fire Falters in Widespread Fighting," *Washington Post*, September 18, 1991, A23; Tony Smith, "Warfare Greets Latest Declared Yugoslav Cease-Fire," Associated Press, September 18, 1991; Jeffrey T. Kuhner, "Zagreb Won't Accept Ex-Army Chief's Indictment," *Washington Times*, October 4, 2002, A15; "Janko Bobetko, 84, Is Dead; Fought to Free Croatians," *New York Times*, April 30, 2003, A1; Jasmina Kuzmanovic, "Croats Worry about Sanctions, Consequences for Carving Up Bosnia," Associated Press, July 21, 1993; Roger Cohen, "U.S. Cooling Ties to Croatia after Winking at Its Buildup," *New York Times*, October 28, 1995, section 1, p. 1; John Pomfret, "Croatia Slips Closer to Renewed War; Zagred Rearming, Moving Up Troops," *Washington Post*, November 14, 1993, A21; Stephen Kinzer, "Conflict in the Balkans: The Strategy," *New York Times*, July 13, 1995, section 1, p. 5; Tony Smith, "Fighting Spreads as Truce Collapses," Associated Press, July 2, 1991, https://apnews.com/ccb54ab4fd591cc781bebc758ec17802; "Croatia Calls Up Reserves, Abandons Vital Stronghold to Serb Militants," *Miami Herald*, August 2, 1991, A6; Blaine Harden, "Croatia Accepts Cease-Fire," *Washington Post*, August 4, 1991, A1; Jasmina Kuzmanovic, "Serb Surrender Defuses Fighting, but Tensions High Elsewhere," Associated Press, May 4, 1995; John Diamond, "Stunned Capital Mourns for Brown," *Chicago Sun-Times*, April 4, 1996, 1; Miroslav Tudjman, "The First Five Years of the Croatian Intelligence Service: 1993–1998," *National Security and the Future* 1 (Summer 2000): 57–58.

39. Vankovska and Wiberg, *Between Past and Future*, 214–15; Zunec, "Democracy and the 'Fog of War,'" 220; Alex J. Bellamy, "'Like Drunken Geese in the Fog': Developing Democratic Control of Armed Forces in Croatia," in Andrew Cottey, Timothy Edmunds, and Anthony Forster, eds., *Democratic Control of the Military in Postcommunist Europe* (New York: Palgrave, 2002), 174–93 at 175, 179.

40. Hislope, "Intra-ethnic Conflict in Croatia and Serbia," 478–81; Tanner, *Croatia*, 265–67; *Balkan Battlegrounds*, 1:133–34; Milan Vego, "The Croatian Forces in Bosnia and Herzegovina," *Jane's Intelligence Review*, March 1993, 100; Jill A. Irvine, "Nationalism and the Extreme Right in the Former Yugoslavia," in Luciano Cheles, Ronnie Ferguson, and Michalina Vaughn, eds., *The Far Right in Western and Eastern Europe* (New York: Longman, 1995), 145–73 at 159–60.

41. MG Griffitts int.; also Vukadinovich and Cehulik, "Development of Civil-Military Relations in Croatia," 80–83. Where necessary, Tudjman was prepared to use force to consolidate

control: in June 1993, the Croatian government arrested Dobroslav Paraga, the leader of the HOS's political wing, on weapons charges, and by the end of the year Tudjman had absorbed Paraga's militia into the HV and eliminated the Party of the Right as a political rival. See Tanner, *Croatia*, 265–67; *Balkan Battlegrounds*, 1:133–34; Vego, "Croatian Forces in Bosnia and Herzegovina," 100; Irvine, "Nationalism and the Extreme Right in the Former Yugoslavia," 159–60.

42. COL Marco Benić int.; LTC Alojzije Hren int.

43. COL J.M. int.

44. MG Richard Griffitts, USA retd, int. See also P. Singer, *Corporate Warriors* 119–36; Avant, *Market for Force*, 98–113; Molly Dunnigan, *Victory for Hire: Private Security Companies' Impact on Military Effectiveness* (Palo Alto, CA: Stanford University Press, 2011), 90–124.

45. Esther Schrader, "U.S. Companies Hired to Train Foreign Armies," *Los Angeles Times*, April 14, 2002, https://www.latimes.com/archives/la-xpm-2002-apr-14-mn-37825-story.html; P. Singer, *Corporate Warriors*, 126–27; Avant, *Market for Force*, 103–4; Dunnigan, *Victory for Hire*, 93–94; "Croatia: Operation Storm 1995," Globalsecurity.org, https://www.globalsecurity.org /intell/ops/croatia.htm.

46. Griffitts int.

47. See, e.g., BG Vlado Hodalj int.

48. BG J. int.; Griffitts int. MPRI found a remarkably receptive student body: MG Richard Griffitts, the MPRI program manager in Croatia in 1995, described them as "sponges": Griffitts int.

49. The MPRI mission was perceived by some as a veiled signal of US support for Tudjman: BG Vlado Hodalj int.

50. Jackovich int.

51. Jackovich int.

52. Tanner, *Croatia*, 279–80; Silber and Little, *Yugoslavia*, 202–4; Walter Zimmermann, *Origins of a Catastrophe: Yugoslavia and Its Destroyers—America's Last Ambassador Tells What Happened and Why* (New York: Times Books, 1996), 160–61; Nesho Djuric, "Lord Carrington Meets Serbian Leader; EC-Backed Talks to Resume," United Press International, February 26, 1992, https://www.upi.com/Archives/1992/02/26/Lord-Carrington-meets-Serbian-leader-EC -backed-talks-to-resume/5305699080400/; John F. Burns, "Serbian Leader in Croatia Agrees to Cooperate with U.N. Troops," *New York Times*, February 24, 1992, 3; Laura Pitter, "Rebel Serbs in Croatia Elect Foe of Patrons in Belgrade," *Christian Science Monitor*, December 21, 1993, 7; Dusan Stojanovic, "Crucial Elections Held in Serb-Occupied Parts of Croatia," Associated Press, January 23, 1994, https://apnews.com/92028cf220be6dca85235fa7b614f200; "Milosevic Protégé Declared Winner in Krajina Elections," Associated Press, January 25, 1994.

53. Slobodan Lekic, "First Elections in Serb-Held Regions of Croatia," Associated Press, December 12, 1993; Filip Svarm, "A Letter of Secession: Hadzic Re-activated," *Vreme News Digest Agency* 192 (June 5, 1995), https://tol.org/client/article/16471.html.

54. Memorandum for the record on anonymous int.; Nigel Thomas and Krunoslav Mikulan, *The Yugoslav Wars*, volume 1, *Slovenia and Croatia, 1991–95* (New York: Osprey, 2006), 42–44; *Balkan Battlegrounds*, 1:85.

55. Memorandum for the record on anonymous int.; *Balkan Battlegrounds*, 1:270.

56. Bjelajac and Zunec, "War in Croatia, 1991–1995," 262; Lekic, "First Elections in Serb-Held Regions of Croatia."

57. COL J.M. int.; BG J. int.; BG Petar Bajan int.; CPT Tihomir Tolić int.; MAJ (retd) Krunoslav Samošćanec int.; COL Marco Benić int.

58. BG Petar Bajan int.; BJ int.; CPT ZG int.; LTC Valentino Rajkovic int.; SGT VS, Pvt VP int.; Private Tomislav Galović int.; MAJ (retd) Krunoslav Samošćanec int.; *Balkan Battlegrounds*, 2:193, 211n17, 211n18.

59. LTC Alojzije Hren int.; BG J. int.; BG Petar Bajan int.; COL Marco Benić int.; see also *Balkan Battlegrounds*, 1:94, 106, 109, 268; 2:113, 225–56.

60. BG J. int.; BG Petar Bajan int.; BJ int.; LTC Valentino Rajkovic int.; MAJ (retd) Krunoslav Samošćanec int.; see also *Balkan Battlegrounds*, vol. 2, and 1:274–76. For the views of UN and NATO observers, see, e.g., Robert Fox, "Secret US Military Advice Helps 'Cocky' Croats in Push towards Eastern Slavonia," *Sunday Telegraph*, October 15, 1995; Juan Carlos Zarate, "The Emergence of a New Dog of War: Private International Security Companies, International Law, and the New World Disorder," *Stanford Journal of International Law* 75, no. 34 (1998): 75–162; P. Singer, *Corporate Warriors*, 126–27. This pattern implies a score of 0.5 on the (0, 1) scale for stealth in the coding system presented in the appendix.

61. DT, AV int.; LTC Valentino Rajkovic int.; SGT VS, Pvt VP int.; Private Tomislav Galović int.; see also *Balkan Battlegrounds*, 2:202.

62. BG Petar Bajan int.; BJ int.; CPT Tihomir Tolić int.; CPT ZG int.; LTC Valentino Rajkovic int.; SGT VS, Pvt VP int.; Private Tomislav Galović int.; MAJ (retd) Krunoslav Samošćanec int.; COL Marco Benić int.; see also *Balkan Battlegrounds*, e.g., 2:88, 193, 195, 196, 198–201, 227. Note that when the rare JNA Guards infantry units were committed in lieu of Serbian militia, combined-arms coordination improved markedly, as in the latter stages of the attack on Vukovar: *Balkan Battlegrounds*, 2:202. This pattern implies a score of 0.5 on the (0, 1) scale for stealth for both the ZNG and the SVK in the coding system presented in the appendix.

63. LTC Rajkovic int.; *Balkan Battlegrounds*, 2:84.

64. Tolić int.; *Balkan Battlegrounds*, 1:99.

65. CPT ZG int.; *Balkan Battlegrounds*, 1:103–5.

66. Galović int.

67. See, e.g., BG Petar Bajan int.; BJ int.; CPT Tihomir Tolić int.; COL Marco Benić int.

68. See, e.g., LTC Valentino Rajkovic int.; BG Petar Bajan int.; BJ int.; CPT Tihomir Tolić int.; COL Marco Benić int.; SGT VS, Pvt VP int.

69. On Operation Storm, see *Balkan Battlegrounds*, 2:367–76.

70. Overall, this pattern implies a score of 1.0 on the "duration of firefights" subscore for holding ground for both the ZNG and the SVK, contributing 0.25 points to the overall index score for the ZNG and the SVK in the coding system presented in the appendix.

71. LTC Valentino Rajkovic int.

72. Private VP int.

73. Private Tomislav Galović int.

74. BG Petar Bajan int.; Private Tomislav Galović int. Overall, this pattern implies a score of 1.0 on the "proximity of attackers to defenders" subscore for holding ground for both the ZNG and the SVK, contributing 0.25 points to the overall index score for the ZNG and the SVK in the coding system presented in the appendix.

75. *Balkan Battlegrounds*, 2:83–84.

76. *Balkan Battlegrounds*, 1:102–3.

77. CPT Tihomir Tolić int.

78. Tomislav Galović int.

79. DT, AV int.

80. LTC Valentino Rajkovic int.

81. Overall, this pattern implies a score of 1.0 on the "incidence of counterattack" subscore for holding ground for both the ZNG and the SVK, contributing 0.25 points to the overall index score for the ZNG and the SVK in the coding system presented in the appendix.

82. BG Petar Bajan int.; also SGT VS, Pvt VP int.

83. See, e.g., BG Petar Bajan int.; BJ int.; CPT Tihomir Tolić int.; LTC Valentino Rajkovic int.; MAJ (retd) Krunoslav Samošćanec int.; also *Balkan Battlegrounds*, 2:192–94, 1:100, 272; Charles M. Winkler and Charles R. Patrick, "Croatian and Serbian Tactics in 1991 Fighting in Former Yugoslavia," in *How They Fight: Armies of the World* (Washington, DC: US Army Intelligence and Threat Analysis Center, 1998), 19–20. Overall, this pattern implies a score of 1.0 on the "incidence of harassing fires and unattended minefields" subscore for holding ground, contributing 0.25 points to the overall index score for both the ZNG and the SVK in the coding system presented in the appendix, and yielding an overall "holding ground" score of 1.0 across its four subcomponents for both actors.

84. See chap. 9, below.

85. Silber and Little, *Yugoslavia*, 187; Vankovska and Wiberg, *Between Past and Future*, 207.

86. *Balkan Battlegrounds*, 2:192, map 2; 2:217, map 4. This pattern corresponds to a value of 0.44 on the (0, 1) scale for dispersion for both actors in the coding system presented in the appendix.

87. See, esp., *Balkan Battlegrounds*, vol. 2, and 1:94–116, 367–76. The First World War–like trench systems adopted by both sides are also strongly suggestive of an emphasis on brute force retention of ground. On defensive entrenchment, see esp. BG Petar Bajan int.; BJ int.; CPT ZG int.; LTC Valentino Rajkovic int.; SGT VS, Pvt VP int.; Private Tomislav Galović int. This pattern implies a value of 1.0 on the (0, 1) scale for "reliance on brute force" in the coding system presented in the appendix for both actors.

88. CPT Tihomir Tolić int.; BG Petar Bajan int.; MAJ (retd) Krunoslav Samošćanec int.; COL J.M. int.

89. BG Petar Bajan int.; Private Tomislav Galović int.; BJ int.; CPT ZG int.; LTC Valentino Rajkovic int.; COL J.M. int.; SGT VS, Pvt VP int.; MAJ (retd) Krunoslav Samošćanec int.

90. BG Petar Bajan int.; LTC Valentino Rajkovic int.; COL Marco Benić int. This pattern implies a score of 1.0 on the "intermingling" subscore for distinguishability, contributing 0.5 points to the overall index score for both actors in the coding system presented in the appendix.

91. MAJ Ivica Tomić int. See also MAJ (retd) Krunoslav Samošćanec int.; COL Marco Benić int.; T.L. int.

92. See, e.g., N. Thomas and Mikulan, *Yugoslav Wars*, 1:43, 61–62; *Balkan Battlegrounds*, vol. 2, cover.

93. MAJ Ivica Tomić int.

94. This pattern implies a score of 1.0 on the "distinguishing markings" subscore for distinguishability, contributing 0.25 points to the overall index score for both actors in the coding system presented in the appendix.

95. This pattern implies a score of 1.0 on the "reliance on heavy weapons" subscore for distinguishability, contributing 0.25 points to the overall index score for both actors in the coding system presented in the appendix.

96. *Balkan Battlegrounds*, vol. 2, maps 4 and 5.

97. *Balkan Battlegrounds*, 1:99–105.

98. On the ZNG's logistical system, see, e.g., BG Petar Bajan int.; BJ int.; LTC Valentino Rajkovic int.; MAJ Ivica Tomić int.; COL Marco Benić int.

99. Taken together, this pattern implies a value of 1.0 on the (0, 1) scale for "articulated theater" for both actors in the coding system presented in the appendix.

100. BG Petar Bajan int.; BJ int.; CPT Tihomir Tolić int.; CPT ZG int.; LTC Valentino Rajkovic int.; SGT VS, Pvt VP int.; Private Tomislav Galović int.; MAJ (retd) Krunoslav Samošćanec int.; COL Marco Benić int.; see also *Balkan Battlegrounds*, e.g., 2:88, 193, 195, 196, 198–201, 227. Note that when the rare JNA Guards infantry units were committed in lieu of Serbian militia, combined-arms coordination improved markedly, as in the latter stages of the attack on Vukovar: *Balkan Battlegrounds*, 2:202.

101. DT, AV int.; LTC Valentino Rajkovic int.; SGT VS, Pvt VP int.; Private Tomislav Galović int.; see also *Balkan Battlegrounds*, 2:202.

102. BG Petar Bajan int.; COL Marco Benić int.; see also *Balkan Battlegrounds*, e.g., 2:12–19, 201.

103. COL J.M. int.; BG J. int.; BG Petar Bajan int.; CPT Tihomir Tolić int.; MAJ (retd) Krunoslav Samošćanec int.; COL Marco Benić int.

104. BG Petar Bajan int.; BJ int.; CPT ZG int.; LTC Valentino Rajkovic int.; SGT VS, Pvt VP int.; Private Tomislav Galović int.; MAJ (retd) Krunoslav Samošćanec int.; *Balkan Battlegrounds*, 2:193, 211n17, 211n18.

105. LTC Alojzije Hren int.; BG J. int.; BG Petar Bajan int.; COL Marco Benić int.; see also *Balkan Battlegrounds*, 1:94, 106, 109, 268; 2:113, 225–26.

106. BG J. int.; BG Petar Bajan int.; BJ int.; LTC Valentino Rajkovic int.; MAJ (retd) Krunoslav Samošćanec int.; see also *Balkan Battlegrounds*, 1:274–76. For the views of UN and NATO observers, see, e.g., Fox, "Secret US Military Advice Helps"; Zarate, "Emergence of a New Dog of War"; P. Singer, *Corporate Warriors*, 126–27.

107. Corresponding to a coding of (0.5, 1, 1, 1, 1, 0.44, 1, 1, 1, 1, 1). For Desert Storm and Goodwood, see chap. 2.

108. As implied by equation [A2], for values of $f = 0.25$, $i = 1$, $s = 0$, and $t = 1995$, per the discussion above.

109. Glenn E. Curtis, ed., *Yugoslavia: A Country Study* (Washington, DC: Library of Congress, 1990), 224–40; Director of Central Intelligence, *Combatant Forces in the Former Yugoslavia*, July 1993 (Washington, DC: Central Intelligence Agency), 14.

110. The ZNG's observed behavior is also not a perfect fit to the functional form presented in the appendix. The ZNG's actual behavior was midspectrum by the terms presented in chaps. 2 and 4 and the coding system in the appendix (with an observed scoring of 4.9); the formal prediction from equation [A2] is close to a midspectrum value but falls short of the 3.0 cutoff for "midspectrum" in table 4.1, with a "slightly Fabian" score of 2.2, as implied by independent variable values of $f = 0.25$, $i = 2$, $s = 1$, and $t = 1991$, per the discussion above. The ZNG prediction is thus more Fabian than the observed value, but it is nevertheless a less Fabian value than for any case considered here except Hezbollah.

Chapter Nine: The Vietcong in the Second Indochina War, 1965–68

1. William J. Duiker, *The Communist Road to Power in Vietnam* (Boulder, CO: Westview, 1996), 133–214; Gerard J. DeGroot, *A Noble Cause? America and the Vietnam War* (London: Longman, 2000), 54, 60, 66–70; Stanley Karnow, *Vietnam: A History*, rev. ed. (New York: Penguin Books, 1997), 253–55; Robert A. Doughty, Ira D. Gruber, Roy K. Flint, Mark Grimsley, George C. Herring, Donald D. Horward, John A. Lynn, and Williamson Murray, *American Military History and the Evolution of Western Warfare* (Lexington, MA: D. C. Heath, 1996), 637–39.

2. Karnow, *Vietnam*, 276–79; DeGroot, *Noble Cause?*, 76–78.

3. Jessica Chapman, *Cauldron of Resistance: Ngo Dinh Diem, the United States, and 1950s Southern Vietnam* (Ithaca, NY: Cornell University Press, 2018), 173–95; Lewy, *America in Vietnam*, 27–28.

4. The relationship between the NLF and the North Vietnamese state, and between the VC and the PAVN, was very close. Not only did North Vietnam provide money and equipment; it also provided military advice and coordinated military planning, culminating in the joint Tet Offensive of 1968. That said, close relationships with state patrons are not unusual among nonstate actors—the SVK in Croatia enjoyed very close relations with the Jugoslav state, for example; Hezbollah is viewed by some as an extension of Iranian foreign policy; and the Jaish al Mahdi received funds, training, and military advising from the Iranian state. Seth Jones estimates that over 80 percent of all insurgencies since 1946 have received external support to varying degrees: S. Jones, *Waging Insurgent Warfare*, 136. Actors with very close relationships to state patrons have displayed wide variations in both their military behavior and their internal politics—from mature natural order, existential stakes, and midspectrum war fighting for Hezbollah to fragile natural order, limited stakes, and maladroit attempts at midspectrum methods for the SVK or fragile natural order, limited stakes, and mostly Fabian war fighting for the JAM; there is no reason to assume that state patrons create effective clients or predetermine their internal politics in any direct or straightforward way. The Vietcong, like the SVK, Hezbollah, and the JAM, received a great deal of state support, but it was still a nonstate actor by the definition presented in chap. 1, and I treat its internal politics as an exogenous independent variable here as elsewhere.

5. Lewy, *America in Vietnam*, 57–78; Spencer C. Tucker, *Vietnam* (London: UCL, 1999), 110–16; Eugenie M. Blang, *Allies at Odds: America, Europe, and Vietnam, 1961–1968* (Plymouth, UK: Rowman and Littlefield, 2011), 82–88; Karnow, *Vietnam*, 320–27, 398; DeGroot, *Noble Cause?*, 80–82, 140, 153, 186; Max Frankel, "More U.S. Strikes Likely in Attempt to Deter Hanoi," *New York Times*, March 3, 1965, https://www.nytimes.com/1965/03/03/archives/more-us-strikes-likely-in-attempt-to-deter-hanoi-more-us-strikes-on.html; Jack Raymond, "3,500 U.S. Marines Going to Vietnam to Bolster Base; 2 Battalions for Danang Are First Land Combat Troops Committed by Washington," *New York Times*, March 7, 1965, https://www.nytimes.com/1965/03/07/archives/3500-us-marines-going-to-vietnam-to-bolster-base-2-battalions-for.html; Addington, *Patterns of War*, 293.

6. DeGroot, *Noble Cause?*, 151–53; Tucker, *Vietnam*, 128–33; Lewy, *America in Vietnam*, 90–97.

7. Karnow, *Vietnam*, 536–61, 616; Doughty, Gruber, Flint, Grimsley, Herring, Horward, Lynn, and Murray, *American Military History*, 654–58; DeGroot, *Noble Cause?*, 162–74; "Troops Fan Out," *New York Times*, April 7, 1968.

8. John Adams and Nancy Hancock, "Land and Economy in Traditional Vietnam," *Journal of Southeast Asian Studies* 1, no. 2 (1970): 93; Gerald Cannon Hickey, *Village in Vietnam* (New Haven, CT: Yale University Press, 1964), 88; Kirsten W. Endres, "Culturalizing Politics: *Doi Moi* and the Restructuring of Ritual in Contemporary Rural Vietnam," in Philip Taylor, *Fragments of the Present: Searching for Modernity in Vietnam's South* (Honolulu: University of Hawai'i Press, 2001), 216; and Mark W. McLeod and Nguyen Thi Dieu, *Culture and Customs of Vietnam* (Westport, CT: Greenwood, 2001), 45.

9. See, for instance, Nancy Wiegersma, *Vietnam: Peasant Land, Peasant Revolution: Patriarchy and Collectivity in the Rural Economy* (New York: St. Martin's, 1988), 77–78; J. Adams and Hancock, "Land and Economy in Traditional Vietnam," 98; Shaun Kingsley Malarney, *Culture, Ritual and Revolution in Vietnam* (New York: RoutledgeCurzon, 2002), 16, 17, 89; McLeod and Nguyen Thi Dieu, *Culture and Customs of Vietnam*, 135; Hickey, *Village in Vietnam*, 82, 91–92; Hy Van Luong, "Vietnamese Kinship: Structural Principles and the Socialist Transformation in Northern Vietnam," *Journal of Asian Studies* 48, no. 4 (1989): 744–47; and Randy Craig Cummings, "Vietnamese Villages in the Mekong: Their Articulations with the Wider Society and the Implications for Local Social Organization" (PhD thesis, State University of New York at Binghamton, 1977), 66–76, cited in John Kleinen, "Is There a 'Village Vietnam'?," in *Vietnamese Villages in Transition: Background and Consequences of Reform Policies in Rural Vietnam*, ed. Bernhard Dahm and Vincent J. Houben (Passau: Passau University Department of Southeast Asian Studies, 1999), 11n9.

10. Dang Nghiem Van, *Ethnological and Religious Problems in Vietnam / Problèmes Ethnologiques et Religiuex du Vietnam* (Hanoi: Social Sciences, 1998), 161–89; Hickey, *Village in Vietnam*, 95–96, 100, 284; Malarney, *Culture, Ritual and Revolution in Vietnam*, 157; Wiegersma, *Vietnam*, 127.

11. Malarney, *Culture, Ritual and Revolution in Vietnam*, 17.

12. Martin Grossheim, "The Impact of Reforms on the Agricultural Sector in Vietnam: The Land Issue," in Dahm and Houben, *Vietnamese Villages in Transition: Background and Consequences of Reform Policies in Rural Vietnam*, 91, 95; J. Adams and Hancock, "Land and Economy in Traditional Vietnam," 90, 97–98; McLeod and Nguyen Thi Dieu, *Culture and Customs of Vietnam*, 29; Wiegersma, *Vietnam*, 14, 20–22, 24, 83, 99, 111–28, 131, 134–35, 220; James B. Hendry, *The Small World of Khanh Hau* (Chicago: Aldine, 1964), 238, quoted in Wiegersma, *Vietnam*, 124–25; Hickey, *Village in Vietnam*, 99, 114–16, 107, 144, 148, 165–66, 169–72, 176–77, 244–45; Hendry, *Small World of Khanh Hau*, 149–50 quoted in Hickey, *Village in Vietnam*, 149.

13. Frances FitzGerald, *Fire in the Lake: The Vietnamese and the Americans in Vietnam* (New York: Little, Brown, 1972), 20, 160–61, 184–86; Lesley Anne Warner, "Vietnam (1959–1972)," in *Money in the Bank—Lessons Learned from Past Counterinsurgency (COIN) Operations*, ed. Angel Rabasa, Lesley Anne Warner, Peter Chalk, Ivan Khilko, and Paraag Shukla (Santa Monica, CA: RAND, 2007), 27–38. Local disputes within families and villages were often resolved by family elders, however: McLeod and Nguyen Thi Dieu, *Culture and Customs of Vietnam*, 136; Hickey, *Village in Vietnam*, 196.

14. Hickey, *Village in Vietnam*, 13, 88–91, 95–96, 99, 280–82; and Wiegersma, *Vietnam*, 112, 126, 209, 256–57n1; Hy Van Luong, "Vietnamese Kinship," 748. See also Guy Gran, "Vietnam and the Capitalist Route to Modernity: Village Cochinchina 1880–1940" (PhD diss., University of Wisconsin–Madison, 1975), cited in P. Taylor, *Fragments of the Present*, 203n6.

15. M. Anderson, M. Arnsten and H. Averch, *Insurgent Organization and Operations: A Case Study of the Viet Cong in the Delta, 1964–1966* (Santa Monica, CA: RAND, 1967); John C. Donnell, *Vietcong Recruitment: Why and How Men Join* (Santa Monica, CA: RAND, 1967); Douglas Pike, *Viet Cong: The Organization and Techniques of the National Liberation Front of South Vietnam* (Cambridge, MA: MIT Press, 1966), 232–40.

16. *MACV Order of Battle Summary*, June 1966, part IV, RG 472, box 39, "Westmoreland vs. CBS Litigation Collection" (Suitland, MD: Washington National Records Center), cited in Lanning and Cragg, *Inside the VC and the NVA*, 51; Pike, *Viet Cong*, 235, 239; Military Institute of Vietnam, *Victory in Vietnam: The Official History of the People's Army of Vietnam 1954–75*, trans. Merle Pribbenow (Lawrence: University of Kansas Press, 2002), 156; Anderson, Arnsten, and Averich, *Insurgent Organization and Operations*, 10; A. J. Tachmindji, *Journal of Defense Research: Series B: Tactical Warfare* 7, no. 3 (Washington, DC: Government Printing Office, 1975), 856–57; Department of Defense, *Know Your Enemy*, 4; George McTurnan Kahin and John W. Lewis, *The United States in Vietnam* (New York: Dell, 1967), 185; Neil Sheehan, *A Bright Shining Lie: John Paul Vann and America in Vietnam* (New York: Random House, 1988), 724, 732–33; Brig. Gen. William A. Stofft, *American Military History* (Washington, DC: US Army Center for Military History, 1989), 627.

17. William C. Westmoreland, *Report on the War in Vietnam* (Washington, DC: Government Printing Office, June 1986), 114, 194–95; see also Kahin and Lewis, *United States in Vietnam*, 185; Lanning and Cragg, *Inside the VC and the NVA*, 43; Kenneth Conboy, *The NVA and the Viet Cong* (Oxford: Osprey, 1991), 9–10.

18. Assuming an area of approximately 174,000 square kilometers for South Vietnam overall, and thus about 58,000 square miles for the VC's primary operating area: Office of Research and Reports, Central Intelligence Agency, *Economic Intelligence Report: A Comparison of the Economies of North and South Vietnam* (December 1961), 5, https://www.cia.gov/library/readingroom/docs/CIA-RDP79R01141A002200070001-8.pdf. For ZNG figures, see chap. 7.

19. Lanning and Cragg, *Inside the VC and the NVA*, 96, 122–28, 140; Truong Nhu Tang, *Viet Cong Memoir*, 159–60; Department of Defense, *Know Your Enemy*, 4; Trullinger, *Village at War*, 82, 121–22; Stuart Herrington, *Stalking the Vietcong: Inside Operation Phoenix* (Novato, CA: Presidio, 1982), 91; Kuno Knoebl, *Victor Charlie: The Face of War in Viet-Nam* (New York: Praeger, 1967), 135–44; Military Institute of Vietnam, *Victory in Vietnam*, 83, 193; Gordon L. Rottman, *The Viet Cong and NVA Tunnels and Fortifications of the Vietnam War* (Oxford: Osprey, 2006), 16–17, 59–60; Wilkins, *Grab Their Belts*, 16–17.

20. Michael A. Hennessy, *Strategy in Vietnam: The Marines and Revolutionary Warfare in I Corps, 1965–1972* (Westport, CT: Praeger, 1997), 48.

21. Jeffrey J. Clarke, *Advice and Support: The Final Years* (Washington DC: Center for Military History, 1988), 109, 145.

22. J. Clarke, *Advice and Support*, 445; Anthony James Joes, *The War for South Vietnam: 1954–1975* (New York: Praeger, 1989), 83.

23. Lieutenant General John J. Tolson, *Vietnam Studies: Airmobility, 1961–1971* (Washington, DC: Government Printing Office, 1999), 39–40, 95, 129, 198–99, 253–54.

24. Nguyen Cao Ky, *How We Lost the Vietnam War* (New York: Stein and Day, 1976), 145.

25. J. Clarke, *Advice and Support*, 113; Stofft, *American Military History*, 630, 686.

26. Military Institute of Vietnam, *Victory in Vietnam*, 49–50; Truong Nhu Tang, *Viet Cong Memoir*, 71; Douglas Pike, *The Viet-Cong Strategy of Terror* (Vietnam: United States Mission, 1970), 5; Jeffrey Race, *War Comes to Long An: Revolutionary Conflict in a Vietnamese Province* (Berkeley: University of California Press, 1972), 105.

27. On the roles of nationalism and Communism in Vietcong motivation, see, e.g., William Darryl Henderson, *Why the Vietcong Fought: A Study of Motivation and Control in a Modern Army in Combat* (Westport, CT: Greenwood, 1979), 49–53; Truong Nhu Tang, *Viet Cong Memoir*, 68–69; Knoebl, *Victor Charlie*, 20–21, 113.

28. R. J. Rummel, *Statistics of Democide: Genocide and Mass Murder since 1900* (Charlottesville, VA: LIT Verlag, 1998), https://www.hawaii.edu/powerkills/SOD.TAB6.1B.GIF; Teddy D. Bitner, *Unreconstructed: Vietnam to Iraq* (Morrisville, NC: Lulu, 1997), 17.

29. Race, *War Comes to Long An*, 110; Tanham, *Communist Revolutionary Warfare*, 98–101; Knoebl, *Victor Charlie*, 42.

30. Lewy, *America in Vietnam*, 459; Directorate of Intelligence, Central Intelligence Agency, *The Effectiveness of the Air Campaign against North Vietnam, 1 January–30 September 1966* (December 1966), A-14, A-23, https://www.cia.gov/library/readingroom/docs/DOC_0003290249.pdf.

31. Of course the Hanoi government eventually did bail out the VC following the latter's decimation in Tet: a mostly NVA post-Tet war effort ultimately toppled the Thieu regime and took over South Vietnam. Instrumental in this was an unexpected political benefit to the VC/ NVA from their military defeat in Tet, however: Tet's effect on US public opinion contributed to an eventual US decision to withdraw, which left the Thieu government vulnerable in ways it would not have been while US troops were still present in strength, yet this US domestic political effect was not anticipated by Communist planners. On the contrary, in 1965 the Communist leadership was looking at an American *escalation* that was only beginning and would continue for years. And the political benefits of Tet for the VC/NVA were largely a function of the VC's own massive exertions—these VC efforts cost them dearly but were what convinced many Americans that the war was far from over. All in all, there would have been no basis between 1965 and 1968 for a reasonable VC planner to assume that they could safely underperform their military potential and rely on others to secure their aims for them. Ironically, whereas the Croatian Serbs between 1991 and 1995 had a reasonable expectation of Jugoslav protection that proved wrong in the clinch, the VC from 1965 to 1968 would have had a reasonable *skepticism* regarding others' ability to protect them that would also have proved wrong in the end.

32. Pike, *Viet Cong*, 218; Lanning and Cragg, *Inside the VC and the NVA*, 93, 95–96, 154; Anderson, Arnsten, and Averich, *Insurgent Organization and Operations*, 7–8.

33. Knoebl, *Victor Charlie*, 116; Anderson, Arnsten, and Averich, *Insurgent Organization and Operations*, 31; Department of Defense, *Know Your Enemy*, 4.

34. Douglas Pike, *Viet Cong*, 148, 233, 237; Department of Defense, *Know Your Enemy*, 11; Michael Conley, *The Communist Insurgent Infrastructure in South Vietnam: A Study of Organization and Strategy* (Washington, DC: Department of the Army, 1966), 145; Lanning and Cragg, *Inside the VC and the NVA*, 91, 108, 109; Wilkins, *Grab Their Belts*, 13; Anderson, Arnsten, and Averich, *Insurgent Organization and Operations*, 20, 33–34.

35. Lanning and Cragg, *Inside the VC and the NVA*, 104–5; William Bredo, "Agrarian in Vietnam: Vietcong and Government of Vietnam Strategies in Conflict," *Asian Survey* 19, no. 8 (August 1970): 745.

36. Pike, *Viet Cong*, 148; Anderson, Arnsten, and Averich, *Insurgent Organization and Operations*, 34, 42; Henderson, *Why the Vietcong Fought*, 33, 36, 46, 56; Lanning and Cragg, *Inside the VC and the NVA*, 99, 108, 113–14. On internal debates, see also Long, *On "Other War,"* 17.

37. North, Wallis, and Weingast, *Violence and Social Orders*, 21–24.

38. Department of the Army, Headquarters, First Brigade, First Infantry Division, APO San Francisco 96345, Combat after Action Report (MACV/RCS/J3/321), December 8, 1967, records housed in the Bud Harton Collection at the Texas Tech Virtual Vietnam Archive.

39. George L. MacGarrigle, *Combat Operations: Taking the Offensive, October 1966–October 1967* (Washington, DC: Center of Military History, 1988), e.g., 107, 241; Rottman, *Viet Cong and NVA Tunnels and Fortifications of the Vietnam War*, 13; Tanham, *Communist Revolutionary Warfare*, 94; Lanning and Cragg, *Inside the VC and the NVA*, 206–7.

40. Tanham, *Communist Revolutionary Warfare*, 92; Anderson, Arnsten, and Averich, *Insurgent Organization and Operations*, 85–87; Lanning and Cragg, *Inside the VC and the NVA*, 204–5. This pattern implies a score of 0.0 on the (0, 1) scale for stealth in the coding system presented in the appendix.

41. For overviews of engagement duration and range in VC tactics, see, e.g., Wilkins, *Grab Their Belts*, 22, 25–29; Lanning and Cragg, *Inside the VC and the NVA*, 203, 209, 223; Tanham, *Communist Revolutionary Warfare*, 80, 85–93; Long, *On "Other War,"* 38; Rottman, *Viet Cong and NVA Tunnels and Fortifications of the Vietnam War*, 13–15; Truong Nhu Tang, *Viet Cong Memoir*, 154; Knoebl, *Victor Charlie*, 144; James H. Willbanks, *Vietnam War: The Essential Reference Guide* (Santa Barbara, CA: ABC-CLIO, 2013), xxvii–xxviii; Nguyen Cao Ky, *How We Lost the Vietnam War*, 158–63; Anderson, Arnsten, and Averich, *Insurgent Organization and Operations*, 96–97.

42. John Albright, "Convoy Ambush on Highway 1," in John A. Cash, John Albright, and Allan W. Sandstrum, *Seven Firefights in Vietnam* (Washington, DC: US Army Office of the Chief of Military History, 1985), 41–58.

43. Gen. Donn A. Starry, *Vietnam Studies: Mounted Combat in Vietnam* (Washington, DC: Department of the Army, 2002), 109–10.

44. Anderson, Arnsten, and Averich, *Insurgent Organization and Operations*, 112.

45. John Albright, "Fight along the Rach Ba Rai," in J. Cash, Albright, and Sandstrum, *Seven Firefights in Vietnam*, 67–84.

46. MacGarrigle, *Combat Operations*, 130–31.

47. Albright, "Fight along the Rach Ba Rai," 77.

48. Tanham, *Communist Revolutionary Warfare*, 90, 93.

49. Overall, this pattern implies a score of 0.0 on the "duration of firefights" subscore for holding ground. But the "proximity of attackers to defenders" subscore cannot be coded for the VC, as it did not sustain contact long enough to meet the criterion in the appendix. Instead, the weights for "duration of firefights," "incidence of counterattack," and "incidence of harassing fires and unattended minefields" are increased from 0.25 to 0.33 for the VC when computing the overall index value, per the coding rules presented in the appendix.

50. Lanning and Cragg, *Inside the VC and the NVA*, 208; Anderson, Arnsten and Averich, *Insurgent Organization and Operations*, 100–101. In fact, VC counterattacks were even less frequent than VC senior leadership would have preferred. As one officer put it: "Our combat plan provided for passive defense and counter-operations and did not provide a plan of attack. Many occasions had not been seized to annihilate the enemy because aggressiveness in counter

operations had not been thoroughly understood by the troops" (Anderson, Arnsten, and Averich, *Insurgent Organization and Operations*, 100). This pattern implies a score of 0.0 on the "incidence of counterattack" subscore for holding ground, contributing 0.0 points to the overall index score for the VC in the coding system presented in the appendix.

51. Wilkins, *Grab Their Belts*, 32–33.

52. For specific types and characteristics, see, e.g., Headquarters, Department of the Army, *Vietcong Booby Traps, Mines, and Mine Warfare Techniques* (Washington, DC: Government Printing Office, 1967), TC-5-31, 8–26; Military Assistance Command Vietnam, *Mines and Booby Traps Used by the Vietcong in South Vietnam* (typescript, 1965), http://www.army.gov.au/Our-history/Primary-Materials/Vietnam-1962-to-1972/~/media/Files/Our%20history/AAHU/Primary%20Materials/Vietnam%201962-1972/Training%20Materials/Min%20Bay%20Do%20Viet%20Cong%20Mines%20and%20Booby%20Traps%20used%20by%20the%20Viet%20Cong%201965.pdf.

53. Cited in Andrew Cooper, "The U.S. Army and Antipersonnel Mines in the Korean and Vietnam Wars," *Human Rights Watch Reports* 9, no. 4 (1997): 9.

54. David Horner, "The Higher Direction of the Army in the Vietnam War," in Peter Dennis and Jeffrey Grey, eds., *The Australian Army and the Vietnam War, 1962–1972* (Canberra: Army History Unit, 2002), 33–57 at 44–46; Cooper, "U.S. Army and Antipersonnel Mines," 10.

55. See, e.g., Headquarters, Department of the Army, *Vietcong Booby Traps, Mines, and Mine Warfare Techniques*, TC-5-31, 27–53; Military Assistance Command Vietnam, *Mines and Booby Traps Used by the Vietcong in South Vietnam*, 145–67.

56. Cooper, "U.S. Army and Antipersonnel Mines," 9.

57. Tanham, *Communist Revolutionary Warfare*, 87; Wilkins, *Grab Their Belts*, 41–44.

58. This pattern implies a score of 0.0 on the "incidence of harassing fires and unattended minefields" subscore for holding ground, contributing 0.0 points to the overall index score for the VC in the coding system presented in the appendix, and yielding an overall value of 0.0 across its four subcomponents for holding ground.

59. See, e.g., MacGarrigle, *Combat Operations*, 57.

60. MacGarrigle, *Combat Operations*, 130–31, 133–34.

61. US relief forces subsequently reported finding 647 enemy bodies on the battlefield and taking 7 prisoners: MacGarrigle, *Combat Operations*, 132. Vietnam body counts were infamously inaccurate, however, and a casualty total of 647 would have constituted more than 90 percent of a two-battalion assault force; actual VC casualties were high, but surely lower than this.

62. Assuming a value of 67 combatants locally at a point of concentration and a midrange estimated average of four fighters per square kilometer theaterwide, this implies a value of 0.16 on the (0, 1) scale for dispersion in the coding system presented in the appendix.

63. Lien-Hang T. Nguyen, *Hanoi's War: An International History of the War for Peace in Vietnam* (Chapel Hill: University of North Carolina Press, 2012), chaps. 2–3; Duiker, *Communist Road to Power in Vietnam*, 273–79; William J. Duiker, *Ho Chi Minh: A Life* (New York: Hyperion, 2001), 551–52; Gary R. Hess, *Vietnam: Explaining American's Lost War* (Malden, MA: John Wiley and Sons, 2015) 155–57; Mitchell K. Hall, *The Vietnam War* (New York: Routledge, 2018), 20–21; Boot, *Road Not Taken*, 332–35.

64. Lewy, *America in Vietnam*, 273.

65. Rottman, *Viet Cong and NVA Tunnels and Fortifications of the Vietnam War*, 13; Tanham, *Communist Revolutionary Warfare*, 81–82, 90; Wilkins, *Grab Their Belts*, 29–33; Lanning and Cragg, *Inside the VC and the NVA*, 217–21; Stephen Hosmer, *Viet Cong Repression and Its Implications for the Future* (Lexington, MA: Heath Lexington Books, 1970), 5–7; Richard Schultz, "The Limits of Terrorism in Insurgency Warfare: The Case of the Viet Cong," *Polity* 11, no. 1 (Autumn 1978): 80–81; Lewy, *America in Vietnam*, 272–79.

66. Nguyen, *Hanoi's War*, chaps. 4–8.

67. Lanning and Cragg, *Inside the VC and the NVA*, 117–18, 203; Trullinger, *Village at War*, 83; Tanham, *Communist Revolutionary Warfare*, 88; Wilkins, *Grab Their Belts*, 18, 35–36. Assuming that all main force combatants but none of the VC's other fighters were thus in uniform, and assuming North Vietnamese figures for relative strength, this implies a value of 0.23 for the "distinguishing markings" subscore of distinguishability, contributing 0.08 points to the index score for the VC in the coding system presented in the appendix (the weight for "distinguishing markings" here is 0.33 rather than 0.25, because as noted below, the VC's lack of heavy weapons makes it impossible to code a value for "reliance on heavy weapons" given the coding rules in the appendix).

68. Pike, *Viet Cong*, 240–43; Kevin Generous, "Irregular Forces in Vietnam," in John S. Bowman, ed., *The Vietnam War: An Almanac* (New York: World Almanac, 1985), 440–69; FitzGerald, *Fire in the Lake*, 43–44.

69. Robert S. Laufer, M. S. Gallops, and Ellen Frey-Wouters, "War Stress and Trauma: The Vietnam Veteran Experience," *Journal of Health and Social Behavior* 25, no. 1 (March 1984), 65–85; Josh Hochgesang, Tracye Lawyer, and Toby Stevenson, "The Psychological Effects of the Vietnam War," Stanford University Ethics of Development in a Global Environment (EDGE) Seminar Series, last modified July 26, 1999, https://web.stanford.edu/class/e297c/war_peace/media/hpsych.html. This pattern implies a value of 0.0 for the "combatant/civilian intermingling" subscore for distinguishability. As the VC lacked heavy weapons, no value can be computed for "reliance on heavy weapons." Across the two codable subscores, "distinguishability" overall thus contributes a total of 0.08 points to the index score for the VC.

70. Stathis Kalyvas and Matthew Kocher, "The Dynamics of Violence in Vietnam: An Analysis of the Hamlet Evaluation System (HES)," *Journal of Peace Research* 46, no. 3 (May 2009): 335–55 at 344.

71. This pattern implies a value of 0.0 on the (0, 1) scale for "articulated theater" in the coding system presented in the appendix.

72. The Battle of Khe Sanh lasted 77 days: Conor Friedersdorf, "The Battle of Khe Sanh and Its Retellings," *Atlantic*, January 27, 2018, https://www.theatlantic.com/politics/archive/2018/01/the-battle-of-khe-sanh-and-its-retellings/551315/. The Battle of Hue lasted 26 days: Pike, *Viet-Cong Strategy of Terror*, 23; "Tet Offensive," History.com, October 19, 2018, https://www.history.com/topics/vietnam-war/tet-offensive#section_4. The Battle of Kontum lasted 14 days: Thomas McKenna, *Kontum: The Battle to Save South Vietnam* (Lexington: University Press of Kentucky Press, 2011). The battle in Saigon lasted 22 days: Anthony Tucker-Jones, *The Vietnam War: The Tet Offensive 1968* (South Yorkshire, UK: Pen and Sword Books, 2014), 124–28.

73. James H. Willbanks, *The Tet Offensive: A Concise History* (New York: Columbia University Press, 2007), 20, 32; Erik Villard, *Staying the Course: October 1967 to September 1968* (Washington, DC: US Army Center of Military History, 2017), 507–8.

74. Peter Brush, "The Battle of Khe Sanh, 1968," in Marc Jason Gilbert and William Head, ed., *The Tet Offensive* (Westport, CT: Praeger, 1996), 191–213; Villard, *Staying the Course*, 387–431, 506–19, 561–96.

75. James H. Willbanks, "Tet 1968: The Turning Point," Foreign Policy Research Institute, May 15, 2012, https://www.fpri.org/article/2012/05/tet-1968-the-turning-point/; Erik Villard, *The 1986 Tet Offensive Battles of Quang Tri City and Hue* (Washington, DC: US Army Center of Military History, 2008), 82.

76. Willbanks, *Tet Offensive*, 81; Villard, *Staying the Course*, 673–80.

77. Dale Andrade, *America's Last Vietnam Battle: Halting Hanoi's 1972 Easter Offensive* (Lawrence: University Press of Kansas, 2001), 5–28.

78. Wilkins, *Grab Their Belts*, 27; Lanning and Cragg, *Inside the VC and the NVA*, 216–17.

79. Tanham, *Communist Revolutionary Warfare*, 86; Lanning and Cragg, *Inside the VC and the NVA*, 214–15; Albright, "Convoy Ambush on Highway 1," 57.

80. Tanham, *Communist Revolutionary Warfare*, 90; Wilkins, *Grab Their Belts*, 23, 24; Anderson, Arnsten, and Averich, *Insurgent Organization and Operations*, xii; Eric Bergerud, *The Dynamics of Defeat: The Vietnam War in Hau Nghia Province* (Boulder CO: Westview, 1991), 96; Rottman, *Viet Cong and NVA Tunnels and Fortifications of the Vietnam War*, 14.

81. See, e.g., Glenn Williams, *Operation ATTLEBORO, 3 to 24 November 1966* (Washington, DC: US Army Center of Military History, 2015), https://history.army.mil/news/2015/151200a_opAttleboro.html.

82. Bernard William Rogers, *Cedar Falls–Junction City: A Turning Point* (Washington, DC: US Army Center of Military History, 1989), 98–99.

83. The SNA score a value of 1.2 before, and 2.5 after Admiral Howe's escalation of the war's stakes. The VC value of 0.2 corresponds to a coding of (0, 0, na, 0, 0, 0.16, 0, 0, 0.23, na, 0). The functional form in the appendix predicts a higher but still mostly Fabian optimum value of 1.45 for a nonstate actor fighting under the VC's circumstances, as implied by equation [A2] for values of $f = 0.25$, $i = 3$, $s = 1$, and $t = 1965$, per the discussion above.

Chapter Ten: Conclusion and Implications

1. For a more exhaustive consideration of possible combinations of material and political variable values, see the comparative statics in the appendix.

2. Note that table 10.1 uses natural-language categorical approximations of actors' location on the Fabian-Napoleonic continuum, per the simplified summary in table 4.1. For the exact, real-valued predicted and observed values, see the discussion in the case studies above. For orthodox materialist and tribal culture views that presuppose a "guerilla-conventional" dichotomy and for which no guidance exists in the literature for relative placement on a continuous spectrum, table entries of "Fabian" and "midspectrum" correspond intuitively to values of ($\phi < 2$) and ($\phi > 2$), respectively, in the new theory's terms. To enable compact presentation, table 10.1 omits the "hybrid" materialist subschool; per the discussion in chaps. 4 through 9, hybrid materialism would predict midspectrum, not Fabian, methods for Hezbollah, the JAM, the SNA, the ZNG, and the SVK, given each actor's access to modern antitank weaponry (if arguably less so for the JAM given the short range of its chief modern antiarmor capability in its Iranian-supplied EFPs) but Fabian methods for the VC given their less modern technology.

These overall predictions fit the Hezbollah, ZNG, and VC cases but not the JAM, SNA, or SVK cases. And in no case does detailed observation of nonstate methods support the hybrid expectation: none of these actors employed archetypically "irregular" methods with modern weapons—each displayed an interpenetrated admixture of Fabian and Napoleonic characteristics albeit in varying proportion.

3. The theory in chaps. 3 and 4 is domain restricted to nonstate actors. The depictions of *state* behavior in figs. 10.1 and 10.2 thus represent assumptions rather than theoretical findings and are presented here for the purpose of setting in context the policy implications of the nonstate findings developed above. These assumptions for state behavior are consistent with the military incentives presented in chap. 3, and they are consistent with the analysis of optimal state military behavior under changing technology presented in my earlier book *Military Power* (see, e.g., 232–35). But the analysis above is not sufficient to sustain rigorous findings on the way states will respond to the military incentives they face. Instead, figs. 10.1 and 10.2 assume that states, like nonstate actors, will vary in their ability to respond to military incentives as a function of some kind of variation in their internal makeup; a plausible hypothesis for further research would hold that states respond in the same way nonstate actors do, and that institutions and stakes have the same effect on states that they have on nonstate actors. Below I argue that this is a promising hypothesis for further research. To establish that hypothesis, however, is beyond my scope in this book, and the depictions of state behavior here thus represent plausible assumptions rather than analytical findings.

4. The importance of nonmaterial factors in interstate warfare is a central finding of S. Biddle, *Military Power*.

5. On the importance of unit-level traits for state military behavior, see S. Biddle, *Military Power*, 48–51. Note that the claim for state military behavior here represents a plausible assumption rather than an analytical finding for a theory whose domain restricts it to nonstate choices.

6. On the Saddam Fedayeen in 2003, see, e.g., S. Biddle, "Speed Kills"; Sharon Otterman, "Iraq: What Is the Fedayeen Saddam?," Council on Foreign Relations, February 3, 2005, accessed October 4, 2018, https://www.cfr.org/backgrounder/iraq-what-fedayeen-saddam; Hosmer, *Why the Iraqi Resistance to the Coalition Invasion Was So Weak*. On Hezbollah in 2006, see chap. 5 above.

7. Jessica Stanton, "Regulating Militias: Governments, Militias, and Civilian Targeting in Civil War," *Journal of Conflict Resolution* 59, no. 5 (2015): 899–923 at 899. In Ukraine, Russia has also deployed state combatants who wore no national insignia and served in nominal militias ostensibly outside state command—in fact, this case has been influential in an emerging redefinition of the concept of "hybrid warfare" to include nominally covert state use of irregulars to destabilize neighbors: see, e.g., David L. Raugh, "Is the Hybrid Threat a True Threat?," *Journal of Strategic Security* 9, no. 2 (Summer 2016): 1–13; Hall Gardner, "Hybrid Warfare: Iranian and Russian Versions of 'Little Green Men' and Contemporary Conflict," *NATO Defense College*, no. 123 (December 2015): 1–16; Tad A. Schnaufer II, "Redefining Hybrid Warfare: Russia's Nonlinear War against the West," *Journal of Strategic Security* 10, no. 1 (Spring 2017): 17–31; Tony Balasevicius, "Looking for Little Green Men: Understanding Russia's Employment of Hybrid Warfare," *Canadian Military Journal* 17, no. 3 (Summer 2017): 17–28. In many ways, however, this case is less novel than, for example, Saddam's use of the Fedayeen in 2003. The Russian "little green men" in Ukraine are clearly well-trained, well-equipped, heavily armed conventional

soldiers in all respects except the absence of national insignia on their camouflaged military uniforms.

8. For state actors, the military incentive for this shift as technology grows more lethal is a major finding of my earlier book *Military Power* (see, e.g., 232–35).

9. See, e.g., Murray and Knox, "Thinking about Revolutions in Warfare"; Deptula, *Effects-Based Operations*; Cebrowski and Garstka, "Network-Centric Warfare"; E. Cohen, "Revolution in Warfare"; Krepinevich, "Cavalry to Computer"; Arquilla, "'Velvet' Revolution in Military Affairs"; N. Davis, "Information-Based Revolution in Military Affairs"; Richard A. Bitzinger, "The Revolution in Military Affairs and the Global Defense Industry: Reactions and Interactions" *Security Challenges* 4, no. 4 (Summer 2008): 1–12; Blank, "Prepping for the Next War."

10. See, e.g., R. Smith, *Utility of Force*; Ucko, *New Counterinsurgency Era*; Vick, Grissom, Rosenau, Grill, and Muller, "Grand Strategy and Counterinsurgency"; Hosmer, *Army's Role in Counterinsurgency and Insurgency*; S. Metz, "Learning from Iraq"; S. Metz and Millen, "Insurgency and Counterinsurgency in the 21st Century."

11. On the latter, in particular, see, e.g., Manatea, "Reflections on the 'Counterinsurgency Decade': *Small Wars Journal* Interview with General David H. Petraeus"; Ucko, "Critics Gone Wild"; R. Evans, "COIN Is Dead, Long Live the COIN"; C. Burke, "Like It or Not"; Andrew Exum, "Amid COIN Debate, U.S. Army Struggles to Find Its Way; Jon R. Lindsay, "Reinventing the Revolution: Technological Visions, Counterinsurgent Criticism, and the Rise of Special Operations," *Journal of Strategic Studies* 36, no. 3 (2013): 422–53; Chris Meserole, "Wars of None: AI, Big Data, and the Future of Insurgency," *Brookings*, July 2, 2018, https://www.brookings.edu/blog/order-from-chaos/2018/07/02/wars-of-none-ai-big-data-and-the-future-of-insurgency/; Judah Grunstein, "COIN, RMA and the Myth of Antiseptic War," *World Politics Review*, April 23, 2010, https://www.worldpoliticsreview.com/trend-lines/5454/coin-rma-and-the-myth-of-antiseptic-war.

12. International Institute for Strategic Studies, *Military Balance, 2001–2002*, 61.

13. "Active Duty Military Strength by Service: Historical Reports," FY 2001, Personnel, Workforce Reports and Publications, Department of Defense, https://www.dmdc.osd.mil/appj/dwp/dwp_reports.jsp. Figures include total enlisted and cadets-midshipmen.

14. International Institute for Strategic Studies, *Military Balance, 2001–2002*, 61; Adam Talaber, *The U.S. Military's Force Structure: A Primer* (Washington, DC: US Congressional Budget Office, 2016), 2, https://www.cbo.gov/sites/default/files/114th-congress-2015-2016/reports/51535-fsprimer.pdf; "Active Duty Military Strength by Service: Historical Reports," FYs 2001 and 2011. Figures include total enlisted and cadets-midshipmen.

15. As the author observed on foot patrols in New Baghdad in March 2007 with soldiers of a US Army artillery battalion that had been retasked to serve, essentially, as dismounted infantry. In Iraq, such units were sometimes referred to as "infantillery."

16. Alex Rogers, "The MRAP: Brilliant Buy, or Billions Wasted?," *Time*, October 2, 2012, http://nation.time.com/2012/10/02/the-mrap-brilliant-buy-or-billions-wasted/.

17. Richard W. Rubright, "Technology and Counterinsurgency Strategy," in *The Role and Limitations of Technology in U.S. Counterinsurgency Warfare* (Lincoln: University of Nebraska Press, 2005), 133–72; Mark F. Cancian, "Military Force Structure: Trade-Offs, Trade-Offs, Trade-Offs," Center for Strategic and International Studies, February 26, 2018, https://www.csis.org/analysis/military-force-structure-trade-offs-trade-offs-trade-offs; Jeremiah Gertler, "U.S. Air

Force Bomber Sustainment and Modernization: Background and Issues," Congressional Research Service, June 4, 2014, https://fas.org/sgp/crs/weapons/R 43049.pdf; "Army Equipment Modernization Strategy," *Department of the Army*, March 27, 2015, http://www.g8.army.mil/pdf/aems_31mar15.pdf.

18. See, e.g., Ben Watson, "USAF, a Bit Rusty in Defended Airspace," *Defense One*, September 10, 2015, http://www.defenseone.com/news/2015/09/the-d-brief-september-10-2015/120656/?oref=d-river; MacFarland, Shields, and Snow, "King and I"; Maj. Julian T. Urquidez, "The King Is Dead: The Current State of the Field Artillery, Core Competency Atrophy, and the Way Ahead" (MA thesis, USMC Staff College, 2011), http://www.dtic.mil/dtic/tr/fulltext/u2/a601899.pdf; Gian P. Gentile, "Misreading the Surge Threatens U.S. Army's Conventional Capabilities," *World Politics Review*, March 4, 2008, https://www.worldpoliticsreview.com/articles/1715/misreading-the-surge-threatens-u-s-armys-conventional-capabilities; Maj. Robert C. Piddock, "The Need for Conventional Warfare as the U.S. Military Addresses the Environment and Threats of the 21st Century" (MA thesis, USMC Staff College, 2009), http://www.dtic.mil/dtic/tr/fulltext/u2/a509847.pdf.

19. See, e.g., Russell, *Innovation, Transformation, and War*; Dale Andrade, *Surging South of Baghdad: The 3d Infantry Division and Task Force Marne in Iraq, 2007–2008* (Washington, DC: US Army Center of Military History, 2010); Ucko, *New Counterinsurgency Era*; O'Hanlon, *Future of Land Warfare*, 141–43; Jon Lindsay and Roger Peterson, "Varieties of Insurgency and Counterinsurgency in Iraq, 2003–2009" (2012), *CIWAG Case Studies*, https://digital-commons.usnwc.edu/ciwag-case-studies/10; David Petraeus, "How We Won in Iraq," *Foreign Policy*, October 29, 2013, https://foreignpolicy.com/2013/10/29/how-we-won-in-iraq/; Rajiv Chandrasekaran, "The Afghan Surge Is Over," *Foreign Policy*, September 25, 2012, https://foreignpolicy.com/2012/09/25/the-afghan-surge-is-over/. Note that this does not imply that the improvements in US COIN capability after 2006 were necessarily enough to win either the Iraq or the Afghanistan war. War outcomes are a function of much more than just military capability at the tactical and operational levels, and the Iraq outcome as of 2011 was ambiguous, with results falling short of the Bush administration's original aims but offering more return to US interests than withdrawal and defeat would have done. Here, I argue only that US military capability to wage tactical- and operational-level COIN had improved substantially between 2006 and 2008. On US methods and outcomes in Iraq, see, e.g., S. Biddle, Friedman, and Shapiro, "Testing the Surge"; James R. Crider, "A View from Inside the Surge," *Military Review* 89, no. 2 (March/April 2009): 81–88; Daniel R. Green, "The Fallujah Awakening: A Case Study in Counter Insurgency," *Small Wars and Insurgencies* 21, no. 4 (December 2010): 591–609. On US methods and outcomes in Afghanistan, see, e.g., Stephen Biddle, "Afghanistan's Legacy: Emerging Lessons of an Ongoing War," *Washington Quarterly* 37, no. 2 (Summer 2014): 73–86; Jerry Meyerle, Megan Katt, and Jim Gavrilis, *On the Ground in Afghanistan: Counterinsurgency in Practice* (Quantico, VA: Marine Corps University Press, 2012); Seth G. Jones, "U.S. Strategy in Afghanistan," Testimony before the House Foreign Affairs Committee, Subcommittee on Middle East and South Asia, US House of Representatives, First Session, 111th Congress, April 2, 2009. On the status of Iraq relative to US interests and war aims, see Stephen Biddle, Michael O'Hanlon, and Kenneth Pollack, "How to Leave a Stable Iraq: Building on Progress," *Foreign Affairs* 87, no. 5 (September/October 2008): 40–58; also Stephen Biddle, "Afghanistan, Iraq, and U.S. Strategy in 2009," Testimony before the Committee on Armed Services, US House of

Representatives, First Session, 111th Congress, February 12, 2009. On the status of the Afghan counterinsurgency campaign as of 2012, see Stephen Biddle, "Ending the War in Afghanistan: How to Avoid Failure on the Installment Plan," *Foreign Affairs*, September/October 2013, 49–58.

20. This is a central finding of S. Biddle, *Military Power*.

21. See, e.g., Ucko, *New Counterinsurgency Era*; Mockaitis, *COIN Conundrum*; Thomas Braun, "Beyond Counterinsurgency: Why the Concept Is Failing," *Connections* 11, no. 3 (Summer 2012): 77–84.

22. Winograd et al., *Final Report*, 212–13; Shelah and Limor, *Captives in Lebanon*, 395–36; Harel and Issacharoff, *34 Days*, 221–24; Exum, *Hizballah at War*, 11.

23. For an argument that improving standoff precision strike technology may actually imply shifting resources away from precision strike and toward close-combat ground forces, see Stephen Biddle, "Future War Up Close: Enemy Can Limit Value of Deep Strike," *Defense News*, October 8–14, 2001, 11.

24. See, e.g., Mansoor, *Baghdad at Sunrise*; David Zucchino, *Thunder Run: The Armored Strike to Capture Baghdad* (New York: Grove, 2004); Jason Conroy, *Heavy Metal: A Tank Company's Battle to Baghdad* (Washington, DC: Potomac Books, 2006); S. Biddle, "Speed Kills," 13.

25. On the "Objective Force," see Eric Shinseki, "Interview: General Eric K. Shinseki," *Frontline*, PBS, https://www.pbs.org/wgbh/pages/frontline/shows/future/interviews/shinseki .html; Bruce R. Nardulli and Thomas L. McNaugher, "The Army: Toward the Objective Force," in Hans Binnendijk, ed., *Transforming America's Military* (Washington, DC: National Defense University Press, 2002), 101–28; Jason A. Pardee, "The Genesis of Transformation: The Rise of the United States Army's Modular Brigade Combat Teams" (MA thesis, Naval Postgraduate School, March 2013), https://apps.dtic.mil/dtic/tr/fulltext/u2/a579873.pdf.

26. As such, it approximates what a game theorist would call a maximin strategy for coping with an uncertain future. (A true maximin option would trade even more midspectrum capability in exchange for greater capability against highly Fabian opponents. In effect, this would yield uniform mediocrity against all possible opponents instead of strength against some with weakness against others. The recommendation here is thus not a strict global maximin choice—it is only maximin relative to the other options presented.)

27. See, e.g., Dan Reiter and Allan C. Stam, *Democracies at War* (Princeton, NJ: Princeton University Press, 2010); Talmadge, *Dictator's Army*; Pilster and Bohmelt, "Coup-Proofing and Military Effectiveness in Interstate Wars," 333–37; Risa Brooks, *Shaping Strategy* (Princeton, NJ: Princeton University Press, 2008).

28. See, e.g., Patricia Sullivan, *Who Wins? Predicting Strategic Success and Failure in Armed Conflict* (New York: Oxford University Press, 2012); Jennifer Kavanaugh et al., *Characteristics of Successful U.S. Military Interventions* (Santa Monica, CA: RAND, 2019); Suzanne Werner, "Negotiating the Terms of Settlement: War Aims and Bargaining Leverage," *Journal of Conflict Resolution* 42, no. 3 (1998): 321–43.

29. For reviews, see, e.g., Kalyvas and Kenny, "Civil Wars"; B. Walter, "New New Civil Wars"; Sambanis, "Terrorism and Civil War"; Jentzsch, Kalyvas, and Schubiger, "Militias in Civil Wars."

30. See, e.g., B. Walter, "New New Civil Wars," 481; Weinstein, *Inside Rebellion*; Kalyvas, *Logic of Violence in Civil War*; Dara Cohen, "Explaining Rape during Civil War: Cross-National Evidence (1980–2009)," *American Political Science Review* 107, no. 3 (August 2013): 461–77;

E. Wood, "Variation in Sexual Violence during War"; Valentino, Huth, and Balch-Lindsay, "'Draining the Sea'"; Carlo Koos, "Sexual Violence in Armed Conflicts: Research Progress and Remaining Gaps," *Third World Quarterly* 38, no. 9 (May 2017): 1935–51; Peter W. Singer, *Children at War* (New York: Pantheon, 2005); David Rosen, *Armies of the Young: Child Soldiers in War and Terrorism* (New Brunswick, NJ: Rutgers University Press, 2005).

31. See, e.g., Kalyvas and Balcells, "International System and Technologies of Rebellion"; Balcells, *Rivalry and Revenge*; Lockyer, "Dynamics of Warfare in Civil War."

32. Headquarters, Department of the Army, *FM 3–24: Counterinsurgency* (Washington, DC: US Government Printing Office, 2006), pages 1–26 to 1–28.

33. See, e.g., Alexander Downes, *Targeting Civilians in War* (Ithaca, NY: Cornell University Press, 2008); P. Singer, *Children at War*; D. Rosen, *Armies of the Young*; Steven P. Remy, *The Malmedy Massacre: The War Crimes Trial Controversy* (Cambridge, MA: Harvard University Press, 2017); Hannes Heer, Walter Manoschek, Alexander Pollak, and Ruth Wodak, *The Discursive Construction of History: Remembering the Wehrmacht's War of Annihilation* (New York: Palgrave Macmillan, 2008), 72–78, 94–95; David Raub Snyder, *Sex Crimes under the Wehrmacht* (Lincoln: University of Nebraska Press, 2007); Alfred M. de Zayas, *The Wehrmacht War Crimes Bureau* (Lincoln: University of Nebraska Press, 1989).

34. See, e.g., Louis Kriesberg, "The Evolution of Conflict Resolution," in Jacob Bercovitch, Victor Kremenyuk, and I. William Zartman, eds., *The Sage Handbook of Conflict Resolution* (Thousand Oaks, CA: Sage, 2009), 15–32.

Appendix

1. While the theory explains nonstate actors' behavior partly in light of the expected behavior of state actors, it is not a complete theory of state behavior—the theory identifies marginal incentives for states in conflict with nonstate rivals, but it is insufficient to account for all important effects on state military choices, especially in warfare against other states.

2. While the theoretical discussion in chaps. 3 and 4 above periodically uses the contrast between post-1900 warfare and pre-1900 warfare to clarify actors' incentives, the theory is not meant to be a dispositive explanation of state or nonstate behavior in the 19th century.

3. S. Biddle, *Military Power*, 72–73.

4. Cf., e.g., Israeli Ministry of Foreign Affairs, "The Second Lebanon War (2006)," July 12, 2006, https://mfa.gov.il/MFA/ForeignPolicy/Terrorism/Hizbullah/Pages/Hizbullah%20attack%20in%20northern%20Israel%20and%20Israels%20response%2012-Jul-2006.aspx; Catherine Bloom, "The Classification of Hezbollah in Both International and Non-international Armed Conflicts," *Annual Survey of International and Comparative Law* 14, no. 1 (2008), http://digitalcommons.law.ggu.edu/annlsurvey/vol14/iss1/5; Kober, "Israel Defense Forces in the Second Lebanon War"; F. Hoffman, *Conflict in the 21st Century*, 35–42.

5. Note that not every individual observation is accorded literally equal weight below. Each of the six primary dimensions of nonstate behavior receives equal weight, but some of the six are coded by reference to more than one observable referent; where this is so, these subdimensions each receive subunity weights to enable the primary dimension to retain a (0, 1) range when all the components are scored. And in one instance, combatant/civilian intermingling, a heavier weight is assigned to this subcomponent for reasons noted below. Each of the six primary dimensions, however, receives equal weight in the overall index.

6. On latent variables models, see, e.g., Christopher J. Fariss, "The Changing Standard of Accountability and the Positive Relationship between Human Rights Treaty Ratification and Compliance," *British Journal of Political Science* 48, no. 1 (January 2018): 239–71. On considerations in the construction of index measures more broadly, see, e.g., Michela Nardo et al., *Handbook on Constructing Composite Indicators: Methodology and User Guide* (OECD, 2008). (The author is indebted to Yonatan Lupu for his insights on latent variable approaches.) Note that table A.1 provides weights for its component subscores; this reflects the use of multiple observable indicators for some behavioral traits. "Holding ground," for example, is coded by reference to four contributing subcomponents; to avoid allowing "holding ground" to receive disproportionate influence on the overall coding, each of the four receives a weight of 0.25. By contrast, "stealth" is coded by one observation type, whose weight is thus 1.0. (The only exception concerns "distinguishability from civilian noncombatants," where physical intermingling is especially important relative to distinguishing markings or reliance on heavy weapons; it thus receives a heaver weighting of 0.5, and the other two receive weights of 0.25.)

7. "Covered" forces are those with impenetrable obstacles between them and likely sources of enemy fire. "Concealed" forces are those with opaque obstacles between them and likely sources of enemy observation.

8. Note that the same firefight, with the same duration, can thus be coded differently for the two sides in the engagement—depending on their respective freedom to persist or break contact. For example, a 30-minute engagement in which a government force assaults an insurgent detachment that fires briefly and then melts away would be coded as Fabian for the insurgent defenders, but as ambiguous for the government attackers, who were not able to choose to continue the firefight after their opponents departed.

9. The one-hour criterion thus excludes brief sallies; reconnaissance patrols that approach hostile positions, draw fire, then withdraw; and surprise ambushes that allow the enemy to reach close range but then break contact immediately after firing. For cases where this subcategory is dropped, the score for "holding ground" is computed as the arithmetic mean of the other three subscores (i.e., "duration of firefights," "incidence of counterattack," and "incidence of harassing fires, unattended minefields").

10. Note that such coding is possible only for tactical defenders.

11. Where "proximity of attackers to defenders" cannot be scored, the "holding ground" subscore is computed as the arithmetic mean of the other three values.

12. Note that the theaterwide density of forces is a material variable, but the local density, and thus the ratio of local to theaterwide density, are behavioral choices in how the available forces will be used and distributed.

13. Chandler, *Campaigns of Napoleon*, 1118.

14. S. Biddle, *Military Power*, 114–20, and assuming an area of 11,500 square kilometers for Normandy.

15. See, e.g., Harry W. Pfanz, *Gettysburg: The First Day* (Chapel Hill: University of North Carolina Press, 2010), 294–330; Antony Beevor, *The Fall of Berlin, 1945* (New York: Viking, 2002), 310–27.

16. As noted in chap. 2, Fabius Maximus's Roman soldiers fought in distinctive Roman equipment; in this sense, modern "Fabian" practice is more distinct from its "conventional" alternative than was its namesake's. Note also that this is not a material distinction in any meaningful sense—it is a free behavioral choice for almost all combatants. All have access to civilian

clothing, and in practical terms almost all actual and potential combatants have access to clothing with distinguishing marks that could differentiate themselves from noncombatant civilians. Arm bands of colored cloth, for example, have been used to identify fighters and are available in any modern society; military-style fatigues have long been widely available in almost all societies. In Bonaparte's day, elaborate, colorful military regalia was used to maximize the distinction between soldiers and civilians and to create unit solidarity among the former—bearskin hats, shakos, epaulettes, and ceremonial sidearms were equipment not widely available to civilian would-be guerillas. But once modern firepower made such plumage dangerous and armies overwhelmingly adopted earth-toned uniforms designed for camouflage rather than display, the distinction between military and civilian clothing became more muted, and military-style clothing became readily available to most. Even here, the theory's dependent variable is thus operationalized in terms of observed behavior, not equipment or materiel.

17. Note that actors who lack access to heavy weapons and equipment thus cannot be scored. Where this is the case, I do not code a value for this dimension of the dependent variable.

18. Where "reliance on heavy weapons and equipment" cannot be scored, the "intermingling" subscore is reweighted to 0.67, and the "distinguishing markings" subscore is reweighted to 0.33.

19. Note that this distinction predates the modern nomenclature of "covering force zones," "main battle areas," "communication zones," and so forth. Even in Bonaparte's day, forward cavalry screens and picket lines were routinely used to perform the distinctive functions of a modern "covering force," and there were clear distinctions between rear-area depots and forward positions in the presence of the enemy: see, e.g., Chandler, *Campaigns of Napoleon*, e.g., 60, 148.

20. S. Biddle, *Military Power*, 252n52.

21. S. Biddle, *Military Power*, 25.

INDEX

Note: Page numbers followed by *f*, *m*, or *t* refer to figures, maps, and tables, respectively.

Aideed, Mohamed Farah, 3, 17–18, 182, 183, 185–88, 190, 193, 195–200, 204–7, 211–17, 220–22, 397n52

air attack, 56, 57*f*, 58*f*

AK-47 assault rifles, 56, 58, 71, 121, 156, 218

Ali Mahdi Mohammed, 185, 190, 193, 199

Allies (World War II), 32

Amal, 114–15, 119–21

ambush: Hezbollah and, 130; JAM and, 173; SNA and, 202–3; Vietcong and, 278–79, 287; as warfare tactic, 29, 77

Amiens, Battle of (1918), 53, 61

Angolan civil war, 102

antiaircraft weapons, 53, 59, 217–18

antitank weapons: comparison of, 401n129; cost of, 402n130; effectiveness of, 53, 56, 58*f*, 359n40; of Hezbollah, 131, 142, 401n129; of JAM, 156; nonstate actors' use of, 59; of SNA, 192–93, 222, 401n129

AQI. *See* Al Qaeda in Iraq

Arab–Israeli War (1973), 61

al-Araji, Hazem and Bahaa, 167

Argentina, 102

Armenian rebels, 59

Army of the Republic of Vietnam (ARVN), 265, 270–71, 279, 283, 285–89

artillery: in combined-arms fighting, 78–79; lethality-survivability trade-off for, 52, 54; range and lethality of, 56, 57*f*

ARVN. *See* Army of the Republic of Vietnam

assassination, 77, 122

asymmetrical warfare, 33–35, 352n43

Atto, Osman, 199–200

Austerlitz, Battle of (1805), 64–65

Ba'ath Party, 148–49, 153–54

Babic, Milan, 235, 243

Baghdad, Iraq, map of, 151*m*

Bao Dai, 264, 272

Baric, Lorraine, 230

Barre, Siad, 18, 183, 185, 188–89, 192–93

basic natural order, 95–96, 97, 237, 240, 241, 261–62

Bassiouni, M. Cherif, 238

Battle of Mogadishu (1993), 194, 198, 202–4, 207, 210–11, 213–16, 218–19, 223

Berri, Nabih, 114

Biafran rebels, 59

Bible, 348n6

Biddle, Stephen, *Military Power*, 43–44

Bin Laden, Osama, 158

Blackhawk Down (film), 182

Bobetko, Janko, 239

Bokan, Dragoslav "Arkan," 244

Bonaparte, Napoleon, 29, 37, 64–65, 354n55, 363n3. *See also* Napoleonic methods

booby-traps, 281

Bosnia, 225, 227, 228

Boutros-Ghali, Boutros, 186
Bowden, Mark, 214–15, 218
Britain, 102
British Special Air Service, 35
Brown, Vahid, 191
brute force vs. coercion: Hezbollah and, 134–38; HV and, 251; JAM and, 174–75; SNA and, 212–14; SVK and, 251; Vietcong and, 282–83; as warfare strategies, 31–33; ZNG and, 251
Buric, Olivera, 230
Bush, George W., 308

Cassino, Battle of (1944), 62
Chechens, 3
Chiang Kai-shek, 101
China, 101
Chinese People's Liberation Army, 50
civilians: as combatants, 192, 211, 214; conventional forces' intermingling with, 41, 42; cooperation or control of, as goal of warfare, 31, 54; in Croatian Wars of Independence, 252–53; fatalities among, 28, 223, 283, 284; guerillas' intermingling with, xv, 2, 4, 9, 12, 27, 35–37, 53; Hezbollah and, 138–39; JAM and, 175–76; nonstate actors' goal of cooperation or control of, 24–26; as shields from fire, 138–39; SNA and, 192, 211, 214–15, 223; state-nonstate competition for allegiance of, 67; SVK and, 252; Vietcong and, 276, 283–84; ZNG and, 252
civil warfare: interstate compared to, xv–xvi, 2, 10, 311–12; military methods in, xv–xvi; scholarship on, 2–5, 10, 311–12
Clausewitz, Carl von, 23, 24, 26, 33, 363n3, 387n45
Clinton, Bill, 187
coercion. See brute force vs. coercion
COIN. See counterinsurgency
collective action: institutional strength and, 89–92, 96–97, 180; JAM and, 180; warfare tactics and, 83–89, 365n21
combined arms: collective action problems linked to, 83–84; Hezbollah and, 128;

JAM and, 178–79; in midspectrum methods, 78–79; SNA and, 219; SVK and, 255–56; ZNG and, 257
concealment. See stealth and concealment; survivability
conventional warfare: features of, 26–39; guerilla/irregular compared to, 6–7, 22–23, 26–39, 43; intermingling with civilians in, 41, 42; nonstate actors' use of, 3, 23, 26; stealth and concealment in, 27–28, 63–65. See also Napoleonic methods; state military methods; warfare spectrum
counterattacks: Hezbollah and, 131–32; JAM and, 171–72; SNA and, 204–8; SVK and, 249; Vietcong and, 280; ZNG and, 249
counterfire, 61–62
counterinsurgency (COIN), 1, 4, 301–6, 311
cover. See stealth and concealment
critical cases, in theory testing, 17, 108, 182
Croatia, map of, 228m
Croatian Army (HV): materiel available to, 232–33; military methods of, 245–62; and MPRI, 227, 237, 240–42, 257; numerical strength of, 233; overview of, 225–29; proficiency of execution by, 254, 257–58; theories applied to case study of, 257; ZNG's transformation into, 224. See also Croatian National Guard
Croatian Democratic Union (HDZ), 225–26, 232, 234, 237–39
Croatian National Guard (ZNG): formation of, 226; institutions of, 239; materiel available to, 50, 231–33; military methods of, 3, 19–20, 245–62; numerical strength of, 232; overview of, 19, 225–29; proficiency of execution by, 254, 256–57; stakes of war for, 19, 233; technology available to, 51, 59; theories applied to case study of, 257; transformation into Croatian Army (HV), 224. See also Croatian Army
Croatian Serbs. See Krajina Serb Army
Croatian Wars of Independence, 19, 224–62
Cunningham, David E., 339n9

al-Darraji, Abd al-Hadi, 166

David, William, 207

Dayton Accords (1995), 224

decisive engagement: defined, 174, 349n18;
Fabian/guerilla acceptance of, 29,
350n23; Fabian/guerilla avoidance of, 12,
28–29, 36–37, 66, 97, 128, 201, 292; Hezbollah and, 128–33, 137; JAM and, 169–75;
Napoleonic/conventional avoidance of,
29, 42–43; Napoleonic/conventional use
of, 12, 203; reasons for avoiding, 72, 97;
SNA and, 182; Vietcong and, 278, 285,
288; ZNG and, 247–48. See also holding
ground

Defense of the Holy Shrines Brigade, 167

delaying actions, 28

Delta Force, 182, 186, 197

Dew, Andrea, 14

Dhi Qar Organization, 167

Diem, Ngo Dihn, 264–65, 273

dispersion: Hezbollah and, 133–34; JAM
and, 173–74; SNA and, 211–12; states'
use of, 64–65; Vietcong and, 281–82; as
warfare tactic, 29–31; ZNG and, 250–51.
See also force-to-space ratio; troop densities

Duan, Le, 282–83

Durant, Michael, 216, 218

duration of firefights: Hezbollah and, 128–
29; HV and, 248; JAM and, 169–70; SNA
and, 201–3; SVK and, 247–48; Vietcong
and, 278–80; ZNG and, 247–48

earth. See terrain

East Africa, 25

Eckstein, Harry, 108, 182

EFPs. See Explosively Formed Projectiles

elites, institutional status/role of, 91, 94–96

empty battlefield, 27

Erdut agreement, 229

Eritrean Liberation Front (ELF), 95

Ethiopia, 95, 183, 193

ethnic cleansing, 25

ethnicity, compared to tribal culture, 231,
402n5

existential threats: defined, 99–100; as extreme stake of war, 101; to Hezbollah, 17,
109, 121–22, 122; to Iraq, 154; responses to,
13, 74–75, 89, 102–3, 105–6; in sectarian
conflicts, 387n45; to SNA, 18, 196, 197–98,
206, 221; to SVK, 19, 234; to Vietcong, 20;
in World War II, 101

Explosively Formed Projectiles (EFPs),
156–57, 178–80

extermination campaigns, 25, 348n6

external support: for Hezbollah, 17, 117, 122,
145; for JAM, 157, 166; for nonstate actors,
357n8, 410n4; from private military
organizations, 224

Fabian methods: advantages and disadvantages of, 36–37, 41–42, 66–68; defined, 7,
12, 36; features of, 77–78; JAM and, 180–81;
lethality-survivability trade-off in, 51–55;
overview of, 36–37; reasons for choosing,
8; SVK and, 260; technology's influence
on, 63–73; theoretical predictions about
use of, 103–6, 105t; Vietcong and, 290.
See also guerilla warfare; warfare spectrum

Fabius Maximus, 36, 353n54

factionalism: as institutional threat, 91–93;
JAM and, 163; SNA and, 199

Falklands War (1982), 102

Farrah, Hussein Mohamed, 188, 199

al-Fartousi, Ahmed, 166

Fedayeen militia, 3

fire and movement, 79–81, 85–86

firefights. See duration of firefights

firepower. See lethality

FNLA rebels, 118

force structure, implications of military
methods for, 301–10

force-to-space ratio: in Croatian Wars of Independence, 232, 233, 250–51; defined, 65;
of nonstate actors, 68–71, 69f; of SNA,
211, 221; of states, 65, 66f, 70–71, 134; of
Vietcong, 270. See also dispersion; troop
densities

Fort Irwin, California, 82

fourth-generation warfare. *See* hybrid (fourth-generation) warfare
fragile natural order, 95, 97, 163, 237, 245
France, 41
fratricide, danger of, 79, 80, 86
front lines. *See* theater of war, organization of
Fuerzas Armadas Revolucionarias de Colombia (FARC), 90

Gaddafi, Muamar, 4
Germany: irregular methods used by, 42; and stakes of war, 101; strategic intent of, 32–33; in World War I, 33, 42; in World War II, 33–34, 42, 101
Giap, Vo Nguyen, 282
Griffitts, Richard, 241
guerilla warfare: combatants in, 35; conventional compared to, 6–7, 22–23, 26–39, 43; defining, 26; features of, 26–39; Hezbollah and, 144; intermingling with civilians as characteristic of, xv, 2, 4, 9, 12, 27, 35–37, 53, 138; as last-resort method, 67–68; states' use of, 3, 23, 26. *See also* Fabian methods; nonstate military methods; warfare spectrum
Gulf War (1991), 30, 32
Gulf War (2003), 30

Hadzic, Goran, 243
al-Haeri, Ayatollah Kazem, 166, 168
Hamzeh, Nizar, 114
Hannibal Barca, 36
harassing fires: Hezbollah and, 132–33; JAM and, 172–73; SNA and, 209–10; SVK and, 250; Vietcong and, 280
hatred, 25
al-Hawza (newspaper), 149
HDZ. *See* Croatian Democratic Union
Hecker, Marc, 347n5
Hezbollah (Party of God), 107–46; fundamental principles of, 119–20; hybrid methods used by, 7; institutions of, 123–26, 124f; internal politics of, 17, 109, 119–26, 180; Iran's support of, 17, 117, 122, 145;

JAM compared to, 109, 147, 159, 164, 180; leadership of, 121, 122; materiel available to, 50, 108–9, 115–19; military expenditures of, 117; military methods of, 3, 7, 17, 108, 126–46, 180; military reputation of, 120–22; numerical strength of, 116, 134; origins of, 119–20; outside support for, 117; overview of 2006 campaign, 3, 17, 110–12; political goals of, 25, 121; proficiency of execution by, 141–44; Shura Council, 123, 125–26; socio-political role/status of, 120–23; stakes of war for, 119–22; technology available to, 50–51, 59, 117; theories applied to case study of, 107–9, 144–46; and tribal culture, 17, 108–9, 112–15, 180
Higgins, William, 120
high-tech, standoff-precision forces, 9–10
Hitler, Adolf, 33, 101
Ho Chi Minh, 282
holding ground: Hezbollah and, 128–33, 137; HV and, 248–50; JAM and, 169–73; SNA and, 201–8; SVK and, 247–50; Vietcong and, 277–81; as warfare tactic, 28–29; ZNG and, 247–50. *See also* decisive engagement
honor, 25
HOS militia, 238–39, 249, 253
Howe, Jonathan, 18, 186, 195, 197–98, 204, 206, 221
Howe, Paul, 218
Huk insurgency, 69
HV. *See* Croatian Army
hybrid (fourth-generation) warfare: Hezbollah and, 17, 26, 108, 146, 392n94; SNA and, 222; SVK and, 258; theory of, 6, 8, 22, 26, 222, 343n25, 392n94, 418n7; ZNG and, 258

IA. *See* Iraqi Army
improvised explosive devices (IEDs), 156, 169, 172–73, 178
indirect fires. *See* harassing fires
infantry: in combined-arms fighting, 78–79; tanks coordinated with, 83–85

infiltration tactics, 30

informal natural order, 94–95, 97–98, 198

Inniskilling Fusiliers, 60

institutions: and collective action problems, 89–92, 96–97; in Croatian Wars of Independence, 237–45; developmental types of, 94–98, 98*t*, 365n25, 368n37, 368n42; efficacy and expertise of, 90; elites' status/role in, 91, 94–96; and factionalism, 91–93; of Hezbollah, 123–26, 124*f*; importance of, for midspectrum methods, xvi, 7–8, 13, 74–75, 89–98, 105–6, 260, 293–94; of JAM, 163–68; of JNA, 242–45; mature, 93–94, 96; of SNA, 198–200; variation in implementation of, 90–91

Iran: Iraq's invasion of (1980), 154; irregular methods used by, 3; Revolutionary Guard Quds Force, 166; support for Hezbollah, 17, 117, 122, 145; support for JAM, 157, 166

Iraq: intrastate violence in, 25; Iran invasion (1980), 154; irregular methods used by, 3; Kuwait invasion (1990), 154; leadership protections in, 367n33; maps of, 150*m*, 151*m*; non-JAM insurgents in, 158–59, 167; Sunni-Shiite conflicts in, 25, 147–52, 155, 161–63, 175–77, 387n45; tribal culture in, 153–55. *See also* Jaish al Mahdi (JAM)

Iraqi Army (IA), 151, 152, 154, 157–59

Iraqi National Police (INP), 151, 157–58

Iraq Security Forces (ISF), 159, 386n36

irregular warfare. *See* guerilla warfare

ISF. *See* Iraq Security Forces

Islamic Supreme Council of Iraq (IS, 158

Israel: Hezbollah campaign (2006), 3, 110–12, 127–41; Hezbollah's attitude toward, 119–20; materiel available to, 50, 117–18; numerical strength of, 117; technology available to, 59

Jackovich, Victor, 242

Jaish al Mahdi (JAM), 147–81; anti-Americanism of, 149, 161–63; conflicts within, 167–68; demise of, 152–53, 181;

formation of, 148–49, 160; Hezbollah compared to, 109, 147, 159, 164, 180; institutions of, 163–68; internal politics of, 17, 109, 147, 160–68, 180; Iran's support of, 157, 166; materiel available to, 155–59, 176; military methods of, 17, 168–81; military organization of, 164–65; numerical strength of, 156, 159; Office of the Martyr Sadr (OMS), 148–49, 164, 166–67, 176; overview of, 17, 148–53; proficiency of execution by, 178–79; revenue of, 157, 163–66; SNA compared to, 399n90; Special Groups, 156, 166–67, 178; stakes of war for, 160–63; Thahabiya (Golden Brigade), 167–68; theories applied to case study of, 179–81; and tribal culture, 17, 109, 153–55, 179

Japan, in World War II, 32, 34, 352n46

Jess, Omar, 190, 196, 205

JNA. *See* Jugoslav National Army

Johnson, Lyndon, 265

Jones, Seth, 340n16, 343n26, 357n8, 368n37, 410n4

Jugoslav National Army (JNA): institutions of, 242–45; materiel available to, 50, 231–33; numerical strength of, 232; overview of, 19, 225–27; stakes of war for, 234–37; SVK and, 19, 234–36; warfare activities of, 245–62; withdrawal of, 234

Junger, Ernst, 63

Kalyvas, Stathis, 67, 284

Karbala Brigade, 167

Karen National Defense Organization (KNDO), 68–69

Khamenei, Ali, 125

Khazali, Qais, 166–68

Kilcullen, David, 343n25

Kocher, Matthew, 284

Kony, Joseph, 25

Kosovo, 32

Krajina Serb Army (SVK): demise of, 229; formation of, 244; internal politics of, 19; JNA and, 19, 234–36; materiel available

Krajina Serb Army (SVK) (*continued*)
to, 231, 233; military methods of, 19–20, 224, 245–62; numerical strength of, 233; overview of, 19, 225–29; proficiency of execution by, 254–56; stakes of war for, 234–37; theories applied to case study of, 257

Kurds, 154–55

Kydd, Andrew, 348n10

land. *See* terrain

landmines. *See* minefields

leaders: of Hezbollah, 121, 122; postwar fates of, 369n50; protective actions taken by, 92–93, 367n33; stakes of war from perspective of, 99–100, 102

Lebanon, map of, 111*m*

Lemke, Douglas, 339n9

lethality: in midspectrum methods, 76; survivability trade-offs with, 47, 51–55, 78–81; technological augmentation of, 55–60; technological-numerical trade-off in, 60–62

Lewy, Guenter, 283

Liberation Tigers of Tamil Eelam (LTTE), 90, 96

Libya, 4

logistics: Hezbollah and, 140; institutional strength and, 97; JAM and, 176–78; in midspectrum methods, 81–82, 86–88; SNA and, 217; Vietcong and, 288

Lord's Resistance Army (LRA), 25

LTTE. *See* Liberation Tigers of Tamil Eelam

Lubnan al-Kafa'at, 114

machine guns, 59, 60

Maginot Line, 41, 134, 379n120

Maliki, Nouri al, 152, 160

Manolic, Jospi, 239

Mao Tse-tung, 50, 68, 101, 283, 284

Martic, Milan, 243, 244

materialist theory: basic principles of, 5–6, 109, 115–16; and Hezbollah, 108, 145–47; hybrid, 17, 108, 146, 222, 258; and JAM,

147, 179–80, 392n94, 392n95; predictions of, 17–19, 108, 109, 126, 145–47, 179–80, 220–22, 258, 290; shortcomings of, 296; and SNA, 220–22; and SVK, 258–59; and Vietcong, 290; and ZNG, 258–59

materiel: defined, 13; Hezbollah and, 50, 108–9, 115–19; HV and, 232–33; Israel and, 50, 117–18; JAM and, 155–59; JNA and, 50, 231–33; military methods influenced by, 5–6, 8, 17–19, 63–73; optimal behavior under constraints of, 46–73; SNA and, 17–18, 191–95, 215; of state vs. nonstate actors, 47–51, 59–60, 63–73; SVK and, 231–33; technological factors in, 47–48, 55–62; United States and, 158, 194–95, 271; Vietcong and, 263–64, 269–71; ZNG and, 50, 231–33. *See also* numerical strength

mature natural order, 96, 123, 146, 273, 275

McKee, Alexander, 61

McNair, Leslie, 86

Menkhaus, Ken, 196

Messines, Battle of (1917), 62

midspectrum methods: advantages of, 8, 68; combined arms in, 78–79, 83–84; defensive strategies for, 10, 307–10; disadvantages of, 8; fire and movement in, 79–81, 85–86; Hezbollah and, 17, 126–46, 180; historical convergence on use of, 297–300, 298f, 307; HV and, 254; implementation challenges of, 73–89; interdependence and collective action in, 83–89; JAM and, 180; lethality-survivability combination in, 76; logistics in, 81–82, 86–88; material incentives for, 48, 63–73; nonstate actors' use of, 17–20, 68–73; political conditions required for, 7–10, 46, 74–75, 89–103, 105–6, 260, 293–94; SNA and, 18, 183, 221; SVK and, 19–20, 259–60; training demands for, 82–83; Vietcong and, 20; ZNG and, 259–60

military expenditures: Hezbollah, 117; United States, 158

military methods. *See* conventional warfare; Fabian methods; guerilla warfare;

midspectrum methods; Napoleonic methods; nonstate military methods; state military methods; warfare spectrum

Military Professional Resources Incorporated (MPRI), 19, 224, 227, 237, 240–42, 257, 261. *See also* private military firms

Milosevic, Slobodan, 32, 226, 229, 234, 235, 243

minefields: Hezbollah and, 132–33; JAM and, 172–73; SNA and, 210; SVK and, 250; Vietcong and, 280–81; ZNG and, 250

missiles: of Hezbollah, 116–17, 131, 135–36; lethality-survivability trade-off for, 52, 54. *See also* antiaircraft weapons; antitank weapons

mobile defense, 29

modernization, socioeconomic, 114, 153, 188

modern-system force employment, 43, 63–64, 208

Mogadishu, map of, *187*

Montevideo Convention (1933), 11

Morgan, Mohammed Said Hersi, 196

mortars and rockets: Hezbollah and, 133; JAM and, 156, 172; nonstate actors' use of, 59; SNA and, 209–10; Vietcong and, 280; as warfare tactic, 54

MPLA rebels, 118

MPRI. *See* Military Professional Resources Incorporated

Mrksic, Mile, 235

al-Musawi, Abbas, 125

al-Musawi, Husayn, 125

Museveni, Yoweri, 25

Myanmar, 68

Napoleonic methods: advantages and disadvantages of, 37–38, 41–42, 60–62; defined, 7, 12–13, 37; features of, 76; lethality-survivability trade-off in, 51–55; overview of, 37–38; reasons for choosing, 8. *See also* Bonaparte, Napoleon; conventional warfare; warfare spectrum

Nasrallah, Hassan, 125, 137

National Liberation Front (NLF), 265, 269, 273–75

Navy SEALs, 182

NLF. *See* National Liberation Front

nonstate actors: cultural factors for, 5–6, 8, 13–14; defined, 11; force-to-space ratio, 69f; importance of, 1; institutions of, xvi, 7–8, 13, 74–75, 89–98, 105–6, 365n25, 368n37; internal politics of, xvi, 7–9, 13, 74–106; material constraints of, 5–6, 8, 47–51; outside support for, 357n8, 410n4; research and policy focus on, xv, 1–5, 8–10, 297–313; stakes of war for, xvi, 7–8, 13, 24–26, 74–75, 99–103, 105–6; technology available to, 50–51, 55–62, 66–73. *See also* nonstate military methods; private military firms

nonstate military methods: atypical, 3, 6, 23, 26, 66–73; common assumptions about, xv, 2–3, 22–23; determinants of, 5–7; Hezbollah, 126–46; historical changes in, 297–98, 298f; JAM, 168–81; new theory applied to, 103–6, 105t, 145–46, 179–81, 220–23, 258–62, 290–91, 294–97, 295t; numerical factors in, 47–50, 69–72; overview of case studies, 17–20; policy implications of new theory for, 297–300; political factors in, 74–106, 294, 299–300; SNA, 182–83, 200–223; state methods compared to, xvi, 2–4, 10, 14–15, 26–39, 298–300, 310–12, 418n3; study of, 4–5, 310–13; SVK, 245–62; technology's influence on, 60–62, 66–73, 104–5, 263–64, 269, 286, 288–89, 291, 298–99; Vietcong, 263, 275–91; ZNG, 245–62. *See also* Fabian methods; guerilla warfare; midspectrum methods

North, Douglass, 93, 94, 368n37, 368n42

North Atlantic Treaty Organization (NATO), 4, 32, 228

Northern Alliance (Afghanistan), 40

North Vietnamese Army (NVA), 265, 267, 268, 270, 274–75, 284–86, 289, 413n31

Novakovic, Mile, 244

numerical strength: Hezbollah, 116, 134; HV and, 233; Israel, 117; JAM, 156, 159; JNA, 232; SNA, 192; of state vs. nonstate actors, 47–50, 49f, 69–72; SVK, 233; technological trade-offs with, 60–62; United States, 157–59, 194, 270–71, 302–3; Vietcong, 118, 270, 289; ZNG, 232. *See also* force-to-space ratio; troop densities

NVA. *See* North Vietnamese Army

Ogaden War (1977–78), 183

OMS. *See* Jaish al Mahdi (JAM): Office of the Martyr Sadr

160th Special Operations Aviation Regiment, 186

Operation Anaconda (2002), 62

Operation Attleboro (1966), 265, 288, 289, 290

Operation Cedar Falls (1967), 265, 288, 289, 290

Operation Change of Direction 8 (2006), 110

Operation Change of Direction 11 (2006), 111

Operation Cobra, 86

Operation Concerto (1943), 41

Operation Desert Shield (1990), 7, 43, 65, 259

Operation Desert Storm (1991), 69

Operation Fard al-Khanoon ("Surge") [2007], 152, 157

Operation Goodwood (1944), 42, 61, 62, 84, 134, 259

Operation Junction City (1967), 265, 279, 288, 289, 290

Operation Restore Hope (1992), 186

Operation Rolling Thunder (1965), 271, 273

Operation Sawlat al-Forsan (2008), 152

Operation Specific Gravity (2006), 110

Operations Together Forward I and II (2007), 151

Operation Storm (1995), 228–29, 232–34, 240, 241, 244, 249, 257

Operation Whirlwind (1991), 257

outside support. *See* external support

Paraga, Dobroslav, 239

Pashtuns, 25

People's Revolutionary Party (PRP), 273–74

personnel. *See* force-to-space ratio; numerical strength; troop densities

persuasive strategy. *See* brute force vs. coercion

Petraeus, David, 152

policy implications of new theory: for force structure, 301–10; for strategy, 297–300

politics, of nonstate actors: conditions for midspectrum methods, 7–10, 46, 74–75, 89–103, 105–6, 260, 293–94; in Croatian Wars of Independence, 224–25, 233–45; defined, 13; Hezbollah, 17, 109, 119–26, 180; HV, 233–42; interaction of military privatization with, 224, 241–42; JAM, 17, 109, 147, 160–68, 180; military behavior made possible by, 74–106, 294, 299–300; purposes of war and, 24–26; SNA, 195–200; SVK, 242–45; technology of war influenced by, 294, 299; Vietcong, 272–75; ZNG, 233–39

Portugal, 118

precision-guided weapons, 59

preemptive fire. *See* counterfire

private military firms, political effects of, 224–25, 240–42, 261–62. *See also* Military Professional Resources Incorporated

proficiency of execution: Hezbollah, 141–44; HV, 254, 257–58; JAM, 178–79; SNA, 217–20, 222; SVK, 254–56; Vietcong, 286–89; ZNG, 254, 256–57

proximity of attackers to defenders: Hezbollah and, 129–31; JAM and, 170–71; SNA and, 203–4; SVK and, 248–49; Vietcong and, 278–80; ZNG and, 248–49

Al Qaeda: conventional methods used by, 3; fighting of, 62; institutions of, 90; political goals of, 25; and Somalia, 193, 218; violence of, 25

Al Qaeda in Iraq (AQI), 149, 158–59

Qassem, Naim, 123

Rassemblement Congolais pour la Demo-
    cratie (RCD), 91, 95
rationalist theory, 15, 181, 260, 346n37
Raznjatovic, Zeljko, 244
RCD. *See* Rassemblement Congolais pour
    la Democratie
Revolutionary United Front (RUF), 39–40,
    91, 95
revolution in military affairs (RMA), 301–2,
    305
Rid, Thomas, 347n5
Rif Rebellion, 118
RMA. *See* revolution in military affairs
roadside bombing, 77
rocket-propelled grenades (RPGs), 210,
    217–18
rockets. *See* mortars and rockets
Rohde, David, 235
Rommel, Erwin, 30
RPGs. *See* rocket-propelled grenades
    (RPGs)
RUF. *See* Revolutionary United Front
Russia/Soviet Union: defeat of Napoleon,
    29; in First Chechen War, 3; irregular
    methods used by, 4, 40–41, 418n7; in
    World War II, 29, 30, 40–41
Rwandan rebels, 3

Saddam Hussein, 3, 32, 148, 154–55, 161, 188,
    367n33
Sadr, Muqtada al, 147–49, 152–53, 155, 160–67,
    175, 180–81
sapper raids, 288
Savimbi, Jonas, 102
Sayyid ash-Shuhada Movement, 167
Schelling, Thomas, 31, 32, 175
scholarship: on civil war, 2–5, 10, 311–12;
    future, 310–13; on nonstate military
    methods, 4–5
self-expression, 25
Serbia, 32
Seselj, Vojislav, 244
73 Easting, Battle of (1991), 61, 75–76
Shapiro, Jacob, 191, 368n37

Shiites: Amal and, 119–20; Hezbollah and,
    17, 109, 114, 119–20, 125, 144; JAM and, 17,
    109; in Lebanon, 113–15, 119–20; in occu-
    pied Iraq, 161–62; Sunnis vs., in Iraq, 25,
    147–52, 155, 161–63, 175–77, 387n45
Shinseki, Eric, 308
Shultz, Richard, 14
Sistani, Ali, 161–62, 166
Slovenian separatists, 69, 225–26
small arms: of Hezbollah, 116; of JAM, 156,
    176, 178–79; lethality of, 56, 58; of SNA,
    192; of Vietcong, 270
SNA. *See* Somali National Alliance
SNF. *See* Somali National Front
Somalia, map of, 184m
Somalia Reconciliation and Restoration
    Council (SRRC), 188
Somali National Alliance (SNA), 182–223;
    civilian allies of, 192, 211, 214–15, 223; and
    civil war, 185–88, 205, 212; disbanding of,
    188; formation of, 185; institutions of,
    198–200; internal politics of, 195–200;
    JAM compared to, 399n90; materiel
    available to, 191–95, 215; military methods
    of, 18, 182–83, 200–223; numerical strength
    of, 192; overview of, 17–18, 183–88; politi-
    cal goals of, 196–97; proficiency of execu-
    tion by, 217–20, 222; revenue of, 193, 196;
    stakes of war for, 18, 195–98, 206, 221;
    technology available to, 59–60; theories
    applied to case study of, 220–23; and
    tribal culture, 17–18, 182, 188–91, 221
Somali National Front (SNF), 189, 192, 194,
    205
Somali National Movement (SNM), 189,
    194
Somali Patriotic Movement (SPM), 189–90,
    194
Somali Salvation Alliance (SSA), 185, 187–88,
    190, 193–94, 199
Somali Salvation Democratic Front
    (SSDF), 189, 194
Somme offensive (1916), 60
South Ossetian separatists, 69

South Vietnam, 118; map of, 266m
sovereignty, 11
Soviet Union. *See* Russia/Soviet Union
Spain, 118
spectrum of warfare. *See* warfare spectrum
SPM. *See* Somali Patriotic Movement
SSA. *See* Somali Salvation Alliance
Stag Hunt game, 365n21
stakes of war: aims of war vs., 100–101; components of, 99–100; in Croatian Wars of Independence, 233–37; for Hezbollah, 119–22; for JAM, 160–63; for JNA, 234–37; as motivating factor for military behavior, xvi, 7–8, 13, 24–26, 74–75, 99–103, 105–6, 293–94; for SNA, 195–98, 206, 221; for SVK, 234–37; variation in, 101–2; for Vietcong, 272–73; for ZNG, 233. *See also* existential threats
state military methods: atypical, 3, 23, 26, 63–66, 259, 300; contingency plans for, 138; nonstate methods compared to, xvi, 2–4, 10, 14–15, 26–39, 298–300, 310–12, 418n3; numerical factors in, 47–50, 69–72; study of, 310; technology's influence on, 60–66, 104–5. *See also* conventional warfare; Napoleonic methods
states: materiel available to, 47–51; as patrons of nonstate actors, 357n8, 410n4; stakes of war for, 24; technology available to, 55–62; Weberian model of, 48, 50. *See also* state military methods
stealth and concealment: Hezbollah and, 127; HV and, 246; JAM and, 168–69; SNA and, 200–220; states' use of, 63–65; SVK and, 246; Vietcong and, 276–77; as warfare tactic, 27–28; ZNG and, 245–46
Stewart, Potter, 26
strategic intent, 31–33
suicide bombing, 352n44
Sunnis: in Saddam's Iraq, 148; Shiites vs., in Iraq, 25, 147–52, 155, 161–63, 175–77, 387n45
suppressive fire, 80–81, 85
survivability: lethality trade-offs with, 47, 51–55, 78–81; in midspectrum methods,

76; state military adaptation for, 63–64. *See also* stealth and concealment
Susak, Gojko, 239
SVK. *See* Krajina Serb Army
symmetrical warfare, 33–35

tanks: in combined-arms fighting, 78–79; infantry coordinated with, 83–85; nonstate actors' use of, 59; vulnerability of, 53, 61, 359n40
Task Force Ranger (TF Ranger), 186–87, 192, 194, 197–202, 208, 211, 213, 214, 216, 218–20, 223
technology of war: Hezbollah and, 50–51, 59, 117; increasing significance of, 48, 55–60, 71–73, 298–99; military methods influenced by, 47–48, 60–73, 104–5, 263–64, 269, 286, 288–89, 291, 298–99; nonstate actors' use of, 50–51, 55–62, 66–73, 104–5; political factors in use of, 294, 299; states' use of, 55–62; theories of high vs. low, 301–10; unmanned weapons, 357n10; Vietcong and, 51, 269, 286–89, 291
terrain: cover offered by, 64; midspectrum methods and, 80
terrorism: Hezbollah, 25; lethality-survivability trade-off in, 53; linked to irregular warfare, 33, 34; political goals of, 25, 348n10; state-sponsored, 23; as war, 11
Tet Offensive (1968), 20, 263, 265, 267, 283, 285–86, 289, 413n31
TF Ranger. *See* Task Force Ranger
Thanh, Nguyen Chi, 282–83
theater of war, organization of: Hezbollah and, 139–41; JAM and, 173, 176–78; SNA and, 215–17; SVK and, 253–54; Vietcong and, 284–85; warfare spectrum and, 35–37, 39–41; ZNG and, 253–54
Thieu, Nguyen Van, 265, 267, 285, 413n31
Tito, Josef Brozip, 225
training: for conventional warfare, 76, 363n3; guerilla fighters' lack of, 77–78; for midspectrum methods, 74, 79, 82–83;

MPRI's provision of, 240–42; in US military, 82, 99, 304

transformation agendas, for US military, 9–10, 301–10

tribal culture: in Arab Middle East, 112; atypical methods of, 8, 19; conflicts and dispute resolution in, 113–15, 154, 190–91, 268; in Croatia, 229–31; defined, 13; ethnicity compared to, 231, 402n5; familist, 229–30; Hezbollah and, 17, 108–9, 112–15, 180; in Iraq, 153–55; JAM and, 17, 109, 155, 179; in Lebanon, 112–15; modern pressures on, 114–15; SNA and, 17–18, 182, 221; in Somalia, 188–91, 198–99; as source of guerilla methods, 5–6, 8, 13–14, 17–19, 115; stability of, 6; theory based on, 5–6, 8, 13, 17–19, 108, 115, 126, 145–47, 221, 229, 258, 290, 296; Vietcong and, 267–69, 290

troop densities: in Fabian methods, 12, 36–37; Hezbollah and, 134; JAM and, 173; in Napoleonic methods, 12, 37, 65; SNA and, 211–12; of state vs. nonstate actors, 68–70, 105; Vietcong and, 282; in World Wars I and II, 65; ZNG and, 251. *See also* force-to-space ratio; numerical strength

Tudjman, Franjo, 19, 237, 238–39, 241–42, 261

Tudjman, Miroslav, 239

Tufayli, Subhi al, 125

Tus, Anton, 232, 239

Twentynine Palms reservation, 82

Uganda, 25

Ukrainian separatists, 51, 59

Ulster Volunteer Force (UVF), 39, 90–91

Unified Task Force (UNITAF), 186, 191–94

uniforms: characteristic of conventional forces, 2, 12, 27–28, 33; Hezbollah's use of, 121, 139; nonstate actors' avoidance of, 35, 138–39; nonstate actors' use of, 35; SVK's use of, 252–53; Vietcong's use of, 283–84; ZNG's use of, 252–53

UNITAF. *See* Unified Task Force (UNITAF)

UNITA rebels, 59, 102, 118

United Nations, 154

United Nations Operations in Somalia (UNOSOM I and II), 185–87, 191–223

United Nations Protection Force (UNPROFOR), 227

United Nations Security Council, 112, 185–86

United Somali Congress (USC), 183, 185, 189–90, 212–13

United States: force structure policy of, 301–10; hybrid methods used by, 7; and Iraq, 3, 7, 30, 32, 43, 148–81; irregular methods used by, 43; in Kuwait, 30; materiel available to, 158, 194–95, 271; military expenditures of, 158; military methods of, 9–10; numerical strength of, 157–59, 194, 270–71, 302–3; and Somalia, 182, 186–87, 193, 194–223; training practices of, 82, 99, 304; and Vietnam War, 263–91, 413n31; in World War II, 33–34, 352n46

unmanned weapons, 357n10

UNOSOM I and II. *See* United Nations Operations in Somalia

urban warfare, 28, 170, 308

Usayran, Ali, 114

USC. *See* United Somali Congress

US Defense Department, 35

US Green Berets, 35

US Rangers, 3, 182, 186, 197. *See also* Task Force Ranger

US Special Forces, 35

UVF. *See* Ulster Volunteer Force

Vance, Cyrus, cease-fire brokered by, 227, 235–36, 243

Vekic, Ivan, 239

Verdun, Battle of (1916), 62

Vietcong, 263–91; civilian allies and adversaries of, 276, 283–84; demise of, 267, 286, 413n31; Hezbollah compared to, 271, 290–91; materiel available to, 263–64, 269–71; military methods of, 20, 263,

Vietcong (*continued*)

275–91; numerical strength of, 118, 270, 289; overview of, 20, 264–67; proficiency of execution by, 286–89; stakes of war for, 272–73; technology available to, 51, 269, 286–89, 291; theories applied to case study of, 290–91; theories of nonstate warfare based on, 20; and tribal culture, 267–69, 290; ZNG compared to, 270, 271, 290–91

violence, purposes of, 25

Wallis, John, 93, 94, 368n37, 368n42

Walter, Barbara, 348n10

war: defining, 11, 345n32; profit as purpose of, 24–25; purposes of, 24–26

warfare spectrum: examples of, 39–44, 40*f*; factors determining position on, 39*t*; historical changes in, 298*f*; index for, 13; midspectrum methods, 7–10; overview of, 6–7, 12, 26, 36–39, 292–93; theoretically superior to categorical distinctions, xvi, 7–8, 10, 44–45, 146, 179–81, 220–23,

259–60, 262, 292, 294–97, 312–13; US defensive capabilities and, 302–10, 303*f*. *See also* conventional warfare; Fabian methods; guerilla warfare; midspectrum methods; Napoleonic methods

Watts, Clint, 191

weapons. *See* antiaircraft weapons; antitank weapons; artillery; materiel; missiles; mortars and rockets; small arms; tanks

Weber, Max, 48, 50

Wehrmacht, 7, 26, 182

Weingast, Barry, 93, 94, 368n37, 368n42

World War I: lethality in, 56; troop densities in, 65

World War II: stakes of war in, 101; strategic intent in, 32–33; symmetrical and asymmetrical warfare in, 34; troop densities in, 65; warfare spectrum in, 41–42

zadrugas (agricultural kinship groups), 230

al-Zayn, Abdulatif, 114

ZNG. *See* Croatian National Guard

zu'ama (land-holding families), 112–15

A NOTE ON THE TYPE

This book has been composed in Arno, an Old-style serif typeface in the classic Venetian tradition, designed by Robert Slimbach at Adobe.

CPSIA information can be obtained
at www.ICGtesting.com
Printed in the USA
JSHW050853040622
26662JS00003B/5

9 780691 216669